HUMAN DEVELOPMENT REPORT 1994

Published
for the United Nations
Development Programme
(UNDP)

New York   Oxford
Oxford University Press
1994

Oxford University Press
Oxford   New York   Toronto
Delhi   Bombay   Calcutta   Madras   Karachi
Kuala Lumpur   Singapore   Hong Kong   Tokyo
Nairobi   Dar es Salaam   Cape Town
Melbourne   Auckland

and associated companies in
Berlin   Ibadan

ISBN 0-19-509170-1 (paper)
ISBN 0-19-509169-8 (cloth)

9 8 7 6 5 4 3 2
Printed in the United States of America on acid-free, recycled paper.

Cover and design: Gerald Quinn, Quinn Information Design, Cabin John, Maryland

Editing, desktop composition and production management: Bruce Ross-Larson, Alison Strong, Kim Bieler, Jennifer Peabody,
Eileen Hanlon, Debbie Sinmao and Markus Bock, all with American Writing Corporation, Washington, D.C.

Foreword

Behind the blaring headlines of the world's many conflicts and emergencies, there lies a silent crisis—a crisis of underdevelopment, of global poverty, of ever-mounting population pressures, of thoughtless degradation of environment. This is not a crisis that will respond to emergency relief. Or to fitful policy interventions. It requires a long, quiet process of sustainable human development.

Sustainable human development is development that not only generates economic growth but distributes its benefits equitably; that regenerates the environment rather than destroying it; that empowers people rather than marginalizing them. It is development that gives priority to the poor, enlarging their choices and opportunities and providing for their participation in decisions that affect their lives. It is development that is pro-people, pro-nature, pro-jobs and pro-women.

It is a great contribution of the *Human Development Reports* that they have stimulated international dialogue on such models of development. The 1994 Report continues this tradition and takes it a step further. It explores the new frontiers of human security in the daily lives of the people. It attempts to discover early warning signals that can spur preventive diplomacy and preventive development in order to save a society from reaching a crisis point. It outlines a new design for development cooperation in the post–cold war era. And it suggests a concrete agenda for the consideration of the World Summit for Social Development that is to meet in Copenhagen in March 1995.

The forthcoming Social Summit offers us a unique opportunity to redefine humanity's development agenda. The Summit will be a time to respond to the new compulsions of human security. It will be a time to reiterate very clearly that without the promotion of people-centred development none of our key objectives can be met—not peace, not human rights, not environmental protection, not reduced population growth, not social integration. It will be a time for all nations to recognize that it is far cheaper and far more humane to act early and to act upstream than to pick up the pieces downstream, to address the root causes of human insecurity rather than its tragic consequences.

From such a diagnosis, it follows that the role of the United Nations must be strengthened significantly in the development field. The peace agenda and the development agenda must finally be integrated. Without peace, there may be no development. But without development, peace is threatened.

There is an urgent need today to establish a more integrated, effective and efficient UN development system to promote the worldwide movement towards sustainable human development. For this purpose, the UN system requires a clearer mandate, integrated policy frameworks and additional resources.

It is our principal goal to restructure and strengthen UNDP so that it can make a critical contribution to these new imperatives of sustainable human development—from assisting countries in the formulation of their own development strategies, to helping donor nations reflect this new development perspective in their aid allocations, to launching global policy initiatives for new designs of development cooperation, to working closely with other UN development programmes and agencies in identifying common missions and complementary approaches so as to help our member countries realize their sustainable human development goals. In other words, we are now poised in UNDP to move from the basic messages of the *Human Development Reports* to their concrete operationalization.

It is in this spirit that I present the *Human Development Report 1994* to the international community. As always, the views set forth in this Report have emerged from the candid, professional analysis of an eminent team working under the able guidance of Mahbub ul Haq, my Special Adviser and the Report's chief architect. They do not necessarily reflect the views of UNDP, its Executive Board or other member governments of UNDP. We have always respected the intellectual independence and professional integrity of these Reports. But there is no question in my mind that the Report will exercise a profound influence on global policy dialogue and on UNDP's future operations.

James Gustave Speth

New York
March 16, 1994

Team for the preparation of
Human Development Report 1994

Special Adviser
Mahbub ul Haq

UNDP Team
Director: Inge Kaul
Members: Saraswathi Menon and Selim Jahan assisted by Babafemi Badejo, Moez Doraid Yusuf, Beth Ebel, Terry McKinley, Melanie Beth Oliviero, Peter Stalker (editing) and Leo Goldstone, World Statistics Ltd., for the statistics, with the assistance of Laura Mourino

Panel of consultants
Sudhir Anand, Meghnad Desai, Keith Griffin, Stephany Griffith-Jones, Edward Laurance, Amartya Sen, Hans Singer, Paul Streeten and Herbert Wulf

Acknowledgements

The preparation of the Report would not have been possible without the support and valuable contributions received from a large number of individuals and organizations.

The authors would like to thank the agencies and offices of the United Nations system who generously shared their extensive practical experience, studies and statistics. The statistical elements of the Report are drawn from the databases and material from the United Nations Statistical Division, United Nations Population Division, United Nations Centre for Social Development and Humanitarian Affairs, Office of the United Nations High Commissioner for Refugees, United Nations Research Institute for Social Development, United Nations Economic Commission for Africa, United Nations Economic and Social Commission for Asia and the Pacific, United Nations Economic Commission for Europe, United Nations Economic Commission for Latin America and the Caribbean, United Nations Economic and Social Commission for Western Asia, ACC Sub-Committee on Nutrition, Food and Agriculture Organization of the United Nations, International Fund for Agricultural Development, International Labour Organisation, International Maritime Organization, International Postal Union, International Telecommunication Union, International Trade Centre, United Nations Children's Fund, United Nations Educational, Scientific and Cultural Organization, United Nations Environment Programme, United Nations Population Fund, United Nations Industrial Development Organization, World Food Programme, World Health Organization, International Monetary Fund, World Bank, Organisation for Economic Co-operation and Development, Statistical Office of the European Communities, International Centre for Urban Studies, Inter-Parliamentary Union, Macro International Inc. (DHS), Penn World Tables, Stockholm International Peace Research Institute, US Arms Control and Disarmament Agency, World Resources Institute and World Priorities Inc.

The authors would also like to thank the many individuals who contributed special studies to the Report. They include Sam O. Adamu, Li An, Tengku Aziz, Russel Lawrence Barsh, Bréhima Béridogo, Keyla Betancourt, Rundheersing Bheenick, Lech Boleslawski, Michael Brzoska, Cristovam Buarque, Radhika Coomaraswamy, Christopher Cosslett, Joseph DiChiaro, Heba El-laithy, Ping Fan, Oscar Fresneda, Mouza Ghubash, Brigitte Hamm, Esther Hanoomanjee, Ralph M. Henry, Michael Hopkins, Angang Hu, Helena Jakubowska, Ruth Klingebiel, Jeni Klugman, Atul Kohli, Michiko Kuroda, Soonwon Kwon, Yeah Kim Leng, Lexi Lenton, Peilin Li, Jianhua Lu, Neva Seidman Makgetla, Gustavo Márquez, Marina Mayer, Jadwiga Mijakowska, Sizwe Mmatli, Petra Müller, Vidula Nababsing, Nehemiah K. Ng'eno, Heinz-Herbert Noll, Franz Nuscheler, Jean Christian Obame, Andrzej Ochocki, Bade Onimode, Fanny Ortiz, Mmakgoshi Phetla, Won Hee Rhee, Kanchana Ruwanpura, Harald Sander, John Shaw, Selby Shezi, Elizabeth Sköns, Dan Smith, Jamil Sofi, Austregésilo Gomes Spíndola, Gabriele Winai Ström, LaMond Tullis, Adam Wagstaff, Rusong Wang, Yoon-Ha Yoo and Cai Zhizhou.

Several UNDP offices provided invaluable information and data that were not otherwise available from international sources. They include UNDP's country offices in Algeria, Argentina, Bolivia, Brazil, Cameroon, China, Colombia, Costa Rica, Ecuador, Egypt, Fiji, Gabon, Ghana, Indonesia, Iran, Kuwait, Kyrgyzstan, Lao People's Democratic Republic, Latvia, Lesotho, Malawi, Malaysia, Mali, Mongolia, Namibia, Nepal, Nicaragua, Niger, Nigeria, Pakistan, Paraguay, Poland, Republic of Korea, Saudi Arabia, Senegal, South Africa, Tanzania, Thailand, Trinidad and Tobago, Tunisia, United Arab Emirates and Venezuela. UNDP's Regional Bureaux, the Bureau for Programme Policy and Evaluation and the United Nations Development Fund for Women also generously provided the team with information and data. The Office for Project Services provided continuous administrative support.

The team is also indebted to colleagues in UNDP who provided useful comments and suggestions during the drafting of the Report. In particular, they would like to express their gratitude to Stephen Adei, Ali Attiga, Denis Benn, Sharon Capeling-Alakija, Shabbir Cheema, Judy Cheng-Hopkins, Desmond Cohen, Ad de Raad, Yves de San, Søren Dyssegaard, Gustaf A. Edgren, Anne Forrester, Peter Gall, Luis Maria Gomez, Luis Gomez-Echeverri, Jean-Jacques Graisse, Reinhart Helmke, Nadia Hijab, Arthur Holcombe, Bruce Jenks, Ellen Johnson-Sirleaf, Henning Karcher, Bahman Kia, Üner Kirdar, Anton Kruiderink, Carlos Lopes, Elena Martinez, Paul Matthews, Toshiyuki Niwa, Linda Pigon-Rebello, Rajeev Pillay, Elizabeth Reid, Ingolf Schuetz Mueller, Ivo Pokorny, Per Arne Stroberg, Sarah L. Timpson, Clay Wescott, David Whaley and Fernando Zumbado.

Secretarial and administrative support were provided by Renuka Corea, Flora Aller, Gabriella Charles and Karin Svadlenak. The team was assisted in background research by Nicole Blakely, Sandeep Kakar, Ulrike Neuhauser, Jasmine Rajbhandary and Maria Ventegodt.

The team has benefited greatly from intellectual advice and professional criticism received from Armeane Choksi, Daan Everts, Dharam Ghai, James Grant, Thomas Homer-Dixon, Richard Jolly, Kees Kingma, Jacky Mathonnat, James H. Michel, Nafis Sadik, Alexander Shakow and Frances Stewart.

The authors also wish to acknowledge their deep debt to James Gustave Speth, UNDP Administrator, whose wholehearted commitment to sustainable human development has been a source of great inspiration for all of us.

ABBREVIATIONS

DAC	Development Assistance Committee
ECOSOC	Economic and Social Council
FAO	Food and Agriculture Organization
GATT	General Agreement on Tariffs and Trade
IBRD	International Bank for Reconstruction and Development
IFAD	International Fund for Agricultural Development
ILO	International Labour Organisation
IMF	International Monetary Fund
ODA	Official development assistance
OECD	Organisation for Economic Co-operation and Development
UNCTAD	United Nations Conference on Trade and Development
UNDP	United Nations Development Programme
UNESCO	United Nations Educational, Scientific and Cultural Organization
UNFPA	United Nations Population Fund
UNICEF	United Nations Children's Fund
UNIDO	United Nations Industrial Development Organization
WFP	World Food Programme
WHO	World Health Organization

Contents

TABLES

FIGURES

SPECIAL CONTRIBUTIONS BY NOBEL PRIZE WINNERS

An agenda for the Social Summit

The world can never be at peace unless people have security in their daily lives. Future conflicts may often be within nations rather than between them—with their origins buried deep in growing socio-economic deprivation and disparities. The search for security in such a milieu lies in development, not in arms.

More generally, it will not be possible for the community of nations to achieve any of its major goals—not peace, not environmental protection, not human rights or democratization, not fertility reduction, not social integration—except in the context of sustainable development that leads to human security.

It is time for humanity to restore its perspective and redesign its agenda. The World Summit for Social Development in March 1995 comes at a time when the world will be celebrating the 50th anniversary of the United Nations—an occasion to review the achievements of the first 50 years and to define the goals for the coming decades.

A world of change

It is easy to lose perspective in today's global uncertainty. As one crisis succeeds another, policy agendas often centre on immediate issues—not the important ones.

It is essential, therefore, to step back a little and to assess the state of affairs in the 50 years since the United Nations was created. What emerges is an arresting picture of unprecedented human progress and unspeakable human misery, of humanity's advance on several fronts mixed with humanity's retreat on several others, of a breathtaking globalization of prosperity side by side with a depressing globalization of poverty. As is so common in human affairs, nothing is simple and nothing is settled for ever. The progress should reassure humankind about its capacity to engineer change, and the present scale of human deprivation should continue to challenge humankind to design a much better world order.

Humanity has advanced on several critical fronts in the past 50 years.

• Most nations have already won their freedom. And the prospects for self-determination have never looked brighter in the few remaining areas, particularly in South Africa and in the Middle East. In the past 50 years, the United Nations family has grown from 51 countries to 184.

• The world is safer today from the threat of nuclear holocaust. With the end of the cold war and the conclusion of several disarmament agreements, it is difficult to recall that so many generations since the Second World War grew up with the constant fear of a sudden, unpredictable nuclear suicide.

• The record of human development during this period is unprecedented, with the developing countries setting a pace three times faster than the industrial countries did a century ago. Rising life expectancy, falling infant mortality, increasing educational attainment and much improved nutrition are a few of the heartening indicators of this human advance.

• While nearly 70% of humanity survived in abysmal human conditions in 1960 (below a human development index of 0.4), only 32% suffered such conditions in 1992. The share of the world population enjoying fairly satisfactory human development levels (above an HDI of 0.6) increased from 25% in 1960 to 60% in 1992.

• The wealth of nations has multiplied in these 50 years. Global GDP has increased

The search for human security lies in development, not in arms

sevenfold—from about $3 trillion to $22 trillion. Since the world population has more than doubled—from 2.5 billion to 5.5 billion—per capita income has more than tripled.

• There have also been dramatic developments in technology. In 1927, the first transatlantic flight by Charles Lindbergh took 33 hours. Today, the Concorde can fly the Atlantic in about a tenth of that time. And most parts of the world are now immediately accessible by telephone, television or fax. Computers move more than a trillion dollars around the world's financial markets every 24 hours.

• Human ingenuity has led to several technological innovations and breathtaking breakthroughs—from an informatics revolution to exciting space explorations, from ever-new medical frontiers to ever-greater additions to knowledge. Sometimes, human institutions have even failed to keep up with technological progress, so fast has been the pace of advance.

• Global military spending has declined significantly in the past six years, after awesome increases in the previous four decades. How intelligently this emerging peace dividend will be used is now up to policy-makers.

• Between one-half and three-quarters of the world's people live under relatively pluralistic and democratic regimes. In 1993 alone, elections were held in 45 countries—in some for the first time.

This recapitulation of human progress is admittedly selective. But it shows that it is possible—indeed mandatory—to engineer change. Today's anxieties should not be allowed to paralyse tomorrow's initiatives. Nor can there be complacency, since a lengthening agenda of human deprivation still awaits us.

• Despite all our technological breakthroughs, we still live in a world where a fifth of the developing world's population goes hungry every night, a quarter lacks access to even a basic necessity like safe drinking water, and a third lives in a state of abject poverty—at such a margin of human existence that words simply fail to describe it.

• We also live in a world of disturbing contrasts—where so many go hungry, there is

How intelligently the emerging peace dividend will be used is now up to policy-makers

so much food to waste; where so many children do not live to enjoy their childhood, there are so many inessential weapons. Global military spending, despite a welcome decline, still equals the combined income of one-half of humanity each year. And the richest billion people command 60 times the income of the poorest billion.

• Poor nations and rich are afflicted by growing human distress—weakening social fabrics, rising crime rates, increasing threats to personal security, spreading narcotic drugs and a growing sense of individual isolation.

• The threats to human security are no longer just personal or local or national. They are becoming global: with drugs, AIDS, terrorism, pollution, nuclear proliferation. Global poverty and environmental problems respect no national border. Their grim consequences travel the world.

• The same speed that has helped unify the world has also brought many problems to our doorsteps with devastating suddenness. Drug dealers can launder money rapidly through many countries—in a fraction of the time it takes their victims to detoxify. And terrorists operating from a remote safe haven can destroy life on a distant continent.

• The basic question of human survival on an environmentally fragile planet has gained in urgency as well. By the middle of the next century—still in the lifetimes of today's children—the world population may double and the world economy may quadruple. Food production must triple if people are to be adequately fed, but the resource base for sustainable agriculture is eroding. Energy must be provided, too, but even at today's level of use, fossil fuels threaten climatic stability. The destruction of the world's forests and the loss of biological wealth and diversity continue relentlessly.

• Several nation-states are beginning to disintegrate. While the threats to national survival may emerge from several sources—ethnic, religious, political—the underlying causes are often the lack of socio-economic progress and the limited participation of people in any such progress.

Against this background of human

achievement and human distress, we must seek a new concept of human security in the decades ahead. We must seek a new paradigm of sustainable human development that can satisfy the expanding frontiers of this human security. We must seek a new framework of development cooperation that brings humanity together through a more equitable sharing of global economic opportunities and responsibilities. And we must seek a new role for the United Nations so that it can begin to meet humanity's agenda not only for peace but also for development.

A new concept of human security

For too long, the concept of security has been shaped by the potential for conflict between states. For too long, security has been equated with the threats to a country's borders. For too long, nations have sought arms to protect their security.

For most people today, a feeling of insecurity arises more from worries about daily life than from the dread of a cataclysmic world event. Job security, income security, health security, environmental security, security from crime—these are the emerging concerns of human security all over the world.

This should not surprise us. The founders of the United Nations had always given equal importance to people's security and to territorial security. As far back as June 1945, the US secretary of state reported this to his government on the results of the San Francisco Conference:

The battle of peace has to be fought on two fronts. The first is the security front where victory spells freedom from fear. The second is the economic and social front where victory means freedom from want. Only victory on both fronts can assure the world of an enduring peace....No provisions that can be written into the Charter will enable the Security Council to make the world secure from war if men and women have no security in their homes and their jobs.

Several insights can help in redefining the basic concept of security:

• Human security is relevant to people everywhere, in rich nations and in poor. The threats to their security may differ—hunger and disease in poor nations and drugs and crime in rich nations—but these threats are real and growing. Some threats are indeed common to all nations—job insecurity and environmental threats, in particular.

• When the security of people is attacked in any corner of the world, all nations are likely to get involved. Famines, ethnic conflicts, social disintegration, terrorism, pollution and drug trafficking are no longer isolated events, confined within national borders. Their consequences travel the globe.

• It is less costly and more humane to meet these threats upstream rather than downstream, early rather than late. Short-term humanitarian assistance can never replace long-term development support.

Most people instinctively understand what security means. It means safety from the constant threats of hunger, disease, crime and repression. It also means protection from sudden and hurtful disruptions in the pattern of our daily lives—whether in our homes, in our jobs, in our communities or in our environment.

It is important to develop some operational indicators of human security. This Report offers various concrete proposals for an early warning system and identifies some countries already in a state of crisis—such as Afghanistan, Angola, Haiti, Iraq, Mozambique, Myanmar, Sudan and Zaire. Determined national and international actions—including both preventive and curative development—are needed to support processes of social integration.

Identifying potential crisis countries is not an indictment of these countries. It is an essential part of preventive diplomacy and preventive development. The Report mentions some of these countries only as an illustration of the potential threats to human security that can eventually lead to social disintegration. What is important for the international community is to recognize that a clear set of human security indicators, and an early warning system based on them, could help these countries avoid reaching a crisis point.

We must seek a new role for the United Nations to meet humanity's agenda not only for peace but also for development

There are several countries where current national and international efforts need to be reinforced to promote human security. The list of such countries extends to all world regions, and it ranges from countries in the midst of ongoing crises—such as Burundi, Georgia, Liberia, Rwanda and Tajikistan—to other countries experiencing either severe internal tensions—such as Algeria—or large regional disparities—such as Egypt, Mexico and Nigeria.

A new paradigm of development

To address the growing challenge of human security, a new development paradigm is needed that puts people at the centre of development, regards economic growth as a means and not an end, protects the life opportunities of future generations as well as the present generations and respects the natural systems on which all life depends.

Such a paradigm of development enables all individuals to enlarge their human capabilities to the full and to put those capabilities to their best use in all fields—economic, social, cultural and political. It also protects the options of unborn generations. It does not run down the natural resource base needed for sustaining development in the future. Nor does it destroy the richness of nature that adds so much to the richness of human life.

Sustainable human development addresses both intragenerational and intergenerational equity—enabling all generations, present and future, to make the best use of their potential capabilities. But it is not indifferent to how present opportunities are actually distributed. It would be odd if we were deeply concerned for the well-being of future—as yet unborn—generations while ignoring the plight of the poor today. Yet, in truth, neither objective today gets the priority it deserves. A major restructuring of the world's income distribution, production and consumption patterns may therefore be a necessary precondition for any viable strategy for sustainable human development.

In the final analysis, sustainable human development is pro-people, pro-jobs and pro-nature. It gives the highest priority to

poverty reduction, productive employment, social integration and environmental regeneration. It brings human numbers into balance with the coping capacities of societies and the carrying capacities of nature. It accelerates economic growth and translates it into improvements in human lives, without destroying the natural capital needed to protect the opportunities of future generations. It also recognizes that not much can be achieved without a dramatic improvement in the status of women and the opening of all economic opportunities to women. And sustainable human development empowers people—enabling them to design and participate in the processes and events that shape their lives.

A new design of development cooperation

The new demands of global human security require a more positive relationship among all nations of the world—leading to a new era of development cooperation. In such a design, economic partnership would be based on mutual interests, not charity; cooperation, not confrontation; equitable sharing of market opportunities, not protectionism; far-sighted internationalism, not stubborn nationalism.

Several fundamental changes will be required in the present framework of development cooperation.

First, foreign assistance must be linked to commonly agreed policy objectives—particularly to poverty reduction strategies, productive employment opportunities and the goals of sustainable human development. During the cold war period, foreign assistance was often given to strategic allies rather than in support of agreed policy objectives. Now is the time for a major restructuring of existing foreign aid allocations.

Second, a certain proportion of existing foreign assistance (equal to, say, 0.1% of the donor countries' GNP) should be channelled to the poorest nations as a global social safety net. This should be clearly earmarked for basic human development priorities (especially basic education and primary health care), and the aim should be to bring all poor nations up to at least a minimum threshold of human development.

Third, the concept of development cooperation should be broadened to include all flows, not just aid—especially trade, investment, technology and labour flows. Greater attention should be paid to the freer movement of non-aid flows, as these are more decisive for the future growth of the developing countries than aid flows. Aid reporting systems should also be recast to include all flows and to monitor them in a comprehensive fashion.

Fourth, new initiatives for development cooperation should be discussed, including the possibility of introducing a payment for services rendered and compensation for damages suffered. For instance, the rich nations should be prepared to pay the poor nations for certain services that are in the global interest and for which the poor countries may not have sufficient resources themselves—instituting environmental controls, regulating narcotics production and trafficking, controlling communicable diseases, destroying nuclear weapons. Industrial nations should also compensate the developing countries for economic damage they suffer from certain market barriers imposed by the industrial countries, particularly trade barriers and restrictions on migration of unskilled labour.

Fifth, a serious search should begin for new sources of international funding that do not rely entirely on the fluctuating political will of the rich nations. Global taxation may become necessary in any case to achieve the goals of global human security. Some of the promising new sources include tradable permits for global pollution, a global tax on non-renewable energy, demilitarization funds and a small transaction tax on speculative international movements of foreign exchange funds.

Sixth, a new design of development cooperation also demands a new framework of global governance. Most international institutions have weakened precisely at a time of growing global interdependence. All existing institutions need considerable strengthening and restructuring if they are to cope with the new challenges to human security—particularly the United Nations system and the Bretton Woods institutions. At the same time, a creative debate must start on the shape of global institutions required for the 21st century.

Chapter 4 offers many concrete proposals on all these aspects of a new development cooperation.

Agenda for the Social Summit

These are the issues the World Summit for Social Development must discuss. It must provide a new vision, a new direction—and lay a solid foundation for a new society.

There are times in the lives of nations when an entirely new vision shapes their destiny. The 1940s were such a watershed—marked by the birth of the United Nations, the launching of the Marshall Plan, the setting up of the Bretton Woods institutions, the initiation of the European Community, the negotiation of new social contracts in the industrial nations and an irresistible movement for the liberation of former colonies. A new world order emerged in the 1940s from the darkness of the Second World War.

Fifty years later, is the world getting ready for yet another profound transition? The initial signs are encouraging: the democratic transition in formerly communist societies as well as in many developing countries, the end of the cold war, a steady fall in global military expenditures, the opening up of economies, the strengthened prospects for peace in South Africa and the Middle East. The unexpected is becoming almost the commonplace.

At this propitious time, can humanity take yet another decisive step? The forthcoming Summit offers such an opportunity. Of course, it cannot resolve all the issues facing humanity. Nor can it provide the political will that national leaders alone can provide. But it can, and must, provide a new sense of direction.

The only practical way of achieving this is to focus on a small, manageable number of issues. It is in this spirit that the following six-point agenda is offered.

• *A new world social charter*—to establish the framework of equality of opportunity among nations and people.

The concept of development cooperation should be broadened to include all flows, not just aid

- *A 20:20 human development compact*—to implement targets for essential human development over a ten-year period (1995–2005).
- *Mobilization of the peace dividend*—to set concrete targets for reducing global military expenditure and for capturing the ensuing peace dividend to enhance human security.

- *A global human security fund*—to address the common threats to global human security.
- *A strengthened UN umbrella for human development*—to establish a more integrated, effective and efficient UN development system.
- *A UN Economic Security Council*—to provide a decision-making forum at the highest level for global issues of human security.

The discussion here summarizes each of these proposals, which are discussed at length in the Report.

A world social charter

To give clear and precise expression to the emerging concept of human security, now is the time to draw up a world social charter. Just as social contracts emerged in the 1930s and 1940s at the national level—the New Deal in the United States and the Beveridge Plan for the welfare state in the United Kingdom—so the growing consensus on the new compulsions of global human security requires social contracts at the global level.

Much of the groundwork for such a charter already exists. The International Covenant on Economic, Social and Cultural Rights—which came into force in 1976—encompassed most of the social goals, including the rights to food, health, shelter, education and work, as well as other non-material aspects of life. World leaders have come together on other occasions at international conferences and summit meetings to give concrete shape to these rights and adopt specific targets for implementation. The most comprehensive international commitments were presented in Agenda 21, adopted at the Earth Summit in 1992.

The challenge now is to translate such general statements and targets into practical action. The Social Summit should request the United Nations to draw up a concrete world social charter, to cost various goals, to set priorities and timetables for their implementation and to monitor the implementation of these goals through the new Economic Security Council proposed

---

BOX 1

A world social charter

WE THE PEOPLE OF THE WORLD SOLEMNLY PLEDGE to build a new global civil society, based on the principles of equality of opportunity, rule of law, global democratic governance and a new partnership among all nations and all people.

WE PROPOSE to build a society where the right to food is as sacrosanct as the right to vote, where the right to a basic education is as deeply enshrined as the right to a free press and where the right to development is considered one of the fundamental human rights.

WE COLLECTIVELY PLEDGE to build new foundations of human security, which ensure the security of people through development, not arms; through cooperation, not confrontation; through peace, not war. We believe that no provision in the Charter of the United Nations will ever ensure global security unless people have security in their homes, in their jobs, in their communities and in their environment.

WE ARE FULLY CONVINCED that diversity in our societies is our strength, not our weakness, and we intend to protect this diversity by ensuring non-discrimination between all our people, irrespective of gender, race, religion or ethnic origin.

WE COLLECTIVELY BELIEVE that our world cannot survive one-fourth rich and three-fourths poor, half democratic and half authoritarian, with oases of human development surrounded by deserts of human deprivation. We pledge to take all necessary actions, nationally and globally, to reverse the present trend of widening disparities within and between nations.

WE ARE CONVINCED that it is possible to overcome the worst aspects of poverty in our lifetime through collective effort. We jointly affirm that our first step towards this goal will be to design a global compact that ensures that no child goes without an education, no human being is denied primary health care or safe drinking water and all willing couples are able to determine the size of their own families.

WE ARE CONSCIOUS of our responsibility to present generations and to future generations, and we are determined to pass on to our children a rich natural heritage and an environment sustained and whole.

WE INTEND to design a pattern of development cooperation based on open global markets, not protectionism; on an equitable sharing of market opportunities, not charity; on an open policy dialogue between sovereign nations, not coercion.

WE PLEDGE our deep commitment to a new social and economic philosophy that puts people at the centre of our concerns and creates unbreakable bonds of human solidarity.

WE STRONGLY BELIEVE that the United Nations must become the principal custodian of our global human security. Towards this end, we are determined to strengthen the development role of the United Nations and to give it wide-ranging decision-making powers in the socio-economic field by establishing an Economic Security Council.

---

later. An illustrative world social charter is given in box 1.

A 20:20 compact for human development

The world social charter would encompass a broad range of human security issues in both industrial and developing countries. Its adoption should be immediately followed by a global compact for human development—whereby all nations pledge to ensure the provision of at least the very basic human development levels for all their people. Most countries can achieve these minimum levels by adjusting their existing development priorities. Some of the poorest countries, however, will require substantial international assistance, in addition to their own domestic efforts.

What should be the global targets in such a compact? The list of international commitments from which to choose is already long, but the most important targets include the following:
• *Universal primary education*—for girls as well as for boys.
• *Adult illiteracy rates to be halved*—with the female rate to be no higher than the male one.
• *Primary health care for all*—with special stress on the immunization of children.
• *Severe malnutrition to be eliminated*—and moderate malnutrition rates to be halved.
• *Family planning services for all willing couples.*
• *Safe drinking water and sanitation for all.*
• *Credit for all*—to ensure self-employment opportunities.

These are the very minimum targets. Much more must be done, particularly to provide sustainable livelihoods. But let the international community start with some commonly agreed and doable basic goals.

A rough estimate of the additional cost of meeting these targets over the next ten years would be $30 to $40 billion a year—a substantial sum, but easily managed by restructuring the priorities in budgets.

Developing countries devote on average only 13% of their national budgets ($57 billion a year) to basic human development concerns. They have considerable scope for changing their budget priorities: by reducing their military spending (around $125 billion a year), by privatizing their loss-making public enterprises and by giving up some low-priority development projects. It is proposed that they earmark at least 20% of their budgets ($88 billion a year) to human priority concerns. The scope for restructuring will differ from one country to another: the target of 20% only suggests an average pattern.

Donor countries also have considerable scope for changing the allocation priorities in their aid budgets in the post–cold war era. On average, bilateral donors allocate only 7% of their aid to the various human priority concerns (basic education, primary health care, mass-coverage water supply systems and family planning services). The problem here is not so much the proportion of aid they give to the social sector (16% on average) as the distribution within the social sector. Less than one-fifth of education aid goes to primary education, and a similar proportion of aid for water supply and sanitation is earmarked for rural areas, with very little for low-cost mass-coverage programmes. If donors also lift their aid allocation for human priority goals to 20%, this would provide $12 billion a year rather than the current $4 billion. Again, the 20% target is an average, with some donors having greater scope for restructuring than others.

Such a 20:20 compact for human development would be based on a sharing of responsibility. Three-fourths of the contributions would come from the developing countries, and one-fourth from the donors. No new money is required, because the compact is based on restructuring existing budget priorities (see chapter 4).

The 20:20 compact could ensure that the essential human development agenda is met in all nations by the turn of this century. The compact would not only give new hope to the majority of humankind—it would also advance many other priority goals.
• It would help slow down population growth, as practical experience shows that human development is the most powerful contraceptive.

The 20:20 compact could ensure that the essential human development agenda is met in all nations

- It would contribute to sustainability, as human capital can replace some forms of natural capital and human development models are the most non-polluting development paradigms.
- It would give the developing countries a good start in the 21st century in competing in the global market-place for their share of development opportunities on the strength of their enhanced human capital.
- It would enable donors to convince their reluctant legislators and skeptical publics that the best use is being made of their aid funds.

Such a compact needs to be managed, monitored and coordinated internationally. The Social Summit should direct the United Nations system to design such a 20:20 compact and to identify institutions and procedures for its implementation.

Capturing the peace dividend

Global military spending declined between 1987 and 1994 at an estimated average annual rate of 3.6%, yielding a cumulative peace dividend of $935 billion—$810 billion in industrial countries and $125 billion in developing countries. But it is difficult to track where these funds went. And there has been no clear link between reduced military spending and enhanced expenditure on human development. Moreover, the poorest regions of the world (especially Sub-Saharan Africa) failed to contain their military spending. Meanwhile, nations continue to compete in the short-sighted business of arms exports.

What is needed now is to continue the pressure for reduced global military spending, to ensure that the poorest regions also cut down their arms spending and to develop a firm link between reduced arms spending and increased social spending.

The next challenge for disarmament is to phase the Third World out of the cold war. This will require new alliances for peace and international and regional forums for disarmament talks. It will also require a defusing of current global tensions and a new resolve on the part of the major powers to address the basic sources of conflicts in the Third World, primarily through the United Nations.

At the same time, the major suppliers of arms must adopt a new ethic of peace, since 86% of the current arms supplies originate from the five permanent members of the Security Council. They must agree to phase out their military assistance and their military bases, regulate the shipment of sophisticated arms and eliminate subsidies to their arms exporters. Foreign assistance must also give the right signals: rather than rewarding high military spenders, as at present, donor countries should reduce allocations of official development assistance (ODA) if a recipient country insists on spending more on its armies than on the social welfare of its people.

Within this perspective, the Social Summit offers an important opportunity to turn from arms to human security. A collective effort must be made at the time of the Summit to:

- Agree on a targeted reduction in military spending for the decade 1995–2005—say, 3% a year.
- Make a clear, explicit link between reduced military spending and increased social spending.
- Persuade all nations to allocate a proportion of the potential savings to a global human security fund (discussed below)—say, 20% of the peace dividend in rich nations and 10% in poor nations.
- Mandate the United Nations to maintain a list of sophisticated weapons and technologies that should not be exported at all, except under international agreement.
- Persuade the industrial nations to close their military bases, phase out their military assistance and eliminate their subsidies to arms exporters over the next three years.
- Request the United Nations to strengthen its reporting system under the UN Register of Conventional Armaments, so that up-to-date information on arms and technology transactions is published regularly.

A global human security fund

Human security is indivisible. Famine, pollution, ethnic violence—their consequences travel the globe. Yet responses are still largely national. The Social Summit should therefore consider setting up a global human security fund to finance an international response. The issues the fund could address would include drug trafficking, international terrorism, nuclear proliferation, transmittable diseases, environmental pollution, natural resource depletion, natural disasters, ethnic conflicts and refugee flows.

Separate global compacts can be negotiated in each of these areas. These compacts will deal with "global goods" and "global bads". Some good precedents are the already-concluded compacts on climate change and biodiversity and the current negotiations for a compact on desertification.

Three main sources should be tapped for such a global fund. First is the peace dividend, discussed above. A fixed proportion of the reductions in global military spending should be credited to the global human security fund—on the grounds that the basic threats to global security have not disappeared but merely taken on new forms.

The peace dividend could be substantial: an annual reduction of 3% in global military spending would yield about $460 billion from 1995 to 2000, of which around $385 billion would be in the industrial world and around $75 billion in the developing world. Not all of this would be available to a global human security fund, because already there are many claims on these savings, including the costs of conversion from military to civilian production.

But if the rich nations were to allocate only 20% of their peace dividend, as suggested, and the poor nations 10%, this would generate at least $85 billion during 1995–2000, or about $14 billion a year. These figures are purely illustrative. The important point is that the contributions should be automatic and shared globally. One form the fund could take is suggested by Nobel Peace Prize winner Oscar Arias (special contribution, p. 59).

A second logical source of funds for a global response to global threats is a set of fees on globally important transactions or

polluting emissions. This is probably some way off, but even at this stage it is worth considering some of the more promising options, two of which are discussed in chapter 4. One is a tax on the international movements of speculative capital suggested by James Tobin, winner of the Nobel Prize for Economics (special contribution, p. 70). Tobin suggests a tax rate of 0.5% on such transactions, but even a tax of 0.05% during 1995–2000 could raise $150 billion a year. Such a tax would be largely invisible and totally non-discriminatory. Another is a global tax on energy: a tax of $1 on each barrel of oil (and its equivalent on coal) during 1995–2000 would yield around $66 billion a year.

A third major source for the fund could be official development assistance. The current target for ODA allocations by industrial countries is 0.7% of each country's GNP, twice their actual contributions. The first 0.1% of GNP contributed to ODA should be earmarked for a social safety net for poor nations (chapter 4). But the balance should be linked to specific objectives—one of which should be global human security. If donors restructured existing ODA and committed some new funds, they could provide around $20 billion a year to a global human security fund.

These three sources together could raise an annual fund of around $250 billion a year during 1995–2000, seemingly ambitious, but still only around 1% of global GDP. Can humanity do less than this for its collective survival when it has been willing until recently to spend more than 4% of global GDP on the military arsenal?

Rather than the specific forms of global taxation, it is the basic notion of designing a global response and raising some global financing that the Social Summit should focus on. What is envisaged here is neither a separate fund nor a new institution. The idea is to establish a global account to pool contributions to meet the needs of global human security.

The Social Summit should approve the basic idea of a global human security fund and give the United Nations the mandate to prepare its concrete blueprint.

The Social Summit should approve the basic idea of a global human security fund

A strengthened United Nations umbrella for human development

The logical forum for the administration of this new global human security fund is the United Nations. But to cope with the increased responsibility, the UN system needs to strengthen its capabilities in the area of sustainable human development.

The development funds of the UN (UNDP, UNICEF, UNFPA, IFAD and WFP) provide substantial resources to developing countries—about $5 billion a year. The pooled resources of these UN funds are nearly as large as those of IDA (the soft-loan window of the World Bank). Moreover, these funds are providing grants, not credits, so that there is a substantial net transfer of resources to developing countries. These development funds are currently discussing how best to strengthen their overall development effort and coordinate their assistance strategies, recognizing the need for a more integrated, effective and efficient UN development system.

Three steps will be essential for the UN development funds to assume the increased responsibilities that may emerge from the Social Summit.

First, the concerned programmes of the UN need to identify common missions and complementary approaches to helping countries realize their sustainable human development goals. Major stimulus will come from the Secretary-General's *Agenda for Development* and from other efforts under way to better define a common sense of purpose and some unifying themes.

Second, much closer cooperation will be necessary in the days ahead among the leaderships of these institutions, both at the headquarters and at the country level. At the same time, a more vigorous leadership from a restructured Economic and Social Council (ECOSOC) will be vital.

Third, if additional resources are generated to support human development strategies—whether through the 20:20 compact or through a global human security fund, as discussed earlier—a strengthened UN development system will be in an excellent position to manage and monitor these additional resources and to assume the new

responsibilities for sustainable human development. The precise institutional modalities can be determined by the restructured ECOSOC. Whatever form a strengthened UN development system takes, it must draw on the relative strengths of each development fund—and their large constituencies and complementary mandates —as well as engineer some critical institutional reforms.

An Economic Security Council

To take this process of strengthening the development mandate of the UN to its logical conclusion, it would also be essential to set up an Economic Security Council. This would be a decision-making forum at the highest level to review the threats to global human security and agree on the necessary actions. In addition to the threats listed earlier, it would consider more basic issues—such as global poverty, unemployment, food security, international migration and a new framework for sustainable human development.

The proposed Economic Security Council would need to include some of the following elements:

• *A focus on sustainable human development*—rather than on political and peacekeeping matters.

• *A small and manageable membership*—say, 11 permanent members from the main industrial and more populous developing countries, and another 11 members on a rotating basis.

• *A protected voting mechanism*—such as a requirement that, beyond an overall majority, all decisions should also be ratified by majorities of both the industrial and the developing countries.

• *A professional secretariat*—small and highly qualified, led by an outstanding person, to prepare policy options for the council's consideration.

• *Expert national delegates*—the regular meetings would involve nationals with economic and financial expertise, but there would also be occasional high-level meetings of ministers of finance and planning, as well as annual sessions at the level of head of state or government.

- *Supervision of global institutions*—the council would act as a watchdog over the policy direction of all international and regional institutions.

The Economic Security Council would thus consist of about 22 members meeting year-round. It would also refer some subjects to smaller negotiating groups.

Establishing an Economic Security Council will be difficult since it would require a change in the UN Charter. So, it would perhaps be more realistic to try for something less ambitious and more manageable administratively.

One possibility is to extend the mandate of the present Security Council so that it could consider not just military threats but also threats to peace from economic and social crises. This would be in line with current attempts to involve the UN not just in peacekeeping but also—as suggested in the *Agenda for Peace*—in actively preventing conflicts.

Another possibility is to use the ECOSOC. Currently rather unwieldy, with 54 members, it could delegate decision-making power to a smaller executive board—with, say, 15 members—that could meet in permanent session. Ministers of finance and planning could be involved for the most important development issues, and decisions could subsequently be ratified by the entire Council and by the General Assembly. Article 65 of the UN Charter contains a provision for the ECOSOC to assume such a mandate at the request of the Security Council.

These are intermediate steps, however, and the fact remains that a full-fledged Economic Security Council would be preferable to less ambitious alternatives. The council's creation need not be such a daunting prospect if the world community agrees on the urgency of the task—and on the need for a much broader international effort. The Social Summit offers an opportunity to agree on the framework for this bold initiative.

The specific proposals for the consideration of the Social Summit are summarized in box 2 for ready reference by policy-makers. These proposals may at first sight seem to demand a great deal from the international community. But they probably are more realistic than they appear.

Let us keep reminding ourselves that the imperatives of human security are bringing people together in all parts of the world. Let us also remember that many heresies of yesterday have become the conventional wisdom of today.

CHAPTER 1

Towards sustainable human development

Human beings are born with certain potential capabilities. The purpose of development is to create an environment in which all people can expand their capabilities, and opportunities can be enlarged for both present and future generations. The real foundation of human development is universalism in acknowledging the life claims of everyone.

Universalism of life claims

The paradigm of sustainable human development values human life for itself. It does not value life merely because people can produce material goods—important though that might be. Nor does it value one person's life more than another's. No newborn child should be doomed to a short life or a miserable one merely because that child happens to be born in the "wrong class" or in the "wrong country" or to be of the "wrong sex".

Development must enable all individuals to enlarge their human capabilities to the fullest and to put those capabilities to the best use in all fields—economic, social, cultural and political.

Universalism of life claims is the common thread that binds the demands of human development today with the exigencies of development tomorrow, especially with the need for environmental preservation and regeneration for the future. The strongest argument for protecting the environment is the ethical need to guarantee to future generations opportunities similar to the ones previous generations have enjoyed. This guarantee is the foundation of "sustainable development".

But sustainability makes little sense if it means sustaining life opportunities that are miserable and indigent: the goal cannot be to sustain human deprivation. Nor should we deny the less privileged today the attention that we are willing to bestow on future generations.

Human development and sustainability are thus essential components of the same ethic of universalism of life claims. There is no tension between the two concepts, for they are a part of the same overall design. In such a conceptual framework, sustainability is, in a very broad sense, a matter of distributional equity—of sharing development opportunities between present and future generations. There would, however, be something distinctly odd if we were deeply concerned for the well-being of future—as yet unborn—generations while ignoring the plight of the poor today. The ethic of universalism clearly demands both intragenerational equity and intergenerational equity.

This equity is, however, in *opportunities*—not necessarily in final achievements. Each individual is entitled to a just opportunity to make the best use of his or her potential capabilities. So is each generation. How they actually use these opportunities, and the results they achieve, are a matter of their own choice. But they must have such a choice—now and in the future.

This universalism of life claims—a powerful idea that provides the philosophical foundations for many contemporary policies—underlies the search for meeting basic human needs. It demands a world where no child goes without an education, where no human being is denied health care and where all people can develop their potential capabilities. Universalism implies the empowerment of people. It protects all basic human rights—economic and social as well as civil and political—and it holds

The real foundation of human development is universalism of life claims

that the right to food is as sacrosanct as the right to vote. It demands non-discrimination between all people, irrespective of gender, religion, race or ethnic origin. And it focuses directly on human beings—respecting national sovereignty but only as long as nation-states respect the human rights of their own people.

Universalism advocates equality of opportunity, not equality of income—though in a civilized society a basic minimum income should be guaranteed to everyone.

The basic thought of universalism of life claims comes from many pioneers. "It is justice, not charity, that is wanting in the world," wrote Mary Wollstonecraft, the pioneering feminist, in *A Vindication of the Rights of Woman,* published in 1792. In the same year, her friend Thomas Paine published the second part of the *Rights of Man.* Both were concerned with giving everyone—women and men—power over their lives and opportunities to live according to their own values and aspirations.

Historical perspective

Interest in the concept of human development is not new. Nor are the concerns of sustainability. Today's belated return to human development means reclaiming an old and established heritage rather than importing or implanting a new diversion.

The roots of the concept of human development can often be traced to early periods in human history and can be found in many cultures and religions. Aristotle wrote that "wealth is evidently not the good we are seeking, for it is merely useful and for the sake of something else". A similar strain was reflected in the writings of the early founders of quantitative economics (William Petty, Gregory King, François Quesnay, Antoine Lavoisier and Joseph Lagrange) and in the works of the pioneers of political economy (Adam Smith, Robert Malthus, Karl Marx and John Stuart Mill). When Adam Smith, that apostle of free enterprise and private initiative, showed his concern that economic development should enable a person to mix freely with others without being "ashamed to appear in publick", he

was expressing a concept of poverty that went beyond counting calories—a concept that integrated the poor into the mainstream of the community.

Throughout this early period, the concept of development treated income and its growth as a means, and directed attention towards a real concern for people—in their individuality and collectivity, in their commonality and diversity. The central concern of development became the quality of people's lives—what they were capable of doing and what they actually did, the discriminations they faced, the struggles they waged and the expanding choices they enjoyed. And this covered not just economic choices but choices in every field in which they could extend control over their lives. The pursuit of material well-being was one of these choices—but it had not yet become the exclusive obsession.

Only during the 20th century did the social sciences become increasingly concerned with economics—and economics with wealth rather than with people, with the economy rather than with the society, with the maximization of income rather than with the expansion of opportunities for people. Although the obsession with materialism may be recent, the preoccupation of economists and policy-makers with augmenting "national treasure", in surplus trade balances, dates back at least to the mercantilists, who preferred to concentrate on material success rather than on the development of human lives.

The dominant contemporary tradition of focusing exclusively on such variables as per capita gross national product or national wealth is a continuation—certainly an intensification—of the old opulence-oriented approach. And it is this low road of regarding humanity as an instrument of production—rather than the high road of acknowledging the universality of life claims—that fits well with the reputation of economics as a "dismal science".

Opulence and human development

Why should there be a tension between wealth maximization and human development? Is not the former indispensable for the latter?

Wealth is important for human life. But to concentrate on it exclusively is wrong for two reasons.

First, accumulating wealth is not necessary for the fulfilment of some important human choices. In fact, individuals and societies make many choices that require no wealth at all. A society does not have to be rich to be able to afford democracy. A family does not have to be wealthy to respect the rights of each member. A nation does not have to be affluent to treat women and men equally. Valuable social and cultural traditions can be—and are—maintained at all levels of income. The richness of a culture can be largely independent of the people's wealth.

Second, human choices extend far beyond economic well-being. Human beings may want to be wealthy. But they may also want to enjoy long and healthy lives, drink deep at the fountain of knowledge, participate freely in the life of their community, breathe fresh air and enjoy the simple pleasures of life in a clean physical environment and value the peace of mind that comes from security in their homes, in their jobs and in their society.

National wealth might expand people's choices. But it might not. The use that nations make of their wealth, not the wealth itself, is decisive. And unless societies recognize that their real wealth is their people, an excessive obsession with the creation of material wealth can obscure the ultimate objective of enriching human lives.

This tension between wealth maximization and human development is not merely academic—it is real. Although there is a definite correlation between material wealth and human well-being, it breaks down in far too many societies. Many countries have a high GNP per capita, but low human development indicators—and vice versa. Countries at similar levels of GNP per capita may have vastly different human development indicators, depending on the use they have made of their national wealth (table 1.1 and figure 1.1). The maximization of wealth and the enrichment of human

lives need not move in the same direction.

Some take the view that opulence should not be valued as an end in itself, but that it still is the most important means for promoting the more basic objectives—even the Aristotelian one of ensuring "flourishing lives". To take a prominent example, W. Arthur Lewis—one of the leading modern development economists and a Nobel Prize winner in economics—had little doubt that the appropriate objective is increasing "the range of human choice". He also acknowledged the causal role of many factors in advancing the freedom to choose. But he decided to concentrate specifically on "the growth of output per head", because it "gives man greater control over his environment, and thereby increases his freedom". Indeed, the focus of his classic book was sufficiently precise to permit him to assert: "Our subject matter is growth, and not distribution." Yet without appropriate distribution and public policy, economic growth may fail to translate into improvements in human lives.

Recent studies confirm that even when intercountry data show a generally positive and statistically significant relationship between GNP per head and indicators of quality of life, much of that relationship depends on the use of extra income for improving public education and health and for reducing absolute poverty.

Accumulating wealth is not necessary for the fulfilment of some important human choices

Country	GNP per capita (US$)	HDI value	HDI rank	Life expectancy (years)	Adult literacy (%)	Infant mortality (per 1,000 live births)
TABLE 1.1 **Similar income, different HDI, 1991/92**						
GNP per capita around $400 to $500						
Sri Lanka	500	0.665	90	71.2	89	24
Nicaragua	400	0.583	106	65.4	78	53
Pakistan	400	0.393	132	58.3	36	99
Guinea	500	0.191	173	43.9	27	135
GNP per capita around $1,000 to $1,100						
Ecuador	1,010	0.718	74	66.2	87	58
Jordan	1,060	0.628	98	67.3	82	37
El Salvador	1,090	0.543	112	65.2	75	46
Congo	1,040	0.461	123	51.7	59	83
GNP per capita around $2,300 to $2,600						
Chile	2,360	0.848	38	71.9	94	17
Malaysia	2,520	0.794	57	70.4	80	14
South Africa	2,540	0.650	93	62.2	80	53
Iraq	2,550	0.614	100	65.7	63	59

FIGURE 1.1
Similar incomes—different human development

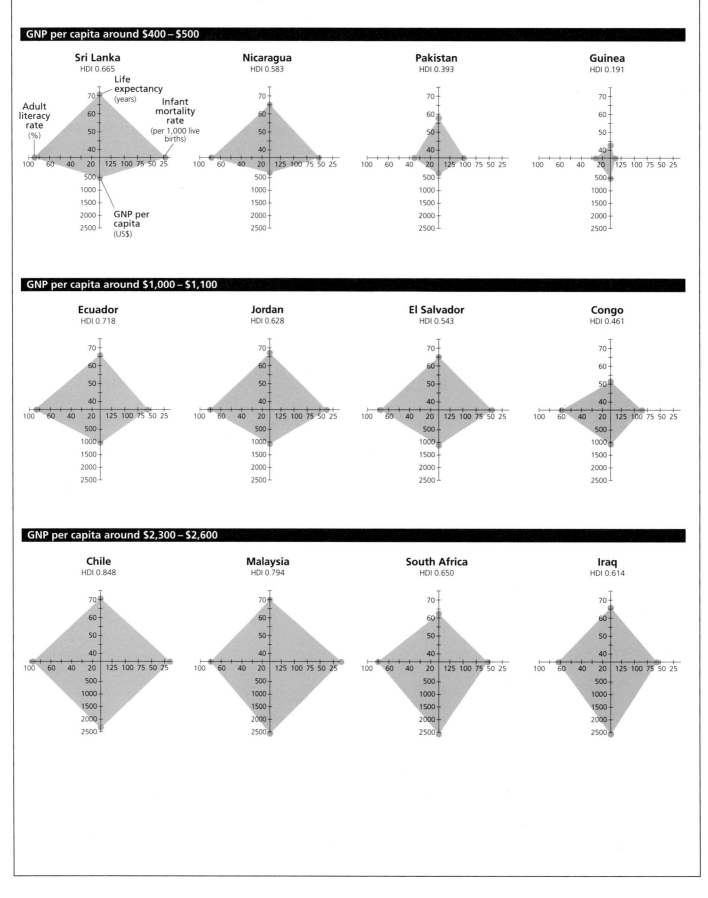

GNP per capita around $400 – $500

Sri Lanka — HDI 0.665
Nicaragua — HDI 0.583
Pakistan — HDI 0.393
Guinea — HDI 0.191

GNP per capita around $1,000 – $1,100

Ecuador — HDI 0.718
Jordan — HDI 0.628
El Salvador — HDI 0.543
Congo — HDI 0.461

GNP per capita around $2,300 – $2,600

Chile — HDI 0.848
Malaysia — HDI 0.794
South Africa — HDI 0.650
Iraq — HDI 0.614

True, countries with higher average incomes tend to have higher average life expectancies, lower rates of infant and child mortality and higher literacy rates—indeed, a higher human development index (HDI). But these associations are far from perfect. In intercountry comparisons, income variations tend to explain not much more than half the variation in life expectancy, or in infant and child mortality. And they explain an even smaller part of the differences in adult literacy rates.

More important is the way the growth of GNP influences human development. There is considerable evidence that the statistical correlation between GNP per head and human development tends to work through the effect of higher GNP in raising public expenditure and in lowering poverty.

This impact should not be interpreted to mean that economic growth does not matter in improving the quality of life. Instead, it indicates that the connections are seriously contingent. Much depends on how the fruits of economic growth are shared—particularly on what the poor get—and how much the additional resources are used to support public services—particularly primary health care and basic education.

In simple terms, it is not the level of income alone that matters—it is also the use that is made of this income. A society can spend its income on arms or on education. An individual can spend his or her income on narcotic drugs or on essential food. What is decisive is not the process of wealth maximization but the choices that individuals and societies make—a simple truth often forgotten.

There is thus no basic conflict between (1) regarding economic growth as very important and (2) regarding it as an insufficient basis for human development. Growth in income will enhance the living conditions of the poor only if they get a share of the additional income, or if it is used to finance public services for sections of society that would otherwise be deprived of them. Again, the central issue turns out to be the need for valuing the enhancement of human capabilities—rather than promoting aggregate growth while overlooking what is needed to make the fruits of growth serve the interests of the least privileged.

Confusion between ends and means

It is often argued (rightly) that investing in people increases their productivity. It is then argued (wrongly) that human development simply means human *resource* development—increasing human capital.

This formulation confuses ends and means. People are not merely instruments for producing commodities. And the purpose of development is not merely to produce more value added irrespective of its use. What must be avoided at all cost is seeing human beings as merely the means of production and material prosperity, regarding the latter to be the end of the causal analysis—a strange inversion of ends and means.

Bestowing value on a human life only to the extent that it produces profits—the "human capital" approach—has obvious dangers. In its extreme form, it can easily lead to slave labour camps, forced child labour and the exploitation of workers by management—as during the industrial revolution.

Human development rejects this exclusive concentration on people as human capital. It accepts the central role of human capital in enhancing human productivity. But it is just as concerned with creating the economic and political environment in which people can expand their human capabilities and use them appropriately. It is also concerned with human choices that go far beyond economic well-being.

Improving human capital does, of course, enhance production and material prosperity—as it has in Japan and East Asia. But it is well to remember Immanuel Kant's injunction "to treat humanity as an end withal, never as means only". The quality of human life is an end.

Sustainable development and economic growth

Sustainable human development means that we have a moral obligation to do at

It is not the level of income alone that matters—it is also the use that is made of this income

least as well for our successor generations as our predecessors did for us.

It means that current consumption cannot be financed for long by incurring economic debts that others must repay. It also means that sufficient investment must be made in the education and health of today's population so as not to create a social debt for future generations. And it means that resources must be used in ways that do not create ecological debts by overexploiting the carrying and productive capacity of the earth.

All postponed debts mortgage sustainability—whether economic debts, social debts or ecological debts. These debts borrow from the future. They rob coming generations of their legitimate options. That is why the strategy for sustainable human development is to replenish all capital—physical, human and natural—so that it maintains the capacity of the future generations to meet their needs at least at the same level as that of the present generations.

But there need not be any tension between economic growth and environmental protection and regeneration. Economic growth, because it provides more options, is vital for poor societies, since much of their environmental degradation arises out of poverty and limited human choices. But the character of their growth and consumption is important.

Poor nations cannot—and should not—imitate the production and consumption patterns of rich nations. That may not, in any case, be entirely possible, despite advances in technology, or entirely desirable. Replicating the patterns of the North in the South would require ten times the present amount of fossil fuels and roughly 200 times as much mineral wealth. And in another 40 years, these requirements would double again as the world population doubles.

The life styles of the rich nations will clearly have to change. The North has roughly one-fifth of the world's population and four-fifths of its income, and it consumes 70% of the world's energy, 75% of its metals and 85% of its wood. If the ecosphere were fully priced, not free, such consumption patterns could not continue.

Sustainable human development is concerned with models of material production and consumption that are replicable and desirable. These models do not regard natural resources as a free good, to be plundered at the free will of any nation, any generation or any individual. They put a price on these resources, reflecting their relative scarcity today and tomorrow. They thus treat exhaustible environmental resources as any other scarce asset and are concerned with policies of sensible asset management.

One important area of asset management is non-renewable energy. There is tremendous scope for reducing energy input per unit of output. For example, the energy consumed for every $100 of GDP is 13 kilogrammes of oil equivalent in Japan, 18 in Germany, 35 in the United States, 50 in Canada and 254 in Romania. Energy use is even more inefficient in developing countries: as high as 187 kilogrammes of oil equivalent for every $100 of GDP in China, 154 in Algeria, 132 in India, 105 in Egypt, 94 in Zimbabwe and 93 in Venezuela. Proper pricing of non-renewable energy can lead to the adoption of new technologies and new patterns of production that can greatly help in reducing energy input per unit of output and in curtailing the environmentally damaging emissions from each unit of energy used.

Sustainability and equity

Obviously, we need to sustain for the next generation the opportunity to enjoy the same kind of well-being that we possess. But we do not know what the next generation's consumption preferences will be. Nor can we anticipate future increases in population that may require more capital to sustain the same opportunities per head. It also is difficult to predict the technological breakthroughs that may reduce the capital that would be required to achieve the same level of well-being. Faced with such uncertainties, the best the present generations can do is to replace the broad stock of capital they consume.

Not every specific resource or form of capital needs to be preserved. If more efficient substitutes are available, they must be used. What must be preserved is the overall capacity to produce a similar level of well-being—perhaps even with an entirely different stock of capital. This difficult issue requires much further research. But one thing is clear: preserving productive capacity intact does not mean leaving the world in every detail as we found it. What needs to be conserved are the opportunities for future generations to lead worthwhile lives.

Attending to the future draws immediate attention to the present. We cannot argue in good conscience that developing countries should be sustained at their current level of poverty, that the present production and consumption patterns of the rich nations are preordained and cannot and must not be changed.

The concept of sustainable development raises the issue of whether present life styles are acceptable and whether there is any reason to pass them on to the next generation. Because intergenerational equity must go hand in hand with intragenerational equity, a major restructuring of the world's income and consumption patterns may be a necessary precondition for any viable strategy of sustainable development.

There is no reason to accept the present way in which rich and poor nations share the common heritage of humankind. Because the environment has been treated as a free resource, the rich nations have taken advantage of this to emit most of the world's pollution. If the environment were correctly priced and tradable permits were issued to all nations (50% on the basis of GDP and 50% on the basis of population), the rich nations might have to transfer as much as 5% of their combined GDP to the poor nations (chapter 4). The global balance of environmental use—and the distribution of present consumption patterns—would begin to shift in a more desirable direction.

The close link between global poverty and global sustainability will also have to be analysed carefully if the concept of sustainable development is to have any real meaning. The very poor, struggling for their daily survival, often lack the resources to avoid degrading their environment. In poor societies, what is at risk is not the quality of life—but life itself.

The poor are not preoccupied with the loud emergencies of global warming or the depletion of the ozone layer. They are preoccupied with the silent emergencies—polluted water or degraded land—that put their lives and their livelihoods at risk. Unless the problems of poverty are addressed, environmental sustainability cannot be guaranteed.

Redistributing resources to the poor by improving their health, education and nutrition is not only intrinsically important because it enhances their capabilities to lead more fulfilling lives. By increasing their human capital, it also has a lasting influence on the future. A general increase in educational levels, for example, will enhance productivity and the ability to generate higher incomes—now and in the future.

Because the accumulation of human capital can replace some forms of exhaustible resources, human development should be seen as a major contribution to sustainability. As argued earlier, there is no tension between human development and sustainable development. Both are based on the universalism of life claims. Development patterns that perpetuate today's inequities are neither sustainable nor worth sustaining. That is why sustainable human development is a more inclusive concept than sustainable development.

Sustainable development may sometimes be interpreted carelessly to mean that the present level and pattern of development should be sustained for future generations as well. This is clearly wrong.

Sustainable human development, by contrast, puts people at the centre of development and points out forcefully that the inequities of today are so great that to sustain the present form of development is to perpetuate similar inequities for future generations. The essence of sustainable human development is that everyone should have equal access to development opportunities—now and in the future.

Individuals and institutions

Universalist concern with the rights and interests of all human beings can be effective only through a combination of individual

Development patterns that perpetuate today's inequities are neither sustainable nor worth sustaining

Poverty reduction

Poverty is the greatest threat to political stability, social cohesion and the environmental health of the planet. Strategies for poverty reduction will certainly embrace all aspects of national policy. Some key lessons of country experience:

• *Basic social services*—The state must help ensure a widespread distribution of basic social services to the poor, particularly basic education and primary health care.

• *Agrarian reform*—Since a large part of poverty in developing countries is concentrated in the rural areas, poverty reduction strategies often require a more equitable distribution of land and agricultural resources.

• *Credit for all*—One of the most powerful ways of opening markets to the poor is to ensure more equal access to credit. The criteria of creditworthiness must change, and credit institutions must be decentralized.

• *Employment*—The best way to extend the benefits of growth to the poor and to involve them in the expansion of output is to rapidly expand productive employment opportunities and to create a framework for ensuring a sustainable livelihood for everyone.

• *Participation*—Any viable strategy for poverty reduction must be decentralized and participatory. The poor cannot benefit from economic development if they do not even participate in its design.

• *A social safety net*—Every country needs an adequate social safety net to catch those whom markets exclude.

• *Economic growth*—The focus of development efforts, in addition to increasing overall productivity, must be to increase the productivity of the poor. This will help ensure that the poor not only benefit from, but also contribute to, economic growth.

• *Sustainability*—Poverty reduces people's capacity to use resources in a sustainable manner, intensifying pressures on the ecosystem. To ensure sustainability, the content of growth must change—becoming less material-intensive and energy-intensive and more equitable in its distribution.

Employment creation

Creating sufficient opportunities for productive employment and sustainable livelihoods is one of the most important—and most difficult—tasks in any society. Based on experience, the central elements of an effective national employment strategy are likely to include:

• *Education and skills*—To compete in a fast-changing global economy, every country has to invest heavily in the education, training and skill formation of its people.

• *An enabling environment*—Most new employment opportunities are likely to be generated by the private sector. But markets cannot work effectively unless governments create an enabling environment—including fair and stable macroeconomic policies, an equitable legal framework, sufficient physical infrastructure and an adequate system of incentives for private investment.

• *Access to assets*—A more equitable distribution of physical assets (land) and better access to means of production (credit and information) are often essential to ensure sustainable livelihoods.

• *Labour-intensive technologies*—Developing countries have to be able to make the most efficient use of their factors of production—and to exploit their comparative advantage of abundant labour. Tax and price policies should, where appropriate, try to encourage labour-intensive employment.

• *Public works programmes*—Where private markets consistently fail to produce sufficient jobs, in certain regions or at certain times of the year, it may be necessary for the state to offer employment through public works programmes to enable people to survive.

• *Disadvantaged groups*—Where markets tend to discriminate against particular groups, such as women or certain ethnic groups, the state may need to consider targeted interventions or programmes of affirmative action.

• *Job-sharing*—With the growing phenomenon of "jobless growth", it has become necessary to rethink the concept of work and to consider more innovative and flexible working arrangements—including job-sharing.

effort and institutional support. Individual initiative needs to be combined both with judicious public policy and with participatory community organizations.

The capabilities that individuals attain depend on many circumstances over which they may not have much control. For example, a child who is not sent to school, is not taught any skills or is not given much support might still do well in life—given unusual initiative, ability or luck. But the cards are stacked very firmly against that child.

If a girl faces discrimination early in life—because she is fed less than her brothers, is sent to school later or not at all or is subjected to physical abuse—the scars she suffers may last all her life and may even be passed on to her offspring. Similarly, the life claims of a black child in the slums of the United States or South Africa are unlikely to be fully honoured.

This is where public policy and community organizations are important. Social policies can make a critical difference in what people can achieve—by preventing discrimination, by enhancing education and skill formation, by expanding employment opportunities and by safeguarding the rewards of individual initiative and enterprise. But states can also seriously limit the choices that the majority of its citizens might otherwise enjoy—by spending more on soldiers than on teachers, more on costly urban hospitals than on primary health care or more on entrenched elitist groups than on the marginalized poor.

This complementarity between individual action and public policy—important for the present generations—is even more important for future generations and for the sustainability of human development. Whether the concern is with restricting pollution, limiting the emissions of greenhouse gases, preventing the destruction of forests and natural habitats or averting premature depletion of exhaustible resources, today's institutions have to persuade today's generations to take adequate note of the interests and rights of the generations yet to come. They can also offer people direct incentives—to encourage people to economize on consumption patterns harmful to future generations—through ownership rights, for example, or through taxes and subsidies.

In a paradigm of sustainable human development, individuals and institutions must become allies in the common cause of enhancing life opportunities—for present and future generations. For this to happen, the foundations of a civil society must be firmly established, with the government fully accountable to the people. The tension between markets and governance—between individual initiative and public policy—must cease if the aim is to widen the range of human choices, for now and for the future.

Policy strategies

Sustainability needs to be ensured in all sectors of the economy and at all levels of developmental action. It would require far-reaching changes in both national and global policies.

At the national level, new balances must be struck between the efficiency of competitive markets, the legal and regulatory frameworks that only governments can provide, the investments to enhance the capabilities of all and the provision of social safety nets for those with unequal access to the markets. Balances between the compulsions of today and the needs of tomorrow, between private initiative and public action, between individual greed and social compassion are sorely needed for this purpose.

The essence and test of sustainable human development strategies must be to ensure a sustainable livelihood for all. These strategies—especially at the national level—will thus have to focus on three core themes: poverty reduction, employment creation and social integration—in short, participation (boxes 1.1, 1.2 and 1.3).

At the global level, sustainable human development requires no less than a new global ethic. Universalism in the recognition of life claims and concern for common survival must lead to policies for a more equitable world order, based on fundamental

global reforms, some of which will be discussed in chapter 4. The concept of sustainability is greatly endangered in a world that is one-fourth rich and three-fourths poor, that is half democratic and half authoritarian, where poor nations are being denied equal access to global economic opportunities, where the income disparity between the richest 20% and the poorest 20% of the world's population has doubled over the past three decades, where one-fourth of humanity is unable to meet its basic human needs and where the rich nations are consuming four-fifths of humanity's natural capital without being obliged to pay for it. The concept of one world and one planet simply cannot emerge from an unequal world. Nor can shared responsibility for the health of the global commons be created without some measure of shared global prosperity. Global sustainability without global justice will always remain an elusive goal.

If this challenge is not met—and met decisively—human security will be at risk all over the world, an issue taken up in chapter 2.

Individuals and institutions must become allies in the common cause of enhancing life opportunities—for present and future generations

---

BOX 1.3

Social integration

One of the main concerns of many countries in the years ahead must be to avoid violent social dislocations—particularly conflicts between ethnic groups. To achieve this, they will have to take decisive measures to promote more equal opportunities for all. Such measures include the following:

• *Equality before the law*—The first essential step towards an integrated society is to ensure that each person enjoys the same basic legal rights.

• *Minority rights*—To protect diversity, the state must ensure that minorities are accorded specific rights by law, including to maintain their culture, and that these rights are respected in practice.

Antidiscrimination policies—Governments need to take firm measures to counter discrimination and to apply stiff

penalties for infringement.

• *Education*—One of the best ways to encourage social integration is to ensure that all sections of society have access to basic educational opportunities that respect diverse cultures and traditions.

• *Employment*—To ensure that employment opportunities are available on a non-discriminatory basis, the state may have to exercise positive discrimination through affirmative action in favour of the most disadvantaged and marginalized groups, including women.

• *Governance*—Social integration can be greatly enhanced by bringing government closer to the people, through devolution, decentralization and accountability, by promoting grass-roots organizations and by creating avenues for direct participation.

CHAPTER 2

New dimensions of human security

We need another profound transition in thinking—from nuclear security to human security

Fifty years ago, Albert Einstein summed up the discovery of atomic energy with characteristic simplicity: "Everything changed." He went on to predict: "We shall require a substantially new manner of thinking if mankind is to survive." Although nuclear explosions devastated Nagasaki and Hiroshima, humankind has survived its first critical test of preventing worldwide nuclear devastation. But five decades later, we need another profound transition in thinking—from nuclear security to human security.

The concept of security has for too long been interpreted narrowly: as security of territory from external aggression, or as protection of national interests in foreign policy or as global security from the threat of a nuclear holocaust. It has been related more to nation-states than to people. The superpowers were locked in an ideological struggle—fighting a cold war all over the world. The developing nations, having won their independence only recently, were sensitive to any real or perceived threats to their fragile national identities. Forgotten were the legitimate concerns of ordinary people who sought security in their daily lives. For many of them, security symbolized protection from the threat of disease, hunger, unemployment, crime, social conflict, political repression and environmental hazards. With the dark shadows of the cold war receding, one can now see that many conflicts are within nations rather than between nations.

For most people, a feeling of insecurity arises more from worries about daily life than from the dread of a cataclysmic world event. Will they and their families have enough to eat? Will they lose their jobs? Will their streets and neighbourhoods be safe from crime? Will they be tortured by a re-pressive state? Will they become a victim of violence because of their gender? Will their religion or ethnic origin target them for persecution (box 2.1)?

In the final analysis, human security is a child who did not die, a disease that did not spread, a job that was not cut, an ethnic tension that did not explode in violence, a dissident who was not silenced. Human security is not a concern with weapons—it is a concern with human life and dignity.

The idea of human security, though simple, is likely to revolutionize society in the 21st century. A consideration of the basic concept of human security must focus on four of its essential characteristics:

• Human security is a *universal* concern. It is relevant to people everywhere, in rich nations and poor. There are many threats that are common to all people—such as unemployment, drugs, crime, pollution and human rights violations. Their intensity may differ from one part of the world to another, but all these threats to human security are real and growing.

• The components of human security are *interdependent*. When the security of people is endangered anywhere in the world, all nations are likely to get involved. Famine, disease, pollution, drug trafficking, terrorism, ethnic disputes and social disintegration are no longer isolated events, confined within national borders. Their consequences travel the globe.

• Human security is *easier to ensure through early prevention* than later intervention. It is less costly to meet these threats upstream than downstream. For example, the direct and indirect cost of HIV/AIDS (human immunodeficiency virus/acquired immune deficiency syndrome) was roughly $240 billion during the 1980s. Even a few billion dollars invested in primary health care and family planning education could have helped contain the spread of this deadly disease.

• Human security is *people-centred.* It is concerned with how people live and breathe in a society, how freely they exercise their many choices, how much access they have to market and social opportunities—and whether they live in conflict or in peace.

Several analysts have attempted rigorous definitions of human security. But like other fundamental concepts, such as human freedom, human security is more easily identified through its absence than its presence. And most people instinctively understand what security means.

Nevertheless, it may be useful to have a more explicit definition. Human security can be said to have two main aspects. It means, first, safety from such chronic threats as hunger, disease and repression. And second, it means protection from sudden and hurtful disruptions in the patterns of daily life—whether in homes, in jobs or in communities. Such threats can exist at all levels of national income and development.

The loss of human security can be a slow, silent process—or an abrupt, loud emergency. It can be human-made—due to wrong policy choices. It can stem from the forces of nature. Or it can be a combination of both—as is often the case when environmental degradation leads to a natural disaster, followed by human tragedy.

In defining security, it is important that human security not be equated with human development. Human development is a broader concept—defined in previous *Human Development Reports* as a process of widening the range of people's choices. Human security means that people can exercise these choices safely and freely—and that they can be relatively confident that the opportunities they have today are not totally lost tomorrow.

There is, of course, a link between human security and human development: progress in one area enhances the chances of progress in the other. But failure in one area also heightens the risk of failure in the other, and history is replete with examples.

Failed or limited human development leads to a backlog of human deprivation—poverty, hunger, disease or persisting disparities between ethnic communities or between regions. This backlog in access to power and economic opportunities can lead to violence.

When people perceive threats to their immediate security, they often become less tolerant, as the antiforeigner feelings and violence in Europe show. Or, where people see the basis of their livelihood erode—such as their access to water—political conflict can ensue, as in parts of Central Asia and the Arab States. Oppression and perceptions of injustice can also lead to violent protest against authoritarianism, as in Myanmar and Zaire, where people despair of gradual change.

BOX 2.1

Human security—as people see it

How individuals regard security depends very much on their immediate circumstances. Here are some views of security gathered from around the world, through a special sample survey by UNDP field offices.

Primary school pupil in Kuwait
"I feel secure because I am living with my family and I have friends. However, I did not feel secure during the Iraqi invasion. If a country is at war, how are people supposed to feel secure?"

Woman in Nigeria
"My security is only in the name of the Lord who has made heaven and earth. I feel secure because I am at liberty to worship whom I like, how I like, and also because I can pray for all the people and for peace all over the country."

Fourth-grade schoolgirl in Ghana
"I shall feel secure when I know that I can walk the streets at night without being raped."

Shoe-mender in Thailand
"When we have enough for the children to eat, we are happy and we feel secure."

Man in Namibia
"Robberies make me feel insecure. I sometimes feel as though even my life will be stolen."

Woman in Iran
"I believe that a girl cannot feel secure until she is married and has someone to depend on."

Public administrator in Cameroon
"Security for me means that my job and position are safe and I can continue to provide for the needs of my family and also have something for investment and friends."

Woman in Kyrgyzstan
"Human security indicates faith in tomorrow, not as much having to do with food and clothing, as with stability of the political and economic situation."

Secondary school pupil in Mongolia
"Before, education in this country was totally free, but from this year every student has to pay. Now I do not feel very secure about finishing my studies."

Woman in Paraguay
"I feel secure because I feel fulfilled and have confidence in myself. I also feel secure because God is great and watches over me."

Man in Ecuador
"What makes you feel insecure above all is violence and delinquency—as well as insecurity with respect to the police. Basic services are also an important part of security."

Ensuring human security does not mean taking away from people the responsibility and opportunity for mastering their lives. To the contrary, when people are insecure, they become a burden on society.

The concept of human security stresses that people should be able to take care of themselves: all people should have the opportunity to meet their most essential needs and to earn their own living. This will set them free and help ensure that they can make a full contribution to development—their own development and that of their communities, their countries and the world. Human security is a critical ingredient of participatory development.

Human security is therefore not a defensive concept—the way territorial or military security is. Instead, human security is an integrative concept. It acknowledges the universalism of life claims that was discussed in chapter 1. It is embedded in a notion of solidarity among people. It cannot be brought about through force, with armies standing against armies. It can happen only if we agree that development must involve all people.

Human security thus has many components. To clarify them, it helps to examine them in detail.

Components of human security

There have always been two major components of human security: freedom from fear and freedom from want. This was recognized right from the beginning of the United Nations. But later the concept was tilted in favour of the first component rather than the second.

The founders of the United Nations, when considering security, always gave equal weight to territories and to people. In 1945, the US secretary of state reported to his government on the results of the conference in San Francisco that set up the United Nations. He was quite specific on this point:

The battle of peace has to be fought on two fronts. The first is the security front where victory spells freedom from fear. The second is the economic and social front where victory means *freedom from want. Only victory on both fronts can assure the world of an enduring peace.... No provisions that can be written into the Charter will enable the Security Council to make the world secure from war if men and women have no security in their homes and their jobs.*

It is now time to make a transition from the narrow concept of national security to the all-encompassing concept of human security.

People in rich nations seek security from the threat of crime and drug wars in their streets, the spread of deadly diseases like HIV/AIDS, soil degradation, rising levels of pollution, the fear of losing their jobs and many other anxieties that emerge as the social fabric disintegrates. People in poor nations demand liberation from the continuing threat of hunger, disease and poverty while also facing the same problems that threaten industrial countries.

At the global level, human security no longer means carefully constructed safeguards against the threat of a nuclear holocaust—a likelihood greatly reduced by the end of the cold war. Instead, it means responding to the threat of global poverty travelling across international borders in the form of drugs, HIV/AIDS, climate change, illegal migration and terrorism. The prospect of collective suicide through an impulsive resort to nuclear weapons was always exaggerated. But the threat of global poverty affecting all human lives—in rich nations and in poor—is real and persistent. And there are no global safeguards against these real threats to human security.

The concept of security must thus change urgently in two basic ways:
• From an exclusive stress on territorial security to a much greater stress on people's security.
• From security through armaments to security through sustainable human development.

The list of threats to human security is long, but most can be considered under seven main categories:
• Economic security
• Food security
• Health security

- Environmental security
- Personal security
- Community security
- Political security.

Economic security

Economic security requires an assured basic income—usually from productive and remunerative work, or in the last resort from some publicly financed safety net. But only about a quarter of the world's people may at present be economically secure in this sense.

Many people in the rich nations today feel insecure because jobs are increasingly difficult to find and keep. In the past two decades, the number of jobs in industrial countries has increased at only half the rate of GDP growth and failed to keep pace with the growth in the labour force. By 1993, more than 35 million people were seeking work, and a high proportion were women.

Young people are more likely to be unemployed: in the United States in 1992, youth unemployment reached 14%, in the United Kingdom 15%, in Italy 33% and in Spain 34%. Often, the unemployment rate also varies with ethnic origin. In Canada, the unemployment rate among indigenous people is about 20%—twice that for other Canadians. And in the United States, the unemployment rate for blacks is twice that for whites.

Even those with jobs may feel insecure if the work is only temporary. In 1991 in Finland, 13% of the employed were temporary workers, and the figures were even higher elsewhere—15% in Greece, 17% in Portugal, 20% in Australia and 32% in Spain. Some people do, of course, choose to work on a temporary basis. But in Spain, Portugal, Greece, Belgium and the Netherlands, more than 60% of workers in temporary jobs accepted them because they could not find full-time employment. To have work for everybody, industrial countries are experimenting with job-sharing.

The problems are even greater in developing countries, where open registered unemployment is commonly above 10%, and total unemployment probably way beyond that. Again, this is a problem especially for young people: for youths in Africa in the 1980s, the open unemployment rate was above 20%. And it is one of the main factors underlying political tensions and ethnic violence in several countries. But unemployment figures understate the real scale of the crisis since many of those working are seriously underemployed. Without the assurance of a social safety net, the poorest cannot survive even a short period without an income. Many of them, however, can rely on family or community support. Yet that system is rapidly breaking down. So, the unemployed must often accept any work they can find, however unproductive or badly paid.

The most insecure working conditions are usually in the informal sector, which has a high proportion of total employment. In 1991, it accounted for 30% of all jobs in Latin America and 60% of those in Africa.

The global shift towards more "precarious" employment reflects changes in the structure of industry. Manufacturing jobs have been disappearing, while many of the new opportunities are in the service sector, where employment is much more likely to be temporary or part-time—and less protected by trade unions.

For many people, the only option is self-employment. But this can be even less secure than wage employment, and those at the bottom of the ladder find it difficult to make ends meet. In the rural areas, the poorest farmers have little access to land, whose distribution can be gauged by the Gini coefficient—a measure of inequality that ranges from 0 (perfect equality) to 1 (absolute inequality). In Kenya, the Gini coefficient for land is 0.77, in Saudi Arabia 0.83 and in Brazil 0.86. And even those who have some land or know of productive investment opportunities often find it difficult to farm and invest effectively because they have little access to credit. This, despite the mounting evidence that the poor are creditworthy. In many developing countries, 40% of the people receive less than 1% of total credit.

The shift to more precarious work has been accompanied by increasing insecurity of incomes. Nominal wages have remained

Only about a quarter of the world's people may at present be economically secure

stagnant, or risen only slowly, but inflation has sharply eroded their value. Some of the worst examples of inflation in the 1980s: Nicaragua 584%, Argentina 417%, Brazil 328% and Uganda 107%; and in the 1990s: Ukraine 1,445%, Russian Federation 1,353% and Lithuania 1,194%.

As a result, real wages in many parts of the world have declined. In Latin America in the 1980s, they fell by 20%, and in many African countries during the same period, the value of the minimum wage dropped sharply—by 20% in Togo, 40% in Kenya and 80% in Sierra Leone. Worse off are women—who typically receive wages 30–40% lower than those of men for doing the same jobs. In Japan and the Republic of Korea, women in manufacturing jobs earn only about half as much as men.

Income insecurity has hit industrial countries as well. In the European Union, 44 million people (some 28% of the workforce) receive less than half the average income of their country. In the United States, real earnings fell by 3% through the 1980s. Minority ethnic groups are usually among the hardest hit: in Canada, nearly half the indigenous people living on reservations now rely on transfer payments for their basic needs.

Some sections of the population face a particularly difficult situation. In 1994, about 65 million disabled people need training and job placement to attain economic security. Only 1% will receive mean-ingful services. The disabled are, by and large, found among the poorest quarter of the population. And their unemployment rate is as high as 84% in Mauritius and 46% in China.

With incomes low and insecure, many people have to look for more support from their governments. But they often look in vain. Most developing countries lack even the most rudimentary forms of social security, and budgetary problems in industrial countries have unravelled social safety nets. In the United States between 1987 and 1990, the real benefits per pensioner declined by 40%, and in Austria by 50%. In Germany, where maternity compensation has already been cut to 25% of full pay, the government decided that over the next three years unemployment and welfare payments will be cut by some $45 billion— the largest cut in postwar German history.

The result: increasing poverty. In both the United States and the European Union, nearly 15% of the people live below the poverty line. The incidence of poverty varies with ethnic origin. In Germany, while the national average has been estimated at 11%, the incidence of poverty among foreign-born residents is 24%. But the most acute problems are in the developing countries, where more than a third of the people live below the poverty line—and more than one billion people survive on a daily income of less than $1.

One of economic insecurity's severest effects is homelessness. Nearly a quarter of a million New Yorkers—more than 3% of the city's population and more than 8% of its black children—have stayed in shelters over the past five years. London has about 400,000 registered homeless people. France has more than 500,000—nearly 10,000 in Paris. The situation is much worse in developing countries. In Calcutta, Dhaka and Mexico City, more than 25% of the people constitute what is sometimes called a "floating population".

Figures 2.1 and 2.2 give selected indicators of economic insecurity. For industrial countries, these indicators refer to job security. But for developing countries, because of data limitations, the data refer only to income security.

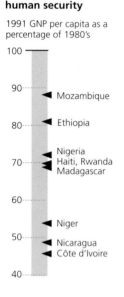

FIGURE 2.1
Falling incomes threaten human security

1991 GNP per capita as a percentage of 1980's

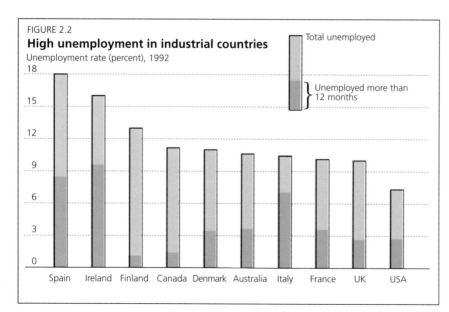

FIGURE 2.2
High unemployment in industrial countries
Unemployment rate (percent), 1992

Total unemployed

Unemployed more than 12 months

Food security

Food security means that all people at all times have both physical and economic access to basic food. This requires not just enough food to go round. It requires that people have ready access to food—that they have an "entitlement" to food, by growing it for themselves, by buying it or by taking advantage of a public food distribution system. The availability of food is thus a necessary condition of security—but not a sufficient one. People can still starve even when enough food is available—as has happened during many famines (box 2.2).

The overall availability of food in the world is not a problem. Even in developing countries, per capita food production increased by 18% on average in the 1980s. And there is enough food to offer everyone in the world around 2,500 calories a day—200 calories more than the basic minimum.

But this does not mean that everyone gets enough to eat. The problem often is the poor distribution of food and a lack of purchasing power. Some 800 million people around the world go hungry. In Sub-Saharan Africa, despite considerable increases in the availability of food in recent years, some 240 million people (about 30% of the total) are undernourished. And in South Asia, 30% of babies are born underweight—the highest ratio for any region in the world and a sad indication of inadequate access to food, particularly for women, who are often the last

to eat in the household. Table 2.1 gives selected indicators of food security in developing countries.

Government and international agencies have tried many ways of increasing food security—at both national and global levels. But these schemes have had only a limited impact. Access to food comes from access to assets, work and an assured income. And unless the question of assets, employment and income security is tackled upstream, state interventions can do little for food insecurity downstream.

Health security

In developing countries, the major causes of death are infectious and parasitic diseases, which kill 17 million people annually, including 6.5 million from acute respiratory infections, 4.5 million from diarrhoeal diseases and 3.5 million from tuberculosis. Most of these deaths are linked with poor nutrition and an unsafe environment—particularly polluted water, which contributes to the nearly one billion cases of diarrhoea a year.

In industrial countries, the major killers are diseases of the circulatory system (5.5 million deaths a year), often linked with diet and life style. Next comes cancer, which

People go hungry not because food is unavailable—but because they cannot afford it

TABLE 2.1
Indicators of food security in selected countries

Country	Food production per capita index (1979/81 =100) 1991	Food import dependency ratio index (1969/71 =100) 1988/90	Daily per capita calorie supply as % of requirements 1988–90
Ethiopia	86	855	71
Afghanistan	71	193	76
Mozambique	77	300	77
Angola	79	366	80
Rwanda	84	322	80
Somalia	78	134	81
Sudan	80	156	83
Burundi	91	165	85
Haiti	84	364	94

BOX 2.2

Starvation amid plenty—the Bengal famine of 1943

Famines are commonly thought of as Nature's revenge on hapless humanity. Although Nature can certainly create local food shortages, human beings turn these shortages into widespread famines. People go hungry not because food is unavailable—but because they cannot afford it.

The Bengal famine of 1943 shows why. Between two million and three million lives were lost, even though there was no overall shortage of food. In fact, the per capita supply of foodgrains in 1943 was 9% higher than in 1941.

The famine was partly a product of an economic boom. Sudden increases in war-related activities exerted powerful inflationary pressures on the economy and caused food prices to rise. In the urban areas, those with work could pay these prices. But in the rural areas, agri-

cultural labourers and other workers found they could no longer afford to eat, and thousands headed for the cities, particularly Calcutta, in the hope of survival. Prices were then driven even higher by speculation and panic buying.

The famine could probably have been averted by timely government action. But the colonial government did nothing to stop hoarding by producers, traders and consumers. The general policy was "wait and see". Relief work was totally inadequate, and the distribution of foodgrains to the rural districts was inefficient. Even in October 1943, with 100,000 sick and destitute people on the streets of Calcutta, the government continued to deny the existence of a famine.

The result was one of the largest man-made catastrophes of our time.

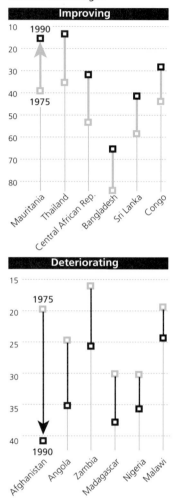

FIGURE 2.3
Children's health

Percentage of children under 5 who are underweight

Improving

Mauritania, Thailand, Central African Rep., Bangladesh, Sri Lanka, Congo

1990 / 1975

Deteriorating

Afghanistan, Angola, Zambia, Madagascar, Nigeria, Malawi

1975 / 1990

in many cases has environmental causes. In the United States, there are considered to be 18 major cancer-causing environmental risks, with indoor pollution at the top of the list.

In both developing and industrial countries, the threats to health security are usually greater for the poorest, people in the rural areas and particularly children (figure 2.3). In the developing countries in 1990, safe water was available to 85% of urban people but to only 62% of rural people. In industrial countries, the poor and the racial minorities are more exposed to disease. In the United States, one-third of whites live in areas polluted by carbon monoxide, but the figure for blacks is nearly 50%. In 1991, life expectancy was 72 years for Canada's indigenous people, compared with 77 years for all Canadians.

The disparities between rich and poor are similar for access to health services. In the industrial countries on average, there is 1 doctor for every 400 people, but for the developing countries there is 1 for nearly 7,000 people (in Sub-Saharan Africa the figure is 1 per 36,000). There also are marked disparities in health spending among developing countries. The Republic of Korea spends $377 per capita annually on health care, but Bangladesh only $7.

People in the industrial countries are much more likely to have access to health care, but even here the disparities in health security are sharp—and for many people getting worse. In the United States between 1989 and 1992, the number of people without health insurance increased from 35 million to 39 million.

While poor people in general have less health security, the situation for women is particularly difficult. One of the most serious hazards they face is childbirth: more than three million women die each year from causes related to childbirth. Most of these deaths could be prevented by ensuring access to safe and affordable family planning and offering the most basic support at home during pregnancy and delivery, with the option of referrals to clinics or hospitals for women with evident complications.

The widest gap between the North and the South in any human indicator is in maternal mortality—which is about 18 times greater in the South. Thus a miracle of life often turns into a nightmare of death just because a society cannot spare the loose change to provide a birth attendant at the time of the greatest vulnerability and anxiety in a woman's life.

Another increasing source of health insecurity for both sexes is the spread of HIV and AIDS (box 2.3). Around 15 million people are believed to be HIV-positive—80% of them in developing countries. By 2000, this figure may rise to 40 million (13 million of them women).

Environmental security

Human beings rely on a healthy physical environment—curiously assuming that whatever damage they inflict on the earth, it will eventually recover. This clearly is not the case, for intensive industrialization and rapid population growth have put the planet under intolerable strain.

The environmental threats countries are facing are a combination of the degradation of local ecosystems and that of the global system. The threats to the global environment are discussed later. Here the focus is environmental threats within countries.

BOX 2.3

HIV and AIDS—a global epidemic

The cumulative number of HIV-infected people worldwide is now around 15 million, with more than 12.5 million in developing countries— 9 million in Sub-Saharan Africa, 1.5 million in Latin America and 2 million in Asia.

Most HIV-infected people live in urban areas, and 70% are in the prime productive ages of 20–40 years. One million are children. In the United States, AIDS is now the prime cause of death for men aged 25–44, and the fourth most important for women in that age group. The cumulative direct and indirect costs of HIV and AIDS in the 1980s have been conservatively estimated at $240 billion. The social and psychological costs of the epidemic for individuals, families, communities and nations are also huge—but inestimable.

Future projections are alarming. By 2000, the number of HIV-infected people is expected to rise to between 30 and 40 million—13 million of them women. By that time, the epidemic would have left more than nine million African children as orphans.

The geographical distribution of HIV and AIDS is changing. In the mid-1980s, the epidemic was well-established in North America and Africa, but by 2000, most of the new infections will be in Asia. In Thailand today, there are an estimated 500,000 HIV-infected people, and in India, more than a million.

The global cost—direct and indirect —of HIV and AIDS by 2000 could be as high as $500 billion a year—equivalent to more than 2% of global GDP.

In developing countries, one of the greatest environmental threats is that to water. Today, the world's supply of water per capita is only one-third of what it was in 1970. Water scarcity is increasingly becoming a factor in ethnic strife and political tension. In 1990, about 1.3 billion people in the developing world lacked access to clean water (figure 2.4). And much water pollution is the result of poor sanitation: nearly two billion people lack access to safe sanitation.

But people in developing countries have also been putting pressure on the land. Some eight to ten million acres of forest land are lost each year—areas the size of Austria. And deforestation combined with overgrazing and poor conservation methods is accelerating desertification. In Sub-Saharan Africa alone in the past 50 years, 65 million hectares of productive land turned to desert.

Even irrigated land is under threat—from salt residues. Salinization damage affects 25% of the irrigated land in Central Asia, and 20% in Pakistan.

In industrial countries, one of the major environmental threats is air pollution. Los Angeles produces 3,400 tons of pollutants each year, and London 1,200 tons. Harmful to health, this pollution also damages the natural environment. The deterioration of Europe's forests from air pollution causes economic losses of $35 billion a year. And the estimated annual loss of agricultural production due to air pollution is $1.5 billion in Sweden, $1.8 billion in Italy, $2.7 billion in Poland and $4.7 billion in Germany.

Although the character of environmental damage differs between industrial and developing countries, the effects are similar almost everywhere. Salinization is also severe in the United States. And air pollution is also acute in cities in the developing world. Mexico City produces 5,000 tons of air pollutants a year, and in Bangkok, air pollution is so severe that more than 40% of the city's traffic police reportedly suffer from respiratory problems.

Many environmental threats are chronic and long-lasting. Others take on a more sudden and violent character. Bhopal and Chernobyl are the more obvious sudden environmental catastrophes. Many chronic "natural" disasters in recent years have also been provoked by human beings. Deforestation has led to more intense droughts and floods. And population growth has moved people into areas prone to cyclones, earthquakes or floods—areas always considered dangerous and previously uninhabited (box 2.4). Poverty and land shortages are doing the same—driving people onto much more marginal territory and increasing their exposure to natural hazards. The result: disasters are more significant and more frequent. During 1967–91, disasters hit three billion people—80% of them in Asia. More than seven million people died, and two million were injured.

Most developing countries have plans to cope with natural emergencies—Bangla-

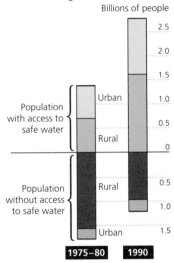

BOX 2.4

The rising tide of disasters

The frequency and severity of disasters have increased sharply over the past two decades. There were 16 major disasters in the 1960s, 29 in the 1970s and 70 in the 1980s.

According to the International Federation of Red Cross and Red Crescent Societies, the major causes of deaths from natural disasters during 1967–91 were droughts (1.3 million), cyclones (0.8 million), earthquakes (0.6 million) and floods (0.3 million). But accounting for the largest number of disaster incidents over the period were floods (1,358), followed by accidents (1,284). A disaster is defined as an event that has killed at least ten people, or affected at least 100.

Probably the most significant cause of the rise in the number and impact of disasters is population growth, which is forcing people to live in more marginal and dangerous places—low-lying land liable to flooding or areas close to active volcanoes. And as more and more of the planet is settled, earthquakes are more likely to strike inhabited areas. Population increases and industrial development also lead to environmental degradation. Deforestation and overgrazing, for example, have increased the number and severity of droughts and floods.

Poor people are much more exposed to disasters than are rich ones. It is they who occupy the steep hillsides vulnerable to landslides. It is they who occupy the fragile delta islands that lie in the paths of cyclones. And it is they who live in the crowded and poorly built slum buildings shaken to the ground by earthquakes.

There also are international disparities. Droughts or floods in Africa do much more damage than those in North America. So, of the global disaster incidents between 1967 and 1991, 22% were in the Americas and 15% in Africa. But 60% of the resulting deaths were in Africa, and only 6% in the Americas. Poor nations obviously are less equipped to cope with natural disasters.

Disasters also cause considerable economic damage, and here too the figures have been rising. Global losses for the 1960s were estimated at $10 billion, for the 1970s at $30 billion and for the 1980s at $93 billion. Most of these losses (over 60%) were in the industrial countries—though as a proportion of GNP, the economic costs were higher for the developing countries.

Disasters in developing countries are an integral part of their poverty cycle. Poverty causes disasters. And disasters exacerbate poverty. Only sustainable human development—which increases the security of human beings and of the planet we inhabit—can reduce the frequency and impact of natural disasters.

FIGURE 2.5
Profile of human distress in industrial countries

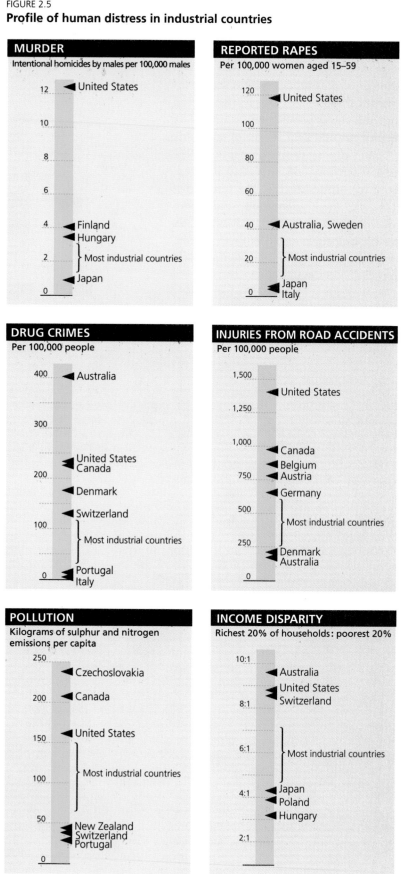

desh, for example, has an elaborate warning system for cyclones arriving in the Bay of Bengal. Sometimes the scale is beyond national resources and calls for international action. Responses, however, are often slow, inadequate and uncoordinated. Current humanitarian efforts, particularly in the UN system, are seriously underfunded. And many of the most vulnerable people perish before any international help arrives.

Personal security

Perhaps no other aspect of human security is so vital for people as their security from physical violence. In poor nations and rich, human life is increasingly threatened by sudden, unpredictable violence. The threats take several forms:
- Threats from the state (physical torture)
- Threats from other states (war)
- Threats from other groups of people (ethnic tension)
- Threats from individuals or gangs against other individuals or gangs (crime, street violence)
- Threats directed against women (rape, domestic violence)
- Threats directed at children based on their vulnerability and dependence (child abuse)
- Threats to self (suicide, drug use).

In many societies, human lives are at greater risk than ever before (figure 2.5). For many people, the greatest source of anxiety is crime, particularly violent crime. Many countries report disturbing trends. In 1992 in the United States, 14 million crimes were reported to the police. These crimes exact a serious economic toll—estimated at $425 billion a year. Reported crimes in Germany in the same year went up by 10%. In the second half of the 1980s, the murder rate in Italy and Portugal doubled, and in Germany it tripled. The increase in crime is often connected with drug trafficking. In Canada, 225 people in every 100,000—and in Australia, 400—suffer each year from drug-related crimes. In the second half of the 1980s, drug-related crimes roughly doubled in Denmark and in Norway—and increased more than thirtyfold in Japan.

Crime and violence are also facts of life in developing countries. Four children are murdered every day in Brazil, where the killing of minors has increased by 40% in the past year. In Kenya in 1993, there were 3,300 reported car thefts—an increase of 200% over 1991. In China, violent crime and rape are on the increase.

Industrial and traffic accidents also present great risks. In industrial countries, traffic accidents are the leading cause of death for people aged 15–30—with some of the highest injury rates in Austria, Belgium, Canada and the United States. And in developing countries, traffic accidents account for at least 50% of total accidental deaths. The highway death toll in South Africa in 1993 was 10,000, three times the number of deaths from political violence.

Violence in the workplace has also increased. In 1992, more than two million US workers were physically attacked at their workplace, nearly 6.5 million others were threatened with violence, and 16 million were harassed in some way. The cost of all this in lost work and legal expenses came to more than $4 billion. About a sixth of the deaths on the job in that year were homicides.

Among the worst personal threats are those to women. In no society are women secure or treated equally to men. Personal insecurity shadows them from cradle to grave. In the household, they are the last to eat. At school, they are the last to be educated. At work, they are the last to be hired and the first to be fired. And from childhood through adulthood, they are abused because of their gender.

True, women are getting better educated and entering employment, often as primary income-earners. Millions of women are now heads of households—one-third of households in the world as a whole, and up to one-half in some African countries, where women produce nearly 90% of the food. But there still are many shocking indicators of gender insecurity and physical violence. It was recently estimated that one-third of wives in developing countries are physically battered. One woman in 2,000 in the world is reported to have been raped. In

the United States, there were more than 150,000 reported rapes in 1993 alone. Sexual harassment on the job is common. In India, women's groups claim that there are about 9,000 dowry-related deaths each year. For 1992, the government estimates that the figure was 5,000.

Children, who should be the most protected in any society, are subject to many abuses. In the United States, nearly three million children were recently reported to be victims of abuse and neglect, and in 1992, nearly 7,000 US children (20 a day) died from gunshot wounds. In developing countries, poverty compels many children to take on heavy work at too young an age—often at great cost to their health. In Brazil, more than 200,000 children spend their lives on the streets. Even conservative estimates put the combined number of child prostitutes in Thailand, Sri Lanka and the Philippines at 500,000.

Community security

Most people derive security from their membership in a group—a family, a community, an organization, a racial or ethnic group that can provide a cultural identity and a reassuring set of values. Such groups also offer practical support. The extended family system, for example, offers protection to its weaker members, and many tribal societies work on the principle that heads of households are entitled to enough land to support their family—so land is distributed accordingly.

But traditional communities can also perpetuate oppressive practices: employing bonded labour and slaves and treating women particularly harshly. In Africa, hundreds of thousands of girls suffer genital mutilation each year because of the traditional practice of female circumcision.

Some of these traditional practices are breaking down under the steady process of modernization. The extended family is now less likely to offer support to a member in distress. Traditional languages and cultures are withering under the onslaught of mass media. On the other hand, many oppressive practices are being fought by people's organizations and through legal action.

In no society are women secure or treated equally to men

Ethnic tensions are
on the rise, often
over limited access
to opportunities

Traditional communities, particularly ethnic groups, can also come under much more direct attack—from each other. About 40% of the world's states have more than five sizable ethnic populations, one or more of which faces discrimination. In several nations, ethnic tensions are on the rise, often over limited access to opportunities—whether to social services from the state or to jobs from the market. Individual communities lose out, or believe they lose out, in the struggle for such opportunities. As a result, about half of the world's states have recently experienced some interethnic strife. And this has been especially serious where national conflict was exacerbated by cold war rivalry.

Ethnic clashes often have brutal results (table 2.2). Since 1983 in Sri Lanka, more than 14,000 people have died in the conflict between the Tamils and the Sinhalese. Since 1981 in former Yugoslavia, more than 130,000 people have been killed and more than 40,000 helpless women reportedly raped in what shamelessly was named "ethnic cleansing", while most of the world watched silently from the sidelines. In Somalia in 1993, there were up to 10,000 casualties—about two-thirds of them women and children—from clashes between rival factions or with UN peacekeepers.

TABLE 2.2
Ethnic and religious conflicts

Country	Group rebellion[a] 1980–89	Major armed conflicts[b] 1989–92	Refugees from the country (thousands) 1992
Afghanistan	yes	yes	4,720
Mozambique	no	yes	1,730
Iraq	yes	yes	1,310
Somalia	yes	yes	870
Ethiopia	yes	yes	840
Liberia	no	yes	670
Angola	yes	yes	400
Myanmar	yes	yes	330
Sudan	yes	yes	270
Sri Lanka	yes	yes	180

a. Group rebellion occurs when non-state communal groups arm themselves and organize more than 1,000 fighters and engage in violent activities against other such groups.
b. Major armed conflicts are defined as contested conflicts that concern government or territory, in which there is use of armed force by the two parties, of which at least one is the government (or parts of government) of a state, and which has resulted in more than 1,000 battle-related deaths during the course of the conflict.

The United Nations declared 1993 the Year of Indigenous People to highlight the continuing vulnerability of the 300 million aboriginal people in 70 countries. In Venezuela in 1986, there were 10,000 Yanomami people—but now their survival is increasingly in danger. Indigenous groups often lose their traditional freedom of movement. During the drought of the 1970s, the one million Tuareg nomads in the Sahara found it much more difficult to move their herds to faraway water holes, and as many as 125,000 people starved to death.

Indigenous people also face widening spirals of violence. In Canada, an indigenous person is six times more likely to be murdered than other Canadians. And symptoms of depression and despair are all too common: in 1988, there were a reported 40 suicides per 100,000 indigenous people, nearly three times the national rate. Nobel Peace Prize winner Rigoberta Menchú gives her view of the importance of the International Decade of Indigenous People (special contribution, facing page).

Political security

One of the most important aspects of human security is that people should be able to live in a society that honours their basic human rights.

In this respect, at least, there has been considerable progress. The 1980s were in many ways a decade of democratic transition—as many military dictatorships ceded power to civilian administrations and one-party states opened themselves up to multiparty elections.

Yet there still is a long way to go in protecting people against state repression. According to a 1993 survey by Amnesty International, political repression, systematic torture, ill treatment or disappearance was still practised in 110 countries.

Human rights violations are most frequent during periods of political unrest. In 1992, Amnesty International concluded that unrest resulted in human rights violations in 112 countries, and in 105 countries there were reports of political detention and imprisonment. Unrest commonly results in military intervention—as in 64 countries. But the police can also be used as agents of repression—they are commonly cited as the perpetrators of human rights violations in both Eastern and Western Europe.

Along with repressing individuals and groups, governments commonly try to exercise control over ideas and information. UNESCO's index of press freedom finds the least free areas to be North Africa, Western Asia and South Asia.

One of the most useful indicators of political insecurity in a country is the priority the government accords military strength—since governments sometimes use armies to repress their own people. If a government is more concerned about its military establishment than its people, this imbalance shows up in the ratio of military to social spending (table 2.3). The two nations with the highest ratios of military spending to education and health spending in 1980 were Iraq (8 to 1) and Somalia (5 to 1). Is it any surprise that these two nations ran into serious trouble during the 1980s and that the same powers that supplied them arms a decade ago are now struggling to disarm them?

Among these seven elements of human security are considerable links and overlaps. A threat to one element of human security is likely to travel—like an angry typhoon—to all forms of human security.

The International Decade of Indigenous People

We believe in the wisdom of our ancestors and wise people who passed on to us their strength and taught us the art of language—enabling us to reaffirm the validity of our thousand-year-old history and the justice of our struggle.

My cause was not born out of something good, it was born out of wretchedness and bitterness. It has been radicalized by the poverty in which my people live. It has been radicalized by the malnutrition which I, as an Indian, have seen and experienced. And by the exploitation and discrimination which I have felt in the flesh. And by the oppression which prevents us from performing our ceremonies, and shows no respect for our way of life, the way we are. At the same time, they've killed the people dearest to me. Therefore, my commitment to our struggle knows no boundaries or limits. That is why I have travelled to so many places where I have had the opportunity to talk about my people.

The international struggle has been of vital importance, especially in the last decade. It has resulted in our achieving a world audience at the United Nations. Promoting the rights of indigenous people has been a tremendous challenge, both for the indigenous peoples themselves and for the member states of the United Nations. But in time and with determination, important successes have been achieved. These include the creation of the Task Force on Indigenous Peoples, the proposed Declaration of the United Nations on Indigenous People, the adoption of 1993 as the International Year of Indigenous People and recently the proclamation by the UN General Assembly of 1994 as the preparatory year for the International Decade of the World's Indigenous People.

The marking of the fifth centenary of the arrival of Columbus in America was an opportunity not only to reiterate the justice of the historic claims of the indigenous people but also to demonstrate our readiness to continue the struggle to achieve them. At the same time, it helped stimulate awareness in international institutions and the communications media of the problems which indigenous people face—as well as explicitly emphasize the significance of our presence within countries and in the world in general.

The International Year of Indigenous People enabled us to strengthen the unity within our organizations, to bring together our aspirations and plans and above all to bear witness to the emptiness and the painful situation of misery, marginalization and humiliation in which we continue to live. The International Year of Indigenous People enabled the indigenous peoples themselves to carry out an enormous number of their own activities and initiatives, including the two summit meetings (Chimaltenango and Oaxtepec). These helped us to bring together our demands and resolutions which we hope the international community will take into account. At the same time, it was possible to disseminate information about the current situation of our people—and start to overcome many of the old cultural and historic prejudices.

I would like to pay my respects to all the organizations, communities, leaders and representatives of indigenous peoples who gave me the wonderful opportunity to bear witness to their aspirations, desires for justice and hopes for peace—in the world of uncertainty, of death and of difficult conditions in which the majority of people currently live. I would also like to reaffirm, together with my fellow indigenous people, our commitment to carry on our own struggle. The International Decade for Indigenous People is one more step towards building new relationships between states and indigenous peoples on the basis of mutual respect.

Rigoberta Menchú, winner of the 1992 Nobel Peace Prize

Global human security

Some global challenges to human security arise because threats within countries rapidly spill beyond national frontiers. Environmental threats are one of the clearest examples: land degradation, deforestation and the emission of greenhouse gases affect climatic conditions around the globe. The trade in drugs is also a transnational phenomenon—drawing millions of people, both producers and consumers, into a cycle of violence and dependency.

Other threats take on a global character because of the disparities between countries—disparities that encourage millions of people to leave their homes in search of a better life, whether the receiving country wants them or not. And in some cases, frustration over inequality can take the form of religious fundamentalism—or even terrorism.

So, when human security is under threat anywhere, it can affect people everywhere. Famines, ethnic conflicts, social disintegration, terrorism, pollution and drug trafficking can no longer be confined within national borders. And no nation can isolate its life from the rest of the world.

This indivisibility of global human security extends to the consequences of both prosperity and poverty. International trade is widening people's range of choices. Instant global communication enables many more to participate in world events as they happen. Every minute, computer networks transfer billions of dollars across international frontiers at the touch of a keyboard.

But if prosperity is becoming globalized, so is poverty, though with much less fanfare. Millions of people migrate to other countries in search of work. Drug traffickers now have one of the best-organized and best-financed international networks. Ethnic tensions can spill over national frontiers. And one person can carry an incurable disease—such as AIDS—to any corner of the world.

Nor does pollution respect borders. And we may yet witness the scary sight of a small nuclear weapon in the hands of a determined international terrorist.

The real threats to human security in the next century will arise more from the actions of millions of people than from aggression by a few nations—threats that will take many forms:

- Unchecked population growth
- Disparities in economic opportunities
- Excessive international migration
- Environmental degradation
- Drug production and trafficking
- International terrorism.

It is in the interest of all nations to discover fresh ways of cooperating to respond to these six emerging threats (and others, should they arise) that constitute the global framework of human insecurity.

Unchecked population growth

The rapid rate of population growth—coupled with a lack of developmental opportunities—is overcrowding the planet, adding to the enormous pressures on diminishing non-renewable resources.

This growth—at the root of global poverty, international migration and environmental degradation—is unprecedented in history. It took one million years to produce the first one billion people on earth. It will now take only ten years to add the next billion to today's 5.5 billion.

The response has to be multifaceted. Certainly, family planning information and services must be available to all those who want them—particularly to the 100 to 200 million couples whose current demand is not being met. But it is folly to treat population growth as a clinical problem. It is a development problem. Indeed, in many societies, human development (especially the education of females) has proven the most powerful contraceptive.

Any plan of action to slow population growth must receive both national and international support, and include both family planning services and targeted human development programmes. A major opportunity to design such a response is the International Conference on Population and Development in Cairo in September 1994.

Despite the considerable international rhetoric on unchecked population growth, population programmes go underfinanced.

TABLE 2.3
Ratios of military to social spending, 1990/91
(military expenditure as % of combined education and health expenditure)

Syrian Arab Rep.	373
Oman	293
Iraq	271
Myanmar	222
Angola	208
Somalia	200
Yemen	197
Qatar	192
Ethiopia	190
Saudi Arabia	151
Jordan	138

The World Bank estimates that if cost-effective methods are adopted, it would take only an additional $2 billion a year to provide family planning services to the 120 million women in developing countries desiring such services. But this amount has yet to be pledged, just like the $2.5 billion a year of additional investment it would take to remove gender disparities in education.

Disparities in economic opportunities

During the past five decades, world income increased sevenfold (in real GDP) and income per person more than tripled (in per capita GDP). But this gain has been spread very unequally—nationally and internationally—and the inequality is increasing. Between 1960 and 1991, the share of world income for the richest 20% of the global population rose from 70% to 85%. Over the same period, all but the richest quintile saw their share of world income fall—and the meagre share for the poorest 20% declined from 2.3% to 1.4% (figure 2.6).

One-fifth of humankind, mostly in the industrial countries, thus has well over four-fifths of global income and other developmental opportunities. These disparities reflect many other disparities—in trade, investment, savings and commercial lending. Overall, they reflect unequal access to global market opportunities. Such disparities entail consequences for other aspects of human security. They encourage overconsumption and overproduction in the North, and they perpetuate the poverty-environment link in the South. Inevitably, they breed resentment and encourage migration from poor countries to rich.

Migration pressures

One of the clearest consequences of population growth and deepening poverty in developing countries is the growth in international migration. At least 35 million people from the South have taken up residence in the North in the past three decades—around one million join them each year. Another million or so are working overseas on contracts for fixed periods. The number of illegal international migrants is

estimated to be around 15 to 30 million.

In addition, there are large numbers of refugees. In the developing countries today, there are nearly 20 million internally displaced people—and worldwide, probably around 19 million refugees (figure 2.7).

These pressures are likely to increase. Expanding populations, limited employment opportunities, closed international markets and continuing environmental degradation will force millions more to leave their own countries. But the affluent nations are closing their doors—since they face stagnating economies, high unemployment and the prospect of "jobless growth".

Sometimes, the policies of the industrial countries intensify migration pressures. First, they restrict employment in developing countries by raising trade and tariff barriers that limit their export potential: if the job opportunities do not move towards the workers, the workers are likely to move towards the job opportunities.

Second, the industrial countries do have a real demand for workers—whether for highly educated scientists or for the unskilled labour to do the difficult manual jobs that their own workers reject. This demand leads to highly ambivalent attitudes towards immigration: official disapproval, with systems of enforcement less effective than they might be so that enough construction workers, fruit pickers or nannies can find their way in.

Control of international migration is not just an administrative issue. It is primarily an economic issue—requiring a new framework of development cooperation that integrates foreign assistance with trade liberalization, technology transfers, foreign investments and labour flows (chapter 4).

Environmental degradation

Most forms of environmental degradation have their most severe impact locally. But other effects tend to migrate. Polluted air drifts inexorably across national frontiers, with sulphur dioxide emissions in one country falling as acid rain in another. About 60% of Europe's commercial forests suffer damaging levels of sulphur deposition. In Sweden, about 20,000 of the country's

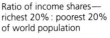

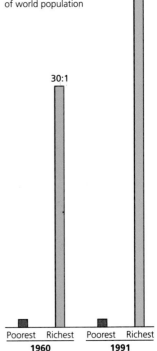

FIGURE 2.6
The widening gap between the rich and the poor

Ratio of income shares—richest 20% : poorest 20% of world population

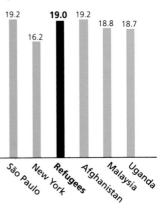

FIGURE 2.7
Refugees of the past three years could populate a major city or a country
Population in millions, 1992

90,000 lakes are acidified to some degree; in Canada, 48,000 are acidic. And the source of the problem in these instances is not only within the country.

The emission of chlorofluorocarbons also has an international, indeed a truly global, effect—as the gases released in individual countries attack the ozone layer. In 1989, research teams found that the ozone layer over Antarctica was reduced to only 50% of its 1979 level. And in 1993, satellite measurements over the heavily populated mid-latitudes of the Northern Hemisphere showed the ozone layer to be at record lows, with serious implications for human health. Ozone filters out ultraviolet radiation, which can lead to various kinds of skin cancer. Between 1982 and 1989 in the United States, the incidence of the most dangerous form of skin cancer, melanoma, rose by more than 80%.

The production of greenhouse gases in individual countries also has a global impact. Layers of these gases, including carbon dioxide and methane, accumulating in the upper atmosphere contribute to global warming because they reflect back infrared radiation that would otherwise escape into space. In 1989, the United States and the former Soviet Union were the largest producers of such gases—respectively responsible for 18% and 14% of total emissions. But the effects will be felt all over the globe—and could have their greatest impact on the poorest countries. With a one-metre rise in sea level partly due to global warming, Bangladesh (which produces only 0.3% of global emissions) could see its land area shrink by 17%.

Biological diversity is more threatened now than at any time in the past. Tropical deforestation is the main culprit, but the destruction of wetlands, coral reefs and temperate forests also figures heavily. Germany and the Netherlands lost nearly 60% of their wetlands between 1950 and 1980. And a recent analysis of tropical forest habitats, which contain 50–90% of the world's species, concluded that, at current rates of loss, up to 15% of the earth's species could disappear over the next 25 years. Today, only 45% of the world's temperate rainforests remain.

The trends of the past 20 years show an accelerated destruction of coastal marine habitats, increases in coastal pollution, and in many areas, a shrinking of the marine fish catch. In 1990, the global fish catch declined for the first time in 13 years—a result of overfishing, coastal habitat destruction and water pollution.

Coral reefs will also come under greater pressure. Approximately one billion people will live in coastal cities by 2000, increasing the danger to reefs from overfishing, pollution and soil erosion.

As habitats are fragmented, altered or destroyed, they lose their ability to provide ecosystem services—water purification, soil regeneration, watershed protection, temperature regulation, nutrient and waste recycling and atmospheric maintenance. All these changes threaten global human security.

Drug trafficking

The trade in narcotic drugs is one of the most corrosive threats to human society. During the past 20 years, the narcotics industry has progressed from a small cottage enterprise to a highly organized multinational business that employs hundreds of thousands of people and generates billions of dollars in profits (box 2.5). The retail value of drugs, as estimated in a recent study, now exceeds the international trade in oil—and is second only to the arms trade. The main producing countries are Afghanistan, Bolivia, Colombia, Iran, Pakistan, Peru and Thailand. And while consumption is rapidly spreading all over the world, the highest per capita use is reported to be in the United States and Canada. In the United States alone, consumer spending on narcotics is thought to exceed the combined GDPs of more than 80 developing countries. In recent times, the countries of Eastern Europe have also become prominent in drug trafficking—at least 25% of the heroin consumed in Western Europe now passes through Eastern Europe.

Despite the magnitude of the threat, the international community has yet to produce a coherent response. But some individual countries have drawn up their own action plans. In Bolivia, coca producers have been paid to take coca out of production—$2,000 a hectare—and since 1989, they have annually converted more than 5,000 hectares of land to other crops.

But such lone efforts are not an effective, durable answer. As long as the demand persists, so will the supply. The real solution has to lie in addressing the causes of drug addiction—and in eradicating the poverty that tempts farmers into drug production.

International terrorism

Violence can travel from one country to another through conventional warfare—and through terrorism.

Between 1975 and 1992, there were an average of 500 international terrorist attacks a year. Bombings are the most common type of incident (60%), followed by armed attacks, and in individual years there have also been large numbers of arson attacks or aircraft hijackings. The peak in recent decades was in 1987, with 672 incidents. In 1992, the number dropped to 362, the lowest since 1975.

Between 1968 and 1992, the number of annual casualties was never less than 1,000, and 1985 was the worst year, with 3,016 casualties—816 people killed and 2,200 wounded. Most of the victims have been the general public—though in 1980–83 the majority were diplomats, and in the past two years most attacks have been made against businesses. While the number of their victims may not look high, the fear that these attacks spread among the world's population at large is immense.

The focus of terrorist activity tends to move around the world. Until the early 1970s, most incidents were in Latin America. Then the focus switched to Europe. In the mid-1980s, most of the incidents were in the Middle East. And now, terrorist incidents take place all over the world. Terrorism, with no particular nationality, is a global phenomenon.

Needed policy action

This discouraging profile of human insecurity demands new policy responses, both na-

tionally and internationally. Over the past five decades, humankind gradually built up an edifice of global security—an edifice of nuclear deterrents, power balances, strategic alliances, regional security pacts and international policing through the superpowers and the United Nations.

Much of this global security framework

BOX 2.5

The international narcotics trade

Narcotic drugs have become one of the biggest items of international trade, with the total volume of drug trafficking estimated at around $500 billion a year. The OECD estimates that $85 billion in drug profits is laundered through financial markets each year, of which $32 billion passes through the United Kingdom.

Since almost all the production and trade in these drugs is illegal, statistics are notoriously unreliable. The largest exporter of cocaine is probably Colombia, followed by Peru and Bolivia, while Myanmar seems to be the leading source of heroin. Pakistan is one of the major exporters of cannabis. One study of the nine major producing countries estimated their annual production of cocaine at around 300 tons, heroin at around 250 tons and cannabis at well over 25,000 tons.

Drug addiction causes immense human distress. And the illegal production and distribution of drugs have spawned worldwide waves of crime and violence. International efforts to stamp out this noxious trade began more than 80 years ago, when opium was brought under international jurisdiction. Since then, there have been numerous conventions and conferences on drug abuse and illicit trafficking. In 1990, the General Assembly of the United Nations declared the 1990s the UN Decade against Drug Abuse.

But thus far, efforts to eliminate the drug menace have prompted rather more righteous indignation than effective action—mainly because the costs of significantly reducing production or consumption are just too high. Successfully eradicating crops like opium or coca demands offering farmers equally valuable alternative crops. But given the high prices for drugs, this is almost impossible. In Bolivia, the coca-cocaine in-

dustry is thought to be worth as much as 20% of GNP.

Most efforts at stifling drug production have brought limited benefits. Eradicating crops in one place tends to shift production elsewhere. When Mexico suppressed marijuana production, it sprang up in Colombia. When Thailand managed to reduce opium crops, producers moved to Myanmar and the Lao People's Democratic Republic.

Reducing consumption is equally difficult. Many wealthy and educated people use small amounts of drugs much as they might use alcohol and tobacco—and are prepared to risk the consequences. But many of the heaviest drug users are poor and desperate—seeking some kind of anaesthesia for the hopelessness of their lives. For them, drugs may be dangerous, but they have little left to lose. This underclass is not limited to the industrial countries. The United States is the largest single market for drugs, but developing countries, particularly those that are drug producers, also have serious addiction problems. Pakistan, for example, is thought to have more than one million heroin users, and Thailand has around 500,000 addicts.

One radical alternative is decriminalization. This would reduce the violence and crime associated with drugs and allow for production and consumption in less squalid and dangerous circumstances. The risk, however, is that it might increase overall consumption.

In the end, probably the only solution will be to remove the kind of social distress that feeds drug addiction and to promote human development, which can strengthen families and communities and offer young people more productive outlets for their time and energies.

now needs change. In its place—or, at least, by its side—must be raised a new, more encompassing structure to ensure the security of all people the world over. Some global concerns require national actions—others, a coordinated international response.

Early warning indicators

Experience shows that where there are multiple problems of personal, economic, political or environmental security, there is a risk of national breakdown (box 2.6).

One question that preoccupies the international community is whether it is possible to get early warning signals of the risk of national breakdown. Such signals could help in agreeing on timely preventive action and avoiding conflict and war, rather than waiting until it is too late, as in Bosnia and Somalia.

One might want to see which countries currently face similar multiple threats.

Some indicators discussed earlier in this chapter can be useful for this purpose: deteriorating food consumption, for example, high unemployment and declining wages, human rights violations, incidents of ethnic violence, widening regional disparities and an overemphasis on military spending.

Identifying potential crisis countries is not an indictment—it is an essential part of preventive diplomacy and an active peace policy. A clear set of indicators, and an early warning system based on them, could help countries avoid reaching the crisis point.

Consider Afghanistan, Angola, Haiti, Iraq, Mozambique, Myanmar, Sudan and Zaire. As analyzed in annex 1, these countries are already in various stages of crisis. Determined national and international actions—including both preventive and curative development—are needed to support processes of social integration.

There are several countries where current national and international efforts need to be reinforced to promote human security. The list of such countries extends to all world regions, and it ranges from countries in the midst of ongoing crises—such as Burundi, Georgia, Liberia, Rwanda and Tajikistan—to other countries experiencing either severe internal tensions—such as Algeria—or large regional disparities—such as Egypt, Mexico and Nigeria.

Preventive action can also avoid larger costs for the world community at a later stage. Today's UN operations in Somalia, for example, cost more than $2 billion in 1993 alone. A similar investment in the socio-economic development of Somalia ten years ago might have averted the current crisis. Soldiers in blue berets are no substitute for socio-economic reform. Nor can short-term humanitarian assistance replace long-term development support.

Policies for social integration

Although the international community can help prevent future crises, the primary responsibility lies with the countries themselves. And often it lies with the people themselves. In Somalia today, where there is no central government, people and their

---

BOX 2.6

Selected indicators of human security

Precise quantification of human security is impossible, but some useful indicators can provide an early warning of whether a country is facing problems of human insecurity and heading towards social disintegration and possible national breakdown. The following indicators are particularly revealing:
- *Food insecurity*—measured by daily calorie supply as a percentage of basic human needs, the index of food production per capita and the trend of the food import dependency ratio.
- *Job and income insecurity*—measured by high and prolonged unemployment rates, a sudden drop in real national income or in real wages, extremely high rates of inflation and wide income disparities between the rich and the poor.
- *Human rights violations*—measured by political imprisonment, torture, disappearance, press censorship and other human rights violations.
- *Ethnic or religious conflicts*—measured by the percentage of population involved in such conflicts and by the number of casualties.
- *Inequity*—measured mainly by the

difference between the HDI values of different population groups.
- *Military spending*—measured by the ratio of military spending to combined expenditure on education and health.

This is only a partial set of indicators. But even though it captures only a few dimensions, if several of the indicators point in the same direction, the country may be heading for trouble.

These indicators would sound an alarm if applied to such countries as Afghanistan, Angola, Haiti, Mozambique, Myanmar, Sudan and Zaire, countries included in the various tables of this chapter and the case studies. They might also sound an alarm if used to measure human security in some of the successor states of the former Soviet Union, notably those in Central Asia.

Ideally, there should also be a set of indicators to identify global threats to human security. And combining national and global indicators would highlight the coincidence of national and global insecurities—as with high unemployment and heavy international migration.

local communities are doing more than government authorities may ever have done. But several countries also offer encouraging examples of what deliberate public policies of social integration can achieve. Malaysia, Mauritius and Zimbabwe, for example, are countries whose governments have taken courageous national actions to overcome potentially dangerous national schisms (annex 2).

The policies pursued by these countries reconfirm many of the policy lessons set forth in chapter 1 and explored further in boxes 2.7 and 2.8. First is the importance of allowing everyone, of whatever race or ethnic group, the opportunity to develop his or her own capacities—particularly through effective health and education services. Second is the need to ensure that economic growth is broadly based—so that everyone has equal access to economic opportunities. Third is the importance of carefully crafted affirmative action programmes designed so that all sections of society gain—but that the weaker groups gain proportionally more. And the most important lesson conveyed by the country case studies on Malaysia and Mauritius is that where human security and social integration are ensured, economic growth and human development can progress too.

Many countries have unfortunately chosen a different path—and allowed inequalities to rise to a disturbing extent. The data presented in chapter 5 on Egypt, Mexico, Nigeria and South Africa show the dangers that this can bring.

The World Summit for Social Development offers a fresh opportunity for the international community to shift its emphasis from the first pillar of territorial security in the past 50 years to the second pillar of human security in the next 50 years. In light of the analysis here, the Summit might wish to consider the following:
• Endorsing the concept of human security as the key challenge for the 21st century.
• Calling on people to make their full contribution to global human security and to bind together in solidarity.
• Requesting national governments in rich and poor countries to adopt policy measures for human security. They should en-

sure that all people have the basic capabilities and opportunities, especially in access to assets and to productive and remunerative work. They should also ensure that people enjoy basic human rights and have political choices.
• Recommending that all countries fully cooperate in this endeavour—regionally and globally. To this end, a new framework of international cooperation for development should be devised, taking into account the indivisibility of global human security—that no one is secure as long as someone is insecure anywhere.
• Requesting that the United Nations step up its efforts in preventive diplomacy —and recognizing that the reasons for conflict and war today are often rooted in

---

Job-sharing

Lavorare meno, lavorare tutti—work less and everybody works—a slogan that recently appeared in Italian workplaces. Indeed, throughout the industrial world, the idea of job-sharing is gathering momentum.

The basic principle is simple. Rather than a five-day work week for some workers, with others remaining unemployed, the work week should be reduced to, say, four days with a corresponding pay cut, so that more people can share the available work.

The German auto-maker BMW in 1990 introduced a four-day, 36-hour week at one of its plants, with an agreement for more flexible working. The productivity gains more than offset the cost of taking on more workers, so there was no need for a wage cut.

A more recent deal at another German car-maker, Volkswagen, involves a four-day week along with a 10% pay cut. This has not created new jobs, but it saved 31,000 jobs that would otherwise have been eliminated.

In France, a subsidiary of the computer company Hewlett-Packard has introduced a more flexible four-day week for workers. This has enabled the plant to be run seven days a week, round the clock, rather than five days on day shifts. Production has tripled, employment has risen 20%, and earnings have remained unchanged.

In Japan, the large steel companies have been closing two days a month and offering workers 80–90% of their pay.

Exactly how many jobs could be saved if countries were to adopt such schemes is difficult to say. But for France, it has been estimated that the universal adoption of a four-day, 33-hour work week with an average 5% reduction in salary would create around two million new jobs—and save $28 billion in unemployment insurance.

Job-sharing has its critics. Some companies may simply use reductions in work time as a way of cutting costs. And it may be harder to implement the plan in smaller companies that have less room for manoeuvre.

Workers and trade unions are concerned, too, that this approach might in the long term concentrate work into a few high-paid, high-productivity jobs, leaving many more workers without jobs or incomes.

Job-sharing could, nevertheless, be the germ of an idea that offers greater freedom for workers, along with an improved private life—while contributing much to reducing unemployment.

Clearly, the question of work and employment needs a basic, fundamental review—nationally and globally. It will no doubt be a central issue for discussion at the 1995 World Summit for Social Development.

Credit for all

Study after study on credit schemes for the poor confirm that the poor are creditworthy:

- The poor can save, even if only a little.
- The poor have profitable investment opportunities to choose from, and they invest their money wisely.
- The poor are very reliable borrowers and hence a very good risk. Repayment rates of 90% and more are not rare.
- The poor are able and willing to pay market interest rates, so that credit schemes for the poor stand a good chance of becoming viable, self-financing undertakings.

The reason credit schemes for the poor work is that they significantly improve the incomes of the poor—typically by more than 20%, and at times even by more than 100%.

Smaller loans are administratively more costly than larger ones. Yet the literature on credit schemes for the poor abounds with examples of how some organizations and programmes manage to keep their administrative costs low. Among the successful measures: lending to peer groups, standardizing loan terms, collaborating with community-based and other developmental non-governmental organizations, eschewing traditional banking requirements and procedures and being located in the community and knowing local people and local investment opportunities.

Many savings schemes for the poor today do mobilize the modest funds that poor communities have to spare. But rarely do they reinvest the money only in poor neighbourhoods. Just the opposite should be the case. Not only should the poor's savings be reinvested in poor neighbourhoods. The savings of the rich should also be encouraged to flow into these neighbourhoods.

Governmental incentive policies can help in this. For example, governments could subsidize, for a defined interim period, the increased overhead costs that banks would incur in lending to the poor. If the aim were to serve about 120 million poor a year—every tenth poor person—this could cost some $10 billion.

The poor know best their opportunities for productive and remunerative work. What they really need are modest amounts of start-up capital for their microenterprises.

As one study put it, the old parable about feeding people for a day by giving them a fish, or feeding them for life by teaching them how to fish, needs a 20th-century postscript: what really matters is who owns the pond.

Small credit can make a difference

Integrated Rural Development Programme, India
- Among beneficiaries, 64% increased their annual family income by 50% or more.
- Seventy percent of the assisted families belonged to the poorest group; however, their share in the benefits of IRDP was only 29%.
- In 71% of cases, the assets procured by the IRDP beneficiaries were found to be intact after two years.

Metro Manila Livelihood Programme, Philippines Business for Social Progress, Philippines
- The average increase in income from an average loan of $94 was 41%.
- Women received 80% of loans.
- Borrowers had an average of 5.7 dependents.

Revolving Loan Fund, Dominican Republic
- The average increase in income from 101 loans was 27% a year.
- The job creation rate among borrowers was more than 20 times that of the control group of non-borrowers.

Revolving Loan Fund, Costa Rica
- The average increase in income from 450 small loans was more than 100% a year.
- A new job was created for every $1,000 lent.

poverty, social injustice and environmental degradation—and back these efforts up through preventive development initiatives.

- Recommending further that today's framework of global institutions be reviewed and redesigned to prepare those institutions fully for doing their part in tackling the urgent challenges of human security, all within the framework of a paradigm of longer-term sustainable human development.

Chapter 4 will return to the question of a new framework for international development cooperation and new global institutions. But before that, chapter 3 addresses one critical source of insecurity that deserves more explicit treatment than it received here, one that arises from the world's previous preoccupation with deterrence and territorial security—excessive militarization and the international arms trade.

Countries in crisis

Afghanistan

Many parts of the country are in the hands of different Mujahedeen factions. A bloody civil war is going on, with no end in sight. Food is scarce, and much of Afghanistan's infrastructure lies in ruins.

• *Food security*—Fourteen years of war have devastated agriculture. Farms have been abandoned and irrigation works destroyed. Agricultural inputs and spare parts are scarce, and armed groups control food supplies. Between 1980 and 1991, per capita food production declined by 29%, and in 1990, Afghans could meet only 76% of their daily per capita calorie requirements. Although food prices tripled in 1992, farmers are unable to fetch remunerative prices for surplus production (due to insecurity and the breakdown of infrastructure), with the exception of opium.
• *Job and income security*—Between 1965 and 1980, per capita income increased by only 0.6% a year.
• *Human rights violations*—Following the change of government in May 1992, thousands of political prisoners were released. But the fate of hundreds of prisoners held in prisons controlled by some Mujahedeen groups remains unknown. Mainly as a consequence of the ongoing civil war, cruel forms of punishment have been introduced by some of the warring factions.
• *Ethnic and other conflicts*—Ethnic and factional conflicts have continued, following the defeat of the communist government by Islamic Mujahedeen in April 1992. Millions of land-mines have disabled one in every six Afghans.
• *Military spending*—Afghanistan is the largest arms recipient per capita among the poorest countries. Between 1983 and 1992, it received more than $600 of conventional arms per capita.

Angola

Angola has been ravaged by years of fighting that has claimed up to 500,000 lives. Tens of thousands of people have been maimed, and 1994 could bring famine to three million of the country's ten million people.

• *Food security*—Between 1980 and 1990, the domestic food production index fell from 100 to 79. In 1990, food availability was only 80% of daily per capita calorie needs. Renewed fighting in 1993 disrupted agriculture and the distribution of relief supplies. Without a cease-fire, some three million people face starvation in 1994.
• *Job and income security*—Between 1980 and 1991, annual inflation was over 90%. Around two-thirds of the population now lives below the poverty line.
• *Human rights violations*—Government forces are responsible for extrajudicial execution of suspected political opponents. And in the areas they control, the opposition UNITA forces kill suspected government supporters.
• *Ethnic and other conflicts*—The Movemento por Popular Libertaçao de Angola (MPLA) derives much of its support from the urban areas, while the Uniao Nacional para Independencia Total de Angola (UNITA) opposition consists largely of the rural Ovimbundu people, who feel threatened by extinction. Elections were held in 1992, but UNITA refused to accept the MPLA victory, and the conflict was resumed. In 1993, starvation, disease and land-mines were reported to be killing thousands of people.
• *Military spending*—In 1990, Angola spent 20% of its GDP on the military. In the late 1980s, there were 200 military personnel for every doctor.

Haiti

Haiti continues in political and economic turmoil, following the failure of recent attempts to ensure the return of the constitutionally elected president.

• *Food security*—Between 1980 and 1991, the index of domestic food production fell from 100 to 84. The current embargo has increased the price of food—and of fuel and other basic necessities. Hunger and malnutrition are widespread: an estimated 1,000 children die every month.
• *Job and income security*—Between 1980 and 1990, per capita income fell on average by 2.4% a year. In 1991, per capita GNP was $380. Unemployment and inflation have risen sharply.
• *Human rights violations*—Following a military coup in 1991, a junta continues to rule through violent repression. All forms of popular organization have been ruthlessly suppressed.
• *Ethnic and other conflicts*—The chief conflict is be-

tween the elite, represented by the military, and the majority of civil society. Some 1,800 people were killed in early 1992 and 300 in early 1993. Fearing civil war, thousands fled to the countryside. In October 1993, the United Nations reimposed its oil and trade embargo aimed at restoring the ousted president.

Iraq

After years of external war and continuing ethnic conflicts, Iraq's infrastructure has been devastated, the country is isolated, and the population is suffering great hardship under an authoritarian government and internationally imposed sanctions.

• *Food security*—Between 1980 and 1991, per capita domestic food production declined by 32%. Large parts of the country have been subjected to blockades to prevent food (as well as fuel and medicines) from reaching the besieged populations. The country normally is highly dependent on food imports, financed by oil exports, and the 1992 harvest was particularly poor, covering only 20% of the 1992–93 needs. Some five million tons of food would have to be imported to fill the gap. Since this is unlikely, hunger and malnutrition will increase. The death rate among Iraqi children under five has tripled since the Gulf War.
• *Job and income security*—Between 1965 and 1980, per capita income grew at an annual average of 0.6%. Though no recent statistics are available, the disruption of war has probably resulted in negative growth.
• *Human rights violations*—Thousands of political opponents are detained. Hundreds have "disappeared", and torture is widespread.
• *Ethnic and other conflicts*—Since 1974, the government has been in conflict with the Kurds—who are around 20% of the population. In 1991, a civil conflict began with Shi'a rebels in the southern marshes. In 1992, there were 1.3 million Iraqi refugees in other countries.
• *Military spending*—Between 1983 and 1992, Iraq spent $28 billion on arms. In 1990, arms imports were nearly $1,500 per capita, and there were 105 military personnel for every doctor. In 1990, military spending was 271% of social spending.

Mozambique

Mozambique's future depends on whether the current peace agreement holds. If it does not, and the civil war continues, the human cost will be enormous.

• *Food security*—Between 1980 and 1991, domestic food production per capita declined by 23%. In 1990, food availability was only 77% of per capita calorie requirements. Even though Mozambique had a good harvest in 1992, it will continue to depend on food aid for a long time, given the social dislocation of the war.

• *Job and income security*—Mozambique has one of the lowest per capita GNPs in the world. In the 1980s, it fell by 1.1% annually, and by 1991, it was just $80. The average annual inflation rate was 38%. About 60% of the population lives below the poverty line.
• *Ethnic and other conflicts*—Since 1976, Mozambique has suffered from civil war between the Frente de Libertaçao de Mozambique (FRELIMO) and Resistência Nacional Moçambicana (RENAMO)—a guerilla group originally supported by Rhodesia and South Africa. A cease-fire was signed in October 1992. Some four million of the population of 16 million have been driven from their homes by a decade and a half of fighting. In 1992, 1.7 million of them were refugees in other countries.
• *Military spending*—Between 1983 and 1992, the country imported $425 million worth of major conventional arms. In 1990, per capita arms imports were $27, and the country had 180 military personnel for every doctor.

Myanmar

Myanmar has a large number of ethnic groups that have been struggling for autonomy or independence for decades. Despite some recent political moves, the conflicts could continue for many years.

• *Food security*—The conflict and its consequences have contributed to severe rates of malnutrition for children, and a third of the children under five are malnourished.
• *Job and income security*—About 35% of the rural population lives in absolute poverty.
• *Human rights violations*—National elections were held in 1990, but the military government refused to accept the results, and the country remains under martial law. More than 1,000 political opponents have been imprisoned. Aung San Suu Kyi, a leader of the opposition and winner of the 1991 Nobel Peace Prize, has been under house arrest for more than four years. Gross and persistent human rights abuses, including torture, are reported from various parts of the country.
• *Ethnic and other conflicts*—Myanmar has more than a dozen significant ethnic minorities, many of which fought the government since independence. The largest are the Karen (10% of the population), the Arakanese (7%) and the Shan (7%). Since 1989, there have been more than 1,000 battle-related deaths. In 1992, over 250,000 of the Muslim minority of Arakan state (the Rohingas) fled to Bangladesh. In total, between 5% and 10% of the population has been displaced, either within Myanmar or to neighbouring countries.
• *Military spending*—The military budget increased by 10% in 1992–93 and now accounts for 35% of the total budget and 6% of GDP. Arms make up more than a fifth of the country's total imports.

Sudan

Sudan faces one of the world's worst humanitarian crises. There is little prospect of ending the relentless cycle of war and famine.

- *Food security*—Between 1980 and 1991, per capita domestic food production declined by 29% in the south. Agricultural production has been devastated by the war—with agricultural lands mined. Both sides use food as a weapon by blocking relief supplies. In the Southern Sudan towns of Kongor, Ame and Ayod, known as the "starvation triangle", undernutrition rates are above 80%, and mortality rates are above 250 per 1,000 people.
- *Human rights violations*—In response to the country's civil war, the military government has banned political parties, and hundreds of suspected government opponents have been detained without trial.
- *Ethnic and other conflicts*—The country has been devastated by two civil wars between the majority in the north (75% of the population) and the minority in the south. The first, between 1955 and 1972, cost 500,000 lives. The present conflict started in 1983 and has killed more than 260,000 people. The main opposition force is the Sudan People's Liberation Army, which in 1992 split into two factions. Conflicts between the factions have also led to thousands of deaths and displaced hundreds of thousands of people. There currently are more than 250,000 Sudanese refugees in other countries.
- *Military expenditure*—Between 1983 and 1992, Sudan imported $532 million worth of major conventional arms.

Zaire

Zaire is dissolving into anarchy as most semblances of responsible government disappear. Looting and riots are common.

- *Food security*—The price of a sack of rice or cassava, doubling every couple of weeks, is now beyond the reach of much of the population. In Kinshasa, the capital, many people rely on relief supplies, and others are leaving for the rural areas in search of food.
- *Job and income security*—During the 1980s, per capita annual income declined by an annual average of 1.3%, and 70% of the population lives below the poverty line. The government has been virtually bankrupt for a decade, largely as a result of rampant corruption and mismanagement. The introduction of a series of new currencies has prompted riots because merchants refused to accept them—the latest, in 1993, caused whole sections of the economy to shut down. Much of the modern sector has been destroyed by looting and violence.
- *Human rights violations*—The central political problem is a lack of effective governance. The president, alleged to have extracted more than $5 billion from the economy, has yielded only marginally to pressure for a transition to democracy, but ultimately refuses to hand over power. He is protected by an elite guard of 20,000 soldiers.
- *Ethnic and other conflicts*—Zaire faces numerous secessionist pressures and has had two prolonged ethnic wars—one in Kivu, to the East, and the other in Shaba, to the South. To prevent secession of the copper-rich Shaba, the government has engaged in a form of "ethnic cleansing", and in late 1993, thousands of people died in ethnic fighting. In total, more than 800,000 people have been displaced by ethnic clashes.

Successes in social integration

Malaysia

*Malaysia presents one of the world's most striking examples of
positive policy action in favour of one disadvantaged ethnic group.
By achieving a broad national consensus for this objective, it has
steadily created a more cohesive and more prosperous society.*

The roots of Malaysia's racial diversity lie in the period of British rule. The colonial government encouraged Chinese immigration to develop trading and mineral extraction. More than four million Chinese came into the country, of whom two million chose to stay. The British also brought in Indian workers for the rubber, sugar cane and coffee plantations—as well as for running public utilities such as water, power and telecommunications. As a result, Malaysia's population today is 61% Bumiputra (groups indigenous to the country), 30% Chinese and 8% Indian.

The colonial policy polarized economic development along racial lines. The Chinese and the Indians eventually dominated the urban modern sector, while most indigenous Malays remained in traditional, largely rural activities such as subsistence rice cultivation and fishing. Of corporate assets in 1970, the Chinese and Indian populations owned 33% while Bumiputras owned only 2% (the rest were held by foreigners). Thus while the more numerous Bumiputra population controlled the political system, it had very little control over the economy.

This imbalance led to increasing tensions, and in May 1969, there were racial riots. These prompted the suspension of Parliament, the creation of a multi-ethnic National Operations Council, and in 1971, the drafting of the New Economic Policy (NEP).

The NEP had two main objectives: first, the restructuring of society so that income and occupations no longer followed ethnic lines, and second, the eradication of poverty.

Bumiputra representation in the economy was to be increased by establishing ethnic ownership quotas, and quotas were established for federal employment, participation in the armed forces, land ownership and educational scholarships.

Since most of the poverty was concentrated in the rural areas, the government established rural development authorities and targeted funds towards rural development—including irrigation projects, social services and rural infrastructure. The government also maintained a strong commitment to investment in education.

The results were impressive. Between 1970 and 1990, the proportion of corporate assets owned by Bumiputras rose from 2.4% to 20.3%. And the incidence of poverty fell dramatically—from 49% of all households to 16%.

Economic growth per capita during 1980–91 averaged 2.9% a year, and much of Malaysia's progress in promoting social integration has been based on distributing the benefits of economic growth as widely as possible.

This improvement is clearly reflected in the country's human development indexes. Between 1970 and 1991, the HDI increased for each group, but the increase was larger for the Bumiputras (38%) than for the Chinese (20%). Even so, the HDI for the Bumiputras, at 0.730, is still lower than that for the Chinese at 0.896.

In 1991, to follow up on this success, the government adopted a New Development Policy (NDP). The NDP relaxed the quotas in favour of Bumiputras but still aimed at redistributing resources towards them. About 56% of the 1.3 million new jobs that the NDP is expected to create between 1990 and 2000 would be taken by the Bumiputras.

Although promoting growth is the main thrust of the NDP, the policy also accepts that some groups and regions still lack equal access to opportunities. Eradicating poverty will therefore also mean focusing on the poorest of the poor, to improve their skills and raise their incomes.

Mauritius

Mauritius is a multiracial society that has made determined efforts to maintain its cultural diversity—while promoting equal opportunities for all through a strong social programme.

Mauritius had no indigenous population, so when the French colonized the island, they enslaved labour from Africa and neighbouring Madagascar to work the sugar plantations. After the abolition of slavery, landowners brought in indentured workers from China and the Indian subcontinent. The legacy of these waves of immigrants is a diverse mixture of ethnic groups. According to the 1990 census, the population was 51% Hindu, 16% Muslim and 2% Sino-Mauritian—the remaining 31% included those of Franco-Mauritian, African or mixed descent.

Mauritius has made a determined effort to ensure equal rights for all its ethnic groups. As in many other countries, equality is enshrined in the law: the constitution explicitly outlaws all forms of discrimination based on race, sex or religion and has provisos to guarantee national representation to minority groups.

The country has also taken steps to preserve its cultural heritage. Language is one clear example. The official language is English, but French and Creole are more widely spoken. In addition, Asian languages, including Hindi, Tamil, Telugu, Urdu and Mandarin, are taught in schools as optional subjects and allocated radio and TV airtime roughly in proportion to the number of people who speak them.

But the main guarantor of social cohesion and economic progress has been education. Primary and secondary education are both free—and enrolment ratios are high. When in 1991 there were still concerns that poorer children were receiving substandard education, the Master Plan for Education set aside special assistance for low-achieving schools.

Mauritius's success in promoting a diverse society does not spring from government action alone. The country also has numerous people's associations representing its myriad social groups—preserving the cultural heritage and providing an important political voice during electoral campaigns.

The government has placed a strong emphasis on social spending and never maintained a standing army. It spends less than 5% of the public budget, and only 0.2% of its GNP, on defence—opening the possibility for a strong social programme. Health care is also widely available—and free to all. Malnutrition persists, but the government has taken measures to reduce it, including providing free milk for pregnant and nursing women and a school lunch programme.

Between 1975 and 1990, the proportion of children under five who were malnourished fell from 32% to 17%. In addition to free education and health care, Mauritius provides an old-age pension plan, price subsidies for rice and flour and some measure of unemployment relief.

This social spending underpins strong economic performance. Between 1960 and 1991, annual per capita income rose from about $300 to $2,380. And following a period of structural adjustment, the economy has become much more diversified. Unemployment at the beginning of the 1980s was around 30%, but by 1992 it had dropped to only 3%.

The achievements should not disguise the fact that there are still wide economic disparities. More than 50% of harvested land is in 19 large estates, controlled by a few powerful families. The rest of the acreage is divided among 33,000 small planters whose plots average around one hectare.

The growth and diversification of the economy have, however, contributed to a rise in real wages and some redistribution of income. Between 1980–81 and 1991–92, the Gini coefficient of income distribution fell from 0.45 to 0.38.

Mauritius still has economic and social problems, but it provides a remarkable model of economic progress with social diversity.

Zimbabwe

Zimbabwe has an impressive record on social integration. After independence, the government reassured the whites that their property would be respected. But it also concentrated public investment on basic social services—which directed resources to the poorer black community.

Despite a long and divisive colonial history, a bitter war of liberation and disputes between the two main political groups, post-independence Zimbabwe has had a relatively smooth transition to black majority rule. Other African countries suffered bloodshed after independence—or saw a massive exodus of whites. But Zimbabwe from the outset offered the white population safety, freedom and legal protection at the same time that it accelerated its investment in the black population.

One of the terms of the treaty that ended the country's civil war was that there was to be no expropriation of white farms. The government honoured that undertaking and gave whites some strategic government posts—including minister of agriculture and minister of commerce and industry. These measures reassured the white community that it was welcome to remain if it was willing to work within the new democratic framework.

The guarantees offered to the whites have, however, also perpetuated considerable inequality. They still own almost half the land and nearly all the investment capital in mining and industry. In 1989, they received 70% of agricultural credit, extension and other services.

In addition to reconciling the black and white communities, the new governing party, ZANU, had to resolve conflicts between itself and ZAPU, the rival group that had also fought for independence. These differences were eventually overcome in 1987 with a Unity Accord, which offered dissidents a general amnesty.

Although there has been no direct redistribution of land or other resources, the government has given priority in social spending to the communal lands that are home to most of the black community. Since 1980, approximately 2,000 primary and 1,200 secondary schools have been built there.

Between 1982 and 1988, the government dramatically expanded primary health care programmes in the rural areas. It also reoriented agricultural services towards the communal lands, and its supportive price policy improved the income of smallholders.

Despite the considerable investment in human development, economic growth in the 1980s was disappointing. Private investment fell as a proportion of GDP, and the labour force grew faster than employment—only one school leaver in three was being absorbed into the formal sector. By the end of the 1980s, it became clear that the government would have to make fundamental economic changes, so in 1991 it introduced a structural adjustment programme.

The programme helped stabilize the economy—but at significant human cost. The government reintroduced school fees, for example, as well as health care charges—and school dropout and infant mortality rates have been rising. Zimbabwe has higher human development levels than the average for Sub-Saharan Africa—life expectancy, for example, is eight years longer. But it does not have an efficient social safety net for the poorest—who have seen their living standards fall in recent years. The government did establish a Social Fund to mitigate the effects of adjustment on the poor, but very few people have benefited. In 1992, their problems worsened after a crippling drought ruined most of the crops in the communal lands.

Zimbabwe has made remarkable progress in social integration. Its major achievement lies in raising the human development levels of the black community without restricting opportunities for the white population—thus avoiding social tension.

CHAPTER 3

Capturing the peace dividend

They shall beat their swords into ploughshares, and their spears into pruning hooks. Nation shall not lift up sword against nation. Neither shall they learn war any more.

It appeared that the time for this prophecy had come with the end of the cold war. But so far this has proved to be an elusive hope. The removal of ideological hostility has prompted some reduction in military expenditure, but not yet on a very significant scale. Around 30 million people are still employed in the world's armed forces. Vast arsenals of nuclear weapons remain, enough to destroy all life on this planet several times over. And at any one time, there are dozens of military conflicts going on in trouble spots around the world (box 3.1).

These conflicts are increasingly a threat not just to the lives of military personnel but also to civilian populations. At the beginning of this century, around 90% of war casualties were military. Today, about 90% are civilian—a disastrous shift in the balance.

Indeed, one of the greatest concerns of this century is the extent to which whole societies have become militarized. In the industrial countries, the development of expensive and sophisticated weapons has meant that technological and military progress have become increasingly intertwined. By 1990, of the five to seven million people engaged in research and development, around 1.5 million were working in the military sector.

There has certainly been opposition to the militarization of the political process— active peace groups in many industrial countries have argued vigorously against the arms race in principle. But the inexorable logic of the balance of terror kept military considerations firmly in the driver's seat, so that the military-industrial complex retained a pervasive influence over whole societies—and encouraged the belief that security essentially meant military security.

In developing countries, the military have also played a central part. Here, however, their role has sometimes been less technological and more directly political. In countries with weakly developed democratic systems, the armed forces have generally been better funded and more organized than other institutions—and have often been in a strong position to direct the political process and subvert democracy.

BOX 3.1

Armed conflicts within states increasing

Global conflicts seem to be changing— from wars between states to wars within them. Of the 82 armed conflicts between 1989 and 1992, only three were between states. Although often cast in ethnic divisions, many also have a political or economic character.

Most conflicts are in developing countries. During 1993, 42 countries in the world had 52 major conflicts, and another 37 countries had political violence. Of these 79 countries, 65 were in the developing world.

But there have been conflicts in all regions. In Europe—Bosnia, Georgia, Turkey and the United Kingdom. In the Middle East—Iraq, Israel and Lebanon. In Latin America—Colombia and Guatemala. In Asia—Bangladesh, India, Indonesia, Iran, the Lao People's Democratic Republic, Myanmar, Pakistan, the Philippines, Sri Lanka and Tajikistan. And in Africa—Angola, Chad, Ethiopia, Morocco, Somalia, South Africa, Sudan, Uganda, Zaire and Zimbabwe.

Many of the conflicts within states are protracted. More than half the conflicts in 1993 had been under way for more than a decade, taking the lives of four to six million people. Between 1989 and 1992, more than a thousand people were dying each year in eight countries: Afghanistan, Angola, India, Peru, the Philippines, Somalia, Sri Lanka and Sudan.

These conflicts have also caused millions of people to flee their borders to avoid repression and death. In 1983, there were nine countries from which more than 50,000 people had fled. But by 1992, there were 31. The major refugee-generating countries in the past decade: Afghanistan (4.3 million), former Yugoslavia (1.8 million) and Mozambique (1.7 million).

Since 1945, more than 20 million people have died in wars and other conflicts. Even in this era of "peace", the numbers show no signs of abating. Unless strong national and international action is taken, the death toll will continue to rise.

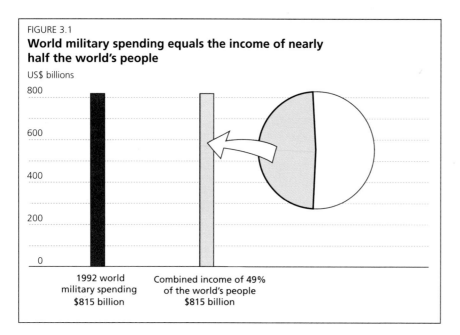

FIGURE 3.1
World military spending equals the income of nearly half the world's people

US$ billions

1992 world
military spending
$815 billion

Combined income of 49%
of the world's people
$815 billion

1991, global military spending fell from $995 billion to $855 billion (table 3.1). In the industrial countries, the drop was from $850 billion to $725 billion (nearly 15%); in the developing countries, from $145 billion to $130 billion (10%).

Disarmament in industrial countries

The dramatic changes in the international political climate have not been matched by correspondingly steep falls in military spending in industrial countries. The general policy is to continue with the programmes of the 1970s and 1980s. Some weapons procurement has been postponed, and some projects have been cancelled. But the principal policy is "a little less of the same", with little effort to design an entirely new security system.

This is a question partly of scale and partly of momentum. The huge commercial and military organizations are fairly inflexible, and cutting arms production and procurement can bring serious problems. Cuts in research and development tend to be even slower since governments generally wish to maintain their capacity to acquire state-of-the-art weapons systems, even if they do not buy as many. Govern-

This pervasive military ethos in both industrial and developing countries was reflected in global military spending, which reached a historical peak in 1987. The reduction in expenditure in recent years is certainly a hopeful sign, but there clearly is a long way to go. Military spending is still very high given the lengthening global agenda of human insecurity (figure 3.1). Most of the reductions in expenditure have been in the industrial countries. Between 1987 and

TABLE 3.1
Global military expenditures and the peace dividend
(US$ billions in 1991 prices and exchange rates)

	1987	1988	1989	1990	1991	1992	1993 (est.)	1994 (est.)	Total 1987–94
Actual military spending									
World	995	970	945	890	855	815	790	767	7,027
Industrial countries[a]	850	835	815	760	725	690	669	649	5,993
Developing countries	145	135	130	130	130	125	121	118	1,034
Actual cumulative peace dividend									
World	0	25	50	105	140	180	205	228	933
Industrial countries[a]	0	15	35	90	125	160	181	201	807
Developing countries	0	10	15	15	15	20	24	27	126

	1995	1996	1997	1998	1999	2000	Total 1995–2000
Projected military spending[b]							
World	744	722	700	679	659	639	4,143
Industrial countries[a]	630	611	593	575	558	541	3,508
Developing countries	114	111	107	104	101	98	635
Potential cumulative peace dividend							
World	23	45	67	88	108	128	459
Industrial countries[a]	19	38	56	74	91	108	386
Developing countries	4	7	11	14	17	20	73

a. China is included in the group of industrial countries for this comparison.
b. Assuming an annual reduction of 3%.

ments are also nervous about potential new threats—particularly ethnic and territorial conflicts in Europe. In these circumstances, decision-makers and military personnel are tempted to hold on to existing structures.

Opposition to change can come from different directions. Arms producers raise the spectre of job losses, so they lobby their governments to buy more weapons, provide higher subsidies and give more support to exports. Local politicians fearing unemployment also argue against the closure of factories and military bases. And within the armed forces, officers and soldiers protest being demobilized.

This opposition has slowed the process but not stopped it—chiefly because of budgetary pressures. In the United States, government policy is to cut military spending as a way of reducing the huge budget deficit. And in the 12 countries of the Commonwealth of Independent States, the mounting economic difficulties have also prompted sharp reductions. The initial cuts are usually the easiest, but domestic budgetary pressures should drive military spending down further. A target reduction of 3% a year during 1993–2000 may be fairly feasible in industrial nations given the actual cuts of about 4% a year during 1987–92.

Western Europe has not yet reduced its spending much. The most expensive arms project—the four-nation Eurofighter, designed to fight the communist enemy—is going ahead despite the disappearance of the East-West conflict. Elsewhere, there have even been increases in arms production. Australia and Japan have long-term commitments to retain or even expand their arms industries.

Nor should one set aside the nuclear threat: although reduced, it has by no means disappeared. The reductions envisaged in the START I and II treaties, for example, called for the removal of more than 20,000 warheads from the arsenals of nuclear weapons states—but not a single warhead has been dismantled so far. Several states continue to pursue nuclear weapons programmes. This could stall hopes of removing the nuclear threat (box 3.2).

Disarmament in developing countries

The developing countries have made even less progress in reducing military expenditure. With surprisingly little international outcry, their military expenditures rose three times as fast as those of the industrial countries between 1960 and 1987—from $24 billion to $145 billion, an increase of 7.5% a year, compared with 2.8% for the industrial countries. As a result, the developing countries' share of global military expenditures rose from 7% to 15%. A significant part of this spending—one-third— was by the countries of the Middle East and

---

BOX 3.2

The continuing nuclear threat

The most welcome effect of the end of the cold war has been the reduced risk of a nuclear catastrophe, but the threat has by no means disappeared. One major concern is the reduction of today's stock of nuclear weapons. The United States and the Soviet Union (or the successor states) have signed the Intermediate-range Nuclear Forces Treaty (1987) and the two treaties on the reduction of strategic offensive arms— START I (1991) and START II (1993). These have helped reduce tension, but they have important limitations. They specify, for example, that warheads be removed from delivery systems, but they do not specify that the warheads be destroyed. Indeed, neither the United States nor Russia has a technically or politically feasible plan to dismantle warheads or dispose of their nuclear components—so the warheads could represent a threat for generations to come. The breakup of the Soviet Union has also complicated matters since agreements now have to be made with the successor states. However, Ukraine has recently ratified START I, which enables START II to come into force.

The other major concern is nuclear proliferation. In addition to the five acknowledged nuclear powers (China, France, Russia, the United Kingdom and the United States) and three successor states of the former Soviet Union with nuclear weapons on their territory (Belarus, Kazakhstan and Ukraine), only three other states are presumed to have nuclear weapons or the ability to deploy them on short notice (India,

Israel and Pakistan). At least four other countries are believed to aspire to nuclear weapons status (Algeria, the Democratic Republic of Korea, Iran and Iraq). Libya and Syria are thought to have similar ambitions but lack the resources to mount a credible threat. On the positive side, three other states appear to have halted nuclear weapons development (Argentina, Brazil and South Africa).

So far, 157 countries have signed the 1967 Non-proliferation Treaty, and there are proposals to extend the treaty indefinitely after 1995. But there are doubts that the treaty will hold. Some countries disagree in principle—complaining that the treaty establishes a "nuclear apartheid" by offering a distinct advantage to the early adopters of nuclear weapons. And some developing countries are also reluctant to agree to restraints that can prevent them from acquiring important technology that also has non-nuclear uses.

There are practical problems, too. The treaty relies heavily on the control of technology transfers, and this has proved difficult to coordinate among exporting countries. It also relies too much on threats by bigger powers and not enough on a shared incentive system.

A more fundamental problem is that some countries still feel threats from their neighbours and regard the possession of nuclear weapons as an effective deterrent. As in the industrial countries, the only way to discourage the production of nuclear weapons is to remove the causes of conflict.

North Africa. But the remainder—a staggering $95 billion a year—was in some of the world's poorest countries.

Developing countries often justified this high military spending on the grounds that it provided an effective deterrent against intervention—either by superpowers or by neighbouring countries—and earned the country respect in the international arena. They have also pointed out that the military have been an important source of employment and technological spin-offs for civilian industry.

Whether this spending brought increased security to the average citizen of these countries is doubtful. In developing countries, the chances of dying from social neglect (from malnutrition and preventable diseases) are 33 times greater than the chances of dying in a war from external aggression. Yet, on average, there are about 20 soldiers for every physician. If anything, the soldiers are more likely to reduce personal security than to increase it. Developing countries have fought few international wars, and many have used their armed forces to repress their people.

Arms spending undermines human security in another way—by eating up precious resources that could have been used for human development (figure 3.2). In 1987 alone, the developing world spent more than $34 billion of its scarce foreign exchange reserves on arms imports (75% of the world's arms trade in that year went to the poor nations).

India and Pakistan together accounted for more than 18% of world arms imports—nearly twice as much as Saudi Arabia's share. Even more disturbing is Sub-Saharan Africa, where the proportion of the regional GDP devoted to military spending increased from 0.7% in 1960 to 3.0% in 1991. At a time of severe structural adjust-

Arms spending undermines human security, eating up precious resources that could have been used for human development

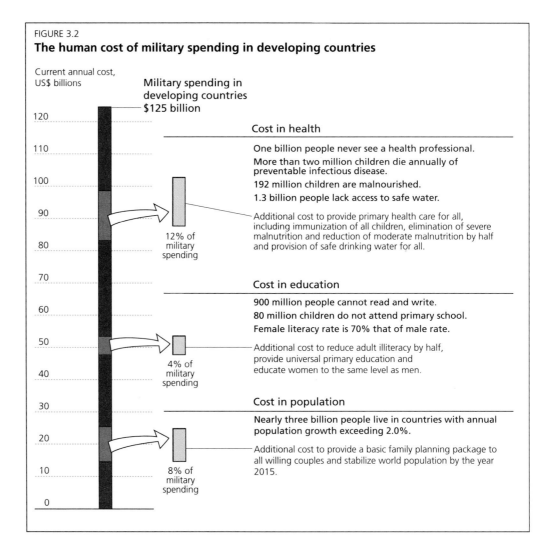

FIGURE 3.2

The human cost of military spending in developing countries

Current annual cost, US$ billions

Military spending in developing countries $125 billion

Cost in health

One billion people never see a health professional.
More than two million children die annually of preventable infectious disease.
192 million children are malnourished.
1.3 billion people lack access to safe water.

12% of military spending — Additional cost to provide primary health care for all, including immunization of all children, elimination of severe malnutrition and reduction of moderate malnutrition by half and provision of safe drinking water for all.

Cost in education

900 million people cannot read and write.
80 million children do not attend primary school.
Female literacy rate is 70% that of male rate.

4% of military spending — Additional cost to reduce adult illiteracy by half, provide universal primary education and educate women to the same level as men.

Cost in population

Nearly three billion people live in countries with annual population growth exceeding 2.0%.

8% of military spending — Additional cost to provide a basic family planning package to all willing couples and stabilize world population by the year 2015.

ment, much deeper cuts were being made in social than in military spending.

The loss of potential spending on human development is enormous. Even some of the poorest countries spend more on their military than on their people's education and health: Angola, Ethiopia, Mozambique, Myanmar, Pakistan, Somalia and Yemen.

It is sobering to reflect that countries spending very little on defence and much more on human development have been more successful at defending their national sovereignty than those spending heavily on arms. Compare the relatively peaceful experiences of Botswana, Costa Rica and Mauritius with the conflicts afflicting Iraq, Myanmar and Somalia.

Some developing regions have nevertheless cut their arms expenditure. Countries in the Middle East in some cases had little choice, since they were facing arms embargoes. There also were cuts in some Latin American countries, where governments undergoing structural adjustment were cutting their spending. But the picture was worse in South Asia and Sub-Saharan Africa, where armies continued to flourish in the midst of human misery (table 3.2). Despite having 800 million people in absolute poverty, the two regions continued to spend heavily on arms: South Asia $19 billion, and Sub-Saharan Africa $8 billion.

Some of the blame for this goes to the industrial countries, which have yet to phase out their military assistance or arms shipments. Indeed, in the past three years, several industrial countries, fearing job losses in defence industries, have increased their subsidies to arms exporters and encouraged them to increase sales to developing countries. Despite rhetoric to the contrary, the heads of state of some industrial countries take a keen interest in promoting international arms sales.

The future of world disarmament

The disappearance of the cold war and the ensuing reduction in military spending led to an initial expectation that world disarmament would follow automatically. Clearly, that is not the case. The removal of one source of antagonism has revealed many others. Some are conflicts that had been suppressed by the larger superpower rivalry. Others are bitter, ongoing struggles that have cost lives for decades but been eclipsed by larger disputes.

Given the diversity of these disputes and the factors that sustain them, promoting human security at a global level will be a long and complex process. There is no simple formula for success. But future progress will clearly demand a higher level of cooperation between industrial and developing countries—to create new forums for peace talks in different parts of the world, to regulate the arms trade and to agree on a new role for the United Nations.

Disarmament is needed more urgently in the Third World. The cold war is not over yet—the job is only half-done. All the disarmament talks so far have been between East and West, not with Third World representatives. In the next phase of world disarmament, therefore, special attention must be paid to the problems of the developing countries.

Some of the most important steps in further world disarmament would be to:
- Establish forums for disarmament
- Defuse tensions around the globe
- Phase out military assistance
- Regulate the arms trade
- Design a new aid policy dialogue
- Agree on criteria for UN mediation in conflicts within nations
- Create more effective information systems.

Establish forums for disarmament

So far, the disarmament talks have been largely among industrial nations. Bilateral

The cold war is not over yet—the job is only half-done

TABLE 3.2
High military spending among poor countries

Country	GNP per capita (US$) 1991	Military expenditure per capita (US$) 1990/91
Sudan	400	23.3
Ethiopia	120	14.9
Chad	210	10.7
Burkina Faso	290	10.5
Mozambique	80	9.5
Mali	270	6.8

or regional negotiations in the developing world have had much less impact. One of the first priorities should be to develop some new institutional frameworks for disarmament. The obvious starting points are existing regional forums, such as the Organization for African Unity (OAU), the Organization of American States (OAS), the South Asian Association for Regional Cooperation (SAARC) and the Association of South-East Asian Nations (ASEAN). The OAU, for example, is already playing a major role in conflict resolution in Liberia. Another alternative, which covers most developing countries, would be the Non-Aligned Movement.

Although some of these forums have specifically excluded any discussion of defence issues, the time may have come to reassess this policy. The forums could be useful umbrellas for some quiet bilateral diplomacy—and enable other neighbouring countries to apply some constructive pressure to normalize relations. The agreement signed in Tegucigalpa in December 1991 by six Central American heads of state is a good precedent (box 3.3).

The United Nations could also be more active—say, by providing strong secretariat support for any concrete moves towards Third World disarmament. So far, disarmament has focused more on high-technology weapons, when the real problems are small weapons. The United Nations has already taken initiatives on one of the worst killers—land-mines.

Defuse tensions around the globe

The defence buildup in many developing countries has been a genuine response to geopolitical tensions, some of which are already being defused—as with the expected settlement of the Israeli-Palestinian conflict, the peace process in Central America and the expected democratic elections in South Africa. Each of these issues has benefited from a strong and constructive interest from the major powers, the Non-Aligned Movement and the United Nations. And there clearly are many other opportunities for similar mediation.

The major powers might consider that they have a moral obligation to create such alliances for peace—to make up for their previous strategy of using the Third World as territory for fighting their proxy wars. Whether the developing countries would welcome such assistance is another matter. Governments may quietly appreciate the enhanced opportunities for peaceful accommodation, but opposition parties and domestic public opinion could consider this to be unwarranted interference.

Since there are often reservations about industrial country involvement, it might be better to use the forum of the United Nations. The UN is likely to be called in only after the outbreak of hostilities—either between or within states. But there is also a strong case for the UN to be involved when it expects major problems. (Chapter 2 of this Report has already identified several crisis spots and underlined the need to engage in preventive diplomacy to defuse any expected crises.)

BOX 3.3

A Central American accord for human development

Central America for decades was one of the world's most conflict-ridden regions. Civil wars, rebellions and cold war confrontations turned many of these small countries into battlefields. By the end of the 1980s, there were more than two million displaced people—10% of the region's population.

Since then, a concerted effort by national leaders and the international community has produced a remarkable transformation. A series of 14 presidential summits has not only helped silence many of the guns but also defused tension and promoted cooperation in human development.

The Esquipulas Declaration of August 1987 was a milestone. This mutual commitment became the basis for an appeal to the international community to support peace and development throughout the region—in every country, regardless of political orientation.

Another milestone was the General Assembly resolution in May 1988 establishing the Special Plan of Economic Cooperation for Central America (PEC). Within this framework, some of the most difficult issues were settled through two internationally supported programmes: the concerted action plan (CIREFCA) and the programme for displaced persons, refugees and returnees (PRODERE), which sought to promote social integration in areas afflicted by poverty and armed conflict. Together, these programmes have helped 210,000 refugees return to their homes and 470,000 benefit from credit and other programmes to rebuild their communities.

These efforts towards sustainable development were further consolidated by the Tegucigalpa Commitment in 1991, which established human development goals for the region up to 2000. Seven National Action Plans were prepared, refocusing budget priorities on the social sectors. The recent summit in Guatemala in October 1993 identified further priorities and called for democratic participation.

Many civil and professional organizations have become more assertive and effective—notably on human rights issues. And several countries are moving towards democratic electoral processes.

Such crises are not necessarily provoked by political unrest: economic collapse and natural disasters can also lead to social breakdown. And on this issue, the UN Secretary-General has been quite explicit in his *Agenda for Peace:*

Drought and disease can decimate no less mercilessly than the weapons of war. So at this moment of renewed opportunity, the efforts of the Organization to build peace, stability and security must encompass matters beyond military threats in order to break the fetters of strife and warfare that have characterized the past.

If the UN is to help prevent such emergencies exploding into violent internal conflicts, its developmental role will have to be considerably strengthened, a subject discussed in chapter 4.

Phase out military assistance

Military assistance to the Third World formed one cornerstone of the cold war—as superpowers bolstered their allies with all manner of expensive hardware. It also had commercial motives, helping sustain the output of the arms industry by subsidizing exports and unloading outdated weaponry.

This kind of assistance declined sharply in recent years (table 3.3). Between 1987 and 1993, it fell from $21 billion to $5 billion. It should be emphasized, however, that most of the decline has been in the sale of larger conventional weapons—sales of small arms continue unabated.

The sharpest fall was from the successor states of the former Soviet Union—whose military aid, chiefly to Eastern Europe and Cuba, has stopped. US mili-

tary assistance has declined more slowly—between 1987 and 1993, it fell from $5.4 billion to $3.4 billion. The reason is that two-thirds of US security assistance is concentrated in Israel and Egypt, which continue to be strategic allies of the United States. The United States has also reduced its military training of personnel in around 100 countries—from 56,000 in 1975 to 4,500 in 1992.

Closely related to military assistance are military bases, which have contributed to the militarization of developing countries and distorted the social and economic development of many cities and regions. Some of these bases are already being phased out.

The most significant moves so far are for two major US installations in the Philippines—although in neither case was the closure a voluntary US decision. The Subic Bay naval facility was closed in 1992, because the Philippine Senate refused to extend the lease, and the Clark air base closure was precipitated by the eruption of nearby Mount Pinatubo in 1991 (box 3.4). But many of the functions of these bases

Drought and disease can decimate no less mercilessly than the weapons of war

---

A new horizon for Subic Bay

The US naval facility at Subic Bay in the Philippines was one of the world's largest overseas military bases. Its transformation illustrates some of the major problems and opportunities of converting bases from military to civilian use.

In addition to the 6,000 US military personnel, the base employed 27,000 Philippine citizens and many local contractors. The adjacent small town of Olongapo depended heavily on the base—providing a range of services to the sailors, including dozens of bars and thousands of prostitutes.

The United States estimated the value of the base on its departure at $1.4 billion. Besides the deep-water port and an airport, there were 1,607 family housing units, a 198-patient hospital, six cinemas and a golf course. But there was also a more sinister legacy of environmental contamination. The residue of chemicals used in fire-fighting flowed directly into the bay. Heavy metals from the shipyard operation also drained into

the bay or were buried in landfills. Chemicals were released into the air by the powerplant. And gasoline and oil leaked into the soil from underground tanks.

By the time the base closed in 1992, the mayor of Olongapo had helped establish a Subic Bay Metropolitan Authority whose aim was to turn the former base into the "Hong Kong" of the Philippines. At the end of 1993, the authority had attracted 33 investors and $340 million to the base—including a US power corporation now running the powerplant, a US petroleum company using the fuel tanks for distribution, Philippine garment manufacturers and international investors interested in creating resort facilities.

But the unknown level of environmental contamination—probably the most significant obstacle to further progress—is already deterring some international investors and could pose serious health problems in the future.

TABLE 3.3
Estimates of worldwide military assistance
(billions of 1993 US$)

Country or region	1987	1993	Total reduction (1987–93)
United States	5.4	3.4	2.0
Western Europe	1.3	0.9	0.4
Arab States	0.3	0.2	0.1
China	0.3	0.1	0.2
Former USSR	13.5	0.0	13.5
Total	20.8	4.6	16.2

---

have been transferred to other countries in the region, including Guam, Japan and Singapore.

Military assistance has many damaging effects for poor countries. In addition to fuelling regional arms races, it has created distortions. Though the weapons may have been supplied cheaply, they have still entailed vast ancillary expenses—for infrastructure, maintenance and spare parts—diverting resources that could have been put to more productive use. Military assistance has also had powerful political and social impacts—greatly strengthening the army, for example, and opening opportunities for considerable corruption by both buyers and sellers. Some countries have also been landed with heavy debts since the former Soviet Union often gave military aid as loans. India owes the successor states $11.3 billion, Viet Nam $11.6 billion, Mongolia $12.1 billion and Cuba $19.7 billion, with more than half the debts apparently resulting from arms transfers.

The current international climate offers a unique opportunity to reach an international agreement to phase out military assistance over, say, a three-year period. There will certainly be opposition to such a proposal, not least from the international arms lobbies. The Social Summit is one place where such an initiative could be launched.

Regulate the arms trade

The arms business is one of the most reprehensible sectors of international trade. Arms traders have no compunction about making profits out of poverty—selling sophisticated jet fighters or nuclear submarines to countries where millions of people lack the most basic means of survival (box 3.5). The top five exporting countries, which sell 86% of the conventional weapons exported to developing countries, in descending order: the former Soviet Union, the United States, France, China and the United Kingdom, all permanent members of the Security Council (figure 3.3). They sell two-thirds of these arms to ten developing countries—among them some of the poorest countries of the world, such as Afghanistan, India and Pakistan, which account for nearly 30% of developing country imports.

Even more regrettable is that arms dealers continue to ship weapons to potential trouble spots, showing little concern about fanning the flames of conflict. More than 40% of the sales of major conventional weapons during the past decade went to such trouble spots (table 3.4). Of the major suppliers, Brazil, China, Egypt, France, Italy, Libya, Romania, the former Soviet Union, Spain and the United States have been among the chief offenders (table 3.5 and figure 3.4). Ironically, the supplier countries lost control of the spread of wea-

---

TABLE 3.5
Deliveries by ten suppliers to countries at war, 1980–89
(as a % of their total deliveries of major conventional weapons)

Syrian Arab Rep.	99
Libyan Arab Jamahiriya	96
Egypt	90
Brazil	47
China	40
Former Soviet Union	35
France	23
United Kingdom	9
USA	5
Germany[a]	2

a. Federal Republic only.

BOX 3.5

The human development cost of arms imports

Many countries continue to import expensive arms, even though they have a long list of more essential items. This is clear from the arms deliveries and orders in the categories covered by the UN's arms register. Some of the choices by developing countries in 1992:

• *China*—purchased 26 combat aircraft from Russia in a deal whose total cost could have provided safe water for one year to 140 million of the 200 million people now without safe water.

• *India*—ordered 20 MiG-29 fighter aircraft from Russia at a cost that could have provided basic education to all the 15 million girls out of school.

• *Iran*—bought two submarines from Russia at a cost that could have provided essential medicines to the whole country many times over; 13% of Iran's population has no access to health care.

• *Republic of Korea*—ordered 28 missiles from the United States for an amount that could have immunized all the 120,000 unimmunized children and provided safe water for three years to the 3.5 million people without safe water.

• *Malaysia*—ordered two warships from the United Kingdom at a cost that could have provided safe water for nearly a quarter century to the five million people without safe water.

• *Nigeria*—purchased 80 battle tanks from the United Kingdom at a cost that could have immunized all of the two million unimmunized children and provided family planning services to nearly 17 million of the more than 20 million couples who lack such services.

• *Pakistan*—ordered 40 Mirage 2000E fighters and three Tripartite aircraft from France at a cost that could have provided safe water for two years for all 55 million people who lack safe water, family planning services for the estimated 20 million couples in need of such services, essential medicines for the nearly 13 million people without access to health care and basic education for the 12 million children out of primary school.

TABLE 3.4
Sales of major conventional weapons
(billions of 1990 US$)

	1985	1992	Average annual change (%) 1985–92
World sales (US$ billions)	40	18	−10.5
Sales to developing countries (%)	57	51	−1.6
Sales to conflict countries/ trouble spots (%)	37	42	1.8

pons and later had to try vigorously to collect the arms they supplied in the first place.

The arms trade is a notoriously murky business. When weapons are being bought and sold, the purpose for which they are intended is rarely clear—whether for legitimate needs of national security, for wars of external aggression, for campaigns of internal repression or for merely satisfying the greed of those who benefit from the transactions (table 3.6). There has never been any satisfactory accounting for arms sales—to the citizens of the buying and selling countries, or to the international community.

These weapons have not just wrought havoc within the buying countries. They have also on occasion been turned against the soldiers from the supplying nations—as in recent conflicts involving Iraq and Somalia.

One major challenge of the post–cold war era must be to design a comprehensive policy framework for arms production and sales. Clearly, much of the pressure for international sales comes from producers promoting overseas sales to recoup overheads and maximize profits. So, if industrial countries genuinely seek world peace, they should be concerned not just about their levels of procurement, but also about their national levels of production. The same should apply to developing countries that also produce arms: Brazil, China, India, the Republic of Korea, South Africa and Turkey

TABLE 3.6
Arms trade, 1988–92

	Exports of major conventional arms (millions of 1990 US$)		
Top arms exporters	1988	1992	Total 1988–92
USA	12,204	8,429	54,968
Former USSR/Russia	14,658	2,043	45,182
France	2,403	1,151	9,349
Germany	1,241	1,928	8,190
China	2,161	1,535	7,658
United Kingdom	1,704	952	7,623
Czechoslovakia	927	779	3,163
Netherlands	626	305	2,048
Italy	693	335	1,613
Sweden	606	113	1,416
Brazil	507	36	1,028
Total	40,034	18,405	151,014

	Imports of conventional arms (millions of 1990 US$)		
Top arms importers	1988	1992	Total 1988–92
India	3,709	1,197	12,235
Japan	2,544	1,095	9,224
Saudi Arabia	2,441	883	8,690
Afghanistan	1,264	1,215[a]	7,515
Greece	814	1,918	6,197
Turkey	1,447	1,511	6,167
Iraq	2,845	596[b]	4,967
Total	40,034	18,405	151,014

a. 1991.
b. 1990.

FIGURE 3.3
The permanent members of the UN Security Council supply the most weapons to developing countries

Biggest suppliers
Percentage of weapons sales to developing countries, 1988–92

Biggest buyers
Percentage of weapons purchases by developing countries, 1988–92

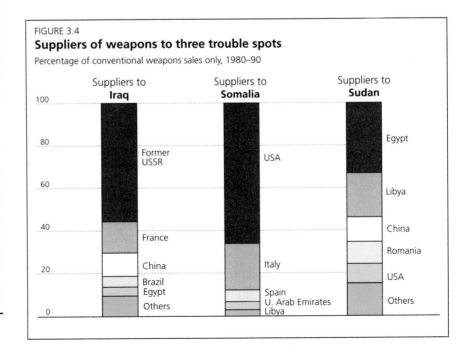

FIGURE 3.4
Suppliers of weapons to three trouble spots
Percentage of conventional weapons sales only, 1980–90

The legacy of land-mines

Strewn liberally in most modern wars, more than 105 million unexploded land-mines are believed to remain buried in at least 62 countries. The UN estimates that 800 people die every month from mines. The countries worst affected: Afghanistan, Angola, Cambodia, El Salvador, Iraq, Kuwait, Nicaragua and Somalia.

Mines continue to kill and maim civilians long after a conflict ends. In Angola, two decades of civil war have left 20 million land-mines in the earth, two for every person in the country. The mines kill 120 Angolans each month. In Afghanistan, 12 million mines were laid during the 1980s war. In Cambodia, one mine remains in the ground for every two people living in the country, killing or maiming 300 people each month. In former Yugoslavia, 60,000 mines are being laid each month.

The increasing use of land-mines reflects the changes in modern conflicts. Armies are more often engaged nowadays in drawn-out, low-intensity conflicts in which one of the objectives is to demoralize not just the opposing army but also the civilian population.

Land-mines are a lucrative part of the arms trade. With around 340 types of mines in production, at least 48 countries now manufacture them, and at least 29 countries export them. China, Italy, Romania and the United States are among the major exporters.

Clearing land-mines is difficult and expensive—between $300 and $1,000 per mine, each of which originally cost perhaps as little as $3. Removing them all will cost $200 to $300 billion—so it is likely to take decades, even generations, to exhume the backlog.

In 1993, the UN General Assembly, concerned "that such mines kill or maim hundreds of people each week, mostly unarmed civilians", called on "States to agree to a moratorium on the export of anti-personnel land-mines that pose grave dangers to civilian populations". Realistically, the only hope for progress lies in an international agreement to stop the production and use of these barbaric weapons.

The United Nations Register of Conventional Armaments

In 1992, the Secretary-General of the United Nations for the first time published a register of conventional armaments. In total, 80 countries (including all the exporters except South Africa and the Democratic Republic of Korea) submitted data on weapons transferred. There were seven categories: battle tanks (1,733 transferred), armoured combat vehicles (1,625), large-calibre artillery systems (1,682), combat aircraft (270), attack helicopters (40), warships (40) and missiles and missile launchers (67,878).

The system still has weaknesses. Some are definitional—it is not completely clear, for example, what exactly constitutes a transfer. And there are problems of incomplete information or insufficient detail (supplier and recipient reports of the same transfer often do not match). Financial data are also excluded, with weapons reported by number and not by value. And several categories of weapons do not have to be reported at all—including bombs, small arms and ground-to-air missiles.

While nearly all exporters reported their sales, far fewer importers reported their purchases. Almost 60% failed to participate—including such importers as Bangladesh, Iran, Kuwait, Saudi Arabia, Syria, Taiwan (province of China) and Thailand.

Since the register excludes local production and procurement, it gives only a partial picture of the quantity of weapons produced and in the possession of armed forces. It nevertheless is an important breakthrough—the first time that governments have made such data public—and it could be the basis for a more complete reporting system.

The register is expected to be even more effective when regional registers are established—for Asia, Africa, Europe and Latin America. The categories of weapons could then more appropriately reflect the security concerns in each region.

are expanding their arms industries.

While cutbacks in production should clearly apply to all arms, special emphasis should be placed on chemical weapons and on land-mines, which cause such terrible suffering to civilian populations: across the world an estimated 100 million land-mines are buried in unmarked locations awaiting their unsuspecting prey (box 3.6). In Cambodia alone, during 20 years of civil war, four million mines were placed. And in Angola, where conflict continues, more than 20,000 people have suffered amputations due to land-mine explosions.

While it is difficult to monitor and control local arms production, a start could be made in controlling international transfers. The United Nations could, for example, set up a mechanism through which the Security Council could:
- Maintain a list of sophisticated weapons and technologies that should not be exported at all, except under international agreement.
- Strengthen the reporting system of the UN arms register, so that up-to-date information on arms and technology transactions is published regularly (box 3.7)
- Regulate and eliminate the use of explicit or hidden subsidies to arms exporters.
- Tax arms sales to finance peacekeeping.

This kind of system would greatly enhance the prospects for action to head off costly conflicts. The Social Summit offers an important opportunity to develop such a framework.

Design a new aid policy dialogue

Many bilateral donors and multilateral agencies are beginning to highlight the issue of military spending—concerned that recipient countries are frittering away aid on weapons, or using up high proportions of their domestic budgets on defence. Germany, Japan, the Netherlands, the IMF and the World Bank have all raised this issue recently, though they have yet to develop a coherent policy for their aid conditionality —or consider any form of international coordination.

Several courses of action are possible. One is to make aid allocations dependent on the recipient country's ratio of military to social spending—progressively reducing aid as the ratio becomes greater than 1. If a country spends more on its army than on its people, this should make donors stop and think. Of course, it would still be possible to keep this ratio below 1 even if social spending were very low or military spending very high, so an additional safeguard would be to set a minimum level of social spending (say, 5% of GNP) and a maximum level of military spending (say, 4% of GNP).

The same principles could be even more effective through positive incentives—giving more aid to countries that reduced their military expenditure.

Agree on criteria for UN mediation in conflicts within nations

The United Nations has intervened in conflicts between countries—to separate the combatants, to arrange cease-fires, to punish aggressors through internationally agreed sanctions and to buy time for a more permanent solution to the underlying dispute. The framework for such interventions is explicitly laid out in Chapter VII of the UN Charter.

Only recently has the UN been drawn into conflicts within nations—the Kurd rebellion in northern Iraq, the Shi'a rebellion in southern Iraq, the ethnic conflict in Bosnia, the disintegration of state authority in Somalia and the overthrow of democratically elected governments in Haiti and Myanmar. These crises raise some delicate questions. Should the UN risk infringing national sovereignty? What form should its intervention take—UN forces, emergency assistance or longer-term development aid?

Some of these issues are addressed in the Secretary-General's report, *An Agenda for Peace.* The report acknowledges that:

The nature of peacekeeping operations has evolved rapidly in recent years. The established principles and practices of peacekeeping have responded flexibly to the new demands of recent years, and the basic conditions of success remain unchanged: a clear and practicable mandate; the cooperation of the parties in im-plementing that mandate; the continuing support of the Security Council; the readiness of member states to contribute the military, police and civilian personnel, including specialists required; effective United Nations command at Headquarters and in the field; and adequate financial and logistic support.

When human security is threatened within nations, UN peacekeeping operations can succeed only when the organization has a clear and workable mandate. Chapter VII may have to be reinterpreted and broadened for this purpose (box 3.8).

The extra resources needed must also be clearly identified. Peacekeeping operations should, as the Secretary-General has recommended, be financed from defence budgets. If the resources are taken from donors' development assistance budgets, they risk upsetting the balance between

---

BOX 3.8

The UN's mandate for conflicts within nations

The UN is being called on to intervene in conflicts within nations—as in Angola, Bosnia, Cambodia, Haiti, Iraq and Somalia. Does it have a mandate and a well-defined strategy for intervening in such circumstances? Chapter VII of the UN Charter (articles 41 to 43) addresses the circumstances in which the UN can take action against individual states. But its provisions have been applied mostly to conflicts between nations. Now they will have to be reviewed and adapted to deal with conflicts within nations.

Three basic issues have to be resolved. When to intervene? In what way? And for how long?

Four situations would appear to warrant international intervention: (1) mass slaughter of the population by the state, (2) decimation through starvation or the withholding of health or other services, (3) forced exodus and (4) occupation and the denial of the right to self-determination. Environmental destruction would appear to be the natural choice for a fifth reason, though international standard-setting has yet to evolve sufficiently. In all such cases, there is a need to establish that the internal situation in a country is a threat not only to its own people but also to international peace and security.

On the form of intervention, soldiers in blue berets will usually be inappropriate in situations that cry out for socio-economic reform. In these situations, it is better to offer humanitarian assistance within a framework of longer-term development—through doctors, engineers or development personnel. Socio-economic interventions will clearly take much longer than military ones, and this should be accepted at the outset. Unless the objectives and time period are clearly specified, disillusionment will rapidly set in.

Nor should there be any attempt to use an occupying force to run the country. Instead, the UN should attempt to build appropriate political alliances.

In short, the traditional forms of UN action need to be critically reviewed to deal with new and different challenges—to decide who the combatants are, what sanctions to impose against each group, or how to enlist popular support for UN intervention.

Chapter VII of the UN Charter clearly needs a fundamental rethink. The Social Summit provides an opportunity to undertake such a review in the interests of global human security.

emergency and long-term development assistance. An important way of mobilizing resources for peacekeeping operations would be to impose taxes on the arms trade and put the money into a separate fund.

The UN will also need greater resources to carry out additional socio-economic development responsibilities. As well as being able to draw on soldiers from various nations, it should also be able to call on a voluntary corps of engineers, doctors, technicians and development personnel from all over the world.

Create more effective information systems

The transition from arms security to human security demands much more accurate information systems. If arms flows are to be slowed or halted, we need to know exactly where they are going and how.

Some data exist on military spending and the international arms trade, but there are also considerable gaps. Some of the most notable:

• *Military expenditure*—Although the military is one of the greatest consumers of public budgets and the earth's resources, few governments have considered it necessary to make military information available to their people or to the international community.

• *Arms transfers*—In 1992, for the first time, the United Nations established an arms register in which 80 countries reported on their imports and exports of major conventional weapons. But the reporting has glaring omissions that should be rectified.

• *Arms production*—Since excessive production of arms is responsible for much of the pressure for international sales, it is important to monitor all arms production.

• *Military assistance*—Neither donors nor recipients publish comprehensive data on military assistance. It would be useful for the Development Assistance Committee of the OECD to include tables on military assistance in its annual reports.

• *Subsidies to arms exporters*—It is almost impossible to find information on such subsidies, either explicit or hidden, making it very difficult to mobilize pressure for their elimination.

• *Military bases*—Information on bases is thin and scattered—whether on location, size or employment. Without such information, it is difficult to assess the impact of existing bases or the real implications of proposed closures.

• *Military debts*—Only in the past three years has the IMF started collecting data on the military debts of developing countries. The people of these countries could be in for a rude shock: the military debts of several countries may exceed their development debts. The IMF would perform a valuable service by regularly collecting and publishing these data.

These are just some of the areas where information is lacking. Indeed, the whole arms industry is surrounded by walls of secrecy that exclude public debate.

The seven-point agenda just outlined is not a detailed plan for Third World disarmament. Instead, it is intended as an invitation for the Social Summit to give the UN the mandate to draw up a time-bound blueprint for global disarmament.

The peace dividend

Reducing military spending is only half the task. A genuine improvement in human security requires that the resources saved—the "peace dividend"—be fully harnessed for human development.

A genuine improvement in human security requires that the "peace dividend" be fully harnessed

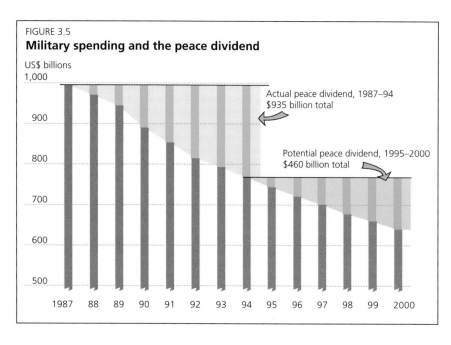

FIGURE 3.5

Military spending and the peace dividend

US$ billions

Actual peace dividend, 1987–94
$935 billion total

Potential peace dividend, 1995–2000
$460 billion total

During 1987–94, the industrial nations appear to have cumulatively saved some $810 billion, and the developing nations $125 billion, producing a sizable peace dividend of $935 billion. But it is difficult to track where these funds went. Most of the savings appear to have been committed to budget deficit reductions and non-development expenditures, rather than to social development or to environmental improvements. It is frustrating that, just as social and human agendas were pushed aside at a time of rising military budgets, they continue to be neglected even when military expenditures are being reduced.

If the world is to seize this opportunity, it will have to be much more positive and precise about future peace dividends. During 1995–2000, if an annual reduction of 3% in military spending is sustained, the peace dividend could be $460 billion (figure 3.5). The first task must be to separate this dividend as an item in national budget accounts—otherwise, it will disappear quietly, frustrating all efforts to track it down. If this had been done earlier, the public probably would have been more vociferous about its destination.

A Global Demilitarization Fund

The recent decline in world military spending presents us with an undeniable challenge. With reductions in military spending between 1987 and 1992 of 3% a year or more, an estimated cumulative dividend of $500 billion was trimmed from defence budgets—$500 billion that could have contributed much to global peace and human security.

What has happened to this peace dividend? Some of it has been absorbed by the costs of conversion from military to civilian activities. Another part has apparently been directed towards the reduction of budget deficits. However, no one knows for sure where the savings from reduced military spending are going. They are not being differentiated in national budgets, nor are they being sufficiently monitored. How long must we wait for the dividends of peace to become visible?

It is in this regard that I would like to propose the establishment of a Global Demilitarization Fund. This fund could add dynamism to the current demilitarization trend by rewarding primarily, but not exclusively, the efforts of developing countries to:

- Disarm and demobilize their armed forces.
- Re-integrate military personnel into society through retraining and re-education programmes in order to expand their range of choices and economic opportunities.
- Promote arms control and the shrinkage of arms production facilities.
- Encourage civic education and participation in fully democratic political life.

In addition, the Global Demilitarization Fund could stimulate the current decline in military spending by linking the reduction in military expenditure to the consolidation of world peace.

There has been a growing tendency for the industrial countries to look inward after the cold war. But they should understand that it is in their own interest to promote demilitarization around the globe.

Let the nations of the world, both rich and poor, commit themselves to at least a 3% a year reduction in their military spending levels over the next five years. The rich nations should agree to earmark at least one-fifth of these savings towards a demilitarization fund which is under international jurisdiction. Developing countries should also agree to contribute a fraction, perhaps one-tenth, of these savings towards such a fund.

The actual numbers are not important. What is important is the principle of committing a portion of the peace dividend to promote global demilitarization. Even those countries which do not reduce their military spending should still be obliged to contribute to the fund according to the prescribed formula.

Who will manage the Global Demilitarization Fund? This is for the 1995 Social Summit to decide. The World Bank and the United Nations agencies should be strongly considered. In any case, the designated institution should have sufficient capacity and authority to administer the Fund's resources justly and efficiently.

We cannot continue to ignore the threats posed by arms proliferation and the declining political and economic incentives to demilitarize. The Global Demilitarization Fund would be an important step towards achieving human security: first, in creating and using the peace dividend; second, by speeding and encouraging the processes of demilitarization, demobilization, and conversion; and third, by helping less developed countries to further their own democratic and human development goals by making a portion of the peace dividend available to them.

Only global cooperation can foster the security which we have sought for so long, but which has eluded us so frequently. Let us make a definitive effort to use the peace dividend for the construction of just, prosperous and demilitarized societies. And let us capitalize on the benefits of disarmament to promote and guarantee the rewards of peace.

Oscar Arias S.

Oscar Arias, winner of the 1987 Nobel Peace Prize

One approach would be for each country to credit the savings from reduced military spending to a separate demilitarization fund. Such a fund is likely to have three main calls on it: reducing budget deficits, paying the costs of military conversion and investing in human development both at home and in other countries. The national funds could be complemented by a global demilitarization fund, as suggested by Nobel Peace Prize winner Oscar Arias (special contribution, p. 59).

Reducing budget deficits is likely to be the most immediate use—since the need to cut government spending has been the motive for most of the defence cuts so far. But a significant proportion of these funds will, of course, have to be spent on the cost of conversion from military to non-military activities. The arms industry worldwide employs 14 million people, of whom four million or more could lose their jobs between 1993 and 1998. Many of these people will find new jobs, but funds will need to be set aside for retraining and for unemployment assistance. The impact of reduction in the arms industry is likely to be concentrated in a few countries, notably France, the United Kingdom and the United States. But the biggest impact will be in the successor states of the former Soviet Union, where the cuts have been taking place while whole economies are in turmoil.

Unemployment can also be anticipated from the demobilization of armed forces. Between 1990 and 1992, some 2.2 million personnel were demobilized (one-third in developing countries), and a similar number are expected to be released in the next few years. In addition are millions of civilian personnel whose jobs depend on the armed forces. Other costs that can be anticipated are those for the conversion of military bases and the destruction or disposal of weapons.

What will this leave for investment in human security? Not much, unless governments make firm commitments at the outset to allocate a significant proportion of the demilitarization fund to human security.

The possibilities for achieving this will vary from country to country. Developing countries should in many cases be able to commit a sizable proportion of their demilitarization funds for human security measures in their own countries. The Western industrial countries should be able to do more—allocate human security funds both domestically and internationally. The successor states of the former Soviet Union, however, will almost certainly absorb all of their peace dividend domestically, to cope with the economic turmoil they face.

The forthcoming Social Summit offers the opportunity to make these kinds of commitments. A collective effort must be made at the time of the Summit to:

• Endorse the principle that no nation should spend more on its military than on the education and health of its people.

• Agree on a targeted reduction in military spending for the decade 1995–2005—say, 3% a year.

• Endorse the establishment of a national demilitarization fund in each country as well as the creation of a global fund for human security.

• Recommend a review of the scope of Chapter VII of the UN Charter.

Focusing the savings from military expenditure more precisely by identifying the peace dividend and allocating it to development requires, however, that the world make good use of such funds. It would be tragic if money saved from military expenditure were dissipated in misdirected social expenditure.

CHAPTER 4

A new design for development cooperation

The new demands of human security will require a new and more positive relationship between North and South—a new era of development cooperation.

Economic relations between North and South have for too long been based on antagonism and confrontation. And it might be thought that the widening income disparities between industrial and developing countries would perpetuate and intensify such disputes into the next century.

In fact, this divide will probably become increasingly irrelevant in the years ahead. The primary reason is that the history of recent international negotiations has exposed yawning gaps between the positions of individual countries within both groups. Many issues bind these groups—many others divide them. The traditional North-South cleavage is no longer a useful basis for negotiations.

Experience has also shown that, even when interests coincide, it would be naive for developing countries to believe that they can negotiate from a position of collective weakness. The only countries that have become major players on the international scene are those that have strong domestic economies.

Developing countries have tended in the past to argue that almost all their economic problems spring from an inequitable international order. There certainly are many changes needed in global economic affairs—including freer flows of trade, technology, capital and labour—but developing countries now recognize that no amount of external assistance can ever substitute for the fundamental reforms needed in their domestic economies.

This more pragmatic and realistic outlook suggests that now is the time to move on from the sterile confrontations of the past and to forge a new and productive economic partnership among the nations of the world—based not on charity but on mutual interest, not on confrontation but on cooperation, not on protectionism but on an equitable sharing of market opportunities, not on stubborn nationalism but on farsighted internationalism.

Development cooperation has often been interpreted narrowly to include little more than foreign aid. But industrial and developing countries interact in numerous other ways—culturally, politically and economically. Indeed, flows of official development assistance (ODA) are often swamped by the other international financial flows. Many of these were considered in *Human Development Report 1992,* which emphasized the importance of opening market opportunities both within and between nations.

Beyond aid

The new design of development cooperation must be broadened to include all the international flows, not just aid. Some of the most significant non-aid flows are private investment, labour and international trade and finance, including debt payments.

Private investment flows

One of the most remarkable developments of the past decade has been the acceleration in private investment flows to developing countries—foreign direct investment, private loans and portfolio equity investment. Between 1970 and 1992, these flows increased from $5 billion to $102 billion (figure 4.1).

No amount of external assistance can ever substitute for fundamental reforms in domestic economies

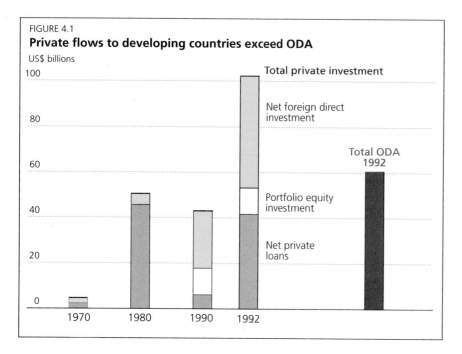

FIGURE 4.1

Private flows to developing countries exceed ODA

US$ billions

Total private investment

Net foreign direct investment

Total ODA 1992

Portfolio equity investment

Net private loans

1970   1980   1990   1992

FIGURE 4.2

More from workers' remittances than from ODA

ODA   • Workers' remittances

US$ billions

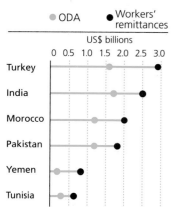

0   0.5   1.0   1.5   2.0   2.5   3.0

Turkey

India

Morocco

Pakistan

Yemen

Tunisia

So far, the private capital flows have been concentrated in just a few countries. Of the total flows during 1989–92, 72% went to just ten countries: in descending order, China, Mexico, Malaysia, Argentina, Thailand, Indonesia, Brazil, Nigeria, Venezuela and the Republic of Korea. The poorer countries received only a very small share: Sub-Saharan Africa received only 6% of foreign direct investment in the late 1980s, and the least developed countries only 2%.

If more developing countries are to benefit from private investment flows, they will have to improve their economic management, invest considerably in their human capital and enlist the support of the regional and international development banks.

Labour flows

International migration has grown significantly in recent years. Around 80 million people now live in foreign lands, and their numbers are rising steadily. One million people emigrate permanently each year, while another million seek political asylum.

The proportion of foreign-born residents is now 21% in Australia, 16% in Canada, 8% in the United States and 4% in Europe. With annual arrivals having doubled since the 1960s, the United States receives more immigrants than any other country—almost more than all other countries put together. Most immigrants in industrial countries today come from developing countries.

Remittances from emigrants have become a major source of income for developing countries—more than $20 billion a year. Among the major beneficiaries: Bangladesh, Egypt, India, Jordan, Morocco, Pakistan, the Philippines, Tunisia, Turkey and Yemen. Remittance flows are equivalent to more than a third of ODA and have the advantage that they come with no conditions attached and do not have to be repaid. In some countries—such as India, Morocco, Pakistan, Tunisia, Turkey and Yemen—annual remittances outweigh ODA by a third or more (figure 4.2).

But the industrial countries are becoming increasingly resistant to immigration. With their economies stagnating and unemployment rising, there is strong public opposition to further arrivals. In the developing countries, however, emigration pressures will remain high, and if global opportunities do not move towards people, people will continue to move towards global opportunities.

If the industrial countries sustain the same immigration policies, there is a strong argument for compensating the developing countries for restrictions on the migration of their unskilled labour. But a better long-term solution would be to offer the developing countries greater trade opportunities—so that their goods move rather than their people.

Trade flows

Since capital and labour markets offer only limited opportunities for developing countries, the burden for equalizing returns between rich and poor countries lies heavily on the trade in goods and services. Despite the barriers, some developing countries have done well in trade in recent years. But the main beneficiaries have been a handful of nations in East Asia and Latin America. The bottom 20% of the world population—in line with its dismal performance in global output and investment—had less than 1% of world trade (figure 4.3).

Developing countries are expected to gain, though only slightly, from the recently concluded Uruguay Round of trade negotiations. The gains to world trade by 2002 are estimated at $275 billion, but the developing countries are expected to see less than a third of this (table 4.1). And even these gains will be long delayed because of the period for phasing out some forms of protection: the Multi-Fibre Arrangement, for example, will be phased out over ten years.

Given the losses that developing countries will continue to sustain over this period, they have a strong case for compensation. Similarly, the developing countries gain little from the new agreements on agriculture since protection has been only slightly dented rather than eliminated.

It is ironic that some industrial countries are becoming more protectionist just as developing countries and the economies in transition are opening their economic systems. In the coming decade, the crucial structural changes will have to take place in the North.

Debt payments

For developing countries, debt is a major constraint on economic growth and on investment in human development. In 1992 alone, they had to pay $160 billion in debt service charges—more than two and a half times the amount of ODA, and $60 billion more than total private flows to developing countries in the same year.

The total external debt of developing countries grew fifteenfold over the past two decades: in 1970, it was $100 billion, in 1980, around $650 billion and in 1992, more than $1,500 billion. Because of the service charges, developing countries now pay more than they receive. In the past decade, net financial transfers on long-term lending to developing countries have been negative, with the industrial world receiving net transfers of $147 billion (figure 4.4). Although there are indications of an upturn, the net transfers to developing countries from the Bretton Woods institutions continue to be negative (figure 4.5). Despite several attempts to find a satisfactory solution, the total debt of developing countries continues to grow.

Their debt service ratio (the ratio of debt service to exports of goods and services), however, has been coming down. Since 1987, the debt service ratio for the

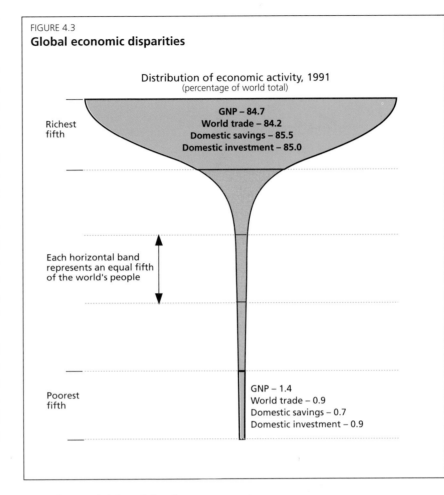

FIGURE 4.3
Global economic disparities

Distribution of economic activity, 1991
(percentage of world total)

Richest fifth

GNP – 84.7
World trade – 84.2
Domestic savings – 85.5
Domestic investment – 85.0

Each horizontal band represents an equal fifth of the world's people

Poorest fifth

GNP – 1.4
World trade – 0.9
Domestic savings – 0.7
Domestic investment – 0.9

TABLE 4.1
Potential benefits from the Uruguay Round in 2002
(billions of 1991 US$)

Country or region	Scenario A[a]	Scenario B[b]
European Union[c]	78.3	71.3
Japan	35.5	42.0
European Free Trade Association[d]	34.2	38.4
USA	26.3	27.6
Canada	5.9	6.6
Australia	1.7	1.9
Total OECD	181.9	187.8
Non-OECD countries	29.9	86.4
Total world	211.8	274.2

a. Scenario A assumes that trade liberalization occurs only in the OECD.
b. Scenario B assumes that trade liberalization occurs in the entire world.
c. Belgium, Denmark, France, Germany, Greece, Ireland, Italy, Luxembourg, Netherlands, Portugal, Spain and the United Kingdom.
d. Austria, Finland, Iceland, Liechtenstein, Norway, Sweden and Switzerland.

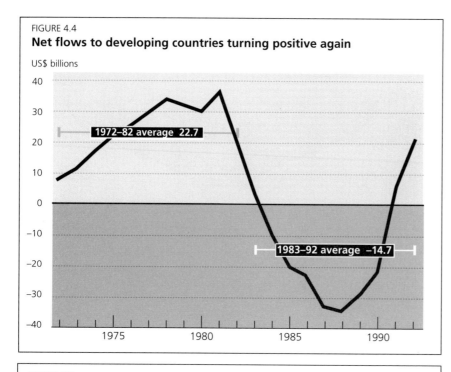

FIGURE 4.4
Net flows to developing countries turning positive again

US$ billions

1972–82 average 22.7

1983–92 average −14.7

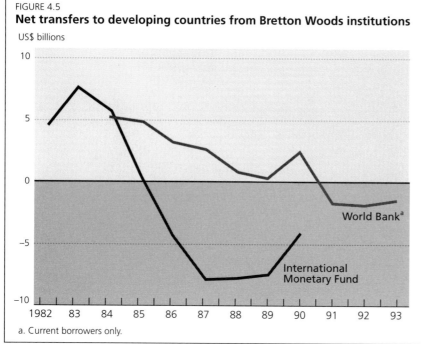

FIGURE 4.5
Net transfers to developing countries from Bretton Woods institutions

US$ billions

World Bank[a]

International
Monetary Fund

a. Current borrowers only.

of the poorest countries—if the money released were earmarked for social development.

New forms of development cooperation

The relationship between industrial and developing countries has often been profoundly unequal, and the losses to developing countries as a result of this inequity have often thwarted the contributions of ODA. That is why a new approach to development cooperation will have to be more inclusive and more coherent. Foreign direct investment, international trade, capital flows and ODA—all should contribute to human development in the South and promote greater global equity.

Even when the industrial countries recognize the inequities in North-South relationships, they may still face many domestic compulsions in removing their restrictions against the developing countries. They may be reluctant to remove trade barriers, for example, before making needed adjustments in their own economies. And they may want time to redirect investment and retrain workers whose jobs may disappear because of competition from developing countries.

Compensation for damages

If industrial countries wish to maintain their restrictive practices, there is a strong case for compensating developing countries. The worst damage usually comes from restrictions on international trade. Free trade normally benefits all countries. Everyone gains in principle from a worldwide flow of goods, services, technology, capital and labour. In any transaction, the benefits might be unequally distributed, but in a liberal trading regime, most parties gain: markets are positive-sum games.

When markets are unfair within a national economy, a legal remedy is usually available. In many countries, it is illegal to discriminate against workers on the basis of their race, gender or religion. It can also be illegal for banks to discriminate against certain borrowers or businesses owned by specific groups. In these cases, the injured

developing world has declined from 24% to 21%—largely as a result of rising exports.

But the debt problem of the poorer nations is nowhere near a solution—and it is hampering their ability to meet urgent human development needs (figure 4.6). The Social Summit would make a significant contribution if it could persuade the industrial countries to respect their agreements at Toronto and Trinidad. Those countries could go even further and cancel the debts

party can take the offender to court and claim damages.

But when it comes to international discrimination, there is no such recourse. Two cases where compensation might be in order are migration and trade.

Restrictions on migration

Rich countries often give immigration permits only to a selected number of technical and highly skilled people, denying entry to large numbers of unskilled workers. This can lead to two forms of damage. First is the brain drain from poor countries that lose the human capital these people embody. Second is the loss of income opportunities for unskilled workers—and the proportion of that income that would have returned to the migrant-sending countries in the form of remittances.

• *Brain drain*—The losses from the brain drain can be seen as the loss of the public investment made in their education or skill, or as a loss in productivity for the country.

African countries are among the hardest hit. Between 1985 and 1990, Africa lost an estimated 60,000 middle and high-level managers. In Ghana, 60% of the doctors trained in the early 1980s have left the country. Latin America and the Caribbean also lose a high proportion of their university graduates: in some countries, over 20% of all graduates choose to emigrate. And some of the smaller countries come off worse, particularly in medicine: to end up with one doctor, a country must train many more. The greatest exodus of trained professionals is from Asia, many of them scientists, with the United States as the principal destination. Between 1972 and 1985, the four major exporting countries (India, the Philippines, China and the Republic of Korea) sent more than 145,000 workers with scientific training to the United States.

One way to compensate partly for brain drain losses would be to require that emigrants, before their departure, should repay any education subsidies they have received. Another option would be a two-tier system of tuition charges: those paying the higher charges would be free to emigrate, while those accepting the subsidy would be required to work in their home country for a set number of years.

A tidier solution, however, would be for the payment to be made by the country receiving the immigration. This would be more consistent with the principle that people should be free to live and work where they please. And if the international community decides that it wishes to discourage the brain drain, it could increase the level of compensation accordingly.

• *Excluding unskilled labour*—It can be argued that the industrial countries are working against their own economic interests by excluding unskilled labour. Fuelling the economic boom in Western Europe in the 1960s and the explosive growth in the oil-producing states of the Middle East in the 1970s and 1980s were large flows of unskilled labour. Such flows result in temporary costs and social dislocations, including racial tensions, and there may be some dampening of wages at the bottom of the scale. But on the whole, immigration stimulates—rather than depresses—expansion and prosperity.

For political or social reasons, industrial countries choose to exclude large numbers of unskilled workers—as do some of the richer developing countries, such as the Republic of Korea and Singapore. If these restrictions on the international migration of unskilled labour were removed, remittances would increase sharply. To make up for the loss of earnings due to the restrictions on labour migration, the migrant-receiving countries might compensate the migrant-sending countries.

For the migrant-receiving countries to be persuaded of the value of such payments, they would need to be assured that the payments were being used to reduce emigration pressures. One way to achieve this objective would be to invest the payments in human development to create employment in the migrant-sending countries and reduce population growth.

Restrictions on trade

The industrial countries also place severe restrictions on the import of some goods

FIGURE 4.6
Burden of debt shifts to poorest regions

Debt service ratio, percent

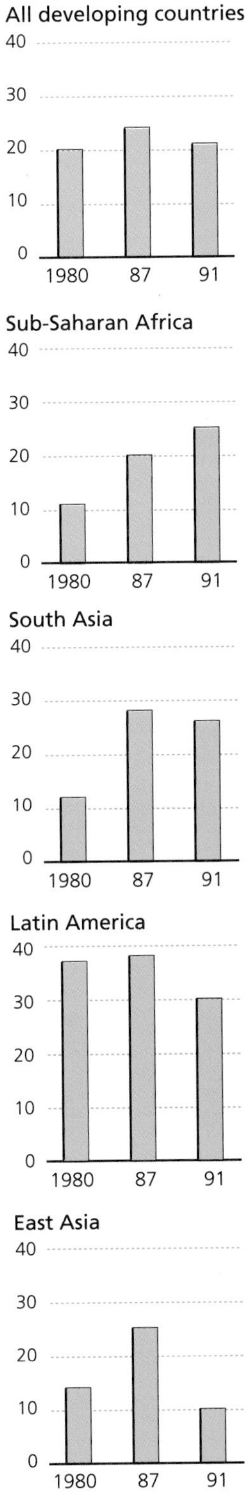

All developing countries

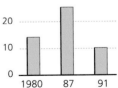
Sub-Saharan Africa

South Asia

Latin America

East Asia

from developing countries, especially clothing, textiles, footwear, processed primary commodities and light manufactured goods. Moreover, protectionism against these goods is rising—frequently in the form of non-tariff barriers, which can more easily circumvent GATT rules. This is particularly galling for the developing countries now that their economies are more open than ever to outside competition. In fact, it is the affluent North, not the poorer South, that is now resisting structural adjustment of its economies.

How much do these restrictions hurt developing countries? Coming up with precise estimates is difficult, but the OECD estimates that their costs to developing countries exceed the value of aid flows to these countries. And *The Economist* reported that if rich countries abolished all their barriers to Third World goods, the increase in developing nations' exports would be worth twice what they receive in aid. For textiles and clothing alone, the damage has been estimated at more than $50 billion a year (box 4.1). Some studies have calculated that liberalizing the trade in agricultural commodities would yield an annual gain of $22 billion (in 1992 dollars) for the developing and formerly centrally planned economies (box 4.2).

So, the case is strong for a compensation scheme—operated perhaps by GATT or by its proposed successor organization, the World Trade Organization (discussed below). In addition to compensating developing countries, this scheme would provide a strong incentive for countries to liberalize their trade. Those that refuse to do this, fearing short-term labour dislocations, would have to pay an immediate price. And those that want to avoid paying compensation would be encouraged to reduce barriers. If such a scheme worked, it would progressively remove the obstacles to trade between rich and poor countries.

Payment for services to ensure global human security

Many projects that the industrial countries support in the Third World have global effects and thus also serve their own interests—as well as those of other developing countries that may not be the direct recipients of their aid. Controlling the flow of drugs is an example, as is halting the spread of communicable diseases. To the extent that these projects serve the interest of industrial countries—and humanity—the funds to support them should be considered not as aid but as payment for services rendered. Although not mediated by markets, the payments are a type of market transaction, and they should not be confused with foreign aid (box 4.3).

Poor countries assist with the security of the rich ones in several ways.

• *Environmental controls*—The developing countries are home to most of the world's tropical forests, and it is in everyone's interest that these be preserved to help slow global warming and maintain biodiversity. So, the world community should share the cost of their preservation.

BOX 4.1

A $50 billion bill for trade barriers on textiles and clothing

The manufacture of textiles and clothing is one area where the developing countries have a comparative advantage—and achieve a trade surplus with the industrial countries. For many developing countries, these labour-intensive industries with simple technologies represent a great opportunity to accelerate the pace of their industrialization and diversify their exports away from primary commodities. In 1992, such exports were worth $60 billion.

But these are precisely the goods against which the industrial countries have raised the highest barriers—tariff and non-tariff—through the Multi-Fibre Arrangement (MFA). Under this arrangement, the industrial countries apply quotas to imports of textiles and clothing from developing countries, but not to those from other industrial countries—a clear breach of the GATT principles of non-discrimination.

The intention of the industrial countries is to preserve jobs in some of their weakest industries. But doing this is very expensive. The short-run gains for textile workers are more than offset by the higher prices that everyone has to pay as consumers. In the United Kingdom, it has been estimated that without the MFA, textiles and clothing (both locally produced and imported) would be 5% cheaper. In the United States, one study concluded that the annual cost of protecting one job was between two and eight times the average annual wage in the industry.

Developing countries pay an even higher cost. A study in the 1980s by the IMF suggested that a complete liberalization would enable developing countries to increase their exports of textiles by 82% and those of clothing by 93%.

In 1992, UNCTAD reported that quantitative restrictions affected 67% of the exports of textiles and clothing from developing countries. Average tariffs also remained high: 18% in the United Kingdom, 20% in Canada, 23% in Austria and 38% for some items in the United States.

Without tariff and non-tariff barriers, the developing countries could nearly double their exports of textiles and clothing. The industrial countries, by violating the principles of free trade, are costing the developing countries an estimated $50 billion a year—nearly equal to the total flow of foreign assistance.

Similarly, the protection of the ozone layer demands global restraint in the production of chlorofluorocarbons (CFCs). The industrial countries have been responsible for most of the ozone destruction to date—through CFCs used as cheap coolants for refrigerators, for example. If the developing countries are to forgo cheap but destructive options, they will need to be compensated—through cash payments, perhaps, or through the provision of alternative technologies or the means to develop them.

A corollary of this principle is that countries that insist on polluting the global environment (usually the industrial ones) should be charged for such irresponsibility. The principle of "making the polluter pay" is already being applied within countries—and now is the time to apply the system internationally. This could be the basis for an international market for tradable permits for various forms of pollution (box 4.4). Some estimates suggest that such a system could transfer as much as 5% of the GNP of the richer nations to the poorer ones. Again, this should be considered not as aid but as a payment for services.

• *Destruction of nuclear weapons*—It is also in everyone's interest that the global nuclear threat be removed. Yet the task of destroying nuclear weapons and converting armaments factories to peaceful use falls disproportionately on some of the weakest countries—particularly the successor states of the former Soviet Union. It is unrealistic to expect them to finance this entirely out of their own resources. Instead, payments should be made on the basis of an international compact. Again, this should not be regarded as aid but as payment for services rendered. At present, however, both bilateral and multilateral donors are financing conversion programmes by raiding ODA funds intended for developing countries.

• *Controlling communicable diseases*—To contain such diseases as malaria, tuberculosis, cholera and HIV/AIDS is clearly in the interest of all countries, and it is much more efficient to do this as a global joint initiative rather than country by country. It makes much more sense to initiate worldwide vaccination campaigns against a contagious

disease than to try to exclude individual carriers at national frontiers. It is easier to clean up the water supply in cholera-prone countries than to monitor all the agricul-

---

The cost of agricultural protection

The industrial countries have long aimed at agricultural self-sufficiency. They have achieved this partly by subsidizing their own farmers—and partly by raising tariff and non-tariff barriers against foreign producers. In most cases, however, this is now resulting in substantial overproduction, with products piling up in grain and butter "mountains".

This strategy is very expensive. In 1991, OECD subsidies for agriculture totalled $180 billion. In the European Union alone, protection costs around $38 billion a year, of which $2.6 billion is spent to store surpluses.

This may benefit farmers, but it is costly for everyone else in the industrial countries. Not only do people have to finance the subsidies by paying higher taxes, they also have to pay higher food bills since import barriers keep out cheaper foreign produce. For the industrial countries in 1990, the average additional bill for each non-farm family was $1,400 a year. In Japan and the European Free Trade Area, the cost was even higher—$3,000 per family.

Industrial country agricultural protectionism also causes damage in developing countries, though in these countries the farmers suffer. When industrial countries dump surpluses of products such as sugar, cereal and beef in developing countries, the local price plummets. In some African countries, where it costs $74 to produce 100 kilos of maize, the local market price has fallen to $21. A similar effect is evident in meat exports. In 1991, the European Community dumped 54 million tons of frozen and chilled beef in Africa—further impoverishing four million Sahelians who depend on cattle farming. In Côte d'Ivoire between 1975 and 1993, the proportion of beef imported from neighbouring countries of the Sahel fell from two-thirds to less than one-quarter. Developing country farmers also lose out because industrial countries use tariff and non-tariff barriers to exclude their produce.

Liberalizing the trade in agricultural commodities would benefit both industrial and developing countries. It has been estimated that complete liberalization would yield an annual gain (in 1992 dollars) of about $25 billion for OECD countries and $22 billion for the developing and formerly centrally planned countries.

Payment for services rendered—forest conservation in Costa Rica

If the industrial countries were to pay Costa Rica not to cut down its forests, how much would this cost? Consider the commercial value of the trees felled. In 1989, Costa Rica felled 10 million cubic metres of forest with an estimated net timber value of $422 million. Clearly, the industrial countries could not be expected to pay the entire cost of the harvest forgone, since Costa Rica would also gain in the long term by establishing sustainable rates of harvesting. But it does indicate an order of magnitude.

Similar, if smaller, payments have already been made to Costa Rica in "debt-for-nature" swaps. In 1988, the Netherlands purchased part of Costa Rica's external debt at a cost of $5 million and then wrote it off on the condition that Costa Rica spend an equivalent amount in local currency on forestry development. In 1989 and 1990, Sweden purchased a further $5.5 million of Costa Rica's debt for a similar purpose.

There is no need, however, to link these payments to debt reduction. They could be made directly—for services rendered.

BOX 4.4

Tradable permits for global pollution

One way of controlling greenhouse gases would be for an international authority to issue tradable permits that entitle the holders to emit a certain quantity of pollutants. The authority could lease the permits for a certain time and use the proceeds for environmental projects—or it could distribute the permits free of charge.

Countries that did not need their full quota could sell or lease their surplus to others. Those generating more pollution would thus pay more, and "ecological space" would be priced for all nations rather than being freely plundered by a few.

This scheme poses two major problems. First, it demands an international consensus on total permissible emissions of greenhouse gases—a consensus that might be difficult to reach. Second, if the distribution of permits were based on income, the largest share would go to industrial countries. If it were based on population, most would go to developing countries—though this would be the most equitable system since each person has an equal right to use the earth's atmosphere. An intermediate solution would be to allocate half the permits on the basis of population and the other half on the basis of GNP.

The industrial countries are the largest polluters, so if they wished to continue emitting at current levels, and a population- and GNP-based distribution were introduced, they would have to buy most of the permits from the developing countries. This could lead to a very significant transfer of resources from the rich to the poor nations: some estimates suggest $500 billion to $1 trillion a year. Such flows would be neither aid nor charity. They would be the outcome of a free market mechanism that penalizes the richer nations' overconsumption of the global commons.

The system would give all countries a strong incentive to reduce pollution—and generate funds that could be earmarked for environmental protection programmes in developing countries.

BOX 4.5

Global human security compacts

The components of human security are indivisible. Famine, pollution, ethnic violence—their consequences can spread rapidly around the globe. Yet the responses to these problems are usually national.

The Social Summit offers an opportunity to deal with global issues globally—through a series of global compacts to tackle the most urgent threats to peace and human development. These threats include:

• Drug trafficking

• International terrorism
• Nuclear proliferation
• Communicable diseases
• Environmental pollution and degradation
• Natural disasters
• Ethnic conflicts
• Excessive international migration.

Separate compacts could be negotiated for each threat. Potential sources of finance for such compacts are indicated in the table below.

Financing a global human security fund
(US$ billions)

Source of finance	Total revenues (1995–2000)	Annual revenues
1. A proportion of the potential peace dividend (20% of the amount saved by industrial countries and 10% of that saved by developing countries through a 3% reduction in global military spending)	85	14
2. A 0.05% tax on speculative international capital movements	900	150
3. A global tax on the consumption of non-renewable energy ($1 per barrel of oil and its equivalent in coal consumption)	395	66
4. One-third of existing ODA	120	20
Grand total	1,500	250

---

tural produce they export. Everyone will gain, too, if the spread of HIV/AIDS worldwide is slowed. This applies to both industrial and developing countries, but HIV/AIDS problems are likely to be greater in developing countries since they have fewer resources to control the epidemic.

The international community has a lot to gain by assisting in dealing with health threats in developing countries—investing money upstream rather than dealing with the consequences downstream. This is not to say that such threats come only from the South. They can come from anywhere. And countries that lack the means to combat them, but are nevertheless willing to take initiatives, act not only in their national interest—but in the global interest, too. They render a "global human security service".

• *Controlling narcotics*—Developing countries are the source of most internationally traded narcotics (see box 2.5). But the trade is fuelled by consumption, not just production, and sellers in the industrial countries get a big chunk of the profits. Poor farmers in developing countries get only around 1% of the street price. It is thus unreasonable to expect developing countries to bear the entire cost of clamping down on production and export. So far, the industrial countries have contributed mainly to administrative control and crop substitution programmes in developing countries, measures that have had limited impact. Experience shows that curbing demand for narcotics is more important than curbing supply. Rather than scattered national plans, a truly global effort is needed.

One paradox of these contributions is that the international community ends up paying in any case—and it pays a lot more downstream than it would have paid upstream. That is why it is important for the international community to address such issues through compacts for global human security (box 4.5).

How much should the industrial countries pay for the services that developing countries render in controlling drug production and export? In theory, they should pay for the costs borne by the developing countries. But these costs are difficult to measure. Payments might be not only directly programme-related but also include compensation for political risks taken by governments. In practice, a more pragmatic solution is simply for industrial countries to be generous in supporting programmes that are vital to global human security and development.

New funding sources

Changing the forms of development cooperation need not entail finding new funds—but it might.

• *Demilitarization funds*—These funds can be created from the cuts in military spending (chapter 3). And while a proportion will inevitably be taken up by the cost of conversion and the need to balance national budgets, many countries should also be able to earmark new funds for development cooperation.

• *Pollution taxes*—Tradable pollution permits, as suggested earlier, could also generate significant North-South financial flows and be an important source of development finance. Alternatively, a global tax of $1 per barrel on oil consumption (and its equivalent on coal consumption) could be considered to discourage excessive and wasteful use of non-renewable energy.

• *Taxing global foreign exchange movements*—Many transactions in the foreign exchange markets are purely speculative, not for international trade. About $1 trillion crosses international frontiers every 24 hours in response to the slightest tremor in interest or currency rates—or in anticipation of such changes. One way of dampening speculation would be to apply a tax (see special contribution by James Tobin, p. 70). Even a tax of 0.05% on the value of each transaction—Tobin suggests 0.5%—could raise around $150 billion a year.

These promising sources could yield the resources to meet many global security needs. And the Social Summit might consider establishing a global human security fund along these lines (see box 4.5).

Restructuring aid

Even though development cooperation in the years ahead will have to be a much more comprehensive concept, open to broader, more innovative approaches, aid will continue to be important. But it will have to be reassessed—with donors and recipients reconsidering why aid should be given and what form it should take. The end of the cold war offers a rare opportunity to make a fresh start and to focus aid much more sharply on strengthening global human security.

A new motivation for aid

The motives for foreign aid programmes have been diverse—sometimes driven by idealism, generosity and international solidarity, but often also by political expediency, ideological confrontation and commercial self-interest.

It is no surprise that such varied motives and objectives have produced some unsatisfactory outcomes—leading to considerable disenchantment on both sides of the ledger, for donors and recipients.

Some critics argue that foreign aid has failed altogether and should be stopped. This argument is obviously incorrect. While some aid has been misspent, and some development has been misdirected, legitimate criticism should lead to improvement, not despair.

The development process—along with foreign assistance—has had more successes than its critics usually concede (box 4.6). A comparison of the performance of industrial and developing countries at similar stages of economic development shows that the developing countries have made more progress in the past 30 years than the industrial countries managed in about a century.

Foreign aid has played a big part in this progress. Development cooperation has enabled vital technologies—from new industrial processes to vaccines for children to hybrid seeds for the Green Revolution—to spread rapidly throughout the developing world.

True, some development models have been wrong, and some technology has been inappropriate or environmentally destructive. And the donors have on occasion placed harsh conditions on their aid or blatantly violated the national sovereignty of

A small tax on global foreign exchange movements could yield $150 billion a year

recipients. But there can be little doubt that, without this transfer of financial resources, technology, expertise and equipment, development in the poorer nations would have been slower.

Aid is not a very popular theme in either donor or recipient countries. The public in donor countries is questioning aid even more persistently now that the industrial countries are experiencing recession and

A tax on international currency transactions

Capital moves ever more freely across national borders, both by direct business investments and by purchases and sales of financial assets. Capital movements certainly can benefit the nations directly involved and the world economy as a whole, by directing world savings to high-productivity projects, wherever they may be. Savers in a capital-intensive economy often find more profitable investment opportunities in capital-poor areas.

However, the capital flows needed to achieve efficient allocation of world savings are today a minuscule fraction of worldwide transactions in currency markets, which are estimated to run at $1 trillion a day. Thanks to modern communications and computers, these deals are easy and cheap. The sun never sets on financial markets, from Hong Kong, to Frankfurt, to London, to New York, to Tokyo. Advanced industrial countries long ago abandoned exchange controls, and many developing countries are relaxing their regulations.

Here, as in so many other dimensions of human life on this globe, technologies have outrun political and social institutions. The bulk of those trillions of currency exchanges are speculations and arbitrages, seeking to make quick money on exchange rate fluctuations and on international interest rate differentials. They contribute little to rational long-term investment allocations. Exchange rates are at the mercy of the opinions of private speculators commanding vast sums. Their activities distort the signals exchange markets give for long-range investments and for trade. Interest rate arbitrages make it difficult for national central banks to follow monetary policies independent of those of major foreign central banks.

The mobility of financial capital across currencies is a problem whether exchange rates float freely in markets or are pegged by agreements among governments. The travails of the world economy since 1973 have inspired nostalgic longings for Bretton Woods, or for an older and purer gold standard. But no system in which parities can be adjusted on occasion eliminates opportunities for speculation or inhibitions on national monetary policies. But the recent crises of the European exchange rate mechanism demonstrated that neither individually nor collectively do central banks have sufficient reserves to withstand concerted pressures from speculators betting on the devaluation of weaker currencies.

A permanent single currency, as among the 50 states of the American union, would escape all this turbulence. The United States example shows that a currency union works to great advantage when sustained not only by centralized monetary authorities but also by other common institutions. In the absence of such institutions, an irrevocably unique world currency is many decades off.

In 1978, I proposed a realistic second-best option. An international uniform tax would be levied on spot transactions in foreign exchange (including deliveries pursuant to futures contracts and options). The proposal has two basic motivations. One is to increase the weight market participants give to long-range fundamentals relative to immediate speculative opportunities. The second is to allow greater autonomy to national monetary policy, by making possible larger wedges between short interest rates in different currencies.

A 0.5% tax on foreign exchange transactions is equivalent to a 4% difference in annual interest rates on three-month bills, a considerable deterrent to persons contemplating a quick round-trip to another currency. The intent is to slow down speculative capital movements; it would be too small to deter commodity trade or serious international capital commitments. The revenue potential is immense, over $1.5 trillion a year for the 0.5% tax.

J. M. Keynes in 1936 pointed out that a transaction tax could strengthen the weight of long-range fundamentals in stock-market pricing, as against speculators' guesses of the short-range behaviours of other speculators. The same is true of the foreign exchange markets.

The tax would have to be worldwide, at the same rate in all markets. Otherwise it could be evaded by executing transactions in jurisdictions with no tax or lower tax. Compliance would depend on the banking and market institutions where the vast bulk of currency exchanges take place. The transaction tax is designed to make international money markets compatible with modest national autonomy in monetary and macroeconomic policy. But it would certainly not permit governments and central banks to ignore the international repercussions of their policies. The G-7 would still need to coordinate policies, and their policies would still be powerful influences and constraints on other economies.

It is appropriate that the proceeds of an international tax be devoted to international purposes and be placed at the disposal of international institutions. This was my suggestion in 1978. Although raising revenues for international purposes was not the primary motivation of my proposal, it has been a major source of the recent upsurge of interest in it.

James Tobin, winner of the 1981 Nobel Prize for Economics

unemployment (box 4.7). Why, they wonder, should they continue to send aid abroad when there is clearly so much poverty at home?

It is sobering to point out how the cake is currently divided. At present, the industrial countries commit an average of 15% of their combined GNPs to providing social safety nets at home, but they allocate only 0.3% of their combined GNPs to foreign aid. And these sums have to cover very different population sizes. The social safety nets in the rich countries serve around 100 million people living below the poverty line (with an average income of less than $5,000 a year). But the rich countries' aid to developing countries has to be shared among 1,300 million people living below the poverty line (with an average income of less than $300 a year).

The impression nevertheless persists that foreign aid is a major diversion of resources. But if all foreign aid were stopped tomorrow, this would enable the industrial countries to increase their domestic social safety nets from an average of 15.0% of GNP to only 15.3% of GNP—hardly the handsomest bargain in history.

The end of the cold war offers an opportunity to discard the ideological baggage that previously encumbered official aid programmes and made it difficult even for non-governmental organizations (NGOs) and commentators who supported aid in principle to justify it in practice. Governments need to ensure that their aid meets specific development objectives and to take care that it is neither misspent nor misappropriated.

Once aid has been targeted properly, it is important that the real purpose of aid be communicated to the public in donor countries. A small proportion of aid—say 2%, or around $1 billion a year—could be earmarked to cultivate public support through better communication of the objectives of aid, in particular, and of development cooperation, in general. The aim would not be to mislead or manipulate public opinion but to fulfil the duty of accountability. Bilateral donors could spend about half of these funds to reach their own people through the mass media (as the

BOX 4.6

Successes of foreign assistance

Foreign aid, often misdirected and misused, has its critics. But it also has many successes.

- *Food production*—Many developing countries have stepped up their food production through the Green Revolution, based on work on maize by US scientists in the 1930s. Plant geneticists extended their findings to wheat and maize in Mexico during the 1940s, and in two decades the country's wheat output tripled. Similarly important research was done at the International Rice Research Institute in the Philippines.

Since the 1960s, aid programmes have introduced the methods to many other countries. As a result, India has almost doubled its output and become self-sufficient in food. The Green Revolution in some cases worked against the interests of smaller farmers who could not afford the high-tech inputs—but it had a dramatic effect on overall production.

- *Infrastructure and communications*—Foreign aid has done much to establish physical infrastructure in developing countries. Loans and technical assistance have been crucial for the construction of roads, embankments and power stations. South Asia's transport and communications systems were developed mainly through foreign aid, as were Africa's airports.

- *Health*—One of the greatest successes of foreign aid in the health field has been the eradication of smallpox. Endemic in 31 countries in 1967, it had disappeared permanently by 1977. Other major successes include the immunization of children against the commonest childhood diseases. Ten years ago, 75 million children contracted measles each year, and 2.5 million died. Today, thanks to improvements in health care and immunization, annual measles cases have been cut to 25 million, and deaths to just over one million.

- *Family planning*—Foreign assistance has also played a major part in population programmes. Bangladesh, with significant foreign funding and technical support, has been remarkably successful in family planning. Between 1970 and 1990, the share of women of reproductive age using contraceptives rose from 3% to 40%, and the fertility rate declined from seven children per woman to less than five.

BOX 4.7

Public opinions on aid

Despite nearly five decades of development assistance, opinion polls suggest that people in the donor countries know little about it.

Most people—around 70% of those polled—approve of aid. But they rarely are aware of how much their country is giving. A survey in the Netherlands found that half the respondents had no idea what the figure might be. And in Canada, people assumed that their country was giving ten times more than it really was. They also typically underestimated the proportion of aid given as loans rather than grants.

Most people see aid as helping the poor and mitigating the consequences of disasters. In a survey in the Netherlands in 1991, respondents identified the major problems they believed aid was combating: 20% said starvation, 15% poverty, 14% overpopulation and 12% drought—while 11% felt aid should be used to improve economic management.

Since most people approve of aid, they do not want their country to be seen as a "bad donor", giving proportionately less than other countries. They also disapprove strongly of tied aid: a survey in Canada found that 70% of respondents considered this an immoral and exploitative practice.

One of the most significant findings was that people do not place aid very high on the list of national priorities. They may approve of it, but they do not pay much attention to it. The donor governments clearly have a lot of work ahead if they are to explain their aid programmes to their constituents.

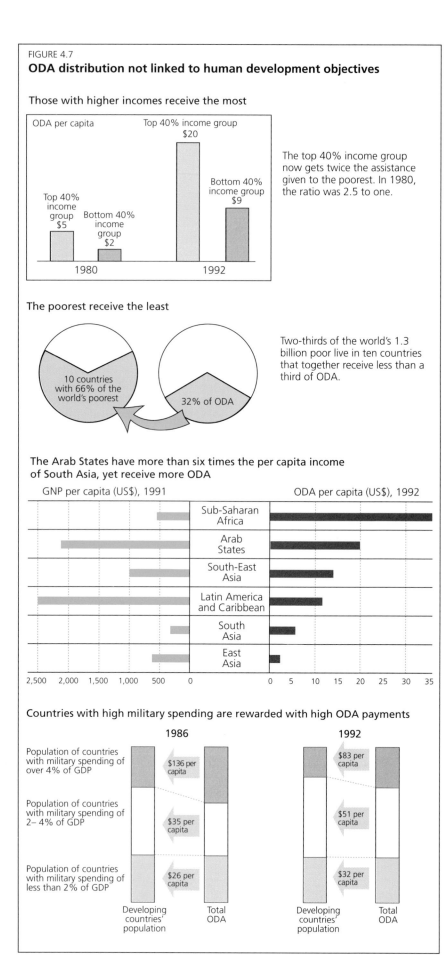

FIGURE 4.7

ODA distribution not linked to human development objectives

Those with higher incomes receive the most

ODA per capita

Top 40% income group
$20

Top 40% income group $5

Bottom 40% income group $2

Bottom 40% income group $9

1980

1992

The top 40% income group now gets twice the assistance given to the poorest. In 1980, the ratio was 2.5 to one.

The poorest receive the least

10 countries with 66% of the world's poorest

32% of ODA

Two-thirds of the world's 1.3 billion poor live in ten countries that together receive less than a third of ODA.

The Arab States have more than six times the per capita income of South Asia, yet receive more ODA

GNP per capita (US$), 1991		ODA per capita (US$), 1992
	Sub-Saharan Africa	
	Arab States	
	South-East Asia	
	Latin America and Caribbean	
	South Asia	
	East Asia	

2,500 2,000 1,500 1,000 500   0   0   5   10 15 20 25 30 35

Countries with high military spending are rewarded with high ODA payments

1986

1992

Population of countries with military spending of over 4% of GDP

$136 per capita

$83 per capita

Population of countries with military spending of 2–4% of GDP

$35 per capita

$51 per capita

Population of countries with military spending of less than 2% of GDP

$26 per capita

$32 per capita

Developing countries' population

Total ODA

Developing countries' population

Total ODA

Netherlands does). The rest could be used to cultivate public support for multilateral assistance.

Aid fatigue has also been growing in the South. Those who have benefited most from aid have often been the elite in the urban areas and the richer peasants or landlords in the rural areas. Indeed, the poorest groups may sometimes suffer from aid programmes, as powerful local establishments pass on harsh aid conditionality and the burden of adjustment to politically weaker sections of society.

If aid is genuinely to benefit the poor, it will have to become much more participatory and people-centred. When there is an open public debate on aid, allowing people to decide whether their country needs aid and who should benefit, aid is likely to be more effective—and to help overcome disparities rather than reinforce them.

In general, aid programmes will have to become much more accountable to people in the South. Negotiation, planning and implementation should be much more open—enabling opposition groups, the media and other elements of civil society to insist on strict standards of accountability. Such transparency in aid negotiations is the best way to build public confidence.

Making aid serve specific objectives

Donor countries usually trot out a large number of objectives for aid. They believe, for example, that aid should help in reducing poverty, promoting human development, guaranteeing human rights, protecting the environment or improving national governance. But their programmes do not appear to be directly linked with these objectives. The main reason is that most aid allocations are country-focused rather than objective-focused—something clear from even a brief analysis of the record of development assistance.

• *Aid and poverty reduction*—Aid is not targeted at the poor. Donors send less than one-third of development assistance to the ten most populous countries, which are home to two-thirds of the world's poor (figure 4.7). As a result of these distortions, the richest 40% of the developing world re-

72

HUMAN DEVELOPMENT REPORT 1994

ceives twice as much aid per capita as the poorest 40%.

The contrasts among regions are even starker. The richer developing countries of the Middle East get $21 per capita, compared with $6 per capita for the poorer countries of South Asia. Egypt receives $280 in aid per poor person, while Bangladesh gets $19 and India only $7. India has 27% of the world's absolute poor, but receives only 5% of ODA (table 4.2).

This misdirection afflicts both bilateral and multilateral assistance. The United States gives $250 per capita to the high-income developing countries but only $1 per capita to the low-income countries. Multilateral donors do slightly better. The International Development Association (the soft-loan affiliate of the World Bank) gives about half of its aid to the ten countries with the highest number of poor people (table 4.3)—but it still has to ration its aid to countries such as India and Pakistan, despite their great poverty and comparatively better economic performance.

• *Aid and priority human development*— Aid is not focused on the priority areas of human development. Bilateral donors direct only 7% of their aid to such priority areas as basic education, primary health care, rural water supplies, nutrition programmes and family planning services (table 4.4). The differences among donors are marked: for Denmark the proportion is 25%, while for Germany it is only 2%. Note, however, that these ratios leave out programme assistance and contributions through multilateral agencies. The Development Assistance Committee of the OECD should present these flows in greater detail and analyse them more fully.

Multilateral institutions do somewhat better: they average around 16% (table 4.5). Again there is a spread, with the highest proportion for UNICEF, which has a specific mandate for development programmes for children. The agency with the lowest proportion is the African Development Bank. Although it serves the world's poorest region, it devotes only 4% of its aid to human development priorities.

The small allocations for priority areas partly reflect the low spending on the social sector in general. And even in the social sector, the higher-status programmes get preference. Urban water supply and sanitation gets preference over rural, which gets only about 20% of total aid expenditures on wa-

Aid is not focused on the priority areas of human development

---

TABLE 4.3
The World Bank and the poorest people, 1989/92
Ten developing countries with two-thirds of the world's poor[a]

Total poor people in these countries (millions)	855
Poor in these countries as a % of total world poor	65.9
Bilateral ODA allocation to these countries as a % of total bilateral ODA	31.7
World Bank allocation to these countries as a % of total World Bank lending	43.9
IDA	51.9
IBRD	40.0

a. Bangladesh, Brazil, China, Ethiopia, India, Indonesia, Nigeria, Pakistan, Philippines, Viet Nam.

TABLE 4.2
ODA to the poorest

Ten developing countries with highest number of poor people	Percentage of population in poverty 1980–90	Number of poor (millions) 1992	Poor as % of total world poor 1992	ODA per poor person (US$) 1992	ODA as % of total ODA 1992
India	40	350.0	26.9	7	5.2
China	9	105.0	8.1	28	6.5
Bangladesh	78	93.2	7.2	19	3.8
Brazil	47	72.4	5.6	3	0.5
Indonesia	25	47.8	3.7	44	4.6
Nigeria	40	46.4	3.6	7	0.5
Viet Nam	54	37.6	2.9	16	1.3
Philippines	54	35.2	2.7	49	3.8
Pakistan	28	35.0	2.7	33	2.6
Ethiopia	60	31.9	2.5	41	2.9
Total	29	854.5	65.9	17	31.7

TABLE 4.4
Human priorities in bilateral aid allocations

Country	ODA (US$ millions) 1992	ODA as % of GNP 1992	Aid social allocation ratio 1989/91	Aid social priority ratio 1989/91	Aid human expenditure ratio 1989/92	Percentage of aid for human priorities[a] 1989/91
Denmark	1,392	1.02	38.7	64.6	0.255	25.0
Norway	1,226	1.12	22.9	78.2	0.200	17.9
Switzerland	1,139	0.46	29.3	50.7	0.068	14.9
Netherlands	2,741	0.86	25.9	53.2	0.118	13.8
United States	10,815	0.18	19.5	58.2	0.020	11.3
Australia	969	0.36	32.0	32.9	0.038	10.5
Canada	2,515	0.46	20.3	44.4	0.042	9.0
Italy	4,122	0.34	21.9	38.6	0.029	8.5
Finland	644	0.62	26.2	32.2	0.052	8.4
Austria	530	0.29	24.3	28.4	0.020	6.9
United Kingdom	3,126	0.30	15.4	42.8	0.020	6.6
France	7,823	0.59	13.1	27.4	0.021	3.6
Japan	11,128	0.30	9.7	35.4	0.010	3.4
Sweden	2,452	1.03	5.7	51.2	0.030	2.9
Germany	6,952	0.36	7.9	42.5	0.012	2.1
Total (15 DAC countries)	57,574	0.32	16.1	43.8	0.023	7.0

a. Human priorities include basic education, primary health care, safe drinking water, adequate sanitation, family planning and nutrition programmes.

Aid has often gone more to strategic allies than to poor nations

ter supply and sanitation. Higher education gets preference over primary education, which gets less than 20% of total aid expenditure on education. Urban hospitals get preference over primary health care, which gets less than 30% of total aid expenditure on health.

Both donors and recipients encourage these distortions. The donors want their assistance to coincide with their commercial interests, so they prefer to use it as a vehicle to deliver their own equipment and con-

sultants. For political reasons, they also want their aid to be highly visible, pushing them to focus more on the construction of buildings than on the recurrent spending needed to make good use of such buildings.

But the recipients must also share the blame (table 4.6). Having yet to recognize the importance of human development, many are tempted to undertake projects they believe will enhance their political prestige. They are particularly reluctant to budget adequate maintenance funds for running their social programmes.

• *Aid and military spending*—Aid has often gone more to strategic allies than to

TABLE 4.5
Human priorities in multilateral aid, 1989/91
(percent)

Agency	Aid social allocation ratio	Aid social priority ratio	ODA for human priorities[a]
UNICEF	91.3	85.2	77.8
IFAD[b]	16.8	100.0	16.8
IDB (including special funds)	22.5	72.9	16.4
IBRD/IDA	22.5	45.3	10.2
AsDB (including special funds)	31.6	30.7	9.7
AfDB/African Dev. Fund	20.7	20.0	4.1
Total	27.3	58.7	16.0

a. Human priorities include basic education, primary health care, safe drinking water, adequate sanitation, family planning and nutrition programmes.
b. 1988–89.

TABLE 4.6
Human priorities in bilateral aid expenditures

Country	Total ODA (US$ millions) 1992	ODA as % of GNP 1992	Percentage of ODA for human priorities 1989/91
Malaysia	213	0.4	30.3
Lesotho	142	13.3	24.4
Uganda	718	22.6	20.9
Namibia	140	6.2	20.1
Burkina Faso	444	16.1	19.6
Bangladesh	1,728	6.6	13.5
Pakistan	1,169	2.3	9.7
India	2,354	0.8	5.2
Indonesia	2,080	1.8	2.9
China	2,945	0.7	2.4

poor nations. And while donors have recently expressed a welcome concern about military spending levels in developing countries, their aid allocations have yet to respond.

Until 1986, bilateral donors on average gave five times as much assistance per capita to high military spenders as they gave to low military spenders (see figure 4.7). And even in 1992, the high military spenders were still getting two and a half times as much per capita as the low military spenders.

El Salvador received 16 times more US aid per poor person than did Bangladesh, even though the GNP per capita of Bangladesh is only one-fifth that of El Salvador. And Israel, because of its special strategic alliance with the United States, continued to receive a hundred times more per poor person than Bangladesh although

it enjoyed a per capita income of over $12,000 (table 4.7).

Multilateral institutions should have been free from cold war considerations. But since the same donors sat on their governing boards, many of the same influences prevailed. For example, recipient countries' military spending seemed to make little difference in the distribution of multilateral funds, such as the World Bank funds (table 4.8).

Some donors have protested that discriminating against high military spenders would have violated the recipients' national sovereignty—a strange argument, since donors have not been so bashful about violating national sovereignty in many other areas of government policy. They have required aid recipients to eliminate food subsidies, to devalue their currency, to privatize public enterprises and to show much greater respect for human rights.

This contrast was particularly noticeable during the structural adjustment period of the 1980s. Many donors were silent witnesses to severe cuts in social spending while military spending continued to rise. In Sub-Saharan Africa between 1960 and 1990, military spending increased from 0.7% of GNP to 3.0%. Developing countries were thus balancing their budgets by unbalancing human lives—not by cutting arms expenditures.

The major powers now seem to be taking a more active interest in disarmament, but with their arms industries attempting to

Many donors were silent witnesses to severe cuts in social spending while military spending continued to rise

TABLE 4.7
US ODA to selected strategic allies and to poor nations

Country	GNP per capita (US$) 1991	US aid per poor person (US$) 1990–91
Strategic allies		
Israel	12,110	176
El Salvador	1,090	28
Bolivia	650	26
Egypt	610	63
Poor countries		
Bangladesh	220	1.7
Madagascar	210	15.0
Tanzania	120	2.7
Mozambique	80	3.6

TABLE 4.8
World Bank lending to countries experiencing a major rise or fall in military spending

Country	Military expenditures as % of GDP		Average annual World Bank loans per capita (US$)		Loans as % of total World Bank loans	
	1960	1990	1960s	1989–91	1960s	1989–91
Major rise in military spending						
Ethiopia	1.6	13.5	10.2	77.4	1.0	0.4
Tanzania	0.1	6.9	5.3	283.0	0.5	1.3
Zambia	1.1	3.2	5.7	92.7	0.5	0.4
Burkina Faso	0.6	2.8	0.1	68.2	0.0	0.3
Major fall in military spending						
Dominican Republic	5.0	0.8	0.0	41.3	0.0	0.2
Costa Rica	1.2	0.5	5.0	53.3	0.5	0.2

Note: IDA and IBRD commitments.

increase sales to developing countries, the effect so far has not been very marked.

• *Aid and human rights*—Many donors have suggested that aid recipients should be required to respect human rights and observe democratic processes. The United States, for example, adopted legislation for this purpose in the 1970s. And other donors —including Germany, Sweden and the Netherlands—have tried to link their assistance to the observance of human rights.

But rhetoric is running far ahead of reality, as a comparison of the per capita ODA received by democratic and authoritarian regimes shows. Indeed, for the United States in the 1980s, the relationship between aid and human rights violations has been perverse.

Multilateral donors also seem not to have been bothered by such considerations. They seem to prefer martial law regimes, quietly assuming that such regimes will promote political stability and improve economic management. After Bangladesh and the Philippines lifted martial law, their shares in the total loans given by the World Bank declined (table 4.9).

• *Aid and national capacity-building*— One central justification for aid is that in the long term it strengthens the capacity of developing countries—enabling them to stand on their own feet. Technical assistance was to be one of the most important instruments for this purpose.

In practice, the record of technical assistance has often been unsatisfactory. For one thing, its distribution has been skewed. The poorest countries, which have the lowest technical capacity, get an even smaller proportion of technical assistance (38%) than of ODA as a whole (46%). And even

the assistance they receive seems to have built little national capacity. Sub-Saharan Africa has been receiving more than $3 billion a year in technical assistance, yet its human development indicators remain among the lowest in the world.

Perhaps most disturbing is that, after 40 years, 90% of the $12 billion a year in technical assistance is still spent on foreign expertise—despite the fact that national experts are now available in many fields.

Often poorly planned and monitored, technical cooperation programmes rarely have clear criteria for assessing the existing technical capacity of recipient countries or for measuring and monitoring additional capacity-building. Nor do they seem able to forecast when each country is expected to graduate from the need for technical assistance.

Technical assistance is clearly in need of reform, and the opportunities for such reform are discussed later in this chapter.

• *Aid and governance*—Donors have also expressed concern in recent years about the need for "good governance"—for democratic pluralism, for the rule of law, for a less regulated economy and for a clean and non-corrupt administration. In general, however, there seems to be little agreement among donors on what good governance entails— or on how it should be monitored or built into aid conditionality.

The donors have also argued for greater decentralization, but they rarely monitor how much of their aid goes through local or provincial governments or NGOs. If anything, as *Human Development Report 1993* concluded, the aid they give has increased centralization, not decreased it.

These are just a few of the goals donors have identified for their aid—goals that their actual programmes do not serve. There are many other objectives as well— perhaps too many. The environment, for example, has become a priority, yet here again there is an awkward gap between declared goals and implementation.

Developing countries protest—reasonably—that they are subject to a host of objectives interpreted differently by different donors and pursued with fitful resolve. Aid could be much more effective if it were fo-

Technical cooperation programmes rarely have clear criteria

TABLE 4.9
World Bank loans and democracy
(annual average, US$ millions)

Philippines	1980–85	1986–93
IBRD	390	532
IDA	—	22
IBRD+IDA	390	554
Share in total IBRD +IDA loans (%)	2.9	2.6
Bangladesh	1988–90	1992–93
IDA	397	213
Share in total IDA loans (%)	8.0	3.2

cused on a few clear global objectives, allocated on that basis and then carefully monitored to ensure a direct connection between intention and outcome.

If aid were directly linked to achieving certain human development priority objectives and emerging global human security threats, this would have a profound impact on its distribution. ODA allocations would be determined by how much each country could contribute towards meeting these objectives. Rather than being doled out to favourite clients, ODA would go where the need was greatest. It would become less a matter of charity and more an investment in global human security.

A compact for human development

One of the most important ways of linking aid to specific objectives is to negotiate a global compact for human development. In this compact, all nations would pledge to ensure that within, say, the next ten years, all their people are provided with at least the very basic human development needs. This would include such social services as primary education and primary health care. It would also give people equitable access to the assets—such as land and credit—needed to permit a decent standard of living. Achieving these objectives would probably require additional expenditure of $30 to $40 billion a year (box 4.8). Many countries can achieve these objectives using their own resources—often by restructuring their expenditure priorities. Others will need outside assistance.

One way to implement the global human development compact would be through a 20:20 formula. Experience shows that countries can achieve decent levels of human development if their governments allocate, on average, 20% of public spending to human development priorities.

Some poor countries may not, however, be able to afford this. And in some, poverty and deprivation may be so severe that governments would have to allocate more than 20% of their spending to achieve the human development targets.

Aid could help fill the gap, with donors allocating a significant share of their aid budgets to human development priorities. Again, 20% would be an appropriate figure.

Developing countries devote on average only 13% of their national budgets ($57 billion a year) to human development pri-

---

BOX 4.8

A 20:20 compact on human development

The global community has long hoped for the time when it could meet the basic needs of every human being. At times this has seemed an unrealistic goal, but it is now clear that it is financially feasible. And the Social Summit now presents the opportunity to turn this hope into reality.

The target over the next ten years should be that:
- Everyone has access to basic education.
- Everyone has access to primary health care, clean drinking water and sanitation.
- All children are immunized.
- Maternal mortality is halved.
- All willing couples have access to family planning services.
- Adult illiteracy is reduced to half the current figure. Female illiteracy is no higher than male illiteracy, and girls' education is on a par with that of boys.
- Severe malnutrition is eliminated, and moderate malnutrition halved.
- World population moves towards stabilization at 7.3 billion by 2015.
- Credit schemes are extended to the poor to enable them to seek self-employment and a sustainable livelihood.

Achieving these goals would require

additional spending on the order of $30 to $40 billion a year. This seems a sizable amount, but it could be marshalled without having to find new money—merely by making better use of existing resources. Required is a 20:20 compact on human development—under which 20% of developing country budgets and 20% of industrial country aid are allocated to human priority expenditure.

For this compact, all countries would have to commit themselves to the following steps:

1. Drawing up national human development profiles—containing all the basic data and the benchmarks against which progress will be measured.

2. Establishing national human development priorities through a participatory national dialogue that includes all elements of civil society, and designing the strategies to achieve them.

3. Participating in annual reviews of the 20:20 compact—to be held as joint donor-recipient meetings on each country as well as annual reviews in the Economic and Social Council.

If the Social Summit were to agree on such a compact, it could give new hope to the majority of humankind.

BOX TABLE
Costing essential human development targets, 1995–2005

Sector	Specific targets	Approximate annual additional costs
Education	• Basic education for all and adult illiteracy reduced by 50%, with female illiteracy no higher than male	$5 to $6 billion
Health	• Primary health care for all, including complete immunization of all children • Reduction of under-five mortality by one-half or to 70 per 1,000 live births, whichever is less • Elimination of severe malnutrition and a 50% reduction in moderate malnutrition	$5 to $7 billion
Population	• Basic family planning package available to all willing couples	$10 to $12 billion
Low-cost water supply and sanitation	• Universal access to safe drinking water	$10 to $15 billion
Total for priority human agenda		$30 to $40 billion

orities. But they have considerable scope for economies in many areas—military expenditure, loss-making public enterprises and wasteful prestige development projects. Diverting funds could raise the proportion of government budgets devoted to human development priorities to at least 20% ($88 billion a year). Obviously, the restructuring would differ from one country to another.

Donor countries likewise have considerable scope for improvement. On average, they allocate only 7% of their aid to human priority concerns. The problem here is not so much the proportion of aid to the social sector (16% on average) as the distribution within the social sector. In education, less than 20% of the $7 billion allocation goes to primary education. And for some countries, the proportion is particularly low: Germany 6%, Canada 4% and the United Kingdom 4%. Similarly, in water supply and sanitation, less than 20% of aid goes to the rural areas and very little to low-cost mass-coverage programmes. The situation is somewhat better in health—with about 30% for basic health facilities.

Donors thus have enormous scope for reallocating their aid. By earmarking more funds for the social sector and by concentrating more on priority areas, they should be able to lift the proportion going to human priority goals to 20%. Again, this is an average. Some donors have greater scope for restructuring than others.

The compact could thus be based on shared responsibility. Developing countries would allocate 20% of their budgets, and donors 20% of their aid, to human development priorities. This mutual 20:20 commitment would mean that three-fourths of extra funds would come from developing countries and one-fourth from the donors.

The political, financial and humanitarian case for such a compact is strong. It could ensure that within the next ten years every nation, poor and rich, would have reached a basic threshold of human development.

A global social safety net

Today, aid contributions are voluntary, and the aid burden is distributed randomly and inequitably. Because the flows are subject to annual appropriations by national parliaments, they can be very unpredictable. Poverty and deprivation, by contrast, are more persistent and enduring.

Even if a 20:20 compact on human development could, within ten years, meet the most basic human needs, this would still leave much inequity and relative poverty. How can international development cooperation be better linked with poverty and deprivation? One way would be to establish a global social safety net.

The size of a global social safety net could be set in terms of essential consumption—perhaps a minimum of $1 per person per day. Or it could be set in terms of certain public goods—such as health, education and nutrition.

However defined, the net would need to be sustained by adequate funding, with the exact contribution a matter of negotiation. But the principle should be that contributions are obligatory and follow a fixed formula so that annual flows are predictable.

One possibility would be to levy a world income tax of around 0.1% on the richest nations (those with a per capita GNP above $10,000). This would yield around $20 billion a year. The rate could be a uniform 0.1% or vary progressively with income per head.

The recipients would also be a clearly defined group of countries—those with a per capita GNP of less than $2,000. Within this group, the basis for distribution could be twofold. First, allocations should be adjusted to the human development index of each country, with the lowest HDI countries making the fastest progress identified as deserving the greatest help. Second, allocations should be modified according to the recipient's spending on defence—to ensure that these fungible funds promote human development rather than merely permit greater arms expenditure. Allocations could, for example, vary inversely with the country's ratio of military to social spending.

The details of such a scheme could be a matter of international negotiation before and during the Social Summit. But the basic idea is to establish for the first time a firm

The political, financial and humanitarian case for a 20:20 compact is strong

social safety net for the poorer nations. This global net should be on top of present ODA. If that is not possible, the first 0.1% of GNP should be earmarked from present ODA contributions for the social safety net—with the balance promoting specific global human security objectives.

Balancing emergency and development assistance

Although many long-term development needs are still unmet, there also seem to be a growing number of immediate emergencies that demand international support—partly because natural disasters have been increasing in number and in impact (see box 2.4). The global community, prompted by the communications media, now accepts a bigger responsibility to assist in such man-made disasters as wars and ethnic strife.

This peacekeeping is becoming expensive. The United Nations, in its first 48 years of existence, committed some $4 billion to peacekeeping operations. It spent the same amount in 1993 alone. Meanwhile, development spending has remained stagnant—or even declined.

Since emergency aid is always more urgent and more easily negotiated with otherwise reluctant legislatures, it seems inevitable that it will continue to draw funds away from long-term development.

The crises may seem to arrive suddenly, but they are the outcome of years of failed development—of environmental degradation leading to a collapse of ecosystems, or of decades of autocratic rule leading to the collapse of the state. The response to such deep-seated problems cannot merely be emergency aid. The crises in Angola, Haiti, Mozambique, Somalia, Sudan, Central Asia or former Yugoslavia cannot be resolved by quick, intensive interventions. Military force can accomplish little on its own if there is no prospect of longer-term development.

By the same token, diverting aid from other parts of the developing world to countries in crisis merely stores up problems for the future—increasing the likelihood of more Somalias and more Yugoslavias in the years ahead.

The only solution is to review emergency aid and long-term development aid together. Today's allocations are based on the assumption that emergency aid tops up development aid. In some cases, this is true—as with the assistance to Pakistan to help with the influx of Afghan refugees. But in many other cases, it is not. Emergency assistance to Bosnia, Liberia and Somalia has had to deal with complete national breakdowns—where there is almost nothing to work with, nothing to build on. This is much more expensive and demands a new level of funding.

To meet current challenges adequately, the UN's emergency fund needs to be raised from its current $50 million to something nearer $5 billion. This would save development funds from raids in the name of emergency.

It is important, therefore, that this be new money rather than funds redirected from development aid. Where should it come from? One obvious source is the defence budgets of the industrial countries—a proposal the Secretary-General has already made in his *Agenda for Peace.* After all, if the United Nations becomes more involved in peacekeeping, it is taking on a role previously played by national armies. But there are also other potential sources apart from the peace dividend, such as a tax on arms trade.

A fundamental reform of technical assistance

The original objective of technical assistance was to close the "gap", particularly the technical capacity gap, between industrial and developing countries—by accelerating the transfer of knowledge, skills and expertise and thus by building national capacity. In a few cases, it has done this. But as the foregoing analysis has shown, in many others, it has had precisely the opposite effect—reining in national capacity rather than unleashing it.

Are there any common factors in the successes? One seems to be that the best projects and programmes have involved well-defined and established technologies that have remained relatively free from

Emergency aid is beginning to draw funds away from long-term development

changes in developmental theory and fashion. These include civil aviation, meteorology, plant protection, various types of education (particularly vocational training) and the eradication of such diseases as malaria. A second common factor is allowing enough time to test alternative approaches—for research, for trial and error, for learning by doing. A third is fostering the participation of enough qualified national counterparts. And a fourth is creating a positive environment in the receiving country.

Many of these conditions have prevailed only at certain times, in certain places and in certain fields. Some Asian countries—whose technical assistance peaked in the 1950s and 1960s—have benefited from better overall economic conditions and from the greater persistence and patience of donors.

On why so many other programmes have failed, there seems to be quite a long list of reasons (box 4.9). Of course, many of the same criticisms can also be applied to capital assistance.

How can technical assistance be improved—taking advantage of the successes of the past and avoiding the many known pitfalls?

One simple and direct solution would be to give the technical assistance funds directly to developing countries—and let them decide how to spend the money. Offering the resources as budgetary support would enable the receiving governments to employ national experts where available or international ones where not. This would have several advantages: the experts would be more appropriate to the country's real needs, and they would probably cost less since their salaries would be determined by international market forces rather than by living costs in the sending country. The result would be a more efficient, effective and equitable allocation of development funds.

Technical assistance could also be improved through regional development cooperation. This may even open up new funding sources and encourage self-financing. Such an approach is described in the proposal by Abdus Salam for an Islamic Science Foundation (special contribution, facing page).

New forms of data on development cooperation

One of the most significant obstacles to reforming development cooperation is the lack of appropriately organized information. It is easy enough to discern from existing data sources who is giving aid and who is receiving it—and the broad sectors to which it is allocated. But it is much more difficult to work out how the aid is being used and what objectives it is serving. It is

---

BOX 4.9

Why failed economists visit

In 1962, the British development economist Dudley Seers wrote an article on "why visiting economists fail" as advisers in developing countries. It is still worth reading. Among his reasons: incompetence in personal relations, getting into a muddle, taking on too much, finding it hard to cope with the ubiquitous xenophobia—and not knowing who not to be seen drinking with. In addition, there were difficulties in finding suitable counterparts, in assembling reliable statistical information and in often having to act as a psychotherapist rather than as an economist.

Seers was too gracious to mention some of the other failures of the visiting experts: being more interested in enjoying the sunshine, buying antiques, being treated as an important person or gathering material for a career-advancing publication than in doing something useful for the country.

Few experts have the characteristics that make a good adviser, and those who do are in great demand in their own countries. A companion piece to Seers's article might therefore be entitled "Why Failed Economists Visit". It could include other reasons for the failure of visiting economists—and the visits of failed economists.
• Technical assistance, unlike turnips, has no independent measure of its value to the recipient. Instead, output is measured by input: salaries or man-months—conveying a deceptive impression of achievement when nothing may have been achieved.
• Developing countries have a limited absorptive capacity, not just for capital but also for technical assistance. Even if foreign experts are good at teaching skills to counterparts (and they usually are not), this is not enough. Unless attitudes and institutions are changed, the assistance "does not take". Without roots, cut flowers wither and die.
• Many UN agencies suffer from a technocratic bias: they believe in technical fixes without much regard for cultural and social factors—assuming, for example, that setting up a seed distribution system or a water supply project requires no knowledge of local patterns of personal relations.
• Technical assistance has not promoted greater self-reliance. Instead, indigenous institutions remain weak. Indeed, in the name of national capacity-building, much national expertise has been displaced.
• Technical assistance can be very costly: in 1989 in Sub-Saharan Africa alone, it cost $3.3 billion—a quarter of the development assistance to the region. Yet Sub-Saharan Africa's human development indicators are the lowest in the world, questionable testimony to the effectiveness of national capacity-building.
• There is salary apartheid for similar expertise—with foreign experts sometimes getting several times as much as national experts.
• There has never been an explicit policy on when countries are ready to graduate from technical assistance. Perversely, the index of success is usually the arrival of ever-greater flows of technical assistance—which should instead be regarded as an index of failure.

---

also difficult to see how aid fits into the general picture of resource flows to and from countries. It would thus be very useful to have comprehensive, integrated country balance sheets of resource flows.

Reshaping aid so that it meets particular objectives will also require reshaping the presentation of data. The first step should be for the Development Assistance Committee of the OECD, and UNDP, to establish a system that itemizes bilateral and multilateral assistance according to commonly agreed national and global objectives (technical note 2). The OECD could do this from the point of view of donors, and UNDP could use its network of country offices to provide reports from the point of view of recipients. Unless donors and recipients establish a clear link between aid and the objectives it is supposed to serve (and regularly monitor performance), the yawning gap between rhetoric and reality is likely to persist.

A new framework of global governance

A new design of development cooperation will be incomplete without a new institutional framework of global governance— one that defends the new frontiers of human security with more democratic partnerships between nations.

Proposal for an Islamic Science Foundation

No Muslim country possesses a high level of scientific and technological competence. While the world economy is getting more and more global, the gap between the industrial countries and the Muslim communities continues to widen, and scientific and technological advances remain confined to the rich countries of the North.

The Islamic countries could make a decisive breakthrough by creating an Islamic Science Foundation. The Foundation would be sponsored by Muslim countries and operate within them. It would be non-political, purely scientific and run by eminent people of science and technology from the Muslim World.

The Foundation would have two principal objectives. First, to build up high-level scientific institutions and personnel— strengthening existing communities of scientists and creating new ones where none currently exist. Second, to build up and strengthen international institutions for advanced scientific research, both pure and applied, relevant to the needs of Muslim countries, and with an emphasis on international standards of quality and attainment.

The Foundation would initially concentrate on five main areas:

• *High-level training*—Scholars would be sponsored abroad to acquire knowledge in areas where gaps exist in the Muslim countries. Some 3,000 would be supported annually with continued support for 1,000 after they return home—about 15% of the Foundation's budget.

• *Enhancing research quality*—Contracts will be awarded to university departments and research centres to strengthen their work in selected scientific fields—about 25% of the budget.

• *Contact with the world scientific community*—To promote the interchange of ideas and criticism on which science thrives, the Foundation will support 3,000 two-way visits of scholars and fellows, as well as the holding of international symposia and conferences—about 10% of the budget.

• *Sponsoring applied research*—To strengthen existing institutions and create new ones devoted to the problems of the Middle East and the Arab World—including health, technology, agriculture, environment and water resources—about 40% of the budget.

• *Popularizing science*—To help make the population of the Islamic countries more scientifically and technologically minded, by making use of the mass media, scientific museums, libraries and exhibitions. It would also help modernize science and technology syllabi, and award prizes for discoveries and inventions.

The Foundation would have its headquarters at the seat of the Islamic Conference and would be open to sponsorship by all its members. Its Board of Trustees would consist of representatives of governments, professors and scientists. It would also have an Executive Council of eminent scientists which would be free from political interference.

The Foundation would be a non-profit tax-free body, which as a non-governmental organization would build up links with the United Nations, UNESCO and the UN University system. It would have an endowment fund of at least $5 billion and a projected annual income of $300 to $350 million. It is envisaged that the sponsoring countries would pledge the endowment fund as a fixed proportion of export earnings and provide it in four annual instalments.

Creating such a Foundation should be an urgent priority for the Muslim World. It would enable Muslim societies to recapture their glorious heritage of scientific pre-eminence and to compete as equals in the world of tomorrow.

Abdus Salam

Abdus Salam, winner of the 1979 Nobel Prize for Physics

The past 50 years of global governance

The edifice of global governance was last rebuilt in the 1940s after the Second World War. With memories of the great depression of the 1930s still fresh, the overarching principle was "never again". Unemployment had been heavy—so the new objective was full employment. Trade and investment rules had broken down—so the new objective was to prevent beggar-thy-neighbour policies and to manage the world economy according to internationally agreed rules. The international monetary system had collapsed—so the new objective was to have stable currencies with agreed procedures for adjustment. Deflation had been prolonged—so the new objective was expansionary economic policies. Commodity prices had crashed—so the new objective was to maintain and stabilize commodity prices. Protectionism had been rising—so the new objective was to move towards liberal and agreed rules for expanding world trade, and to support countries that had balance of payments deficits.

On the political front, the 1930s had seen the withering away of the League of Nations—so the objective was to build a new and stronger organization, the United Nations, to provide the political and social security indispensable for an expanding world economy.

The international institutions that emerged in the 1940s were largely a reaction to the 1930s and partly the fruits of an inspired vision of the future.

The institutions of global governance created in the 1940s (UN, World Bank, IMF, GATT) have played a major role in the past five decades in keeping the world at peace and in accelerating global economic growth and trade liberalization. They certainly succeeded in avoiding any recurrence of the experience of the pre-1940s. No world war broke out. No worldwide depression occurred. But they were far less successful in narrowing world income disparities or in reducing global poverty. The role of the Bretton Woods institutions was undermined considerably after 1970 as global economic decision-making shifted either to smaller groups, such as the G-7, or to the workings of the international capital markets. The United Nations, for its part, started with enormous promise but was never allowed to play its role as the fourth pillar of development (box 4.10).

BOX 4.10

Does the United Nations work in the development field?

So much attention has focused on the weaknesses of the UN system that its successes are generally forgotten. While it is true that the development role of the United Nations has never been fully recognized or strengthened, UN agencies still have a number of notable achievements to their credit. To mention but a few:

WHO helped mobilize worldwide action for the eradication of smallpox. FAO created an early warning and monitoring network for food production. UNESCO has helped countries launch literacy campaigns and expand education. ILO, in the 1970s, launched the World Employment Programme and has since undertaken other pioneering work in the employment field. UNICEF has been very effective at promoting universal immunization and focusing world attention on the needs of children. UNFPA put the issue of balanced population growth on the world's agenda. And UNDP has been a respected partner of many developing countries because of its multidisciplinarity and neutrality.

The smaller specialized agencies have also made significant contributions, if in a much quieter fashion. The International Telecommunication Union, the World Meteorological Organization, the International Civil Aviation Organization and the Universal Postal Union have not only helped regulate important aspects of international cooperation, they have also provided technical assistance to the poorer (or weaker) countries.

The United Nations Statistical Office and other specialized agencies have helped build many of the statistical systems used to track economic and social developments—including the standardized system of national accounts underlying the statistics on GNP, production, consumption, trade and transfers throughout the world.

Moreover, many important policy initiatives, even if subsequently implemented elsewhere, started within the United Nations:

• *The International Development Association*—The World Bank set up its soft-loan facility, IDA, in 1960 as a response to the proposal for a Special United Nations Fund for Economic Development (SUNFED).
• *The Compensatory Finance Facility*—The IMF created this facility in 1963 to finance export shortfalls in response to a proposal in 1962 by the UN Commission on International Commodity Trade.
• *Special Drawing Rights*—The IMF created SDRs following an UNCTAD report (the Hart-Kaldor-Tinbergen Report) that proposed the creation of a new form of international liquidity.
• *The Generalized System of Preferences*—This followed continuing pressure from the UN, especially UNCTAD, for developing countries to receive special consideration when the rules of a global trading system were being formulated.
• *Changes in policy dialogue*—Publications such as UNICEF's *Adjustment with a Human Face* and UNDP's *Human Development Reports* have had considerable influence on donors—including the Bretton Woods institutions.

Despite these successes, the inadequacies of the UN system have grown increasingly apparent.

A series of international conferences in the past three decades identified many of the priority needs—for children, women, population, food, nutrition, health, education, employment, human settlements, science and technology, environment and energy. The Alma Ata Conference on primary health care for all in 1978, the Jomtien Conference on basic education for all in 1990, the Children's Summit in 1990, the Earth Summit in 1992 and the Women's Conferences in 1975, 1980 and 1985 have been important milestones in identifying key human priorities. But followup has been weak, and the UN system has often failed to generate the focus, organization or resources needed to support accelerated international action. This needs to change in the future.

A major problem for the United Nations has been inadequacy of financial resources. To put it quite bluntly, many donors have always preferred the Bretton Woods system of one-dollar, one-vote over the one-country, one-vote system at the UN. So, they gave the UN far fewer resources than the Bretton Woods organizations, or the multilateral development banks or the bilateral agencies. This lack of resources reduced the UN's effectiveness—and in a vicious circle this became a further reason to deny it resources.

The need for strengthened institutions of global governance is much greater today than ever before. Markets have become globalized. Issues of prosperity, as well as of poverty, are linking the concerns of all people. Nation-states are weakening as decision-making becomes either local or global. In such a milieu, the long-term perspective for global governance needs to be re-examined.

New institutions for the 21st century

The imperatives of global human security and development in the 21st century will require a wave of creative innovations similar to that in the 1940s. At least three institutional changes are needed urgently:
• The design of a strengthened United Nations role in sustainable human development.
• The creation of an Economic Security Council to reflect a much broader concept of security.
• The restructuring and strengthening of the existing institutions for global economic management.

The only feasible strategy is to enlarge the scope of existing institutions—step by step—to cope with the challenges of the 21st century.

A United Nations human development umbrella

The new compulsions of human security demand a strong role from the United Nations in promoting sustainable human development. Some of the elements for such an effort are already in place. Others can be developed in an agreed step-by-step approach. The final objective should be to enable the United Nations to serve the international community as its strongest human development pillar.

The following evolution may be necessary for this purpose:
• *A sustainable human development paradigm*—The concerned agencies of the UN need to identify common missions and complementary approaches to helping countries realize their sustainable human development goals. Stimulus will come from the Secretary-General's *Agenda for Development* and from other efforts under way to better define a common sense of purpose and unifying themes.
• *A coordinated effort by development funds*—The development funds of the UN (UNDP, UNICEF, UNFPA, IFAD, WFP) provide substantial resources to developing countries—about $5 billion a year. The pooled resources of these UN funds are nearly as large as those of IDA (the soft-loan window of the World Bank). Moreover, these funds are providing grants, not credits, so that there is a substantial net transfer of resources to developing countries. These development funds are now discussing how best to strengthen their overall development effort and coordinate their assistance strategies, recognizing the need for a more integrated, effective and efficient UN development system. Much closer cooperation among the leadership of these institutions, both at headquarters and at the country level, as well as with the leadership of the Economic and Social Council, will be necessary in the days ahead.
• *Additional resources and responsibilities*—If additional resources are generated to support human development strategies—whether through the 20:20 compact or a global human security fund, as discussed earlier—a strengthened UN development system would be in an excellent position to manage and monitor these additional resources and to assume the new responsibilities for social development that could emerge from the Social Summit.

Some analysts have gone so far as to suggest the establishment of an integrated Human Development Agency. It would be

The United Nations must serve the international community as its strongest human development pillar

An Economic
Security Council
can provide the
highest-level
decision-making
forum for global
human security

far better, however, to take advantage of the relative strengths of each UN development fund—drawing on the large constituencies and complementary development mandates each has created over time—than to aim at an outright merger. More critical than any superficial administrative merger are a substantive merger of the development funds' policy frameworks and some restructuring and management reforms— as well as the overall umbrella of sustainable human development. But this consideration does place a major responsibility on all the existing UN development funds to get together on a common platform and a well-considered structure.

Economic Security Council

A further step in strengthening the UN role in sustainable human development would be the creation of an Economic Security Council—a decision-making forum at the highest level to review the threats to global human security and agree on required actions.

The council must be kept small and manageable. Its membership could consist of 11 permanent members from the main industrial and more populous developing countries. Another 11 members could be added on a rotating basis from various geographical and political constituencies.

An intermediate alternative would be to extend the mandate of the present Security Council so that it could consider not just military threats but also threats to peace from economic and social crises. For this purpose, it may be necessary to establish a separate entity within the council—one with an enlarged membership and a new role in socio-economic security.

Another possibility would be to use the Economic and Social Council—establishing within it a small and manageable executive board that could meet in permanent session and make decisions to be ratified later by the entire body.

The voting system in an Economic Security Council should not include a veto. But to reassure all constituencies that their legitimate interests would be protected, the voting system should be to have all decisions ratified not just by a majority of all members but also by majorities of the industrial and the developing countries.

As well as coordinating the activities of the UN agencies, the Economic Security Council would act as a watchdog over the policy direction of all international and regional financial institutions. To implement its decisions effectively, the council should have access to the global human security fund proposed earlier. The council would need to be backed by a professional secretariat to prepare policy options for its consideration.

World Central Bank

A World Central Bank is essential for the 21st century—for sound macroeconomic management, for global financial stability and for assisting the economic expansion of the poorer nations. It would perform five functions:

- Help stabilize global economic activity.
- Act as a lender of last resort to financial institutions.
- Calm the financial markets when they become jittery or disorderly.
- Regulate financial institutions, particularly the deposit banks.
- Create and regulate new international liquidity.

The IMF was supposed to perform all these functions, but the industrial countries have been reluctant to give it the responsibility for them, weakening its role considerably over the past two decades.

It will take some time—and probably some international financial crisis—before a full-scale World Central Bank can be created. In the meantime, four steps could convert the IMF into an embryonic central bank.

1. A RENEWED ISSUE OF SPECIAL DRAW-ING RIGHTS. A new issue of SDRs by the IMF—in the range of 30 to 50 billion SDRs—could help fuel world recovery at a time when inflationary pressures are low, primary commodity prices are at rock bottom and most of the world is in the grip of deflationary policies.

This issue of SDRs would also help meet

the reserve requirements of poor countries. Today, 25 developing countries hold non-gold international resources equal to less than eight weeks of imports. An SDR allocation would enable them to increase their reserves without further borrowing or without adopting deflationary policies that would retard economic growth and impose unnecessary human costs.

There could also be some innovations in the distribution of SDRs. If they were initially allocated on the basis of IMF quotas, the poor countries would get less than they need for their reserve requirements, while the industrial countries would get more than they need. The industrial countries could thus pass on some of their allocation to developing countries through overdraft facilities.

The private sector should also be able to make use of SDRs. Commercial banks, for example, could deposit national currencies with their central banks and receive SDRs for use in international transactions.

2. AN EXPANDED COMPENSATORY AND CONTINGENCY FINANCIAL FACILITY. The CCFF needs to be changed—in three ways. First, there should be no quota restriction. At present, a country's access to the CCFF is limited to a percentage of its quota, so the country may not be able to get full compensation for a shortfall in exports. Second, the loan period needs to be extended so that countries do not have to repay before the contingency is over. Third, there should be no conditions attached to borrowing. If a country is suffering from external factors outside its control, it seems strange that it should be subjected to the additional burden of IMF conditionality.

3. GLOBAL MACROECONOMIC MANAGEMENT. An enhanced IMF should be central in global macroeconomic management—reviewing the policies of all countries, whether or not they are active borrowers. If major countries have unsustainable policies—such as high budget deficits or inappropriate interest rates—the IMF should request the Bank for International Settlements (BIS) to link the level of reserves that banks are required to hold

against loans to these countries to the IMF's evaluation. This would affect the industrial countries' ability to raise funds from private banks and give the IMF an important lever on their policies.

The IMF already has considerable leverage over developing countries through the conditions of its lending—but the form of conditionality should change. Rather than rely exclusively on short-run demand management and on deflationary policies in poor countries (where there is so little to deflate), it should place more emphasis on supply expansion to promote economic growth, employment and human development.

4. SUPERVISION OF INTERNATIONAL BANKING. In collaboration with the BIS, the IMF should acquire some regular control over international banking activities. Flows of capital sweep with hurricane force across international frontiers, sometimes creating havoc in international markets. Just as domestic capital markets are regulated, so there is a need for a minimum of regulation in international capital markets.

These four steps would not turn the IMF into a full-fledged World Central Bank, but they would help it to move in that direction. Given the needs of global governance for the 21st century, the Social Summit can provide a valuable service by inviting a serious debate on this issue.

International Investment Trust

As discussed earlier, private capital markets have become very active in recycling funds to emerging markets in developing countries. But most of these funds are going to a handful of creditworthy nations, particularly in East Asia and Latin America.

The World Bank is already playing a very useful role in helping developing countries obtain greater access to these market funds—particularly for countries that may not be able to get these funds on the basis of their own limited creditworthiness. The World Bank's intervention in the market helps the developing countries by raising funds on less expensive terms, by lengthen-

A World Central Bank is essential for the 21st century

ing maturities, by lending to social sectors that private markets might not touch otherwise (education, health, nutrition, family planning) and by combining the provision of funds with policy advice on macroeconomic management. But the total scale of the Bank's recycling is rather modest: in net terms, the resource transfers to developing countries are negative, at –$1 to –$2 billion a year.

In the face of declining resource transfers, some creative new thinking is needed to recycle international surpluses to developing countries. One possibility would be for the World Bank to take on the role of an International Investment Trust—selling bonds to nations with a surplus and lending the proceeds to developing countries.

Such bonds, to compete with those issued by governments, would have to be attractive. They could, for example, be guaranteed against currency fluctuations and perhaps indexed against inflation. Although the bonds might have a lower rate of return, they could be safer than government bonds, which carry no such guarantees.

Developing countries could borrow from the trust on terms appropriate to their level of development. The newly industrializing countries could pay commercial rates, while low-income countries would pay less—a subsidy that richer members of the international community would have to cover. If some of the proposals regarding international fees or taxes prove to be acceptable to the international community, a pool of resources will become available for such a subsidized recycling of market funds.

These innovations would also require more automatic replenishing of the World Bank's capital, and its capital-gearing ratio would have to increase to enable it to make loans equivalent to a higher proportion of its capital.

Since the evolution of an International Investment Trust would probably be a long process, it might be worthwhile in the meantime to consider establishing a new loan window at the World Bank. Today, developing countries taking World Bank loans fall into two categories: those developed enough to afford the stiff terms demanded

by the IBRD, and those poor enough to qualify for concessionary funds from IDA. But many countries, such as those in South Asia, are poised uncertainly between the two extremes. The World Bank has tried to cope with the limitations of its lending instruments by blending IBRD and IDA resources. But since IDA now represents only about 30% of total World Bank lending, this restricts such juggling.

A further limitation on both the IBRD and the IDA is the amount of funds available. The United States is the largest contributor to both—and so has the most votes. But it is not only reluctant to increase its own contribution—it is also unwilling to let other countries give more, since this would reduce US voting power. If not for this constraint, Japan, for example, might be able to contribute much more.

A solution to both problems would be to create a new loan window—an Intermediate Assistance Facility, with its own board of governors and a separate voting structure. It would be able to receive funds directly from donors and to lend to countries, such as India and Pakistan, that are ready to graduate from IDA terms but not yet sufficiently creditworthy to meet the hard terms of the IBRD. Borrowers could pay, say, two-thirds of the going interest rate over 25 years.

This facility would allow the World Bank to concentrate its IDA resources mainly on the long-term development of Africa—in a fashion similar to its focus on Asia for the first 25 years of the IDA's existence. The World Bank would then be able to concentrate IBRD funds on the most creditworthy of the newly industrializing countries, and thus protect the credit rating of IBRD bonds in the international capital markets.

World Trade Organization

One of the most important outcomes of the Uruguay Round of trade negotiations has been to transform GATT from a provisional agreement into a full institution—to be headed by a ministerial conference. This new World Trade Organization (WTO) will negotiate rules for international trade—to level the playing field—and deal with legal aspects of dispute regulation.

A more systematic approach to the management of world trade is certainly welcome. But there still are many inequities to be addressed. Trade needs to be further liberalized in areas of primary interest to developing countries, such as labour services. And several fundamental issues have yet to be resolved, notably the need to promote environmentally sound trade without resorting to protectionism.

This new WTO should also have other responsibilities. It is, for example, one of the institutions that could help negotiate and implement the new types of development cooperation suggested earlier, such as compensation for damages and payment for services rendered.

And for the future, one could think of expanding a WTO into a WPTO—a world production and trade organization—to cover investment and technology transfers, too. A strong WTO could be of great benefit to developing countries. But a level playing field is of little use if one team is overwhelmingly stronger than the other. Developing countries will thus have to invest much more in their own national capacities if they are to compete internationally.

World Anti-Monopoly Authority

Transnational corporations (TNCs) control more than 70% of world trade and dominate the production, distribution and sale of many goods from developing countries, especially in the cereal and tobacco markets. An estimated 25% of world trade is conducted as intrafirm trade within TNCs.

These corporations thus have great power, which, if harnessed for sustainable human development, could be of great benefit. There is a growing consensus that governments and TNCs should work closely together to promote national and international economic welfare.

This concentration of power can also be damaging. To some extent, transnationals have escaped regulation by national authorities, and the speed and ease with which they can restructure their assets, relocate production, transfer their assets, transfer technology and indulge in transfer pricing have become a matter of international concern. TNCs have also engaged in oligopolistic practices and shown insensitivity to environmental concerns (more than 50% of greenhouse gases are thought to be generated by their operations).

There is thus a strong case for some international supervision of TNCs. A useful starting point would be to complete the UN Code of Conduct for Transnationals, which after 20 years' work has now been negotiated. This could be followed by the creation within the UN of a World Anti-Monopoly Authority—to monitor observance of the new code and to ensure that TNCs do not resort to monopolistic and restrictive practices, particularly in their dealings with developing countries.

New institutions of a global civil society

The shape our societies take does not depend exclusively on governments. Individuals, families, community groups, international foundations, transnational corporations, the communications media—these and many others help mould civil society.

There also are thousands of nongovernmental organizations operating nationally and internationally—monitoring human rights, organizing humanitarian aid and promoting the interests of such groups as women, the disabled or indigenous people. And new organizations emerge each year, often sprouting up spontaneously in response to felt needs and forming new alliances for change. They can powerfully influence government policy, as many women's organizations and environmental groups have demonstrated.

One of the more significant new international NGOs is the Earth Council, established in 1992 after the Earth Summit in Brazil, where nearly 10,000 NGOs played a very important part. The Earth Council will act as a global ombudsman on the issues of environment and development. It intends to issue an annual earth report to remind the global community of significant successes and failures in the field of sustainable development and to generate pressure for change in global policies.

The shape our societies take does not depend exclusively on governments

One significant gap in NGO activity at the national and international level has been in the area of corruption, which is spreading like a cancer all over the world—in government bureaucracies, among political leaders, in military procurement, in transnational corporations, in international banking. *Human Development Report 1992* proposed setting up Honesty International, similar to Amnesty International, to research and publicize cases of corruption. A new NGO, Transparency International, has since been set up on these lines, though it is too soon to judge how effective it is likely to be.

This chapter has included just a few of the institutions that the world is likely to need in the 21st century. Some people may consider them overly ambitious, but others may consider them timid. Jan Tinbergen, the first Nobel Prize winner in economics, believes that we need nothing less than a world government (special contribution, this page). This may appear to be totally utopian today. But he points out: "The idealists of today often turn out to be the realists of tomorrow."

A pragmatic approach would be to take some practical steps now and to initiate further reviews of some of the longer-term

SPECIAL CONTRIBUTION

Global governance for the 21st century

Mankind's problems can no longer be solved by national governments. What is needed is a World Government.

This can best be achieved by strengthening the United Nations system. In some cases, this would mean changing the role of UN agencies from advice-giving to implementation. Thus, the FAO would become the World Ministry of Agriculture, UNIDO would become the World Ministry of Industry, and the ILO the World Ministry of Social Affairs.

In other cases, completely new institutions would be needed. These could include, for example, a permanent World Police which would have the power to subpoena nations to appear before the International Court of Justice, or before other specially created courts. If nations do not abide by the Court's judgement, it should be possible to apply sanctions, both non-military and military.

Other institutions could include an Ocean Authority (based on the new Law of the Seas), and an analogous Outer Space Authority, to deal with matters such as outer space, aviation and information satellites.

But some of the most important new institutions would be financial—a World Treasury and a World Central Bank. The World Treasury would serve as a world ministry of finance. Its main task would be to collect the resources needed by the other world ministries through one or more systems of global automatic taxation. If there were any delay in contributions from member governments, it would have to make funds available where they are most urgently needed. In addition, there should be a World Central Bank based on a reformed IMF to deal, among other things, with monetary, banking and stock exchange policies.

Just as each nation has a system of income redistribution, so there should be a corresponding "world financial policy" to be implemented by the World Bank and the World Central Bank. Redistribution is the core political issue of the 20th century.

Here it is useful to make a comparison with well-governed nations. The proportion of GDP distributed through social security benefits varies greatly from one country to another. It is typically lower in developing countries: 0.3% in Rwanda, 2.1% in Bangladesh, 2.3% in Bolivia. In industrial countries, it is generally higher but does vary considerably: 6.0% in Japan, 12.6% in the United States, 33.7% in Sweden. Two main factors explain the difference: the level of development and the sociopolitical policy of the country. The low level in developing countries reflects their underdeveloped condition and the fact that many are living in a feudal state: the rich are accustomed to ruling the people, and also feel poor in relation to the rich in the high-income countries. But this is no justification for the present callous neglect: there is a strong case for much more redistribution within developing countries.

But there should also be redistribution at the international level through development cooperation. How much should the industrial nations make available to the developing countries? In 1970, the UN General Assembly decided that 0.7% was needed. By 1991, the actual average for the OECD countries was only 0.33%. But the UN target figure is itself too low. In the 1970s and 1980s, the gap between the developing and industrial countries widened. To have prevented this would have required aid equivalent to 1.3% of GDP. As the world economy becomes increasingly integrated, so the redistribution of world income should become similar to that within well-governed nations.

Some of these proposals are, no doubt, far-fetched and beyond the horizon of today's political possibilities. But the idealists of today often turn out to be the realists of tomorrow.

J. Tinbergen

Jan Tinbergen, winner of the 1969 Nobel Prize for Economics

measures. Thus, to help create a new framework for international development cooperation, the World Summit for Social Development might want to consider the following:

- Recommending the design of a 20:20 global human development compact.
- Recommending, furthermore, the design of global human security compacts to address the major challenges currently facing humankind.
- Endorsing the proposal for the creation of an Economic Security Council within the United Nations.
- Urging the international community—beyond these measures—to undertake a comprehensive review of the existing framework of international development cooperation, and in this connection, to undertake studies on the practicability of such measures as establishing a global social safety net, introducing a world income tax and supporting the Tobin tax (on foreign exchange movements) as a potential source of financing for a more effective United Nations.

CHAPTER 5

The human development index revisited

One way the HDI has been improved is through disaggregation

The first *Human Development Report* (1990) introduced a new way of measuring human development—by combining indicators of life expectancy, educational attainment and income into a composite human development index, the HDI (box 5.1). The Report acknowledged that no single index could ever completely capture such a complex concept. It acknowledged, too, that the HDI would remain subject to improvements, corrections and refinements—both as a result of a growing awareness of its deficiencies, and to accommodate criticisms and suggestions from academics and policy-makers. Also to be emphasized is that the HDI is not intended to replace the other detailed socioeconomic indicators in this Report, for these are essential for a fuller understanding of individual countries.

One way the index has been improved is through disaggregation. A country's overall index can conceal the fact that different groups within the country have very different levels of human development—men and women, for example, or different ethnic groups, regions or social classes. The 1993 Report therefore constructed separate HDIs for different population groups in five countries.

This Report adds nine more countries. The results, discussed in greater detail later in this chapter, show how different population groups in the same country seem to be living in different worlds. They also show how powerful the disaggregated HDI can be for detecting societal strains and potential conflicts.

The 1993 Report identified the vast disparities between black and white communities in the United States. It also identified the disparities in Mexico between people in the state of Chiapas and those in richer parts of the country—a year ahead of the political upheaval there.

Another way of highlighting national disparities and comparing them across countries is by reducing the country's overall HDI in proportion to its internal disparities. Since 1991, these Reports have offered two disparity-adjusted HDIs—one for gender, one for income distribution—the construction of which is discussed below. These HDIs illustrate how socioeconomic disparities diminish the overall human development record of some countries.

In the income-distribution-adjusted HDI, more egalitarian countries, such as the Nordic countries, rise in the rankings, while others fall—notably Brazil, with its unequal income distribution. In the gender-disparity-adjusted HDI, the Nordic countries again improve their position, while Japan, where women earn much less than men, slips in the ranking.

A further possibility for adjusting the HDI would be to reflect a country's environmental performance. Exploratory work has shown that, for the time being, there does not seem to be sufficient agreement on which indicators would be appropriate or how this might be done. Work will therefore continue in this area.

Modifications to the basic HDI

In addition to the two "adjusted" HDIs, there have been modifications to components of the basic index—specifically, the indicators of educational attainment and of income.

Educational attainment was originally measured only through the adult literacy rate, but the 1991 Report broadened this measure to incorporate mean years of schooling.

For income, the HDI starts from the premise that a $300 increase in per capita income clearly makes a significant difference in a country where the average is currently $600—but that it will matter much less in a country where it is $20,000. The HDI originally used a threshold value beyond which the marginal increase in income was considered less significant and was therefore heavily discounted. Until 1993, this threshold was derived from the poverty-level income of the industrial countries in the Luxembourg Income Study, with values updated and translated into purchasing power parity dollars (PPP$).

It was always questionable, however, whether the poverty level of industrial countries was an appropriate income target for developing countries. So, for the 1994 HDI, the threshold value has been taken to be the current average global value of real GDP per capita in PPP$. Once a country gets beyond the world average, any further increases in per capita income are considered to make a sharply diminishing marginal contribution to human development.

The HDI emphasizes sufficiency rather than satiety. On the new basis of real GDP per capita, the threshold is $5,120. The method of discounting remains the same, however: the discount rate increases as incomes exceed higher multiples of the threshold. In 1994, after appropriate discounting, the incomes of countries range from $370 to $5,371 in real purchasing power (PPP$).

One innovative feature of the HDI is the way its components are combined. Each indicator is measured in different units: life expectancy in years of life, schooling in mean years of schooling, income in purchasing-power-adjusted dollars and adult literacy as a percentage. To combine these indicators, the range of values for each one is put onto a scale of 0 to 1, where 0 is the minimum and 1 is the maximum. So, if the minimum life expectancy is 25 years and the maximum is 85 years, and the actual value for a country is halfway between the two at

55 years, its index value for life expectancy is 0.5.

In previous years, the minimum value of each dimension—longevity, educational attainment and income—was set at the level of the poorest-performing country, and the maximum at that of the best-performing country. The HDI for any country was thus its position between the best and the worst countries, but maximums and minimums changed each year—following the perfor-

BOX 5.1

A primer on the human development index

Why do we need a human development index?
Because national progress tends otherwise to be measured by GNP alone, many people have looked for a better, more comprehensive socio-economic measure. The human development index is a contribution to this search.

What does the HDI include?
The HDI is a composite of three basic components of human development: longevity, knowledge and standard of living. *Longevity* is measured by life expectancy. *Knowledge* is measured by a combination of adult literacy (two-thirds weight) and mean years of schooling (one-third weight). *Standard of living* is measured by purchasing power, based on real GDP per capita adjusted for the local cost of living (purchasing power parity, or PPP).

Why only three components?
The ideal would be to reflect all aspects of human experience. The lack of data imposes some limits on this, and more indicators could perhaps be added as the information becomes available. But more indicators would not necessarily be better. Some might overlap with existing indicators: infant mortality, for example, is already reflected in life expectancy. And adding more variables could confuse the picture and detract from the main trends.

How to combine indicators measured in different units?
The measuring rod for GNP is money. The breakthrough for the HDI, however, was to find a common measuring rod for the socio-economic distance travelled. The HDI sets a minimum and a

maximum for each dimension and then shows where each country stands in relation to these scales—expressed as a value between 0 and 1. So, since the minimum adult literacy rate is 0% and the maximum is 100%, the literacy component of knowledge for a country where the literacy rate is 75% would be 0.75. Similarly, the minimum for life expectancy is 25 years and the maximum 85 years, so the longevity component for a country where life expectancy is 55 years would be 0.5. For income the minimum is $200 (PPP) and the maximum is $40,000 (PPP). Income above the average world income is adjusted using a progressively higher discount rate. The scores for the three dimensions are then averaged in an overall index.

Is it not misleading to talk of a single HDI for a country with great inequality?
National averages can conceal much. The best solution would be to create separate HDIs for the most significant groups: by gender, for example, or by income group, geographical region, race or ethnic group. Separate HDIs would reveal a more detailed profile of human deprivation in each country, and disaggregated HDIs are already being attempted for countries with sufficient data.

How can the HDI be used?
The HDI offers an alternative to GNP for measuring the relative socio-economic progress of nations. It enables people and their governments to evaluate progress over time—and to determine priorities for policy intervention. It also permits instructive comparisons of the experiences in different countries.

mance of the countries at the extreme ends of the scale.

This scaling could produce a frustrating outcome, since a country might improve its performance on life expectancy or educational attainment but see its HDI score fall because the top or bottom countries had done even better—in effect, moving the goal posts. Some efforts were made to change this by using the maximum and minimum for a longer period, say 1960–90, but this did not overcome the original objection.

The main problem with shifting the goal posts annually is that it precludes meaningful comparisons over time: a country's HDI could change from year to year for reasons that have nothing to do with its performance. So, this year, we fix "normative" values for life expectancy, adult literacy, mean years of schooling and income. These minimums and maximums are not the observed values in the best- or worst-performing countries today but the most extreme values observed or expected over a long period (say, 60 years).

The minimums are those observed historically, going back about 30 years. The maximums are the limits of what can be envisioned in the next 30 years. Demographic and medical information suggests that the maximum average life expectancy for the foreseeable future is 85 years. Similarly, recent economic growth rates indicate that the maximum income that the richest countries are likely to achieve by 2020 is $40,000 (in 1990 PPP$).

With the new fixed goal posts (table 5.1), the greatest differences from previous values are in the much lower minimums for life expectancy (25 years rather than 42 years) and for literacy rates (0% rather than 12%) and in the higher maximums for life expectancy (85 years rather than 78.6 years) and mean years of schooling (15 years rather than 12.3 years).

From now on, therefore, the HDI value will permit more meaningful comparisons across countries and over time. Using the new maximums and minimums, and recalculating the HDIs for previous years accordingly, it will be legitimate to suggest, for example, that the Republic of Korea's cur-

rent level of human development is similar to that of the United Kingdom 30 years ago. And it can now be asserted that while there were 16 countries in the high human development category in 1960, among the countries for which it was possible to make a comparison over time, there were 40 in 1992.

In addition to the methodological changes, there has been a major change in one of the sources of data—that for income. The HDI uses the GNP per capita based on purchasing power parity (PPP$) to reflect not just income but also what that income can buy. Housing and food are cheaper in Bangladesh than in Switzerland, so a dollar is worth more in Bangladesh than in Switzerland. Purchasing power parity adjusts for this.

Until this year, the main source of PPP data has been the Penn World Tables. For the 1994 HDI, however, we are replacing these data, where feasible, with estimates from the World Bank. Most of the large increases in estimates are in developing countries, notably in Latin America, and most of the large decreases are in the successor states of the former Soviet Union.

Despite these changes, the underlying principle of the HDI remains the same. It is based on a country's position in relation to a final target—expressed as a value between 0 and 1. Countries with an HDI below 0.5 are considered to have a low level of human development, those between 0.5 and 0.8 a medium level and those above 0.8 a high level.

We have been modifying the HDI in response to constructive reviews and criticisms to make the index a steadily more valuable measure of human progress. Following this year's changes, we do not propose any major modifications to the basic method in the near future—though next

TABLE 5.1
Fixed maximums and minimums for HDI values

	Minimum	Maximum
Life expectancy (years)	25	85
Adult literacy (%)	0	100
Mean years of schooling	0	15
Income (real GDP per capita in PPP$)	200	40,000

year's Report will review the gender-disparity-adjusted HDI in preparation for the Fourth World Conference on Women in Beijing in 1995.

A priority in the years ahead must be to improve human development statistics—at country, regional and international levels. The statistical map of human development still has far too many blanks. Too many indicators are missing. Too much information is outdated. And too many statistics are not collected or analysed separately for different population groups—for men and women, for urban and rural, for rich and poor (particularly the growing populations of urban poor) or for different races or ethnic groups.

To encourage the collection and analysis of comprehensive statistics, governments could undertake to prepare human development country profiles—annually or every other year. They already collect information regularly on trade and finance. Why should they not do so for human development? The Social Summit could perhaps agree that all countries should produce such profiles and use them to formulate policy and to monitor social programmes.

A priority in the years ahead must be to improve human development statistics

What the 1994 HDI reveals

Some of the most significant changes in the HDI estimates arise from the new fixed goal posts (tables 5.2 and 5.3). Since the maximum values have increased, they are now beyond the levels already attained by the industrial countries. This change tends to reduce each country's HDI value: in 1993, the value for the top-ranked country was 0.983, but now it is only 0.932—even the richest countries still have a fair distance to travel. Yet the minimums are also lower, which tends to increase all HDI values, particularly those of countries in the bottom category. In 1993, 62 countries were classified as having low human development, but in 1994 there are only 55.

In 1994, Canada has returned to the top of the human development index (it was also on top in 1992). Switzerland has moved up to second place, from fourth in 1993. And Japan, which occupied the top spot in 1990, 1991 and 1993, is now in third place. Among the developing countries, there is no change either at the top (Barbados) or at the bottom (Guinea).

This year's HDI rankings underline some of the messages from previous years, with the relationship between the HDI and GNP per capita the most significant one. Although there is some correlation between the two (richer countries usually have

TABLE 5.2
HDI ranking for industrial countries

	HDI value	HDI rank	GNP per capita rank	GNP per capita rank minus HDI rank[a]
Canada	0.932	1	11	10
Switzerland	0.931	2	1	−1
Japan	0.929	3	3	0
Sweden	0.928	4	4	0
Norway	0.928	5	5	0
France	0.927	6	13	7
Australia	0.926	7	18	11
USA	0.925	8	9	1
Netherlands	0.923	9	16	7
United Kingdom	0.919	10	19	9
Germany	0.918	11	12	1
Austria	0.917	12	14	2
Belgium	0.916	13	15	2
Iceland	0.914	14	8	−6
Denmark	0.912	15	7	−8
Finland	0.911	16	6	−10
Luxembourg	0.908	17	2	−15
New Zealand	0.907	18	24	6
Israel	0.900	19	25	6
Ireland	0.892	21	27	6
Italy	0.891	22	17	−5
Spain	0.888	23	23	0
Greece	0.874	25	35	10
Czechoslovakia	0.872	27	56	29
Hungary	0.863	31	55	24
Malta	0.843	41	32	−9
Portugal	0.838	42	38	−4
Bulgaria	0.815	48	76	28
Poland	0.815	49	79	30
Romania	0.729	72	89	17
Albania	0.714	76	86	10
Successor states of the former Soviet Union				
Lithuania	0.868	28	63	35
Estonia	0.867	29	43	14
Latvia	0.865	30	47	17
Russian Fed.	0.858	34	48	14
Belarus	0.847	40	49	9
Ukraine	0.823	45	68	23
Armenia	0.801	53	73	20
Kazakhstan	0.774	61	71	10
Georgia	0.747	66	80	14
Azerbaijan	0.730	71	92	21
Moldova, Rep. of	0.714	75	81	6
Turkmenistan	0.697	80	88	8
Kyrgyzstan	0.689	82	95	13
Uzbekistan	0.664	91	104	13
Tajikistan	0.629	97	116	19

a. A positive figure shows that the HDI rank is better than the GNP per capita rank, a negative the opposite.

TABLE 5.3
HDI ranking for developing countries

	HDI value	HDI rank	GNP per capita rank	GNP per capita rank minus HDI rank[a]		HDI value	HDI rank	GNP per capita rank	GNP per capita rank minus HDI rank[a]
Barbados	0.894	20	34	14	Morocco	0.549	111	101	−10
Hong Kong	0.875	24	22	−2	El Salvador	0.543	112	97	−15
Cyprus	0.873	26	30	4	Bolivia	0.530	113	119	6
Korea, Rep. of	0.859	32	36	4	Gabon	0.525	114	42	−72
Uruguay	0.859	33	53	20	Honduras	0.524	115	123	8
Trinidad and Tobago	0.855	35	46	11	Viet Nam	0.514	116	150	34
Bahamas	0.854	36	26	−10	Swaziland	0.513	117	96	−21
Argentina	0.853	37	43	6	Maldives	0.511	118	132	14
Chile	0.848	38	66	28	Vanuatu	0.489	119	93	−26
Costa Rica	0.848	39	75	36	Lesotho	0.476	120	124	4
Singapore	0.836	43	21	−22	Zimbabwe	0.474	121	118	−3
Brunei Darussalam	0.829	44	29	−15	Cape Verde	0.474	122	112	−10
Venezuela	0.820	46	55	9	Congo	0.461	123	100	−23
Panama	0.816	47	70	23	Cameroon	0.447	124	111	−13
Colombia	0.813	50	91	41	Kenya	0.434	125	146	21
Kuwait	0.809	51	28	−23	Solomon Islands	0.434	126	115	−11
Mexico	0.804	52	51	−1	Namibia	0.425	127	84	−43
Thailand	0.798	54	82	28	São Tomé and Principe	0.409	128	138	10
Antigua and Barbuda	0.796	55	40	−15	Papua New Guinea	0.408	129	108	−21
Qatar	0.795	56	20	−36	Myanmar	0.406	130	149	19
Malaysia	0.794	57	61	4	Madagascar	0.396	131	162	31
Bahrain	0.791	58	33	−25	Pakistan	0.393	132	140	8
Fiji	0.787	59	74	15	Lao People's Dem. Rep.	0.385	133	157	24
Mauritius	0.778	60	65	5	Ghana	0.382	134	133	−1
United Arab Emirates	0.771	62	10	−52	India	0.382	135	147	12
Brazil	0.756	63	52	−11	Côte d'Ivoire	0.370	136	117	−19
Dominica	0.749	64	62	−2	Haiti	0.354	137	141	4
Jamaica	0.749	65	87	22	Zambia	0.352	138	134	−4
Saudi Arabia	0.742	67	31	−36	Nigeria	0.348	139	145	6
Turkey	0.739	68	78	10	Zaire	0.341	140	160	20
Saint Vincent	0.732	69	77	8	Comoros	0.331	141	131	−10
Saint Kitts and Nevis	0.730	70	47	−23	Yemen	0.323	142	126	−16
Syrian Arab Rep.	0.727	73	94	21	Senegal	0.322	143	114	−29
Ecuador	0.718	74	102	28	Liberia	0.317	144	130	−14
Saint Lucia	0.709	77	57	−20	Togo	0.311	145	136	−9
Grenada	0.707	78	67	−11	Bangladesh	0.309	146	159	13
Libyan Arab Jamahiriya	0.703	79	41	−38	Cambodia	0.307	147	164	17
Tunisia	0.690	81	85	4	Tanzania, U. Rep. of	0.306	148	170	22
Seychelles	0.685	83	39	−44	Nepal	0.289	149	166	17
Paraguay	0.679	84	90	6	Equatorial Guinea	0.276	150	154	4
Suriname	0.677	85	48	−37	Sudan	0.276	151	137	−14
Iran, Islamic Rep. of	0.672	86	64	−22	Burundi	0.276	152	158	6
Botswana	0.670	87	58	−29	Rwanda	0.274	153	152	−1
Belize	0.666	88	69	−19	Uganda	0.272	154	168	14
Cuba	0.666	89	110	21	Angola	0.271	155	120	−35
Sri Lanka	0.665	90	128	38	Benin	0.261	156	142	−14
Oman	0.654	92	38	−54	Malawi	0.260	157	156	−1
South Africa	0.650	93	60	−33	Mauritania	0.254	158	127	−31
China	0.644	94	143	49	Mozambique	0.252	159	173	14
Peru	0.642	95	98	3	Central African Rep.	0.249	160	135	−25
Dominican Rep.	0.638	96	107	11	Ethiopia	0.249	161	171	10
Jordan	0.628	98	99	1	Bhutan	0.247	162	165	3
Philippines	0.621	99	113	14	Djibouti	0.226	163	125	−38
Iraq	0.614	100	59	−41	Guinea-Bissau	0.224	164	167	3
Korea, Dem. Rep. of	0.609	101	109	8	Somalia	0.217	165	172	7
Mongolia	0.607	102	103	1	Gambia	0.215	166	144	−22
Lebanon	0.600	103	83	−20	Mali	0.214	167	155	−12
Samoa	0.596	104	105	1	Chad	0.212	168	161	−7
Indonesia	0.586	105	121	16	Niger	0.209	169	148	−21
Nicaragua	0.583	106	139	33	Sierra Leone	0.209	170	163	−7
Guyana	0.580	107	151	44	Afghanistan	0.208	171	169	−2
Guatemala	0.564	108	106	−2	Burkina Faso	0.203	172	153	−19
Algeria	0.553	109	72	−37	Guinea	0.191	173	129	−44
Egypt	0.551	110	122	12					

a. A positive figure shows that the HDI rank is better than the GNP per capita rank, a negative the opposite.

higher HDIs), it clearly breaks down in many cases.

For some countries—such as Angola, Gabon, Guinea, Namibia, Saudi Arabia and the United Arab Emirates—the income rank is far ahead of the HDI rank, showing that they still have considerable potential for translating their income into improved well-being for their people.

For other countries—such as China, Colombia, Costa Rica, Cuba, Guyana, Madagascar and Sri Lanka—the HDI rank is far ahead of their income rank, showing that they have made more judicious use of their income to improve the capabilities of their people. The highest positive difference between HDI and GNP ranks is for China (+49 places), and the highest negative difference is for Gabon (–72 places)—a striking demonstration of the differences between two development strategies.

Many countries in Latin America and East Asia and among the Arab States have already moved beyond the basic threshold of human development and are now in the medium or high HDI categories. Most countries in Sub-Saharan Africa and South Asia, by contrast, are still classified as having low human development.

As discussed earlier, the HDI is a composite score of three indicators. So, even countries with a high HDI may have a low score on one indicator, which is offset by a high score on another. Among the industrial countries, for example, Switzerland ranks number 2 on the HDI but only 21 when it comes to tertiary enrolment. Similarly, among the developing countries, the Republic of Korea ranks number 4 on the HDI but only 18 when it comes to life expectancy (annex tables 5.1 and 5.2). Careful analysis of the tables will show where improvements are still necessary and achievable.

Changes in the HDI over time

The main advantage in fixing the goal posts is that it permits comparisons of the HDI over time—though, because of data limitations, this can be done for only 114 countries for 1960–92 (annex table 5.3).

The comparisons reveal interesting trends. All countries have made substantial progress in human development. Between 1960 and 1992, the overall HDI for the developing countries increased from 0.260 to 0.541—more than doubling. Even the least developed countries, and those in Sub-Saharan Africa, made clear progress. True, they started from very low levels, but they managed as a group to increase their HDI values by around 80%.

Many countries have shifted into higher human development categories: 30 countries have moved from low to medium, 20 from medium to high, and four all the way from low to high. The number of countries in the low group has shrunk from 76 to 42, while that in the medium category has increased from 22 to 32 and that in the high category from 16 to 40 (table 5.4 and figures 5.1 and 5.2).

In East Asia, the region with the largest absolute increase in HDI, the HDI value increased two and half times between 1960 and 1992—from 0.255 to 0.653 (table 5.5). This shows that the fast pace of economic

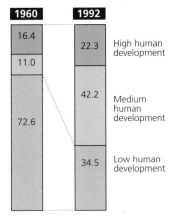

FIGURE 5.1
The majority of the world's people have shifted from low to medium and high human development

Percentage shares of world population

TABLE 5.4
Distribution of countries by human development group, 1960–92

	1960	1970	1980	1992
High human development	16	23	30	40
Medium human development	22	26	28	32
Low human development	76	65	56	42
Total	114	114	114	114

TABLE 5.5
HDI values by region, 1960–92

	1960	1970	1980	1992	Absolute increase in HDI value 1960–92
All developing countries	0.260	0.347	0.428	0.541	0.281
Least developed countries	0.165	0.209	0.251	0.307	0.142
Industrial[a]	0.799	0.859	0.889	0.918	0.119
World	0.392	0.460	0.519	0.605	0.213
Sub-Saharan Africa	0.200	0.255	0.306	0.357	0.156
Middle East and North Africa	0.277	0.363	0.480+	0.631	0.354
South Asia	0.202	0.248	0.290	0.376	0.174
South Asia excl. India	0.188	0.231	0.270	0.358	0.170
East Asia	0.255	0.379	0.484+	0.653	0.397
East Asia excl. China	0.416+	0.547	0.686>	0.861	0.446
South-East Asia and Oceania	0.284	0.373	0.469+	0.613	0.329
Latin America and the Caribbean	0.467+	0.568	0.682	0.757	0.290
excl. Mexico and Brazil	0.504	0.586	0.654	0.735	0.231

+ Region moving from low to medium human development.
> Region moving from medium to high human development.
a. Excluding Eastern Europe and the former Soviet Union.

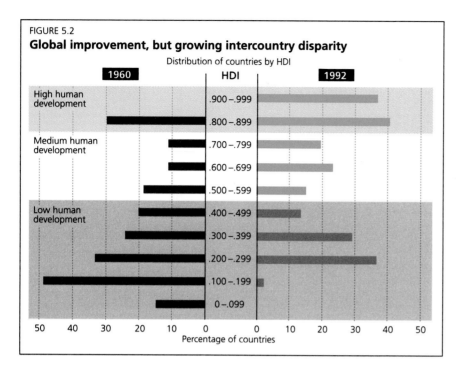

FIGURE 5.2

Global improvement, but growing intercountry disparity

Distribution of countries by HDI

	1960	HDI	1992
High human development		.900–.999	
		.800–.899	
Medium human development		.700–.799	
		.600–.699	
		.500–.599	
Low human development		.400–.499	
		.300–.399	
		.200–.299	
		.100–.199	
		0–.099	

Percentage of countries

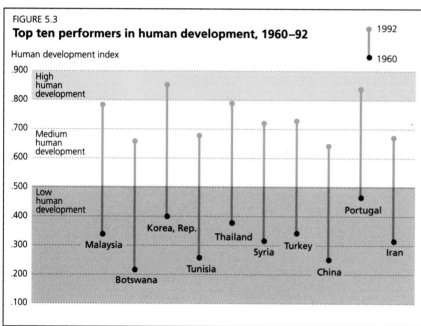

FIGURE 5.3

Top ten performers in human development, 1960–92

Human development index

● 1992
● 1960

Malaysia · Botswana · Korea, Rep. · Tunisia · Thailand · Syria · Turkey · China · Portugal · Iran

---

growth in East Asia was built on a solid foundation of human development.

Some countries have made spectacular leaps. Japan jumped from a rank of 23 in 1960 to 3 in 1992. The four countries that made a double jump from low to high human development ranks were Portugal (among the industrial countries) and Colombia, Panama and the Republic of Korea (in the developing world).

The five countries showing the largest absolute increases in HDI were Malaysia (+0.463), Botswana (+0.463), the Republic of Korea (+0.462), Tunisia (+0.432) and Thailand (+0.424)—see table 5.6 and figure 5.3.

No country saw its HDI value fall over this period, unlike GDP, which has on occasion fallen in several countries. Human capital, once it is built up, is more likely to be sustainable.

A gender-disparity-adjusted HDI

One of the most significant differences within the overall HDI score for any country is between males and females. Men generally fare better than women on almost every socio-economic indicator (except life expectancy since, for biological reasons, women tend to live longer than men).

One way to illustrate this difference is to adjust the HDI ranking for gender disparities, expressing the female value of each component as a percentage of the male value. These percentages can be calculated separately for income, educational attainment and life expectancy—and then averaged to give an overall gender disparity factor. A country's overall HDI can then be

---

TABLE 5.6

Top performers in human development, 1960–92

Top ten performers 1960–70	Absolute increase in HDI value	Top ten performers 1970–80	Absolute increase in HDI value	Top ten performers 1980–92	Absolute increase in HDI value	Top ten performers 1960–92	Absolute increase in HDI value
Japan	0.190	Syrian Arab Rep.	0.239	Botswana	0.256	Malaysia	0.463
Spain	0.184	Malaysia	0.216	Thailand	0.247	Botswana	0.463
Hong Kong	0.176	Malta	0.187	Korea, Rep. of	0.193	Korea, Rep. of	0.462
Singapore	0.163	Brazil	0.166	Tunisia	0.191	Tunisia	0.432
Cyprus	0.154	Tunisia	0.159	Egypt	0.191	Thailand	0.424
Greece	0.150	Algeria	0.153	Turkey	0.190	Syrian Arab Rep.	0.408
Barbados	0.146	Portugal	0.148	Iran, Islamic Rep. of	0.175	Turkey	0.406
Malaysia	0.141	Jordan	0.148	China	0.169	China	0.396
Jamaica	0.132	Korea, Rep. of	0.143	Indonesia	0.168	Portugal	0.378
Portugal	0.128	Hungary	0.133	Morocco	0.166	Iran, Islamic Rep. of	0.366

multiplied by this factor to give a gender-disparity-adjusted HDI figure—if the relevant data are available.

For life expectancy and educational attainment, data are generally collected and analysed by gender. But for income, there is no way to determine how males and females share GDP. The distribution would be affected not just by the different earning capacities of men and women but also by the distribution of resources within households.

The only internationally comparable data on this are the wage rates in the industrial sector and the labour force participation rates outside agriculture. For the 43 countries with data, the female-male wage ratio ranges from a low of 51% (Japan) to a high of 90% (Sweden). Similarly, the female-male ratio in non-agricultural labour force participation rates varies from 22% (Bahrain) to 89% (Finland).

Multiplying these two ratios gives an overall "female-male income ratio" (annex table 5.4). Such ratios can paint only a partial picture, but they still reveal a remarkable pattern of discrimination. The combined ratios range from 21% (Bahrain) to 83% (Sweden). Of the 43 countries, 14 have a ratio below 40%, and only 11 a ratio above 60%. Even these disparities underestimate discrimination since male-female income differences are generally greater in agriculture and services than in manufacturing.

The differences along the other HDI dimensions are also significant. For life expectancy, women in industrial countries (and in most developing countries) live longer than men. In educational achievement, however, women are likely to lose out—not so much in the industrial countries, where there are relatively few differences between men and women, but certainly in the developing countries, where women's literacy levels and years of schooling are much lower than men's.

For the 43 countries (24 industrial and 19 developing) with data, no country improves its HDI value after it is adjusted for gender disparities. All countries treat women worse than men—unconscionable, after so many years of debate on gender equality, so many changes in national legislation and so many years of struggle.

But some countries do less badly than others, so the gender-disparity adjustment makes a considerable difference to rankings. Slipping down the list are Japan, from 3 to 19, Canada from 1 to 9, Switzerland from 2 to 17, and Hong Kong from 22 to 30. Improving their rankings are Sweden from 4 to 1, Denmark from 15 to 4, Finland from 16 to 3 and New Zealand from 18 to 8.

In the industrial countries, gender discrimination shows up in the HDI mainly in employment and wages—with women often getting less than two-thirds of the employment opportunities and about half the earnings of men.

In developing countries, the discrimination is more broadly based. It occurs not only in employment but also in education, nutritional support and health care. Illiteracy is always higher for women—who make up two-thirds of the illiterate population. And neglect of women's health and nutrition is so serious in some countries, particularly in Asia, that it even outweighs women's natural biological tendency to live longer than men. Considering these early deaths, as well as those from the infanticide of girl babies, some studies estimate that up to 100 million women are "missing".

An income-distribution-adjusted HDI

Another way the HDI can usefully be adjusted is for income distribution. The overall HDI reflects national income, but in many countries, particularly in the developing world, the distribution is badly skewed. This makes it important to discount the income component of the HDI to reflect maldistributions of income.

For the income disparity factor, we have divided the share of the income of the bottom 20% of the population by the share of the top 20%. Multiplying this ratio by the country's overall HDI gives the income-distribution-adjusted HDI. This information is available for 55 countries.

No country has a perfect income distribution, so adjusting the HDI for income distribution reduces the score for all. But

Men generally fare better than women on almost every socio-economic indicator

the effect is greater for some countries (annex table 5.5).

Among the industrial countries, Belgium improves its ranking in this group by nine places and Germany by seven. But other countries slip significantly: Canada and Switzerland by seven places, and Australia by eight.

In developing countries, the income disparities can be even greater. In Brazil, the ratio between the income share of the bottom 20% of the population and that of the top 20% is 1 to 32, and in Botswana it is 1 to 47. As the table indicates, this causes their HDI rankings to slip significantly: Brazil by seven places and Botswana by eight places. Countries with more egalitarian income distributions climb several places: China by six, Sri Lanka by seven and Jamaica by eight.

One might also consider disaggregating the other HDI dimensions—educational achievement and longevity. But the range within a country is much greater for income than for the other dimensions: a rich person can earn 1,000 times more than a poor one but cannot live 1,000 times longer. So, having a small number of healthy people in a population in which most people are un-

healthy cannot inflate the average life expectancy figure by much—certainly not to the extent that a small number of fabulously wealthy people can inflate average national income.

Disaggregated HDIs

These adjustments to the overall HDI are particularly useful for international comparisons of disparities among countries. For comparisons within countries, a more useful approach is to calculate separate HDIs for different groups—by region, perhaps, or by gender or race. Previous *Human Development Reports* have included such disaggregations: for the United States, by race and gender, for India and Mexico, by state, for Swaziland, by region, and for Turkey, by region and gender.

Case studies were prepared for this Report, and summaries of nine of them appear here: for South Africa, Brazil, Nigeria, Egypt, China, Malaysia, Canada, Germany and Poland.

• *South Africa*—The very fact of apartheid has made it difficult to obtain reliable data on disparities between blacks and whites. In the mid-1970s, the government stopped publishing data on the nominally independent "homelands" (home to one-quarter of the black population). But even the data available give a striking picture of inequality (figure 5.4). The overall HDI for South Africa is 0.650—but that for whites is 0.878, while for blacks it is 0.462. If white South Africa were a separate country, it would rank 24 in the world (just after Spain). Black South Africa would rank 123 in the world (just above Congo). Not just two different peoples, these are almost two different worlds.

There are also significant gender differences, though these are due almost entirely to disparities within the black community—the HDI for black males is 0.530, while for black females it is 0.426. The poorest group of all is black rural females, whose HDI of 0.356 is only around 40% of that of the white population.

The wide disparities between black and white raise delicate issues. The major challenge for policy-makers will be to promote

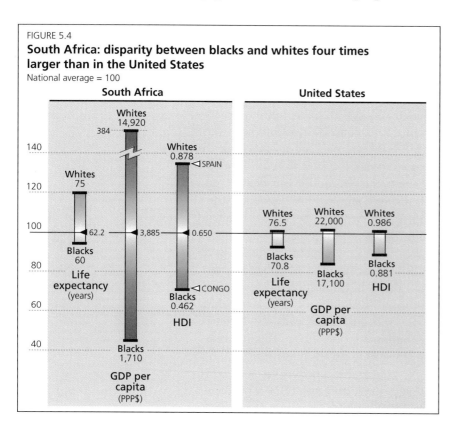

FIGURE 5.4

South Africa: disparity between blacks and whites four times larger than in the United States

National average = 100

HUMAN DEVELOPMENT REPORT 1994

social integration without provoking racial violence. As an indication of the scale of the task, the HDI disparity between blacks and whites in South Africa is four times that between blacks and whites in the United States, where racial violence remains a threat. Zimbabwe's experience may also be relevant for South Africa. Zimbabwe at the time of independence had similar disparities, if on a smaller scale, but it has achieved a considerable degree of social integration without inciting racial trouble.

• *Brazil*—Some of Brazil's greatest inequalities are between different income groups, but there are also striking regional disparities (figure 5.5). Brazil's overall HDI is 0.756, ranked 63 in the world. But if the South of Brazil were a separate country, its HDI of 0.838 would rank it number 42 (equal to Portugal), while the North-East, with an HDI of 0.549, would rank number 111 (on a par with El Salvador and Bolivia)—this, despite the fact that since 1970 the disparity between the two regions has been halved.

The socio-economic indicators in North-East Brazil point to the potential for considerable trouble. The region lags behind the more prosperous South in every respect: the disparity between the two regions is 17 years in life expectancy, 33 percentage points in adult literacy and $2,000 (40%) in

real GDP per capita. These disparities are much greater than those between Mexico's state of Chiapas and the national average, and the recent trouble there should serve as a timely warning for policy-makers elsewhere.

• *Nigeria*—Regional disparities in Nigeria are among the worst in the world. Ranking the 19 states of Nigeria by HDI puts the state of Bendel on top with an HDI of 0.666, ahead of a progressive country like Sri Lanka (figure 5.6). At the bottom is Borno, with an HDI of 0.156, lower than that of any country in the world. Average life expectancy in Borno is only 40 years (18 years less than in Bendel), and adult literacy at 12% is less than one-quarter of the national average. Kaduna is another poor state, with a per capita GDP less than one-fifth of that in Bendel. These disparities contain the potential for major social, economic and political unrest—and deserve the urgent attention of policy-makers.

• *Egypt*—One of the most disturbing contrasts in Egypt is that between rural Upper Egypt and the Cairo Governate (figure 5.7). The Cairo Governate, with its HDI of 0.738, would rank 69 in the world (just behind Turkey). But rural Upper Egypt, with an HDI of 0.444, would rank 125 (behind Cameroon). These contrasts extend to all

Separate HDIs should be calculated for separate groups— by region, by gender or by race

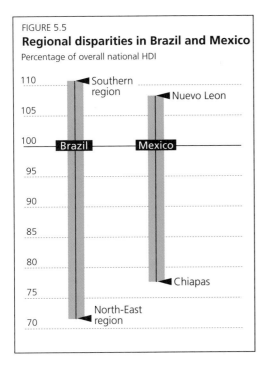

FIGURE 5.5
Regional disparities in Brazil and Mexico
Percentage of overall national HDI

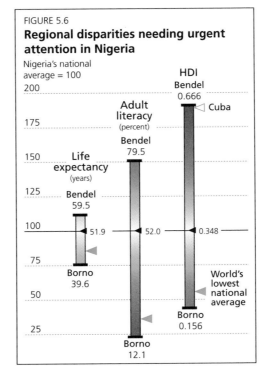

FIGURE 5.6
Regional disparities needing urgent attention in Nigeria

Nigeria's national average = 100

the major indicators of human development. Adult literacy in rural Upper Egypt is less than half that in the Cairo Governate, average life expectancy is six years less and real per capita GDP, at $2,680, is 45% less. Regional disparities in Egypt may not be as extreme as those in Brazil and Nigeria, but they are still large enough to deserve immediate policy attention.

- *China*—Over a long period of time, China has invested liberally in human development. So, despite its low per capita income, it falls in the medium HDI category. China also has the largest positive gap (+49) between its HDI rank and its GNP per capita rank—showing that it has made judicious use of its national income. But there are large regional disparities (figure 5.8). At the top of the regional HDI ranking are Shanghai (0.865) and Beijing (0.861), whose HDI would give them a rank of 31. At the bottom are Qinghai (0.550) and Tibet (0.404), which would rank 110 and 131 respectively. Now that China has embarked on rapid, market-led economic growth, it will need to take care that existing regional disparities do not widen further. Thoughtful state intervention will be required to ensure a more equitable distribution of social services.

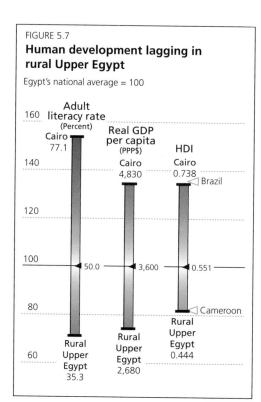

FIGURE 5.7

Human development lagging in rural Upper Egypt

Egypt's national average = 100

- *Malaysia*—There are major disparities between the Malay and Chinese communities (figure 5.9). Malaysia's overall HDI is 0.794, and it ranks number 57 in the world. But the Chinese community has an HDI of 0.896—which, taken alone, would rank it number 20 in the world (five places above Hong Kong). The Malays have an HDI of 0.730, which would rank them 70. The ethnic gaps have nevertheless been narrowing: in 1970, the Malay HDI was only 70% of that of the Chinese, but by 1991, it had reached 81%.

After racial riots in 1969, Malaysia embarked on a remarkably successful strategy for social integration, as discussed in chapter 2. The government made large investments in education, health and other services for all classes of society—but with a focus on the Malays as the more disadvantaged group (between 1970 and 1991, the HDI of the Malays increased nearly one and a half times as fast as that of the Chinese).

- *Canada*—The available data do not allow the construction of a separate HDI for different social groups in Canada. But they do show that the "aboriginals"(the Indians, the Inuit and the Metis, constituting 2.3% of the population) have a life expectancy 5.6 years lower than that of the rest of the population, and their real income is one-third less.

- *Germany*—Now that Germany has been reunified after 47 years, formerly international disparities have become regional ones. For life expectancy and education, these are not very great, since the former East Germany had invested significantly in human development. There is, however, a striking difference in income, which is three and a half times greater in the west than in the east. This gap is likely to be eroded fairly rapidly following the opening of market opportunities, since there do not seem to be significant differences in human capabilities.

- *Poland*—Poland offers a refreshing contrast to most other countries in regional distribution. The country has 49 regions but the HDI of Ostrolec, the least advanced region, is about 80% of that of Warsaw, the most advanced—a clear benefit of the egalitarian model of development that Poland followed in the past.

Using the HDI

The HDI, though only five years old, has already had a major impact on policy-making on human development. It seems the world was ready for a measure of development that went beyond per capita GNP. So far, the HDI has been used in five main ways:

• *To stimulate national political debate*— The reaction of most countries when the index is published is to see how well they are doing this year in comparison with everyone else. People have used the HDI for advocacy and to hold their representatives accountable—fuelling a national debate involving political parties and the press as well as NGOs.

• *To give priority to human development*— The HDI has emphasized that even the poorest countries can afford improvements in human development. An analysis of the three components of the HDI can identify areas requiring policy attention. Specific human development strategies have been formulated by Bangladesh, Botswana, Colombia, Egypt, Ghana, Mexico, Pakistan, Tunisia, the Pacific Islands and several Central American countries.

• *To highlight disparities within countries*— These disparities may already be well known, but the HDI can reveal them even more starkly. The disaggregation prepared for the 1993 Report on the differences in living conditions in the United States among blacks, hispanics and whites spurred a great deal of policy debate. Disaggregation by social group or region can also enable local community groups to press for more resources, making the HDI a tool for participatory development.

• *To open new avenues for analysis*— Widely used for academic analysis and for country reports and statistics, the HDI allows new types of international comparison—for example, between countries that have effectively translated economic growth into human development and those less successful: between Japan and the United States, perhaps, or between the Republic of Korea and Pakistan. And development theories that previously relied on GNP growth as an indicator of success or failure can instead consider changes in the HDI.

• *To stimulate dialogue on aid policy*— Some donor countries have contemplated using the HDI as the basis for aid allocations. But it is not obvious how this should be done. Should aid go to countries with low HDIs—to the needy? Or should it go to countries showing the fastest rate of improvement in HDI over time—to the speedy? Or should it go as a reward to countries that already have high HDIs? A case is sometimes made for each option. The best use for the HDI, however, is to stimulate a constructive aid policy dialogue rather than to serve as a basis for aid allocations.

This Report has focused on the emerging concept of human security and a specific action agenda for the forthcoming World Summit for Social Development in Copenhagen in March 1995. One of the key issues in this analysis is the dark shadow of insecurity cast on the majority of the world's population: women. Although an attempt has been made to point out women's concerns in this Report, gender issues deserve a much more detailed analysis. In fact, a major effort is needed to analyse both the policies and the politics necessary for gender equality. This will be the principal focus of *Human Development Report 1995.* It is hoped that the next Report, to be released in May 1995, will make a useful contribution to the deliberations of the Fourth World Conference on Women in Beijing in September 1995.

FIGURE 5.8
China: good overall performance, extreme regional differences

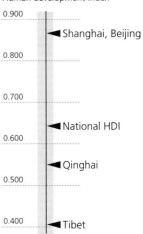

FIGURE 5.9
Malaysia: all improve, but some faster

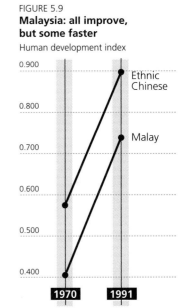

How developing countries rank on human development indicators

		HDI 1992	Life expectancy 1992	Access to safe water 1988-91	Infant mortality 1992	Daily calorie supply 1988-90	Child malnutrition 1990	Adult literacy 1992	Mean years of schooling 1992	Radios 1990	Real GDP per capita (PPP$) 1991	GNP per capita (US$) 1991
20	Barbados	1	5	1	4	16	6	1	1	2	7	7
24	Hong Kong	2	1	8	1	15	10	15	10	5	1	3
26	Cyprus	3	2	1	3	20	15	8	12	25	6	5
32	Korea, Rep. of	4	18	18	13	21	3	3	2	1	10	8
33	Uruguay	5	10	26	12	66	11	4	5	9	17	15
35	Trinidad and Tobago	6	14	13	11	26	20	5	4	10	9	12
37	Argentina	7	13	21	20	12	1	6	3	4	22	16
38	Chile	8	11	24	10	45	2	9	7	19	15	23
39	Costa Rica	9	3	17	5	25	16	11	16	27	23	26
43	Singapore	10	7	1	2	2	9	12	39	6	3	2
46	Venezuela	11	19	21	24	53	8	18	15	11	11	17
47	Panama	12	9	27	13	54	24	16	13	38	24	24
50	Colombia	13	23	16	21	44	22	21	9	51	18	33
51	Kuwait	14	6	1	9	11	6	43	20	20	4	4
52	Mexico	15	20	32	26	9	37	20	27	30	14	13
54	Thailand	16	25	33	18	56	34	10	42	48	19	29
57	Malaysia	17	17	36	5	18	45	33	18	12	12	20
60	Mauritius	18	21	1	13	13	42	34	33	17	13	21
62	United Arab Emirates	19	15	1	16	1	12	50	19	21	2	1
63	Brazil	20	35	25	38	32	13	27	37	16	20	14
65	Jamaica	21	8	1	5	30	14	2	21	13	30	31
67	Saudi Arabia	22	24	15	23	24	32	51	40	24	5	6
68	Turkey	23	31	19	38	19	23	28	43	55	25	27
73	Syrian Arab Rep.	24	33	35	29	17	31	47	32	27	21	34
74	Ecuador	25	34	56	41	42	34	22	17	21	29	40
79	Libyan Arab Jamahiriya	26	46	14	51	3	4	48	45	38	16	10
81	Tunisia	27	29	9	32	4	18	46	59	45	27	30
84	Paraguay	28	28	83	34	31	5	13	25	51	34	32
86	Iran, Islamic Rep. of	29	32	47	31	6	87	59	40	35	28	22
87	Botswana	30	50	48	45	52	66	38	55	63	26	19
89	Cuba	31	4	12	5	5	17	7	6	18	52	43
90	Sri Lanka	32	12	37	17	60	92	17	11	45	44	57
92	Oman	33	22	30	21	36	54	85	81	7	8	9
94	China	34	16	28	19	33	52	32	22	50	39	68
95	Peru	35	43	54	53	81	36	23	14	30	37	39
96	Dominican Rep.	36	30	44	38	59	27	25	30	51	38	41
98	Jordan	37	27	10	27	35	33	26	22	30	40	37
99	Philippines	38	41	29	29	38	76	14	8	57	47	46
100	Iraq	39	36	20	43	8	26	54	24	38	32	18
103	Lebanon	40	26	11	25	14	18	31	29	3	46	28
105	Indonesia	41	47	65	49	23	83	24	34	56	43	51
106	Nicaragua	42	38	60	36	57	47	36	28	27	45	60
108	Guatemala	43	42	50	35	50	61	58	35	78	36	42
109	Algeria	44	37	39	47	27	29	55	51	35	41	25
110	Egypt	45	48	23	41	7	21	70	49	21	31	51
111	Morocco	46	45	34	51	10	27	64	48	43	35	38
112	El Salvador	47	40	72	33	48	48	41	31	14	51	36
113	Bolivia	48	49	63	60	89	25	35	37	8	49	49
114	Gabon	49	64	43	67	41	39	53	53	57	33	11
115	Honduras	50	39	31	45	78	50	39	36	15	54	53
116	Viet Nam	51	44	90	27	47	91	19	26	65	64	73
120	Lesotho	52	51	71	54	75	44	36	46	78	60	53
121	Zimbabwe	53	56	82	43	72	38	45	47	74	50	49
123	Congo	54	69	92	57	40	69	56	60	65	42	35
124	Cameroon	55	60	57	48	73	41	57	71	57	48	44
125	Kenya	56	53	69	50	85	43	44	57	62	63	70
129	Papua New Guinea	57	59	86	37	29	81	49	80	78	57	45
130	Myanmar	58	55	88	57	28	74	29	54	74	87	73
131	Madagascar	59	61	94	79	74	85	30	58	45	83	83
132	Pakistan	60	54	53	70	49	90	83	67	72	53	63

How developing countries rank on human development indicators (continued)

	HDI 1992	Life expectancy 1992	Access to safe water 1988-91	Infant mortality 1992	Daily calorie supply 1988-90	Child malnutrition 1990	Adult literacy 1992	Mean years of schooling 1992	Radios 1990	Real GDP per capita (PPP$) 1991	GNP per capita (US$) 1991
133 Lao People's Dem. Rep.	61	75	81	69	34	78	61	50	63	55	80
134 Ghana	62	58	61	56	79	65	52	44	26	75	63
135 India	63	52	67	64	43	96	71	56	74	68	72
136 Côte d'Ivoire	64	70	40	65	22	29	60	66	57	58	48
137 Haiti	65	57	78	62	70	60	61	69	86	76	68
138 Zambia	66	90	70	59	82	64	40	52	74	72	59
139 Nigeria	67	67	66	68	77	80	66	75	51	62	70
140 Zaire	68	71	85	66	64	75	42	72	71	95	80
142 Yemen	69	68	40	77	76	67	76	82	93	61	55
143 Senegal	70	76	73	55	69	49	79	82	65	56	47
144 Liberia	71	62	59	89	63	51	75	61	35	78	57
145 Togo	72	63	51	60	61	46	72	73	43	82	62
146 Bangladesh	73	66	77	78	71	97	82	64	88	67	80
147 Cambodia	74	74	80	81	67	82	81	65	65	64	87
148 Tanzania, U. Rep. of	75	73	64	73	80	59	61	63	93	91	95
149 Nepal	76	65	75	71	46	95	92	62	93	69	88
151 Sudan	77	72	74	71	88	77	91	87	30	66	63
152 Burundi	78	77	52	76	86	70	66	89	82	89	83
153 Rwanda	79	83	45	79	91	72	65	79	82	85	78
154 Uganda	80	96	95	74	87	62	68	76	65	70	91
155 Angola	81	89	84	88	92	79	74	74	82	73	91
156 Benin	82	87	58	63	51	56	95	88	72	59	67
157 Malawi	83	92	62	93	83	56	73	68	38	79	79
158 Mauritania	84	80	40	82	37	40	85	89	57	74	56
159 Mozambique	85	83	91	95	94	94	87	70	86	77	97
160 Central African Rep.	86	81	96	75	93	73	78	78	78	88	66
161 Ethiopia	87	85	89	84	96	88	69	77	48	97	93
162 Bhutan	88	79	87	90	55	83	77	93	97	90	88
164 Guinea-Bissau	89	94	79	92	65	54	80	89	88	81	88
165 Somalia	90	85	49	84	90	86	93	93	88	80	95
167 Mali	91	91	76	96	39	53	84	89	88	94	77
168 Chad	92	82	97	84	97	71	88	93	34	96	83
169 Niger	93	88	55	87	62	93	90	96	82	92	73
170 Sierra Leone	94	97	67	94	84	63	96	82	38	71	83
171 Afghanistan	95	94	93	97	95	89	89	82	65	84	93
172 Burkina Faso	96	78	38	82	68	68	97	96	93	86	76
173 Guinea	97	93	46	91	58	58	94	82	88	93	60

Note: Ninety-seven developing countries have been given ranks that reflect their comparative performance in the selected aspects of human development illustrated in this table. To make the ranks comparable across indicators, countries have been ranked only if they have estimates for all the indicators. Countries with equal performance in an indicator are given the same rank.

How industrial countries rank on human development indicators

		HDI 1992	Life expectancy 1992	Population per doctor 1990	Maternal mortality 1988	Mean years of schooling 1992	Overall enrolment 1991	Tertiary enrolment 1990	News-paper circulation 1990	Televi-sions 1990	Real GDP per capita (PPP$) 1991	GNP per capita (US$) 1991
1	Canada	1	6	17	9	2	1	2	19	2	5	8
2	Switzerland	2	2	25	6	7	10	21	6	19	2	1
3	Japan	3	1	24	23	15	11	20	2	3	4	2
4	Sweden	4	3	10	9	9	20	15	4	10	10	3
5	Norway	5	9	20	2	3	7	5	1	14	11	4
6	France	6	11	8	16	4	5	6	20	18	6	10
7	Australia	7	10	16	5	5	17	11	16	8	14	15
8	USA	8	17	15	16	1	2	1	16	1	1	7
9	Netherlands	9	6	13	18	12	17	10	13	7	13	13
10	United Kingdom	10	13	27	14	6	15	19	8	13	15	16
11	Germany	11	16	10	13	8	11	8	9	4	3	8
12	Austria	12	15	2	14	10	25	12	11	9	8	11
13	Belgium	13	14	4	2	11	9	7	14	11	9	12
15	Denmark	14	20	12	2	13	7	13	10	5	7	6
16	Finland	15	18	13	21	14	3	3	3	6	16	5
18	New Zealand	16	19	22	24	16	5	4	12	12	17	18
19	Israel	17	12	8	6	17	11	14	15	23	18	19
21	Ireland	18	21	25	1	20	11	18	22	22	20	20
22	Italy	19	8	1	6	22	15	17	25	15	12	14
23	Spain	20	4	3	9	26	4	9	26	20	19	17
25	Greece	21	5	22	9	25	15	22	23	25	22	21
27	Czechoslovakia	22	24	4	18	19	21	25	5	16	23	24
31	Hungary	23	27	7	25	18	25	26	18	17	24	23
42	Portugal	24	22	18	18	27	23	23	28	27	21	22
48	Bulgaria	25	25	6	26	24	21	16	7	24	25	25
49	Poland	26	26	18	21	21	17	24	24	21	26	26
72	Romania	27	28	21	28	23	28	27	21	25	27	28
76	Albania	28	23	28	27	28	23	28	27	28	27	27

Note: Twenty-eight industrial countries have been given ranks that reflect their comparative performance in the selected aspects of human development illustrated in this table. To make the ranks comparable across indicators, countries have been ranked only if they have estimates for all the indicators. Countries with equal performance in an indicator are given the same rank.

HDI values, 1960–92

	1960	1970	1980	1992		1960	1970	1980	1992
Canada	0.865	0.887	0.911	0.932	Peru	0.420+	0.528	0.590	0.642
Switzerland	0.853	0.872	0.897	0.931	Dominican Rep.	0.385	0.455+	0.541	0.638
Japan	0.686>	0.875	0.906	0.929	Jordan	0.296	0.405+	0.553	0.628
Sweden	0.867	0.881	0.899	0.928	Philippines	0.419	0.489+	0.557	0.621
Norway	0.865	0.878	0.901	0.928	Iraq	0.348	0.452+	0.581	0.614
France	0.853	0.871	0.895	0.927	Indonesia	0.223	0.306	0.418+	0.586
Australia	0.850	0.862	0.890	0.926	Nicaragua	0.344	0.462+	0.534	0.583
USA	0.865	0.881	0.905	0.925	Guatemala	0.311	0.392	0.477+	0.564
Netherlands	0.855	0.867	0.888	0.923	Algeria	0.264	0.323	0.476+	0.553
United Kingdom	0.857	0.873	0.892	0.919	Egypt	0.210	0.269	0.360+	0.551
Germany	0.841	0.856	0.881	0.918	Morocco	0.198	0.282	0.383+	0.549
Austria	0.797>	0.857	0.880	0.917	El Salvador	0.339	0.422	0.454+	0.543
Belgium	0.826	0.851	0.873	0.916	Bolivia	0.308	0.369	0.442+	0.530
Iceland	0.853	0.863	0.890	0.914	Gabon	0.259	0.378	0.468+	0.525
Denmark	0.857	0.879	0.888	0.912	Honduras	0.280	0.350	0.435+	0.524
Finland	0.811	0.855	0.880	0.911	Lesotho	0.245	0.307	0.404	0.476
Luxembourg	0.826	0.843	0.869	0.908	Zimbabwe	0.284	0.326	0.386	0.474
New Zealand	0.852	0.861	0.877	0.907	Congo	0.241	0.307	0.368	0.461
Israel	0.719>	0.827	0.862	0.900	Cameroon	0.191	0.253	0.332	0.447
Barbados	0.678>	0.824	0.856	0.894	Kenya	0.192	0.254	0.340	0.434
Ireland	0.710>	0.829	0.862	0.892	Papua New Guinea	0.208	0.325	0.348	0.408
Italy	0.755>	0.831	0.857	0.891	Myanmar	0.243	0.318	0.356	0.406
Spain	0.636>	0.820	0.851	0.888	Madagascar	0.237	0.291	0.344	0.396
Hong Kong	0.561	0.737>	0.830	0.875	Pakistan	0.183	0.244	0.287	0.393
Greece	0.573	0.723>	0.839	0.874	Ghana	0.233	0.283	0.323	0.382
Cyprus	0.579	0.733>	0.844	0.873	India	0.206	0.254	0.296	0.382
Hungary	0.625	0.705>	0.838	0.863	Côte d'Ivoire	0.168	0.243	0.330	0.370
Korea, Rep. of	0.398+	0.523	0.666>	0.859	Haiti	0.174	0.218	0.295	0.354
Uruguay	0.737	0.762>	0.830	0.859	Zambia	0.258	0.315	0.342	0.352
Trinidad and Tobago	0.737	0.789>	0.816	0.855	Nigeria	0.184	0.230	0.297	0.348
Argentina	0.667	0.748	0.790>	0.853	Zaire	0.179	0.235	0.286	0.341
Chile	0.584	0.682	0.753>	0.848	Yemen	0.092	0.138	0.253	0.323
Costa Rica	0.550	0.647	0.746>	0.848	Senegal	0.146	0.176	0.233	0.322
Malta	0.517	0.615>	0.802	0.843	Liberia	0.166	0.229	0.277	0.317
Portugal	0.460+	0.588	0.736>	0.838	Togo	0.123	0.183	0.255	0.311
Singapore	0.519	0.682	0.780>	0.836	Bangladesh	0.166	0.199	0.234	0.309
Venezuela	0.600	0.728	0.784>	0.820	Tanzania, U. Rep. of	0.162	0.211	0.282	0.306
Panama	0.485+	0.592	0.687>	0.816	Nepal	0.128	0.162	0.209	0.289
Colombia	0.469+	0.554	0.656>	0.813	Sudan	0.160	0.188	0.229	0.276
Mexico	0.517	0.642	0.758>	0.804	Burundi	0.131	0.157	0.219	0.276
Thailand	0.373	0.465+	0.551	0.798	Rwanda	0.185	0.215	0.244	0.274
Malaysia	0.330	0.471+	0.687	0.794	Uganda	0.185	0.213	0.215	0.272
Mauritius	0.486+	0.524	0.626	0.778	Angola	0.139	0.195	0.212	0.271
United Arab Emirates	0.515	0.601	0.719	0.771	Benin	0.130	0.162	0.197	0.261
Brazil	0.394+	0.507	0.673	0.756	Malawi	0.144	0.176	0.216	0.260
Jamaica	0.529	0.662	0.654	0.749	Mozambique	0.169	0.248	0.247	0.252
Saudi Arabia	0.448+	0.511	0.629	0.742	Central African Rep.	0.160	0.196	0.226	0.249
Turkey	0.333	0.441+	0.549	0.739	Guinea-Bissau	0.091	0.125	0.148	0.224
Syrian Arab Rep.	0.318	0.419+	0.658	0.727	Somalia	0.111	0.124	0.162	0.217
Ecuador	0.422	0.485+	0.613	0.718	Gambia	0.068	0.107	0.148	0.215
Tunisia	0.258	0.340	0.499+	0.690	Mali	0.083	0.102	0.146	0.214
Paraguay	0.474+	0.511	0.602	0.679	Chad	0.112	0.135	0.151	0.212
Iran, Islamic Rep. of	0.306	0.406	0.497+	0.672	Niger	0.090	0.134	0.163	0.209
Botswana	0.207	0.284	0.414+	0.670	Sierra Leone	0.095	0.155	0.177	0.209
Sri Lanka	0.475+	0.506	0.552	0.665	Afghanistan	0.101	0.131	0.165	0.208
South Africa	0.464+	0.591	0.629	0.650	Burkina Faso	0.086	0.116	0.151	0.203
China	0.248	0.372	0.475+	0.644	Guinea	0.083	0.111	0.148	0.191

> Country moving from medium to high human development.
+ Country moving from low to medium human development.

Gender-disparity-adjusted HDI

	HDI value	Females as % of males			Average female-male ratio for the three HDI components (%)	Gender-disparity-adjusted HDI	Percentage difference between HDI and gender-disparity-adjusted HDI	Difference between HDI and gender-disparity-adjusted HDI ranks[b]
		Life expectancy[a]	Educational attainment	Adjusted real income				
Sweden	0.928	101.0	100.0	83.4	94.8	0.880	−4.8	3
Norway	0.927	102.2	99.2	71.1	90.8	0.843	−8.5	3
Finland	0.911	104.1	99.4	69.4	91.0	0.829	−8.2	13
Denmark	0.912	101.2	99.4	71.0	90.5	0.826	−8.6	11
France	0.927	104.0	100.6	61.0	88.5	0.820	−10.7	1
Iceland	0.914	100.0	100.7	68.3	89.7	0.820	−9.4	8
Australia	0.926	101.7	99.4	63.8	88.3	0.818	−10.8	0
New Zealand	0.907	101.5	101.3	61.0	87.9	0.797	−11.0	10
Canada	0.932	102.1	98.9	51.5	84.2	0.785	−14.7	−8
Netherlands	0.923	101.7	101.5	51.6	84.9	0.784	−13.9	−1
United Kingdom	0.919	100.3	100.6	53.0	84.6	0.778	−14.1	−1
USA	0.925	102.4	100.5	48.3	83.7	0.775	−15.0	−4
Germany	0.918	101.9	97.0	54.0	84.3	0.774	−14.4	−2
Austria	0.917	102.1	96.7	54.2	84.3	0.773	−14.4	−2
Czechoslovakia	0.872	103.4	95.9	62.6	87.3	0.761	−11.1	10
Belgium	0.916	102.0	100.0	46.6	82.9	0.759	−15.7	−3
Switzerland	0.931	102.1	97.8	41.7	80.5	0.750	−18.1	−15
Italy	0.891	101.8	98.6	47.0	82.5	0.735	−15.6	2
Japan	0.929	100.9	99.4	35.3	78.5	0.730	−19.9	−16
Luxembourg	0.908	103.2	98.5	30.9	77.5	0.704	−20.4	−3
Spain	0.888	101.3	97.7	37.6	78.8	0.700	−18.8	0
Ireland	0.892	100.8	100.8	33.3	78.3	0.698	−19.4	−3
Portugal	0.838	102.7	86.8	59.7	83.1	0.696	−14.2	5
Greece	0.874	100.4	90.6	38.8	76.6	0.669	−20.5	−1
Thailand	0.798	100.1	89.6	60.5	83.4	0.666	−13.2	5
Costa Rica	0.848	99.5	98.9	33.2	77.2	0.654	−19.4	1
Cyprus	0.873	99.2	85.5	37.7	74.1	0.647	−22.6	−3
Korea, Rep. of	0.859	101.4	83.7	37.3	74.1	0.637	−22.2	−2
Singapore	0.836	100.8	66.2	47.6	71.5	0.598	−23.8	0
Hong Kong	0.875	100.4	62.8	39.9	67.7	0.592	−28.3	−8
Mauritius	0.778	102.5	80.9	35.2	72.9	0.567	−21.1	1
Paraguay	0.679	99.1	93.3	48.5	80.3	0.545	−13.4	2
Bahrain	0.791	99.4	79.4	20.9	66.6	0.527	−26.4	−2
Turkey	0.739	100.3	69.1	40.6	70.0	0.517	−22.2	−1
Sri Lanka	0.665	99.0	86.5	43.7	76.4	0.508	−15.7	0
Philippines	0.621	98.2	96.7	35.2	76.7	0.476	−14.5	1
China	0.644	97.6	69.4	52.4	73.1	0.471	−17.3	−1
El Salvador	0.543	101.5	88.6	69.5	86.5	0.470	−8.7	1
Bolivia	0.530	99.3	75.8	63.8	79.6	0.422	−10.8	1
Swaziland	0.513	97.6	81.8	32.3	70.6	0.362	−15.1	1
Egypt	0.551	95.8	48.8	32.5	59.0	0.325	−22.6	−3
Kenya	0.434	98.0	63.7	58.5	73.4	0.318	−11.6	0
Myanmar	0.406	97.1	76.7	56.8	76.8	0.312	−9.4	0

a. Adjusted for natural biological life expectancy advantage for females.
b. A positive figure shows that the gender-disparity-adjusted HDI rank is better than the unadjusted HDI rank, a negative the opposite.

Income-distribution-adjusted HDI

	HDI value 1992	Income-distribution-adjusted HDI value 1992	Difference between HDI and income-distribution-adjusted ranks[a]
Japan	0.929	0.875	2
Sweden	0.928	0.829	2
Belgium	0.916	0.817	9
Germany	0.918	0.797	7
Netherlands	0.923	0.773	4
Norway	0.928	0.772	−1
France	0.926	0.765	−1
Canada	0.932	0.763	−7
Switzerland	0.931	0.749	−7
Finland	0.911	0.740	4
USA	0.925	0.740	−3
United Kingdom	0.919	0.731	−2
Denmark	0.912	0.730	0
Italy	0.891	0.730	3
Australia	0.926	0.695	−8
Israel	0.900	0.689	0
Spain	0.884	0.683	1
Hong Kong	0.875	0.668	1
New Zealand	0.907	0.668	−4
Hungary	0.863	0.655	0
Poland	0.815	0.598	5
Singapore	0.836	0.593	1
Costa Rica	0.848	0.546	−1
Jamaica	0.749	0.542	8
Chile	0.848	0.540	−4
Venezuela	0.820	0.534	−2
Panama	0.816	0.511	−2
Sri Lanka	0.665	0.510	7
Colombia	0.813	0.508	−2
Thailand	0.798	0.508	−1
Mexico	0.804	0.503	−3
Malaysia	0.794	0.499	−2
Philippines	0.621	0.485	5
China	0.644	0.484	6
Peru	0.642	0.461	1
Dominican Rep.	0.638	0.455	1
Indonesia	0.586	0.447	2
Brazil	0.756	0.436	−7
Tunisia	0.690	0.427	−6
Honduras	0.524	0.412	3
Lesotho	0.476	0.386	3
Botswana	0.670	0.374	−8
Guatemala	0.564	0.366	−2
Morocco	0.549	0.365	−2
Kenya	0.434	0.351	0
Ghana	0.382	0.332	1
India	0.382	0.324	1
Pakistan	0.393	0.294	−2
Côte d'Ivoire	0.370	0.290	0
Tanzania, U. Rep. of	0.306	0.271	1
Bangladesh	0.309	0.253	−1
Rwanda	0.274	0.241	1
Nepal	0.289	0.233	−1
Ethiopia	0.249	0.230	0
Uganda	0.272	0.219	0

a. A positive figure indicates that the income-distribution-adjusted rank is better than the HDI rank, a negative the opposite.

Technical notes

1. Computing the human development index

The HDI for 1994 is calculated on a different basis from that in previous years. Maximum and minimum values have been fixed for the four basic variables—life expectancy (85.0 and 25.0 years), adult literacy (100% and 0%), mean years of schooling (15 and 0 years) and income (PPP$40,000 and $200). For income, the threshold value is taken to be the global average real GDP per capita of PPP$5,120. Multiples of income beyond the threshold are discounted using a progressively higher rate.

To illustrate, take a pair of countries, one industrial, one developing—Greece and Gabon. Their basic variables are as follows:

Country	Life expectancy (years)	Adult literacy (%)	Mean years of schooling	Income (PPP$)
Greece	77.3	93.8	7.0	7,680
Gabon	52.9	62.5	2.6	3,498

Life expectancy

$$\text{Greece} \quad \frac{77.3 - 25.0}{85.0 - 25.0} = \frac{52.3}{60.0} = 0.872$$

$$\text{Gabon} \quad \frac{52.9 - 25.0}{85.0 - 25.0} = \frac{27.9}{60.0} = 0.465$$

Adult literacy

$$\text{Greece} \quad \frac{93.8 - 0.0}{100.0 - 0.0} = \frac{93.8}{100.0} = 0.938$$

$$\text{Gabon} \quad \frac{62.5 - 0.0}{100.0 - 0.0} = \frac{62.5}{100.0} = 0.625$$

Mean years of schooling

$$\text{Greece} \quad \frac{7.0 - 0.0}{15.0 - 0.0} = \frac{7.0}{15.0} = 0.467$$

$$\text{Gabon} \quad \frac{2.6 - 0.0}{15.0 - 0.0} = \frac{2.6}{15.0} = 0.173$$

Educational attainment

Greece $= 2\,(0.938) + 0.467 = 2.343 \div 3 = 0.781$
Gabon $= 2\,(0.625) + 0.173 = 1.423 \div 3 = 0.473$

Adjusted income

Greece's income is above the threshold, but less than twice the threshold. Thus,

$$\begin{aligned}
\text{Greece} &= 5,120 + 2\,(7,680 - 5,120)^{\frac{1}{2}} \\
&= 5,120 + 101 \\
&= 5,221
\end{aligned}$$

Gabon's income is below the threshold, so it needs adjusting. To calculate the distance for income, use the maximum adjusted income (5,385) and the minimum (200).

$$\text{Greece} \quad \frac{5,221 - 200}{5,385 - 200} = \frac{5,021}{5,185} = 0.968$$

$$\text{Gabon} \quad \frac{3,498 - 200}{5,385 - 200} = \frac{3,298}{5,185} = 0.636$$

Country	Indexed life expectancy	Indexed educational attainment	Indexed adjusted income	Σ	HDI
Greece	0.872	0.781	0.968 =	2.621	0.874
Gabon	0.465	0.473	0.636 =	1.574	0.525

2. A new aid reporting system

While aid concerns have been changing in recent years, the ways in which statistics are recorded have remained largely unchanged. This makes analysing and accounting for aid extremely difficult.

Whether one uses the aid statistics produced in the reports of the Development Assistance Committee (DAC) of the OECD, or the Development Cooperation Reports produced by UNDP, the picture is more or less the same. Aid flows are recorded primarily according to country (donor and recipient) and by sector (such as agriculture, industry, transport, health or education).

If, on the other hand, one wants to know what proportion of available resources are going towards priority concerns such as poverty reduction, the integration of women in development, democratization or environmental protection and regeneration, it is usually possible to make only rough estimates. More accurate information requires special research.

Another shortcoming of aid reporting is that the statistics are presented in isolation from other resource flows, such as trade, foreign investment, debt payments or remittances from workers abroad.

Clearly, there is an urgent need for a new aid reporting system. This system should provide information on at least three sets of issues.

• *Human development priorities*—showing the allocations to such concerns as primary health care (including family planning), basic education, nutrition support, and low-cost rural and peri-urban water and sanitation.

• *Distribution by target groups*—showing how much aid reaches the poorest, and how much is spent at the local level.

• *Military spending*—allowing examination of the link between aid flows and reduction in military spending.

Aid should also be shown in the context of overall resource flows to each country—in effect, presenting a total financial resource flow balance sheet.

DAC is probably the organization best able to take the lead. It has already made a start on revising the existing system. And preliminary work shows that it is possible and useful to report on aid according to its objectives.

We suggest that the Annual Report of the Chairman of DAC should include tables along the lines of those below.

TABLE 1
Human development aid profile of donor countries

	Official development assistance (ODA) given						Aid social allocation ratio (%)	Aid social priority ratio (%)	Aid human expenditure ratio (%)	Human priority aid (as % of total aid)	Aid to least developed countries (as % of total)
Donor country	US$ millions	As % of GNP	As % of central government budget	As % of military exports	Per capita (US$)	Per poor person (US$)					

TABLE 2
Human development aid profile of recipient countries

	Official development assistance (ODA) received				Aid social allocation ratio (%)	Aid social priority ratio (%)	Aid human expenditure ratio (%)	Human priority aid (as % of total aid)
Recipient country	US$ millions	As % of GNP	Per capita (US$)	Per poor person (US$)				

TABLE 3
Human development aid profile of multilateral donor agencies

Donor agency	Aid social allocation ratio (%)	Social priority ratio (%)	Share of total ODA for human priorities (%)

TABLE 4
Aid to human development priorities— overview of donor-country allocations

Human development priority	US$ millions	As % of total aid
Primary health care (including family planning)		
Basic education		
Low-cost rural and peri-urban water and sanitation		
Nutrition support		
Total aid to social sector		
Memo items		
Income enhancement and other poverty alleviation activities		
Local environment and sustainable development activities		

TABLE 5
Aid to human development priorities—overview of recipient-country expenditure

Human development priority	US$ millions	As % of total aid
Primary health care (including family planning)		
Basic education		
Low-cost rural and peri-urban water and sanitation		
Nutrition support		
Total aid to social sector		
Memo items		
Income enhancement and other poverty alleviation activities		
Local environment and sustainable development activities		

TABLE 8
ODA de-concentration ratios

ODA target groups in recipient countries	ODA (US$)	Percentage of total
Government		
Central government		
State/provincial government		
Local government		
Private sector		
National NGOs		
Memo items		
ODA channelled through international NGOs		
ODA spent in donor countries—for example, on aid-related communication purposes		
Total		

TABLE 6
Aid allocations to human development priorities, by donor country

Donor country	Primary health care (including family planning) (US$ millions)	Basic education (US$ millions)	Nutrition (US$ millions)	Rural and peri-urban water and sanitation (US$ millions)	Total (US$ millions)	Human development priorities as % of total ODA

TABLE 9
ODA and military spending

Military spending	Number of countries in group	Share of total ODA (%)	Share of population (%)	ODA share as % of population share
Low (<2% of GDP)				
Medium (2–4% of GDP)				
High (>4% of GDP)				
Total				

TABLE 7
ODA to the poor

Recipient country	Number of poor (millions)	Poor as % of total population	ODA per poor person (US$)	ODA to the poor as % of total ODA

Bibliographic note

Chapter 1 draws on the following: Anand 1992 and 1993, Anand and Ravallion 1993, Anand and Sen forthcoming, Hartwick 1977, Nussbaum and Sen 1993, Pronk and Haq 1992, Repetto 1985, Sen 1970, 1985a, 1985b and 1992 and Solow 1974a and 1992.

Chapter 2 draws on the following: Barsh 1993, Baverman 1993, Bowser and others 1992, Bread for the World Institute 1993, Brown, Kane and Ayres 1993, Clarke 1991, Cohen 1993, Cuhane 1993, Deng 1993, End Child Prostitution in Asian Tourism 1992, Gurr 1993, Hamm, Nuscheler and Sander 1993, Homer-Dixon 1991, Human Rights Watch 1993, International Labour Office 1993, Kakar 1993, Kaplan 1994, Mackay 1993, Mandel and others 1993, Mann, Tarantola and Netter 1992, OECD 1993c, Pear 1993, Remenyi 1991, Sen 1981, Sköns and Ström 1993, Smith 1993, Speth 1993, Tullis 1993, UNDP 1993a, UNFPA 1991, United Nations 1993c, U.S. Department of State 1945, WHO 1993a, Wilford 1994, World Bank 1993c and World Resources Institute 1992.

References for the boxes are as follows: box 2.1, materials from UNDP country offices; box 2.2, Sen 1981; box 2.3, Mann, Tarantola and Netter 1992; box 2.4, Kakar 1993; box 2.5, Tullis 1993; box 2.7, Cohen 1993; box 2.8, Kieschnick and Parzen 1992, Remenyi 1991 and Yaron 1994.

References for the tables are as follows: table 2.2, Sköns and Ström 1993 and UNHCR 1993.

References for the figures are as follows: figure 2.1, World Bank 1993c; figure 2.2, OECD 1993d; figure 2.6, UNHCR 1993.

References for the current crisis spots in annex 1 are as follows: Amnesty International 1993; Human Rights Watch 1993; Sköns and Ström 1993; United Nations 1993c; World Bank 1993c; Bread for the World Institute 1993 and Kuroda 1993.

References for the country studies in social integration are as follows: Mauritius, Bheenick, Hanoomanjee and Nababsing 1993; Malaysia, Demery and Demery 1992 and ISIS 1993b; Zimbabwe, de Waal 1990 and Klugman, Stewart and Helmsing 1992.

Chapter 3 draws on the following: Boutros-Ghali 1992, Brzoska 1993, DiChiaro and Laurance 1993, Eliasson 1993, Physicians for Human Rights and the Arms Project of Human Rights Watch 1993, Sivard 1993, Sköns and Ström 1993, Smith 1993, United Nations 1945, 1993a, 1993b and 1994, Urquhart 1993 and Wulf 1993a, 1993b, 1993c and 1993d.

References for the boxes are as follows: box 3.1, Sköns and Ström 1993; box 3.2, DiChiaro and Laurance 1993; box 3.4, Cunningham 1994; box 3.5, DiChiaro and Laurance 1994; box 3.6, Physicians for Human Rights and the Arms Project of Human Rights Watch 1993; box 3.7, Laurance and Wulf 1993; box 3.8, United Nations 1945.

References for the tables are as follows: table 3.3, Brzoska 1993; tables 3.4 and 3.5, Sköns and Ström 1993.

References for the figures are as follows: figures 3.3 and 3.4, Sköns and Ström 1993; figure 3.5, Wulf 1993b.

Chapter 4 draws on the following: Cassen and others 1987, Chickering and Salahdine 1991, Griffin and McKinley 1993, Kaul and Savio 1993, Krueger 1993, North-South Roundtable forthcoming, OECD 1993a, Ogata, Volcker and others 1993, Randel and German 1993, UNDP 1992, 1993a and 1993b, UNICEF 1994 and World Bank 1992a, 1992b, 1993a and 1993c.

References for the boxes are as follows: boxes 4.1, 4.2 and 4.3, Griffin and McKinley 1993; box 4.4, World Bank 1992b; box 4.5, Ofstad, Tostensen and Vraalsen 1991; box 4.6, UNDP 1993b and UNICEF 1994; box 4.7, Kamphius 1993 and Randel and German 1993; box 4.8, Parker and Jesperson 1994, World Bank 1993c and UNICEF 1990; box 4.9, Streeten 1994b.

References for the tables are as follows: table 4.1, OECD 1993a; table 4.9, UNDP 1992 and World Bank 1993a.

References for the figures are as follows: figure 4.1, World Bank 1993b; figures 4.4 and 4.5, UNDP 1992, World Bank 1992a and 1993a; figure 4.6, World Bank 1993b.

Chapter 5 draws on the following: Adamu 1993, Akder 1993, Aturupane, Glewwe and Isenman 1994, Barsh 1993, El-laithy 1993, ISIS 1993a, Khatib 1993, Makgetla 1993, Noll 1993, Obame 1993, Osman 1993, Spíndola 1993, Srinivasan 1994, Streeten 1994a and Zhizhou 1993.

References for the figures are as follows: figure 5.4, Makgetla 1993 and UNDP 1993a; figure 5.5, Spíndola 1993 and UNDP 1993a; figure 5.6, Adamu 1993; figure 5.7, El-laithy 1993; figure 5.8, Zhizhou 1993; figure 5.9, ISIS 1993a and 1993b.

References

Adamu, Sam O. 1993. "Disaggregated Human Development Index within Nigeria." Background paper for *Human Development Report 1994.* UNDP, New York.

Akder, A. Halis. 1993. "Disaggregated Human Development Index: A Means to Closing Gaps." Paper presented at seminar on the Uses of the Human Development Index, February 17–18, UNDP, New York.

Amnesty International. 1993. *Amnesty International Report 1993.* London.

Anand, Sudhir. 1992. "Review of *Hunger and Public Action* by Jean Drèze and Amartya Sen." *Journal of Economic Literature* 30 (June): 919–21.

———. 1993. "Inequality Between and Within Nations." Harvard University, Center for Population and Development Studies, Cambridge, Mass. Mimeo.

———. 1994. "Population, Well-being, and Freedom." In G. Sen, A. Germain and L.C. Chen, eds., *Population Policies Reconsidered.* Cambridge, Mass.: Harvard University Press.

Anand, Sudhir, and S.M.R. Kanbur. 1991. "Public Policy and Basic Needs Provision: Intervention and Achievement in Sri Lanka." In J.P. Drèze and A.K. Sen, eds., *The Political Economy of Hunger,* vol. 3. Oxford: Clarendon Press.

Anand, Sudhir, and Martin Ravallion. 1993. "Human Development in Poor Countries: On the Role of Private Incomes and Public Services." *Journal of Economic Perspectives* 7 (1): 133–50.

Anand, Sudhir, and Amartya Sen. Forthcoming. "Sustainable Human Development: Concepts and Priorities." HDRO Occasional Paper 8. UNDP, New York.

Aturupane, Harsha, Paul Glewwe and Paul Isenman. 1994. "Poverty, Human Development and Growth: An Emerging Consensus?" Paper presented at American Economic Association meeting, January 3, Boston, Mass.

Bank for International Settlements. 1993. *Annual Report.* Basle.

Barsh, Russel Lawrence. 1993. "Canada's Aboriginal Peoples: Social Integration or Disintegration." Background paper for *Human Development Report 1994.* UNDP, New York.

Baverman, Mark. 1993. "Violence: The Newest Worry on the Job." *New York Times,* December 15.

Béridogo, Bréhima. 1993. "Social Integration: Mali's Case." Background paper for *Human Development Report 1994.* UNDP, New York.

Betancourt, Keyla, and Gustavo Márquez. 1993. "Venezuela: Un estudio de caso en integración social." Background paper for *Human Development Report 1994.* UNDP, New York.

Bheenick, Rundheersing, Esther Hanoomanjee and Vidula Nababsing. 1993. "Mauritius: A Case Study on Social Integration from a Human Development Perspective." Background paper for *Human Development Report 1994.* UNDP, New York.

Boutros-Ghali, Boutros. 1992. *An Agenda for Peace: Peacemaking and Peace-keeping.* Report of the Secretary-General Pursuant to the Statement Adopted by the Summit Meeting of the Security Council, January 31. New York: United Nations. DPI/1247.

Bowser, Rene, Susan Conbere, Bella Maranion and Alan Miller. 1992. *Southern Exposure: Global Climate Change and Developing Countries.* Center for Global Change, University of Maryland, College Park.

Bread for the World Institute. 1993. *Hunger 1994: Transforming the Politics of Hunger.* Fourth Annual Report on the State of World Hunger. Washington, D.C.

Brown, Lester R., Hal Kane and Ed Ayres. 1993. *Vital Signs 1993.* New York: W.W. Norton and Company.

Brown, Lester R., and others. 1993. *State of the World— A Worldwatch Institute Report on Progress toward a Sustainable Society.* New York: W.W. Norton and Company.

Brundtland, Gro Harlem. 1993. "Population, Environment and Development." The Rafael M. Salas Memorial Lecture, United Nations Population Fund, September 28, New York.

Brzoska, Michael. 1993. "Military Aid—Selected Issues and Data." Background paper for *Human Development Report 1994.* UNDP, New York.

Buarque, Cristovam. 1993. "Brazil: From Inequality to Apartation." Background paper for *Human Development Report 1994.* UNDP, New York.

Carlson, Beverley A. Forthcoming. "Indicators Concerning Children in the Countries of the Former Soviet Union." *Journal of Development Studies.*

Cassen, Robert, and others. 1987. *Does Aid Work?* New York: Oxford University Press.

Chickering, Lawrence A., and Mohamed Salahdine, eds. 1991. *The Silent Revolution: The Informal Sector in Five Asian and Near Eastern Countries.* San Francisco: ICS Press.

Clarke, Robin. 1991. *Water: The International Crisis.* Cambridge, Mass.: MIT Press.

Cohen, Roger. 1993. "Europeans Ponder Working Less So More of Them Can Have Jobs." *New York Times,* November 22, section A, p. 6.

Coomaraswamy, Radhika. 1993. "Sri Lanka: A Case Study in Social Integration." Background paper for *Human Development Report 1994.* UNDP, New York.

Cosslett, Christopher. 1993. "Environmental Degradation, Resource Scarcity and the Implications for Human Security." Background paper for *Human Development Report 1994.* UNDP, New York.

Cuhane, Dennis. 1993. "Where Should the Homeless Sleep?" *New York Times,* December 19, section E, p. 13.

Cunningham, Keith. 1994. "U.S. Foreign Base Closure with European and Pacific Case Studies." Background paper for *Human Development Report 1994.* UNDP, New York.

Demery, David, and Lionel Demery. 1992. *Adjustment and Equity in Malaysia.* Paris: OECD.

Deng, Francis M. 1993. *Protecting the Dispossessed: A Challenge for the International Community.* Washington, D.C.: The Brookings Institute.

Desai, Meghnad. 1994. "Greening of the HDI?" Background paper for *Human Development Report 1994.* UNDP, New York.

de Waal, Victor. 1990. *The Politics of Reconciliation: Zimbabwe's First Decade.* London: Hirst and Company.

DiChiaro, Joseph, and Edward J. Laurance. 1993. "Nuclear Weapons in a Changing World: Consequences for Development." Background paper for *Human Development Report 1994.* UNDP, New York.

———. 1994. "Arms Transfer Cost Data." Background note prepared for *Human Development Report 1994.* UNDP, New York.

Dore, Ronald. Forthcoming. "Why Visiting Sociologists Fail." *World Development* 22.

Dowd, John E., and Laurance D. Haber. 1994. "A Human Development Agenda for Disability: Statistical Considerations." United Nations Statistical Division (UNSTAT), New York.

Eliasson, Jan. 1993. "End the Grim Harvest." *New York Times,* October 22.

El-laithy, Heba. 1993. "The Disaggregated Human Development Index for Egypt." Background paper for *Human Development Report 1994.* UNDP, New York.

End Child Prostitution in Asian Tourism. 1992. "Child Prostitution in Asia." Bangkok. Mimeo.

Food and Agriculture Organization of the United Nations. 1992. *The State of Food and Agriculture.* Rome.

Fresneda, Oscar. 1993. "Informe de avance sobre recopilacion de indicatores de desarrollo humano para Colombia." Background paper for *Human Development Report 1994.* UNDP, New York.

Ghubash, Mouza. 1993. "Human Development Report 1994: United Arab Emirates." Background paper for *Human Development Report 1994.* UNDP, New York.

Goldstone, Leo. 1993. "The Use of Composite Indexes for Ranking Countries by Their Level of Development." Working paper. World Bank, Washington, D.C.

Griffin, Keith, and Terry McKinley. 1993. "A New Framework for Development Cooperation." Background paper for *Human Development Report 1994.* UNDP, New York.

Gurr, Tedd Robert. 1993. *Minorities at Risk: A Global View of Ethnic Conflicts.* Washington, D.C.: United States Institute of Peace Press.

Hamm, Brigitte, Franz Nuscheler and Harald Sander. 1993. "Social Needs and Social (Dis-) Integration in Industrial Countries." Background paper for *Human Development Report 1994.* UNDP, New York.

Haq, Mahbub ul. 1993a. "Bretton Woods Institutions: The Vision and the Reality." Paper presented at the Bretton Woods Conference, September 1–3, Bretton Woods, N.H.

———. 1993b. "New Compulsions of Human Security." Paper presented at the Forty-sixth NGO/DPI Annual Conference, September 8, New York.

———. 1993c. "A New Framework of Development Cooperation." Paper presented at the Tidewater Meeting, July 19–20, Zacatecas, Mexico.

———. Forthcoming. "New Perspectives on Human Development." HDRO Occasional Paper 9. UNDP, New York.

Hartwick, John M. 1977. "Intergenerational Equity and the Investing of Rents from Exhaustible Resources." *American Economic Review* 67 (5): 972–74.

Henry, Ralph M. 1993. "Trinidad and Tobago: Human Development Index 1993." Background paper for *Human Development Report 1994.* UNDP, New York.

Hicks, John R. 1946. *Value and Capital.* 2nd ed. Oxford: Clarendon Press.

Homer-Dixon, Thomas F. 1991. "On the Threshold: Environmental Changes as Causes of Acute Conflict." *International Security* 16 (2): 76–116.

Human Rights Watch. 1993. *Human Rights Watch World Report 1993.* New York.

International Fund for Agricultural Development. 1992. *The State of the World Rural Poverty: An Inquiry into Its Causes and Consequences.* New York: New York University Press.

International Labour Office. 1992. *World Labour Report.* Geneva.

———. 1993. *World Labour Report.* Geneva.

International Monetary Fund. 1993. *World Economic Outlook.* Washington, D.C. October.

ISIS (Institute of Strategic and International Studies). 1993a. "Disaggregated Human Development Index of Malaysia." Background paper for *Human Development Report 1994.* UNDP, New York.

———. 1993b. "Social Integration and Social Tension and Disintegration in Malaysia." Background paper for *Human Development Report 1994.* UNDP, New York.

IUCN (International Union for the Conservation of Nature and Natural Resources). 1980. *World Conservation Strategy: Living Resource Conservation for Sustainable Development.* Gland, Switzerland: IUCN-UNEP-WWF.

Jahan, Selim. 1992. "The US Foreign Aid in the Nineties." *Journal of International and Strategic Studies* (October): 136–59.

Kakar, Sandip. 1993. "Natural Disaster Trends in Relation to Vulnerability and Development." Background paper for *Human Development Report 1994*. UNDP, New York.

Kamphius, Elise. 1993. "Hidden Trade Barriers: Tied Aid Credits." Paper presented at the workshop on Aid and Conditionality, European Association of Development Research and Norwegian Institute of International Affairs, September 13, Berlin.

Kaplan, Robert D. 1994. "The Coming of Anarchy." *Atlantic Monthly* (February).

Kaul, Inge, and Roberto Savio. 1993. "Global Human Security: A New Political Framework for North-South Relations." Society for International Development, Rome and New York. Mimeo.

Khatib, Hisham. 1993. "The Human Development Index as a Policy and Planning Tool." Paper presented at seminar on the Uses of the Human Development Index, February 17–18, UNDP, New York.

Kieschnick, Michael Hall, and Julia Ann Parzen. 1992. *Credit Where It's Due: Development Banking for Communities*. Philadelphia: Temple University Press.

Kirdar, Üner, and Leonard Silk, eds. 1994. *A World Fit for People*. New York: New York University Press.

Klugman, Jeni. 1993. "The Russian Federation: Case Study on Social Integration." Background paper for *Human Development Report 1994*. UNDP, New York.

Klugman, Jeni, Frances Stewart and A.H. Helmsing. 1992. "Decentralization in Zimbabwe." Background paper for *Human Development Report 1993*. UNDP, New York.

Krueger, Anne O. 1993. *Economic Policies at Crossroads: The United States and Developing Countries*. Washington, D.C.: Brookings Institute.

Kuroda, Michiko. 1993. "Potential Emergency Conflicts." Background paper for *Human Development Report 1994*. UNDP, New York.

Lamb, Geoffrey, with Valeriana Kallab, eds. 1992. *Military Expenditure and Economic Development: A Symposium on Research Issues*. World Bank Discussion Paper 185. Washington, D.C.

Laurance, Edward J., and Herbert Wulf. 1993. "United Nations Register of Conventional Armaments 1992." Background note for *Human Development Report 1994*. UNDP, New York.

Lewis, W. Arthur. 1955. *The Theory of Economic Growth*. Chicago, Ill.: Richard D. Irwin, Inc.

Mackay, Judith. 1993. *The State of Health Atlas*. New York: Touchtone Books.

Makgetla, Neva Seidman. 1993. "South Africa: Submission on Human Development Index." Background paper for *Human Development Report 1994*. UNDP, New York.

Mandel, Michael J., Paul Magnusson, James E. Ellis, Gail DeGeorge and Keith L. Alexander. 1993. "The Economics of Crime." *Business Week*, December 13, pp. 72–81.

Mann, Jonathan, Daniel Tarantola and Thomas Netter, eds. 1992. *AIDS in the World: A Global Report 1992*. Cambridge, Mass.: Harvard University Press.

Ng'eno, Nehemiah. 1993. "Social Integration and Disintegration in Kenya: An Economic Analysis." Background paper for *Human Development Report 1994*. UNDP, New York.

Noll, Heinz-Herbert. 1993. "Disaggregated Human Development Index for Germany." Background paper for *Human Development Report 1994*. UNDP, New York.

North-South Roundtable. Forthcoming. *The United Nations and Bretton Woods Institutions: Challenges for the Twenty-first Century*. London: Macmillan.

Nussbaum, Martha, and Amartya K. Sen, eds. 1993. *The Quality of Life*. Oxford: Clarendon Press.

Obame, Jean Christian. 1993. "Étude sur les indices sectoriels du développement humain au Gabon." Background paper for *Human Development Report 1994*. UNDP, New York.

Ochocki, Hab Andrzej. 1993. "National Human Development Report: Poland." Background paper for *Human Development Report 1994*. UNDP, New York.

OECD (Organisation for Economic Co-operation and Development). 1992. *Development Cooperation Report*. Paris.

———. 1993a. *Assessing the Effects of the Uruguay Round*. Trade Policy Issues 2. Paris.

———. 1993b. *Development Cooperation Report*. Paris.

———. 1993c. *Education at a Glance*. Paris.

———. 1993d. *Employment Outlook*. Paris.

Ofstad, Arve, Arne Tostensen and Tom Vraalsen. 1991. "Towards a 'Development Contract': A New Model for International Agreements with African Countries?" Working paper. Christian Michelsen Institute, Development Research and Action Programme, Fantoft.

Ogata, Shijuro, Paul Volcker and others. 1993. "Financing an Effective United Nations: A Report of the Independent Advisory Group on the U.N. Financing." A Project of the Ford Foundation. February.

Onimode, Bade. 1993. "Nigeria: Case Study on Social Integration, Social Tension and Disintegration." Background paper for *Human Development Report 1994*. UNDP, New York.

Osman, Osman M. 1993. "The Uses of the HDI as a Statistical Tool of Policy Planning." Paper presented at seminar on the Uses of the Human Development Index, February 17–18, UNDP, New York.

Pardo, Candido M. Lopez. 1994. "Indice de Desarrollo Humano: El Caso Cuba." Background paper for *Human Development Report 1994*. UNDP, New York.

Parker, David, and Eva Jesperson. 1994. *20/20: Mobilizing Resources for Children in the 1990s*. UNICEF Staff working paper. New York.

Pear, Robert. 1993. "Fewer Are Insured for Medical Care." *New York Times*, December 15, section A, p. 24.

Pearce, David W. 1993. *Economic Values and the Natural World*. Cambridge, Mass.: MIT Press.

Pearce, David W., and Jeremy J. Warford. 1993. *World without End: Economics, Environment, and Sustainable Development*. New York: Oxford University Press.

Physicians for Human Rights and the Arms Project of Human Rights Watch. 1993. *Landmines: A Deadly Legacy*. New York: Human Rights Watch.

Preparatory Committee for the International Conference

on Population and Development. 1994. "Draft Programme of Action of the Conference: Note by the Secretary-General." United Nations, New York. No. A/Conf. 171/PC/5.

Pronk, Jan, and Mahbub ul Haq. 1992. "Sustainable Development: From Concept to Action." The Hague Report. Ministry of Development Cooperation, the Hague, and UNDP, New York.

Randel, Judith, and Tony German. 1993. *The Reality of Aid: An Independent View of Aid.* London: Action Aid.

Remenyi, Joe. 1991. *Where Credit Is Due: Income-Generating Programs of the Poor in Developing Countries.* Boulder, Colo.: Westview Press.

Repetto, Robert, ed. 1985. *The Global Possible: Resources, Development, and the New Century.* A World Resources Institute Book. New Haven, Conn.: Yale University Press.

Rupesinghe, Kumar, and Michiko Kuroda, eds. 1992. *Early Warning and Conflict Resolution.* New York: St. Martin's Press in association with the International Peace Research Institute, Oslo.

Schultz, Theodore W. 1980. *Investing in People.* San Francisco: University of California Press.

Seers, Dudley. 1962. "Why Visiting Economists Fail." *Journal of Political Economy* 70 (August): 325–38.

Sen, Amartya K. 1970. *Collective Choice and Social Welfare.* San Francisco: Holden-Day. Reprint. Amsterdam: North-Holland, 1979.

———. 1980. "Equality of What?" In S.M. McMurrin, ed., *Tanner Lectures on Human Values,* vol. 1. Salt Lake City: University of Utah Press, and Cambridge, UK: Cambridge University Press. Reprinted in Sen 1982.

———. 1981. *Poverty and Famines: An Essay on Entitlement and Deprivation.* London: Oxford University Press.

———. 1982. *Choice, Welfare and Measurement.* Oxford: Basil Blackwell, and Cambridge, Mass.: MIT Press.

———. 1985a. *Commodities and Capabilities.* Amsterdam: North-Holland.

———. 1985b. "Well-being, Agency and Freedom: The Dewey Lectures 1984." *Journal of Philosophy* 82 (4): 169–221.

———. 1987. *The Standard of Living.* Cambridge, UK: Cambridge University Press.

———. 1992. *Inequality Reexamined.* Oxford: Clarendon Press, and Cambridge, Mass.: Harvard University Press.

Shaw, John. 1993. "Study on Social Integration in Australia." Background paper for *Human Development Report 1994.* UNDP, New York.

Sivard, Ruth Leger. 1993. *World Military and Social Expenditures 1993.* Leesburg, Va.: World Priorities Inc.

Sköns, Elisabeth, and Gabriele Winai Ström. 1993. "Weapon Supplies to Trouble Spots." Background paper for *Human Development Report 1994.* UNDP, New York.

Smith, Dan. 1993. "War, Peace and Third World Development." Background paper for *Human Development Report 1994.* UNDP, New York.

Sofi, Jamil. 1993. "Study on Social Integration in the Kingdom of Saudi Arabia." Background paper for *Human Development Report 1994.* UNDP, New York.

Solow, Robert M. 1974a. "The Economics of Resources or the Resources of Economics." *American Economic Review* 64 (2): 1–14.

———. 1974b. "Intergenerational Equity and Exhaustible Resources." *Review of Economic Studies,* Symposium on the Economics of Exhaustible Resources.

———. 1992. "An Almost Practical Step toward Sustainability." Invited lecture on the occasion of the fortieth anniversary of Resources for the Future, October 8, Washington, D.C.

Speth, James Gustave. 1992. "A Post-Rio Compact." *Foreign Policy* 88 (fall).

———. 1993. "Towards Sustainable Food Security." Sir John Crawford Memorial Lecture, Consultative Group on International Agricultural Research, October 25, Washington, D.C.

Spíndola, Austregésilo Gomes. 1993. "The Human Development Index and Other Development Indicators of Brazil." Background paper for *Human Development Report 1994.* UNDP, New York.

Srinivasan, T.N. 1994. "Human Development: A Paradigm or Reinvention of the Wheel?" Paper presented at American Economic Association meeting, January 3, Boston, Mass.

Stalker, Peter. 1994. *The Work of Strangers: A Survey of International Labour Migration.* Geneva: ILO.

Stiftung Entwicklung und Frieden. 1993. *Entwicklung und Frieden: Globale Trends 93/94—Daten zur Weltentwicklung.* Frankfurt: Fischer Taschenbuch Verlag GmbH.

Stockholm International Peace Research Institute. 1992. *World Armaments and Disarmament.* New York: Oxford University Press.

Streeten, Paul. 1994a. "Human Development: Means and Ends." Paper presented at American Economic Association meeting, January 3, Boston, Mass.

———. 1994b. "Why Failed Economists Visit." Background note for *Human Development Report 1994.* UNDP, New York.

Taylor, Charles. 1985. *Human Agency and Language: Philosophical Papers,* vol. 1. Cambridge, UK: Cambridge University Press.

Transparency International. 1993. "Good Governance and Third World Development." With contributions from Ulrich Albrecht, Peter Eigen, Thomas F. Gallagher and Johan Galtung. Background paper for *Human Development Report 1994.* UNDP, New York.

Tullis, LaMond. 1993. "Illicit Drugs: Socioeconomic and Political Impacts in Nine Countries." Background paper for *Human Development Report 1994.* UNDP, New York.

UNCTAD (United Nations Conference on Trade and Development). 1992a. *Combating Global Warming: Study on a Global System of Tradable Carbon Emission Entitlements.* Geneva: United Nations.

———. 1992b. *Trade and Development Report 1992.* Report by the Secretariat of the United Nations Conference on Trade and Development. New York: United Nations.

———. 1993. *Trade and Development Report 1993.* Report by the Secretariat of the United Nations Conference on Trade and Development. New York: United Nations.

UNDP (United Nations Development Programme). 1990. *Human Development Report 1990.* New York: Oxford University Press.

———. 1991. *Human Development Report 1991.* New York: Oxford University Press.

———. 1992. *Human Development Report 1992.* New York: Oxford University Press.

———. 1993a. *Human Development Report 1993.* New York: Oxford University Press.

———. 1993b. *Rethinking Technical Cooperation: Reforms for Capacity Building in Africa.* New York.

UNESCO (United Nations Educational, Scientific and Cultural Organization). 1992. *World Education Report.* Paris.

———. 1993. *World Education Report.* Paris.

UNFPA (United Nations Population Fund). 1991. *Population and the Environment: The Challenges Ahead.* New York.

———. 1993. *The State of the World Population.* New York.

UNHCR (Office of the United Nations High Commissioner for Refugees). 1993. *The State of the World's Refugees.* London: Penguin.

UNICEF (United Nations Children's Fund). 1990. *Children and Development in the 1990s: A UNICEF Sourcebook.* New York.

———. 1993. *Progress of Nations.* New York.

———. 1994. *The State of the World's Children 1994.* New York: Oxford University Press.

United Nations. 1945. *Charter of the United Nations.* New York.

———. 1991. *The World's Women 1970–1990: Trends and Statistics.* New York.

———. 1992. *World Economic Survey 1992: Current Trends and Policies in the World Economy.* Department of Economic and Social Development. New York. E/1992/40.ST/ESA/231.

———. 1993a. *Assistance in Mine Clearance.* New York. A/RES/48/7.

———. 1993b. *General and Complete Disarmament.* Resolution. New York. A/C.1/48/L.42.

———. 1993c. *Report on the World Social Situation 1993.* New York.

———. 1993d. *World Economic Survey 1993: Current Trends and Policies in the World Economy.* New York.

———. 1994. *Convention on Prohibitions or Restrictions on the Use of Certain Conventional Weapons which May Be Deemed To Be Excessively Injurious or To Have Indiscriminate Effects.* New York. A/RES/48/79.

United Nations International Drug Control Programme. 1994. *The Opiate Industry of Pakistan—Summary.* Islamabad.

Urquhart, Brian. 1993. "A UN Volunteer Force—The Prospects." *New York Review of Books,* July 15, pp. 52–56.

U.S. Committee for Refugees. 1993. *World Refugee Survey.* Washington, D.C.: World Refugee Survey.

U.S. Department of State. 1945. Report to the President on the results of the San Francisco Conference by the Secretary of State. Publication 2343. June 26. Washington, D.C.

Wagstaff, Adam. 1993. "Human Development Indicators for the United Kingdom." Background paper for *Human Development Report 1994.* UNDP, New York.

Wang, Rusong. 1993. "Country Case Study on Social Integration in China: Its Past, Present and Prospect." Background paper for *Human Development Report 1994.* UNDP, New York.

Weston, Barus H., ed. 1990. *Alternative Security: Living without Nuclear Deterrence.* Boulder, Colo.: Westview Press.

WHO (World Health Organization). 1993a. *Global Health Situation and Projections.* Division of Epidemiological Surveillance and Health Situation and Trend Assessment. Geneva.

———. 1993b. *Implementation of the Global Strategy for Health for All by the Year 2000.* Geneva.

Wilford, John Noble. 1994. "Among the Dying Species Are Lost Tribes of Mankind." *New York Times,* January 2, section 4.

Wollstonecraft, Mary. 1792. *Vindication of the Rights of Woman: with Strictures on Political and Moral Subjects.* London: Joseph Johnson.

World Bank. 1992a. *The World Bank Annual Report.* Washington, D.C.

———. 1992b. *World Development Report 1992: Development and the Environment.* New York: Oxford University Press.

———. 1993a. *The World Bank Annual Report.* Washington, D.C.

———. 1993b. *World Debt Tables.* Washington, D.C.

———. 1993c. *World Development Report 1993: Investing in Health.* New York: Oxford University Press.

World Commission on Environment and Development. 1987. *Our Common Future.* (The Brundtland Report.) New York: Oxford University Press.

World Resources Institute. 1992. *World Resources 1992–1993.* New York: Oxford University Press.

Wulf, Herbert. 1993a. "Conversion: Managing the Disarmament Process." Background paper for *Human Development Report 1994.* UNDP, New York.

———. 1993b. "Peace Dividend." Background paper for *Human Development Report 1994.* UNDP, New York.

———. 1993c. "Suggestions for a Concrete Agenda of Action." Background paper for *Human Development Report 1994.* UNDP, New York.

———. 1993d. "Transparency in Armaments and Armed Forces." Background paper for *Human Development Report 1994.* UNDP, New York.

Yaron, Jacob. 1994. "What Makes Rural Finance Institutions Successful?" *World Bank Research Observer* 9 (1): 49–70.

Yoo, Yoon-Ha, Soon Wonkwon and Won Hee Rhee. 1993. "Human Development Index of Korea." Background paper for *Human Development Report 1994.* UNDP, New York.

Zhizhou, Cai. 1993. "Human Development of China." Background paper for *Human Development Report 1994.* UNDP, New York.

HUMAN
DEVELOPMENT
INDICATORS

Indicator	Indicator tables[a]	Original international source
A		
Agricultural production	13,26,49	FAO,WBANK
Aid for human priority	19,41	OECD*
Aid human expenditure ratio	19,41	OECD*
Aid social allocation ratio, bilateral	19,41	OECD*
Aid social priority ratio, bilateral	19,41	OECD*
AIDS	12,35	WHO
Alcohol consumption	35	WHO,WBANK
Anemia, pregnant women	11	WHO,WBANK
Armed forces per person	21,43	WPI*
per doctor	21,43	WPI*
per teacher	21,43	WPI*
Arms exports, to dev. countries, total	43	SIPRI
% of exports to dev. countries	43	SIPRI*
Arms imports, total	21	SIPRI
% of national imports	21	SIPRI*
Asylum applications	30	UNHCR
B		
Birth rate, crude	23	UNPOP
Births attended by health personnel	11	WHO
Births outside marriage	30	EUROSTAT,OECD
Birth-weight, low	11	WHO
Book titles published	16,37	UNESCO
Breast-feeding, median duration	11	MACRO,WHO
Budget surplus/deficit	27,50	IMF
C		
Calorie supply as % of requirements	2,13	FAO*
South-North gap	6	FAO*
Calorie supply per capita	13	FAO
Cancers, malignant	35	WHO
Cereal imports	13	FAO
Cinema attendances	16,37	UNESCO
Circulatory system diseases	35	WHO
Consumption, government	26,49	WBANK*
private	26,49	WBANK*
Contraceptive prevalence	23,45	UNPOP,UNFPA
Current account balance	20,42	IMF
D		
Death rate, crude	23	UNPOP
Debt, external	20	WBANK,OECD
% of GNP	20	WBANK,OECD
public	42	OECD
government interest payments	42	OECD*
Debt service	20	WBANK,OECD
Deforestation	24	FAO,WRI
Dependency ratio	45	UNPOP
Divorces	30	EUROSTAT,OECD*
Doctors	12,28,35	WHO,WBANK
Drug crimes	30	UNCSDHA
E		
Earnings disparity	38	OECD*
Earnings per employee	17,38	UNIDO,WBANK
Education expenditure, total	31,36,40	OECD
public	15,18,36	UNESCO,OECD
primary and secondary combined	15	UNESCO*
tertiary	15,36	UNESCO,OECD
Educational attainment, lower secondary	29	OECD

Indicator	Indicator tables[a]	Original international source
Energy consumption, total	25,47	UNSTAT,WBANK
per capita	25,47	UNSTAT,WBANK
share of world consumption	47	UNSTAT,WBANK*
rate of change	25,47	UNSTAT,WBANK*
Energy efficiency	25,47	OECD,WBANK*
Energy imports	25	UNSTAT,WBANK*
Enrolment, primary, total	14	UNESCO
primary, female	8	UNESCO
primary, female-male gap	9	UNESCO*
Enrolment, secondary, total	14	UNESCO
secondary, female	8,33	UNESCO
secondary, female-male gap	9,34	UNESCO*
secondary technical	15	UNESCO*
upper secondary	36	OECD
upper secondary, female	33	OECD
upper secondary technical	36	OECD*
Enrolment, tertiary, total	14,31	UNESCO,OECD
tertiary, female	8	UNESCO
tertiary, female-male gap	9	UNESCO*
tertiary science	15,36	UNESCO,OECD*
tertiary science, female	8,33	UNESCO,OECD*
tertiary science, female-male gap	34	OECD*
tertiary, full-time equivalent, total	28,36	OECD
female	28,33	OECD
female-male gap	34	OECD*
tertiary students abroad	15	UNESCO*
university, full-time, female-male gap	34	OECD*
Enrolment, 19-year-olds	36	OECD
Enrolment, all levels, total	2,4,28,36	UNESCO
South-North gap	7	UNESCO*
Export to import growth rate	42	UNSTAT*
Export-import ratio	20,42	UNSTAT*
Exports, % of GDP	26,49	UNSTAT*
% of GDP growth rate	27,50	UNSTAT*
F		
Fertility rate, total	23,45	UNPOP
South-North gap	7	UNPOP*
rates of change	23,45	UNPOP*
Food aid	13	OECD,WFP*
Food import dependency ratio	13	FAO*
Food production	13	FAO
Fuel wood production	24	FAO,WRI
G		
GDP, total	26,49	WBANK
GDP, real per capita (PPP$)	1,2,4,18,28, 31,40	WBANK,PENN
South-North gap	7	WBANK,PENN*
GNP, total	27,50	WBANK
annual growth rate	27,50	WBANK
industrial, percentage share	40	WBANK*
GNP per capita	2,18,28,31, 40	WBANK
GNP per capita annual growth rate	27,50	WBANK
Government expenditure, central	26,49	IMF,WBANK
Graduates, upper secondary, total	32	OECD*
upper secondary, female	33	OECD*
upper secondary, female-male gap	34	OECD*
Graduates, tertiary	5,32	UNESCO,OECD*
tertiary science	5,32	UNESCO,OECD*
Greenhouse index, global emissions	24,48	WRI*

Indicator	Indicator tables[a]	Original international source
H		
Health aid flows	12	WBANK
Health bills paid by public	35	OECD
Health expenditure, total	12,18,31,35, 40	WBANK,OECD
public	12,18,35	WHO,WBANK
private	35	OECD
Health services, % with access	2	WHO
population without access	3	WHO*
rural/urban access	10	WHO
rural-urban gap	10	WHO*
Homicides by men, intentional	29,30	WHO,UNCSDHA
Human development index	1	UNDP
I, J, K		
Illiterates, total/female	3	UNESCO*
Immunization	11	WHO,UNICEF*
Imports	26,49	UNSTAT*
Income share, lowest 40% of households	18,40	WBANK*
highest 20% to lowest 20%	18,29,40	WBANK*
Industrial production	26,49	UNSTAT,WBANK
Infant mortality	4,11	UNPOP
Inflation	27,29,50	IMF,WBANK
International reserves, gross	20,42	IMF
Investment, gross domestic	26,49	WBANK
L		
Labour force, total	17,38	ILO
agriculture	17,38	ILO
industry	17,38	ILO
services	17,38	ILO
female-male gap	9,34	ILO*
future replacement ratio	38	UNPOP*
Labour market programmes, expenditure	38	OECD
Land area, total	24,46	FAO
arable	24,46	FAO
irrigated	24,46	FAO
forest	24,46	FAO
permanent grasslands	46	OECD
Letters posted	16,37	UPU
Libraries, registered users	37	UNESCO
Life expectancy, total	1,2,4,28,31	UNPOP
South-North gap	6	UNPOP*
female	8,33	UNPOP
female-male gap	9,34	UNPOP*
at age 60	45	OECD
Literacy, total	1,2,4,5	UNESCO
South-North gap	6	UNESCO*
female/male	5	UNESCO
female-male gap	9	UNESCO*
age 15-19	5	UNESCO
female, age 15-24	8	UNESCO
M		
Malaria	12	WHO
Malnourished children, underweight	3,4,11	SCN,MACRO*
rural-urban gap	10	MACRO,UNICEF*
Maternal mortality	11,28,33	WHO
Military expenditure, % of GDP	21,43	SIPRI,USACDA*
% of education and health	21,43	SIPRI,USACDA*
Motor vehicles	16,37	UNSTAT
Museum attendances	37	UNESCO

Indicator	Indicator tables[a]	Original international source
N		
Newspaper circulation	2,16,28,37	UNESCO
Nurses, per person	12	WHO,WBANK
per doctor	12	WHO*,WBANK*
O		
ODA disbursed, total	41	OECD
% of GNP	41	OECD
per capita	41	OECD*
to least developed countries	41	OECD
% of central government budget	41	OECD
% of military expenditure	43	OECD*
multilateral	41	OECD
ODA received, bilateral, total	19	OECD
% of GNP	19	OECD
per capita	19	OECD*
per poor person	19	OECD*
ORS access	11	WHO
Out-of-school children, primary	3	UNESCO*
P, Q		
Pesticides	24,48	FAO,OECD
Population, total	23,45	UNPOP
annual growth rate	23,45	UNPOP
rates of change	23	UNPOP*
doubling date	23	UNPOP,WBANK
female-male gap	9,34	UNPOP*
age 60 and over	45	OECD,UNPOP
rural	10	UNPOP
urban	22,44	UNPOP
urban annual growth rate	22,44	UNPOP
major cities	22,44	UNPOP,ICUS
Population density, total	24,46	UNPOP
major cities	22,44	UNPOP,ICUS
Post offices	16	UPU
Poverty, people in, total/rural	3	WBANK,IFAD*
% population, total/rural/urban	18	WBANK,IFAD*
Premature death, years lost	12,29,35	WBANK
Prenatal care	11	WHO
Primary education, intake	14	UNESCO
repeaters	14	UNESCO
completers	14	UNESCO
transition to secondary	14	UNESCO*
Primary entrants to secondary	14	UNESCO*
Printing and writing paper	16,37	UNESCO
Prisoners, total	30	UNCSDHA
juvenile	30	UNCSDHA
Pupil-teacher ratio, primary	15	UNESCO
secondary	15	UNESCO
R		
Radios	16,37	UNESCO
Rapes reported	29,30	UNSTAT
Refugees	3	UNHCR
Research and development, scientists and technicians	5,32	UNESCO
expenditure	32	UNESCO
Road accidents, injuries	29	WHO
Road traffic noise	44	OECD

Indicator	Indicator tables[a]	Original international source
S		
Safe water, % with access	2,4	WHO
% with access, South-North gap	6	WHO*
population without access	3	WHO*
rural/urban access	10	WHO
rural-urban gap	10	WHO*
Sanitation, % with access	2	WHO
population without access	3	WHO*
rural/urban access	10	WHO
rural-urban gap	10	WHO*
Savings, gross domestic	26,49	WBANK
Schooling, mean years, total	1,5,32	UNESCO*
South-North gap	7	UNESCO*
female/male	5,32	UNESCO*
female-male gap	9,34	UNESCO*
Scientists and technicians	5,28,32	UNESCO
Secondary education, repeaters	14	UNESCO
Services	26,49	UNSTAT,WBANK
Single-female-parent homes	30	OECD
Social security benefits expenditure	18,40	ILO
Suicides by men	30	WHO
Sulfur and nitrogen emissions	29,48	OECD,UNEP
Sulfur dioxide concentration, major cities	48	OECD
T		
Tax revenue, % of GNP	26,49	IMF*
% of GNP growth	27,50	IMF*
Taxes, direct	27,50	IMF*
Telephones	16,37	UNSTAT,ITU
South-North gap	7	UNSTAT,ITU*
international calls	37	ITU
Televisions	2,16,28,37	UNESCO
Tobacco consumption	35	WHO,WBANK
Trade dependency	20,42	UNSTAT*
Trade, terms of	20,42	UNSTAT
Tuberculosis	12	WHO,WBANK
U, V		
Under-five mortality	3,11	UNPOP*
South-North gap	6	UNPOP*
Unemployment, total	29,39	OECD
discouraged workers	39	OECD*
female	39	OECD
female-male gap	34	OECD*
youth	29,39	OECD*
male youth	39	OECD*
long-term, more than 6 months	39	OECD
more than 12 months	39	OECD
regional disparity	39	OECD*
educational attainment disparity	39	OECD*
Unemployment benefits expenditure	39	OECD
Unionization	38	OECD
W, X, Y, Z		
Waste, hazardous	48	WRI
municipal	48	OECD
nuclear	48	OECD
Waste recycling	48	OECD,UNEP
Water resources, internal renewable	24,46	WRI
Water withdrawals, fresh	24,46	WRI

Indicator	Indicator tables[a]	Original international source
Women, labour force	17,33	ILO*
administrators and managers	8,33	UNSTAT
parliament	8,33	IPU
average age at first marriage	8,33	UNPOP
wages, female-male gap	29,34	ILO*
Workers' remittances from abroad	20,42	IMF*
Working hours	38	ILO

a. In addition to being shown in the tables as listed, all indicators in tables 2 to 27 are also shown in aggregated form in tables 51 and 52. The aggregates include global, regional, HDI and income aggregates. A few of these aggregates are also included in the subject tables themselves. The industrial subregional aggregates for all indicators in tables 28 to 50 are shown in the industrial subject tables.

* The first source listed is the main international source for the indicator. Whenever data come originally from more than one international source or when a second agency has published the data in a more convenient form, the leading secondary source follows the main source. When the original data have been specially commissioned, have not been published by the original international source or have been reanalysed by Leo Goldstone of World Statistics Ltd., the original international source is followed by an asterisk.

Key to international source abbreviations

EUROSTAT	Statistical Office of the European Communities
FAO	Food and Agriculture Organization of the United Nations
ICUS	International Centre for Urban Studies
IFAD	International Fund for Agricultural Development
ILO	International Labour Organisation
IMF	International Monetary Fund
IPU	Inter-Parliamentary Union
ITU	International Telecommunication Union
MACRO	Macro International, Inc. (Demographic Health Surveys)
OECD	Organisation for Economic Co-operation and Development
PENN	Penn World Tables
SCN	ACC SubCommittee on Nutrition
SIPRI	Stockholm International Peace Research Institute
UNCSDHA	United Nations Centre for Social Development and Humanitarian Affairs
UNDP	United Nations Development Programme
UNEP	United Nations Environment Programme
UNESCO	United Nations Educational, Scientific and Cultural Organization
UNFPA	United Nations Population Fund
UNHCR	United Nations High Commissioner for Refugees
UNICEF	United Nations Children's Fund
UNIDO	United Nations Industrial Development Organization
UNPOP	United Nations Population Division
UNSTAT	United Nations Statistical Division
UPU	Universal Postal Union
USACDA	US Arms Control and Disarmament Agency
WBANK	World Bank
WFP	World Food Programme
WHO	World Health Organization
WPI	World Priorities, Inc.
WRI	World Resources Institute

171	Afghanistan	11	Germany	5	Norway
76	Albania	134	Ghana	92	Oman
109	Algeria	25	Greece	132	Pakistan
155	Angola	78	Grenada	47	Panama
55	Antigua and Barbuda	108	Guatemala	129	Papua New Guinea
37	Argentina	173	Guinea	84	Paraguay
53	Armenia	164	Guinea-Bissau	95	Peru
7	Australia	107	Guyana	99	Philippines
12	Austria	137	Haiti	49	Poland
71	Azerbaijan	115	Honduras	42	Portugal
36	Bahamas	24	Hong Kong	56	Qatar
58	Bahrain	31	Hungary	72	Romania
146	Bangladesh	14	Iceland	34	Russian Federation
20	Barbados	135	India	153	Rwanda
40	Belarus	105	Indonesia	70	Saint Kitts and Nevis
13	Belgium	86	Iran, Islamic Rep. of	77	Saint Lucia
88	Belize	100	Iraq	69	Saint Vincent
156	Benin	21	Ireland	104	Samoa
162	Bhutan	19	Israel	128	São Tomé and Principe
113	Bolivia	22	Italy	67	Saudi Arabia
87	Botswana	65	Jamaica	143	Senegal
63	Brazil	3	Japan	83	Seychelles
44	Brunei Darussalam	98	Jordan	170	Sierra Leone
48	Bulgaria	61	Kazakhstan	43	Singapore
172	Burkina Faso	125	Kenya	126	Solomon Islands
152	Burundi	101	Korea, Dem. Rep. of	165	Somalia
147	Cambodia	32	Korea, Rep. of	93	South Africa
124	Cameroon	51	Kuwait	23	Spain
1	Canada	82	Kyrgyzstan	90	Sri Lanka
122	Cape Verde	133	Lao People's Dem. Rep.	151	Sudan
160	Central African Rep.	30	Latvia	85	Suriname
168	Chad	103	Lebanon	117	Swaziland
38	Chile	120	Lesotho	4	Sweden
94	China	144	Liberia	2	Switzerland
50	Colombia	79	Libyan Arab Jamahiriya	73	Syrian Arab Rep.
141	Comoros	28	Lithuania	97	Tajikistan
123	Congo	17	Luxembourg	148	Tanzania, U. Rep. of
39	Costa Rica	131	Madagascar	54	Thailand
136	Côte d'Ivoire	157	Malawi	145	Togo
89	Cuba	57	Malaysia	35	Trinidad and Tobago
26	Cyprus	118	Maldives	81	Tunisia
27	Czechoslovakia*	167	Mali	68	Turkey
15	Denmark	41	Malta	80	Turkmenistan
163	Djibouti	158	Mauritania	8	USA
64	Dominica	60	Mauritius	154	Uganda
96	Dominican Rep.	52	Mexico	45	Ukraine
74	Ecuador	75	Moldova, Rep. of	62	United Arab Emirates
110	Egypt	102	Mongolia	10	United Kingdom
112	El Salvador	111	Morocco	33	Uruguay
150	Equatorial Guinea	159	Mozambique	91	Uzbekistan
29	Estonia	130	Myanmar	119	Vanuatu
161	Ethiopia**	127	Namibia	46	Venezuela
59	Fiji	149	Nepal	116	Viet Nam
16	Finland	9	Netherlands	142	Yemen
6	France	18	New Zealand	140	Zaire
114	Gabon	106	Nicaragua	138	Zambia
166	Gambia	169	Niger	121	Zimbabwe
66	Georgia	139	Nigeria		

* Includes data for Czech Republic and Slovakia.
** Includes data for Eritrea.

In the human development indicators, the countries and areas are ranked in descending order of their human development index (HDI). Reference numbers indicating that rank are in the alphabetical list of countries provided here.

To help the reader use these tables, the indicators are indexed alphabetically in the key to indicators, with table locations and sources.

Official government data received by the responsible United Nations system agencies or other international organizations have been used whenever possible. For cases in which there are no reliable official figures, estimates by the responsible agency have been used if available. In some cases, UNDP has made its own estimates, based on field information or comparable country data. Only comprehensive or representative national data have been used. The data in the human development indicators, derived from so many sources, inevitably cover a wide range of data reliability.

Unless otherwise stated, the summary measures for the various human development, income and regional groups of countries are the appropriately weighted values for each group (see the lists following the indicators for the composition of each group). Where the summary measure is a total, the letter T appears after the figure. In the absence of the phrase "annual", "annual rate" or "growth rate", a hyphen between two years indicates that the data refer to a range of years, and a slash between two years indicates an average for that period. The following signs have been used:

.. Data not available
(.) Less than half the unit shown
T Total
Italicized figures are UNDP estimates.

Contents

TABLE 1   Human development index   129   **All countries**

TABLE 2   Profile of human development   132   **Developing countries**

- Life expectancy at birth
- Population with access to health services
- Population with access to safe water
- Population with access to sanitation
- Daily calorie supply as % of requirements
- Adult literacy rate
- Enrolment ratio for all levels
- Daily newspapers
- Televisions
- Real gross domestic product (GDP) per capita
- Gross national product (GNP) per capita

TABLE 3   Profile of human deprivation   134   **Developing countries**

- People in absolute poverty: total and rural
- Refugees
- Population without access to health services
- Population without access to safe water
- Population without access to sanitation
- Illiterate adults
- Illiterate females
- Children not in primary school
- Malnourished children under five
- Children dying before age five

TABLE 4   Trends in human development   136   **Developing countries**

- Life expectancy at birth
- Infant mortality rate
- Population with access to safe water
- Malnourished children, % underweight
- Adult literacy rate
- Enrolment ratio for all levels
- Real GDP per capita

TABLE 5   Human capital formation   138   **Developing countries**

- Adult literacy rate
- Literacy rate, age 15–19
- Mean years of schooling
- Scientists and technicians
- R & D scientists and technicians
- Tertiary graduates
- Science graduates

TABLE 6   Narrowing South-North gaps   140   **Developing countries**

- Life expectancy
- Adult literacy
- Daily calorie supply
- Access to safe water
- Under-five mortality

TABLE 7   Widening South-North gaps   142   **Developing countries**

- Real GDP per capita
- Mean years of schooling
- Overall enrolment
- Fertility
- Telephones

TABLE 8   Status of women   144   **Developing countries**

- Life expectancy at birth
- Average age at first marriage
- Literacy rate, age 15–24
- Enrolment ratios by level
- Tertiary science enrolment
- Administrators and managers
- Parliament

TABLE 18 Wealth, poverty and social investment 164 Developing countries

- Real GDP per capita
- GNP per capita
- Income share of lowest 40% of households
- Ratio of income of highest 20% of households to income of lowest 20%
- People in absolute poverty, total, rural and urban
- Social security benefits expenditure
- Public expenditure on education
- Public expenditure on health
- Total expenditure on health

TABLE 19 Aid flows 166 Developing countries

- Official development assistance (ODA) received
- ODA as % of GNP
- ODA per capita
- ODA per poor person
- Bilateral aid social allocation ratio
- Bilateral aid social priority ratio
- Bilateral aid human expenditure ratio
- Human priority aid as % of total

TABLE 20 Resource flow imbalances 168 Developing countries

- Total external debt
- Total external debt as % of GNP
- Debt service ratio
- Export-import ratio
- Trade dependency
- Terms of trade
- Workers' remittances from abroad
- Gross international reserves
- Current account balance

TABLE 21 Military expenditure and resource use imbalances 170 Developing countries

- Military expenditure as % of GDP
- Military expenditure as % of combined education and health expenditure
- Arms imports
- Arms imports as % of national imports
- Armed forces per 1,000 people
- Armed forces per teacher
- Armed forces per doctor

TABLE 22 Growing urbanization 172 Developing countries

- Urban population as % of total
- Urban population annual growth rate
- Population in cities of more than 1 million as % of urban population
- Population in largest city
- Population in cities of more than 1 million as % of total population
- Major city with highest population density

TABLE 23 Demographic profile 174 Developing countries

- Estimated population
- Annual population growth rate
- Population growth rates over time
- Population doubling date
- Crude birth rate
- Crude death rate
- Fertility rate
- Fertility rates over time
- Contraceptive prevalence rate

TABLE 24 Natural resources balance sheet 176 Developing countries

- Land area
- Population density
- Arable land
- Pesticide consumption
- Forest area
- Production of fuel wood
- Deforestation
- Internal renewable water resources
- Fresh water withdrawals as % of water resources
- Fresh water withdrawals per capita
- Irrigated land
- Global emissions share

TABLE 25 Energy consumption 178 Developing countries

- Total commercial energy consumption
- Commercial energy consumption per capita
- Energy imports
- Rate of change in commercial energy consumption
- Commercial energy efficiency

TABLE 26 National income accounts 180 Developing countries

- Total GDP
- Agricultural production
- Industrial production
- Services
- Private consumption
- Government consumption
- Gross domestic investment
- Gross domestic savings
- Tax revenue
- Central government expenditure
- Exports
- Imports

TABLE 35 Health profile 191 Industrial countries

- Years of life lost to premature death
- Deaths from circulatory system diseases
- Deaths from malignant cancers
- AIDS cases
- Alcohol consumption
- Tobacco consumption
- Population per doctor
- Health bills paid by public insurance
- Public expenditure on health
- Total health expenditure
- Private expenditure on health

TABLE 36 Education profile 192 Industrial countries

- Enrolment ratio for all levels
- Upper-secondary enrolment ratio
- Upper-secondary technical enrolment
- Nineteen-year-olds in full-time education
- Tertiary enrolment ratio
- Tertiary science enrolment
- Expenditure on tertiary education
- Public expenditure per tertiary student
- Total education expenditure
- Public expenditure on education

TABLE 37 Communication profile 193 Industrial countries

- Radios
- Televisions
- Cinema attendances
- Museum attendances
- Registered library users
- Daily newspapers
- Book titles published
- Printing and writing paper
- Letters posted
- Telephones
- International telephone calls
- Motor vehicles

TABLE 38 Employment 194 Industrial countries

- Labour force as % of total population
- Percentage of labour force in agriculture
- Percentage of labour force in industry
- Percentage of labour force in services
- Future labour force replacement ratio
- Earnings per employee annual growth rate
- Earnings disparity
- Percentage of labour force unionized
- Weekly hours of work
- Expenditure on labour market programmes

TABLE 39 Unemployment 195 Industrial countries

- Unemployed persons
- Total unemployment rate
- Total rate including discouraged workers
- Female unemployment rate
- Youth unemployment rate
- Male youth unemployment rate
- Unemployment benefits expenditure
- Incidence of long-term unemployment
- Regional unemployment disparity
- Unemployment by educational level

TABLE 40 Wealth, poverty and social investment 196 Industrial countries

- Real GDP per capita
- GNP per capita
- Share of industrial GNP
- Income share of lowest 40% of households
- Ratio of income of highest 20% of households to lowest 20%
- Social security benefits expenditure
- Education expenditure
- Health expenditure

TABLE 41 Aid flows 197 Industrial countries

- Official development assistance (ODA) disbursed
- ODA as % of GNP
- ODA as % of central government budget
- ODA per capita
- Bilateral aid social allocation ratio
- Bilateral aid social priority ratio
- Bilateral aid human expenditure ratio
- Bilateral aid for human priorities
- Aid to least developed countries
- Multilateral aid

TABLE 42 Resource flow imbalances 198 Industrial countries

- Export-import ratio
- Export growth rate as % of import growth rate
- Trade dependency
- Terms of trade
- Workers' remittances from abroad
- Public debt
- Government debt interest payments
- Gross international reserves
- Current account balance

HUMAN DEVELOPMENT INDICATORS

Human development index

HDI rank	Life expectancy at birth (years) 1992	Adult literacy rate (%) 1992	Mean years of schooling 1992	Literacy index	Schooling index	Educational attainment 1992	Real GDP per capita (PPP$) 1991	Adjusted real GDP per capita	Human development index 1992	GNP per capita rank minus HDI rank[a]
High human development	74.1	97.3	9.8				14,000		0.886	
1 Canada	77.2	99.0	12.2	0.99	0.82	2.80	19,320	5,347	0.932	10
2 Switzerland	77.8	99.0	11.6	0.99	0.77	2.75	21,780	5,370	0.931	-1
3 Japan	78.6	99.0	10.8	0.99	0.72	2.70	19,390	5,347	0.929	0
4 Sweden	77.7	99.0	11.4	0.99	0.76	2.74	17,490	5,342	0.928	0
5 Norway	76.9	99.0	12.1	0.99	0.80	2.78	17,170	5,341	0.928	0
6 France	76.6	99.0	12.0	0.99	0.80	2.78	18,430	5,345	0.927	7
7 Australia	76.7	99.0	12.0	0.99	0.80	2.78	16,680	5,339	0.926	11
8 USA	75.6	99.0	12.4	0.99	0.83	2.81	22,130	5,371	0.925	1
9 Netherlands	77.2	99.0	11.1	0.99	0.74	2.72	16,820	5,340	0.923	7
10 United Kingdom	75.8	99.0	11.7	0.99	0.78	2.76	16,340	5,337	0.919	9
11 Germany	75.6	99.0	11.6	0.99	0.77	2.75	19,770	5,347	0.918	1
12 Austria	75.7	99.0	11.4	0.99	0.76	2.74	17,690	5,343	0.917	2
13 Belgium	75.7	99.0	11.2	0.99	0.75	2.73	17,510	5,342	0.916	2
14 Iceland	78.1	99.0	9.2	0.99	0.61	2.59	17,480	5,342	0.914	-6
15 Denmark	75.3	99.0	11.0	0.99	0.73	2.71	17,880	5,343	0.912	-8
16 Finland	75.4	99.0	10.9	0.99	0.72	2.70	16,130	5,336	0.911	-10
17 Luxembourg	75.2	99.0	10.5	0.99	0.70	2.68	20,800	5,364	0.908	-15
18 New Zealand	75.3	99.0	10.7	0.99	0.71	2.69	13,970	5,310	0.907	6
19 Israel	76.2	95.0	10.2	0.95	0.68	2.58	13,460	5,307	0.900	6
20 Barbados	75.3	99.0	9.4	0.99	0.63	2.61	9,667	5,255	0.894	14
21 Ireland	75.0	99.0	8.9	0.99	0.60	2.58	11,430	5,295	0.892	6
22 Italy	76.9	97.4	7.5	0.97	0.50	2.45	17,040	5,340	0.891	-5
23 Spain	77.4	98.0	6.9	0.98	0.46	2.42	12,670	5,303	0.888	0
24 Hong Kong	77.4	90.0	7.2	0.90	0.48	2.28	18,520	5,345	0.875	-2
25 Greece	77.3	93.8	7.0	0.94	0.46	2.34	7,680	5,221	0.874	10
26 Cyprus	76.7	94.0	7.0	0.94	0.47	2.35	9,844	5,257	0.873	4
27 Czechoslovakia	72.1	99.0	9.2	0.99	0.62	2.60	6,570	5,196	0.872	29
28 Lithuania	72.6	98.4	9.0	0.98	0.60	2.57	5,410	5,154	0.868	35
29 Estonia	71.2	99.0	9.0	0.99	0.60	2.58	8,090	5,229	0.867	15
30 Latvia	71.0	99.0	9.0	0.99	0.60	2.58	7,540	5,218	0.865	15
31 Hungary	70.1	99.0	9.8	0.99	0.65	2.63	6,080	5,182	0.863	23
32 Korea, Rep. of	70.4	96.8	9.3	0.97	0.62	2.55	8,320	5,233	0.859	4
33 Uruguay	72.4	96.5	8.1	0.97	0.54	2.47	6,670	5,199	0.859	20
34 Russian Federation	70.0	98.7	9.0	0.99	0.60	2.57	6,930	5,205	0.858	15
35 Trinidad and Tobago	70.9	96.0	8.4	0.96	0.56	2.48	8,380	5,234	0.855	11
36 Bahamas	71.9	99.0	6.2	0.99	0.41	2.39	12,000	5,299	0.854	-10
37 Argentina	71.1	95.5	9.2	0.96	0.62	2.53	5,120	5,120	0.853	6
38 Chile	71.9	93.8	7.8	0.94	0.52	2.39	7,060	5,208	0.848	28
39 Costa Rica	76.0	93.2	5.7	0.93	0.38	2.24	5,100	5,100	0.848	36
40 Belarus	71.0	97.9	7.0	0.98	0.47	2.42	6,850	5,203	0.847	10
41 Malta	75.7	87.0	6.1	0.87	0.41	2.15	7,575	5,219	0.843	-9
42 Portugal	74.4	86.2	6.4	0.86	0.43	2.15	9,450	5,252	0.838	-5
43 Singapore	74.2	92.0	4.0	0.92	0.27	2.11	14,734	5,313	0.836	-22
44 Brunei Darussalam	74.0	86.0	5.0	0.86	0.33	2.05	14,000	5,310	0.829	-15
45 Ukraine	70.0	95.0	6.0	0.95	0.40	2.30	5,180	5,135	0.823	23
46 Venezuela	70.1	89.0	6.5	0.89	0.43	2.21	8,120	5,230	0.820	9
47 Panama	72.5	89.6	6.8	0.90	0.45	2.25	4,910	4,910	0.816	23
48 Bulgaria	71.9	94.0	7.0	0.93	0.47	2.33	4,813	4,813	0.815	28
49 Poland	71.5	99.0	8.2	0.99	0.54	2.52	4,500	4,500	0.815	30
50 Colombia	69.0	87.4	7.5	0.87	0.50	2.25	5,460	5,157	0.813	41
51 Kuwait	74.6	73.9	5.5	0.74	0.37	1.85	13,126	5,306	0.809	-23
52 Mexico	69.9	88.6	4.9	0.89	0.32	2.10	7,170	5,211	0.804	-1
53 Armenia	72.0	98.8	5.0	0.99	0.33	2.31	4,610	4,610	0.801	20
Medium human development	68.0	80.4	4.8				3,420		0.649	
54 Thailand	68.7	93.8	3.9	0.94	0.26	2.14	5,270	5,144	0.798	28
55 Antigua and Barbuda	74.0	96.0	4.6	0.96	0.31	2.23	4,500	4,500	0.796	-15
56 Qatar	69.6	79.0	5.8	0.79	0.39	1.97	14,000	5,310	0.795	-36
57 Malaysia	70.4	80.0	5.6	0.80	0.37	1.97	7,400	5,215	0.794	4
58 Bahrain	71.0	79.0	4.3	0.79	0.29	1.87	11,536	5,296	0.791	-25
59 Fiji	71.1	87.0	5.1	0.87	0.34	2.08	4,858	4,858	0.787	15
60 Mauritius	69.6	79.9	4.1	0.80	0.28	1.87	7,178	5,211	0.778	5
61 Kazakhstan	69.0	97.5	5.0	0.98	0.33	2.28	4,490	4,490	0.774	10
62 United Arab Emirates	70.8	65.0	5.6	0.65	0.37	1.67	17,000	5,340	0.771	-52
63 Brazil	65.8	82.1	4.0	0.82	0.27	1.91	5,240	5,142	0.756	-11
64 Dominica	72.0	97.0	4.7	0.97	0.31	2.25	3,900	3,900	0.749	-2
65 Jamaica	73.3	98.5	5.3	0.99	0.35	2.32	3,670	3,670	0.749	22
66 Georgia	73.0	99.0	5.0	0.99	0.33	2.31	3,670	3,670	0.747	14
67 Saudi Arabia	68.7	64.1	3.9	0.64	0.26	1.54	10,850	5,289	0.742	-36
68 Turkey	66.7	81.9	3.6	0.82	0.24	1.88	4,840	4,840	0.739	10

HDI rank	Life expectancy at birth (years) 1992	Adult literacy rate (%) 1992	Mean years of schooling 1992	Literacy index	Schooling index	Educational attainment 1992	Real GDP per capita (PPP$) 1991	Adjusted real GDP per capita	Human development index 1992	GNP per capita rank minus HDI rank[a]
69 Saint Vincent	71.0	98.0	4.6	0.98	0.31	2.27	3,700	3,700	0.732	8
70 Saint Kitts and Nevis	70.0	99.0	6.0	0.99	0.40	2.38	3,550	3,550	0.730	-23
71 Azerbaijan	71.0	96.3	5.0	0.96	0.33	2.26	3,670	3,670	0.730	21
72 Romania	69.9	96.9	7.1	0.97	0.47	2.41	3,500	3,500	0.729	17
73 Syrian Arab Rep.	66.4	66.6	4.2	0.67	0.28	1.61	5,220	5,140	0.727	21
74 Ecuador	66.2	87.4	5.6	0.87	0.37	2.12	4,140	4,140	0.718	28
75 Moldova, Rep. of	69.0	96.0	6.0	0.96	0.40	2.32	3,500	3,500	0.714	6
76 Albania	73.0	85.0	6.2	0.85	0.41	2.11	3,500	3,500	0.714	10
77 Saint Lucia	72.0	93.0	3.9	0.93	0.26	2.12	3,500	3,500	0.709	-20
78 Grenada	70.0	98.0	4.7	0.98	0.31	2.27	3,374	3,374	0.707	-11
79 Libyan Arab Jamahiriya	62.4	66.5	3.5	0.66	0.24	1.57	7,000	5,207	0.703	-38
80 Turkmenistan	66.0	97.7	5.0	0.98	0.33	2.29	3,540	3,540	0.697	8
81 Tunisia	67.1	68.1	2.1	0.68	0.14	1.50	4,690	4,690	0.690	4
82 Kyrgyzstan	68.0	97.0	5.0	0.97	0.33	2.27	3,280	3,280	0.689	13
83 Seychelles	71.0	77.0	4.6	0.77	0.31	1.85	3,683	3,683	0.685	-44
84 Paraguay	67.2	90.8	4.9	0.91	0.33	2.14	3,420	3,420	0.679	6
85 Suriname	69.9	95.6	4.2	0.96	0.28	2.19	3,072	3,072	0.677	-37
86 Iran, Islamic Rep. of	66.6	56.0	3.9	0.56	0.26	1.38	4,670	4,670	0.672	-22
87 Botswana	60.3	75.0	2.5	0.75	0.17	1.67	4,690	4,690	0.670	-29
88 Belize	68.0	96.0	4.6	0.96	0.31	2.23	3,000	3,000	0.666	-19
89 Cuba	75.6	94.5	8.0	0.95	0.53	2.42	2,000	2,000	0.666	21
90 Sri Lanka	71.2	89.1	7.2	0.89	0.48	2.26	2,650	2,650	0.665	38
91 Uzbekistan	69.0	97.2	5.0	0.97	0.33	2.28	2,790	2,790	0.664	13
92 Oman	69.1	35.0	0.9	0.35	0.06	0.76	9,230	5,248	0.654	-54
93 South Africa	62.2	80.0	3.9	0.80	0.26	1.86	3,885	3,885	0.650	-33
94 China	70.5	80.0	5.0	0.80	0.33	1.93	2,946	2,946	0.644	49
95 Peru	63.6	86.2	6.5	0.86	0.44	2.16	3,110	3,110	0.642	3
96 Dominican Rep.	67.0	84.3	4.3	0.84	0.29	1.97	3,080	3,080	0.638	11
97 Tajikistan	70.0	96.7	5.0	0.97	0.33	2.27	2,180	2,180	0.629	19
98 Jordan	67.3	82.1	5.0	0.82	0.33	1.98	2,895	2,895	0.628	1
99 Philippines	64.6	90.4	7.6	0.90	0.51	2.31	2,440	2,440	0.621	14
100 Iraq	65.7	62.5	5.0	0.62	0.33	1.58	3,500	3,500	0.614	-41
101 Korea, Dem. Rep. of	70.7	95.0	6.0	0.95	0.40	2.30	1,750	1,750	0.609	8
102 Mongolia	63.0	95.0	7.2	0.95	0.48	2.38	2,250	2,250	0.607	1
103 Lebanon	68.1	81.3	4.4	0.81	0.29	1.92	2,500	2,500	0.600	-20
104 Samoa	66.0	98.0	5.8	0.98	0.39	2.35	1,869	1,869	0.596	1
105 Indonesia	62.0	84.4	4.1	0.84	0.27	1.96	2,730	2,730	0.586	16
106 Nicaragua	65.4	78.0	4.5	0.78	0.30	1.86	2,550	2,550	0.583	33
107 Guyana	64.6	96.8	5.1	0.97	0.34	2.28	1,862	1,862	0.580	44
108 Guatemala	64.0	56.4	4.1	0.56	0.27	1.40	3,180	3,180	0.564	-2
109 Algeria	65.6	60.6	2.8	0.61	0.19	1.40	2,870	2,870	0.553	-37
110 Egypt	60.9	50.0	3.0	0.50	0.20	1.20	3,600	3,600	0.551	12
111 Morocco	62.5	52.5	3.0	0.52	0.20	1.25	3,340	3,340	0.549	-10
112 El Salvador	65.2	74.6	4.2	0.75	0.28	1.77	2,110	2,110	0.543	-15
113 Bolivia	60.5	79.3	4.0	0.79	0.27	1.85	2,170	2,170	0.530	6
114 Gabon	52.9	62.5	2.6	0.63	0.17	1.42	3,498	3,498	0.525	-72
115 Honduras	65.2	74.9	4.0	0.75	0.27	1.77	1,820	1,820	0.524	8
116 Viet Nam	63.4	88.6	4.9	0.89	0.33	2.10	1,250	1,250	0.514	34
117 Swaziland	57.3	71.0	3.8	0.71	0.25	1.67	2,506	2,506	0.513	-21
118 Maldives	62.6	92.0	4.5	0.92	0.30	2.14	1,200	1,200	0.511	14
Low human development	55.8	47.4	2.0				1,170		0.355	
119 Vanuatu	65.0	65.0	3.7	0.65	0.25	1.55	1,679	1,679	0.489	-26
120 Lesotho	59.8	78.0	3.5	0.78	0.23	1.79	1,500	1,500	0.476	4
121 Zimbabwe	56.1	68.6	3.1	0.69	0.21	1.58	2,160	2,160	0.474	-3
122 Cape Verde	67.3	66.5	2.2	0.67	0.15	1.48	1,360	1,360	0.474	-10
123 Congo	51.7	58.5	2.1	0.59	0.14	1.31	2,800	2,800	0.461	-23
124 Cameroon	55.3	56.5	1.6	0.57	0.11	1.24	2,400	2,400	0.447	-13
125 Kenya	58.6	70.5	2.3	0.71	0.15	1.56	1,350	1,350	0.434	21
126 Solomon Islands	70.0	24.0	1.0	0.24	0.07	0.55	2,113	2,113	0.434	-11
127 Namibia	58.0	40.0	1.7	0.40	0.11	0.91	2,381	2,381	0.425	-43
128 São Tomé and Principe	67.0	60.0	2.3	0.60	0.15	1.35	600	600	0.409	10
129 Papua New Guinea	55.3	65.3	1.0	0.65	0.07	1.37	1,550	1,550	0.408	-21
130 Myanmar	56.9	81.5	2.5	0.82	0.17	1.80	650	650	0.406	19
131 Madagascar	54.9	81.4	2.2	0.81	0.14	1.77	710	710	0.396	31
132 Pakistan	58.3	36.4	1.9	0.36	0.12	0.85	1,970	1,970	0.393	8
133 Lao People's Dem. Rep.	50.3	55.0	2.9	0.55	0.20	1.30	1,760	1,760	0.385	24
134 Ghana	55.4	63.1	3.5	0.63	0.24	1.50	930	930	0.382	-1
135 India	59.7	49.8	2.4	0.50	0.16	1.16	1,150	1,150	0.382	12
136 Côte d'Ivoire	51.6	55.8	1.9	0.56	0.13	1.24	1,510	1,510	0.370	-19
137 Haiti	56.0	55.0	1.7	0.55	0.11	1.21	925	925	0.354	4
138 Zambia	45.5	74.8	2.7	0.75	0.18	1.68	1,010	1,010	0.352	-4

HDI rank	Life expectancy at birth (years) 1992	Adult literacy rate (%) 1992	Mean years of schooling 1992	Literacy index	Schooling index	Educational attainment 1992	Real GDP per capita (PPP$) 1991	Adjusted real GDP per capita	Human development index 1992	GNP per capita rank minus HDI rank[a]
139 Nigeria	51.9	52.0	1.2	0.52	0.08	1.12	1,360	1,360	0.348	6
140 Zaire	51.6	74.0	1.6	0.74	0.11	1.59	469	469	0.341	20
141 Comoros	55.4	55.0	1.0	0.55	0.07	1.17	700	700	0.331	-10
142 Yemen	51.9	41.1	0.9	0.41	0.06	0.88	1,374	1,374	0.323	-16
143 Senegal	48.7	40.0	0.9	0.40	0.06	0.86	1,680	1,680	0.322	-29
144 Liberia	54.7	42.5	2.1	0.42	0.14	0.99	850	850	0.317	-14
145 Togo	54.4	45.5	1.6	0.45	0.11	1.02	738	738	0.311	-9
146 Bangladesh	52.2	36.6	2.0	0.37	0.13	0.87	1,160	1,160	0.309	13
147 Cambodia	50.4	37.8	2.0	0.38	0.13	0.89	1,250	1,250	0.307	17
148 Tanzania, U. Rep. of	51.2	55.0	2.0	0.55	0.14	1.24	570	570	0.306	22
149 Nepal	52.7	27.0	2.1	0.27	0.14	0.68	1,130	1,130	0.289	17
150 Equatorial Guinea	47.3	51.5	0.8	0.52	0.05	1.08	700	700	0.276	4
151 Sudan	51.2	28.2	0.8	0.28	0.05	0.62	1,162	1,162	0.276	-14
152 Burundi	48.2	52.0	0.4	0.52	0.03	1.07	640	640	0.276	6
153 Rwanda	46.5	52.1	1.1	0.52	0.07	1.11	680	680	0.274	-1
154 Uganda	42.6	50.5	1.1	0.51	0.07	1.08	1,036	1,036	0.272	14
155 Angola	45.6	42.5	1.5	0.43	0.10	0.95	1,000	1,000	0.271	-35
156 Benin	46.1	25.0	0.7	0.25	0.05	0.55	1,500	1,500	0.261	-14
157 Malawi	44.6	45.0	1.7	0.45	0.12	1.02	800	800	0.260	-1
158 Mauritania	47.4	35.0	0.4	0.35	0.03	0.73	962	962	0.254	-31
159 Mozambique	46.5	33.5	1.6	0.34	0.11	0.78	921	921	0.252	14
160 Central African Rep.	47.2	40.2	1.1	0.40	0.07	0.88	641	641	0.249	-25
161 Ethiopia	46.4	50.0	1.1	0.50	0.07	1.07	370	370	0.249	10
162 Bhutan	47.8	40.9	0.3	0.41	0.02	0.84	620	620	0.247	3
163 Djibouti	48.3	19.0	0.4	0.19	0.03	0.41	1,000	1,000	0.226	-38
164 Guinea-Bissau	42.9	39.0	0.4	0.39	0.03	0.81	747	747	0.224	3
165 Somalia	46.4	27.0	0.3	0.27	0.02	0.56	759	759	0.217	7
166 Gambia	44.4	30.0	0.6	0.30	0.04	0.64	763	763	0.215	-22
167 Mali	45.4	35.9	0.4	0.36	0.03	0.74	480	480	0.214	-12
168 Chad	46.9	32.5	0.3	0.33	0.02	0.67	447	447	0.212	-7
169 Niger	45.9	31.2	0.2	0.31	0.01	0.64	542	542	0.209	-21
170 Sierra Leone	42.4	23.7	0.9	0.24	0.06	0.53	1,020	1,020	0.209	-7
171 Afghanistan	42.9	31.6	0.9	0.32	0.06	0.69	700	700	0.208	-2
172 Burkina Faso	47.9	19.9	0.2	0.20	0.01	0.41	666	666	0.203	-19
173 Guinea	43.9	26.9	0.9	0.27	0.06	0.60	500	500	0.191	-44

a. A positive figure shows that the HDI rank is better than the GNP per capita rank, a negative the opposite.

Note: Figures in italics are UNDP estimates.

2 Profile of human development

HDI rank		Life expectancy at birth (years) 1992	Population with access to			Daily calorie supply (as % of requirements) 1988-90	Adult literacy rate (%) 1992	Enrolment ratio for all levels (% age 6-23) 1990	Daily newspapers (copies per 100 people) 1990	Tele-visions (per 100 people) 1990	Real GDP per capita (PPP$) 1991	GNP per capita (US$) 1991
			Health services (%) 1985-91	Safe water (%) 1988-91	Sanitation (%) 1988-91							
High human development		70.5	95	86	76	122	92	66	27.8	17.7	7,290	3,830
20	Barbados	75.3	100	100	100	128	..	67	11.7	26.5	9,667	6,650
24	Hong Kong	77.4	99	100	88	129	..	69	64.8	28.0	18,520	13,580
26	Cyprus	76.7	95	100	100	..	..	..	11.0	15.0	9,844	8,670
32	Korea, Rep. of	70.4	100	92	100	123	97	74	27.7	20.7	8,320	6,350
33	Uruguay	72.4	90	85	..	96	..	73	23.3	23.3	6,670	2,880
35	Trinidad and Tobago	70.9	99	97	99	120	..	66	7.7	31.3	8,380	3,790
36	Bahamas	71.9	100	100	100	..	..	74	13.7	22.4	..	11,790
37	Argentina	71.1	..	..	89	130	96	82	12.4	22.2	5,120	3,790
38	Chile	71.9	97	88	88	104	94	66	45.5	20.5	7,060	2,360
39	Costa Rica	76.0	97	92	97	120	93	56	8.1	14.8	5,100	1,870
43	Singapore	74.2	100	100	96	144	..	68	28.2	37.8	14,734	14,140
44	Brunei Darussalam	74.0	96	95	95	..	..	67	3.9	24.1	..	..
46	Venezuela	70.1	..	90	94	100	89	63	14.5	17.1	8,120	2,720
47	Panama	72.5	80	84	92	100	90	62	7.0	16.5	4,910	2,130
50	Colombia	69.0	100	93	63	104	87	55	6.2	11.8	5,460	1,250
51	Kuwait	74.6	100	100	98	130	74	..	21.0	27.1	13,126	..
52	Mexico	69.9	90	77	55	132	89	62	13.3	14.6	7,170	3,080
Medium human development		68.0	88	77	80	109	80	50	4.6	6.6	3,420	970
Excluding China		65.4	85	70	59	107	79	58	6.0	10.7	4,000	1,680
54	Thailand	68.7	70	76	74	100	94	45	7.3	11.4	5,270	1,650
55	Antigua and Barbuda	74.0	100	100	100	..	..	..	7.9	30.3	..	4,720
56	Qatar	69.6	100	89	97	..	..	78	18.7	44.5	..	15,040
57	Malaysia	70.4	90	72	94	124	80	58	14.0	14.8	7,400	2,520
58	Bahrain	71.0	100	100	100	..	79	75	5.7	41.4	11,536	7,150
59	Fiji	71.1	100	79	75	108	..	70	3.7	..	4,858	1,920
60	Mauritius	69.6	100	100	98	129	80	57	7.4	21.7	7,178	2,380
62	United Arab Emirates	70.8	100	100	94	151	..	73	15.7	11.0	17,000	22,180
63	Brazil	65.8	..	86	78	114	82	60	5.4	21.5	5,240	2,920
64	Dominica	72.0	100	96	99	100	..	..	..	6.1	..	2,440
65	Jamaica	73.3	90	100	90	115	99	62	6.4	13.2	3,670	1,490
67	Saudi Arabia	68.7	98	93	82	120	64	50	4.0	26.9	10,850	7,900
68	Turkey	66.7	..	92	..	124	82	52	7.1	17.4	4,840	1,790
69	Saint Vincent	71.0	80	89	100	99	..	..	..	12.9	..	1,840
70	Saint Kitts and Nevis	70.0	100	100	98	..	..	..	..	20.5	..	3,780
73	Syrian Arab Rep.	66.4	99	73	83	126	67	66	2.3	6.0	5,220	1,170
74	Ecuador	66.2	88	54	48	106	87	68	8.7	8.3	4,140	1,010
77	Saint Lucia	72.0	100	..	..	102	..	..	..	16.7	..	2,700
78	Grenada	70.0	..	..	..	..	..	..	..	35.3	3,374	2,300
79	Libya	62.4	100	93	95	140	66	..	1.5	9.9	..	..
81	Tunisia	67.1	91	99	96	137	68	62	3.7	8.1	4,690	1,500
83	Seychelles	71.0	99	99	65	100	..	..	4.6	8.7	3,683	5,070
84	Paraguay	67.2	..	36	60	115	91	52	3.9	5.8	3,420	1,270
85	Suriname	69.9	91	89	52	..	96	69	9.5	13.0	3,072	3,650
86	Iran, Islamic Rep. of	66.6	87	61	51	134	56	61	2.6	6.5	4,670	2,410
87	Botswana	60.3	89	60	42	100	75	64	1.5	1.6	4,690	2,580
88	Belize	68.0	95	75	48	114	..	..	..	16.6	..	2,180
89	Cuba	75.6	100	98	92	137	95	63	12.4	20.7	..	..
90	Sri Lanka	71.2	90	71	60	99	89	68	3.2	3.5	2,650	500
92	Oman	69.1	87	79	44	..	..	61	4.0	75.5	9,230	6,140
93	South Africa	62.2	..	..	..	128	..	..	3.5	9.7	3,885	2,540
94	China	70.5	90	83	97	112	80	43	4.2	3.0	2,946	370
95	Peru	63.6	95	56	59	89	86	74	7.9	9.7	3,110	1,070
96	Dominican Rep.	67.0	100	67	60	100	84	66	3.2	8.4	3,080	940
98	Jordan	67.3	97	99	76	111	82	73	5.6	8.1	2,895	1,060
99	Philippines	64.6	75	82	69	108	90	64	5.4	4.8	2,440	740
100	Iraq	65.7	99	91	70	133	62	62	3.6	7.2	..	..
101	Korea, Dem. Rep. of	70.7	100	..	..	123	..	..	23.0	1.5	..	..
102	Mongolia	63.0	100	79	73	97	..	56	7.4	4.1	..	..
103	Lebanon	68.1	95	98	81	129	81	65	11.7	32.5	..	..
104	Samoa	66.0	100	83	94	..	..	..	..	3.7	1,869	960
105	Indonesia	62.0	80	51	44	122	84	58	2.8	6.0	2,730	610
106	Nicaragua	65.4	..	54	52	100	..	53	6.8	6.5	2,550	400
107	Guyana	64.6	96	64	90	108	97	65	10.1	3.8	1,862	300
108	Guatemala	64.0	50	60	60	101	56	41	2.1	5.2	3,180	940
109	Algeria	65.6	90	70	60	118	61	60	5.1	7.4	2,870	1,990
110	Egypt	60.9	99	88	51	133	50	66	5.7	10.9	3,600	610
111	Morocco	62.5	63	73	57	131	52	37	1.3	7.4	3,340	1,030
112	El Salvador	65.2	60	47	58	102	75	51	8.8	9.2	2,110	1,090
113	Bolivia	60.5	63	52	35	83	79	55	5.6	10.5	2,170	650

| HDI rank | Life expectancy at birth (years) 1992 | Population with access to | | | Daily calorie supply (as % of requirements) 1988-90 | Adult literacy rate (%) 1992 | Enrolment ratio for all levels (% age 6-23) 1990 | Daily newspapers (copies per 100 people) 1990 | Tele-visions (per 100 people) 1990 | Real GDP per capita (PPP$) 1991 | GNP per capita (US$) 1991 |
		Health services (%) 1985-91	Safe water (%) 1988-91	Sanitation (%) 1988-91							
114 Gabon	52.9	90	68	..	107	62	..	1.7	3.7	3,498	3,980
115 Honduras	65.2	66	78	67	91	75	50	3.9	7.2	1,820	590
116 Viet Nam	63.4	90	27	18	102	89	52	0.9	3.9	..	..
117 Swaziland	57.3	55	35	40	105	..	64	1.3	2.1	2,506	1,130
118 Maldives	62.6	75	51	28	80	..	..	0.8	2.5	..	470
Low human development	55.8	..	..	22	99	49	42	2.1	2.4	1,170	330
Excluding India	51.9	62	45	30	93	47	33	1.0	1.5	1,200	320
119 Vanuatu	65.0	82	74	46	..	..	58	2.0	..	1,679	1,180
120 Lesotho	59.8	80	48	25	93	..	58	1.1	0.6	..	570
121 Zimbabwe	56.1	83	36	42	94	69	66	2.1	3.0	2,160	670
122 Cape Verde	67.3	..	72	17	125	67	49	1.0	..	1,360	750
123 Congo	51.7	..	21	..	107	59	..	0.8	0.6	2,800	1,040
124 Cameroon	55.3	41	54	78	93	57	52	0.7	2.3	2,400	860
125 Kenya	58.6	77	50	43	86	71	58	1.5	1.0	1,350	340
126 Solomon Islands	70.0	80	60	..	84	..	..	..	..	2,113	700
127 Namibia	58.0	70	52	15	..	..	..	15.3	2.1	2,381	1,520
128 São Tomé and Principe	67.0	..	..	..	103	..	..	2.0	..	..	400
129 Papua New Guinea	55.3	97	32	56	116	65	30	1.3	..	1,550	930
130 Myanmar	56.9	48	31	36	116	82	39	0.5	0.2	..	210
131 Madagascar	54.9	65	20	5	93	81	40	0.4	2.0	710	210
132 Pakistan	58.3	90	56	24	101	36	24	1.5	1.8	1,970	400
133 Lao People's Dem. Rep.	50.3	67	37	24	111	..	42	0.3	0.7	1,760	220
134 Ghana	55.4	60	54	42	91	63	46	1.3	1.5	930	420
135 India	59.7	..	..	15	105	50	50	3.2	3.2	1,150	330
136 Côte d'Ivoire	51.6	45	70	35	122	56	37	0.8	6.1	1,510	680
137 Haiti	56.0	50	39	27	94	55	..	0.7	0.5	925	380
138 Zambia	45.5	74	48	43	87	75	47	1.2	3.1	1,010	420
139 Nigeria	51.9	72	50	15	93	52	37	1.6	3.2	1,360	350
140 Zaire	51.6	40	33	25	97	74	38	..	0.1	469	..
141 Comoros	55.4	82	75	83	90	..	34	..	(.)	..	490
142 Yemen	51.9	30	..	68	93	41	43	1.1	2.9	1,374	520
143 Senegal	48.7	40	47	54	95	40	30	0.7	3.6	1,680	730
144 Liberia	54.7	39	54	15	97	42	..	1.4	1.8	..	..
145 Togo	54.4	60	59	21	99	45	54	0.3	0.6	738	410
146 Bangladesh	52.2	60	..	32	94	37	32	0.6	0.5	1,160	220
147 Cambodia	50.4	53	37	15	96	38	..	..	0.8	1,250	200
148 Tanzania, U. Rep. of	51.2	80	51	66	91	..	32	0.8	0.2	570	120
149 Nepal	52.7	..	42	8	103	27	41	0.8	0.2	1,130	180
150 Equatorial Guinea	47.3	..	32	37	..	52	64	0.6	0.9	..	290
151 Sudan	51.2	60	45	70	83	28	27	2.4	7.1	1,162	..
152 Burundi	48.2	80	56	48	85	52	30	0.4	0.1	640	220
153 Rwanda	46.5	80	66	58	80	52	39	(.)	..	680	290
154 Uganda	42.6	70	15	31	83	51	41	0.2	1.0	1,036	170
155 Angola	45.6	30	34	18	80	43	32	1.3	0.6	..	380
156 Benin	46.1	30	54	42	101	25	30	0.5	0.5	1,500	380
157 Malawi	44.6	80	53	..	87	..	38	0.3	..	800	230
158 Mauritania	47.4	40	70	23	109	35	25	0.1	2.3	962	510
159 Mozambique	46.5	39	24	24	77	34	24	0.6	0.3	921	80
160 Central African Rep.	47.2	30	12	21	77	40	35	0.1	0.4	641	410
161 Ethiopia	46.4	46	28	16	71	..	17	0.1	0.2	370	120
162 Bhutan	47.8	70	31	9	..	41	11	..	..	620	190
163 Djibouti	48.3	99	86	59	..	..	24	2.0	5.2	..	..
164 Guinea-Bissau	42.9	80	39	25	97	39	25	0.6	..	747	180
165 Somalia	46.4	27	60	17	81	27	..	..	1.2	759	..
166 Gambia	44.4	90	77	44	103	30	29	0.2	..	763	360
167 Mali	45.4	35	41	23	107	36	..	0.1	0.1	480	270
168 Chad	46.9	30	..	..	69	33	29	(.)	0.1	447	210
169 Niger	45.9	30	55	10	98	31	14	0.1	0.5	542	310
170 Sierra Leone	42.4	37	50	62	86	24	29	0.2	1.0	1,020	200
171 Afghanistan	42.9	48	21	..	76	32	13	1.1	0.8	..	..
172 Burkina Faso	47.9	60	71	12	95	20	17	(.)	0.5	666	290
173 Guinea	43.9	40	64	24	100	27	19	..	0.7	500	500
All developing countries	63.0	81	70	56	109	69	46	4.4	5.5	2,730	880
Least developed countries	50.1	54	45	32	91	46	31	0.6	0.9	880	240
Sub-Saharan Africa	51.1	59	45	31	92	51	35	1.2	2.5	1,250	540
Industrial countries	74.5	..	..	..	..	..	79	30.3	54.4	14,860	14,920
World	65.6	..	..	..	..	..	49	9.2	14.7	5,490	4,160

Note: Data for industrial countries for this subject area are in table 28.

3 Profile of human deprivation

		People in absolute poverty		Refugees (thousands)	Without access to health services	Without access to safe water	Without access to sanitation	Illiterate adults (15+)	Illiterate females (15+)	Children not in primary school (thousands)	Mal-nourished children under five (thousands)	Children dying before age five (thousands)
		Total 1992	Rural 1992	1992	1992	1992	1992	1992	1992	1992	1992	1992
HDI rank												
High human development		..	..	..	..	..	..	..	..	..	..	..
20	Barbados	(.)	(.)	..	..	..	..	..	..	3	..	..
24	Hong Kong	..	..	45	0.1	(.)	0.7	..	..	..	..	1
26	Cyprus	..	(.)	..	(.)	..	..	..	..	..	5	0
32	Korea, Rep. of	2.1	0.5	(.)	..	3.5	..	1.0	0.8	..	..	16
33	Uruguay	0.4	0.1	(.)	0.3	0.5	..	0.2	(.)	35	25	1
35	Trinidad and Tobago	..	0.2	..	(.)	(.)	(.)	..	..	20	14	1
36	Bahamas	..	..	..	..	..	..	..	..	..	..	..
37	Argentina	5.2	0.9	12	..	..	3.5	1.0	..	..	39	22
38	Chile	..	0.5	(.)	0.4	1.6	1.6	0.6	0.3	285	30	6
39	Costa Rica	0.9	0.6	114	0.1	0.3	0.1	0.1	0.1	56	33	1
43	Singapore	..	..	(.)	..	..	0.1	..	..	..	..	0
44	Brunei Darussalam	..	..	..	(.)	(.)	(.)	..	..	4	..	0
46	Venezuela	6.3	1.1	2	..	2.0	1.1	1.3	0.5	461	148	21
47	Panama	1.1	0.8	1	0.5	0.4	0.2	0.2	0.1	30	33	2
50	Colombia	14.0	4.4	1	..	2.5	12.2	2.6	1.4	1,010	387	31
51	Kuwait	..	..	125	..	..	(.)	0.4	0.2	..	15	1
52	Mexico	26.4	11.7	361	8.8	20.1	39.8	6.0	3.8	..	1,585	105
Medium human development		..	..	..	..	..	..	..	..	..	..	..
Excluding China		..	..	..	..	..	..	..	..	..	..	..
54	Thailand	16.8	14.7	64	16.8	13.5	14.7	2.3	1.6	..	726	41
55	Antigua and Barbuda	..	(.)	..	..	..	..	..	..	..	..	..
56	Qatar	..	..	..	..	0.1	(.)	..	..	3	..	0
57	Malaysia	3.0	2.3	10	1.9	5.3	1.1	2.2	1.6	..	459	10
58	Bahrain	..	..	..	..	..	..	0.1	(.)	65	..	0
59	Fiji	..	0.1	..	..	0.2	0.2	..	..	..	..	1
60	Mauritius	0.1	0.1	..	..	..	(.)	0.2	0.1	..	17	1
62	United Arab Emirates	..	..	..	..	..	0.1	..	..	..	12	1
63	Brazil	72.4	25.9	5	..	21.4	33.5	17.4	9.3	3,215	1,250	278
64	Dominica	..	(.)	..	..	(.)	(.)	..	..	..	..	..
65	Jamaica	..	0.9	..	0.2	..	0.2	(.)	(.)	..	20	1
67	Saudi Arabia	..	..	29	0.4	1.1	2.9	3.0	1.7	952	309	24
68	Turkey	..	2.9	29	..	4.7	..	6.5	5.0	..	768	122
69	Saint Vincent	..	(.)	..	(.)	(.)	..	..	..	..	..	..
70	Saint Kitts and Nevis	..	..	..	..	..	(.)	..	..	..	..	..
73	Syrian Arab Rep.	..	3.5	6	0.1	3.6	2.3	2.1	1.5	22	294	30
74	Ecuador	6.2	3.0	(.)	1.3	5.0	5.7	0.8	0.5	..	193	25
77	Saint Lucia	..	..	..	..	..	..	..	..	..	..	..
78	Grenada	..	..	..	..	..	..	..	..	..	..	0
79	Libya	..	..	..	..	0.3	0.2	0.8	0.5	..	33	21
81	Tunisia	1.4	0.5	(.)	0.8	0.1	0.3	1.6	1.0	48	92	12
83	Seychelles	..	..	..	(.)	(.)	(.)	..	..	..	..	..
84	Paraguay	1.6	1.2	..	..	2.9	1.8	0.2	0.1	33	28	8
85	Suriname	..	0.1	(.)	(.)	(.)	0.2	(.)	(.)	..	..	0
86	Iran, Islamic Rep. of	..	7.8	4,150	8.3	23.8	30.0	13.9	8.6	200	4,145	120
87	Botswana	0.6	0.5	1	0.1	0.5	0.8	0.2	0.1	9	57	4
88	Belize	..	0.1	20	(.)	0.1	0.1	..	..	..	..	..
89	Cuba	..	0.9	5	..	0.2	0.9	0.4	0.3	66	75	3
90	Sri Lanka	7.0	6.3	..	1.8	5.1	7.2	1.3	0.9	..	762	11
92	Oman	..	0.1	..	0.2	0.3	0.9	..	..	50	..	3
93	South Africa	..	..	..	..	..	..	..	..	..	..	85
94	China	105.0	105.0	288	120.0	205.0	40.1	167.5	130.5	2,375	24,315	866
95	Peru	7.2	4.9	1	1.1	10.0	9.2	1.9	1.3	159	373	65
96	Dominican Rep.	4.1	2.0	1	..	2.5	3.0	0.7	0.4	..	118	16
98	Jordan	0.7	0.2	(.)	0.1	(.)	1.0	0.4	0.3	60	87	8
99	Philippines	35.2	23.4	7	16.3	11.9	20.0	3.6	1.8	..	3,045	108
100	Iraq	..	1.6	95	0.2	1.7	5.8	3.8	2.4	180	373	61
101	Korea, Dem. Rep. of	..	1.9	..	..	..	..	..	..	..	..	15
102	Mongolia	..	..	..	..	0.5	0.6	..	..	..	..	6
103	Lebanon	..	0.1	6	0.1	0.1	0.6	0.3	0.2	..	31	3
104	Samoa	..	0.1	..	..	(.)	(.)	..	..	..	..	..
105	Indonesia	47.8	35.9	16	38.2	94.2	106.7	18.5	13.7	516	8,660	484
106	Nicaragua	0.8	0.3	15	..	1.8	1.9	..	..	155	128	12
107	Guyana	..	0.3	..	(.)	0.3	0.1	(.)	(.)	..	17	1
108	Guatemala	6.9	4.3	225	4.9	3.9	3.9	2.2	1.3	735	402	28
109	Algeria	5.9	3.1	220	2.6	7.9	10.5	5.5	3.7	534	470	60
110	Egypt	12.6	7.7	6	0.3	6.3	27.0	15.9	10.2	..	759	139
111	Morocco	9.7	6.3	(.)	9.8	7.0	11.3	7.1	4.5	1,645	453	81
112	El Salvador	2.8	2.2	20	2.2	2.8	2.3	0.7	0.5	379	153	11
113	Bolivia	4.5	3.1	1	2.8	3.6	4.9	0.9	0.6	286	125	32

		People in absolute poverty		Refugees	Without access to health services	Without access to safe water	Without access to sanitation	Illiterate adults	Illiterate females	Children not in primary school	Mal-nourished children under five	Children dying before age five
		Total	Rural	(thousands)				(15+)	(15+)	(thousands)	(thousands)	(thousands)
HDI rank		1992	1992	1992	1992	1992	1992	1992	1992	1992	1992	1992
114	Gabon	..	0.3	(.)	0.1	0.4	..	0.3	0.2	60	26	6
115	Honduras	2.0	1.7	100	1.9	1.2	1.8	0.7	0.4	61	173	16
116	Viet Nam	37.6	33.4	16	7.0	51.1	57.4	4.7	3.5	..	3,860	101
117	Swaziland	0.4	0.3	56	0.4	0.5	0.5	..	..	23	11	3
118	Maldives	..	0.1	..	0.1	0.1	0.2	..	..	..	..	1
Low human development		..	..	..	..	..	..	..	..	..	..	..
Excluding India		..	..	..	..	..	..	..	..	..	..	..
119	Vanuatu	..	..	..	(.)	(.)	0.1	..	..	..	..	..
120	Lesotho	1.0	0.8	(.)	0.4	1.0	1.4	..	..	102	48	7
121	Zimbabwe	..	4.4	135	1.8	6.8	6.1	1.7	1.1	..	252	35
122	Cape Verde	..	0.1	..	..	0.1	0.3	0.1	..	3	..	1
123	Congo	..	1.1	10	..	1.9	..	0.5	0.3	..	113	14
124	Cameroon	4.5	2.8	42	7.2	5.6	2.6	2.8	1.8	466	335	57
125	Kenya	13.2	10.4	400	5.8	12.7	14.5	3.5	2.4	..	782	90
126	Solomon Islands	..	0.2	..	0.1	0.1	..	..	..	..	..	..
127	Namibia	..	..	(.)	0.5	0.7	1.3	..	..	50	75	7
128	São Tomé and Principe	..	(.)	..	..	..	..	..	..	..	..	..
129	Papua New Guinea	3.0	2.6	7	0.1	2.8	1.8	0.8	0.6	165	210	10
130	Myanmar	15.3	13.1	..	22.7	30.2	28.0	4.8	3.6	..	1,985	154
131	Madagascar	5.6	4.8	..	4.5	10.3	12.2	1.2	0.9	613	834	91
132	Pakistan	35.0	24.3	1,630	12.9	55.0	94.9	42.3	24.7	..	3,725	652
133	Lao People's Dem. Rep.	..	3.0	..	1.5	2.8	3.4	..	..	183	255	28
134	Ghana	6.7	5.6	12	6.4	7.4	9.2	3.0	1.9	..	733	84
135	India	350.0	270.0	260	..	..	750.0	271.8	169.3	..	69,345	3,505
136	Côte d'Ivoire	..	..	175	7.1	3.9	8.4	2.7	1.8	963	297	78
137	Haiti	5.1	3.8	..	3.4	4.1	5.0	1.7	1.0	70	241	29
138	Zambia	5.5	4.0	140	2.2	4.4	5.0	1.1	0.7	301	419	58
139	Nigeria	46.4	37.2	5	32.5	58.0	98.5	27.4	17.2	..	7,480	791
140	Zaire	28.0	25.5	390	24.0	26.7	30.2	5.1	3.8	722	2,425	260
141	Comoros	..	0.2	..	0.1	0.1	0.1	..	..	..	..	4
142	Yemen	..	2.6	60	8.8	..	4.1	3.5	2.2	..	645	103
143	Senegal	..	3.2	72	4.7	4.1	3.6	2.4	1.5	626	259	49
144	Liberia	0.6	0.3	100	1.7	1.3	2.3	0.8	0.5	..	95	24
145	Togo	..	0.8	3	1.5	1.6	3.0	1.1	0.7	148	119	22
146	Bangladesh	93.2	84.3	245	47.8	..	81.5	42.3	24.8	4,785	11,480	659
147	Cambodia	..	..	..	4.1	5.5	7.5	3.1	2.1	..	522	63
148	Tanzania, U. Rep. of	16.2	13.1	290	5.7	13.6	9.5	..	..	2,405	1,220	208
149	Nepal	12.4	11.1	76	..	11.9	19.0	8.1	4.7	1,100	1,665	120
150	Equatorial Guinea	0.2	0.2	..	..	0.3	0.2	0.1	(.)	..	..	3
151	Sudan	..	17.5	725	10.7	14.6	8.0	9.9	6.1	..	1,525	175
152	Burundi	4.9	4.7	270	1.2	2.6	3.0	1.4	0.9	437	300	44
153	Rwanda	6.4	6.4	25	1.5	2.6	3.2	1.7	1.1	511	457	68
154	Uganda	..	13.2	195	5.6	15.9	12.8	4.5	2.9	..	896	162
155	Angola	..	4.7	11	7.0	6.6	8.2	2.8	1.8	..	641	106
156	Benin	..	1.9	(.)	3.5	2.3	2.9	1.9	1.0	366	212	33
157	Malawi	8.4	8.2	1,060	2.1	4.8	..	..	..	1,060	466	121
158	Mauritania	..	0.9	38	1.3	0.6	1.7	0.7	0.4	..	58	20
159	Mozambique	8.9	6.9	(.)	9.2	11.4	11.4	5.3	3.2	1,045	1,195	158
160	Central African Rep.	..	1.5	19	2.2	2.8	2.5	..	..	216	..	24
161	Ethiopia	31.9	29.3	430	28.7	38.4	44.8	..	..	5,660	3,810	499
162	Bhutan	..	1.4	..	0.5	1.1	1.5	0.5	0.2	..	93	12
163	Djibouti	..	(.)	28	(.)	0.1	0.2	..	..	45	..	3
164	Guinea-Bissau	..	0.6	12	0.2	0.6	0.8	0.3	0.2	78	37	10
165	Somalia	5.6	4.3	1	6.8	3.5	7.7	3.4	2.0	..	656	94
166	Gambia	..	0.6	4	0.1	0.2	0.5	0.3	0.2	67	27	9
167	Mali	5.3	4.4	13	6.4	5.8	7.6	3.1	1.8	1,165	390	92
168	Chad	3.2	2.2	..	4.1	..	..	2.1	1.3	551	296	52
169	Niger	..	2.3	4	5.8	3.7	7.5	2.8	1.7	959	676	85
170	Sierra Leone	..	2.0	6	2.8	2.2	1.6	1.8	1.0	..	196	51
171	Afghanistan	10.2	9.3	60	9.9	15.2	..	6.6	4.0	527	1,195	242
172	Burkina Faso	..	7.1	6	3.8	2.8	8.4	4.0	2.3	980	444	83
173	Guinea	..	3.1	480	3.7	2.2	4.6	2.2	1.3	693	268	65
All developing countries		1,300T	1,000T	19,000T	1,000T	1,300T	1,900T	900T	600T	80,000T	192,000T	12,200T
Least developed countries		350T	300T	..	250T	330T	370T	150T	100T	42,000T	38,000T	400T
Sub-Saharan Africa		..	..	..	..	..	..	..	..	..	..	..
Industrial countries		..	..	..	..	..	..	..	..	..	..	..
World		..	..	..	..	..	..	..	..	..	..	..

Trends in human development

HDI rank	Life expectancy at birth (years)		Infant mortality rate (per 1,000 births)		Population with access to safe water (%)		Underweight children (as % of children under five)		Adult literacy rate (%)		Enrolment ratio for all levels (% age 6-23)		Real GDP per capita (PPP$)	
	1960	1992	1960	1992	1975-80	1988-91	1975	1990	1970	1992	1980	1990	1960	1991
High human development	58.5	70.5	83	30	68	86	14	10	83	92	64	66	3,140	7,290
20 Barbados	64.3	75.3	74	10	98	100	..	..	..	..	67	67	3,443	9,667
24 Hong Kong	66.2	77.4	44	6	99	100	..	..	..	..	59	69	2,323	18,520
26 Cyprus	68.7	76.7	30	9	100	100	8	8	..	..	..	..	2,039	9,844
32 Korea, Rep. of	53.9	70.4	85	21	66	92	..	..	88	97	66	74	690	8,320
33 Uruguay	67.7	72.4	51	20	..	..	6	7	93	97	63	73	4,401	6,670
35 Trinidad and Tobago	63.5	70.9	56	18	93	97	14	9	..	..	59	66	4,754	8,380
36 Bahamas	63.2	71.9	..	..	..	..	..	..	..	..	70	74		
37 Argentina	64.9	71.1	60	29	..	..	3	1	93	96	65	82	3,381	5,120
38 Chile	57.1	71.9	114	17	70	88	2	2	89	94	65	66	3,130	7,060
39 Costa Rica	61.6	76.0	85	14	72	92	10	8	88	93	55	56	2,160	5,100
43 Singapore	64.5	74.2	36	8	..	..	..	..	..	..	53	68	2,409	14,734
44 Brunei Darussalam	62.3	74.0	63	8	..	..	..	..	..	..	64	67		
46 Venezuela	59.6	70.1	81	33	79	90	14	6	75	89	58	63	3,899	8,120
47 Panama	60.7	72.5	69	21	77	84	14	11	81	90	66	62	1,533	4,910
50 Colombia	56.6	69.0	99	30	64	93	19	10	78	87	53	55	1,874	5,460
51 Kuwait	59.6	74.6	89	15	..	..	14	5	54	74	..	..		
52 Mexico	57.1	69.9	92	36	62	77	19	14	74	89	68	62	2,870	7,170
Medium human development	48.5	68.0	139	40	..	..	29	22	..	..	51	56	1,010	3,420
Excluding China	50.4	65.4	124	51	42	70	32	23	60	79	52	58	1,680	4,000
54 Thailand	52.3	68.7	103	26	25	76	36	13	79	94	49	45	985	5,270
55 Antigua and Barbuda	..	..	..	..	..	..	..	..	..	..	..	..		
56 Qatar	53.0	69.6	145	26	..	..	..	..	..	..	60	78	..	..
57 Malaysia	53.9	70.4	73	14	..	..	31	18	60	80	54	58	1,783	7,400
58 Bahrain	55.5	71.0	130	12	100	100	..	..	..	..	58	75	..	..
59 Fiji	59.0	71.1	71	24	..	..	..	..	..	..	63	70	2,354	4,858
60 Mauritius	59.2	69.6	70	21	99	100	32	17	..	..	48	57	2,113	7,178
62 United Arab Emirates	53.0	70.8	145	23	..	..	9	7	..	..	44	73		
63 Brazil	54.7	65.8	116	57	62	86	18	7	66	82	54	60	1,404	5,240
64 Dominica	..	..	..	..	79	96	..	..	..	..	..	..		
65 Jamaica	62.8	73.3	63	14	86	100	14	7	97	99	67	62	1,829	3,670
67 Saudi Arabia	44.4	68.7	170	31	64	93	25	13	9	64	36	50	7,612	10,850
68 Turkey	50.1	66.7	190	57	68	92	15	11	52	82	44	52	1,669	4,840
69 Saint Vincent	..	..	..	..	..	..	..	..	..	..	..	..		
70 Saint Kitts and Nevis	..	..	..	..	..	..	..	..	..	..	..	..		
73 Syrian Arab Rep.	49.8	66.4	135	40	..	..	20	13	40	67	60	66	1,787	5,220
74 Ecuador	53.1	66.2	124	58	36	54	20	13	72	87	69	68	1,461	4,140
77 Saint Lucia	..	..	..	..	..	..	..	..	..	..	..	..		
78 Grenada	..	..	..	..	..	..	..	..	..	..	..	..		
79 Libyan Arab Jamahiriya	46.7	62.4	160	70	87	93	7	4	37	66	..	..		
81 Tunisia	48.4	67.1	159	44	35	99	17	9	31	68	50	62	1,394	4,690
83 Seychelles	..	..	..	..	79	99	..	..	..	..	..	..		
84 Paraguay	63.8	67.2	66	47	13	36	9	4	80	91	49	52	1,220	3,420
85 Suriname	60.2	69.9	70	26	88	89	..	..	..	..	61	69	2,234	3,072
86 Iran, Islamic Rep. of	49.6	66.6	169	41	51	61	43	39	29	56	46	61	1,985	4,670
87 Botswana	45.5	60.3	116	61	..	..	37	27	41	75	51	64	474	4,690
88 Belize	..	..	..	..	..	..	..	..	..	..	..	..		
89 Cuba	63.8	75.6	65	14	..	..	10	8	87	95	72	63	..	..
90 Sri Lanka	62.0	71.2	71	24	19	71	58	42	77	89	58	68	1,389	2,650
92 Oman	40.1	69.1	214	30	..	..	..	..	..	..	28	61	2040	9,230
93 South Africa	49.0	62.2	89	53	..	..	..	..	..	..	..	..	2,984	3,885
94 China	47.1	70.5	150	27	..	..	26	21	..	..	50	53	723	2,946
95 Peru	47.7	63.6	142	77	..	..	17	13	71	86	65	74	2,130	3,110
96 Dominican Rep.	51.8	67.0	125	57	55	67	17	12	67	84	60	66	1,227	3,080
98 Jordan	47.0	67.3	135	37	..	..	18	13	47	82	75	73	1,328	2,895
99 Philippines	52.8	64.6	80	40	..	..	39	34	83	90	61	64	1,183	2,440
100 Iraq	48.5	65.7	139	59	66	91	19	12	34	62	67	62	..	..
101 Korea, Dem. Rep. of	53.9	70.7	85	25	..	..	..	..	..	..	..	..	..	..
102 Mongolia	46.7	63.0	128	61	..	..	..	..	..	..	60	56	..	..
103 Lebanon	59.6	68.1	68	35	..	..	17	9	69	81	67	65	..	..
104 Samoa	..	..	..	..	95	83	..	..	..	..	..	..	..	..
105 Indonesia	41.2	62.0	139	66	11	51	51	38	54	84	51	58	490	2,730
106 Nicaragua	47.0	65.4	140	53	46	54	20	19	..	..	53	53	1,756	2,550
107 Guyana	56.1	64.6	100	49	72	64	23	18	..	..	61	65	1,630	1,862
108 Guatemala	45.6	64.0	125	49	39	60	30	25	44	56	35	41	1,667	3,180
109 Algeria	47.0	65.6	168	62	77	70	23	12	25	61	52	60	1,676	2,870
110 Egypt	46.2	60.9	179	58	75	88	17	10	35	50	51	66	557	3,600
111 Morocco	46.7	62.5	163	70	..	..	19	12	22	52	38	37	854	3,340
112 El Salvador	50.5	65.2	130	46	53	47	22	19	57	75	47	51	1,305	2,110
113 Bolivia	42.7	60.5	167	86	34	52	17	11	57	79	54	55	1,142	2,170

HDI rank	Life expectancy at birth (years)		Infant mortality rate (per 1,000 births)		Population with access to safe water (%)		Underweight children (as % of children under five)		Adult literacy rate (%)		Enrolment ratio for all levels (% age 6-23)		Real GDP per capita (PPP$)	
	1960	1992	1960	1992	1975-80	1988-91	1975	1990	1970	1992	1980	1990	1960	1991
114 Gabon	40.8	52.9	171	95	..	..	20	15	33	62	..	..	1,373	3,498
115 Honduras	46.5	65.2	160	61	41	78	23	20	53	75	47	50	901	1,820
116 Viet Nam	44.2	63.4	147	37	..	..	55	42	..	..	52	52	..	..
117 Swaziland	40.2	57.3	157	74	43	35	14	9	..	..	59	64	1,182	2,506
118 Maldives	43.6	62.6	158	56	..	..	..	..	..	..	..	..	..	..
Low human development	42.6	55.8	165	98	..	..	57	48	31	49	37	42	670	1,170
Excluding India	41.4	51.9	166	104	28	45	42	37	28	47	33	33	740	1,200
119 Vanuatu	..	..	..	..	55	74	..	..	..	..	..	..	..	..
120 Lesotho	42.9	59.8	149	80	17	48	20	18	..	..	52	58	346	1,500
121 Zimbabwe	45.3	56.1	110	59	..	..	25	14	55	69	41	66	937	2,160
122 Cape Verde	52.0	67.3	110	41	40	72	..	..	..	..	45	49	..	..
123 Congo	41.7	51.7	143	83	38	21	43	28	35	59	..	..	1,092	2,800
124 Cameroon	39.3	55.3	163	64	..	..	19	17	33	57	48	52	736	2,400
125 Kenya	44.7	58.6	124	67	17	50	25	17	32	71	62	58	635	1,350
126 Solomon Islands	50.3	70.0	..	..	27	60	..	..	..	..	..	..	..	..
127 Namibia	42.5	58.0	146	71	..	..	..	..	..	..	..	..	..	..
128 São Tomé and Principe	..	..	..	..	..	..	..	..	..	..	..	..	..	..
129 Papua New Guinea	40.7	55.3	165	54	20	32	39	36	32	65	28	30	1,136	1,550
130 Myanmar	43.8	56.9	158	83	17	31	41	33	71	82	39	39	341	650
131 Madagascar	40.7	54.9	220	110	..	..	30	38	50	81	60	40	1,013	710
132 Pakistan	43.1	58.3	163	99	25	56	47	42	21	36	19	24	820	1,970
133 Lao People's Dem. Rep.	40.4	50.3	155	98	..	..	41	34	..	..	44	42	..	..
134 Ghana	45.0	55.4	132	82	35	54	35	27	31	63	48	46	1,049	930
135 India	44.0	59.7	165	89	..	..	71	63	34	50	40	50	617	1,150
136 Côte d'Ivoire	39.2	51.6	166	91	..	..	18	12	18	56	39	37	1,021	1,510
137 Haiti	42.2	56.0	182	87	12	39	26	24	22	55	..	..	921	925
138 Zambia	41.6	45.5	135	84	42	48	17	26	52	75	46	47	1,172	1,010
139 Nigeria	39.5	51.9	190	97	..	..	30	35	25	52	50	37	1,133	1,360
140 Zaire	41.3	51.6	158	93	19	33	28	33	42	74	46	38	379	469
141 Comoros	42.5	55.4	165	90	..	..	..	..	..	..	45	34	..	..
142 Yemen	36.4	51.9	214	107	..	..	33	27	8	41	22	43	..	..
143 Senegal	37.3	48.7	172	81	36	47	19	20	12	40	24	30	1,136	1,680
144 Liberia	41.3	54.7	184	127	..	..	24	20	18	42	..	..	967	800
145 Togo	39.3	54.4	182	86	16	59	25	18	17	45	61	54	411	738
146 Bangladesh	39.6	52.2	156	109	..	..	84	66	24	37	30	32	621	1,160
147 Cambodia	42.4	50.4	146	117	..	..	43	38	..	..	..	..	..	..
148 Tanzania, U. Rep. of	40.5	51.2	147	103	39	51	25	24	..	..	44	32	272	570
149 Nepal	38.4	52.7	187	100	8	42	63	51	13	27	28	41	584	1,130
150 Equatorial Guinea	36.8	47.3	188	118	..	..	..	..	..	..	57	64	..	..
151 Sudan	38.7	51.2	170	100	..	..	36	34	17	28	25	27	975	1,162
152 Burundi	41.3	48.2	153	106	29	56	27	29	20	52	11	30	473	640
153 Rwanda	42.3	46.5	150	111	68	66	37	32	32	52	33	39	538	680
154 Uganda	43.0	42.6	133	104	35	15	28	26	41	51	25	41	371	1,036
155 Angola	33.0	45.6	208	126	17	34	24	35	12	43	54	32	880	1,000
156 Benin	35.0	46.1	185	88	34	54	34	24	16	25	34	30	1,075	1,500
157 Malawi	37.8	44.6	207	143	51	53	19	24	..	..	33	38	423	800
158 Mauritania	35.3	47.4	191	118	..	..	39	16	..	..	19	25	930	962
159 Mozambique	37.3	46.5	190	148	..	..	44	47	22	34	29	24	1,368	921
160 Central African Rep.	38.5	47.2	175	105	..	..	53	32	16	40	33	35	806	641
161 Ethiopia	36.0	46.4	175	123	8	28	45	40	..	..	16	17	262	370
162 Bhutan	37.3	47.8	203	131	..	..	..	..	..	..	7	11	..	..
163 Djibouti	36.0	48.3	186	113	42	86	..	..	..	..	19	24	..	..
164 Guinea-Bissau	34.0	42.9	201	141	10	39	..	..	..	27	27	25	..	..
165 Somalia	36.0	46.4	175	123	38	62	47	39	3	27	..	..	891	759
166 Gambia	32.3	44.4	213	133	..	..	28	17	..	..	23	29	411	763
167 Mali	34.8	45.4	210	160	..	..	36	22	8	36	..	..	541	480
168 Chad	34.8	46.9	195	123	..	..	34	31	11	33	16	29	785	447
169 Niger	35.3	45.9	192	125	..	..	50	44	4	31	12	14	604	542
170 Sierra Leone	31.5	42.4	219	144	14	50	22	26	13	24	30	29	871	1,020
171 Afghanistan	33.4	42.9	215	164	9	21	19	40	8	32	20	13	775	700
172 Burkina Faso	36.2	47.9	205	118	25	71	34	27	8	20	8	17	290	666
173 Guinea	33.6	43.9	203	135	14	64	28	24	14	27	21	19	444	500
All developing countries	46.2	63.0	149	69	36	70	40	35	46	69	45	46	950	2,730
Least developed countries	39.0	50.1	170	112	21	45	46	40	29	46	31	32	580	880
Sub-Saharan Africa	40.0	51.1	165	101	25	45	31	31	28	51	39	35	..	..
Industrial countries	69.0	74.5	35	13	..	..	..	..	..	..	..	..	..	..
World	53.4	65.6	128	60	..	..	..	..	..	..	..	..	..	..

Note: Data for industrial countries for this subject area are in table 31.

5 Human capital formation

HDI rank	Adult literacy rate (as % of age 15+)			Literacy rate (% of age 15-19) 1990	Mean years of schooling (25+)			Scientists and technicians (per 1,000 people) 1986-91	R & D scientists and technicians (per 10,000 people) 1986-89	Tertiary graduates (as % of corresponding age group) 1987-90	Science graduates (as % of total graduates) 1988-90
	Total 1992	Female 1992	Male 1992		Total 1992	Female 1992	Male 1992				
High human development	92	90	93	97	7.0	6.5	7.4	50.7	8.2	2.7	31
20 Barbados	..	..	..	..	9.4	9.1	9.7	11.6	..	..	11
24 Hong Kong	..	..	..	..	7.2	5.5	8.8	56.3	..	6.7	39
26 Cyprus	..	..	..	..	7.0	6.5	7.6	61.2	2.0	..	21
32 Korea, Rep. of	97	95	99	100	9.3	7.1	11.6	45.9	22.0	..	29
33 Uruguay	97	97	98	99	8.1	8.6	7.7	..	..	..	44
35 Trinidad and Tobago	..	..	..	..	8.4	8.5	8.4	..	4.5	1.2	33
36 Bahamas	..	..	..	..	6.2	6.0	6.4	..	..	..	33
37 Argentina	96	96	97	97	9.2	9.5	9.0	28.4	5.4	..	32
38 Chile	94	94	95	98	7.8	7.4	8.1	..	5.9	3.1	27
39 Costa Rica	93	93	93	97	5.7	5.6	5.8	..	..	2.7	20
43 Singapore	..	..	..	..	4.0	3.2	4.8	22.9	18.7	5.8	53
44 Brunei Darussalam	..	..	..	..	5.0	4.5	5.5	21.7	6.3	..	0
46 Venezuela	89	91	88	97	6.5	6.4	6.6	104.1	4.4	2.7	32
47 Panama	90	90	90	95	6.8	7.0	6.6	8.0	..	2.3	42
50 Colombia	87	86	88	94	7.5	7.7	7.3	..	0.8	2.6	28
51 Kuwait	74	68	78	82	5.5	4.8	6.1	69.2	12.7	4.2	18
52 Mexico	89	86	91	96	4.9	4.8	5.0	..	6.1	2.5	32
Medium human development	80	70	89	91	4.8	3.8	5.9	10.7		1.4	29
Excluding China	79	73	85	90	4.6	3.8	5.4	15.4	3.2	2.4	25
54 Thailand	94	92	96	99	3.9	3.4	4.4	1.2	1.6	5.0	18
55 Antigua and Barbuda	..	..	..	..	4.6	4.1	5.1	..	..	..	24
56 Qatar	..	..	..	..	5.8	5.6	6.0	19.6	9.3	4.3	13
57 Malaysia	80	72	89	94	5.6	5.2	5.9	..	4.0	1.4	28
58 Bahrain	79	71	84	93	4.3	3.6	5.2	44.7	..	2.3	52
59 Fiji	..	..	..	..	5.1	4.6	5.6	13.0	1.8	1.1	22
60 Mauritius	80	75	85	..	4.1	3.3	4.9	15.9	3.4	0.7	26
62 United Arab Emirates	..	..	..	..	5.6	5.7	5.6	..	..	1.7	12
63 Brazil	82	81	84	92	4.0	3.9	4.1	29.5	..	2.5	19
64 Dominica	..	..	..	..	4.7	4.5	4.9	..	..	..	33
65 Jamaica	99	99	99	100	5.3	5.2	5.3	6.2	0.1	2.0	19
67 Saudi Arabia	64	50	76	..	3.9	1.6	6.3	..	..	2.5	14
68 Turkey	82	72	91	91	3.6	2.4	4.9	26.3	3.7	2.1	36
69 Saint Vincent	..	..	..	..	4.6	4.5	4.7	..	..	..	37
70 Saint Kitts and Nevis	..	..	..	..	6.0	5.9	6.1	..	..	..	(.)
73 Syrian Arab Rep.	67	53	82	82	4.2	3.1	5.2	3.6	..	4.0	33
74 Ecuador	87	85	89	95	5.6	5.3	5.8	9.1	..	2.3	..
77 Saint Lucia	..	..	..	..	3.9	3.8	4.0	..	10.4	..	(.)
78 Grenada	..	..	..	..	4.7	4.5	4.9	..	..	..	26
79 Libyan Arab Jamahiriya	66	52	78	89	3.5	1.4	5.7	10.8	..	..	..
81 Tunisia	68	59	77	95	2.1	1.2	3.1	1.4	..	0.9	36
83 Seychelles	..	..	..	..	4.6	4.4	4.8	..	3.8	..	..
84 Paraguay	91	89	93	96	4.9	4.6	5.2	..	..	..	31
85 Suriname	96	96	96	..	4.2	4.0	4.3	..	..	..	3
86 Iran, Islamic Rep. of	56	45	67	79	3.9	3.1	4.6	7.6	1.1	0.9	61
87 Botswana	75	66	85	..	2.5	2.5	2.6	1.2	..	0.6	3
88 Belize	..	..	..	..	4.6	4.4	4.8	..	..	..	..
89 Cuba	95	94	96	100	8.0	8.1	7.9	..	19.8	3.8	26
90 Sri Lanka	89	85	94	96	7.2	6.3	8.0	..	2.2	1.4	12
92 Oman	..	..	..	..	0.9	0.3	1.4	6.6	..	..	24
93 South Africa	..	..	..	..	3.9	3.7	4.1	..	..	..	..
94 China	80	68	92	93	5.0	3.8	6.3	8.1	..	0.5	43
95 Peru	86	80	93	96	6.5	5.8	7.3	20.3	..	..	38
96 Dominican Rep.	84	83	86	94	4.3	4.0	4.6	..	..	..	..
98 Jordan	82	72	91	97	5.0	4.0	6.0	..	1.3	5.6	25
99 Philippines	90	90	90	96	7.6	7.2	8.0	..	1.3	6.7	30
100 Iraq	62	51	73	85	5.0	4.0	5.9	3.6	..	..	20
101 Korea, Dem. Rep. of	..	..	..	..	6.0	4.6	7.4	..	..	..	..
102 Mongolia	..	..	..	..	7.2	7.0	7.4	0.9	..	..	44
103 Lebanon	81	74	89	..	4.4	3.5	5.3	..	..	2.9	24
104 Samoa	..	..	..	..	5.8	5.1	6.6	..	..	..	..
105 Indonesia	84	77	91	95	4.1	3.1	5.3	12.1	..	0.6	11
106 Nicaragua	..	..	..	..	4.5	4.7	4.3	..	2.9	0.9	37
107 Guyana	97	96	99	100	5.1	4.9	5.4	2.3	3.5	1.1	19
108 Guatemala	56	48	65	67	4.1	3.8	4.4	1.4	2.1	..	..
109 Algeria	61	49	74	88	2.8	0.9	4.8	..	..	2.2	42
110 Egypt	50	35	66	65	3.0	1.7	4.2	..	6.0	3.8	19
111 Morocco	52	40	64	80	3.0	1.6	4.4	..	..	1.1	27
112 El Salvador	75	70	80	88	4.2	4.0	4.4	1.4	3.4	1.7	9
113 Bolivia	79	72	86	94	4.0	3.0	5.0	9.0	..	..	..

HDI rank	Adult literacy rate (as % of age 15+)			Literacy rate (% of age 15-19) 1990	Mean years of schooling (25+)			Scientists and technicians (per 1,000 people) 1986-91	R & D scientists and technicians (per 10,000 people) 1986-89	Tertiary graduates (as % of corresponding age group) 1987-90	Science graduates (as % of total graduates) 1988-90
	Total 1992	Female 1992	Male 1992		Total 1992	Female 1992	Male 1992				
114 Gabon	62	50	76	..	2.6	1.3	3.9	..	..	0.8	20
115 Honduras	75	73	78	90	4.0	3.8	4.1	1.9	..	0.5	36
116 Viet Nam	89	84	93	93	4.9	3.6	6.2	..	..	..	..
117 Swaziland	..	..	..	..	3.8	3.4	4.1	..	..	0.7	16
118 Maldives	..	..	..	..	4.5	3.9	5.1	..	..	..	38
Low human development	49	35	62	64	2.0	1.0	2.9	2.9	..	..	19
Excluding India	47	35	59	63	1.6	0.9	2.4	1.7	..	0.3	19
119 Vanuatu	..	..	..	..	3.7	3.1	4.3	..	..	..	30
120 Lesotho	..	..	..	..	3.5	4.1	2.8	..	..	0.7	5
121 Zimbabwe	69	61	76	81	3.1	1.8	4.5	..	..	0.5	12
122 Cape Verde	67	..	..	..	2.2	1.3	3.2	..	..	..	..
123 Congo	59	45	72	..	2.1	1.1	3.1	..	12.4	1.2	20
124 Cameroon	57	45	70	77	1.6	0.8	2.6	..	..	0.3	..
125 Kenya	71	60	82	..	2.3	1.3	3.1	1.3	..	0.2	24
126 Solomon Islands	..	..	..	..	1.0	0.8	1.2	..	..	..	..
127 Namibia	..	..	..	..	1.7	..	..	..	..	..	..
128 São Tomé and Principe	..	..	..	..	2.3	1.3	3.3	..	..	..	33
129 Papua New Guinea	65	48	82	..	1.0	0.7	1.3	3.2	..	0.6	23
130 Myanmar	82	72	90	90	2.5	2.1	3.0	..	..	..	..
131 Madagascar	81	74	90	..	2.2	1.7	2.6	..	1.1	0.4	32
132 Pakistan	36	22	49	50	1.9	0.7	2.9	4.0	1.5	..	..
133 Lao People's Dem. Rep.	..	..	..	..	2.9	2.1	3.6	..	..	0.5	17
134 Ghana	63	54	74	88	3.5	2.2	4.9	1.5	..	..	23
135 India	50	35	64	66	2.4	1.2	3.5	3.5	2.5	..	20
136 Côte d'Ivoire	56	41	69	..	1.9	0.9	2.9	..	..	..	..
137 Haiti	55	49	61	..	1.7	1.3	2.0	4.7	..	0.2	..
138 Zambia	75	67	83	90	2.7	1.7	3.7	4.4	..	0.2	10
139 Nigeria	52	41	63	78	1.2	0.5	1.7	1.0	0.7	0.3	23
140 Zaire	74	63	86	91	1.6	0.8	2.4	..	..	0.2	27
141 Comoros	..	..	..	..	1.0	0.8	1.2	..	..	..	..
142 Yemen	41	28	56	..	0.9	0.2	1.5	0.2	..	0.2	3
143 Senegal	40	26	55	..	0.9	0.5	1.5	..	..	1.0	22
144 Liberia	42	31	53	67	2.1	0.8	3.3	..	..	0.3	17
145 Togo	45	33	59	63	1.6	0.8	2.4	0.2	..	..	18
146 Bangladesh	37	23	49	46	2.0	0.9	3.1	0.5	..	0.6	16
147 Cambodia	38	24	52	..	2.0	1.7	2.3	..	..	..	..
148 Tanzania, U. Rep. of	..	..	..	..	2.0	1.3	2.8	..	..	0.1	20
149 Nepal	27	14	39	39	2.1	1.0	3.2	0.5	..	0.3	13
150 Equatorial Guinea	52	38	66	..	0.8	0.3	1.3	..	..	..	..
151 Sudan	28	13	45	37	0.8	0.5	1.0	0.4	..	0.4	3
152 Burundi	52	42	63	80	0.4	0.3	0.7	..	0.6	0.2	31
153 Rwanda	52	39	67	65	1.1	0.5	1.5	0.2	0.2	0.1	25
154 Uganda	51	37	65	..	1.1	0.6	1.6	..	..	0.1	26
155 Angola	43	29	57	..	1.5	1.0	2.0	..	..	..	45
156 Benin	25	17	35	41	0.7	0.3	1.1	..	2.3	..	19
157 Malawi	..	..	..	..	1.7	1.1	2.4	..	..	0.1	23
158 Mauritania	35	22	48	..	0.4	0.1	0.7	..	..	..	..
159 Mozambique	34	21	46	53	1.6	1.2	2.2	..	..	0.0	21
160 Central African Rep.	40	26	55	..	1.1	0.5	1.6	..	2.2	0.4	16
161 Ethiopia	..	..	..	..	1.1	0.7	1.5	..	..	0.2	24
162 Bhutan	41	26	55	..	0.3	0.2	0.5	..	..	0.1	..
163 Djibouti	..	..	..	..	0.4	0.3	0.7	0.1	..	..	4
164 Guinea-Bissau	39	25	53	..	0.4	0.1	0.7	..	..	..	..
165 Somalia	27	16	41	..	0.3	0.2	0.5	..	..	..	13
166 Gambia	30	18	43	..	0.6	0.2	0.9	..	..	..	..
167 Mali	36	27	46	67	0.4	0.1	0.7	..	..	0.2	9
168 Chad	33	20	46	..	0.3	0.2	0.5	..	..	0.1	11
169 Niger	31	18	44	..	0.2	0.2	0.4	..	..	0.2	4
170 Sierra Leone	24	12	35	..	0.9	0.4	1.4	..	..	..	..
171 Afghanistan	32	15	48	51	0.9	0.2	1.6	..	..	0.2	32
172 Burkina Faso	20	10	31	33	0.2	0.2	0.3	..	..	0.3	28
173 Guinea	27	15	39	..	0.9	0.3	1.5	..	4.2	0.3	62
All developing countries	69	58	79	80	3.9	3.0	4.9	8.8	3.2	1.2	28
Least developed countries	46	34	58	59	1.6	0.9	2.2	..	..	0.3	18
Sub-Saharan Africa	51	40	63	73	1.6	1.0	2.2	..	..	0.3	21
Industrial countries	..	..	..	..	10.0	..	..	84.9	40.5	19.2	24
World	..	..	..	..	5.2	..	..	25.0	12.0	3.8	24

Note: Data for industrial countries for this subject area are in table 32.

	Index: North=100 (see note)								
	Life expectancy		Adult literacy		Daily calorie supply		Access to safe water		Under-five mortality	
HDI rank	1960	1992	1970	1992	1965	1988-90	1975-80	1988-91	1960	1992
High human development	85	95	87	95	86	90	68	86	92	98
20 Barbados	93	100+	..	..	..	..	98	100	96	100+
24 Hong Kong	96	100+	..	..	..	..	99	100	98	100+
26 Cyprus	99	100+	..	..	..	..	100	100	100+	100+
32 Korea, Rep. of	78	94	95	100	77	95	66	92	93	99
33 Uruguay	98	97	100+	99	85	74	..	..	99	99
35 Trinidad and Tobago	92	95	..	..	83	92	93	97	98	100
36 Bahamas	91	96	..	..	..	..	..	..	..	..
37 Argentina	94	95	100+	98	96	100	..	..	97	98
38 Chile	83	96	96	97	87	80	70	88	90	100
39 Costa Rica	89	100+	95	96	84	92	72	92	92	100
43 Singapore	93	99	..	..	70	100+	..	..	100+	100+
44 Brunei Darussalam	90	99	..	..	..	..	..	..	..	..
46 Venezuela	86	94	81	92	76	77	..	..	93	98
47 Panama	88	97	88	92	79	77	77	84	94	99
50 Colombia	82	92	84	90	76	80	64	93	89	98
51 Kuwait	86	100+	58	76	..	..	..	..	92	100
52 Mexico	83	94	80	91	90	100+	62	77	84	97
Medium human development	70	91	..	..	71	81	..	..	84	96
Excluding China	73	88	63	81	74	79	42	70	86	95
54 Thailand	76	92	85	97	77	77	25	76	90	98
55 Antigua and Barbuda	..	..	..	..	..	..	..	..	..	..
56 Qatar	77	93	..	..	..	..	..	..	86	98
57 Malaysia	78	94	65	82	81	96	..	..	94	100
58 Bahrain	80	95	..	..	..	..	100	100	84	100+
59 Fiji	85	95	..	..	..	..	..	..	95	99
60 Mauritius	86	93	..	..	83	99	99	100	94	99
62 United Arab Emirates	77	95	..	..	..	..	..	..	81	99
63 Brazil	79	88	71	85	81	88	62	86	89	94
64 Dominica	..	..	..	..	..	..	..	..	..	..
65 Jamaica	91	98	100+	100	81	89	86	100+	96	100
67 Saudi Arabia	64	92	10	66	64	92	64	93	75	97
68 Turkey	73	89	56	84	85	95	..	..	79	94
69 Saint Vincent	..	..	..	..	..	..	..	..	..	..
70 Saint Kitts and Nevis	..	..	..	..	..	..	..	..	..	..
73 Syrian Arab Rep.	72	89	43	69	72	97	..	..	83	96
74 Ecuador	77	89	78	90	67	82	36	54	86	94
77 Saint Lucia	..	..	..	..	..	..	..	..	..	..
78 Grenada	..	..	..	..	..	..	..	..	..	..
79 Libyan Arab Jamahiriya	68	84	40	68	67	100+	87	93	78	91
81 Tunisia	70	90	33	70	76	100+	35	99	79	96
83 Seychelles	..	..	..	..	..	..	..	..	..	..
84 Paraguay	92	90	86	93	90	88	13	36	91	96
85 Suriname	87	94	..	..	..	..	88	89	95	98
86 Iran, Islamic Rep. of	72	89	31	58	70	100+	51	61	79	97
87 Botswana	66	81	44	77	71	77	..	..	87	93
88 Belize	..	..	..	..	..	..	..	..	..	..
89 Cuba	92	100+	94	97	82	100+	..	..	96	100
90 Sri Lanka	90	95	83	92	81	76	19	71	93	99
92 Oman	58	93	..	..	..	..	..	..	67	98
93 South Africa	71	83	..	..	86	99	..	..	85	95
94 China	68	94	..	..	69	86	..	..	84	98
95 Peru	69	85	77	89	79	69	..	..	81	91
96 Dominican Rep.	75	90	72	87	69	77	55	67	85	94
98 Jordan	68	90	51	85	75	85	..	..	83	97
99 Philippines	76	87	90	93	66	83	..	..	91	96
100 Iraq	70	88	37	64	72	100+	66	91	82	93
101 Korea, Dem. Rep. of	78	95	..	..	80	95	..	..	93	99
102 Mongolia	68	84	..	..	85	75	..	..	86	93
103 Lebanon	86	91	75	84	80	99	..	..	95	97
104 Samoa	..	..	..	..	..	..	95	83	..	..
105 Indonesia	60	83	58	87	65	94	11	51	82	92
106 Nicaragua	68	88	..	..	86	77	46	54	84	94
107 Guyana	81	87	..	..	..	..	72	64	92	95
108 Guatemala	66	86	48	58	75	78	39	60	82	94
109 Algeria	68	88	27	62	58	91	77	70	78	95
110 Egypt	67	82	38	51	78	100+	75	88	74	93
111 Morocco	68	84	24	54	74	100+	..	..	78	92
112 El Salvador	73	87	62	77	65	78	53	47	84	96
113 Bolivia	62	81	62	82	62	63	34	52	76	89

	Life expectancy		Adult literacy		Daily calorie supply		Access to safe water		Under-five mortality	
HDI rank	1960	1992	1970	1992	1965	1988-90	1975-80	1988-91	1960	1992
114 Gabon	59	71	36	64	65	82	..	..	76	86
115 Honduras	67	87	57	77	70	70	41	78	81	93
116 Viet Nam	64	85	..	..	78	78	..	..	81	97
117 Swaziland	58	77	..	..	..	..	..	..	82	90
118 Maldives	63	84	..	..	..	..	..	..	..	..
Low human development	62	75	32	50	72	73	..	..	76	86
Excluding India	60	70	29	48	72	69	28	45	77	85
119 Vanuatu	..	..	..	..	..	..	55	74	..	..
120 Lesotho	62	80	..	..	72	72	17	48	84	89
121 Zimbabwe	65	75	59	71	70	72	..	..	86	93
122 Cape Verde	75	90	..	..	..	..	40	72	88	96
123 Congo	60	69	38	60	81	82	38	21	80	88
124 Cameroon	57	74	38	60	81	82	..	..	77	89
125 Kenya	65	79	35	73	79	66	17	50	84	93
126 Solomon Islands	73	94	..	..	..	..	27	60	..	..
127 Namibia	61	78	..	..	..	..	..	..	78	90
128 São Tomé and Principe	..	..	..	..	..	..	..	..	..	..
129 Papua New Guinea	59	74	35	67	58	89	20	32	80	94
130 Myanmar	63	76	77	84	72	90	17	31	82	90
131 Madagascar	59	74	54	84	87	72	..	..	68	85
132 Pakistan	62	78	23	38	61	78	25	56	77	88
133 Lao People's Dem. Rep.	58	67	..	..	69	85	..	..	81	87
134 Ghana	65	74	33	65	70	70	35	54	82	88
135 India	64	80	37	51	72	81	..	..	76	88
136 Côte d'Ivoire	57	69	19	57	82	94	..	..	78	88
137 Haiti	61	75	24	57	71	73	12	39	78	89
138 Zambia	60	61	56	77	73	67	42	48	82	86
139 Nigeria	57	70	27	54	77	71	..	..	73	86
140 Zaire	60	69	45	76	79	75	19	33	78	87
141 Comoros	62	74	..	..	..	..	..	..	77	87
142 Yemen	53	70	9	42	..	..	..	..	..	..
143 Senegal	54	65	13	41	84	73	36	47	75	86
144 Liberia	60	73	19	44	76	75	..	..	74	82
145 Togo	57	73	18	47	81	76	16	59	74	87
146 Bangladesh	57	70	26	38	73	72	..	..	78	86
147 Cambodia	61	67	..	..	79	74	..	..	83	83
148 Tanzania, U. Rep. of	59	69	..	..	69	70	39	51	..	..
149 Nepal	55	71	14	28	70	79	8	42	75	86
150 Equatorial Guinea	53	63	..	..	..	..	..	..	73	81
151 Sudan	56	69	18	29	64	64	..	..	75	85
152 Burundi	60	65	22	54	83	65	29	56	79	84
153 Rwanda	61	62	35	54	59	62	68	66	80	83
154 Uganda	62	57	44	52	77	64	35	15	82	83
155 Angola	48	61	13	44	65	62	17	34	70	79
156 Benin	51	62	17	26	71	77	34	54	74	87
157 Malawi	55	60	..	..	73	67	..	..	68	78
158 Mauritania	51	64	..	..	71	84	..	..	72	80
159 Mozambique	54	62	24	34	69	59	..	..	71	77
160 Central African Rep.	56	63	17	41	73	59	..	..	74	84
161 Ethiopia	52	62	..	..	62	54	8	28	75	81
162 Bhutan	54	64	..	..	..	..	..	..	75	81
163 Djibouti	52	65	..	..	..	..	42	86	..	..
164 Guinea-Bissau	49	58	..	..	..	..	10	39	71	77
165 Somalia	52	62	3	28	74	63	..	..	75	80
166 Gambia	47	60	..	..	..	..	..	..	67	78
167 Mali	50	61	9	37	67	83	..	..	68	80
168 Chad	50	63	12	33	80	53	..	..	72	80
169 Niger	51	62	4	32	69	76	..	..	72	80
170 Sierra Leone	46	57	14	24	64	66	..	..	66	76
171 Afghanistan	48	58	9	33	73	59	9	21	66	74
172 Burkina Faso	52	64	9	20	73	73	25	71	68	82
173 Guinea	49	59	15	28	65	77	14	64	71	79
All developing countries	67	84	41	71	72	81	36	70	80	92
Least developed countries	57	67	29	47	71	67	21	45	75	85
Sub-Saharan Africa	58	68	28	53	74	68	25	45	75	85
Industrial countries	100	100	100	100	100	100	100	100	100	100
World	..	..	..	..	..	..	..	..	..	..

Note: All figures are expressed in relation to the North average, which is indexed to equal 100. The smaller the figure the bigger the gap, the closer the figure to 100 the smaller the gap, and a figure of 100+ indicates that the country is better than the North average.

7 Widening South-North gaps

	Real GDP per capita		Mean years of schooling		Overall enrolment		Fertility		Telephones	
				Index: North=100 (see note)						
HDI rank	1960	1990	1980	1992	1980	1990	1965	1992	1980	1990-92
High human development	50	48	59	68	92	87	63	68	48	37
20 Barbados	54	63	69	92	96	88	..	..	97	84
24 Hong Kong	36	100+	68	70	85	91	67	100+	46	100+
26 Cyprus	32	65	76	68	..	..	..	..	44	100+
32 Korea, Rep. of	..	..	73	90	95	97	61	100+	33	83
33 Uruguay	69	44	67	79	90	96	100+	82	92	37
35 Trinidad and Tobago	74	55	67	82	85	87	70	69		
36 Bahamas	..	..	68	60	100+	97	..	..	99	100+
37 Argentina	53	34	66	90	93	100+	97	68	98	28
38 Chile	49	46	68	76	93	87	62	72	38	22
39 Costa Rica	34	33	62	56	79	74	48	60	19	30
43 Singapore	38	97	38	39	76	89	64	100+	63	78
44 Brunei Darussalam	..	..	55	49	92	88	..	..	30	40
46 Venezuela	61	53	58	63	83	83	49	60	93	18
47 Panama	24	32	65	67	95	82	53	65	36	22
50 Colombia	29	36	57	73	76	72	46	70	27	25
51 Kuwait	..	..	49	54	..	..	41	51	37	35
52 Mexico	45	47	44	47	97	82	45	59	28	23
Medium human development	20	21	49	47	73	66	48	69	10	7
Excluding China	25	25	43	43	74	76	54	52	21	12
54 Thailand	15	35	38	38	70	59	48	83	20	6
55 Antigua and Barbuda	..	..	51	45	..	..	..	..	..	..
56 Qatar	..	..	49	57	86	100+	..	..	58	68
57 Malaysia	28	49	44	54	77	76	48	52	14	22
58 Bahrain	..	..	22	42	83	99	..	..	66	68
59 Fiji	37	32	54	50	90	92	..	..	75	21
60 Mauritius	33	47	41	40	69	75	62	95	35	14
62 United Arab Emirates	..	..	34	54	63	96	44	42	23	100+
63 Brazil	22	34	36	39	77	79	54	67	32	18
64 Dominica	..	..	52	46	..	..	..	..	18	41
65 Jamaica	29	24	56	51	96	82	53	78	..	..
67 Saudi Arabia	100+	71	30	38	52	66	41	30	32	16
68 Turkey	26	32	31	35	63	68	53	54	26	41
69 Saint Vincent	..	..	51	45	..	..	..	..	62	31
70 Saint Kitts and Nevis	..	..	66	59	..	..	..	..	..	..
73 Syrian Arab Rep.	28	34	33	41	86	87	39	31	49	11
74 Ecuador	23	27	59	54	99	89	44	51	..	..
77 Saint Lucia	..	..	43	38	..	..	..	..	..	..
78 Grenada	..	..	52	46	..	..	..	..	42	59
79 Libyan Arab Jamahiriya	..	..	30	34	..	..	41	30	..	..
81 Tunisia	22	31	20	21	72	82	43	54	20	10
83 Seychelles	..	..	51	45	..	..	..	..	..	..
84 Paraguay	19	22	51	48	70	68	45	44	17	7
85 Suriname	35	20	44	41	87	91	..	..	64	29
86 Iran, Islamic Rep. of	31	31	38	38	66	80	42	32	16	10
87 Botswana	7	31	22	24	73	84	43	37	8	10
88 Belize	..	..	51	45	..	..	..	..	..	..
89 Cuba	..	..	63	78	100+	83	..	..	41	11
90 Sri Lanka	22	17	60	70	83	89	61	76	13	2
92 Oman	..	..	6	9	40	80	42	28	4	32
93 South Africa	47	25	41	38	..	..	49	46	23	26
94 China	11	19	53	49	72	57	47	86	4	3
95 Peru	33	20	63	64	93	97	45	52	34	7
96 Dominican Rep.	19	20	47	42	86	87	43	56	..	..
98 Jordan	21	19	55	49	100+	96	38	33	..	..
99 Philippines	18	16	73	74	87	84	44	48	10	3
100 Iraq	..	..	44	49	96	82	42	33	..	..
101 Korea, Dem. Rep. of	..	..	66	59	..	..	..	..	..	..
102 Mongolia	..	..	66	70	86	74	51	41	..	..
103 Lebanon	..	..	48	43	96	86	48	61	..	..
104 Samoa	..	..	55	57	..	..	..	..	..	..
105 Indonesia	..	..	34	40	73	76	55	60	5	1
106 Nicaragua	27	17	38	44	76	70	42	37	..	..
107 Guyana	25	12	55	50	87	86	..	..	..	..
108 Guatemala	26	21	44	40	50	54	45	35	..	..
109 Algeria	26	19	14	28	74	79	41	38	47	9
110 Egypt	9	24	19	29	73	87	44	45	35	9
111 Morocco	13	22	20	30	54	49	42	43	16	5
112 El Salvador	20	14	37	41	67	67	45	46	42	11
113 Bolivia	18	14	44	39	77	72	45	41	..	..

HDI rank	Real GDP per capita		Mean years of schooling		Overall enrolment		Fertility		Telephones	
	1960	1990	1980	1992	1980	1990	1965	1992	1980	1990-92
114 Gabon	21	23	27	25	..	..	73	37	..	..
115 Honduras	14	12	33	39	67	66	41	38	11	4
116 Viet Nam	..	..	35	48	74	68	..	..	15	1
117 Swaziland	18	16	33	37	85	84	..	..	19	6
118 Maldives	..	..	49	44	..	..	..	..	..	..
Low human development	11	8	23	22	53	55	47	39	8	1
Excluding India	11	8	22	20	47	43	45	31	14	1
119 Vanuatu	..	..	41	36	..	..	..	..	31	4
120 Lesotho	..	..	30	34	74	76	52	40	1	2
121 Zimbabwe	15	14	22	30	59	87	38	35	7	6
122 Cape Verde	..	..	22	22	64	64	..	..	5	5
123 Congo	17	18	22	20	..	..	53	31	..	..
124 Cameroon	11	16	15	16	69	68	58	33	7	1
125 Kenya	10	9	22	22	89	76	38	30	6	3
126 Solomon Islands	..	..	11	10	..	..	..	..	..	..
127 Namibia	..	..	19	17	..	..	49	32	..	..
128 São Tomé and Principe	..	..	25	22	..	..	..	..	21	5
129 Papua New Guinea	18	10	10	10	40	39	48	39	9	3
130 Myanmar	..	..	27	25	56	51	52	45	..	..
131 Madagascar	16	5	22	21	86	53	45	29	21	1
132 Pakistan	13	13	19	18	27	32	43	30	12	2
133 Lao People's Dem. Rep.	..	..	27	29	63	55	49	29	..	..
134 Ghana	16	6	36	35	69	61	44	32	21	1
135 India	10	8	24	23	57	66	48	49	5	2
136 Côte d'Ivoire	16	10	19	19	56	49	41	26	..	..
137 Haiti	14	6	16	16	..	..	49	40	..	..
138 Zambia	18	7	29	26	66	62	45	30	5	2
139 Nigeria	18	9	11	11	72	49	43	29	..	..
140 Zaire	6	3	16	16	66	50	50	29	8	(.)
141 Comoros	..	..	11	10	64	45	..	..	..	..
142 Yemen	..	..	8	9	31	57	43	26	..	..
143 Senegal	18	11	8	9	34	39	47	31	..	..
144 Liberia	..	..	18	20	..	..	47	28	..	..
145 Togo	6	5	16	15	87	71	46	29	..	..
146 Bangladesh	10	8	22	20	43	42	44	40	..	..
147 Cambodia	..	..	22	20	..	..	48	43	..	..
148 Tanzania, U. Rep. of	4	4	22	20	63	42	45	28	..	..
149 Nepal	9	7	20	20	40	54	50	34	..	..
150 Equatorial Guinea	..	..	9	8	82	84	..	..	..	..
151 Sudan	15	8	8	7	36	36	45	31	23	1
152 Burundi	7	4	3	4	16	39	47	28	..	..
153 Rwanda	8	4	11	10	47	51	40	23	2	(.)
154 Uganda	6	7	11	11	36	54	43	26	5	1
155 Angola	..	..	16	15	77	42	47	27	..	..
156 Benin	17	10	7	7	49	39	44	27	..	..
157 Malawi	7	5	19	17	47	50	38	25	6	1
158 Mauritania	15	6	3	4	27	33	46	30	..	..
159 Mozambique	21	6	18	16	42	32	44	30	3	1
160 Central African Rep.	13	4	11	11	47	46	67	31	6	(.)
161 Ethiopia	4	2	11	11	23	22	52	28	4	1
162 Bhutan	..	..	2	3	10	14	51	33	..	..
163 Djibouti	..	..	3	4	27	32	..	..	12	6
164 Guinea-Bissau	..	..	3	4	39	33	..	..	..	..
165 Somalia	14	5	2	3	..	..	45	28	..	..
166 Gambia	6	5	5	6	33	38	..	..	..	..
167 Mali	8	3	3	4	..	..	46	27	..	..
168 Chad	12	3	2	3	23	38	50	33	..	..
169 Niger	9	4	1	2	17	18	42	27	4	(.)
170 Sierra Leone	14	7	9	9	43	38	47	30	..	..
171 Afghanistan	..	..	9	9	29	17	42	28	..	..
172 Burkina Faso	..	..	1	2	11	22	47	30	4	(.)
173 Guinea	..	..	9	9	30	25	51	28	..	..
All developing countries	18	17	38	36	64	61	50	59	12	6
Least developed countries	9	6	17	15	45	42	47	32	7	1
Sub-Saharan Africa	14	8	17	15	56	46	46	29	10	3
Industrial countries	100	100	100	100	100	100	100	100	100	100
World	..	..	..	..	..	..	..	..	..	..

Note: All figures are expressed in relation to the North average, which is indexed to equal 100. The smaller the figure the bigger the gap, the closer the figure to 100 the smaller the gap, and a figure of 100+ indicates that the country is better than the North average.

HDI rank	Life expectancy at birth (years) 1992	Average age at first marriage (years) 1980-90	Literacy rate (% of age 15-24) 1980-89	Enrolment ratios Primary (net) 1990	Enrolment ratios Primary (gross) 1990	Enrolment ratios Secondary (gross) 1990	Enrolment ratios Tertiary (gross) 1990	Tertiary natural and applied science enrolment (as % of female tertiary) 1990-91	Administrators and managers (% female) 1980-89	Parliament (% of seats occupied by women) 1992
High human development	73.7	22.4	..	..	..	..	..	27	14	6
20 Barbados	77.6	30.4	..	92	110	92	19.6	16	31	4
24 Hong Kong	80.2	..	..	..	..	77	..	..	12	..
26 Cyprus	79.0	24.2	..	100	103	91	16.0	23	7	5
32 Korea, Rep. of	73.3	24.7	..	100	109	85	24.9	19	3	..
33 Uruguay	75.6	22.9	99	92	107	..	..	32	25	5
35 Trinidad and Tobago	73.5	22.3	99	90	96	85	4.9	18	..	..
36 Bahamas	75.6	24.8	..	..	..	..	..	..	..	4
37 Argentina	74.6	22.9	97	..	115	74	43.1	35	..	5
38 Chile	75.5	23.4	97	86	97	75	..	34	18	6
39 Costa Rica	78.3	22.2	98	87	100	43	..	..	22	12
43 Singapore	77.1	26.2	96	100	107	71	..	..	22	4
44 Brunei Darussalam	76.0	25.0	93	89	107	71	4.7	..	6	..
46 Venezuela	73.3	21.2	94	90	98	40	25.5	..	15	9
47 Panama	74.7	21.4	93	92	105	62	24.6	22	22	8
50 Colombia	71.9	22.6	..	..	112	60	14.7	27	21	5
51 Kuwait	77.1	23.0	76	..	..	..	16.7	25	4	0
52 Mexico	73.2	20.6	91	..	113	56	12.1	26	15	7
Medium human development	69.9	22.0	81	93	111	45	4.2	..	12	15
Excluding China	67.6	22.0	80	90	101	49	10.6	25	13	8
54 Thailand	71.3	22.7	96	..	88	32	..	..	21	4
55 Antigua and Barbuda	..	22.5	..	..	..	..	..	(.)	..	..
56 Qatar	72.9	22.7	..	91	100	87	43.3	6	..	..
57 Malaysia	72.6	23.5	83	..	93	58	6.8	16	8	8
58 Bahrain	73.7	..	82	92	102	95	19.8	36	4	..
59 Fiji	73.3	22.5	91	100	127	62	..	26	9	4
60 Mauritius	73.1	23.8	..	94	108	54	1.5	6	15	3
62 United Arab Emirates	73.7	18.0	56	100	114	71	18.1	13	1	0
63 Brazil	68.7	22.6	85	..	..	..	11.3	..	..	5
64 Dominica	..	30.8	..	..	..	..	..	(.)	24	13
65 Jamaica	75.5	29.7	..	100	108	66	5.2	28	..	12
67 Saudi Arabia	70.4	..	..	56	72	42	11.3	15	..	..
68 Turkey	69.4	..	75	..	111	38	9.1	28	3	2
69 Saint Vincent	..	28.2	..	..	..	..	..	1	20	10
70 Saint Kitts and Nevis	..	31.3	..	..	..	..	..	1	14	7
73 Syrian Arab Rep.	68.5	21.5	..	94	103	44	14.8	31	33	8
74 Ecuador	68.4	21.1	93	..	117	57	..	15	15	5
77 Saint Lucia	..	31.4	..	..	..	..	..	6	19	14
78 Grenada	..	29.4	..	..	..	..	..	..	..	..
79 Libyan Arab Jamahiriya	64.3	18.7	..	..	..	..	15.3	..	..	..
81 Tunisia	68.0	24.3	63	92	109	42	6.8	34	..	4
83 Seychelles	..	23.0	..	..	..	..	..	(.)	12	..
84 Paraguay	69.4	21.8	94	94	106	31	7.6	39	..	6
85 Suriname	72.4	18.6	..	100	125	58	9.5	3	..	6
86 Iran, Islamic Rep. of	67.1	20.2	42	94	105	43	..	41	..	3
87 Botswana	63.3	26.4	..	99	119	45	2.8	..	36	5
88 Belize	..	23.9	..	..	..	..	..	(.)	12	5
89 Cuba	77.4	19.9	99	94	99	97	24.5	21	..	23
90 Sri Lanka	73.4	24.4	90	..	105	77	4.1	26	7	5
92 Oman	71.2	..	..	79	95	53	4.3	..	..	..
93 South Africa	65.2	26.1	..	..	..	..	..	..	17	3
94 China	72.1	22.0	82	95	120	42	1.1	..	11	21
95 Peru	65.6	22.7	90	..	..	..	..	..	8	6
96 Dominican Rep.	69.3	19.7	..	..	96	..	..	..	21	12
98 Jordan	69.2	22.8	77	92	98	62	23.5	26	14	1
99 Philippines	66.5	22.4	92	100	111	75	..	..	25	11
100 Iraq	67.2	22.3	..	88	102	37	9.8	28	..	11
101 Korea, Dem. Rep. of	73.5	..	..	..	100	..	..	..	..	20
102 Mongolia	64.3	..	..	..	100	..	..	43	..	4
103 Lebanon	70.1	..	..	..	110	64	..	17	..	2
104 Samoa	..	23.2	..	..	..	..	..	..	19	4
105 Indonesia	63.8	21.1	82	96	114	41	..	21	7	12
106 Nicaragua	67.8	20.2	..	77	101	46	8.3	29	..	16
107 Guyana	67.4	23.7	..	..	111	59	4.4	10	13	..
108 Guatemala	66.4	21.4	..	..	74	..	..	..	16	5
109 Algeria	66.6	21.0	60	83	88	53	..	35	..	10
110 Egypt	62.1	21.9	38	..	93	73	12.6	18	14	2
111 Morocco	64.3	22.3	..	46	53	28	7.3	26	..	1
112 El Salvador	68.2	19.4	71	72	79	26	12.9	14	16	8
113 Bolivia	62.8	22.8	76	78	81	31	..	..	..	..

HDI rank	Life expectancy at birth (years) 1992	Average age at first marriage (years) 1980-90	Literacy rate (% of age 15-24) 1980-89	Enrolment ratios				Tertiary natural and applied science enrolment (as % of female tertiary) 1990-91	Administrators and managers (% female) 1980-89	Parliament (% of seats occupied by women) 1992
				Primary (net) 1990	Primary (gross) 1990	Secondary (gross) 1990	Tertiary (gross) 1990			
114 Gabon	54.6	17.7	..	..	..	..	2.2	21	..	6
115 Honduras	67.4	20.0	..	..	107	34	6.6	..	..	12
116 Viet Nam	65.6	23.2	94	..	..	..	..	..	..	19
117 Swaziland	59.1	..	75	87	108	46	3.7	..	..	..
118 Maldives	61.3	17.9	87	..	..	..	..	..	10	4
Low human development	56.4	18.8	38	..	68	22	..	25	3	6
Excluding India	52.9	18.9	34	48	55	14	1.2	25	5	6
119 Vanuatu	..	22.6	68	..	..	..	..	..	..	..
120 Lesotho	62.3	20.5	..	77	116	31	5.3	5	..	2
121 Zimbabwe	57.7	20.4	..	..	116	46	2.4	..	15	12
122 Cape Verde	68.2	23.6	..	94	111	15	..	..	..	7
123 Congo	54.2	21.9	..	..	..	..	1.8	8	..	..
124 Cameroon	56.8	18.8	59	71	95	23	..	..	6	12
125 Kenya	60.5	20.3	..	..	93	25	0.9	10	..	3
126 Solomon Islands	72.3	21.1	..	..	..	..	..	..	..	0
127 Namibia	59.3	..	..	..	126	47	4.0	..	..	7
128 São Tomé and Principe	..	15.6	74	41	49	..	..	..	9	11
129 Papua New Guinea	56.1	20.6	..	..	66	10	..	54	..	0
130 Myanmar	58.6	22.4	81	..	..	23	..	..	..	..
131 Madagascar	56.4	20.3	..	63	91	18	2.9	40	..	..
132 Pakistan	58.3	19.8	25	..	30	13	1.5	41	..	1
133 Lao People's Dem. Rep.	51.8	..	..	53	84	17	0.8	29	..	9
134 Ghana	57.2	19.4	..	..	70	29	0.6	9	9	8
135 India	59.9	18.7	40	..	84	32	..	25	2	7
136 Côte d'Ivoire	53.1	18.9	..	..	58	14	..	..	..	5
137 Haiti	57.7	23.8	51	26	54	21	..	27	33	3
138 Zambia	46.2	19.4	..	80	92	15	1.1	5	11	7
139 Nigeria	53.7	18.7	..	..	63	17	1.9	..	..	2
140 Zaire	53.2	20.1	..	51	64	15	..	..	..	5
141 Comoros	55.9	19.5	55	..	68	15	..	10	..	..
142 Yemen	52.2	17.8	..	..	44	10	1.5	..	..	1
143 Senegal	49.7	18.3	..	..	..	11	1.2	44	..	12
144 Liberia	56.1	19.4	..	..	..	..	1.2	10	..	6
145 Togo	56.2	18.5	36	62	87	12	0.7	17	8	6
146 Bangladesh	51.9	16.7	27	64	71	12	1.1	24	2	10
147 Cambodia	51.7	21.3	..	..	..	..	..	4	..	4
148 Tanzania, U. Rep. of	52.7	19.1	54	51	68	4	0.1	8	..	11
149 Nepal	52.2	17.9	15	41	54	17	2.4	..	..	3
150 Equatorial Guinea	49.0	..	..	..	..	..	..	8	..	..
151 Sudan	52.4	20.9	..	..	43	20	2.3	10	..	5
152 Burundi	49.8	21.7	..	46	66	4	0.4	13	..	10
153 Rwanda	48.1	21.2	45	67	70	7	0.2	16	..	17
154 Uganda	43.9	17.7	..	..	..	..	0.6	11	..	13
155 Angola	47.4	17.9	..	..	70	..	0.3	..	..	10
156 Benin	47.7	18.3	18	36	45	7	0.7	16	..	6
157 Malawi	45.3	17.8	..	49	60	3	0.3	10	..	12
158 Mauritania	49.1	19.5	..	..	43	10	0.9	15	..	0
159 Mozambique	48.2	17.6	25	40	52	6	0.1	44	..	16
160 Central African Rep.	49.7	18.4	18	44	52	7	0.4	44	..	4
161 Ethiopia	48.1	18.1	..	24	30	11	0.3	13	..	..
162 Bhutan	48.4	..	..	..	19	2	..	..	..	0
163 Djibouti	50.0	..	..	31	36	11	..	..	..	0
164 Guinea-Bissau	44.5	18.3	18	32	42	4	..	8	..	13
165 Somalia	48.0	20.1	..	..	..	..	..	10	..	..
166 Gambia	46.0	..	..	45	53	13	..	..	15	8
167 Mali	47.0	16.4	14	14	17	4	0.2	15	..	2
168 Chad	48.5	16.5	..	23	35	3	..	..	..	..
169 Niger	47.5	15.8	..	19	21	4	0.2	15	..	6
170 Sierra Leone	44.0	..	..	..	39	12	0.5	..	..	..
171 Afghanistan	43.4	17.8	11	..	17	6	1.0	56	..	3
172 Burkina Faso	49.6	18.4	7	23	28	5	0.3	14	..	6
173 Guinea	44.4	16.0	..	17	24	5	0.3	46	..	..
All developing countries	64.5	20.8	67	81	90	34	4.3	25	9	11
Least developed countries	51.0	18.7	36	47	55	12	0.9	20	5	8
Sub-Saharan Africa	52.8	19.0	37	43	60	15	1.1	16	13	6
Industrial countries	78.0	24.5	..	..	..	..	..	23	24	10
World	67.5	21.0	..	..	..	..	..	24	12	11

Note: Data for industrial countries for this subject area are in table 33.

145

			Females as a percentage of males (see note)							
HDI rank	Life expectancy 1992	Population 1992	Literacy 1970	Literacy 1992	Years of schooling 1992	Primary enrolment 1960	Primary enrolment 1990	Secondary enrolment 1990	Tertiary enrolment 1990	Labour force 1990-92
High human development	109	100	90	97	91	95	100	109	85	58
20 Barbados	107	109	..	..	93	..	105	107	136	92
24 Hong Kong	107	94	71	..	63	85	..	105	..	59
26 Cyprus	106	101	..	..	86	..	100	102	114	61
32 Korea, Rep. of	109	100	86	95	61	90	100	96	49	67
33 Uruguay	109	103	100	99	111	100	102	..	..	69
35 Trinidad and Tobago	107	101	94	..	101	98	100	102	62	56
36 Bahamas	111	106	..	..	94	..	..	..	..	89
37 Argentina	110	102	98	99	105	101	..	109	117	39
38 Chile	110	102	98	99	92	96	98	109	..	47
39 Costa Rica	106	98	99	100	97	98	100	105	..	43
43 Singapore	108	97	60	..	66	93	100	103	..	67
44 Brunei Darussalam	105	94	..	..	82	..	100	109	115	..
46 Venezuela	109	98	90	103	97	100	102	143	92	47
47 Panama	106	97	100	100	106	96	100	111	..	41
50 Colombia	109	99	96	98	106	100	..	120	107	75
51 Kuwait	106	76	65	87	78	78	..	..	129	32
52 Mexico	110	100	88	94	96	94	..	104	76	45
Medium human development	105	96	..	78	63	..	94	80	58	67
Excluding China	105	98	59	85	68	83	..	84	..	55
54 Thailand	108	99	84	96	77	90	..	94	..	89
55 Antigua and Barbuda	..	..	..	..	80	..	..	..	..	..
56 Qatar	107	60	..	..	93	..	96	110	..	8
57 Malaysia	106	98	68	80	89	77	..	107	89	56
58 Bahrain	107	73	..	84	68	..	100	100	122	22
59 Fiji	106	99	..	..	82	..	100	103	..	23
60 Mauritius	110	102	77	..	69	90	104	104	52	43
62 United Arab Emirates	106	48	29	..	102	..	100	113	..	6
63 Brazil	109	101	91	96	95	96	..	..	100	56
64 Dominica	..	..	..	..	92	..	..	..	..	72
65 Jamaica	106	101	101	101	98	101	100	114	79	89
67 Saudi Arabia	104	84	13	66	25	..	82	84	82	8
68 Turkey	108	95	49	79	49	64	..	66	..	45
69 Saint Vincent	..	..	..	..	96	..	..	..	..	..
70 Saint Kitts and Nevis	..	..	..	..	97	..	..	..	..	..
73 Syrian Arab Rep.	106	98	33	..	60	44	90	73	71	22
74 Ecuador	107	99	91	95	91	91	..	104	..	35
77 Saint Lucia	..	106	..	..	95	..	..	..	..	..
78 Grenada	..	..	..	..	92	..	..	..	..	96
79 Libyan Arab Jamahiriya	106	91	22	67	24	26	..	..	87	10
81 Tunisia	103	98	39	76	40	49	92	84	68	27
83 Seychelles	..	101	..	..	92	..	..	..	..	75
84 Paraguay	107	97	88	96	88	86	98	107	88	69
85 Suriname	107	102	..	100	93	..	100	116	107	69
86 Iran, Islamic Rep. of	101	97	43	66	67	48	92	70	..	11
87 Botswana	110	109	..	77	96	..	106	110	82	61
88 Belize	..	..	..	..	92	..	..	..	..	49
89 Cuba	105	97	101	98	103	100	100	117	..	47
90 Sri Lanka	106	99	81	90	79	90	..	108	65	49
92 Oman	106	91	..	..	21	..	95	87	81	9
93 South Africa	110	101	..	..	90	90	..	..	..	64
94 China	105	94	..	74	60	..	94	78	48	75
95 Peru	106	99	74	86	80	75	..	..	..	64
96 Dominican Rep.	107	97	94	96	87	99	..	..	..	18
98 Jordan	105	95	45	79	67	63	102	97	118	11
99 Philippines	106	99	96	100	90	95	100	106	..	59
100 Iraq	105	96	36	70	68	38	88	63	64	6
101 Korea, Dem. Rep. of	109	101	..	..	62	..	..	..	..	85
102 Mongolia	104	99	85	..	94	99	..	..	..	82
103 Lebanon	106	106	73	83	66	94	..	103	..	37
104 Samoa	..	..	..	..	78	..	..	..	..	..
105 Indonesia	106	101	64	85	58	67	96	84	..	67
106 Nicaragua	107	100	98	..	110	102	103	135	81	49
107 Guyana	109	99	..	97	91	..	..	104	76	27
108 Guatemala	108	98	73	75	86	78	..	..	..	35
109 Algeria	103	100	28	66	18	67	89	79	..	..
110 Egypt	104	97	40	54	41	65	..	82	52	41
111 Morocco	106	100	29	62	37	40	68	70	58	35
112 El Salvador	110	104	87	92	100	..	103	100	74	82
113 Bolivia	108	103	68	84	60	64	91	84	..	69

			Females as a percentage of males (see note)							
	Life expectancy	Population	Literacy		Years of schooling	Primary enrolment		Secondary enrolment	Tertiary enrolment	Labour force
HDI rank	1992	1992	1970	1992	1992	1960	1990	1990	1990	1990-92
114 Gabon	106	103	51	66	33	..	..	..	42	61
115 Honduras	107	98	91	93	93	99	..	121	66	45
116 Viet Nam	107	104	..	90	59	..	..	..	..	89
117 Swaziland	106	103	..	..	83	..	105	96	73	52
118 Maldives	96	..	..	..	76	..	..	..	..	25
Low human development	102	96	44	55	36	50	..	59	..	47
Excluding India	104	99	45	55	37	50	..	61	34	55
119 Vanuatu	..	92	..	..	72	..	..	..	..	85
120 Lesotho	109	108	..	..	..	..	..	148	..	79
121 Zimbabwe	106	102	75	81	40	..	85	36	92	..
122 Cape Verde	103	112	..	..	41	..	..	98	88	59
123 Congo	110	103	38	63	35	51	..	..	20	64
124 Cameroon	106	103	40	64	32	49	88	70	..	43
125 Kenya	107	100	43	..	41	47	..	76	43	67
126 Solomon Islands	106	..	..	..	67	..	..	..	..	..
127 Namibia	104	101	..	..	..	..	..	134	167	32
128 São Tomé and Principe	..	..	..	..	39	..	..	..	..	..
129 Papua New Guinea	103	93	62	58	50	12	..	71	..	64
130 Myanmar	106	101	67	81	70	85	..	92	..	59
131 Madagascar	106	102	77	83	65	78	97	100	83	67
132 Pakistan	100	92	37	45	23	28	..	45	41	16
133 Lao People's Dem. Rep.	106	99	76	..	58	47	82	63	50	82
134 Ghana	107	101	42	73	46	48	..	62	27	67
135 India	101	93	43	55	34	50	..	57	..	41
136 Côte d'Ivoire	106	97	38	60	31	35	..	47	..	47
137 Haiti	106	104	65	80	65	84	100	91	..	67
138 Zambia	103	103	56	80	46	67	95	60	41	41
139 Nigeria	107	102	40	65	28	59	..	74	37	49
140 Zaire	107	102	36	73	33	36	78	45	..	56
141 Comoros	102	102	..	..	67	..	..	71	..	69
142 Yemen	101	108	15	51	15	..	..	29	40	15
143 Senegal	104	102	28	48	31	..	..	52	26	35
144 Liberia	105	98	30	58	25	40	..	..	32	45
145 Togo	107	102	26	55	33	38	70	35	16	59
146 Bangladesh	99	94	33	47	29	39	86	46	19	69
147 Cambodia	106	101	..	46	74	..	..	..	..	127
148 Tanzania, U. Rep. of	106	102	38	..	46	55	100	67	20	92
149 Nepal	98	95	13	34	31	5	51	40	32	52
150 Equatorial Guinea	107	103	..	..	23	..	..	..	..	56
151 Sudan	105	99	21	28	45	40	..	83	70	41
152 Burundi	107	104	34	66	40	33	85	50	40	113
153 Rwanda	107	102	49	58	31	..	100	78	20	117
154 Uganda	106	102	58	56	38	..	..	..	38	69
155 Angola	107	103	44	52	50	..	..	..	27	64
156 Benin	107	103	35	50	27	39	51	47	15	32
157 Malawi	103	103	43	..	46	..	96	60	27	104
158 Mauritania	107	102	..	45	20	23	..	45	17	28
159 Mozambique	107	103	48	47	57	60	80	60	33	92
160 Central African Rep.	111	106	23	48	31	23	65	41	17	89
161 Ethiopia	107	102	..	..	47	27	75	85	23	69
162 Bhutan	102	93	..	..	33	..	..	25	..	47
163 Djibouti	107	98	..	..	40	..	72	65	..	..
164 Guinea-Bissau	108	105	..	48	20	..	55	40	..	72
165 Somalia	107	110	20	39	33	..	..	..	..	64
166 Gambia	107	103	..	41	22	..	71	57	..	69
167 Mali	107	106	36	59	20	43	58	40	14	19
168 Chad	107	103	10	43	33	14	43	27	..	20
169 Niger	107	102	33	85	50	43	61	40	17	89
170 Sierra Leone	108	104	44	35	29	..	..	60	22	49
171 Afghanistan	102	94	15	32	14	13	..	50	50	9
172 Burkina Faso	107	102	23	32	67	42	66	45	27	96
173 Guinea	102	102	33	37	23	36	49	38	12	43
All developing countries	104	96	54	71	55	61	91	72	51	58
Least developed countries	104	100	38	54	42	44	80	60	30	..
Sub-Saharan Africa	107	102	42	60	40	52	..	67	35	62
Industrial countries	108	104	..	..	95	..	..	..	..	73
World	105	98	..	..	74	..	..	..	..	62

Note: All figures are expressed in relation to the male average, which is indexed to equal 100. The smaller the figure the bigger the gap, the closer the figure to 100 the smaller the gap, and a figure above 100 indicates that the female average is higher than the male average. Data for industrial countries for this subject area are in table 34.

10 Rural-urban gaps

	Rural population (as % of total) 1992	Population with access to services (%)						Rural-urban disparity (100=rural-urban parity: see note)			
		Health		Water		Sanitation		Health	Water	Sani- tation	Child nutrition
HDI rank		Rural 1985-91	Urban 1985-91	Rural 1988-91	Urban 1988-91	Rural 1988-91	Urban 1988-91	1985-91	1988-91	1988-91	1980-92
High human development	22	..	..	70	91	42	87	..	77	48	..
20 Barbados	54	100	100	100	100	100	100	100	100	100	..
24 Hong Kong	6	..	..	96	100	50	90	..	96	56	..
26 Cyprus	46	95	95	100	100	100	100	100	100	100	..
32 Korea, Rep. of	26	100	100	79	97	100	100	100	81	100	..
33 Uruguay	11	..	..	..	100	..	..	..	..	..	..
35 Trinidad and Tobago	34	..	..	91	99	98	99	..	92	99	96
36 Bahamas	..	100	100	75	98	..	..	100	77	..	..
37 Argentina	13	..	..	..	..	29	100	..	..	29	..
38 Chile	15	..	..	21	100	20	100	..	21	20	..
39 Costa Rica	52	..	..	86	100	94	100	..	86	94	..
43 Singapore	0	100	100	100	100	..	99	100	100	..	..
44 Brunei Darussalam	42	..	..	..	..	..	..	..	..	..	..
46 Venezuela	9	..	..	36	..	72	97	..	..	74	..
47 Panama	46	..	..	66	100	84	100	..	66	84	..
50 Colombia	29	..	..	76	100	18	84	..	76	21	95
51 Kuwait	4	100	100	100	100	98	98	100	100	100	..
52 Mexico	26	..	..	68	81	17	70	..	84	24	..
Medium human development	62	..	..	70	87	76	90	..	80	84	86
Excluding China	51	..	..	51	88	40	82	..	58	49	87
54 Thailand	77	..	..	72	89	72	80	..	82	90	81
55 Antigua and Barbuda	53	100	100	..	100	100	100	100	..	100	..
56 Qatar	21	100	100	48	100	85	100	100	48	85	..
57 Malaysia	55	..	..	50	96	94	94	..	52	100	..
58 Bahrain	17	100	100	100	100	100	100	100	100	100	..
59 Fiji	63	..	..	69	96	65	91	..	72	71	..
60 Mauritius	59	100	100	100	100	96	100	100	100	96	93
62 United Arab Emirates	18	100	100	..	100	77	100	100	..	77	..
63 Brazil	23	..	..	61	95	48	89	..	64	54	94
64 Dominica	43	100	100	95	97	98	100	100	98	98	..
65 Jamaica	46	..	..	100	100	80	100	..	100	80	98
67 Saudi Arabia	26	100	97	74	100	30	100	103	74	30	..
68 Turkey	36	..	..	..	..	..	..	..	..	..	..
69 Saint Vincent	75	..	..	85	100	100	100	..	85	100	..
70 Saint Kitts and Nevis	59	100	100	100	100	98	98	100	100	100	..
73 Syrian Arab Rep.	49	99	100	58	90	82	84	99	64	98	..
74 Ecuador	42	..	..	44	63	38	56	..	69	68	..
77 Saint Lucia	..	100	100	..	100	..	..	100	..	..	..
78 Grenada	..	..	..	..	..	..	..	..	..	..	..
79 Libyan Arab Jamahiriya	16	100	100	80	100	85	100	100	80	85	..
81 Tunisia	43	80	100	99	100	94	98	80	99	96	93
83 Seychelles	..	99	99	98	100	..	..	100	98	..	..
84 Paraguay	51	..	..	24	50	..	56	..	48	..	99
85 Suriname	57	91	91	94	82	43	64	100	115	67	..
86 Iran, Islamic Rep. of	42	70	100	16	98	9	86	70	16	10	..
87 Botswana	73	..	..	46	98	20	98	..	47	20	..
88 Belize	49	90	100	53	95	28	67	90	56	42	..
89 Cuba	25	100	100	91	100	68	100	100	91	68	..
90 Sri Lanka	78	..	..	64	100	56	73	..	64	84	85
92 Oman	89	85	100	77	91	40	75	85	85	53	..
93 South Africa	50	..	..	..	..	..	..	..	..	..	..
94 China	72	..	..	81	87	95	100	..	93	95	86
95 Peru	29	..	..	10	77	20	77	..	13	26	88
96 Dominican Rep.	38	100	100	45	82	36	77	100	55	47	93
98 Jordan	31	..	..	98	100	32	100	..	98	32	95
99 Philippines	56	..	..	79	85	63	78	..	93	81	90
100 Iraq	27	96	100	72	100	..	96	96	72	..	100
101 Korea, Dem. Rep. of	41	100	100	..	..	..	..	100	..	..	..
102 Mongolia	51	100	100	58	100	47	100	100	58	47	..
103 Lebanon	15	..	..	..	..	18	94	..	..	19	..
104 Samoa	73	100	100	77	100	92	100	100	77	92	..
105 Indonesia	70	..	..	43	68	36	64	..	64	56	76
106 Nicaragua	39	..	..	21	78	16	78	..	27	21	..
107 Guyana	66	..	..	51	90	89	90	..	56	99	..
108 Guatemala	60	..	..	41	91	52	72	..	45	73	85
109 Algeria	47	80	100	55	85	40	80	80	65	50	..
110 Egypt	56	99	100	82	96	26	80	99	85	33	91
111 Morocco	53	30	100	50	100	19	100	30	50	19	91
112 El Salvador	55	..	..	19	85	36	86	..	22	42	94
113 Bolivia	48	..	..	27	77	..	..	..	35	..	94

HDI rank	Rural population (as % of total) 1992	Population with access to services (%)						Rural-urban disparity (100=rural-urban parity: see note)			
		Health		Water		Sanitation		Health	Water	Sanitation	Child nutrition
		Rural 1985-91	Urban 1985-91	Rural 1988-91	Urban 1988-91	Rural 1988-91	Urban 1988-91	1985-91	1988-91	1988-91	1980-92
114 Gabon	53	..	..	50	90	..	..	..	56	..	..
115 Honduras	55	..	..	63	98	43	98	..	64	44	..
116 Viet Nam	80	..	..	21	47	13	34	..	45	38	94
117 Swaziland	72	..	..	..	100	10	100	..	..	10	..
118 Maldives	69	..	..	33	100	4	95	..	33	4	..
Low human development	74	..	..	..	..	..	54	..	..	..	..
Excluding India	74	..	..	33	72	22	55	..	46	40	87
119 Vanuatu	73	75	100	64	100	33	82	75	64	40	..
120 Lesotho	79	..	..	45	59	..	..	..	76	..	92
121 Zimbabwe	70	80	90	14	95	22	95	89	15	23	92
122 Cape Verde	70	..	..	65	87	9	35	..	75	26	..
123 Congo	58	..	..	7	42	..	..	..	17	..	..
124 Cameroon	58	..	..	27	95	64	100	..	29	64	95
125 Kenya	75	..	..	43	74	35	69	..	58	51	89
126 Solomon Islands	92	..	..	58	82	..	73	..	71	..	..
127 Namibia	71	..	..	35	98	11	24	..	36	46	85
128 São Tomé and Principe	74	..	..	..	..	..	..	..	..	..	..
129 Papua New Guinea	84	96	100	20	94	56	57	96	21	98	..
130 Myanmar	75	..	..	29	37	35	39	..	79	90	93
131 Madagascar	75	..	..	9	55	3	12	..	16	25	88
132 Pakistan	67	85	100	45	80	10	55	85	56	18	82
133 Lao People's Dem. Rep.	80	..	..	33	54	8	97	..	61	8	..
134 Ghana	65	..	..	35	93	32	64	..	38	50	90
135 India	74	..	..	..	..	..	53	..	..	..	..
136 Côte d'Ivoire	58	..	..	..	70	62	..	..	..	..	96
137 Haiti	70	..	..	33	55	16	55	..	60	29	..
138 Zambia	58	50	100	28	70	12	75	50	40	16	90
139 Nigeria	63	62	87	30	81	5	30	71	37	17	83
140 Zaire	71	..	..	17	59	11	46	..	29	24	..
141 Comoros	71	..	..	66	98	80	90	..	67	89	..
142 Yemen	69	22	50	30	..	60	87	44	..	69	73
143 Senegal	59	..	..	26	84	36	85	..	31	42	87
144 Liberia	53	..	..	22	93	55	..	..	24	..	..
145 Togo	71	..	60	53	77	10	56	..	68	18	84
146 Bangladesh	82	..	..	..	..	26	63	..	..	41	89
147 Cambodia	88	..	..	33	65	..	81	..	51	..	..
148 Tanzania, U. Rep. of	78	73	94	45	65	62	74	78	69	84	95
149 Nepal	88	..	..	39	67	3	52	..	59	6	..
150 Equatorial Guinea	71	..	..	14	70	10	95	..	20	11	..
151 Sudan	77	..	..	43	55	65	89	..	78	73	..
152 Burundi	94	..	..	54	99	47	71	..	54	66	77
153 Rwanda	94	..	..	65	75	56	77	..	86	73	91
154 Uganda	88	..	..	12	43	28	63	..	28	44	88
155 Angola	73	..	..	20	71	15	25	..	28	60	..
156 Benin	60	..	..	43	73	31	60	..	59	52	..
157 Malawi	88	..	..	..	..	..	..	..	..	..	89
158 Mauritania	50	..	..	..	65	13	34	..	..	38	91
159 Mozambique	70	30	..	17	44	11	61	..	39	18	88
160 Central African Rep.	52	..	..	11	14	9	36	..	79	25	..
161 Ethiopia	87	..	..	19	91	7	76	..	20	9	..
162 Bhutan	95	..	..	30	60	7	50	..	50	14	..
163 Djibouti	14	95	100	70	88	24	64	95	80	38	88
164 Guinea-Bissau	80	..	..	35	56	..	27	..	62	..	..
165 Somalia	65	15	50	..	..	5	41	30	..	12	..
166 Gambia	76	..	..	48	..	27	100	..	..	27	..
167 Mali	75	..	..	38	53	10	81	..	72	12	89
168 Chad	66	..	..	25	..	..	..	..	..	..	..
169 Niger	81	17	86	45	98	3	39	20	46	8	88
170 Sierra Leone	69	13	88	33	..	49	92	15	..	53	89
171 Afghanistan	81	45	65	17	39	..	..	69	44	..	..
172 Burkina Faso	83	..	..	70	78	6	77	..	90	8	..
173 Guinea	73	..	..	56	87	5	84	..	65	6	..
All developing countries	65	..	..	62	85	45	75	..	73	60	87
Least developed countries	79	..	..	30	60	25	61	..	50	41	89
Sub-Saharan Africa	70	..	..	31	74	23	55	..	42	42	88
Industrial countries	27	..	..	..	..	..	..	..	..	..	..
World	56	..	..	..	..	..	..	..	..	..	..

Note: The figures in the last four columns are expressed in relation to the urban estimate, which is indexed to equal 100. The smaller the figure the bigger the gap, the closer the figure to 100 the smaller the gap, and a figure above 100 indicates that the rural estimate is higher than the urban estimate.

11 Child survival and development

HDI rank		Pregnant women Receiving prenatal care (%) 1988-90	Pregnant women With anemia (%) 1975-90	Births attended by health personnel (%) 1985-90	Low-birth-weight babies (%) 1985-90	Maternal mortality rate (per 100,000 live births) 1988	Infant mortality rate (per 1,000 live births) 1992	Median duration of breast-feeding (months) 1985-92	One-year-olds immunized (%) 1992	ORS access rate (%) 1992	Under-weight children (as % of children under five) 1990	Under-five mortality rate (per 1,000 live births) 1992
	High human development	70	34	67	7	130	30	7	87	81	10	35
20	Barbados	98	..	98	..	35	10	..	90	85	..	11
24	Hong Kong	..	..	100	4	6	6	..	79	..	..	7
26	Cyprus	100	..	100	5	10	9	..	85	35	8	11
32	Korea, Rep. of	96	..	95	4	80	21	..	83	..	..	23
33	Uruguay	..	..	100	8	50	20	..	95	84	7	23
35	Trinidad and Tobago	95	..	95	13	120	18	6	85	100	9	20
36	Bahamas	100	..	100	8	..	..	..	..	98	..	..
37	Argentina	..	..	92	6	140	29	..	87	60	1	33
38	Chile	91	20	98	7	67	17	..	93	80	2	20
39	Costa Rica	91	..	97	7	36	14	7	89	90	8	16
43	Singapore	95	18	100	7	14	8	..	90	..	..	9
44	Brunei Darussalam	100	..	97	5	..	8	..	..	..	..	9
46	Venezuela	74	29	82	10	130	33	3	70	95	6	40
47	Panama	83	..	85	8	60	21	4	84	80	11	28
50	Colombia	59	24	51	17	150	30	9	80	62	10	38
51	Kuwait	99	..	99	7	30	15	..	92	100	5	17
52	Mexico	60	41	45	5	150	36	8	92	90	14	43
	Medium human development	..	38	78	9	200	40	..	90	55	22	55
	Excluding China	57	51	64	11	260	51	15	87	83	23	70
54	Thailand	53	52	71	10	180	26	15	86	90	13	34
55	Antigua and Barbuda	..	..	86	8	..	..	..	93	100	..	..
56	Qatar	100	..	100	6	140	26	..	90	75	..	32
57	Malaysia	84	34	92	9	120	14	3	90	95	18	18
58	Bahrain	99	..	99	4	80	12	16	92	100	..	15
59	Fiji	100	..	98	18	150	24	9	96	100	..	29
60	Mauritius	90	..	91	8	130	21	..	87	..	17	27
62	United Arab Emirates	76	..	97	6	130	23	..	89	95	7	29
63	Brazil	75	34	73	15	230	57	5	78	68	7	75
64	Dominica	96	..	96	11	..	..	..	97	100	..	..
65	Jamaica	67	..	88	11	120	14	..	77	90	7	18
67	Saudi Arabia	70	24	82	7	220	31	..	90	100	13	43
68	Turkey	..	74	83	8	200	57	13	72	100	11	75
69	Saint Vincent	60	..	73	10	..	..	..	99	100	..	..
70	Saint Kitts and Nevis	..	..	97	9	..	..	..	99	100	..	..
73	Syrian Arab Rep.	40	52	80	8	200	40	11	89	95	13	55
74	Ecuador	47	46	26	10	200	58	14	83	55	13	75
77	Saint Lucia	95	..	98	10	..	..	..	96	100	..	..
78	Grenada	..	..	81	..	..	30	..	80	100	..	36
79	Libyan Arab Jamahiriya	76	..	76	5	200	70	..	69	80	4	105
81	Tunisia	60	38	60	7	200	44	15	89	100	9	55
83	Seychelles	99	..	99	10	..	..	..	96	..	..	..
84	Paraguay	57	63	30	5	200	47	11	89	91	4	55
85	Suriname	100	..	91	12	120	26	..	77	66	..	32
86	Iran, Islamic Rep. of	25	28	70	12	250	41	..	97	85	39	50
87	Botswana	71	..	78	8	300	61	18	75	95	27	80
88	Belize	92	..	87	13	..	23	..	80	100	..	26
89	Cuba	100	..	100	7	54	14	..	95	100	8	17
90	Sri Lanka	86	62	85	22	180	24	20	88	95	42	30
92	Oman	98	..	90	8	220	30	..	97	100	..	40
93	South Africa	..	28	..	12	250	53	..	..	..	..	70
94	China	..	25	94	6	130	27	..	94	25	21	35
95	Peru	60	53	78	9	300	77	17	81	28	13	100
96	Dominican Rep.	43	..	44	14	200	57	6	59	13	12	75
98	Jordan	75	50	86	10	200	37	12	95	95	13	48
99	Philippines	77	48	76	15	250	40	13	92	85	34	55
100	Iraq	65	..	74	15	250	59	..	82	100	12	85
101	Korea, Dem. Rep. of	..	..	..	..	130	25	..	96	100	..	28
102	Mongolia	98	..	99	5	250	61	..	85	70	..	80
103	Lebanon	85	..	45	10	200	35	..	74	95	9	45
104	Samoa	52	..	52	4	..	..	..	91	50	..	..
105	Indonesia	47	74	44	8	300	66	23	92	92	38	95
106	Nicaragua	87	..	42	8	200	53	..	78	75	19	75
107	Guyana	95	..	93	12	200	49	5	82	100	18	65
108	Guatemala	34	..	23	10	250	49	21	62	40	25	75
109	Algeria	..	42	..	9	210	62	12	89	84	12	70
110	Egypt	40	47	24	12	300	58	19	90	95	10	80
111	Morocco	25	46	31	9	270	70	16	87	70	12	95
112	El Salvador	69	14	66	8	200	46	15	66	84	19	60
113	Bolivia	38	36	29	9	600	86	16	82	58	11	125

HDI rank	Pregnant women Receiving prenatal care (%) 1988-90	Pregnant women With anemia (%) 1975-90	Births attended by health personnel (%) 1985-90	Low-birth-weight babies (%) 1985-90	Maternal mortality rate (per 100,000 live births) 1988	Infant mortality rate (per 1,000 live births) 1992	Median duration of breast-feeding (months) 1985-92	One-year-olds immunized (%) 1992	ORS access rate (%) 1992	Under-weight children (as % of children under five) 1990	Under-five mortality rate (per 1,000 live births) 1992
114 Gabon	70	..	92	10	600	95	..	82	70	15	155
115 Honduras	78	..	63	9	220	61	17	92	65	20	80
116 Viet Nam	73	..	90	17	400	37	..	90	88	42	50
117 Swaziland	76	..	67	7	400	74	16	92	90	9	110
118 Maldives	47	..	..	20	..	56	..	98	100	..	80
Low human development	64	65	55	23	640	98	..	70	68	48	150
Excluding India	59	46	40	19	700	104	21	56	61	37	160
119 Vanuatu	98	..	67	5	..	..	..	89	95	..	..
120 Lesotho	50	..	40	10	350	80	19	64	54	18	120
121 Zimbabwe	83	34	65	6	330	59	19	74	70	14	85
122 Cape Verde	99	..	49	..	200	41	..	94	81	..	55
123 Congo	..	..	..	15	900	83	..	75	75	28	135
124 Cameroon	56	..	25	13	550	64	17	41	50	17	120
125 Kenya	..	57	28	15	400	67	20	62	65	17	85
126 Solomon Islands	92	..	85	20	..	..	..	77	92	..	..
127 Namibia	82	..	71	14	400	71	17	71	..	29	115
128 São Tomé and Principe	76	..	63	7	..	..	..	77	100	..	..
129 Papua New Guinea	68	..	20	23	700	54	..	76	95	36	75
130 Myanmar	90	58	94	13	600	83	..	74	57	33	110
131 Madagascar	77	..	71	10	600	110	17	34	62	38	165
132 Pakistan	70	57	70	30	600	99	20	81	85	42	130
133 Lao People's Dem. Rep.	..	62	..	13	750	98	..	36	65	34	145
134 Ghana	65	64	42	17	700	82	21	46	78	27	130
135 India	70	88	75	30	550	89	..	90	77	63	130
136 Côte d'Ivoire	..	34	50	15	680	91	18	38	26	12	130
137 Haiti	43	64	40	15	600	87	18	30	52	24	125
138 Zambia	80	34	43	14	600	84	19	45	89	26	150
139 Nigeria	86	43	45	17	750	97	20	43	60	35	155
140 Zaire	..	42	..	10	700	93	..	40	50	33	145
141 Comoros	76	..	24	13	500	90	..	34	84	..	145
142 Yemen	17	..	11	10	800	107	..	50	16	27	175
143 Senegal	21	55	40	10	750	81	19	51	16	20	150
144 Liberia	50	..	89	..	600	127	16	44	30	20	195
145 Togo	83	47	56	32	600	86	22	51	60	18	140
146 Bangladesh	40	51	7	34	650	109	27	69	75	66	150
147 Cambodia	..	..	..	..	800	117	..	37	25	38	185
148 Tanzania, U. Rep. of	90	80	60	16	600	103	22	87	75	24	165
149 Nepal	9	33	6	26	850	100	24	73	80	51	155
150 Equatorial Guinea	15	..	58	10	800	118	..	75	80	..	200
151 Sudan	40	36	60	15	700	100	19	69	22	34	160
152 Burundi	80	68	26	14	800	106	24	81	90	29	170
153 Rwanda	82	..	28	16	700	111	21	86	80	32	185
154 Uganda	86	..	..	10	700	104	19	77	30	26	180
155 Angola	27	29	16	15	900	126	16	33	60	35	220
156 Benin	69	55	51	10	800	88	19	75	75	24	145
157 Malawi	76	49	41	11	500	143	..	88	56	24	230
158 Mauritania	39	..	20	10	800	118	16	48	30	16	210
159 Mozambique	54	58	29	11	800	148	..	58	30	47	240
160 Central African Rep.	38	67	66	18	650	105	..	52	49	32	175
161 Ethiopia	40	..	10	10	900	123	..	14	50	40	200
162 Bhutan	63	..	11	..	800	131	..	85	85	38	200
163 Djibouti	76	..	79	9	740	113	..	84	80	..	160
164 Guinea-Bissau	29	..	39	12	1,000	141	..	73	80	23	240
165 Somalia	..	73	..	..	900	123	..	24	31	39	210
166 Gambia	72	..	65	10	1,000	133	..	88	80	17	230
167 Mali	11	65	14	10	850	160	18	45	95	22	210
168 Chad	22	37	21	11	800	123	..	21	65	31	210
169 Niger	33	47	21	20	850	125	21	28	65	44	210
170 Sierra Leone	30	45	25	13	1,000	144	..	69	55	26	250
171 Afghanistan	8	..	8	19	1,000	164	..	35	32	40	270
172 Burkina Faso	49	24	33	12	750	118	..	46	65	27	195
173 Guinea	36	..	76	11	1,000	135	..	55	30	24	220
All developing countries	62	52	66	16	420	69	..	80	63	35	100
Least developed countries	50	44	31	18	730	112	23	55	57	40	160
Sub-Saharan Africa	64	43	40	14	700	101	20	49	56	31	160
Industrial countries	..	..	..	..	24	13	..	..	..	..	15
World	..	..	..	..	290	60	..	..	..	..	90

HDI rank	Years of life lost to premature death (per 1,000 people) 1990	Tuberculosis cases (per 100,000 people) 1990	Malaria cases (per 100,000 people exposed to malaria-infected environments) 1991	AIDS cases (per 100,000 people) 1992	Population per doctor 1990	Population per nurse 1990	Nurses per doctor 1990	External aid flows to health (as % of total health expenditure) 1990	Public expenditure on health As % of GNP 1960	As % of GDP 1990	Total expenditure on health (as % of GDP) 1990
High human development	13	97	230	2.7	1,320	1,790	0.7	0.5	1.2	2.1	4.7
20 Barbados	..	..	..	29.4	1,120	220	5.0	..	3.0	..	..
24 Hong Kong	7	140	..	..	1,080	240	4.5	..	..	1.1	5.7
26 Cyprus	..	..	..	0.1	750	280	2.7	..	0.6	4.2	..
32 Korea, Rep. of	10	162	..	..	1,370	1,370	1.0	0.2	0.2	2.7	6.6
33 Uruguay	15	15	..	2.8	350	1,750	0.2	1.4	2.6	2.5	4.6
35 Trinidad and Tobago	..	..	..	19.4	940	250	3.7	..	1.7	2.6	..
36 Bahamas	..	..	..	105.7	1,060	210	5.1	..	..	3.5	..
37 Argentina	12	50	20	1.8	330	1,650	0.2	0.2	1.3	2.5	4.2
38 Chile	13	67	..	1.1	2,170	2,710	0.8	0.7	2.0	3.4	4.7
39 Costa Rica	..	..	390	3.7	1,030	490	2.1	..	3.0	5.6	..
43 Singapore	9	82	..	0.6	920	240	3.8	0.1	1.0	1.1	1.9
44 Brunei Darussalam	..	..	..	..	1,460	260	5.6	..	..	2.2	..
46 Venezuela	13	44	270	1.5	650	1,300	0.5	0.1	2.6	2.0	3.6
47 Panama	..	..	50	3.9	840	320	2.6	..	3.0	..	..
50 Colombia	11	67	810	1.3	1,150	1,920	0.6	1.6	0.4	1.8	4.0
51 Kuwait	..	..	..	..	690	220	3.2	..	..	..	..
52 Mexico	17	110	70	3.4	1,850	2,310	0.8	0.9	1.9	1.6	3.2
Medium human development	..	155	190	..	1,980	2,600	0.8	1.4	0.8	2.3	3.9
Excluding China	29	141	460	..	3,410	3,940	0.9	1.8	0.7	2.4	4.0
54 Thailand	22	173	410	1.2	5,000	910	5.5	0.9	0.4	1.1	5.0
55 Antigua and Barbuda	..	..	..	..	..	..	..	..	..	..	..
56 Qatar	16	..	..	0.2	530	200	2.6	..	..	3.1	..
57 Malaysia	15	67	210	0.2	2,700	690	3.9	0.2	1.1	1.3	3.0
58 Bahrain	..	..	..	0.7	930	420	2.2	..	..	6.0	..
59 Fiji	..	..	..	..	2,030	500	4.1	..	..	..	..
60 Mauritius	..	..	..	0.5	1,180	360	3.3	..	1.5	2.0	..
62 United Arab Emirates	..	..	210	..	1,020	390	2.6	..	..	9.0	..
63 Brazil	26	56	930	4.8	670	6,700	0.1	0.4	0.6	2.8	4.2
64 Dominica	..	..	..	..	2,950	..	..	..	..	..	..
65 Jamaica	..	..	..	3.8	2,040	490	4.2	..	2.0	2.9	..
67 Saudi Arabia	37	22	200	..	660	1,040	0.6	..	0.6	3.1	4.8
68 Turkey	31	57	20	..	1,260	970	1.3	0.5	0.8	1.5	4.0
69 Saint Vincent	..	..	..	5.2	3,760	..	..	..	..	..	..
70 Saint Kitts and Nevis	..	..	..	8.7	2,180	..	..	..	..	..	..
73 Syrian Arab Rep.	25	58	..	..	1,160	1,550	0.8	7.1	0.4	0.4	2.1
74 Ecuador	21	166	920	0.5	960	3,200	0.3	7.0	0.4	2.6	4.1
77 Saint Lucia	..	..	..	14.6	3,830	..	..	..	..	..	..
78 Grenada	..	..	..	3.8	2,120	..	..	..	..	..	..
79 Libyan Arab Jamahiriya	..	12	..	..	690	350	2.0	..	1.3	..	..
81 Tunisia	21	55	..	0.2	1,870	11,660	0.2	3.0	1.6	3.3	4.9
83 Seychelles	..	..	..	1.5	2,170	..	..	..	..	..	..
84 Paraguay	22	166	80	0.4	1,610	950	1.7	6.4	0.5	1.2	2.8
85 Suriname	..	..	480	6.9	1,260	270	4.6	..	..	5.7	..
86 Iran, Islamic Rep. of	32	83	210	..	3,140	8,570	0.4	..	0.8	1.5	2.6
87 Botswana	..	..	..	13.7	5,150	530	9.8	..	1.5	3.2	..
88 Belize	..	..	1,710	6.8	2,220	490	4.5	..	..	2.2	..
89 Cuba	..	10	..	0.5	270	160	1.7	..	3.0	3.4	..
90 Sri Lanka	14	167	3,150	..	7,140	1,400	5.1	7.4	2.0	1.8	3.7
92 Oman	..	..	1,350	0.3	1,060	2,810	0.4	..	..	2.1	..
93 South Africa	40	250	..	1.7	1,640	360	4.5	..	0.5	3.2	5.6
94 China	..	166	10	..	730	1,460	0.5	0.6	1.3	2.1	3.5
95 Peru	32	250	460	0.3	970	1,080	0.9	2.7	1.1	1.9	3.2
96 Dominican Rep.	24	110	10	2.5	930	1,330	0.7	4.1	1.3	2.1	3.7
98 Jordan	18	14	..	0.1	770	1,190	0.6	12.4	0.6	1.8	3.8
99 Philippines	27	280	530	..	8,330	2,690	3.1	7.8	0.4	1.0	2.0
100 Iraq	..	111	10	..	1,810	1,650	1.1	..	1.0	..	..
101 Korea, Dem. Rep. of	..	162	..	..	370	..	..	..	0.5	..	..
102 Mongolia	..	..	..	..	..	..	..	..	..	..	..
103 Lebanon	..	..	..	0.1	670	..	..	..	..	..	..
104 Samoa	..	..	..	..	3,570	410	8.7	..	..	5.6	..
105 Indonesia	36	220	10	..	7,140	2,550	2.8	7.4	0.3	0.7	2.0
106 Nicaragua	45	110	690	0.1	1,670	3,340	0.5	20.0	0.4	6.7	8.6
107 Guyana	..	..	5,280	14.9	6,220	890	7.0	..	..	..	..
108 Guatemala	41	110	1,500	0.9	2,270	910	2.5	11.1	0.6	2.1	3.7
109 Algeria	27	53	..	0.1	2,330	16,450	0.1	0.1	1.2	5.4	7.0
110 Egypt	33	78	..	..	1,320	3,560	0.4	12.1	0.6	1.0	2.6
111 Morocco	43	125	..	0.1	4,840	22,310	0.2	3.0	1.0	0.9	2.6
112 El Salvador	28	110	120	2.0	1,560	1,040	1.5	13.9	0.9	2.6	5.9
113 Bolivia	59	335	630	0.1	2,080	2,970	0.7	20.3	0.4	2.4	4.0

HDI rank	Years of life lost to premature death (per 1,000 people) 1990	Tuberculosis cases (per 100,000 people) 1990	Malaria cases (per 100,000 people exposed to malaria-infected environments) 1991	AIDS cases (per 100,000 people) 1992	Population per doctor 1990	Population per nurse 1990	Nurses per doctor 1990	External aid flows to health (as % of total health expenditure) 1990	Public expenditure on health As % of GNP 1960	Public expenditure on health As % of GDP 1990	Total expenditure on health (as % of GDP) 1990
114 Gabon	..	..	..	14.1	2,790	270	10.3		0.5	3.2	
115 Honduras	27	133	1,960	13.0	3,130	3,130	1.0	15.1	1.0	2.9	4.5
116 Viet Nam	..	166	390	..	2,860	580	4.9	15.9	..	1.1	2.1
117 Swaziland	..	..	..	18.4	18,820	1,050	17.9	..	..	5.8	..
118 Maldives	..	..	..	..	15,000	..	..	..	..	5.0	..
Low human development	..	213	330	..	13,550	4,650	2.9	9.4	0.6	1.6	4.9
Excluding India	83	207	..	9.8	25,320	7,230	4.0	16.2	0.7	1.9	3.6
119 Vanuatu	..	..	10,520	..	5,000	450	11.2	..	..	2.9	..
120 Lesotho	..	..	..	6.9	18,610	..	..	..	1.0	1.2	..
121 Zimbabwe	37	207	..	33.5	62,500	10,250	6.1	10.0	1.2	3.2	6.2
122 Cape Verde	..	..	..	3.2	5,130	710	7.2	..	..	..	..
123 Congo	..	..	..	84.7	8,320	590	14.2	..	1.6	3.0	..
124 Cameroon	67	194	..	11.3	12,500	1,950	6.4	13.4	1.0	1.0	2.6
125 Kenya	45	140	..	24.7	71,430	22,320	3.2	22.3	1.5	2.7	4.3
126 Solomon Islands	..	..	..	..	7,420	..	..	..	..	5.0	..
127 Namibia	..	..	..	..	4,620	..	..	..	..	5.0	..
128 São Tomé and Principe	..	..	..	1.7	1,940	280	6.9	..	..	..	..
129 Papua New Guinea	79	275	2,290	0.1	12,500	1,540	8.1	4.9	..	2.8	4.4
130 Myanmar	..	189	330	..	12,500	3,130	4.0	..	0.7	0.8	..
131 Madagascar	63	310	..	..	8,330	2,380	3.5	21.5	1.4	1.3	2.6
132 Pakistan	61	150	60	..	2,940	1,720	1.7	5.4	0.3	1.8	3.4
133 Lao People's Dem. Rep.	93	235	1,010	..	4,350	740	5.9	22.7	0.5	1.0	2.5
134 Ghana	55	222	..	16.8	25,000	2,750	9.1	14.2	1.1	1.7	3.5
135 India	..	220	260	..	2,440	2,220	1.1	1.6	0.5	1.3	6.0
136 Côte d'Ivoire	50	196	..	28.3	16,670	3,470	4.8	3.4	1.5	1.7	3.3
137 Haiti	69	333	430	..	7,140	8,930	0.8	17.0	1.0	3.2	7.0
138 Zambia	86	345	..	14.0	11,110	1,850	6.0	4.9	1.0	2.2	3.2
139 Nigeria	98	222	..	0.1	66,670	11,110	6.0	6.4	0.3	1.2	2.7
140 Zaire	..	333	..	3.0	..	..	2.1	26.7	..	0.8	2.4
141 Comoros	..	..	..	..	12,290	2,280	5.4	..	..	3.3	..
142 Yemen	104	96	210	..	..	..	..	11.6	..	1.5	3.2
143 Senegal	99	166	..	4.1	20,000	7,690	2.6	16.9	1.5	2.3	3.7
144 Liberia	..	..	..	0.1	9,340	1,370	6.8	..	0.8	3.5	..
145 Togo	79	244	..	18.3	12,500	2,020	6.2	21.0	1.3	2.5	4.1
146 Bangladesh	69	220	50	..	6,670	8,340	0.8	17.9	..	1.4	3.2
147 Cambodia	..	235	5,040	..	25,000	3,130	8.0	..	..	..	..
148 Tanzania, U. Rep. of	112	140	..	15.5	33,330	4,570	7.3	48.3	0.5	3.2	4.7
149 Nepal	67	167	240	..	16,670	6,170	2.7	23.6	0.2	2.2	4.5
150 Equatorial Guinea	..	..	..	2.5	..	..	..	..	..	..	..
151 Sudan	84	211	..	0.6	11,110	4,120	2.7	13.0	1.0	0.5	3.3
152 Burundi	81	367	..	27.4	16,670	3,880	4.3	42.7	0.8	1.7	3.3
153 Rwanda	124	260	..	37.5	50,000	29,410	1.7	39.5	0.5	1.9	3.5
154 Uganda	107	300	..	22.3	25,000	2,980	8.4	48.4	0.7	1.6	3.4
155 Angola	..	225	..	1.7	14,290	870	16.4	6.0	..	1.8	..
156 Benin	89	135	..	4.3	14,290	2,460	5.8	41.8	1.5	2.8	4.3
157 Malawi	110	173	..	51.6	50,000	17,860	2.8	23.3	0.2	2.9	5.0
158 Mauritania	..	..	..	0.6	11,900	1,180	10.1	..	0.5	5.5	..
159 Mozambique	141	189	..	1.9	50,000	3,820	13.1	52.9	..	4.4	5.9
160 Central African Rep.	74	139	..	13.5	25,000	5,560	4.5	35.8	1.3	2.6	4.2
161 Ethiopia	107	155	..	5.5	33,330	13,890	2.4	18.8	0.7	2.3	3.8
162 Bhutan	..	..	11,060	..	13,110	3,970	3.3	..	..	4.2	..
163 Djibouti	..	..	..	33.3	4,180	500	8.3	..	..	..	..
164 Guinea-Bissau	..	..	..	11.2	7,260	1,130	6.4	..	..	1.3	..
165 Somalia	..	222	..	..	14,290	2,010	7.1	45.6	0.6	0.9	1.5
166 Gambia	..	..	..	5.1	11,690	..	..	..	..	1.6	..
167 Mali	108	289	..	4.6	20,000	8,000	2.5	27.7	1.0	2.8	5.2
168 Chad	106	167	..	6.0	33,330	37,030	0.9	43.0	0.5	4.7	6.3
169 Niger	121	144	..	3.8	33,330	2,950	11.3	34.0	0.2	3.4	5.0
170 Sierra Leone	188	167	..	0.7	14,290	2,860	5.0	33.0	..	1.7	2.4
171 Afghanistan	..	278	3,170	..	6,430	9,190	0.7	..	..	1.6	..
172 Burkina Faso	114	289	..	..	33,330	4,070	8.2	19.4	0.6	7.0	8.5
173 Guinea	125	166	..	..	50,000	11,630	4.3	23.8	1.0	2.3	3.9
All developing countries	49	176	240	5.7	6,670	3,390	2.0	2.2	0.9	2.2	4.2
Least developed countries	92	220	..	10.2	19,110	7,430	2.6	24.9	0.8	2.0	3.8
Sub-Saharan Africa	89	220	..	9.3	35,680	8,190	4.4	19.9	0.7	2.5	4.4
Industrial countries	13	..	..	7.8	390	..	..	..	..	..	9.4
World	35	..	..	6.7	5,260	..	..	..	..	..	8.6

Note: Data for industrial countries for this subject area are in table 35.

13 Food security

HDI rank	Food production per capita index (1979-81=100) 1991	Agricultural production (as % of GDP) 1991	Daily calorie supply Per capita 1988-90	As % of requirements 1988-90	Food import dependency ratio (%) 1969/71	1988/90	Cereal imports (thousands of metric tons) 1991	Food aid (US$ millions) 1992
High human development	99	8	2,840	122	19.2	36.4	20,980T	44T
20 Barbados	80	..	3,220	128	68.8	71.7	..	..
24 Hong Kong	..	(.)	2,860	129	104.6	141.8	785	..
26 Cyprus	100	..	..	..	..	..	..	..
32 Korea, Rep. of	95	8	2,830	123	26.2	50.8	10,410	..
33 Uruguay	109	10	2,690	96	9.2	8.8	83	2.3
35 Trinidad and Tobago	..	3	2,770	120	70.7	80.8	201	..
36 Bahamas	..	..	2,780	..	71.7	63.5	..	..
37 Argentina	95	15	3,070	130	1.3	0.4	31	..
38 Chile	117	..	2,480	104	23.1	10.5	588	0.9
39 Costa Rica	92	18	2,710	120	23.4	30.2	320	1.5
43 Singapore	..	(.)	3,120	144	..	..	780	..
44 Brunei Darussalam	..	..	2,860	..	81.2	93.5	..	..
46 Venezuela	102	5	2,440	100	32.3	43.2	1,470	..
47 Panama	88	10	2,270	100	19.2	24.8	101	1.2
50 Colombia	111	17	2,450	104	9.3	10.2	780	6.1
51 Kuwait	..	..	3,040	130	110.6	97.3	..	..
52 Mexico	96	9	3,060	132	3.2	24.8	5,430	31.7
Medium human development	118	17	2,480	109	6.1	10.4	99,440T	3,130T
Excluding China	110	15	2,410	107	12.2	18.0	86,010T	3,080T
54 Thailand	106	12	2,280	100	1.4	3.8	521	2.8
55 Antigua and Barbuda	..	..	2,310	..	83.0	83.4	..	0.1
56 Qatar	..	..	..	..	..	..	..	..
57 Malaysia	159	..	2,670	124	46.1	51.3	3,010	..
58 Bahrain	..	..	..	..	..	..	..	..
59 Fiji	..	..	2,770	108	50.6	70.1	..	..
60 Mauritius	104	11	2,900	129	57.0	95.3	183	4.0
62 United Arab Emirates	..	..	3,290	151	93.2	136.5	..	..
63 Brazil	132	10	2,730	114	4.6	3.1	6,330	10.6
64 Dominica	..	..	2,910	100	50.1	66.4	..	0.2
65 Jamaica	96	5	2,560	115	59.9	63.7	413	66.5
67 Saudi Arabia	..	7	2,930	120	57.3	72.4	5,890	..
68 Turkey	99	18	3,200	124	3.4	10.9	638	3.4
69 Saint Vincent	..	..	2,460	99	56.8	113.1	..	0.5
70 Saint Kitts and Nevis	..	..	2,440	..	56.8	86.4	..	0.4
73 Syrian Arab Rep.	77	30	3,120	126	31.8	31.7	1,740	10.8
74 Ecuador	115	15	2,400	106	7.1	13.9	481	4.0
77 Saint Lucia	..	..	2,420	102	52.0	75.7	..	..
78 Grenada	..	..	2,400	..	61.3	77.5	..	0.4
79 Libyan Arab Jamahiriya	80	..	3,290	140	69.1	77.9	..	..
81 Tunisia	113	18	3,120	137	38.8	59.9	920	42.5
83 Seychelles	..	..	2,360	100	83.1	86.8	..	0.1
84 Paraguay	114	22	2,680	115	6.0	1.1	24	2.3
85 Suriname	..	..	2,440	..	32.6	39.6	..	..
86 Iran, Islamic Rep. of	116	21	3,020	134	10.1	31.6	5,030	17.7
87 Botswana	68	5	2,260	100	47.5	74.8	99	5.4
88 Belize	..	..	2,580	114	46.8	40.4	..	..
89 Cuba	96	..	3,130	137	..	..	..	7.4
90 Sri Lanka	90	27	2,250	99	37.8	30.4	918	63.2
92 Oman	..	4	..	..	..	..	345	..
93 South Africa	82	5	3,130	128	6.5	9.7	1,350	..
94 China	138	27	2,640	112	1.7	4.7	13,430	41.3
95 Peru	92	..	2,040	89	17.5	27.1	1,430	86.5
96 Dominican Rep.	95	18	2,310	100	16.1	38.3	712	4.3
98 Jordan	89	7	2,710	111	61.0	87.2	1,540	34.8
99 Philippines	88	21	2,340	108	8.6	11.4	1,850	43.6
100 Iraq	68	..	3,100	133	30.7	64.5	..	24.2
101 Korea, Dem. Rep. of	104	..	2,840	123	9.1	8.0	..	..
102 Mongolia	78	..	2,360	97	21.3	12.2	..	1.5
103 Lebanon	136	..	3,140	129	80.7	74.9	..	9.4
104 Samoa	..	..	..	..	31.7	31.2	..	0.1
105 Indonesia	135	19	2,610	122	4.7	5.7	2,800	20.8
106 Nicaragua	61	30	2,240	100	11.3	26.9	176	27.5
107 Guyana	65	..	2,500	108	28.9	22.6	..	7.3
108 Guatemala	88	26	2,250	101	11.0	18.5	410	34.1
109 Algeria	107	14	2,940	118	34.2	76.8	5,440	11.0
110 Egypt	114	18	3,310	133	19.8	42.6	7,810	410.9
111 Morocco	140	19	3,030	131	18.1	21.1	1,960	74.9
112 El Salvador	100	10	2,330	102	15.9	24.5	324	61.2
113 Bolivia	124	..	2,010	83	20.0	11.6	219	41.0

HDI rank	Food production per capita index (1979-81=100) 1991	Agricultural production (as % of GDP) 1991	Daily calorie supply Per capita 1988-90	As % of requirements 1988-90	Food import dependency ratio (%) 1969/71	1988/90	Cereal imports (thousands of metric tons) 1991	Food aid (US$ millions) 1992
114 Gabon	82	9	2,440	107	19.5	32.8	70	..
115 Honduras	92	22	2,210	91	11.4	13.7	284	27.9
116 Viet Nam	124	..	2,220	102	19.3	1.8	..	13.0
117 Swaziland	85	..	2,630	105	25.9	30.5	..	9.2
118 Maldives	..	..	2,400	80	61.9	68.6	..	1.1
Low human development	109	32	2,180	99	5.9	7.8	12,110T	1,850T
Excluding India	98	33	2,130	93	8.5	12.9	12,060T	1,760T
119 Vanuatu	..	..	2,740	..	27.8	16.6	..	..
120 Lesotho	70	14	2,120	93	30.5	59.0	100	11.7
121 Zimbabwe	78	20	2,260	94	5.0	4.6	131	59.8
122 Cape Verde	..	..	2,780	125	75.7	71.3	..	18.1
123 Congo	92	12	2,300	107	13.2	25.1	96	3.3
124 Cameroon	78	27	2,210	93	6.7	17.7	532	2.6
125 Kenya	103	27	2,060	86	7.4	9.6	330	68.9
126 Solomon Islands	..	..	2,280	84	15.4	29.8	..	..
127 Namibia	..	10	1,970	..	36.4	30.8	18	6.4
128 São Tomé and Principe	..	..	2,150	103	51.6	40.1	..	5.5
129 Papua New Guinea	..	26	2,590	116	19.7	27.5	287	0.1
130 Myanmar	100	..	2,450	116	1.0	0.9	..	..
131 Madagascar	86	33	2,160	93	4.5	5.2	114	14.0
132 Pakistan	106	26	2,280	101	3.5	14.1	972	190.4
133 Lao People's Dem. Rep.	111	..	2,470	111	9.8	5.6	44	3.6
134 Ghana	116	53	2,140	91	12.4	11.3	344	26.9
135 India	119	31	2,230	105	2.8	1.8	58	99.4
136 Côte d'Ivoire	93	38	2,570	122	14.7	18.4	644	22.2
137 Haiti	84	..	2,010	94	7.2	26.2	348	16.1
138 Zambia	96	16	2,020	87	22.0	7.0	104	27.6
139 Nigeria	123	37	2,200	93	2.6	3.7	763	..
140 Zaire	94	..	2,130	97	4.9	4.8	..	24.7
141 Comoros	..	..	1,760	90	27.2	37.5	..	2.8
142 Yemen	67	22	2,230	93	29.4	66.0	..	35.1
143 Senegal	98	20	2,320	95	31.4	38.1	784	19.8
144 Liberia	66	..	2,260	97	18.6	23.9	..	68.4
145 Togo	95	33	2,270	99	5.5	21.0	238	4.3
146 Bangladesh	96	36	2,040	94	8.3	12.3	1,630	239.7
147 Cambodia	141	..	2,120	96	1.8	3.2	..	2.8
148 Tanzania, U. Rep. of	78	61	2,200	91	4.9	3.3	130	6.6
149 Nepal	127	59	2,210	103	..	2.3	6	5.7
150 Equatorial Guinea	..	..	..	..	..	..	..	1.7
151 Sudan	80	..	2,040	83	9.5	14.8	1,190	113.1
152 Burundi	91	55	1,950	85	2.0	3.3	31	1.8
153 Rwanda	84	38	1,910	80	2.3	7.4	19	12.3
154 Uganda	98	51	2,180	83	2.2	1.4	26	14.8
155 Angola	79	..	1,880	80	9.8	35.9	..	43.9
156 Benin	119	37	2,380	101	5.8	12.0	216	7.0
157 Malawi	75	35	2,050	87	4.4	5.6	120	148.8
158 Mauritania	80	22	2,450	109	33.4	59.4	342	14.3
159 Mozambique	77	64	1,810	77	7.3	21.9	479	154.6
160 Central African Rep.	94	41	1,850	77	6.1	9.4	27	3.3
161 Ethiopia	86	47	1,700	71	1.1	9.4	802	217.8
162 Bhutan	..	43	..	..	..	..	26	3.0
163 Djibouti	..	..	2,360	..	90.9	87.7	..	1.9
164 Guinea-Bissau	..	46	2,240	97	24.6	26.6	64	5.0
165 Somalia	78	..	1,870	81	12.7	17.0	..	37.8
166 Gambia	90	..	2,290	103	18.8	64.2	..	5.7
167 Mali	96	44	2,260	107	6.6	7.7	226	16.3
168 Chad	102	43	1,740	69	3.8	4.8	73	7.5
169 Niger	78	38	2,240	98	2.0	9.9	143	20.2
170 Sierra Leone	84	43	1,900	86	15.3	19.0	183	6.6
171 Afghanistan	71	..	1,770	76	7.4	14.3	..	5.1
172 Burkina Faso	119	44	2,220	95	3.8	8.9	177	17.2
173 Guinea	90	29	2,240	100	4.8	17.2	296	7.8
All developing countries	118	17	2,480	109	6.7	10.5	99,440T	3,130T
Least developed countries	92	37	2,070	91	..	11.3	7,250T	1,320T
Sub-Saharan Africa	96	21	2,170	92	6.5	10.2	10,440T	1,270T
Industrial countries	..	..	..	..	..	..	..	..
World	..	..	..	..	..	..	..	..

HDI rank	First-grade intake rate (%) 1990	Primary enrolment ratio		Primary repeaters (as % of primary enrolment) 1990	Completing primary level (as % of first-grade entrants) 1990	Transition to secondary level (as % of primary completers) 1988	Primary entrants proceeding to secondary schooling (%) 1990	Secondary enrolment ratio		Secondary repeaters (as % of secondary enrolment) 1989-91	Tertiary enrolment ratio (gross) 1990
		Net 1990	Gross 1990					Net 1990	Gross 1990		
High human development	100	93	110	10	73	82	59	48	61	5	22.4
20 Barbados	..	90	106	..	75	..	..	84	89	..	17.0
24 Hong Kong	100	..	108	..	97	..	..	..	75	..	..
26 Cyprus	100	100	103	0	100	99	99	86	90	2	15.0
32 Korea, Rep. of	100	100	107	..	99	99	98	79	87	0	37.7
33 Uruguay	99	91	108	9	93	..	..	..	81	..	30.1
35 Trinidad and Tobago	..	90	96	3	89	73	65	73	84	2	6.4
36 Bahamas	..	..	..	..	100	..	..	..	93	..	19.5
37 Argentina	..	..	111	..	..	..	..	..	71	..	39.9
38 Chile	..	87	98	..	77	..	..	55	72	..	20.6
39 Costa Rica	100	87	101	11	79	61	48	36	42	12	26.3
43 Singapore	..	100	108	..	100	..	..	..	70	..	..
44 Brunei Darussalam	100	89	110	10	..	..	..	63	68	9	4.4
46 Venezuela	100	89	97	11	48	88	42	18	34	6	26.6
47 Panama	100	92	107	10	79	85	67	48	59	8	20.9
50 Colombia	100	74	111	11	56	60	34	38	55	20	14.2
51 Kuwait	92	..	..	3	90	70	63	..	..	12	14.8
52 Mexico	100	100	115	9	72	81	58	46	55	2	14.0
Medium human development	98	95	116	8	77	65	54	..	49	5	7.4
Excluding China	96	92	107	10	67	72	..	37	51	9	13.3
54 Thailand	85	..	99	4	87	..	..	..	33	..	15.7
55 Antigua and Barbuda	..	..	..	3	..	..	..	..	..	14	..
56 Qatar	..	93	104	7	97	84	81	69	83	10	27.8
57 Malaysia	88	..	93	..	96	..	..	..	56	..	7.2
58 Bahrain	..	92	..	5	98	95	93	81	95	5	18.0
59 Fiji	100	100	126	..	..	29	..	..	61	7	12.0
60 Mauritius	99	92	106	5	97	48	47	..	53	14	2.2
62 United Arab Emirates	100	100	116	4	94	94	88	60	67	9	10.4
63 Brazil	100	88	108	19	20	..	..	16	39	..	11.3
64 Dominica	..	..	..	..	85	79	67	..	..	5	..
65 Jamaica	100	100	106	4	85	..	..	61	62	2	5.9
67 Saudi Arabia	76	62	77	10	88	..	..	33	46	12	12.5
68 Turkey	100	100	114	7	96	47	45	42	48	15	..
69 Saint Vincent	..	..	..	15	..	..	..	..	..	..	..
70 Saint Kitts and Nevis	..	..	..	..	88	..	..	..	..	..	..
73 Syrian Arab Rep.	100	99	109	7	59	72	42	46	52	14	17.8
74 Ecuador	100	..	118	..	63	..	..	..	56	..	19.1
77 Saint Lucia	..	..	..	..	95	34	32	..	..	3	..
78 Grenada	..	..	..	..	..	..	..	..	..	..	..
79 Libyan Arab Jamahiriya	..	..	..	..	..	..	..	..	..	..	16.4
81 Tunisia	100	96	116	20	78	43	34	44	46	16	8.4
83 Seychelles	..	..	..	..	78	..	..	..	..	..	..
84 Paraguay	100	95	108	9	59	..	..	25	30	..	8.1
85 Suriname	100	100	127	23	93	..	..	45	54	..	9.2
86 Iran, Islamic Rep. of	100	98	112	9	91	74	67	47	52	14	9.3
87 Botswana	100	96	117	5	80	45	36	34	43	0	3.1
88 Belize	..	..	..	..	..	..	..	..	..	..	..
89 Cuba	100	94	100	3	89	96	85	70	90	3	20.8
90 Sri Lanka	99	..	107	8	97	92	89	..	74	11	5.2
92 Oman	92	81	100	11	91	86	78	50	57	9	4.8
93 South Africa	..	..	..	..	..	..	..	..	..	..	..
94 China	100	98	125	6	85	62	53	..	48	2	1.7
95 Peru	100	95	126	..	..	..	..	42	67	10	33.1
96 Dominican Rep.	100	..	95	..	14	..	..	..	..	..	..
98 Jordan	..	91	97	5	87	91	79	42	63	6	21.7
99 Philippines	100	100	112	2	70	93	65	54	73	2	24.4
100 Iraq	100	94	111	19	58	56	32	40	48	32	12.6
101 Korea, Dem. Rep. of	..	..	100	..	..	..	..	..	..	..	..
102 Mongolia	..	..	98	..	..	..	..	..	86	..	14.4
103 Lebanon	..	..	112	..	..	..	..	..	63	..	27.3
104 Samoa	..	..	..	..	..	..	..	..	..	..	..
105 Indonesia	100	98	117	10	77	..	..	38	45	1	9.2
106 Nicaragua	100	76	98	17	41	94	39	25	40	7	9.3
107 Guyana	69	..	112	..	97	..	..	..	58	11	5.1
108 Guatemala	100	..	79	..	36	..	..	..	28	..	..
109 Algeria	94	88	95	9	90	82	74	53	60	14	10.9
110 Egypt	87	..	101	8	..	..	..	..	81	..	18.4
111 Morocco	71	57	65	12	75	61	46	28	34	20	9.9
112 El Salvador	100	71	79	8	24	..	..	15	26	4	15.2
113 Bolivia	100	82	85	3	44	..	..	27	34	5	20.6

HDI rank	First-grade intake rate (%) 1990	Primary enrolment ratio Net 1990	Primary enrolment ratio Gross 1990	Primary repeaters (as % of primary enrolment) 1990	Completing primary level (as % of first-grade entrants) 1990	Transition to secondary level (as % of primary completers) 1988	Primary entrants proceeding to secondary schooling (%) 1990	Secondary enrolment ratio Net 1990	Secondary enrolment ratio Gross 1990	Secondary repeaters (as % of secondary enrolment) 1989-91	Tertiary enrolment ratio (gross) 1990
114 Gabon	..	..	..	33	44	37	16	..	..	25	3.7
115 Honduras	100	93	104	12	34	..	..	19	31	10	8.3
116 Viet Nam	..	..	..	..	58	..	..	..	..	..	..
117 Swaziland	100	85	108	15	73	70	51	..	47	9	4.4
118 Maldives	..	..	..	..	..	..	..	..	..	..	..
Low human development	..	..	81	8	52	..	..	..	30	..	..
Excluding India	75	54	67	16	52	..	..	..	19	..	2.5
119 Vanuatu	..	..	..	..	..	59	30	14	26	6	3.7
120 Lesotho	100	70	107	22	50	..	..	..	50	..	4.5
121 Zimbabwe	100	..	116	..	94	..	..	..	..	..	..
122 Cape Verde	100	95	115	19	51	45	23	11	16	20	..
123 Congo	..	..	..	37	54	62	33	..	..	44	5.3
124 Cameroon	85	76	103	29	69	30	21	..	28	19	3.2
125 Kenya	..	..	95	..	..	..	..	..	29	..	1.5
126 Solomon Islands	..	..	..	..	..	..	..	..	..	..	..
127 Namibia	..	81	119	..	38	..	..	..	41	..	3.2
128 São Tomé and Principe	55	..	..	30	88	..	..	..	..	..	..
129 Papua New Guinea	92	..	72	..	61	..	..	..	12	..	..
130 Myanmar	..	..	97	..	..	..	..	..	24	..	4.8
131 Madagascar	92	64	92	36	38	38	14	..	18	20	3.2
132 Pakistan	77	..	42	..	48	..	..	..	21	..	2.6
133 Lao People's Dem. Rep.	..	59	98	30	..	..	..	15	22	8	1.2
134 Ghana	83	..	77	3	..	..	..	..	38	1	1.4
135 India	..	..	99	4	62	..	..	..	44	..	..
136 Côte d'Ivoire	60	52	69	24	71	23	16	..	22	17	..
137 Haiti	71	26	56	13	39	61	24	..	22	8	1.9
138 Zambia	..	82	97	..	84	..	..	16	20	..	..
139 Nigeria	..	..	72	..	58	..	..	..	20	..	3.5
140 Zaire	77	58	76	21	64	..	..	17	24	..	1.9
141 Comoros	68	..	75	..	31	30	9	..	18	33	..
142 Yemen	..	..	79	..	67	..	..	..	23	..	2.6
143 Senegal	52	48	58	16	85	39	33	13	16	11	2.9
144 Liberia	..	..	..	..	..	..	..	..	..	..	2.5
145 Togo	97	75	111	36	59	27	16	..	23	37	2.5
146 Bangladesh	98	69	77	7	47	..	..	17	19	..	3.4
147 Cambodia	..	..	..	..	..	..	..	..	..	..	..
148 Tanzania, U. Rep. of	78	51	69	5	73	..	..	..	5	..	0.3
149 Nepal	..	61	82	21	..	..	..	23	30	9	5.0
150 Equatorial Guinea	..	..	..	..	..	..	..	..	..	..	..
151 Sudan	55	..	50	..	76	..	..	..	22	..	2.8
152 Burundi	68	50	73	22	77	10	8	..	6	14	0.7
153 Rwanda	95	67	71	12	50	4	2	7	8	7	0.6
154 Uganda	84	..	80	..	..	..	..	..	14	..	1.1
155 Angola	75	..	91	33	34	..	..	..	12	..	0.7
156 Benin	75	53	67	26	40	38	15	..	11	31	2.7
157 Malawi	98	50	66	21	42	7	3	2	4	2	0.7
158 Mauritania	70	..	51	17	68	26	18	..	16	11	3.1
159 Mozambique	72	45	64	27	40	34	14	..	8	29	0.2
160 Central African Rep.	66	56	68	31	62	31	19	..	12	29	1.4
161 Ethiopia	63	28	39	9	28	78	22	..	12	13	0.8
162 Bhutan	28	..	25	17	..	..	..	..	5	6	..
163 Djibouti	41	37	44	14	88	27	24	12	14	11	..
164 Guinea-Bissau	61	45	60	..	8	73	6	..	7	20	..
165 Somalia	..	..	..	..	..	..	..	..	..	..	..
166 Gambia	73	54	64	16	..	32	31	15	18	2	..
167 Mali	24	19	24	28	50	44	22	5	7	26	0.8
168 Chad	61	38	57	33	71	40	28	..	7	20	0.8
169 Niger	27	25	29	14	82	31	25	6	7	19	0.7
170 Sierra Leone	..	..	48	..	..	..	..	..	16	..	1.4
171 Afghanistan	34	..	24	..	28	..	..	..	9	4	1.5
172 Burkina Faso	36	29	37	18	71	33	23	7	8	25	0.7
173 Guinea	43	26	37	20	67	58	39	7	9	23	1.4
All developing countries	92	86	99	8	71	65	51	33	41	5	6.8
Least developed countries	75	53	67	15	51	39	17	15	16	14	2.2
Sub-Saharan Africa	71	48	69	19	57	36	18	..	18	..	2.0
Industrial countries	..	..	..	..	..	..	..	..	..	..	..
World	..	..	..	..	..	..	..	..	..	..	..

HDI rank	Pupil-teacher ratio Primary 1990	Pupil-teacher ratio Secondary 1990	Secondary technical enrolment (as % of total secondary) 1988-91	Tertiary natural and applied science enrolment (as % of total tertiary) 1990	Tertiary students abroad (as % of those at home) 1987-88	Education (as % of GNP) 1960	Education (as % of GNP) 1990	Education (as % of total public expenditure) 1990	Primary and secondary education (as % of all levels) 1990	Higher education (as % of all levels) 1990	Ratio of current expenditure per tertiary student to GNP per capita 1990
High human development	28	17	17.2	46	1	2.2	3.7	..	74	15	0.2
20 Barbados	17	..	..	30	13	..	8.0	..	75	19	0.8
24 Hong Kong	27	23	10.0	..	32	..	3.0	17.4	71	29	..
26 Cyprus	21	12	6.6	31	..	..	3.6	11.3	89	4	0.1
32 Korea, Rep. of	34	25	18.6	42	2	2.0	3.6	22.4	79	7	0.1
33 Uruguay	22	..	16.3	..	1	3.7	3.1	15.9	68	23	0.3
35 Trinidad and Tobago	26	..	0.8	48	62	2.8	4.1	11.6	79	12	0.8
36 Bahamas	..	..	..	..	..	..	..	..	..	..	..
37 Argentina	19	7	..	54	(.)	2.1	..	..	..	..	..
38 Chile	29	17	37.5	46	1	2.7	3.7	..	72	22	0.3
39 Costa Rica	32	19	22.2	24	2	4.1	4.6	20.8	48	36	0.7
43 Singapore	26	..	..	..	25	2.8	3.4	..	65	31	0.6
44 Brunei Darussalam	15	12	4.6	16	..	..	..	..	50	10	..
46 Venezuela	23	9	17.6	..	1	3.7	4.1	18.8	..	..	..
47 Panama	20	19	25.6	39	3	3.6	5.5	..	60	21	0.5
50 Colombia	30	20	21.5	39	1	1.7	2.9	21.4	60	21	0.4
51 Kuwait	18	13	0.3	43	16	..	5.0	..	..	..	..
52 Mexico	31	17	12.2	46	1	1.2	4.1	..	..	..	..
Medium human development	24	17	10.2	40	4	2.2	4.1	14.0	66	21	1.6
Excluding China	26	18	11.4	37	4	2.5	4.7	19.3	65	21	0.7
54 Thailand	18	18	18.5	22	1	2.3	3.8	20.0	78	15	0.3
55 Antigua and Barbuda	..	..	..	..	..	..	..	..	58	7	..
56 Qatar	11	8	2.7	10	20	..	3.4	..	..	..	..
57 Malaysia	20	19	2.2	30	38	2.9	6.9	18.8	76	15	1.2
58 Bahrain	19	14	12.7	53	45	..	..	..	..	..	..
59 Fiji	31	17	9.1	42	54	..	5.0	15.4	88	9	0.9
60 Mauritius	21	..	1.4	29	..	3.0	3.7	11.8	81	7	1.2
62 United Arab Emirates	18	13	0.8	15	25	..	1.9	14.6	..	..	..
63 Brazil	23	14	..	31	1	1.9	4.6	..	56	26	1.1
64 Dominica	29	..	1.1	60	..	..	5.8	10.6	87	3	0.5
65 Jamaica	31	26	3.5	35	22	2.3	6.1	12.9	71	21	1.6
67 Saudi Arabia	16	13	2.8	26	6	3.2	6.2	17.8	..	..	..
68 Turkey	30	24	24.5	33	3	2.6	..	..	..	..	..
69 Saint Vincent	20	25	2.8	44	..	..	..	..	..	..	..
70 Saint Kitts and Nevis	21	15	..	50	..	..	..	..	..	..	..
73 Syrian Arab Rep.	25	17	5.9	40	9	2.0	4.1	17.3	74	23	0.5
74 Ecuador	29	..	33.8	32	1	1.9	2.8	19.1	74	14	0.2
77 Saint Lucia	29	..	..	40	..	..	..	..	74	10	2.4
78 Grenada	27	20	..	..	..	..	..	..	..	..	..
79 Libyan Arab Jamahiriya	12	12	17.2	..	7	2.8	..	..	..	..	..
81 Tunisia	28	17	3.5	35	25	3.3	6.1	14.3	76	19	1.2
83 Seychelles	19	12	29.0	..	..	..	8.5	11.9	79	..	..
84 Paraguay	25	..	6.9	32	1	1.3	..	..	73	22	0.3
85 Suriname	23	12	27.1	14	..	..	8.3	..	75	9	0.7
86 Iran, Islamic Rep. of	28	24	4.6	63	16	2.4	4.1	22.4	72	14	0.5
87 Botswana	32	17	4.6	22	24	2.7	8.4	15.9	80	12	2.8
88 Belize	25	14	1.3	..	..	..	6.0	..	..	..	..
89 Cuba	13	10	32.2	33	1	5.0	6.6	12.8	65	14	0.4
90 Sri Lanka	29	..	..	42	6	3.8	2.7	8.1	84	13	0.5
92 Oman	28	16	2.2	32	..	..	3.5	11.1	91	7	0.6
93 South Africa	..	..	..	..	1	3.0	..	..	..	..	..
94 China	22	15	9.1	57	3	1.8	2.3	12.4	67	19	1.9
95 Peru	28	21	..	49	1	2.3	..	..	55	..	..
96 Dominican Rep.	41	..	..	..	1	2.1	..	..	..	..	..
98 Jordan	25	15	23.3	33	41	3.0	5.9	13.3	64	33	1.0
99 Philippines	33	33	(.)	37	0	2.3	2.9	10.1	73	15	0.1
100 Iraq	25	22	13.7	36	3	5.8	..	..	77	21	..
101 Korea, Dem. Rep. of	26	..	..	..	..	..	..	..	..	..	..
102 Mongolia	28	..	..	..	1	..	..	..	83	17	..
103 Lebanon	..	..	..	..	21	..	..	11.7	..	..	..
104 Samoa	..	..	..	..	..	..	5.3	10.7	..	..	..
105 Indonesia	23	13	12.0	..	2	2.5	..	..	..	..	..
106 Nicaragua	33	24	9.1	56	10	1.5	..	..	..	..	..
107 Guyana	34	..	3.4	50	31	..	4.7	..	..	..	..
108 Guatemala	34	15	..	..	2	1.4	1.4	11.8	..	..	..
109 Algeria	28	17	7.0	63	7	5.6	9.1	27.0	..	..	..
110 Egypt	24	18	20.9	28	2	4.1	6.7	..	70	30	0.8
111 Morocco	27	14	1.5	37	14	3.1	5.5	26.1	84	16	0.8
112 El Salvador	40	28	..	34	2	2.3	1.8	..	..	..	..
113 Bolivia	25	18	..	52	2	1.5	3.0	20.1	66	23	0.4

HDI rank	Pupil-teacher ratio Primary 1990	Pupil-teacher ratio Secondary 1990	Secondary technical enrolment (as % of total secondary) 1988-91	Tertiary natural and applied science enrolment (as % of total tertiary) 1990	Tertiary students abroad (as % of those at home) 1987-88	Public expenditure on Education (as % of GNP) 1960	Public expenditure on Education (as % of GNP) 1990	Education (as % of total public expenditure) 1990	Primary and secondary education (as % of all levels) 1990	Higher education (as % of all levels) 1990	Ratio of current expenditure per tertiary student to GNP per capita 1990
114 Gabon	44	..	20.6	34	26	2.1	5.7	..	..	..	..
115 Honduras	38	..	30.2	46	4	2.2	4.6	15.9	73	21	1.0
116 Viet Nam	..	..	5.6	..	4	..	..	..	..	..	..
117 Swaziland	33	..	1.4	36	12	..	6.4	22.5	62	21	2.6
118 Maldives	..	..	1.0	..	..	..	9.2	10.0	..	..	..
Low human development	45	..	2.6	..	..	2.3	3.6	14.1	72	17	2.3
Excluding India	43	23	4.7	33	10	2.3	3.6	15.7	74	16	4.6
119 Vanuatu	..	..	6.9	..	..	..	..	..	..	..	..
120 Lesotho	55	20	3.6	..	11	3.2	3.8	13.8	76	18	1.9
121 Zimbabwe	36	28	1.7	27	8	0.5	10.6	..	85	10	1.4
122 Cape Verde	33	24	7.5	..	..	..	4.1	19.9	72	3	..
123 Congo	66	27	6.7	18	28	2.5	5.6	14.4	..	..	..
124 Cameroon	51	26	18.0	30	40	1.7	3.4	19.6	70	30	3.2
125 Kenya	31	..	1.6	32	17	4.6	6.8	16.7	77	15	6.8
126 Solomon Islands	..	..	17.3	..	..	..	..	..	..	..	..
127 Namibia	..	..	1.9	17	..	..	4.7	..	57	10	1.6
128 São Tomé and Principe	35	..	1.4	..	..	..	..	..	..	..	..
129 Papua New Guinea	32	22	11.6	..	6	2.5	..	..	..	..	..
130 Myanmar	35	..	1.2	..	(.)	2.2	1.9	..	86	13	0.4
131 Madagascar	40	21	5.0	42	12	2.3	..	..	..	..	..
132 Pakistan	43	19	1.6	..	9	1.1	3.4	..	70	18	1.6
133 Lao People's Dem. Rep.	28	12	2.9	..	14	..	1.1	..	..	..	..
134 Ghana	29	18	2.5	41	15	3.8	3.3	24.3	64	11	2.5
135 India	47	..	1.6	..	1	2.3	3.5	11.2	71	17	0.8
136 Côte d'Ivoire	36	..	9.8	..	20	4.6	..	..	..	..	..
137 Haiti	29	..	..	..	31	1.4	1.8	20.0	72	9	1.4
138 Zambia	44	25	2.8	29	14	1.6	2.9	8.7	66	17	2.1
139 Nigeria	39	22	3.9	43	7	1.5	..	..	..	..	..
140 Zaire	..	..	27.4	..	15	2.4	0.9	6.4	77	23	1.4
141 Comoros	36	..	1.4	29	..	..	..	..	..	..	..
142 Yemen	35	32	3.6	13	33	..	..	..	..	..	..
143 Senegal	58	23	3.3	38	23	2.4	3.7	24.1	60	23	3.4
144 Liberia	..	..	..	39	18	0.7	..	..	..	..	..
145 Togo	59	28	6.7	25	26	1.9	5.7	24.7	56	29	6.8
146 Bangladesh	63	27	0.7	27	1	0.6	2.0	10.3	88	9	0.4
147 Cambodia	..	..	..	..	..	..	..	..	..	..	..
148 Tanzania, U. Rep. of	35	21	..	62	31	2.1	5.8	11.4	63	17	28.4
149 Nepal	37	29	..	17	2	0.4	..	..	..	..	..
150 Equatorial Guinea	..	..	..	..	..	..	1.7	3.9	..	..	..
151 Sudan	34	22	4.1	21	27	1.9	..	..	..	..	..
152 Burundi	67	22	12.8	40	19	2.4	3.5	16.7	76	22	11.5
153 Rwanda	57	14	..	26	38	0.3	4.2	25.4	82	16	12.8
154 Uganda	35	17	2.5	22	10	3.2	2.9	22.5	81	13	4.7
155 Angola	32	..	5.9	40	30	0.3	..	10.7	96	4	..
156 Benin	35	..	6.1	19	25	2.5	..	..	..	..	..
157 Malawi	64	26	2.4	25	14	2.1	3.4	10.3	55	30	10.3
158 Mauritania	47	18	2.6	12	34	2.1	4.7	22.0	66	24	4.3
159 Mozambique	55	34	6.0	60	11	..	6.3	12.0	66	10	22.2
160 Central African Rep.	..	37	7.1	36	45	2.0	2.8	..	67	22	4.1
161 Ethiopia	30	..	0.5	40	17	0.8	4.8	9.4	82	12	7.1
162 Bhutan	37	..	..	..	20	..	3.7	..	..	..	..
163 Djibouti	43	20	15.9	..	..	..	3.3	10.5	80	12	..
164 Guinea-Bissau	25	..	10.3	58	..	..	2.8	..	..	..	..
165 Somalia	..	..	..	..	10	0.9	..	..	..	..	..
166 Gambia	32	..	..	..	..	..	3.8	11.0	63	18	..
167 Mali	42	14	13.4	55	39	2.0	3.2	17.3	..	..	..
168 Chad	67	36	4.8	..	50	0.9	2.3	..	68	8	1.9
169 Niger	42	26	1.1	31	28	0.5	..	..	..	..	..
170 Sierra Leone	31	17	5.3	17	49	..	1.4	..	53	35	3.7
171 Afghanistan	..	..	..	46	10	..	..	..	..	..	..
172 Burkina Faso	57	..	7.6	28	30	1.5	2.3	17.5	68	32	11.3
173 Guinea	40	14	9.5	61	20	1.5	..	21.5	42	31	..
All developing countries	34	18	7.9	41	4	2.2	3.9	14.2	68	19	1.9
Least developed countries	45	24	5.9	28	9	1.3	3.0	14.1	76	15	5.6
Sub-Saharan Africa	40	22	6.7	37	15	2.4	4.6	15.7	..	..	8.2
Industrial countries	..	..	..	21	..	..	4.9	..	..	26	..
World	..	..	..	31	..	..	4.8	..	..	26	..

Note: Data for industrial countries for this subject area are in table 36.

HDI rank	Radios (per 100 people) 1990	Televisions (per 100 people) 1990	Annual cinema atten- dances (per person) 1988-91	Daily newspapers (copies per 100 people) 1990	Book titles published (per 100,000 people) 1988-91	Printing and writing paper consumed (metric tons per 1,000 people) 1990	Post offices (per 100,000 people) 1991	Letters posted (per capita) 1991	Telephones (per 100 people) 1990-92	Motor vehicles (per 100 people) 1989-90
High human development	47	17.7	1.6	27.8	19.8	16.9	..	48.9	18.7	11.4
20 Barbados	88	26.5	..	11.7	29.8	9.7	..	..	42.1	..
24 Hong Kong	67	28.0	10.3	64.8	..	94.0	..	..	60.5	6.0
26 Cyprus	29	15.0	..	11.0	..	12.7	..	..	51.7	35.6
32 Korea, Rep. of	99	20.7	1.3	27.7	66.7	31.3	7.7	59.7	41.4	7.7
33 Uruguay	60	23.3	..	23.3	36.5	7.3	..	..	18.5	13.7
35 Trinidad and Tobago	49	31.3	..	7.7	..	16.0	19.6	13.6	18.5	25.6
36 Bahamas	54	22.4	..	13.7	..	12.5	..	..	53.3	31.5
37 Argentina	68	22.2	0.6	12.4	..	13.4	..	..	14.0	17.5
38 Chile	34	20.5	0.7	45.5	14.5	11.7	8.4	17.8	11.0	7.9
39 Costa Rica	26	14.8	..	8.1	7.6	3.8	..	..	15.2	8.3
43 Singapore	65	37.8	12.5	28.2	..	54.0	24.2	..	39.2	15.0
44 Brunei Darussalam	27	24.1	13.0	3.9	9.3	6.2	4.6	18.4	19.8	43.8
46 Venezuela	45	17.1	1.0	14.5	17.1	10.9	..	..	8.9	10.1
47 Panama	22	16.5	..	7.0	..	8.2	..	..	10.9	7.0
50 Colombia	17	11.8	1.3	6.2	4.4	6.3	..	..	12.3	..
51 Kuwait	33	27.1	0.6	21.0	41.0	16.2	..	..	17.5	32.3
52 Mexico	25	14.6	..	13.3	3.0	12.0	..	..	11.5	11.2
Medium human development	21	6.6	..	4.6	6.2	4.8	..	..	3.5	..
Excluding China	23	10.7	1.6	5.0	..	5.4	7.6	11.6	5.8	4.8
54 Thailand	19	11.4	..	7.3	13.7	5.9	7.3	11.6	3.1	3.9
55 Antigua and Barbuda	34	30.3	..	7.9	..	..	17.3	16.9	27.7	..
56 Qatar	44	44.5	0.7	18.7	..	8.2	..	..	34.1	33.7
57 Malaysia	43	14.8	..	14.0	20.0	23.8	12.4	43.9	10.8	12.0
58 Bahrain	55	41.4	..	5.7	..	4.2	..	..	34.2	23.0
59 Fiji	61	..	..	3.7	..	6.7	..	..	10.5	9.8
60 Mauritius	36	21.7	0.6	7.4	5.1	7.4	9.4	22.4	6.8	5.7
62 United Arab Emirates	32	11.0	..	15.7	16.9	..	10.0	29.6	62.7	..
63 Brazil	38	21.5	0.7	5.4	..	9.0	7.9	22.7	9.2	8.5
64 Dominica	51	6.1	..	..	..	..	..	..	20.4	..
65 Jamaica	42	13.2	..	6.4	..	5.7	..	..	7.8	3.9
67 Saudi Arabia	30	26.9	..	4.0	..	3.9	..	..	8.1	18.8
68 Turkey	16	17.4	0.3	7.1	10.9	4.7	..	..	20.3	3.6
69 Saint Vincent	64	12.9	..	..	..	31.9	..	..	15.4	7.4
70 Saint Kitts and Nevis	61	20.5	..	..	7.0	..	18.2	27.1	9.0	13.7
73 Syrian Arab Rep.	26	6.0	0.6	2.3	..	2.4	..	..	5.3	1.8
74 Ecuador	32	8.3	0.6	8.7	6.5	4.7	4.9	1.0	4.9	3.4
77 Saint Lucia	67	16.7	..	..	..	..	..	15.7	12.3	10.5
78 Grenada	64	35.3	..	..	..	..	..	..	29.5	..
79 Libyan Arab Jamahiriya	22	9.9	..	1.5	3.0	2.1	..	..	5.5	15.7
81 Tunisia	20	8.1	..	3.7	4.0	5.3	..	..	4.9	..
83 Seychelles	46	8.7	..	4.6	..	..	7.1	45.3	14.3	7.6
84 Paraguay	17	5.8	..	3.9	..	2.8	7.2	1.0	3.4	4.2
85 Suriname	64	13.0	..	9.5	..	5.7	..	..	14.4	11.5
86 Iran, Islamic Rep. of	23	6.5	1.1	2.6	8.1	2.0	..	..	4.8	4.7
87 Botswana	12	1.6	..	1.5	12.0	..	12.8	22.4	5.0	3.6
88 Belize	58	16.6	..	..	..	2.7	..	..	10.1	2.3
89 Cuba	35	20.7	2.8	12.4	17.2	10.5	..	..	5.7	..
90 Sri Lanka	20	3.5	2.3	3.2	14.3	1.8	23.0	26.0	1.0	1.8
92 Oman	64	75.5	..	4.0	..	4.9	..	..	16.0	..
93 South Africa	30	9.7	..	3.5	12.1	14.1	..	..	13.1	12.8
94 China	18	3.0	..	4.2	6.2	4.2	..	..	1.3	..
95 Peru	25	9.7	1.9	7.9	2.0	8.5	..	..	3.6	2.7
96 Dominican Rep.	17	8.4	..	3.2	..	4.9	..	..	8.5	..
98 Jordan	25	8.1	0.3	5.6	..	4.4	..	..	12.9	5.6
99 Philippines	14	4.8	..	5.4	1.3	1.4	4.0	12.6	1.7	1.9
100 Iraq	22	7.2	..	3.6	..	3.9	..	..	3.5	5.4
101 Korea, Dem. Rep. of	12	1.5	9.2	23.0	..	(.)	..	..	3.5	..
102 Mongolia	13	4.1	9.4	7.4	31.0	3.2	..	..	3.0	..
103 Lebanon	83	32.5	..	11.7	..	9.1	..	..	15.4	..
104 Samoa	44	3.7	..	..	..	0.6	..	..	2.6	3.6
105 Indonesia	15	6.0	..	2.8	0.9	3.3	5.4	2.8	0.7	1.4
106 Nicaragua	26	6.5	1.8	6.8	..	1.9	..	..	1.2	1.9
107 Guyana	49	3.8	..	10.1	..	1.0	..	..	2.0	4.1
108 Guatemala	7	5.2	0.9	2.1	..	2.5	6.5	6.7	2.6	1.9
109 Algeria	23	7.4	0.9	5.1	1.9	3.8	10.6	13.0	4.7	4.6
110 Egypt	32	10.9	0.5	5.7	3.0	4.6	12.4	3.1	4.6	2.6
111 Morocco	21	7.4	1.2	1.3	..	1.7	..	..	2.7	3.6
112 El Salvador	41	9.2	..	8.8	..	5.2	5.2	1.4	5.5	2.2
113 Bolivia	61	10.5	0.7	5.6	6.0	1.1	2.8	0.9	2.6	4.2

HDI rank	Radios (per 100 people) 1990	Televisions (per 100 people) 1990	Annual cinema attendances (per person) 1988-91	Daily newspapers (copies per 100 people) 1990	Book titles published (per 100,000 people) 1988-91	Printing and writing paper consumed (metric tons per 1,000 people) 1990	Post offices (per 100,000 people) 1991	Letters posted (per capita) 1991	Telephones (per 100 people) 1990-92	Motor vehicles (per 100 people) 1989-90
114 Gabon	14	3.7	..	1.7	..	1.4	8.5	12.7	2.1	..
115 Honduras	39	7.2	..	3.9	..	1.3	..	..	2.0	1.4
116 Viet Nam	11	3.9	3.8	0.9	..	1.1	..	..	0.3	..
117 Swaziland	16	2.1	..	1.3	..	..	8.3	16.2	3.2	6.7
118 Maldives	12	2.5	..	0.8	..	1.9	..	..	3.7	..
Low human development	9	2.4	3.9	2.1	1.6	1.3	13.8	12.5	0.7	0.7
Excluding India	11	1.5	..	1.0	..	0.6	..	4.5	0.5	0.6
119 Vanuatu	28	..	..	2.0	..	..	..	..	1.9	3.8
120 Lesotho	7	0.6	..	1.1	..	..	..	..	1.2	..
121 Zimbabwe	8	3.0	0.2	2.1	3.3	2.2	2.8	16.7	3.0	3.5
122 Cape Verde	16	..	..	1.0	2.6	..	16.8	3.3	2.4	..
123 Congo	11	0.6	..	0.8	..	0.2	..	..	0.8	1.9
124 Cameroon	14	2.3	..	0.7	..	0.7	..	..	0.4	0.8
125 Kenya	13	1.0	..	1.5	1.4	2.2	..	..	1.5	1.2
126 Solomon Islands	12	..	..	..	..	..	..	..	1.3	..
127 Namibia	17	2.1	..	15.3	12.5	..	..	..	6.0	..
128 São Tomé and Principe	26	..	..	2.0	..	..	9.1	0.6	2.5	..
129 Papua New Guinea	7	..	..	1.3	..	..	..	..	1.6	..
130 Myanmar	8	0.2	..	0.5	..	0.2	..	..	0.2	0.3
131 Madagascar	20	2.0	..	0.4	(.)	0.2	8.0	2.0	0.3	..
132 Pakistan	9	1.8	..	1.5	..	1.3	11.5	6.1	1.0	0.8
133 Lao People's Dem. Rep.	12	0.7	0.2	0.3	2.4	..	4.9	0.8	0.2	..
134 Ghana	27	1.5	0.3	1.3	..	0.3	6.5	5.0	0.5	0.8
135 India	8	3.2	5.0	3.2	1.6	1.9	17.6	16.6	0.8	0.7
136 Côte d'Ivoire	14	6.1	..	0.8	..	0.9	3.0	2.9	1.2	1.9
137 Haiti	5	0.5	0.4	0.7	4.0	0.2	2.0	44.7	0.8	0.5
138 Zambia	8	3.1	..	1.2	..	0.8	..	..	1.2	..
139 Nigeria	17	3.2	0.1	1.6	1.5	0.5	4.0	4.2	0.5	..
140 Zaire	10	0.1	..	..	..	0.1	1.3	1.0	0.1	..
141 Comoros	13	(.)	..	..	..	..	..	..	0.9	..
142 Yemen	3	2.9	2.5	1.1	..	..	..	..	1.1	..
143 Senegal	11	3.6	..	0.7	..	1.1	1.9	0.9	0.6	..
144 Liberia	23	1.8	..	1.4	..	0.1	..	..	0.2	..
145 Togo	21	0.6	..	0.3	..	..	..	..	0.6	..
146 Bangladesh	4	0.5	..	0.6	1.0	0.7	..	..	0.2	0.1
147 Cambodia	11	0.8	..	..	..	..	..	..	0.1	..
148 Tanzania, U. Rep. of	3	0.2	0.1	0.8	0.6	0.8	3.7	1.9	0.5	0.3
149 Nepal	3	0.2	..	0.8	0.6	(.)	..	1.7	0.3	..
150 Equatorial Guinea	42	0.9	..	0.6	5.0	..	..	..	0.4	..
151 Sudan	25	7.1	0.6	2.4	..	0.3	..	..	0.3	..
152 Burundi	6	0.1	(.)	0.4	..	0.2	0.6	0.5	0.2	0.4
153 Rwanda	6	..	..	(.)	..	0.2	..	..	0.2	0.2
154 Uganda	11	1.0	..	0.2	..	(.)	..	..	0.3	..
155 Angola	6	0.6	0.4	1.3	..	0.1	0.7	0.6	0.7	1.6
156 Benin	9	0.5	0.4	0.3	..	0.1	3.9	0.7	0.4	0.7
157 Malawi	22	..	..	0.3	1.4	0.2	..	..	0.5	0.3
158 Mauritania	14	2.3	..	0.1	..	..	..	..	0.4	..
159 Mozambique	5	0.3	0.7	0.6	..	0.1	1.6	0.2	0.4	..
160 Central African Rep.	7	0.4	..	0.1	..	..	..	..	0.2	0.5
161 Ethiopia	19	0.2	..	0.1	(.)	0.2	..	..	0.3	0.1
162 Bhutan	2	..	..	..	..	..	5.5	1.9	0.3	..
163 Djibouti	8	5.2	..	2.0	..	..	..	..	3.1	..
164 Guinea-Bissau	4	..	..	0.6	..	0.2	..	..	0.6	..
165 Somalia	4	1.2	..	..	..	(.)	..	..	0.2	..
166 Gambia	17	..	..	0.2	2.3	..	..	..	1.3	0.8
167 Mali	4	0.1	..	0.1	..	(.)	..	..	0.1	0.3
168 Chad	24	0.1	..	(.)	..	(.)	0.6	0.3	0.1	..
169 Niger	6	0.5	..	0.1	..	0.1	0.8	0.3	0.2	..
170 Sierra Leone	22	1.0	..	0.2	..	0.1	2.0	0.3	0.8	..
171 Afghanistan	11	0.8	..	1.1	14.5	(.)	..	..	0.2	0.3
172 Burkina Faso	3	0.5	0.5	(.)	..	..	..	..	0.2	0.3
173 Guinea	4	0.7	0.7	..	..	..	..	..	0.3	..
All developing countries	18	5.5	3.0	4.4	5.2	4.0	..	13.4	3.1	3.1
Least developed countries	10	0.9	..	0.6	1.8	0.3	..	3.2	0.3	0.2
Sub-Saharan Africa	15	2.5	..	1.2	2.7	1.5	3.4	3.3	1.5	2.6
Industrial countries	113	54.4	2.3	30.3	74.4	95.2	..	401.0	47.8	50.1
World	35	14.7	2.8	9.2	15.1	20.3	..	104.9	13.0	15.4

Note: Data for industrial countries for this subject area are in table 37.

17 Employment

HDI rank	Labour force (as % of total population) 1990-92	Women in labour force (as % of total labour force) 1990-92	Percentage of labour force in						Earnings per employee annual growth rate (%)	
			Agriculture		Industry		Services			
			1965	1990-92	1965	1990-92	1965	1990-92	1970-80	1980-90
High human development	44	34	28	17	32	29	40	54	..	-0.2
20 Barbados	66	48	..	7	..	11	..	82	..	..
24 Hong Kong	50	37	6	1	53	35	41	64	6.4	4.9
26 Cyprus	48	38	..	15	..	21	..	64	..	..
32 Korea, Rep. of	61	40	55	17	15	36	30	47	10.0	7.4
33 Uruguay	45	41	20	5	29	22	51	73	..	0.8
35 Trinidad and Tobago	39	36	20	10	35	33	45	57	..	-0.7
36 Bahamas	45	47	..	5	..	4	..	91	..	..
37 Argentina	38	28	18	13	34	34	48	53	-1.5	-0.8
38 Chile	38	32	27	19	29	26	44	55	8.2	-1.0
39 Costa Rica	37	30	47	25	19	27	34	48	..	-2.2
43 Singapore	65	40	6	(.)	27	35	67	65	3.0	5.0
44 Brunei Darussalam	..	..								
46 Venezuela	37	32	30	13	24	25	46	62	3.8	-5.2
47 Panama	48	29	46	27	16	14	38	59	0.2	2.2
50 Colombia	45	43	45	10	21	24	34	66	-0.2	1.6
51 Kuwait	39	24	2	..	34	26	64	73	..	3.8
52 Mexico	38	31	49	23	22	29	29	48	1.2	-3.9
Medium human development	50	39	73	46	11	25	16	29	..	2.7
Excluding China	41	34	53	38	18	21	29	41	..	1.6
54 Thailand	56	47	82	67	5	11	13	22	1.0	5.9
55 Antigua and Barbuda	..	..	..	..	..	..	..	..	..	..
56 Qatar	42	7	..	3	..	28	..	69	..	..
57 Malaysia	38	36	58	26	13	28	29	46	2.0	2.6
58 Bahrain	45	18	..	3	..	14	..	83	..	..
59 Fiji	35	19	..	44	..	20	..	36	..	..
60 Mauritius	41	30	37	16	25	30	38	54	1.8	-0.1
62 United Arab Emirates	50	6	21	5	32	38	47	57	..	..
63 Brazil	44	36	49	25	20	25	31	47	4.0	4.8
64 Dominica	38	42	..	31	..	13	..	56	..	..
65 Jamaica	45	47	37	26	20	24	43	50	-0.2	-0.8
67 Saudi Arabia	29	7	68	48	11	14	21	37	..	..
68 Turkey	37	31	75	47	11	20	14	33	6.1	-1.2
69 Saint Vincent	..	..	..	..	..	..	..	..	..	..
70 Saint Kitts and Nevis	..	..	..	..	..	..	..	..	..	..
73 Syrian Arab Rep.	28	18	52	23	20	29	28	48	2.8	-5.4
74 Ecuador	35	26	55	33	19	19	26	48	3.3	-1.5
77 Saint Lucia	..	..	..	..	..	..	..	..	..	..
78 Grenada	40	49	..	..	..	..	..	..	..	..
79 Libyan Arab Jamahiriya	24	9	41	20	21	30	38	50	..	..
81 Tunisia	30	21	50	26	21	34	29	40	4.2	-0.8
83 Seychelles	44	43	..	..	..	..	..	..	..	..
84 Paraguay	43	41	54	48	20	21	26	31	..	..
85 Suriname	56	41	..	20	..	20	..	60	..	..
86 Iran, Islamic Rep. of	26	10	49	30	26	26	25	44	..	-8.2
87 Botswana	33	38	88	28	4	11	8	61	2.6	-5.5
88 Belize	31	33	..	..	..	..	..	..	..	..
89 Cuba	44	32	33	24	25	29	42	47	..	..
90 Sri Lanka	41	33	56	49	14	21	30	30	..	1.8
92 Oman	28	8	62	49	15	22	23	29	..	..
93 South Africa	38	39	32	13	30	25	38	62	2.7	0.2
94 China	59	43	81	73	8	14	11	13	..	3.5
95 Peru	40	39	49	35	19	12	32	53	..	-3.5
96 Dominican Rep.	30	15	59	46	14	15	27	39	-1.1	-4.4
98 Jordan	23	10	37	10	26	26	37	64	..	-3.9
99 Philippines	56	37	58	45	16	16	26	39	-3.7	5.6
100 Iraq	24	6	50	14	20	19	30	67	..	..
101 Korea, Dem. Rep. of	45	46	57	43	23	30	20	27	..	..
102 Mongolia	46	45	54	40	20	21	26	39	..	..
103 Lebanon	30	27	29	14	24	27	47	59	..	..
104 Samoa	..	..	..	..	..	..	..	..	..	..
105 Indonesia	43	40	70	56	9	14	21	30	5.0	5.1
106 Nicaragua	35	33	56	46	16	16	28	38	..	-10.0
107 Guyana	36	21	..	27	..	26	..	47	..	..
108 Guatemala	34	26	64	50	15	18	21	32	-3.2	-1.9
109 Algeria	24	4	57	18	17	33	26	49	-1.0	..
110 Egypt	31	29	55	42	15	21	30	37	4.1	-2.1
111 Morocco	33	26	61	46	15	25	24	29	..	-3.5
112 El Salvador	41	45	58	11	16	23	26	66	2.4	-9.4
113 Bolivia	38	41	54	47	20	19	26	34	(.)	-6.4

HDI rank	Labour force (as % of total population) 1990-92	Women in labour force (as % of total labour force) 1990-92	Percentage of labour force in						Earnings per employee annual growth rate (%)	
			Agriculture		Industry		Services			
			1965	1990-92	1965	1990-92	1965	1990-92	1970-80	1980-90
114 Gabon	48	38	..	75	..	11	..	14	..	..
115 Honduras	35	31	68	38	12	15	20	47	..	0.9
116 Viet Nam	49	47	79	67	6	12	15	21	..	..
117 Swaziland	24	34	..	74	..	9	..	17	..	..
118 Maldives	27	20	..	25	..	32	..	43	..	..
Low human development	38	31	74	64	10	10	16	26	..	2.9
Excluding India	38	34	75	66	9	10	16	24	..	1.8
119 Vanuatu	47	46	..	68	..	8	..	24	..	..
120 Lesotho	46	44	91	23	3	33	6	44	..	..
121 Zimbabwe	41	48	79	71	8	8	13	21	1.6	0.5
122 Cape Verde	35	37	..	31	..	6	..	63	..	..
123 Congo	40	39	66	62	11	12	23	26	..	-2.6
124 Cameroon	39	30	87	79	4	7	9	14	..	..
125 Kenya	40	40	86	81	5	7	9	12	-3.4	-0.7
126 Solomon Islands	..	..	..	..	..	..	..	..	..	..
127 Namibia	29	24	..	43	..	22	..	35	..	..
128 São Tomé and Principe	..	..	..	..	..	..	..	..	..	..
129 Papua New Guinea	47	39	87	76	6	10	7	14	2.9	-1.5
130 Myanmar	41	37	63	70	14	9	23	21	..	..
131 Madagascar	43	40	85	81	4	6	11	13	-0.9	6.6
132 Pakistan	28	14	60	47	18	20	22	33	3.4	6.6
133 Lao People's Dem. Rep.	55	45	80	76	5	7	15	17	..	..
134 Ghana	38	40	61	59	15	11	24	30	0.4	7.8
135 India	38	29	73	62	12	11	15	27	-0.9	3.4
136 Côte d'Ivoire	39	32	80	65	5	8	15	27	-0.9	..
137 Haiti	41	40	77	68	7	9	16	23	-3.3	4.6
138 Zambia	32	29	79	38	8	8	13	54	-3.2	3.1
139 Nigeria	31	33	72	48	10	7	18	45	-0.8	..
140 Zaire	37	36	82	71	9	13	9	16	..	..
141 Comoros	38	41	..	83	..	6	..	11	..	..
142 Yemen	25	13	73	63	8	11	19	26	..	..
143 Senegal	34	26	83	81	6	6	11	13	-4.9	0.5
144 Liberia	36	31	79	75	10	9	11	16	..	1.7
145 Togo	41	37	78	65	9	6	13	29	-3.0	0.6
146 Bangladesh	47	41	84	59	5	13	11	28	-3.0	0.6
147 Cambodia	43	56	80	74	4	7	16	19	..	..
148 Tanzania, U. Rep. of	47	48	91	85	3	5	6	10	..	-13.5
149 Nepal	40	34	94	93	2	1	4	6	..	..
150 Equatorial Guinea	39	36	..	77	..	2	..	21	..	..
151 Sudan	35	29	81	72	5	5	14	23	..	..
152 Burundi	53	53	94	92	2	2	4	6	-7.5	..
153 Rwanda	46	54	95	90	2	2	3	8	..	..
154 Uganda	45	41	91	86	3	4	6	10	..	..
155 Angola	41	39	79	73	8	10	13	17	..	..
156 Benin	35	24	83	70	5	7	12	23	..	..
157 Malawi	43	51	92	87	3	5	5	8	..	-0.8
158 Mauritania	33	22	89	69	3	9	8	22	..	..
159 Mozambique	55	48	87	85	6	7	7	8	..	..
160 Central African Rep.	48	47	88	81	3	3	9	16	..	..
161 Ethiopia	41	41	86	88	5	2	9	10	-4.6	0.5
162 Bhutan	46	32	94	92	2	3	4	5	..	..
163 Djibouti	..	..	..	..	..	..	..	..	..	..
164 Guinea-Bissau	30	42	..	82	..	4	..	14	..	..
165 Somalia	29	39	81	76	6	8	13	16	-5.1	..
166 Gambia	36	41	..	84	..	7	..	9	..	..
167 Mali	32	16	91	85	1	2	8	13	..	..
168 Chad	37	17	92	83	3	5	5	12	..	..
169 Niger	51	47	95	85	1	3	4	12	..	0.4
170 Sierra Leone	35	33	78	70	11	14	11	16	..	..
171 Afghanistan	30	8	69	61	11	14	20	25	..	..
172 Burkina Faso	51	49	90	87	3	4	7	9	..	..
173 Guinea	39	30	87	78	6	1	7	21	..	..
All developing countries	45	35	72	58	11	15	17	27	1.3	2.6
Least developed countries	42	38	83	73	6	8	11	19	..	..
Sub-Saharan Africa	39	37	79	67	8	8	13	25	-1.5	1.2
Industrial countries	48	43	22	9	37	33	41	58	2.2	1.2
World	45	37	57	13	19	31	24	56	1.6	2.3

Note: Data for industrial countries for this subject area are in table 38.

18 Wealth, poverty and social investment

HDI rank	Real GDP per capita (PPP$) 1991	GNP per capita (US$) 1991	Income share Lowest 40% of house-holds (%) 1980-91	Income share Ratio of highest 20% to lowest 20% 1980-91	People in absolute poverty Total (%) 1980-90	People in absolute poverty Rural (%) 1980-90	People in absolute poverty Urban (%) 1980-90	Social security benefits expenditure (as % of GDP) 1985-90	Public expenditure on Education (as % of GNP) 1990	Public expenditure on Health (as % of GDP) 1990	Total expenditure on health (as % of GDP) 1990
High human development	**7,290**	**3,830**	..	..	**25**	**37**	**21**	**2.7**	**3.7**	**2.1**	**4.7**
20 Barbados	9,667	6,650	..	..	15	23	..	0.9	8.0	..	..
24 Hong Kong	18,520	13,580	16.2	8.7	..	..	..	..	3.0	1.1	5.7
26 Cyprus	9,844	8,670	..	..	..	9	..	2.3	3.6	4.2	..
32 Korea, Rep. of	8,320	6,350	..	..	5	4	5	..	3.6	2.7	6.6
33 Uruguay	6,670	2,880	..	..	13	29	10	7.5	3.1	2.5	4.6
35 Trinidad and Tobago	8,380	3,790	..	..	..	39	..	2.1	4.1	2.6	..
36 Bahamas	..	11,790	..	..	..	..	..	0.5	..	3.5	..
37 Argentina	5,120	3,970	..	..	16	20	15	..	..	2.5	4.2
38 Chile	7,060	2,360	10.5	17.0	..	25	..	9.9	3.7	3.4	4.7
39 Costa Rica	5,100	1,870	13.1	12.7	29	34	24	6.3	4.6	5.6	..
43 Singapore	14,734	14,140	15.0	9.6	..	..	..	7.1	3.4	1.1	1.9
44 Brunei Darussalam	..	..	..	..	..	..	..	..	..	2.2	..
46 Venezuela	8,120	2,720	14.3	10.3	31	58	28	1.1	4.1	2.0	3.6
47 Panama	4,910	2,130	8.3	29.9	42	65	21	9.4	5.5	..	..
50 Colombia	5,460	1,250	12.7	13.3	42	45	40	1.5	2.9	1.8	4.0
51 Kuwait	13,126	..	..	..	..	..	..	..	5.0	..	..
52 Mexico	7,170	3,080	11.9	13.6	30	51	23	1.5	4.1	1.6	3.2
Medium human development	**3,420**	**970**	..	..	**20**	**23**	..	**3.3**	**4.1**	**2.3**	**3.9**
Excluding China	**4,000**	**1,680**	..	..	**37**	**41**	**29**	**3.3**	**4.7**	**2.4**	**4.0**
54 Thailand	5,270	1,650	15.5	8.3	30	34	17	..	3.8	1.1	5.0
55 Antigua and Barbuda	..	4,720	..	..	..	50	..	..	..	..	..
56 Qatar	..	15,040	..	..	..	..	..	..	3.4	3.1	..
57 Malaysia	7,400	2,520	12.9	11.7	16	22	8	0.5	6.9	1.3	3.0
58 Bahrain	11,536	7,150	..	..	..	..	..	0.1	..	6.0	..
59 Fiji	4,858	1,920	..	..	..	20	..	0.6	5.0	..	..
60 Mauritius	7,178	2,380	..	..	8	12	..	5.6	3.7	2.0	..
62 United Arab Emirates	17,000	22,180	..	..	..	..	..	..	1.9	9.0	..
63 Brazil	5,240	2,920	7.0	32.1	47	73	38	4.6	4.6	2.8	4.2
64 Dominica	..	2,440	..	..	..	70	..	..	5.8	..	..
65 Jamaica	3,670	1,490	15.9	8.1	..	80	..	1.2	6.1	2.9	..
67 Saudi Arabia	10,850	7,900	..	..	..	..	..	1.4	6.2	3.1	4.8
68 Turkey	4,840	1,790	..	..	..	14	..	4.5	..	1.5	4.0
69 Saint Vincent	..	1,840	..	..	..	50	..	..	..	..	..
70 Saint Kitts and Nevis	..	3,780	..	..	46	50	40	..	..	..	..
73 Syrian Arab Rep.	5,220	1,170	..	..	..	54	..	..	4.1	0.4	2.1
74 Ecuador	4,140	1,010	..	..	56	65	40	1.6	2.8	2.6	4.1
77 Saint Lucia	..	2,700	..	..	..	50	..	..	..	..	..
78 Grenada	3,374	2,300	..	..	..	25	..	..	..	..	..
79 Libyan Arab Jamahiriya	..	..	..	..	..	..	..	..	..	..	..
81 Tunisia	4,690	1,500	16.3	7.8	17	15	20	3.6	6.1	3.3	4.9
83 Seychelles	3,683	5,070	..	..	..	20	..	1.7	8.5	..	..
84 Paraguay	3,420	1,270	..	..	35	50	19	..	..	1.2	2.8
85 Suriname	3,072	3,650	..	..	..	57	..	0.6	8.3	5.7	..
86 Iran, Islamic Rep. of	4,670	2,410	..	..	..	30	..	..	4.1	1.5	2.6
87 Botswana	4,690	2,580	6.0	47.4	43	55	30	..	8.4	3.2	..
88 Belize	..	2,180	..	..	..	65	..	..	6.0	2.2	..
89 Cuba	..	..	..	..	..	35	..	7.1	6.6	3.4	..
90 Sri Lanka	2,650	500	13.3	11.5	39	46	15	2.0	2.7	1.8	3.7
92 Oman	9,230	6,140	..	..	..	6	..	..	3.5	2.1	..
93 South Africa	3,885	2,540	..	..	..	..	..	..	..	3.2	5.6
94 China	2,946	370	17.4	6.5	9	13	..	3.4	2.3	2.1	3.5
95 Peru	3,110	1,070	14.1	10.5	32	75	13	..	..	1.9	3.2
96 Dominican Rep.	3,080	940	12.1	13.2	55	70	45	0.5	..	2.1	3.7
98 Jordan	2,895	1,060	..	..	16	17	14	(.)	5.9	1.8	3.8
99 Philippines	2,440	740	16.6	7.4	54	64	40	0.7	2.9	1.0	2.0
100 Iraq	..	..	..	..	..	30	..	..	..	..	..
101 Korea, Dem. Rep. of	..	..	..	..	..	20	..	..	..	..	..
102 Mongolia	..	..	..	..	..	..	..	..	..	..	..
103 Lebanon	..	..	..	..	..	15	..	1.2	..	..	..
104 Samoa	1,869	960	..	..	..	60	..	..	5.3	5.6	..
105 Indonesia	2,730	610	20.8	4.9	25	27	20	..	..	0.7	2.0
106 Nicaragua	2,550	400	..	..	20	19	21	1.5	..	6.7	8.6
107 Guyana	1,862	300	..	..	..	60	..	0.8	4.7	..	..
108 Guatemala	3,180	940	7.9	30.0	71	74	66	0.8	1.4	2.1	3.7
109 Algeria	2,870	1,990	..	..	23	25	20	..	9.1	5.4	7.0
110 Egypt	3,600	610	..	..	23	25	21	1.1	6.7	1.0	2.6
111 Morocco	3,340	1,030	17.1	7.0	37	45	28	1.5	5.5	0.9	2.6
112 El Salvador	2,110	1,090	..	..	51	75	20	1.0	1.8	2.6	5.9
113 Bolivia	2,170	650	..	..	60	86	30	2.3	3.0	2.4	4.0

HDI rank	Real GDP per capita (PPP$) 1991	GNP per capita (US$) 1991	Income share Lowest 40% of house-holds (%) 1980-91	Income share Ratio of highest 20% to lowest 20% 1980-91	People in absolute poverty Total (%) 1980-90	People in absolute poverty Rural (%) 1980-90	People in absolute poverty Urban (%) 1980-90	Social security benefits expenditure (as % of GDP) 1985-90	Public expenditure on Education (as % of GNP) 1990	Public expenditure on Health (as % of GDP) 1990	Total expenditure on health (as % of GDP) 1990
114 Gabon	3,498	3,980	..	..	..	41	..	2.0	5.7	3.2	..
115 Honduras	1,820	590	8.7	23.5	37	55	14	..	4.6	2.9	4.5
116 Viet Nam	..	..	..	..	54	60	..	..	..	1.1	2.1
117 Swaziland	2,506	1,130	..	..	48	50	45	..	6.4	5.8	..
118 Maldives	..	470	..	..	..	40	..	..	9.2	5.0	..
Low human development	1,170	330	..	..	46	52	30	0.6	3.6	1.6	4.9
Excluding India	1,200	320	..	..	53	62	25	1.0	3.6	1.9	3.6
119 Vanuatu	1,679	1,180	..	..	..	..	..	..	..	2.9	..
120 Lesotho	..	570	11.0	13.6	54	55	50	..	3.8	1.2	..
121 Zimbabwe	2,160	670	..	..	..	60	..	0.1	10.6	3.2	6.2
122 Cape Verde	1,360	750	..	..	..	40	..	..	4.1	..	..
123 Congo	2,800	1,040	..	..	..	80	..	..	5.6	3.0	..
124 Cameroon	2,400	860	..	..	37	40	15	..	3.4	1.0	2.6
125 Kenya	1,350	340	9.1	22.6	52	55	10	0.6	6.8	2.7	4.3
126 Solomon Islands	2,113	700	..	..	..	60	..	..	..	5.0	..
127 Namibia	2,381	1,520	..	..	..	..	..	..	4.7	5.0	..
128 São Tomé and Principe	..	400	..	..	..	50	..	..	..	..	..
129 Papua New Guinea	1,550	930	..	..	73	75	10	..	..	2.8	4.4
130 Myanmar	..	..	..	..	35	40	..	..	1.9	0.8	..
131 Madagascar	710	210	..	..	43	50	21	..	..	1.3	2.6
132 Pakistan	1,970	400	21.3	4.7	28	29	26	..	3.4	1.8	3.4
133 Lao People's Dem. Rep.	1,760	220	..	..	..	85	..	..	1.1	1.0	2.5
134 Ghana	930	420	18.3	6.3	42	54	20	..	3.3	1.7	3.5
135 India	1,150	330	21.3	4.7	40	42	33	0.5	3.5	1.3	6.0
136 Côte d'Ivoire	1,510	680	19.2	5.8	..	..	30	0.5	..	1.7	3.3
137 Haiti	925	380	..	..	76	80	65	..	1.8	3.2	7.0
138 Zambia	1,010	420	..	..	64	80	47	..	2.9	2.2	3.2
139 Nigeria	1,360	350	..	..	40	51	21	..	..	1.2	2.7
140 Zaire	469	..	..	..	70	90	..	..	0.9	0.8	2.4
141 Comoros	..	490	..	..	..	50	..	..	..	3.3	..
142 Yemen	1,374	520	..	..	..	30	..	..	..	1.5	3.2
143 Senegal	1,680	730	..	..	..	70	..	1.4	3.7	2.3	3.7
144 Liberia	..	..	..	..	20	23	..	..	..	3.5	..
145 Togo	738	410	..	..	..	30	..	0.8	5.7	2.5	4.1
146 Bangladesh	1,160	220	22.9	4.1	78	86	..	2.1	2.0	1.4	3.2
147 Cambodia	1,250	200	..	..	..	..	..	..	..	..	..
148 Tanzania, U. Rep. of	570	120	8.1	26.1	58	60	10	..	5.8	3.2	4.7
149 Nepal	1,130	180	22.0	4.3	60	61	51	..	..	2.2	4.5
150 Equatorial Guinea	..	290	..	..	67	70	60	..	1.7	..	..
151 Sudan	1,162	..	..	..	..	85	..	(.)	..	0.5	3.3
152 Burundi	640	220	..	..	84	85	55	0.7	3.5	1.7	3.3
153 Rwanda	680	290	22.8	4.0	85	90	30	0.3	4.2	1.9	3.5
154 Uganda	1,036	170	20.6	4.9	..	80	..	..	2.9	1.6	3.4
155 Angola	..	..	..	..	..	65	..	..	..	1.8	..
156 Benin	1,500	380	..	..	..	65	..	0.6	..	2.8	4.3
157 Malawi	800	230	..	..	82	90	25	..	3.4	2.9	5.0
158 Mauritania	962	510	..	..	..	80	..	..	4.7	5.5	..
159 Mozambique	921	80	..	..	59	65	40	..	6.3	4.4	5.9
160 Central African Rep.	641	410	..	..	..	90	..	..	2.8	2.6	4.2
161 Ethiopia	370	120	21.3	4.8	60	63	..	1.4	4.8	2.3	3.8
162 Bhutan	620	190	..	..	..	90	..	..	3.7	4.2	..
163 Djibouti	..	..	..	..	..	70	..	1.4	3.3	..	..
164 Guinea-Bissau	747	180	..	..	..	75	..	..	2.8	1.3	..
165 Somalia	759	..	..	..	60	70	..	..	..	0.9	1.5
166 Gambia	763	360	..	..	..	85	..	..	3.8	1.6	..
167 Mali	480	270	..	..	54	60	27	0.5	3.2	2.8	5.2
168 Chad	447	210	..	..	54	56	30	..	2.3	4.7	6.3
169 Niger	542	310	..	..	..	35	..	0.3	..	3.4	5.0
170 Sierra Leone	1,020	200	..	..	..	65	..	..	1.4	1.7	2.4
171 Afghanistan	..	..	..	..	53	60	18	..	..	1.6	..
172 Burkina Faso	666	290	..	..	..	90	..	0.4	2.3	7.0	8.5
173 Guinea	500	500	..	..	..	70	..	..	..	2.3	3.9
All developing countries	2,730	880	..	..	31	37	28	2.7	3.9	2.2	4.2
Least developed countries	880	240	..	..	64	71	31	1.2	3.0	2.0	3.8
Sub-Saharan Africa	1,250	540	..	..	54	65	23	0.9	4.6	2.5	4.4
Industrial countries	14,860	14,920	..	..	..	..	..	16.2	4.9	..	9.4
World	5,490	4,160	..	..	..	..	..	14.7	4.8	..	8.6

Note: Data for industrial countries for this subject area are in table 40.

19 Aid flows

HDI rank	Bilateral official development assistance (ODA) received				Bilateral aid			Human priority aid (as % of total bilateral aid) (%) 1989-91
	US$ millions 1992	As % of GNP 1992	Per capita (US$) 1992	Per poor person (US$) 1992	Social allocation ratio (%) 1989-91	Social priority ratio (%) 1989-91	Human expenditure ratio (%) 1989-92	
High human development	1,170T	0.2	4	23	31.3	44.0	0.028	13.8
20 Barbados	2	0.1	8	..	..	..	..	..
24 Hong Kong	37	(.)	(.)	..	33.9	..	..	..
26 Cyprus	27	0.4	38	..	60.2	18.6	0.049	11.2
32 Korea, Rep. of	-106	-(.)	-2	..	..	..	..	..
33 Uruguay	70	0.8	22	174	6.1	70.1	0.033	4.2
35 Trinidad and Tobago	8	0.2	6	..	..	..	..	..
36 Bahamas	2	0.1	8	..	..	..	..	..
37 Argentina	286	0.3	9	55	17.6	63.2	0.035	11.1
38 Chile	137	0.5	10	..	41.1	34.9	0.067	14.3
39 Costa Rica	136	2.3	43	147	13.3	17.3	0.053	2.3
43 Singapore	20	0.1	7	..	..	..	..	..
44 Brunei Darussalam	5	..	19	..	..	..	..	..
46 Venezuela	31	0.1	2	6	53.7	..	..	..
47 Panama	157	2.9	62	149	8.3	..	..	..
50 Colombia	240	0.6	7	17	33.9	12.3	0.024	4.2
51 Kuwait	-199	..	-103	..	..	..	..	..
52 Mexico	317	0.1	4	12	2.4	30.1	0.001	0.7
Medium human development	18,920T	1.0	9	46	20.3	61.5	0.125	12.5
Excluding China	15,970T	1.0	16	53	21.3	63.7	0.136	13.6
54 Thailand	789	0.9	14	47	8.7	17.8	0.014	1.5
55 Antigua and Barbuda	5	1.7	76	..	..	..	..	..
56 Qatar	2	(.)	4	..	..	..	..	..
57 Malaysia	213	0.4	11	71	39.3	77.1	0.136	30.3
58 Bahrain	71	1.9	133	..	..	..	..	..
59 Fiji	63	4.4	85	..	43.7	18.5	0.357	8.1
60 Mauritius	47	1.7	43	534	10.1	2.0	0.000	0.2
62 United Arab Emirates	-566	-1.7	-333	..	21.7	37.0	0.004	8.1
63 Brazil	236	0.1	2	3	21.7	37.0	0.004	8.1
64 Dominica	14	8.0	196	..	52.5	..	..	..
65 Jamaica	126	3.7	51	..	16.6	56.0	0.343	9.3
67 Saudi Arabia	-703	-0.6	-44	..	..	..	..	..
68 Turkey	323	0.3	6	..	9.3	69.9	0.020	6.5
69 Saint Vincent	28	14.8	257	..	5.2	..	..	..
70 Saint Kitts and Nevis	7	4.2	168	366	..	..	..	..
73 Syrian Arab Rep.	163	1.1	12	..	6.6	..	..	..
74 Ecuador	249	2.3	23	40	22.6	56.0	0.285	12.6
77 Saint Lucia	7	2.1	51	..	48.1	..	..	..
78 Grenada	12	6.0	131	..	9.6	..	..	..
79 Libyan Arab Jamahiriya	22	..	4	..	..	..	..	..
81 Tunisia	407	3.2	48	285	13.5	10.9	0.047	1.5
83 Seychelles	20	5.4	277	..	5.7	18.7	0.058	1.1
84 Paraguay	99	1.7	22	62	8.9	59.7	0.091	5.3
85 Suriname	79	5.0	180	..	49.9	..	..	..
86 Iran, Islamic Rep. of	169	0.1	3	..	4.6	..	..	..
87 Botswana	113	3.4	86	202	38.8	48.5	0.640	18.8
88 Belize	23	5.8	117	..	30.4	48.3	0.854	14.7
89 Cuba	30	..	3	..	8.0	..	..	..
90 Sri Lanka	658T	7.4	37	94	20.3	45.9	0.694	9.3
92 Oman	54	0.5	33	..	..	..	..	..
93 South Africa	..	..	..	..	..	..	..	..
94 China	2,945	0.7	3	28	13.2	18.2	0.017	2.4
95 Peru	419	1.8	19	58	9.4	74.3	0.128	7.0
96 Dominican Rep.	62	0.9	8	15	21.9	55.7	0.108	12.2
98 Jordan	379	8.4	88	550	9.0	28.0	0.210	2.5
99 Philippines	1,738	3.7	27	49	13.6	62.3	0.309	8.4
100 Iraq	187	..	10	..	..	..	..	..
101 Korea, Dem. Rep. of	12	..	1	..	..	..	..	..
102 Mongolia	105	..	45	..	23.4	7.4	..	1.7
103 Lebanon	81	..	28	..	22.2	3.5	..	0.8
104 Samoa	60	39.5	379	..	..	..	..	..
105 Indonesia	2,080	1.8	11	44	12.6	23.4	0.053	2.9
106 Nicaragua	662	36.2	166	832	9.8	58.0	2.046	5.7
107 Guyana	95	27.2	117	..	0.7	..	..	..
108 Guatemala	210	2.3	22	30	24.4	54.6	0.308	13.3
109 Algeria	412	0.8	16	69	9.8	98.5	0.076	9.7
110 Egypt	3,538	10.6	64	280	18.7	81.2	1.602	15.2
111 Morocco	996	3.7	38	111	9.6	62.5	0.220	6.0
112 El Salvador	399	6.8	74	144	25.7	20.9	0.367	5.4
113 Bolivia	679	13.9	90	66	15.5	51.6	1.109	8.0

HDI rank	Bilateral official development assistance (ODA) received				Bilateral aid			Human priority aid (as % of total bilateral aid) (%) 1989-91
	US$ millions 1992	As % of GNP 1992	Per capita (US$) 1992	Per poor person (US$) 1992	Social allocation ratio (%) 1989-91	Social priority ratio (%) 1989-91	Human expenditure ratio (%) 1989-92	
114 Gabon	69	1.5	56	..	6.2	8.0	0.007	0.5
115 Honduras	355	11.2	65	178	18.6	43.9	0.913	8.2
116 Viet Nam	586	..	8	16	45.8	21.7	..	9.9
117 Swaziland	49	5.9	62	129	41.9	28.7	0.708	12.0
118 Maldives	39	37.3	172	..	34.2	8.7	1.118	3.0
Low human development	25,120T	4.3	14	25	22.5	53.2	0.515	12.0
Excluding India	22,770T	8.2	26	45	23.2	53.8	1.023	12.5
119 Vanuatu	45	24.8	286	..	31.6	33.6	2.634	10.6
120 Lesotho	142	13.3	77	143	30.4	80.3	3.247	24.4
121 Zimbabwe	735	10.7	69	..	8.2	58.7	0.517	4.8
122 Cape Verde	120	41.5	311	..	15.9	73.9	4.869	11.7
123 Congo	115	4.3	48	..	13.2	62.8	0.358	8.3
124 Cameroon	727	7.0	59	161	13.9	36.8	0.359	5.1
125 Kenya	780	9.1	31	59	19.2	30.5	0.530	5.8
126 Solomon Islands	44	18.6	128	..	17.6	40.1	1.311	7.1
127 Namibia	140	6.2	91	..	40.9	49.2	1.253	20.1
128 São Tomé and Principe	54	108.3	433	..	24.5	..	..	..
129 Papua New Guinea	483	14.3	119	163	43.0	18.9	1.165	8.1
130 Myanmar	126	..	3	8	2.1	..	..	..
131 Madagascar	359	13.3	28	64	12.0	29.3	0.468	3.5
132 Pakistan	1,169	2.3	9	33	20.1	48.4	0.227	9.7
133 Lao People's Dem. Rep.	173	17.6	39	..	21.6	44.3	1.681	9.6
134 Ghana	626	9.8	39	93	13.3	44.0	0.573	5.9
135 India	2,354	0.8	3	7	12.0	43.0	0.043	5.2
136 Côte d'Ivoire	763	8.5	59	210	4.8	47.3	0.196	2.3
137 Haiti	106	4.2	16	21	32.4	58.1	0.797	18.8
138 Zambia	1,016	29.9	118	184	10.1	50.6	..	5.1
139 Nigeria	265	0.8	3	7	8.7	9.0	0.006	0.8
140 Zaire	269	3.3	7	10	6.1	27.0	..	1.6
141 Comoros	48	16.4	82	..	7.2	..	..	..
142 Yemen	262	4.0	21	..	21.1	49.1	0.415	10.4
143 Senegal	673	12.1	87	..	24.8	55.0	1.642	13.6
144 Liberia	118	..	43	210	7.7	..	..	..
145 Togo	225	14.5	60	..	15.0	68.3	1.492	10.3
146 Bangladesh	1,728	6.6	14	19	17.4	77.8	0.887	13.5
147 Cambodia	148	8.4	17	..	7.7	..	..	..
148 Tanzania, U. Rep. of	1,344	48.2	48	83	19.2	52.9	4.897	10.2
149 Nepal	467	12.6	23	38	27.6	38.7	1.346	10.7
150 Equatorial Guinea	63	51.4	170	253	20.3	..	..	..
151 Sudan	608	6.0	23	..	15.2	46.9	..	7.1
152 Burundi	316	25.8	54	65	19.9	52.9	2.723	10.6
153 Rwanda	352	17.3	47	55	24.3	73.9	3.104	18.0
154 Uganda	718	22.6	38	..	31.2	67.0	4.722	20.9
155 Angola	322	..	32	..	19.8	22.6	..	4.5
156 Benin	269	14.4	55	..	30.1	59.7	2.581	18.0
157 Malawi	521	22.1	51	62	16.3	36.8	1.326	6.0
158 Mauritania	210	19.2	98	..	7.4	31.0	0.441	2.3
159 Mozambique	1,393	115.6	92	157	24.2	36.3	10.165	8.8
160 Central African Rep.	179	14.4	56	..	11.0	67.6	1.077	7.5
161 Ethiopia	1,301	20.4	24	41	9.3	40.9	0.779	3.8
162 Bhutan	63	21.7	39	..	24.0	39.1	2.034	9.4
163 Djibouti	117	..	250	..	19.5	4.6	..	0.9
164 Guinea-Bissau	107	59.0	106	..	30.7	66.4	12.016	20.4
165 Somalia	577	..	62	103	23.4	..	..	..
166 Gambia	116	35.5	128	..	36.7	11.5	1.493	4.2
167 Mali	439	15.9	45	83	26.7	44.5	1.892	11.9
168 Chad	248	20.1	42	78	30.3	28.0	1.703	8.5
169 Niger	362	14.6	44	..	23.5	51.9	1.777	12.2
170 Sierra Leone	134	14.5	31	..	17.0	98.6	2.441	16.8
171 Afghanistan	174	..	9	17	38.6	12.3	..	4.7
172 Burkina Faso	444	16.1	47	..	36.2	54.1	3.143	19.6
173 Guinea	463	16.4	75	..	29.7	49.0	2.390	14.6
All developing countries	45,210T	1.3	11	32	22.0	56.3	0.161	12.4
Least developed countries	16,180T	13.6	30	42	23.5	56.6	1.801	13.3
Sub-Saharan Africa	18,080T	10.4	35	69	22.5	52.2	1.221	11.7
Industrial countries	..	..	..	..	..	..	..	..
World	..	..	..	..	..	..	..	..

Note: Data for industrial countries for this subject area are in table 41.

HDI rank	Total external debt US$ billions 1991	Total external debt As % of GNP 1991	Debt service ratio (debt service as % of exports of goods and services) 1970	Debt service ratio 1991	Export-import ratio (exports as % of imports) 1991	Trade dependency (exports plus imports as % of GDP) 1991	Terms of trade (1987=100) 1991	Net workers' remittances from abroad (as % of GNP) 1991	Gross international reserves (months of import coverage) 1991	Current account balance (US$ millions) 1991
High human development	293T	35	..	19.0	71	62	103	0.5	4.1	-17,770T
20 Barbados	..	..	..	..	17	..	115	..	..	-31
24 Hong Kong	..	..	..	..	30	192	101	..	..	2,490
26 Cyprus	..	..	..	..	21	..	98	..	..	-200
32 Korea, Rep. of	40.5	14	19.5	7.1	88	54	108	..	1.8	-8,550
33 Uruguay	4.2	45	21.7	38.2	101	33	105	..	5.9	65
35 Trinidad and Tobago	2.3	48	4.6	16.2	119	74	97	0.1	1.9	-20
36 Bahamas	..	..	..	..	..	..	..	..	..	-208
37 Argentina	63.7	49	21.6	48.4	148	18	113	..	5.5	-2,830
38 Chile	17.9	61	19.2	33.9	115	51	122	(.)	7.8	-158
39 Costa Rica	4.0	75	10.0	18.4	80	60	109	(.)	4.5	-165
43 Singapore	..	..	..	..	89	312	101	..	5.4	4,350
44 Brunei Darussalam	..	..	..	..	175	..	96	..	4.8	..
46 Venezuela	34.4	65	2.9	18.7	149	47	101	-1.2	10.8	1,700
47 Panama	6.8	130	7.7	3.9	20	36	112	..	0.9	-105
50 Colombia	17.4	44	12.0	35.2	146	29	84	2.1	8.6	2,360
51 Kuwait	..	..	..	..	..	..	..	..	..	..
52 Mexico	101.7	37	23.6	30.9	71	23	100	0.7	3.7	-13,470
Medium human development	608T	38	..	21.0	108	41	98	..	4.8	8,330T
Excluding China	547T	46	11.0	24.5	106	42	94	-0.2	3.2	-4,560T
54 Thailand	35.8	39	3.3	13.1	76	70	91	(.)	4.8	-7,610
55 Antigua and Barbuda	..	..	..	..	10	..	115	..	..	-37
56 Qatar	..	..	..	..	389	..	85	..	..	..
57 Malaysia	21.4	48	3.8	8.3	97	148	93	(.)	3.2	-4,620
58 Bahrain	..	..	..	..	85	..	96	..	..	-840
59 Fiji	..	..	..	..	47	..	147	..	..	-6
60 Mauritius	1.0	37	3.2	8.8	76	123	104	..	5.5	-39
62 United Arab Emirates	..	..	..	..	153	..	85	..	..	..
63 Brazil	116.5	29	12.5	30.0	138	13	119	(.)	2.7	-3,070
64 Dominica	..	..	..	..	41	..	112	..	..	..
65 Jamaica	4.5	135	2.8	29.4	59	84	91	4.2	0.5	-303
67 Saudi Arabia	..	..	..	..	214	74	79	-11.0	2.4	-19,250
68 Turkey	50.3	48	21.9	30.5	65	36	108	2.7	2.9	-1,970
69 Saint Vincent	..	..	..	..	..	..	..	..	..	-16
70 Saint Kitts and Nevis	..	..	..	..	27	..	115	..	..	-49
73 Syrian Arab Rep.	16.8	104	11.3	..	186	50	..	2.4	..	..
74 Ecuador	12.5	115	8.6	32.2	127	46	90	(.)	3.2	-577
77 Saint Lucia	..	..	..	..	88	..	115	..	..	-86
78 Grenada	..	..	..	..	40	..	112	..	..	-48
79 Libyan Arab Jamahiriya	..	..	..	..	146	..	85	..	..	..
81 Tunisia	8.3	66	19.7	22.7	72	77	95	4.5	1.6	-322
83 Seychelles	..	..	..	..	10	..	128	..	..	-24
84 Paraguay	2.2	35	11.8	11.9	50	35	117	(.)	5.2	-476
85 Suriname	..	..	..	..	..	..	..	..	..	..
86 Iran, Islamic Rep. of	11.5	12	..	3.9	73	39	88	..	..	-7,810
87 Botswana	0.5	16	1.0	3.4	..	..	..	(.)	17.6	-251
88 Belize	..	..	..	..	38	..	96	..	..	-60
89 Cuba	..	..	..	..	..	..	..	..	..	..
90 Sri Lanka	6.6	73	11.0	13.9	68	79	87	5.0	2.5	-472
92 Oman	2.7	29	..	..	20	37	..	-8.4	5.5	..
93 South Africa	..	..	..	..	138	46	86	..	1.5	2,700
94 China	60.8	16	..	12.1	114	37	111	(.)	10.1	12,890
95 Peru	20.7	44	11.6	27.7	118	13	67	..	6.1	-1,800
96 Dominican Rep.	4.5	66	4.5	11.6	38	33	112	4.7	2.2	-115
98 Jordan	8.6	227	3.6	20.9	35	96	116	9.9	3.4	-876
99 Philippines	31.9	70	7.5	23.2	72	47	91	0.7	3.3	-1,390
100 Iraq	..	..	..	..	..	..	..	..	..	..
101 Korea, Dem. Rep. of	..	..	..	..	..	..	..	..	..	..
102 Mongolia	..	..	..	..	..	..	..	..	..	-155
103 Lebanon	..	..	..	..	30	..	108	..	..	..
104 Samoa	..	..	..	..	8	..	147	..	..	-41
105 Indonesia	73.6	66	7.0	32.7	112	47	101	0.1	3.3	-4,210
106 Nicaragua	10.4	154	10.6	..	36	15	99	0.5	..	-849
107 Guyana	..	..	..	..	70	..	105	..	..	-31
108 Guatemala	2.7	30	7.4	15.3	65	33	103	1.4	4.8	-186
109 Algeria	28.6	70	4.0	73.7	153	60	95	0.5	3.5	2,560
110 Egypt	40.6	133	38.0	16.7	49	39	93	11.2	4.4	-2,440
111 Morocco	21.2	80	8.7	27.8	62	40	98	7.3	4.5	-676
112 El Salvador	2.2	37	3.6	17.2	41	21	103	8.0	3.1	-369
113 Bolivia	4.1	85	11.3	34.0	77	35	73	(.)	3.7	-422

HDI rank	Total external debt US$ billions 1991	Total external debt As % of GNP 1991	Debt service ratio (debt service as % of exports of goods and services) 1970	Debt service ratio 1991	Export-import ratio (exports as % of imports) 1991	Trade dependency (exports plus imports as % of GDP) 1991	Terms of trade (1987=100) 1991	Net workers' remittances from abroad (as % of GNP) 1991	Gross international reserves (months of import coverage) 1991	Current account balance (US$ millions) 1991
114 Gabon	3.8	88	5.7	6.5	395	82	79	-2.7	1.6	-185
115 Honduras	3.2	114	2.8	30.6	77	59	113	(.)	1.0	-368
116 Viet Nam	..	..	..	..	..	..	..	..	..	-552
117 Swaziland	..	..	..	..	..	..	..	..	..	-77
118 Maldives	..	..	..	..	..	..	..	..	..	..
Low human development	267T	53	11.3	27.8	88	27	90	1.2	2.6	-10,690T
Excluding India	196T	84	9.0	26.2	90	42	84	1.6	2.2	-7,210T
119 Vanuatu					20	..	147			-49
120 Lesotho	0.4	39	4.5	4.6	..	..	..	(.)	1.3	-443
121 Zimbabwe	3.4	57	2.3	27.2	84	70	101	(.)	1.4	-693
122 Cape Verde	..	..	..	..	8	..	77	..	..	-72
123 Congo	4.7	182	11.5	21.3	278	68	84	-2.0	0.1	-231
124 Cameroon	6.3	58	3.2	18.7	88	23	81	(.)	0.2	-658
125 Kenya	7.0	90	6.0	32.7	59	45	87	(.)	0.6	-435
126 Solomon Islands	..	..	..	..	87	..	147	..	..	-73
127 Namibia	..	..	..	..	..	..	..	..	..	-256
128 São Tomé and Principe	..	..	..	..	..	..	..	..	..	-40
129 Papua New Guinea	2.8	85	1.1	29.6	84	80	80	1.7	1.6	1,050
130 Myanmar					..	..	..			..
131 Madagascar	3.7	148	3.7	32.0	66	35	85	(.)	1.2	-318
132 Pakistan	23.0	50	23.8	21.1	77	37	80	3.7	1.2	-2,170
133 Lao People's Dem. Rep.	1.1	110	..	7.6	..	..	..	..	3.3	-121
134 Ghana	4.2	67	5.5	26.9	70	38	62	(.)	4.4	-442
135 India	71.6	29	22.2	30.7	87	17	100	0.9	3.3	-3,480
136 Côte d'Ivoire	18.8	223	7.1	43.4	180	64	67	-5.5	0.1	-1,610
137 Haiti	0.7	29	7.2	6.6	28	18	77	3.4	0.6	-176
138 Zambia	7.3	..	6.4	50.3	86	61	116	(.)	1.4	-487
139 Nigeria	34.5	109	4.3	25.2	185	54	82	(.)	4.4	470
140 Zaire	..	..	4.4	..	100	..	109	..	..	..
141 Comoros	..	..	..	..	..	..	..	..	..	-46
142 Yemen	6.5	88	..	7.3	..	..	..	12.2	..	-106
143 Senegal	3.5	63	2.9	19.9	69	41	93	0.6	0.1	-503
144 Liberia	..	..	8.0	..	135	..	97	..	..	..
145 Togo	1.4	85	3.1	7.3	53	51	80	0.3	5.0	-170
146 Bangladesh	13.1	56	..	19.9	50	22	105	2.9	4.0	-932
147 Cambodia	..	..	..	..	..	..	..	..	..	..
148 Tanzania, U. Rep. of	6.5	251	5.3	24.6	28	80	84	..	1.4	-832
149 Nepal	1.8	54	3.2	13.6	32	32	85	(.)	5.9	-380
150 Equatorial Guinea	..	..	..	..	..	..	..	..	..	-87
151 Sudan	15.9	..	10.6	..	23	..	94	..	..	-1,860
152 Burundi	1.0	84	2.3	31.5	36	33	43	..	5.0	-214
153 Rwanda	0.8	54	1.5	17.6	..	..	..	-0.5	3.7	-194
154 Uganda	2.8	109	2.9	70.0	36	30	48	..	1.0	-393
155 Angola	..	..	..	..	..	..	..	..	..	..
156 Benin	1.3	70	2.5	6.2	83	39	85	3.7	3.6	-174
157 Malawi	1.7	79	7.8	25.0	65	60	87	(.)	2.5	-244
158 Mauritania	2.3	215	3.4	16.8	93	88	109	(.)	1.2	-209
159 Mozambique	4.7	426	..	10.6	..	..	..	-2.5	2.3	-783
160 Central African Rep.	0.9	72	5.1	11.4	68	27	111	-2.9	4.4	-219
161 Ethiopia	3.5	53	11.4	18.6	27	22	60	3.2	1.0	-585
162 Bhutan	0.1	39	..	7.2	..	..	..	(.)	9.3	-36
163 Djibouti	..	..	..	..	..	..	..	..	..	..
164 Guinea-Bissau	0.7	324	..	..	36	50	138	-1.1	..	..
165 Somalia	..	..	2.1	..	22	..	72	..	..	..
166 Gambia	..	..	..	..	19	..	87	..	..	..
167 Mali	2.5	105	1.4	4.6	56	40	99	2.8	4.5	-344
168 Chad	0.6	47	4.2	4.5	48	49	95	-3.2	2.6	-347
169 Niger	1.7	73	4.0	50.4	89	36	82	-1.5	5.3	-164
170 Sierra Leone	1.3	168	10.8	..	89	41	116	..	0.2	..
171 Afghanistan	..	..	..	..	24	..	80	..	..	..
172 Burkina Faso	1.0	35	7.1	9.1	19	27	89	2.9	..	-426
173 Guinea	2.6	95	..	17.9	..	..	..	(.)	..	-329
All developing countries	1,168T	40	13.3	21.3	90	45	99	0.2	4.3	9,030T
Least developed countries	88T	81	4.5	25.2	51	33	92	2.4	2.9	-9,280T
Sub-Saharan Africa	152T	101	4.7	25.3	120	48	85	..	2.1	-7,740T
Industrial countries	..	..	..	..	96	30	101	..	2.7	310T
World	..	..	..	..	91	32	100	..	4.2	9,340T

Note: Data for industrial countries for this subject area are in table 42.

HDI rank	Military expenditure (as % of GDP)		Military expenditure (as % of combined education and health expenditure)		Average annual imports of non-nuclear arms		Armed forces		
					US$ millions	As % of national imports	Per 1,000 people	Per teacher	Per doctor
	1960	1990-91	1960	1990-91	1988-92	1991	1990	1990	1990
High human development	1.9	2.3	115	39	1,850T	0.7	5.8	0.8	6
20 Barbados	..	0.6	..	5	..	..	..	..	..
24 Hong Kong	..	0.4	..	10	..	..	..	..	..
26 Cyprus	..	1.3	..	17	89	3.4	14.2	1.7	11
32 Korea, Rep. of	6.0	3.8	273	60	705	0.9	17.5	2.7	19
33 Uruguay	2.5	2.1	40	38	23	1.5	8.1	0.8	4
35 Trinidad and Tobago	..	0.6	..	9	..	..	2.4	0.3	3
36 Bahamas	..	..	..	..	9	..	..	..	..
37 Argentina	2.1	3.3	62	51	92	1.1	2.3	0.2	1
38 Chile	2.8	4.8	60	68	166	2.2	7.3	1.0	7
39 Costa Rica	1.2	0.5	17	5	..	..	..	..	..
43 Singapore	0.4	5.8	11	129	263	0.4	18.6	2.9	16
44 Brunei Darussalam	..	9.0	..	125	..	..	15.6	1.0	20
46 Venezuela	2.5	2.0	40	33	123	1.2	3.6	0.3	2
47 Panama	0.1	2.5	2	34	7	0.4	0.4	(.)	(.)
50 Colombia	1.2	2.7	57	57	73	1.5	4.2	0.6	5
51 Kuwait	..	6.5	..	88	249	..	10.3	0.7	8
52 Mexico	0.7	0.3	23	5	45	0.1	1.7	0.2	2
Medium human development	6.9	4.0	162	67	10,200T	1.7	5.1	0.6	9
Excluding China	2.6	3.7	97	54	8,970T	2.5	7.9	0.8	17
54 Thailand	2.6	3.5	96	71	654	1.7	5.1	0.6	25
55 Antigua and Barbuda	..	..	..	..	..	..	..	..	..
56 Qatar	..	12.5	..	192	57	3.0	18.2	1.0	13
57 Malaysia	1.9	3.1	48	38	26	0.1	7.3	0.7	19
58 Bahrain	..	4.7	..	41	148	3.6	11.9	0.6	5
59 Fiji	..	2.6	..	37	..	..	6.7	0.4	8
60 Mauritius	0.2	0.2	4	4	..	..	..	..	..
62 United Arab Emirates	..	4.8	..	44	413	3.0	27.6	2.1	15
63 Brazil	1.8	1.7	72	23	-15	-0.1	2.2	0.2	2
64 Dominica	..	..	..	..	..	..	..	..	..
65 Jamaica	..	0.7	..	8	..	..	1.2	0.2	3
67 Saudi Arabia	5.7	14.0	150	151	1,738	6.8	4.6	0.4	4
68 Turkey	5.2	4.0	153	87	1,233	5.9	11.5	1.9	13
69 Saint Vincent	..	..	..	..	..	..	..	..	..
70 Saint Kitts and Nevis	..	..	..	..	..	..	..	..	..
73 Syrian Arab Rep.	7.9	16.8	329	373	524	17.4	32.7	2.7	47
74 Ecuador	2.4	1.4	104	26	53	2.3	5.6	0.6	5
77 Saint Lucia	..	..	..	..	..	..	..	..	..
78 Grenada	..	..	..	..	..	..	..	..	..
79 Libyan Arab Jamahiriya	1.2	7.8	29	71	140	2.8	18.7	1.1	15
81 Tunisia	2.2	2.9	45	31	14	0.3	4.7	0.5	10
83 Seychelles	..	..	..	..	..	..	..	..	..
84 Paraguay	1.7	1.0	94	42	..	..	3.7	0.4	6
85 Suriname	..	3.8	..	27	..	..	..	..	..
86 Iran, Islamic Rep. of	4.5	2.1	141	38	726	3.3	9.0	0.9	30
87 Botswana	..	2.5	..	22	15	..	3.2	0.3	20
88 Belize	..	..	..	..	..	..	..	..	..
89 Cuba	5.1	12.5	64	125	123	..	17.0	1.3	5
90 Sri Lanka	1.0	4.8	17	107	33	0.8	3.8	0.4	25
92 Oman	..	16.4	..	293	94	3.0	19.3	1.9	21
93 South Africa	0.9	3.5	26	41	7	0.0	2.1	0.3	4
94 China	12.0	5.0	387	114	-1,228	-1.9	2.7	0.4	3
95 Peru	2.0	2.1	59	39	76	2.7	5.5	0.5	6
96 Dominican Rep.	5.0	0.8	147	22	..	..	3.3	0.5	6
98 Jordan	16.7	10.6	464	138	73	2.9	26.9	2.0	24
99 Philippines	1.2	1.6	44	41	25	0.2	1.8	0.3	12
100 Iraq	8.7	16.0	128	271	993	..	52.9	5.7	105
101 Korea, Dem. Rep. of	11.0	8.9	..	..	514	..	51.5	..	..
102 Mongolia	4.2	10.0	..	..	..	..	10.3	1.2	4
103 Lebanon	..	3.5	..	..	13	0.5	8.2	0.5	7
104 Samoa	..	..	..	..	..	..	..	..	..
105 Indonesia	5.8	1.7	207	49	235	0.9	1.6	0.1	12
106 Nicaragua	1.9	9.0	100	97	41	5.6	16.6	2.7	27
107 Guyana	..	1.9	..	21	..	..	2.5	0.3	10
108 Guatemala	0.9	1.1	45	31	..	..	4.7	0.8	12
109 Algeria	2.1	1.6	31	11	199	2.6	5.0	0.5	12
110 Egypt	5.5	4.0	117	52	659	8.4	8.6	0.9	7
111 Morocco	2.0	4.6	49	72	103	1.5	7.7	1.1	39
112 El Salvador	1.1	2.9	34	66	..	..	4.7	0.8	12
113 Bolivia	2.0	3.1	105	57	15	1.5	3.9	0.5	6

HDI rank	Military expenditure (as % of GDP)		Military expenditure (as % of combined education and health expenditure)		Average annual imports of non-nuclear arms		Armed forces		
					US$ millions	As % of national imports	Per 1,000 people	Per teacher	Per doctor
	1960	1990-91	1960	1990-91	1988-92	1991	1990	1990	1990
114 Gabon	..	4.5	..	51	29	3.6	4.4	0.8	13
115 Honduras	1.2	6.9	38	92	14	1.6	3.5	0.7	6
116 Viet Nam	..	4.8	..	..	..	..	15.9	2.2	47
117 Swaziland	..	1.4	..	11	..	..	..	..	..
118 Maldives	..	..	..	..	..	..	..	..	..
Low human development	2.2	3.3	94	65	5,780T	10.4	2.3	0.7	32
Excluding India	2.5	3.6	138	65	3,340T	9.2	3.1	1.0	59
119 Vanuatu	..	..	..	..	..	..	..	..	2
120 Lesotho	..	2.4	..	48	..	..	1.1	0.2	20
121 Zimbabwe	..	9.1	..	66	27	1.3	5.6	0.7	42
122 Cape Verde	..	..	..	..	..	..	..	..	..
123 Congo	0.3	3.2	7	37	..	..	4.0	0.7	18
124 Cameroon	1.7	2.1	63	48	..	..	1.0	0.2	15
125 Kenya	0.5	2.3	8	24	14	0.7	1.0	0.1	7
126 Solomon Islands	..	..	..	..	..	..	..	..	..
127 Namibia	..	2.2	..	23	..	..	5.1	0.7	30
128 São Tomé and Principe	..	..	..	..	..	..	..	..	..
129 Papua New Guinea	..	3.0	..	41	7	0.4	1.0	0.3	10
130 Myanmar	7.0	6.0	241	222	102	..	5.5	0.8	19
131 Madagascar	0.3	1.4	8	37	..	..	1.8	0.4	18
132 Pakistan	5.5	6.5	393	125	697	8.3	4.9	1.5	9
133 Lao People's Dem. Rep.	5.8	..	..	..	..	..	13.3	1.8	92
134 Ghana	1.1	0.6	22	12	..	..	0.8	0.1	6
135 India	1.9	3.1	68	65	2,447	12.0	1.5	0.3	4
136 Côte d'Ivoire	0.5	1.2	8	14	..	..	0.6	0.1	12
137 Haiti	2.4	1.5	100	30	..	..	1.1	0.2	8
138 Zambia	1.1	3.2	42	63	..	..	2.0	0.4	18
139 Nigeria	0.2	0.9	11	33	87	1.3	0.8	0.2	6
140 Zaire	..	1.2	..	71	..	..	1.4	0.3	20
141 Comoros	..	..	..	..	..	..	..	..	..
142 Yemen	..	14.4	..	197	50	..	5.9	1.0	31
143 Senegal	0.5	2.0	13	33	..	..	1.4	0.5	20
144 Liberia	1.1	3.5	73	47	..	..	3.1	1.1	40
145 Togo	..	3.2	..	39	..	..	1.6	0.4	30
146 Bangladesh	..	1.4	..	41	221	6.4	1.0	0.3	6
147 Cambodia	..	..	..	..	54	..	13.2	2.1	187
148 Tanzania, U. Rep. of	0.1	6.9	4	77	..	..	1.9	0.4	39
149 Nepal	0.4	1.6	67	35	..	..	1.9	0.4	35
150 Equatorial Guinea	..	..	..	..	..	..	2.4	0.5	..
151 Sudan	1.5	2.0	52	44	20	1.4	3.0	1.0	32
152 Burundi	..	2.2	..	42	..	..	1.3	0.6	35
153 Rwanda	..	1.5	..	25	..	..	0.7	0.2	25
154 Uganda	..	0.8	..	18	6	1.1	4.3	0.7	100
155 Angola	..	20.0	..	208	402	..	10.0	2.8	200
156 Benin	1.1	2.0	28	..	..	..	0.8	0.3	13
157 Malawi	..	1.5	..	24	..	..	0.8	0.3	35
158 Mauritania	..	4.1	..	40	..	..	5.6	2.2	55
159 Mozambique	..	13.0	..	121	..	..	4.6	2.9	180
160 Central African Rep.	..	1.8	..	33	..	..	2.0	1.2	60
161 Ethiopia	1.6	13.5	107	190	99	9.6	8.6	4.8	548
162 Bhutan	..	..	..	..	..	..	..	..	..
163 Djibouti	..	..	..	..	..	..	..	..	..
164 Guinea-Bissau	..	..	..	..	12	15.9	..	..	..
165 Somalia	..	3.0	..	200	..	..	8.2	5.8	128
166 Gambia	..	0.6	..	11	..	..	1.1	0.3	10
167 Mali	1.7	3.2	57	53	6	1.0	0.8	0.5	23
168 Chad	..	5.2	..	74	11	2.6	3.0	1.7	170
169 Niger	0.3	0.8	43	11	..	..	0.4	0.3	10
170 Sierra Leone	..	0.7	..	23	..	..	0.7	0.2	10
171 Afghanistan	..	..	..	..	1,503	150.3	2.8	2.4	19
172 Burkina Faso	0.6	2.8	29	30	..	..	1.0	0.8	45
173 Guinea	1.3	1.3	52	37	17	..	1.7	0.7	100
All developing countries	4.2	3.5	143	60	17,830T	2.0	4.0	0.6	19
Least developed countries	2.1	3.5	..	..	2,120T	..	3.2	1.2	88
Sub-Saharan Africa	0.7	3.0	27	43	750T	1.0	2.6	1.0	83
Industrial countries	6.3	3.4	97	33	..	..	8.7	0.8	4
World	6.0	3.4	104	37	..	..	4.7	0.7	16

Note: Data for industrial countries for this subject area are in table 43.

HDI rank	Urban population (as % of total)			Urban population annual growth rate (%)		Population in cities of more than 1 million (as % of urban) 1990	Population in largest city (as % of urban) 1990	Population in cities of more than 1 million (as % of total) 1990	Major city with highest population density	
	1960	1992	2000	1960-1992	1992-2000				City	Population per km² 1980-90
High human development	53	78	81	3.8	2.2	49	32	38	..	..
20 Barbados	30	46	57	1.1	1.7	..	..	..	..	..
24 Hong Kong	90	94	96	2.4	1.0	100	100	94	Hong Kong	5,050
26 Cyprus	38	54	63	2.0	2.1	..	..	..	..	..
32 Korea, Rep. of	28	74	81	5.1	2.1	65	35	51	Seoul	15,930
33 Uruguay	79	89	88	0.9	0.8	47	47	42	Montevideo	6,950
35 Trinidad and Tobago	22	66	77	5.3	2.3	..	..	..	..	..
36 Bahamas	..	..	..	..	..	..	..	..	..	..
37 Argentina	74	87	89	2.0	1.4	..	..	..	Buenos Aires	14,620
38 Chile	68	85	89	2.6	1.8	44	44	37	Santiago	9,880
39 Costa Rica	36	48	53	3.9	3.2	53	53	25	..	..
43 Singapore	98	100	100	1.7	1.0	100	100	100	Singapore	4,160
44 Brunei Darussalam	..	58	..	..	..	..	..	..	..	..
46 Venezuela	67	91	94	4.3	2.6	34	16	31	..	..
47 Panama	39	54	59	3.4	2.8	64	64	34	Panama	3,890
50 Colombia	48	71	75	3.7	2.5	40	21	28	Medellin	3,110
51 Kuwait	78	96	96	7.9	2.8	53	53	51	..	..
52 Mexico	51	74	77	4.1	2.6	43	25	31	Guadalajara	10,290
Medium human development	24	38	56	4.0	4.3	40	16	15	..	..
Excluding China	30	49	56	4.3	3.6	41	24	20	..	..
54 Thailand	13	23	29	4.6	4.0	58	58	13	Bangkok	3,490
55 Antigua and Barbuda	..	47	..	..	..	49	49	42	..	..
56 Qatar	73	79	84	8.0	3.3	..	..	..	..	..
57 Malaysia	25	45	51	4.5	3.9	22	22	9	Kuala Lumpur	3,770
58 Bahrain	75	83	91	4.1	3.1	..	..	..	..	..
59 Fiji	30	37	43	3.2	2.3	..	..	..	..	..
60 Mauritius	35	41	43	2.3	1.3	..	..	..	Port Louis	3,800
62 United Arab Emirates	44	82	79	12.5	2.1	..	..	..	..	..
63 Brazil	45	77	81	4.2	2.5	51	16	39	Recife	6,230
64 Dominica	..	57	..	..	..	..	..	..	..	..
65 Jamaica	33	54	60	2.9	2.2	..	..	..	..	..
67 Saudi Arabia	30	74	82	7.6	4.5	28	17	21	..	..
68 Turkey	30	64	74	4.9	3.7	37	19	22	Ankara	3,440
69 Saint Vincent	..	25	..	..	..	..	..	..	..	..
70 Saint Kitts and Nevis	..	41	..	..	..	..	..	..	..	..
73 Syrian Arab Rep.	37	51	56	4.5	4.6	54	29	27	..	..
74 Ecuador	34	58	64	4.6	3.7	52	28	29	..	..
77 Saint Lucia	..	..	..	..	..	..	..	..	..	..
78 Grenada	..	..	..	..	..	..	..	..	..	..
79 Libyan Arab Jamahiriya	22	84	76	8.1	4.5	93	69	77	..	..
81 Tunisia	36	57	59	3.6	2.7	39	39	22	..	..
83 Seychelles	..	..	..	..	..	..	..	..	..	..
84 Paraguay	37	49	54	4.0	4.0	48	48	23	..	..
85 Suriname	49	43	54	1.3	3.0	..	..	..	..	..
86 Iran, Islamic Rep. of	34	58	63	5.0	3.5	38	20	22	Mashhad	21,130
87 Botswana	2	27	43	13.5	7.9	..	..	..	..	..
88 Belize	..	51	..	..	..	..	..	..	..	..
89 Cuba	55	75	80	2.5	1.5	27	27	20	Havana	2,750
90 Sri Lanka	18	22	24	2.5	2.5	..	..	..	..	..
92 Oman	4	11	15	7.5	7.5	..	..	..	..	..
93 South Africa	47	50	66	3.2	3.2	42	12	21	..	..
94 China	19	28	47	3.8	4.9	38	4	10	Beijing	4,040
95 Peru	46	71	75	4.1	2.7	43	43	30	Lima	1,380
96 Dominican Rep.	30	62	68	5.1	3.1	70	51	42	..	..
98 Jordan	43	69	74	4.5	4.2	35	35	24	Amman	11,100
99 Philippines	30	44	49	3.9	3.6	36	33	16	Manila	45,840
100 Iraq	43	73	75	5.2	3.9	31	31	22	Baghdad	5,380
101 Korea, Dem. Rep. of	40	59	63	3.7	2.4	17	17	10	..	..
102 Mongolia	38	49	54	4.1	3.2	..	..	..	..	..
103 Lebanon	41	85	87	3.8	2.5	..	..	..	..	..
104 Samoa	..	27	..	..	..	..	..	..	..	..
105 Indonesia	15	30	40	4.7	4.4	40	17	11	..	..
106 Nicaragua	40	61	66	4.7	4.1	44	44	26	..	..
107 Guyana	31	34	43	1.7	3.1	..	..	..	..	..
108 Guatemala	32	40	44	3.5	4.0	23	23	9	..	..
109 Algeria	30	53	60	4.7	4.3	23	23	12	Algiers	7,930
110 Egypt	38	44	54	3.1	3.6	55	37	24	Cairo	29,390
111 Morocco	29	47	55	4.3	3.8	35	24	16	Casablanca	12,130
112 El Salvador	38	45	50	2.9	3.6	..	..	..	..	..
113 Bolivia	39	52	58	3.5	4.2	28	28	14	Cochabamba	6,560

HDI rank	Urban population (as % of total)			Urban population annual growth rate (%)		Population in cities of more than 1 million (as % of urban) 1990	Population in largest city (as % of urban) 1990	Population in cities of more than 1 million (as % of total) 1990	Major city with highest population density	
	1960	1992	2000	1960-1992	1992-2000				City	Population per km² 1980-90
114 Gabon	17	47	54	6.3	4.9	..	..	..	..	..
115 Honduras	23	45	52	5.6	4.7	34	34	15	..	..
116 Viet Nam	15	20	27	3.6	4.3	33	24	7	..	..
117 Swaziland	4	28	46	10.5	6.7	..	..	..	..	..
118 Maldives	..	31	..	..	..	..	..	..	..	..
Low human development	15	26	33	4.6	4.7	38	17	10	..	..
Excluding India	12	26	33	5.7	5.5	39	30	10	..	..
119 Vanuatu	..	27	..	..	..	..	..	..	..	..
120 Lesotho	3	21	28	8.6	6.3	..	..	..	..	..
121 Zimbabwe	13	30	35	5.9	5.4	30	30	9	..	..
122 Cape Verde	16	30	38	4.1	5.6	..	..	..	..	..
123 Congo	32	42	47	3.6	4.9	..	..	..	..	..
124 Cameroon	14	42	51	6.5	5.7	39	22	16	..	..
125 Kenya	7	25	32	7.7	7.0	27	27	6	Nairobi	1,590
126 Solomon Islands	..	8	..	..	..	..	..	..	..	..
127 Namibia	14	29	35	4.8	5.4	..	..	..	..	..
128 São Tomé and Principe	..	26	..	..	..	..	..	..	..	..
129 Papua New Guinea	3	16	20	8.6	4.8	..	..	..	..	..
130 Myanmar	19	25	28	3.0	3.5	32	32	8	..	..
131 Madagascar	11	25	31	5.6	6.0	..	..	..	..	..
132 Pakistan	22	33	38	4.3	4.6	51	21	16	Karachi	3,990
133 Lao People's Dem. Rep.	8	20	25	5.1	5.9	..	..	..	..	..
134 Ghana	23	35	38	3.9	4.6	28	28	9	..	..
135 India	18	26	32	3.6	3.9	36	6	9	Calcutta	88,140
136 Côte d'Ivoire	19	42	47	6.5	5.5	45	45	18	Abidjan	3,030
137 Haiti	16	30	34	3.8	4.1	56	56	16	Port-au-Prince	6,990
138 Zambia	17	42	59	7.1	5.5	29	29	12	..	..
139 Nigeria	14	37	43	6.3	5.4	24	20	8	..	..
140 Zaire	22	29	46	4.8	5.0	33	33	9	..	..
141 Comoros	9	29	35	6.8	5.8	..	..	..	..	..
142 Yemen	9	31	37	5.8	6.2	..	..	..	..	..
143 Senegal	32	41	45	3.5	4.4	55	55	22	..	..
144 Liberia	18	47	58	6.2	5.5	..	..	..	..	..
145 Togo	10	29	33	6.2	6.0	..	..	..	..	..
146 Bangladesh	5	18	23	6.8	6.2	53	35	9	Dhaka	9,930
147 Cambodia	10	12	15	1.8	4.3	100	100	12	..	..
148 Tanzania, U. Rep. of	5	22	47	10.3	7.5	27	27	6	..	..
149 Nepal	3	12	14	6.3	6.5	..	..	..	..	..
150 Equatorial Guinea	30	29	37	1.5	4.0	..	..	..	..	..
151 Sudan	10	23	27	5.4	4.8	34	34	8	..	..
152 Burundi	2	6	7	5.5	6.1	..	..	..	..	..
153 Rwanda	2	6	11	7.4	7.6	..	..	..	..	..
154 Uganda	5	12	14	6.1	6.6	39	39	4	..	..
155 Angola	10	27	36	5.9	5.4	63	63	18	..	..
156 Benin	9	40	45	7.4	5.0	45	45	17	..	..
157 Malawi	4	12	16	6.5	6.5	..	..	..	..	..
158 Mauritania	6	50	59	9.8	5.3	..	..	..	..	..
159 Mozambique	4	30	41	9.5	7.2	41	41	11	..	..
160 Central African Rep.	22	48	56	4.8	4.6	..	..	..	..	..
161 Ethiopia	6	13	17	4.8	5.8	30	30	4	..	..
162 Bhutan	3	5	8	4.4	6.3	..	..	..	..	..
163 Djibouti	63	86	85	7.3	3.5	..	..	..	..	..
164 Guinea-Bissau	13	20	25	3.2	4.7	..	..	..	..	..
165 Somalia	17	35	44	5.8	4.7	37	37	9	..	..
166 Gambia	15	24	30	5.2	5.3	..	..	..	..	..
167 Mali	11	25	23	4.4	5.2	..	..	..	..	..
168 Chad	7	34	39	7.1	5.4	..	..	..	..	..
169 Niger	6	19	27	7.4	6.7	..	..	..	..	..
170 Sierra Leone	13	31	40	5.2	5.1	..	..	..	..	..
171 Afghanistan	8	19	22	4.3	6.9	52	52	9	..	..
172 Burkina Faso	5	17	12	4.6	6.3	..	..	..	..	..
173 Guinea	10	27	33	5.3	5.8	76	76	20	Conakry	6,910
All developing countries	22	35	49	4.3	4.4	40	18	14	..	..
Least developed countries	9	21	28	5.9	5.8	41	37	8	..	..
Sub-Saharan Africa	14	29	38	6.0	5.6	34	28	10	..	..
Industrial countries	61	74	78	1.2	0.7	43	17	33	..	..
World	34	44	57	3.8	3.8	41	18	21	..	..

Note: Data for industrial countries for this subject area are in table 44.

HDI rank	Estimated population (millions) 1960	1992	2000	Annual population growth rate (%) 1960-1992	1992-2000	Population growth rates over time (1985-90 as % of 1955-60)	Population doubling date (at current rate)	Crude birth rate 1992	Crude death rate 1992	Total fertility rate 1992	Fertility rates over time (1992 as % of 1960)	Contra-ceptive prevalence rate (%) 1985-92
High human development	130T	260T	290T	2.2	1.5	61	2040	24	6	2.8	51	61
20 Barbados	0.2	0.3	0.3	0.4	0.4	90	2100+	16	9	1.7	39	55
24 Hong Kong	3.1	5.8	6.1	2.0	0.7	21	2081	13	6	1.4	28	81
26 Cyprus	0.6	0.7	0.8	0.7	0.8	69	2064	18	8	2.3	66	..
32 Korea, Rep. of	25.0	44.1	46.9	1.8	0.8	40	2076	16	6	1.7	30	79
33 Uruguay	2.5	3.1	3.3	0.7	0.6	42	2100+	17	10	2.4	82	..
35 Trinidad and Tobago	0.8	1.3	1.4	1.3	1.0	41	2055	24	6	2.8	54	53
36 Bahamas	0.1	0.3	0.3	2.8	1.4	43	2033	20	5	2.1	54	62
37 Argentina	20.6	33.1	36.2	1.5	1.1	74	2050	21	9	2.8	91	..
38 Chile	7.6	13.5	15.3	1.8	1.5	71	2036	23	6	2.7	51	56
39 Costa Rica	1.2	3.2	3.8	3.0	2.2	74	2020	27	4	3.2	46	75
43 Singapore	1.6	2.8	3.0	1.7	0.9	26	2058	16	5	1.7	32	74
44 Brunei Darussalam	0.1	0.3	0.3	3.8	2.1	49	2021	25	4	3.2	46	..
46 Venezuela	7.5	20.2	23.6	3.1	2.0	59	2024	27	5	3.2	50	49
47 Panama	1.1	2.5	2.9	2.5	1.8	82	2027	25	5	3.0	50	58
50 Colombia	15.9	33.4	37.8	2.3	1.6	62	2033	25	6	2.7	41	66
51 Kuwait	0.3	1.9	1.7	6.2	-1.4	66	..	28	2	3.8	52	35
52 Mexico	36.5	88.2	102.6	2.8	1.9	72	2025	29	6	3.3	49	53
Medium human development	1,190T	2,320T	2,630T	2.1	1.6	93	2035	25	7	3.0	48	68
Excluding China	470T	1,040T	1,210T	2.4	1.9	88	2025	30	8	3.8	59	51
54 Thailand	26.4	56.1	61.2	2.4	1.1	45	2046	21	6	2.3	36	66
55 Antigua and Barbuda	0.1	0.1	0.1	0.6	0.7	56	2068	..	..	..	..	53
56 Qatar	(.)	0.5	0.5	7.5	2.3	70	2016	24	4	4.5	65	32
57 Malaysia	8.1	18.8	22.3	2.6	2.1	88	2020	30	5	3.7	55	48
58 Bahrain	0.2	0.5	0.7	3.9	2.6	105	2016	27	4	3.8	54	53
59 Fiji	0.4	0.7	0.8	2.0	1.0	24	2063	24	5	3.0	48	..
60 Mauritius	0.7	1.1	1.2	1.6	0.9	36	2060	19	7	2.0	35	75
62 United Arab Emirates	0.1	1.7	2.0	9.6	2.1	126	2021	22	4	4.6	66	..
63 Brazil	72.6	154.0	172.8	2.4	1.5	64	2035	24	8	2.9	47	66
64 Dominica	0.1	0.1	0.1	0.6	-0.1	..	..	..	..	..	..	50
65 Jamaica	1.6	2.5	2.7	1.3	1.0	84	2059	23	6	2.5	46	66
67 Saudi Arabia	4.1	16.0	20.7	4.4	3.3	146	2012	36	5	6.5	90	..
68 Turkey	27.5	58.4	68.2	2.4	1.9	75	2025	29	7	3.6	56	63
69 Saint Vincent	0.1	0.1	0.1	1.0	0.9	52	2067	..	..	..	..	58
70 Saint Kitts and Nevis	0.1	(.)	(.)	-0.6	-0.2	..	..	..	..	..	..	41
73 Syrian Arab Rep.	4.6	13.3	17.5	3.4	3.5	127	2010	43	6	6.3	87	20
74 Ecuador	4.4	11.1	13.1	2.9	2.1	84	2021	30	7	3.8	55	53
77 Saint Lucia	0.1	0.1	0.2	1.5	1.3	197	2044	..	..	..	..	47
78 Grenada	0.1	0.1	0.1	(.)	0.4	19	2100+	..	..	..	..	54
79 Libyan Arab Jamahiriya	1.3	4.9	6.4	4.1	3.4	101	2011	43	8	6.5	92	..
81 Tunisia	4.2	8.4	9.8	2.2	1.9	116	2025	28	7	3.6	50	50
83 Seychelles	(.)	0.1	0.1	1.7	0.8	58	2075	..	..	..	..	..
84 Paraguay	1.8	4.5	5.5	3.0	2.6	110	2017	34	6	4.4	65	48
85 Suriname	0.3	0.4	0.5	1.3	1.7	65	2028	26	6	2.8	42	55
86 Iran, Islamic Rep. of	21.6	61.6	77.9	3.3	3.0	140	2017	41	7	6.1	85	65
87 Botswana	0.5	1.3	1.7	3.2	2.9	141	2015	39	10	5.2	76	33
88 Belize	0.1	0.2	0.2	2.4	1.9	84	2025	..	..	..	..	47
89 Cuba	7.0	10.8	11.5	1.4	0.8	60	2069	17	7	1.9	45	70
90 Sri Lanka	9.9	17.7	19.4	1.8	1.2	53	2046	21	6	2.5	48	62
92 Oman	0.5	1.6	2.2	3.8	3.5	180	2010	41	5	6.8	96	9
93 South Africa	17.4	39.9	47.9	2.6	2.3	99	2020	32	9	4.2	64	50
94 China	657.5	1,187.4	1,309.7	1.9	1.2	97	2040	21	7	2.3	40	83
95 Peru	9.9	22.5	26.3	2.6	2.0	77	2025	30	8	3.7	54	59
96 Dominican Rep.	3.2	7.5	8.6	2.7	1.8	67	2026	29	6	3.5	47	56
98 Jordan	1.7	4.3	5.6	3.0	3.4	103	2011	39	6	5.8	76	35
99 Philippines	27.6	65.2	76.1	2.7	2.0	84	2024	31	7	4.0	59	40
100 Iraq	6.8	19.3	24.8	3.3	3.1	113	2013	39	7	5.8	81	14
101 Korea, Dem. Rep. of	10.8	22.6	25.9	2.3	1.7	52	2028	24	5	2.4	42	..
102 Mongolia	1.0	2.3	2.8	2.8	2.6	114	2017	35	8	4.7	79	..
103 Lebanon	1.9	2.9	3.3	1.4	1.9	19	2026	27	7	3.2	51	53
104 Samoa	0.1	0.2	0.2	1.1	0.3	..	2100+	..	..	..	..	..
105 Indonesia	96.2	191.2	218.0	2.2	1.7	91	2030	27	9	3.2	58	50
106 Nicaragua	1.5	4.0	5.2	3.1	3.3	84	2010	41	7	5.2	70	49
107 Guyana	0.6	0.8	0.9	1.1	1.1	..	2065	26	7	2.6	41	31
108 Guatemala	4.0	9.8	12.2	2.9	2.8	100	2015	39	8	5.5	80	23
109 Algeria	10.8	26.4	32.7	2.8	2.7	128	2017	34	7	5.0	69	51
110 Egypt	25.9	54.9	64.8	2.4	2.1	100	2023	32	10	4.2	60	46
111 Morocco	11.6	26.3	31.7	2.6	2.3	94	2020	33	9	4.5	63	42
112 El Salvador	2.6	5.4	6.4	2.4	2.2	59	2023	34	8	4.2	61	47
113 Bolivia	3.4	7.5	9.0	2.5	2.3	112	2020	35	10	4.7	70	30

HDI rank		Estimated population (millions)			Annual population growth rate (%)		Population growth rates over time (1985-90 as % of 1955-60)	Population doubling date (at current rate)	Crude birth rate 1992	Crude death rate 1992	Total fertility rate 1992	Fertility rates over time (1992 as % of 1960)	Contra- ceptive prevalence rate (%) 1985-92
		1960	1992	2000	1960-1992	1992-2000							
114	Gabon	0.5	1.2	1.6	3.0	3.2	..	2012	41	16	5.2	..	..
115	Honduras	1.9	5.5	6.8	3.3	2.8	96	2014	38	7	5.1	71	41
116	Viet Nam	34.7	69.5	81.5	2.2	2.0	131	2025	30	9	4.0	66	53
117	Swaziland	0.3	0.8	1.0	2.8	2.7	115	2017	37	11	5.0	77	20
118	Maldives	0.1	0.2	0.3	2.6	2.9	159	2014	39	9	6.3	90	..
Low human development		**810T**	**1,760T**	**2,130T**	**2.4**	**2.5**	**105**	**2020**	**37**	**13**	**5.1**	**79**	**30**
	Excluding India	370T	880T	1,110T	2.7	3.1	126	2015	44	15	6.2	92	16
119	Vanuatu	0.1	0.2	0.2	2.8	2.4	106	2020	..	..	..	..	..
120	Lesotho	0.9	1.8	2.2	2.4	2.5	139	2019	35	10	4.8	82	23
121	Zimbabwe	3.8	10.6	13.2	3.2	2.8	110	2014	41	11	5.5	73	43
122	Cape Verde	0.2	0.4	0.5	2.1	2.8	77	2015	36	7	4.4	64	..
123	Congo	1.0	2.4	3.0	2.8	2.9	140	2014	45	15	6.3	107	..
124	Cameroon	5.3	12.2	15.3	2.6	2.8	162	2016	41	13	5.8	101	16
125	Kenya	8.3	25.3	32.8	3.5	3.3	116	2012	44	11	6.4	81	33
126	Solomon Islands	0.1	0.3	0.4	3.4	3.3	117	2012	38	4	5.5	86	..
127	Namibia	0.6	1.5	2.0	2.8	3.1	137	2013	43	11	6.0	100	29
128	São Tomé and Principe	0.1	0.1	0.1	2.1	2.0	364	2022	..	..	..	..	..
129	Papua New Guinea	1.9	4.1	4.9	2.4	2.3	118	2021	34	11	5.0	79	..
130	Myanmar	21.7	43.7	51.6	2.2	2.1	102	2023	33	12	4.3	71	5
131	Madagascar	5.3	12.9	16.6	2.8	3.2	135	2012	46	13	6.6	100	17
132	Pakistan	50.0	124.9	154.8	2.9	2.7	130	2017	42	11	6.3	92	12
133	Lao People's Dem. Rep.	2.2	4.5	5.6	2.3	2.8	138	2014	45	16	6.7	109	..
134	Ghana	6.8	16.0	20.2	2.7	2.9	97	2014	42	12	6.1	88	13
135	India	442.3	880.1	1,018.7	2.2	1.8	87	2027	30	10	4.0	67	43
136	Côte d'Ivoire	3.8	12.9	17.1	3.9	3.5	113	2010	50	15	7.4	103	3
137	Haiti	3.8	6.8	8.0	1.8	2.1	124	2025	36	12	4.9	77	10
138	Zambia	3.1	8.6	10.7	3.2	2.7	129	2015	47	17	6.5	98	15
139	Nigeria	42.3	115.9	147.7	2.7	5.1	126	2013	46	14	6.6	96	6
140	Zaire	15.3	40.0	51.0	3.0	3.1	139	2013	48	15	6.7	112	29
141	Comoros	0.2	0.6	0.8	3.2	3.6	172	2010	49	12	7.1	104	..
142	Yemen	5.2	12.6	16.4	2.8	3.4	175	2011	49	14	7.3	97	7
143	Senegal	3.2	7.8	9.6	2.8	2.7	111	2017	44	17	6.2	89	7
144	Liberia	1.0	2.8	3.6	3.1	3.2	123	2012	47	15	6.8	103	6
145	Togo	1.5	3.8	4.8	2.9	3.1	225	2013	45	13	6.6	100	12
146	Bangladesh	51.4	119.5	144.3	2.7	2.4	98	2020	39	14	4.8	73	40
147	Cambodia	5.4	8.8	10.6	1.5	2.4	112	2019	40	15	4.5	72	..
148	Tanzania, U. Rep. of	10.2	27.9	35.9	3.2	3.2	127	2012	48	15	6.8	100	10
149	Nepal	9.4	20.6	24.9	2.5	2.4	165	2019	39	14	5.6	97	23
150	Equatorial Guinea	0.3	0.4	0.5	1.2	2.5	211	2018	44	18	5.9	107	..
151	Sudan	11.2	26.7	33.2	2.8	2.7	151	2016	43	15	6.2	92	9
152	Burundi	2.9	5.8	7.2	2.2	2.7	161	2015	46	17	6.8	100	9
153	Rwanda	2.7	7.5	9.8	3.2	3.3	120	2011	52	18	8.5	113	21
154	Uganda	6.6	18.7	23.4	3.3	2.8	93	2014	51	21	7.3	106	5
155	Angola	4.8	9.9	13.1	2.3	3.5	173	2010	51	20	7.2	113	..
156	Benin	2.2	4.9	6.3	2.5	3.0	257	2013	49	18	7.1	103	9
157	Malawi	3.5	10.3	12.6	3.4	2.6	248	2012	55	21	7.6	110	13
158	Mauritania	1.0	2.1	2.7	2.4	2.8	143	2015	46	18	6.5	100	3
159	Mozambique	7.5	15.1	19.4	2.2	3.2	47	2015	45	18	6.5	103	..
160	Central African Rep.	1.5	3.2	3.9	2.3	2.5	164	2017	45	18	6.2	110	..
161	Ethiopia	24.2	53.1	67.2	2.5	3.0	133	2014	49	19	7.0	104	4
162	Bhutan	0.9	1.6	1.9	2.0	2.3	137	2021	40	17	5.9	98	..
163	Djibouti	0.1	0.5	0.6	5.7	2.9	99	2014	47	17	6.6	100	..
164	Guinea-Bissau	0.5	1.0	1.2	2.0	2.1	264	2023	43	22	5.8	114	..
165	Somalia	3.8	9.3	11.9	2.8	3.1	91	2013	50	19	7.0	100	1
166	Gambia	0.4	0.9	1.1	3.0	2.5	123	2018	45	20	6.2	97	..
167	Mali	4.4	9.8	12.6	2.6	3.1	136	2013	51	20	7.1	100	5
168	Chad	3.1	5.9	7.3	2.1	2.8	132	2017	44	18	5.9	99	..
169	Niger	3.0	8.3	10.6	3.2	3.2	132	2012	51	19	7.1	100	4
170	Sierra Leone	2.2	4.4	5.4	2.1	2.6	168	2017	48	22	6.5	104	4
171	Afghanistan	10.8	19.2	26.8	1.8	4.2	129	2001	52	22	6.9	99	2
172	Burkina Faso	4.5	9.5	11.8	2.4	2.7	127	2016	47	18	6.5	102	8
173	Guinea	3.1	6.1	7.8	2.1	3.0	138	2014	51	21	7.0	100	..
All developing countries		**2,070T**	**4,240T**	**4,930T**	**2.2**	**1.9**	**96**	**2030**	**30**	**9**	**3.8**	**60**	**53**
	Least developed countries	240T	540T	670T	2.6	2.8	125	2015	44	16	6.1	92	18
	Sub-Saharan Africa	230T	560T	710T	2.8	3.4	129	2015	46	15	6.5	96	15
Industrial countries		**930T**	**1,210T**	**1,400T**	**0.8**	**0.6**	..	..	..	..	**2.0**	**65**	**60**
World		**3,000T**	**5,450T**	**6,330T**	**1.8**	**1.6**	..	..	..	..	**3.4**	**61**	**52**

Note: Data for industrial countries for this subject area are in table 45.

24 Natural resources balance sheet

HDI rank	Land area (thousands of km²)	Population density (people per km²) 1992	Arable land (as % of land area) 1987-90	Pesticide consumption (metric tons per 1,000 people) 1982-84	Forest area (as % of land area) 1987-90	Production of fuel wood (% change) 1979-90	Annual rate of deforestation (%) 1981-85	Internal renewable water resources per capita (1,000 m³ per year) 1990	Annual fresh water withdrawals As % of water resources 1980-89	Annual fresh water withdrawals Per capita (m³) 1980-89	Irrigated land (as % of arable land area) 1987-90	Share of global emissions (greenhouse index per 10 million people) 1989
High human development	8,000T	32	8.3	..	..	..	..	15.8	14	760	15	0.24
20 Barbados	(.)	601	76.7	..	(.)	..	..	0.2	51	120	..	(.)
24 Hong Kong	1	5,798	6.1	..	12	..	..	..	..	..	29	0.14
26 Cyprus	9	80	11.3	0.28	13	-24	..	1.3	60	810	21	0.28
32 Korea, Rep. of	99	445	20.1	0.28	66	-34	..	1.4	17	300	64	0.17
33 Uruguay	177	18	7.2	0.48	4	24	..	18.9	1	240	8	0.16
35 Trinidad and Tobago	5	253	14.4	..	43	38	0.4	4.0	3	150	18	0.63
36 Bahamas	14	19	0.8	..	32	..	..	..	..	..	..	(.)
37 Argentina	2,770	12	9.5	0.43	22	-25	..	21.5	3	1,060	5	0.18
38 Chile	757	18	5.7	0.13	12	18	0.7	35.5	4	1,630	29	0.08
39 Costa Rica	51	63	5.6	1.15	32	33	3.6	31.5	1	780	22	0.25
43 Singapore	1	2,767	1.6	..	5	..	..	0.2	32	80	..	0.40
44 Brunei Darussalam	6	47	0.6	..	45	..	..	..	..	..	14	0.74
46 Venezuela	912	22	3.6	0.40	35	33	0.7	43.4	(.)	390	7	0.27
47 Panama	77	33	5.8	0.95	44	8	0.9	59.6	1	740	5	0.24
50 Colombia	1,140	29	3.7	0.48	49	24	1.7	33.6	(.)	180	10	0.42
51 Kuwait	18	107	0.2	..	(.)	..	..	(.)	..	240	50	0.57
52 Mexico	1,960	45	12.1	0.31	23	27	1.3	4.0	15	900	21	0.23
Medium human development	44,160T	52	8.0	0.18	29	20	..	6.6	16	490	25	0.11
Excluding China	34,600T	33	7.3	0.23	34	21	0.8	11.2	16	530	16	0.16
54 Thailand	513	109	37.2	0.40	28	21	2.5	2.0	18	600	20	0.27
55 Antigua and Barbuda	(.)	150	18.2	..	11	..	..	..	..	..	..	(.)
56 Qatar	11	41	0.5	..	..	..	..	0.1	663	420	..	0.88
57 Malaysia	330	57	3.2	0.52	58	26	1.2	26.3	2	770	7	0.39
58 Bahrain	1	533	1.5	..	6	..	..	(.)	..	610	..	0.75
59 Fiji	18	41	8.3	..	65	118	0.2	38.1	(.)	40	..	0.14
60 Mauritius	2	549	54.1	0.89	31	-14	3.3	2.0	16	420	16	(.)
62 United Arab Emirates	84	20	0.3	..	(.)	..	..	0.2	299	570	13	1.08
63 Brazil	8,510	18	7.9	0.30	65	25	0.5	34.5	1	210	3	0.26
64 Dominica	1	72	9.3	..	41	..	..	..	..	..	..	(.)
65 Jamaica	11	225	19.1	0.57	17	86	3.0	3.3	4	160	13	0.12
67 Saudi Arabia	2,150	7	0.5	..	1	..	..	0.2	164	260	36	0.37
68 Turkey	779	75	32.3	0.15	26	-31	..	3.5	8	320	8	0.07
69 Saint Vincent	(.)	321	10.3	..	36	..	..	..	..	..	..	(.)
70 Saint Kitts and Nevis	(.)	155	22.2	..	17	..	..	..	..	..	..	(.)
73 Syrian Arab Rep.	185	72	26.6	0.37	4	-4	..	0.6	9	450	12	0.08
74 Ecuador	284	39	6.1	0.28	41	39	2.3	29.1	2	560	20	0.44
77 Saint Lucia	1	220	8.2	..	13	..	..	..	..	..	..	(.)
78 Grenada	(.)	269	14.7	..	9	..	..	..	..	..	..	(.)
79 Libyan Arab Jamahiriya	1,760	3	1.0	0.41	(.)	1	..	0.2	404	620	11	0.25
81 Tunisia	164	51	19.5	(.)	4	29	1.7	0.5	53	330	6	0.06
83 Seychelles	(.)	159	3.7	..	19	..	..	..	..	..	..	(.)
84 Paraguay	407	11	5.3	0.76	36	26	1.1	22.0	(.)	110	3	0.42
85 Suriname	163	3	0.4	..	95	-43	(.)	496.3	(.)	1,180	84	0.23
86 Iran, Islamic Rep. of	1,650	37	8.6	..	11	6	0.5	2.1	39	1,360	39	0.10
87 Botswana	582	2	2.4	..	19	42	0.1	0.8	1	100	..	0.15
88 Belize	23	9	1.9	..	44	64	0.6	..	(.)	..	4	(.)
89 Cuba	111	97	23.7	0.89	25	21	0.1	3.3	23	870	26	0.12
90 Sri Lanka	66	268	14.3	0.04	27	18	3.5	2.5	15	500	29	0.06
92 Oman	212	8	0.1	..	..	..	..	1.4	24	330	85	0.24
93 South Africa	1,220	33	10.1	0.28	4	(.)	..	1.4	18	400	9	0.27
94 China	9,560	124	10.3	0.13	14	19	..	2.5	16	460	46	0.08
95 Peru	1,290	17	2.7	0.12	54	30	0.4	1.8	15	290	33	0.21
96 Dominican Rep.	49	152	20.7	0.44	13	106	0.6	2.8	15	450	15	0.05
98 Jordan	89	48	3.5	..	1	44	..	0.2	41	170	15	0.09
99 Philippines	300	217	15.3	0.07	35	31	1.0	5.2	9	690	19	0.12
100 Iraq	438	44	12.0	..	4	37	..	1.8	43	4,580	47	0.13
101 Korea, Dem. Rep. of	121	187	14.1	..	75	16	..	2.9	21	1,650	50	0.22
102 Mongolia	1,570	1	0.9	..	9	(.)	..	11.0	2	270	3	0.17
103 Lebanon	10	286	20.3	..	8	2	..	1.6	16	270	29	0.07
104 Samoa	3	53	19.4	..	47	..	..	..	..	..	..	(.)
105 Indonesia	1,910	100	8.7	0.09	63	21	0.5	14.0	1	100	35	0.09
106 Nicaragua	130	31	9.3	0.50	29	38	2.7	45.2	1	370	7	0.43
107 Guyana	215	4	2.4	0.81	83	51	(.)	231.7	2	4,620	26	0.12
108 Guatemala	109	90	12.8	0.52	35	33	2.0	12.6	1	140	4	0.15
109 Algeria	2,380	11	3.0	0.81	2	36	2.3	0.7	16	160	5	0.08
110 Egypt	1,000	55	2.3	0.36	(.)	31	..	(.)	97	1,200	100	0.06
111 Morocco	447	59	19.4	0.13	18	36	0.4	1.2	37	500	14	0.04
112 El Salvador	21	258	27.3	0.52	5	15	3.2	3.6	5	240	16	0.04
113 Bolivia	1,100	7	3.0	0.11	51	31	0.2	41.0	(.)	180	5	0.19

HDI rank	Land area (thousands of km²)	Population density (people per km²) 1992	Arable land (as % of land area) 1987-90	Pesticide consumption (metric tons per 1,000 people) 1982-84	Forest area (as % of land area) 1987-90	Production of fuel wood (% change) 1979-90	Annual rate of deforestation (%) 1981-85	Internal renewable water resources per capita (1,000 m³ per year) 1990	Annual fresh water withdrawals As % of water resources 1980-89	Annual fresh water withdrawals Per capita (m³) 1980-89	Irrigated land (as % of arable land area) 1987-90	Share of global emissions (greenhouse index per 10 million people) 1989
114 Gabon	268	5	1.1	..	78	49	0.1	140.1	(.)	50	..	0.40
115 Honduras	112	49	14.3	0.16	30	41	2.3	19.9	1	510	5	0.24
116 Viet Nam	332	209	17.5	0.01	30	25	0.6	5.6	1	80	28	0.10
117 Swaziland	17	47	9.3	..	6	10	..	8.8	4	410	38	(.)
118 Maldives	(.)	757	10.0	..	3	..	..	..	..	..	..	(.)
Low human development	29,410T	59	12.8	0.06	29	29	0.8	5.8	17	540	22	0.07
Excluding India	26,120T	33	7.4	0.06	30	34	0.9	9.4	16	470	18	0.10
119 Vanuatu	12	13	1.6	..	75	..	..	..	..	..	..	(.)
120 Lesotho	30	61	10.5	..	66	32	..	2.3	1	30	..	(.)
121 Zimbabwe	391	27	7.0	0.02	50	31	0.4	2.4	5	130	8	0.10
122 Cape Verde	4	96	9.2	..	(.)	..	..	0.5	20	150	5	(.)
123 Congo	342	7	0.4	..	62	31	0.1	90.8	(.)	20	2	0.17
124 Cameroon	475	26	12.8	..	53	31	0.4	18.5	(.)	30	..	0.25
125 Kenya	580	44	3.4	0.05	4	47	1.7	0.6	7	50	2	0.04
126 Solomon Islands	29	12	1.4	..	92	39	(.)	149.0	(.)	20	..	(.)
127 Namibia	824	2	0.8	..	22	..	0.2	..	2	80	1	(.)
128 São Tomé and Principe	1	125	2.1	..	(.)	..	..	..	..	..	..	(.)
129 Papua New Guinea	463	9	0.1	..	84	8	0.1	199.7	(.)	30	..	0.05
130 Myanmar	677	65	14.5	0.35	49	23	0.3	26.0	(.)	100	10	0.27
131 Madagascar	587	22	4.4	0.13	27	36	1.2	3.3	41	1,680	29	0.31
132 Pakistan	771	162	26.3	0.01	5	43	0.4	2.4	33	2,050	75	0.04
133 Lao People's Dem. Rep.	237	19	3.8	..	56	23	1.0	66.3	(.)	230	13	1.50
134 Ghana	239	67	5.0	..	35	71	0.8	3.5	1	40	..	0.07
135 India	3,290	268	55.6	0.06	22	24	0.3	2.2	18	610	25	0.05
136 Côte d'Ivoire	322	40	7.6	..	24	52	5.2	5.9	1	70	2	0.73
137 Haiti	28	242	20.1	..	2	20	3.7	1.7	(.)	50	8	0.01
138 Zambia	753	11	7.1	..	39	44	0.2	11.4	(.)	90	1	0.10
139 Nigeria	924	107	31.6	0.04	13	40	2.7	2.3	1	40	3	0.12
140 Zaire	2,350	17	3.2	..	77	37	0.2	28.3	(.)	20	..	0.09
141 Comoros	2	294	35.0	..	16	..	3.1	2.0	1	20	..	(.)
142 Yemen	528	24	2.6	..	8	31	..	..	..	1,170	..	0.02
143 Senegal	197	39	27.1	..	31	24	0.5	3.1	4	200	3	0.06
144 Liberia	111	25	1.3	0.11	18	30	2.3	90.8	(.)	50	1	0.40
145 Togo	57	66	25.3	..	30	34	0.7	3.3	1	40	..	0.03
146 Bangladesh	144	830	69.3	(.)	15	31	0.9	11.7	1	210	24	0.04
147 Cambodia	181	49	16.5	0.09	76	22	0.2	10.7	(.)	70	3	0.09
148 Tanzania, U. Rep. of	945	30	4.7	0.21	46	44	0.3	2.8	1	40	3	0.04
149 Nepal	141	146	19.1	..	18	29	4.0	8.9	2	160	28	0.07
150 Equatorial Guinea	28	13	4.6	..	46	10	0.2	68.2	(.)	10	..	(.)
151 Sudan	2,510	11	5.2	..	19	36	1.1	1.2	14	1,090	15	0.13
152 Burundi	28	208	43.7	0.01	3	31	2.7	0.7	3	20	5	(.)
153 Rwanda	26	290	34.4	..	23	12	2.2	0.9	2	20	..	0.01
154 Uganda	236	79	25.1	..	28	40	0.8	3.6	(.)	20	..	0.02
155 Angola	1,250	8	2.4	..	43	31	0.2	15.8	(.)	40	..	0.12
156 Benin	113	44	12.7	..	32	35	1.7	5.5	(.)	30	..	0.06
157 Malawi	118	87	25.3	..	40	37	3.5	1.1	2	20	1	0.17
158 Mauritania	1,030	2	0.2	..	5	40	2.4	0.2	10	470	6	0.09
159 Mozambique	802	19	3.7	..	18	33	0.8	3.7	1	50	4	0.06
160 Central African Rep.	623	5	3.1	..	58	29	0.2	48.4	(.)	30	..	0.13
161 Ethiopia	1,220	43	12.0	0.02	25	21	0.3	2.4	2	50	1	0.03
162 Bhutan	47	34	2.4	..	55	7	0.1	62.7	(.)	20	26	(.)
163 Djibouti	23	20	..	..	(.)	..	..	0.7	2	30	..	(.)
164 Guinea-Bissau	36	28	10.7	..	38	2	2.7	31.4	(.)	20	..	0.50
165 Somalia	638	15	1.6	..	15	47	0.1	1.5	7	170	11	0.06
166 Gambia	11	83	17.8	0.11	16	6	2.4	3.5	(.)	30	7	0.11
167 Mali	1,240	8	1.7	0.07	6	32	0.5	6.6	2	160	10	0.04
168 Chad	1,280	5	2.5	..	10	26	0.6	6.8	(.)	40	..	0.10
169 Niger	1,270	7	2.8	0.02	2	33	2.6	2.0	1	40	1	0.05
170 Sierra Leone	72	61	23.1	..	29	26	0.3	38.5	(.)	100	2	0.05
171 Afghanistan	652	29	12.1	0.03	3	-6	..	3.0	52	1,440	33	0.02
172 Burkina Faso	274	35	13.0	..	24	29	1.7	3.1	1	20	..	0.06
173 Guinea	246	25	2.5	..	60	26	0.8	32.9	(.)	120	3	0.20
All developing countries	78,110T	54	9.8	0.14	29	23	0.9	6.8	16	520	22	0.10
Least developed countries	19,930T	27	6.1	0.08	29	30	0.9	11.4	6	260	12	0.09
Sub-Saharan Africa	24,300T	22	6.2	0.09	29	34	0.9	7.2	5	120	6	0.12
Industrial countries	53,620T	22	12.9	..	..	..	..	9.7	21	1,200	9	0.47
World	131,730T	41	10.7	..	..	..	..	7.3	17	650	18	0.18

Note: Data for industrial countries for this subject area are in table 46.

		Commercial energy consumption				Energy imports (as % of total merchandise exports)	Annual rate of change in commercial energy consumption (%)		Commercial energy efficiency (energy consumption in kg of oil equivalent per $100 GDP)	
		Total (billion kg of oil equivalent)		Per capita (kg of oil equivalent)						
HDI rank		1965	1991	1965	1991	1991	1970-80	1980-90	1965	1991
High human development		110T	390T	780	1,570	11	7.5	5.3	140	41
20	Barbados	..	..	..	..	..	..	..	..	..
24	Hong Kong	2.0	8.3	584	1,440	7	5.4	3.1	51	12
26	Cyprus	..	..	..	..	..	..	..	..	..
32	Korea, Rep. of	7.0	83.8	238	1,940	18	10.1	7.9	197	30
33	Uruguay	2.0	2.5	765	816	15	1.0	0.8	191	27
35	Trinidad and Tobago	4.0	6.4	4,490	4,910	..	4.5	1.7	309	130
36	Bahamas	..	..	..	..	..	..	..	..	..
37	Argentina	22.0	57.7	975	1,760	6	3.3	3.6	107	50
38	Chile	6.0	12.0	652	892	13	0.1	3.1	85	38
39	Costa Rica	(.)	1.8	267	570	21	6.6	3.7	65	32
43	Singapore	4.0	17.3	2,210	6,180	16	2.8	5.6	124	43
44	Brunei Darussalam	..	..	..	..	..	..	..	..	..
46	Venezuela	21.0	49.9	2,320	2,520	1	4.4	2.3	195	93
47	Panama	4.0	4.2	3,070	1,660	..	-6.6	0.2	101	75
50	Colombia	8.0	25.5	412	778	4	5.9	3.1	125	61
51	Kuwait	8.0	..	16,780	..	..	..	..	..	..
52	Mexico	26.0	115.2	605	1,380	5	8.7	1.4	113	41
Medium human development		550T	1,430T	240	700	12	6.7	6.6	170	85
Excluding China		420T	740T	330	820	14	6.4	7.7	162	56
54	Thailand	3.0	25.1	82	438	12	7.9	7.4	65	27
55	Antigua and Barbuda	..	..	..	..	..	..	..	..	..
56	Qatar	..	..	..	..	..	..	..	..	..
57	Malaysia	3.0	19.4	313	1,070	5	5.4	7.9	96	41
58	Bahrain	..	..	..	..	..	..	..	..	..
59	Fiji	..	..	..	..	..	..	..	..	..
60	Mauritius	(.)	0.4	160	389	24	4.9	3.4	59	19
62	United Arab Emirates	(.)	..	126	..	..	..	..	..	..
63	Brazil	24.0	137.5	286	908	19	8.8	4.7	123	33
64	Dominica	..	..	..	..	..	..	..	..	..
65	Jamaica	1.0	2.1	703	858	35	3.6	-1.4	131	59
67	Saudi Arabia	8.0	74.9	1,760	4,870	..	4.5	9.3	276	69
68	Turkey	8.0	46.4	258	809	32	7.4	6.5	103	48
69	Saint Vincent	..	..	..	..	..	..	..	..	..
70	Saint Kitts and Nevis	..	..	..	..	..	..	..	..	..
73	Syrian Arab Rep.	1.0	11.9	212	955	10	14.4	3.9	71	69
74	Ecuador	1.0	6.5	162	598	1	13.5	3.7	63	56
77	Saint Lucia	..	..	..	..	..	..	..	..	..
78	Grenada	..	..	..	..	..	..	..	..	..
79	Libyan Arab Jamahiriya	(.)	..	222	..	..	..	..	..	..
81	Tunisia	1.0	4.6	170	556	13	8.7	4.5	94	39
83	Seychelles	..	..	..	..	..	..	..	..	..
84	Paraguay	(.)	1.0	84	231	24	9.7	4.9	34	16
85	Suriname	..	..	..	..	..	..	..	..	..
86	Iran, Islamic Rep. of	..	62.2	..	1,080	..	5.2	4.5	267	64
87	Botswana	(.)	0.5	191	408	..	10.5	3.0	162	15
88	Belize	..	..	..	..	..	..	..	..	..
89	Cuba	..	..	..	..	..	..	..	..	..
90	Sri Lanka	1.0	3.0	106	177	17	1.2	4.9	59	37
92	Oman	(.)	4.6	14	2,860	..	5.9	10.1	12	45
93	South Africa	35.0	88.0	1,740	2,260	..	3.7	2.9	311	97
94	China	130.0	692.0	178	602	3	7.5	5.3	195	187
95	Peru	5.0	9.9	395	451	9	4.4	1.4	62	20
96	Dominican Rep.	(.)	2.5	127	341	..	6.7	0.9	57	34
98	Jordan	1.0	3.2	393	856	41	13.1	5.3	..	90
99	Philippines	5.0	13.7	158	218	20	4.0	1.9	87	31
100	Iraq	3.0	..	399	..	..	..	..	..	..
101	Korea, Dem. Rep. of	..	..	..	..	..	..	..	..	..
102	Mongolia	1.0	..	461	..	..	..	..	..	..
103	Lebanon	2.0	..	713	..	..	..	..	..	..
104	Samoa	..	..	..	..	..	..	..	..	..
105	Indonesia	10.0	50.6	91	279	8	9.9	4.8	241	43
106	Nicaragua	(.)	1.0	172	254	36	4.1	2.7	..	14
107	Guyana	..	..	..	..	..	..	..	..	..
108	Guatemala	1.0	1.5	150	155	26	6.5	0.6	39	16
109	Algeria	3.0	50.3	226	1,960	2	16.9	15.1	..	154
110	Egypt	9.0	31.8	313	594	5	10.9	4.6	224	105
111	Morocco	2.0	6.5	124	252	25	6.8	2.9	54	23
112	El Salvador	(.)	1.2	140	230	31	7.7	2.4	50	21
113	Bolivia	1.0	1.8	156	251	1	9.5	-0.1	76	37

		Commercial energy consumption			Energy imports (as % of total merchandise exports)	Annual rate of change in commercial energy consumption (%)		Commercial energy efficiency (energy consumption in kg of oil equivalent per $100 GDP)	
		Total (billion kg of oil equivalent)		Per capita (kg of oil equivalent)					
HDI rank		1965	1991	1965	1991	1991	1970-80	1980-90	1965	1991
114	Gabon	(.)	1.4	153	1,150	..	11.3	2.5	33	28
115	Honduras	(.)	1.0	111	181	20	6.1	2.0	46	36
116	Viet Nam	4.0	..	97	..	..	..	..	..	..
117	Swaziland	..	..	..	..	..	..	..	..	..
118	Maldives	..	..	..	..	..	..	..	..	..
Low human development		72T	370T	87	240	23	7.2	7.0	132	92
	Excluding India	22T	79T	68	120	21	10.2	5.8	74	40
119	Vanuatu	..	..	..	..	..	..	..	..	..
120	Lesotho	(.)	..	(.)	..	..	..	..	..	..
121	Zimbabwe	2.0	5.2	441	517	28	1.0	3.0	200	94
122	Cape Verde	..	..	..	..	..	..	..	..	..
123	Congo	(.)	0.5	90	214	1	6.2	3.3	54	18
124	Cameroon	(.)	1.7	67	147	1	6.2	4.4	48	15
125	Kenya	1.0	2.6	110	104	25	3.0	1.6	140	36
126	Solomon Islands	..	..	..	..	..	..	..	..	..
127	Namibia	..	..	..	..	..	..	..	..	..
128	São Tomé and Principe	..	..	..	..	..	..	..	..	..
129	Papua New Guinea	(.)	0.9	56	231	11	8.4	2.4	32	25
130	Myanmar	1.0	..	39	..	..	..	..	..	..
131	Madagascar	(.)	0.5	34	39	36	-2.5	1.8	29	19
132	Pakistan	8.0	28.1	135	243	23	5.3	6.5	129	70
133	Lao People's Dem. Rep.	(.)	0.2	24	42	..	-4.0	2.3	..	18
134	Ghana	1.0	2.0	76	130	44	2.3	0.4	54	31
135	India	50.0	292.0	100	337	26	6.4	7.2	169	132
136	Côte d'Ivoire	(.)	2.1	101	170	12	6.5	2.7	66	29
137	Haiti	(.)	0.3	23	49	43	9.8	1.7	28	12
138	Zambia	2.0	3.1	464	369	21	7.7	1.3	129	80
139	Nigeria	2.0	15.2	34	154	1	16.0	4.4	30	45
140	Zaire	1.0	..	75	..	..	..	..	..	..
141	Comoros	..	..	..	..	..	..	..	..	..
142	Yemen	(.)	1.2	6	96	..	23.3	7.9	..	16
143	Senegal	1.0	0.8	342	105	28	-2.9	-1.6	25	14
144	Liberia	(.)	..	179	..	..	..	..	..	..
145	Togo	(.)	0.2	27	47	14	9.4	0.8	25	11
146	Bangladesh	..	6.3	..	57	26	8.8	7.7	..	27
147	Cambodia	(.)	..	19	..	..	..	..	..	..
148	Tanzania, U. Rep. of	(.)	0.9	37	37	65	-0.2	2.0	48	42
149	Nepal	(.)	0.4	6	22	38	6.0	8.0	7	14
150	Equatorial Guinea	..	..	..	..	..	..	..	..	..
151	Sudan	1.0	1.4	67	54	..	-4.3	0.6	..	..
152	Burundi	(.)	0.1	5	24	20	6.9	7.4	12	13
153	Rwanda	(.)	0.2	8	29	..	12.3	1.8	17	13
154	Uganda	(.)	0.4	36	25	..	-6.4	4.1	27	17
155	Angola	1.0	..	114	..	..	..	..	..	..
156	Benin	(.)	0.2	21	46	29	2.8	3.7	24	12
157	Malawi	(.)	0.4	25	41	24	7.8	1.3	35	18
158	Mauritania	(.)	0.2	48	111	7	4.7	0.3	30	22
159	Mozambique	1.0	0.9	81	59	..	-1.6	1.0	..	78
160	Central African Rep.	(.)	0.1	22	29	10	-1.6	3.3	27	7
161	Ethiopia	(.)	1.1	10	20	37	0.9	3.4	23	18
162	Bhutan	..	..	..	15	..	..	..	..	..
163	Djibouti	..	..	..	..	..	..	..	..	..
164	Guinea-Bissau	..	..	..	38	..	4.0	2.2	..	..
165	Somalia	(.)	..	11	..	..	..	..	..	..
166	Gambia	..	..	..	..	..	..	..	..	..
167	Mali	(.)	0.2	14	23	..	7.8	2.1	24	8
168	Chad	(.)	0.1	12	17	31	4.0	0.4	..	8
169	Niger	(.)	0.3	8	41	22	11.8	2.3	5	14
170	Sierra Leone	(.)	0.3	109	75	32	-1.7	0.1	92	42
171	Afghanistan	(.)	..	30	..	..	..	..	..	..
172	Burkina Faso	(.)	0.2	7	17	35	12.0	1.1	12	6
173	Guinea	(.)	0.4	64	68	..	2.3	1.4	..	14
All developing countries		710T	2,110T	200	550	13	6.9	6.5	156	73
	Least developed countries	6T	20T	42	52	31	14.7	6.4	41	23
	Sub-Saharan Africa	48T	130T	200	280	20	6.6	3.2	..	..
Industrial countries		2,520T	4,380T	3,360	4,840	..	2.6	1.6	166	26
World		3,230T	6,490T	1,030	1,350	..	4.6	4.8	164	34

Note: Data for industrial countries for this subject area are in table 47.

HDI rank		Total GDP (US$ billions) 1991	Agri-cultural production (as % of GDP) 1991	Industrial produc-tion (as % of GDP) 1991	Services (as % of GDP) 1991	Consumption Private (as % of GDP) 1991	Consumption Govern-ment (as % of GDP) 1991	Gross domestic investment (as % of GDP) 1991	Gross domestic savings (as % of GDP) 1991	Tax revenue (as % of GNP) 1991	Central government expen-diture (as % of GNP) 1991	Exports (as % of GDP) 1991	Imports (as % of GDP) 1991
	High human development	940T	8	37	55	64	9	26	26	15	18	26	37
20	Barbados	..	..	..	..	..	..	19	16	..	..	..	..
24	Hong Kong	67.6	(.)	25	75	60	8	..	..	..	..	44	148
26	Cyprus	..	..	..	..	..	..	..	..	..	..	..	..
32	Korea, Rep. of	283.0	8	45	47	53	11	39	37	16	17	25	29
33	Uruguay	9.5	10	32	58	70	13	13	17	26	27	17	16
35	Trinidad and Tobago	4.9	3	39	58	59	15	18	26	..	..	40	34
36	Bahamas	..	..	..	..	..	..	..	..	..	..	..	..
37	Argentina	114.3	15	40	45	81	4	13	15	12	13	10	7
38	Chile	31.3	..	..	..	66	10	19	24	..	..	27	24
39	Costa Rica	5.6	19	25	56	61	16	23	22	21	26	27	34
43	Singapore	40.0	(.)	38	62	43	11	..	..	16	22	147	165
44	Brunei Darussalam	..	..	..	..	..	..	..	..	..	..	..	..
46	Venezuela	53.4	5	47	48	67	9	19	23	19	24	28	19
47	Panama	5.5	10	11	79	72	21	15	7	22	30	6	30
50	Colombia	41.7	17	35	48	66	11	15	23	12	15	17	12
51	Kuwait	..	..	..	..	..	..	..	..	..	..	..	..
52	Mexico	282.5	9	30	61	72	8	23	20	14	18	10	14
	Medium human development	1,760T	17	39	44	63	11	27	28	19	..	21	20
	Excluding China	1,400T	14	38	48	67	12	24	22	19	30	22	20
54	Thailand	93.3	12	39	49	58	10	39	32	19	16	30	40
55	Antigua and Barbuda	..	..	..	..	..	..	..	..	..	..	..	..
56	Qatar	..	..	..	..	..	..	..	..	..	..	..	..
57	Malaysia	47.0	..	..	..	56	14	36	30	21	31	73	75
58	Bahrain	..	..	..	..	..	..	..	..	..	..	..	..
59	Fiji	..	..	..	..	..	..	16	17	..	..	..	..
60	Mauritius	2.3	11	33	56	65	12	28	23	23	24	53	70
62	United Arab Emirates	..	..	..	..	..	..	..	..	..	..	..	..
63	Brazil	414.1	10	39	51	70	9	19	..	19	35	8	6
64	Dominica	..	..	..	..	..	..	..	..	..	..	..	..
65	Jamaica	3.5	5	39	56	68	12	20	20	..	..	31	53
67	Saudi Arabia	108.6	7	52	41	..	..	..	..	..	..	50	24
68	Turkey	95.8	18	33	49	66	17	20	17	18	30	14	22
69	Saint Vincent	..	..	..	..	..	..	..	..	..	..	..	..
70	Saint Kitts and Nevis	..	..	..	..	..	..	..	..	..	..	..	..
73	Syrian Arab Rep.	17.2	30	23	47	..	..	..	..	19	24	32	17
74	Ecuador	11.6	15	35	50	70	8	22	22	18	16	26	20
77	Saint Lucia	..	..	..	..	..	..	..	..	..	..	..	..
78	Grenada	..	..	..	..	..	..	..	..	..	..	..	..
79	Libyan Arab Jamahiriya	..	..	..	..	..	..	..	..	..	..	..	..
81	Tunisia	11.6	18	32	50	66	16	23	18	25	35	32	45
83	Seychelles	..	..	..	..	..	..	20	19	..	..	..	..
84	Paraguay	6.3	22	24	54	75	8	25	17	9	9	12	23
85	Suriname	..	..	..	..	..	..	16	8	..	..	..	..
86	Iran, Islamic Rep. of	97.0	21	21	58	77	13	21	10	15	23	16	22
87	Botswana	3.6	5	54	41	..	..	..	..	34	42	..	..
88	Belize	..	..	..	..	..	..	..	..	..	..	..	..
89	Cuba	..	..	..	..	..	..	..	..	..	..	..	..
90	Sri Lanka	8.2	27	25	48	77	10	23	13	18	29	32	47
92	Oman	10.2	4	52	44	38	35	17	..	9	45	6	30
93	South Africa	91.2	5	44	51	58	21	..	..	30	34	27	19
94	China	369.7	26	42	32	52	9	36	39	16	..	20	17
95	Peru	48.4	..	..	..	82	5	16	13	8	9	7	6
96	Dominican Rep.	7.2	18	25	57	77	9	17	14	11	12	9	24
98	Jordan	3.5	7	26	67	78	23	25	2	22	41	25	71
99	Philippines	44.9	22	34	44	72	9	20	19	15	19	19	27
100	Iraq	..	..	..	..	..	..	..	..	..	..	..	..
101	Korea, Dem. Rep. of	..	..	..	..	..	..	..	..	..	..	..	..
102	Mongolia	..	..	..	..	..	..	26	2	..	..	..	..
103	Lebanon	..	..	..	..	..	..	..	..	..	..	..	..
104	Samoa	..	..	..	..	..	..	33	-17	..	..	..	..
105	Indonesia	116.5	19	42	39	55	9	35	36	20	21	25	22
106	Nicaragua	7.0	30	23	47	89	21	21	-10	16	34	4	11
107	Guyana	..	..	..	..	..	..	22	26	..	..	..	..
108	Guatemala	9.4	25	20	55	84	6	14	10	8	12	13	20
109	Algeria	32.7	14	50	36	48	16	30	36	..	..	36	24
110	Egypt	30.3	18	30	52	83	10	20	7	23	40	13	26
111	Morocco	27.7	19	31	50	68	15	22	17	..	..	15	25
112	El Salvador	5.9	10	24	66	88	11	14	2	9	10	6	15
113	Bolivia	5.0	..	..	..	77	15	14	9	10	19	15	20

HDI rank	Total GDP (US$ billions) 1991	Agricultural production (as % of GDP) 1991	Industrial production (as % of GDP) 1991	Services (as % of GDP) 1991	Consumption Private (as % of GDP) 1991	Consumption Government (as % of GDP) 1991	Gross domestic investment (as % of GDP) 1991	Gross domestic savings (as % of GDP) 1991	Tax revenue (as % of GNP) 1991	Central government expenditure (as % of GNP) 1991	Exports (as % of GDP) 1991	Imports (as % of GDP) 199
114 Gabon	4.9	9	45	46	41	17	26	42	25	38	65	17
115 Honduras	2.7	22	27	51	70	10	24	20	..	..	26	33
116 Viet Nam	..	..	..	..	..	..	..	..	..	..	..	..
117 Swaziland	..	..	..	..	..	..	..	..	..	..	..	..
118 Maldives	..	..	..	..	..	..	..	..	..	..	..	..
Low human development	430T	32	26	42	72	13	21	17	12	19	13	15
Excluding India	210T	33	24	43	75	14	16	10	14	23	20	22
119 Vanuatu	..	..	..	..	..	..	..	..	..	..	..	..
120 Lesotho	0.6	14	38	48	95	18	93	-13	23	32	..	..
121 Zimbabwe	5.5	19	32	49	61	21	22	18	29	36	32	38
122 Cape Verde	..	..	..	..	..	..	26	-3	..	..	..	..
123 Congo	2.9	12	37	51	58	22	11	20	..	..	50	18
124 Cameroon	11.7	27	22	51	71	14	15	15	18	22	11	12
125 Kenya	7.1	27	22	51	63	17	21	19	19	28	17	29
126 Solomon Islands	..	..	..	..	..	..	28	-2	..	..	..	..
127 Namibia	2.0	10	28	62	64	27	14	9	34	48	..	..
128 São Tomé and Principe	..	..	..	..	..	..	..	..	..	..	..	..
129 Papua New Guinea	3.7	26	36	38	63	24	29	13	..	..	36	43
130 Myanmar	..	..	..	..	..	..	..	..	..	..	..	..
131 Madagascar	2.5	33	14	53	92	9	8	-1	7	16	14	21
132 Pakistan	40.2	26	25	49	75	13	19	12	12	22	16	21
133 Lao People's Dem. Rep.	1.0	..	..	..	..	11	..	..	..	..	..	..
134 Ghana	6.4	53	17	30	83	9	17	8	..	..	15	22
135 India	221.9	31	28	41	69	12	24	23	11	18	8	9
136 Côte d'Ivoire	7.3	38	22	40	67	18	10	15	24	30	41	23
137 Haiti	2.6	..	..	..	..	..	..	..	..	..	4	14
138 Zambia	3.8	16	47	37	78	10	14	12	11	22	28	33
139 Nigeria	34.1	37	37	26	65	13	16	23	..	..	35	19
140 Zaire	..	..	..	..	..	..	..	..	..	..	..	..
141 Comoros	..	..	..	..	..	..	16	-6	..	..	..	..
142 Yemen	7.5	22	26	52	70	28	13	2	..	..	..	..
143 Senegal	5.8	19	19	62	78	13	14	9	..	..	17	24
144 Liberia	..	..	..	..	..	..	..	..	..	..	..	..
145 Togo	1.6	33	23	44	74	15	19	10	..	..	18	34
146 Bangladesh	23.4	36	16	48	86	11	10	3	9	15	7	15
147 Cambodia	..	..	..	..	..	..	..	..	..	..	..	..
148 Tanzania, U. Rep. of	2.2	61	5	34	96	16	22	-11	..	..	18	62
149 Nepal	3.1	59	14	27	85	10	19	5	8	18	8	24
150 Equatorial Guinea	..	..	..	..	..	..	52	-3	..	..	..	..
151 Sudan	..	..	..	..	..	..	13	-3	..	..	..	..
152 Burundi	1.0	55	16	29	85	16	17	-1	..	..	9	25
153 Rwanda	1.6	38	22	40	78	20	13	1	..	..	..	..
154 Uganda	2.5	51	12	37	93	8	12	-1	..	..	8	22
155 Angola	..	..	..	..	..	..	..	..	..	..	..	..
156 Benin	1.9	37	14	49	85	12	12	3	..	..	18	21
157 Malawi	2.0	35	20	45	77	14	20	9	21	29	24	36
158 Mauritania	1.0	22	31	47	81	9	16	10	..	..	43	46
159 Mozambique	1.2	64	15	21	90	20	42	-10	..	..	11	16
160 Central African Rep.	1.2	42	16	42	86	15	11	-1	..	..	11	16
161 Ethiopia	6.0	47	13	40	78	21	10	0	..	..	5	17
162 Bhutan	0.2	43	27	30	..	..	..	..	5	43	..	..
163 Djibouti	..	..	..	..	..	..	..	..	..	..	..	..
164 Guinea-Bissau	0.2	46	12	42	85	17	30	-3	..	63	13	37
165 Somalia	..	..	..	..	..	..	..	..	..	..	..	..
166 Gambia	..	..	..	..	..	..	19	8	..	..	..	..
167 Mali	2.5	45	12	43	82	12	23	6	..	..	14	26
168 Chad	1.2	43	18	39	97	20	8	-17	7	31	16	33
169 Niger	2.3	38	20	42	86	8	9	7	..	..	17	19
170 Sierra Leone	0.7	43	14	43	85	11	11	4	6	10	20	22
171 Afghanistan	..	..	..	..	..	..	..	..	..	..	..	..
172 Burkina Faso	2.6	43	20	37	79	17	23	4	..	..	4	23
173 Guinea	2.9	29	35	36	76	10	18	14	14	25	..	..
All developing countries	3,100T	17	36	47	65	11	26	25	16	24	21	24
Least developed countries	80T	37	20	43	83	14	15	2	..	..	11	22
Sub-Saharan Africa	230T	21	34	45	66	17	17	12	27	32	26	22
Industrial countries	17,000T	4	37	59	61	17	22	22	24	30	15	16
World	20,100T	7	37	56	61	16	23	23	23	29	16	17

Note: Data for industrial countries for this subject area are in table 49.

HDI rank	Total GNP US$ billions 1991	Total GNP Annual growth rate (%) 1980-91	GNP per capita annual growth rate (%) 1965-80	GNP per capita annual growth rate (%) 1980-91	Average annual rate of inflation (%) 1980-91	Average annual rate of inflation (%) 1992	Exports as % of GDP (% annual growth rate) 1980-91	Tax revenue as % of GNP (% annual growth rate) 1980-91	Direct taxes as % of total taxes 1980	Direct taxes as % of total taxes 1991	Overall budget surplus/deficit (as % of GNP) 1980	Overall budget surplus/deficit (as % of GNP) 1991
High human development	920T	4.7	3.9	1.5	..	..	-2.8	-0.3	36	37	-2.0	0.4
20 Barbados	1.7	1.6	3.5	1.3	5.2	3.0	..	..	..	..	..	..
24 Hong Kong	77.9	6.9	6.2	5.6	7.5	..	-7.0	..	..	..	..	..
26 Cyprus	6.2	6.0	..	4.9	5.5	..	..	..	..	..	..	..
32 Korea, Rep. of	279.1	10.0	7.3	8.7	5.6	6.3	-9.3	-0.2	25	35	-2.3	-1.7
33 Uruguay	8.9	0.2	2.5	-0.4	64.4	62.3	2.5	1.7	12	7	(.)	0.4
35 Trinidad and Tobago	4.6	-3.9	3.1	-5.2	6.5	8.9	-5.7	..	85	..	7.8	..
36 Bahamas	3.1	3.3	1.0	1.3	5.9	..	..	..	..	..	..	..
37 Argentina	92.3	-0.2	1.7	-1.5	416.9	15.4	5.0	0.7	..	6	-3.6	-0.5
38 Chile	29.2	3.4	(.)	1.6	20.5	13.8	4.3	..	22	..	5.6	..
39 Costa Rica	5.9	3.4	3.3	0.7	22.9	18.6	2.7	1.7	15	10	-7.8	-1.4
43 Singapore	39.3	7.1	8.3	5.3	1.9	..	-2.0	-1.2	47	45	2.2	11.2
44 Brunei Darussalam	..	..	..	..	..	..	..	..	..	..	..	..
46 Venezuela	55.1	1.1	2.3	-1.3	21.2	28.3	-1.7	0.2	79	78	(.)	4.5
47 Panama	5.4	0.3	2.8	-1.8	2.4	-4.4	-4.8	0.4	29	23	-5.8	3.5
50 Colombia	42.1	3.2	3.7	1.2	25.0	29.1	2.5	1.6	29	30	-1.8	-2.0
51 Kuwait	..	..	0.6	..	-2.7	..	..	..	..	..	..	..
52 Mexico	267.1	1.5	3.6	-0.5	66.5	14.7	0.4	-0.8	39	40	-3.1	0.8
Medium human development	2,110T	4.4	4.0	5.1	87.1	286.2	2.9	..	..	..	..	..
Excluding China	1,670T	3.1	3.8	1.5	110.3	377.2	0.4	1.0	35	35	-4.6	-2.7
54 Thailand	88.1	7.8	4.4	5.9	3.7	4.1	4.2	3.2	19	28	-4.9	5.0
55 Antigua and Barbuda	0.3	4.4	-1.4	3.8	6.9	..	..	..	..	..	..	..
56 Qatar	6.7	-6.6	..	-12.2	..	..	..	..	..	..	..	..
57 Malaysia	47.3	5.6	4.7	2.9	1.7	4.4	2.1	-1.4	42	44	-6.2	-2.3
58 Bahrain	3.8	0.1	..	-3.8	-0.3	..	..	..	..	..	..	..
59 Fiji	1.4	1.5	4.2	-0.2	6.1	13.7	..	..	..	..	..	..
60 Mauritius	2.6	7.2	3.7	6.1	8.1	7.4	..	1.9	17	15	-10.4	(.)
62 United Arab Emirates	33.6	-1.8	0.6	-6.3	1.1	..	..	..	..	..	..	..
63 Brazil	452.7	2.5	6.3	0.5	327.6	991.4	-1.0	0.0	17	24	-2.5	-5.9
64 Dominica	0.2	4.4	-0.8	4.7	6.0	2.5	..	..	..	..	..	..
65 Jamaica	3.4	1.0	-0.1	(.)	19.6	75.0	-1.2	..	35	..	-17.1	..
67 Saudi Arabia	124.8	0.4	0.6	-3.4	-2.4	..	..	..	..	..	..	..
68 Turkey	104.0	5.4	3.6	2.9	44.7	59.9	9.2	0.2	62	51	-3.8	-7.6
69 Saint Vincent	0.2	6.1	0.2	5.2	4.4	3.1	..	..	..	..	..	..
70 Saint Kitts and Nevis	0.2	4.5	4.0	5.8	7.2	9.2	..	..	..	..	..	..
73 Syrian Arab Rep.	15.5	1.4	5.1	-1.4	14.3	..	6.5	5.3	25	40	-9.7	0.4
74 Ecuador	11.1	2.0	5.4	-0.6	38.0	50.3	1.7	3.0	47	58	-1.5	2.1
77 Saint Lucia	0.3	4.8	2.7	..	..	2.2	..	..	..	..	..	..
78 Grenada	0.2	4.9	0.1	..	..	2.0	..	..	..	..	..	..
79 Libyan Arab Jamahiriya	..	..	0.6	..	0.2	..	..	..	..	..	..	..
81 Tunisia	12.6	3.5	4.7	1.1	7.3	5.8	0.5	-0.2	19	18	-2.9	-4.3
83 Seychelles	0.4	3.2	4.6	3.2	3.5	-0.1	..	..	..	..	..	..
84 Paraguay	5.7	2.3	4.1	-0.8	25.1	14.7	4.8	-0.6	17	13	0.3	3.0
85 Suriname	1.6	-2.2	5.5	-4.5	9.0	..	..	..	..	..	..	..
86 Iran, Islamic Rep. of	133.8	2.5	2.9	-1.3	13.8	18.9	..	7.2	12	16	-13.8	-2.8
87 Botswana	3.3	9.3	9.9	5.6	13.2	..	..	2.3	45	72	-0.2	14.0
88 Belize	0.4	5.3	3.4	2.5	2.9	3.3	..	..	..	..	..	..
89 Cuba	..	..	0.6	..	..	..	..	..	..	..	..	..
90 Sri Lanka	8.8	4.0	2.8	2.5	11.2	10.1	2.4	-0.5	16	14	-18.4	-9.5
92 Oman	10.1	9.3	9.0	4.4	-3.1	..	..	-2.4	92	82	0.5	-8.1
93 South Africa	102.1	3.3	3.2	0.7	14.4	..	-2.5	2.9	64	50	-2.5	-0.3
94 China	439.3	9.4	4.1	7.8	5.8	8.1	9.6	..	..	..	..	..
95 Peru	22.9	-0.4	0.8	2.4	287.3	73.5	-8.2	-6.3	28	9	-2.5	-0.5
96 Dominican Rep.	7.0	1.9	3.8	-0.2	24.5	1.4	-3.4	0.0	25	24	-2.7	..
98 Jordan	4.5	0.6	5.8	-1.7	1.6	5.3	-0.5	..	17	22	..	-4.0
99 Philippines	47.6	1.2	3.2	-1.2	14.6	7.8	1.4	1.4	24	33	-1.4	-2.1
100 Iraq	..	..	0.6	..	10.3	..	..	..	..	..	..	..
101 Korea, Dem. Rep. of	..	..	0.6	..	..	..	..	..	..	..	..	..
102 Mongolia	..	..	0.6	..	1.0	195.8	..	..	..	..	..	..
103 Lebanon	..	..	0.6	..	..	..	..	..	..	..	..	..
104 Samoa	0.2	6.0	..	..	11.6	8.8	..	..	..	..	..	..
105 Indonesia	116.6	5.8	5.2	3.9	8.5	6.2	-2.1	-0.5	82	65	-2.3	0.4
106 Nicaragua	1.8	-1.4	-0.7	-4.4	583.7	23.1	..	-3.1	9	18	-7.3	-15.2
107 Guyana	0.3	-3.8	0.7	-4.5	35.0	10.8	..	..	..	..	..	..
108 Guatemala	9.1	1.0	3.0	-1.8	15.9	10.4	-3.7	-2.2	12	22	-3.9	-1.8
109 Algeria	52.3	..	4.2	-0.7	10.1	21.3	1.4	..	25	25	-12.5	-6.8
110 Egypt	33.5	4.5	2.8	1.9	12.5	19.5	-0.3	-2.7	..	..	..	..
111 Morocco	27.1	4.3	2.7	1.6	7.1	4.8	1.3	..	22	..	-10.0	..
112 El Salvador	5.8	1.1	1.5	-0.3	17.4	10.0	-13.0	-2.4	24	24	-5.9	-2.1
113 Bolivia	4.9	0.5	1.7	-2.0	263.4	10.2	-1.0	..	..	8	(.)	-0.1

HDI rank	Total GNP US$ billions 1991	Total GNP Annual growth rate (%) 1980-91	GNP per capita annual growth rate (%) 1965-80	GNP per capita annual growth rate (%) 1980-91	Average annual rate of inflation (%) 1980-91	Average annual rate of inflation (%) 1992	Exports as % of GDP (% annual growth rate) 1980-91	Tax revenue as % of GNP (% annual growth rate) 1980-91	Direct taxes as % of total taxes 1980	Direct taxes as % of total taxes 1991	Overall budget surplus/deficit (as % of GNP) 1980	Overall budget surplus/deficit (as % of GNP) 1991
114 Gabon	4.7	-0.9	5.6	-4.2	1.5	4.2	..	-0.3	60	39	6.8	-2.0
115 Honduras	3.2	2.6	1.1	-0.5	6.8	8.4	-3.1	..	33	..	..	..
116 Viet Nam	..	..	0.6	..	..	34.4	..	..	..	..	..	..
117 Swaziland	0.8	6.8	3.7	3.1	10.3	-4.8	..	..	..	..	..	..
118 Maldives	0.1	10.2	1.8	6.7	..	..	..	..	..	..	..	..
Low human development	540T	4.5	1.8	1.9	10.0	14.2	3.3	1.1	23	21	-5.6	-6.2
Excluding India	250T	3.2	2.0	0.2	12.5	19.6	0.8	0.0	24	24	-4.2	-4.5
119 Vanuatu	0.2	2.6	..	..	5.0	..	..	..	..	..	..	..
120 Lesotho	1.1	2.7	6.8	-0.5	13.6	13.2	..	4.1	16	20	-3.7	-0.3
121 Zimbabwe	6.9	3.6	1.7	-0.2	12.5	34.6	..	3.5	58	49	-11.1	-6.9
122 Cape Verde	0.3	4.8	..	2.3	9.4	9.1	..	..	..	..	..	..
123 Congo	2.7	3.1	2.7	-0.2	0.4	3.6	7.4	..	64	..	-5.8	..
124 Cameroon	10.4	2.1	2.4	-1.0	4.5	-1.4	-6.6	1.7	24	48	0.5	-3.5
125 Kenya	8.6	4.1	3.1	0.3	9.2	25.1	-2.3	-0.4	33	33	-4.6	-5.8
126 Solomon Islands	0.2	6.7	5.0	3.5	12.4	10.6	..	..	..	..	..	..
127 Namibia	2.2	1.6	0.6	-1.2	12.6	..	..	..	..	27	..	-7.6
128 São Tomé and Principe	(.)	-1.2	3.3	-3.3	21.5	14.1	..	..	..	..	..	..
129 Papua New Guinea	3.4	1.7	0.6	-0.6	5.2	3.5	-1.2	..	68	..	-2.0	..
130 Myanmar	..	..	1.6	..	..	..	..	..	..	..	..	..
131 Madagascar	2.7	0.5	-0.4	-2.5	16.8	12.2	-0.6	-5.1	17	19	..	-5.9
132 Pakistan	49.9	6.5	1.8	3.2	7.0	9.1	2.7	-0.8	17	14	-5.8	-6.2
133 Lao People's Dem. Rep.	1.0	4.2	0.6	..	..	10.3	..	..	..	..	..	..
134 Ghana	6.4	3.1	-0.8	-0.3	40.0	12.6	8.7	..	22	..	-4.2	..
135 India	290.4	5.5	1.5	3.2	8.2	10.1	4.9	1.5	22	19	-6.5	-7.0
136 Cote d'Ivoire	8.9	0.3	2.8	-4.6	3.8	0.5	0.7	0.9	14	18	-11.1	-3.6
137 Haiti	2.5	-0.6	0.9	-2.4	7.1	..	-19.5	..	16	..	-4.7	..
138 Zambia	3.4	0.7	-1.2	..	..	67.4	..	-6.9	41	..	-20.0	-5.0
139 Nigeria	33.7	1.4	4.2	-2.3	18.1	48.4	2.0	..	..	..	..	..
140 Zaire	8.1	1.6	-1.3	..	60.9	65.0	..	..	..	..	..	..
141 Comoros	0.3	2.6	0.6	-1.0	..	-0.4	..	..	..	..	..	..
142 Yemen	6.5	..	5.1	..	..	..	..	..	..	..	..	..
143 Senegal	5.6	2.9	-0.5	0.1	6.0	1.3	-1.3	..	20	..	0.9	..
144 Liberia	..	..	0.5	..	..	..	..	..	..	..	..	..
145 Togo	1.5	1.8	1.7	-1.3	4.4	2.2	-10.5	..	40	..	-2.0	..
146 Bangladesh	26.3	4.2	-0.3	1.9	9.3	4.2	0.7	1.2	15	11	2.5	-0.4
147 Cambodia	1.8	..	0.6	..	..	108.1	..	..	..	..	..	..
148 Tanzania, U. Rep. of	2.8	2.0	0.8	-0.8	25.7	28.2	3.8	..	35	..	-8.4	..
149 Nepal	3.7	4.7	(.)	2.1	9.1	20.4	..	1.7	7	12	-3.0	-6.2
150 Equatorial Guinea	0.1	5.8	..	2.8	-0.9	1.3	..	..	..	..	..	..
151 Sudan	10.1	0.3	0.8	..	..	..	..	..	17	..	-3.3	..
152 Burundi	1.2	4.3	2.4	1.3	4.3	6.0	0.7	..	20	..	-3.9	..
153 Rwanda	2.0	0.5	1.6	-2.4	4.1	4.7	..	..	21	..	-1.7	..
154 Uganda	3.2	5.9	-2.2	..	..	43.7	7.7	..	12	..	-3.1	..
155 Angola	..	..	0.6	..	..	..	..	..	..	..	..	..
156 Benin	1.9	2.1	-0.3	-0.9	1.6	3.4	10.7	..	..	..	..	..
157 Malawi	2.4	3.5	3.2	0.1	14.9	15.3	0.5	1.2	39	40	-17.3	-1.9
158 Mauritania	1.1	0.6	-0.1	-1.8	8.7	8.8	0.6	..	..	..	..	..
159 Mozambique	1.2	-1.1	0.6	-1.1	37.6	35.0	..	..	..	..	..	..
160 Central African Rep.	1.2	1.2	0.8	-1.4	5.1	1.9	-0.3	..	18	..	-3.5	..
161 Ethiopia	6.4	1.5	0.4	-1.6	2.4	10.3	-6.4	..	25	..	-4.5	..
162 Bhutan	0.3	9.0	0.6	..	8.4	10.1	..	-2.3	25	30	0.9	-2.6
163 Djibouti	..	..	..	..	..	3.0	..	..	..	..	..	..
164 Guinea-Bissau	0.2	3.3	-2.7	1.1	56.2	91.9	..	..	..	..	..	-17.7
165 Somalia	..	..	-0.1	..	49.7	..	..	..	..	..	..	..
166 Gambia	0.3	3.2	2.3	-0.1	18.2	11.4	..	..	..	..	..	..
167 Mali	2.8	2.5	2.1	-0.1	4.4	2.4	0.2	..	19	..	-4.7	..
168 Chad	1.2	6.3	-1.9	3.8	1.1	-4.7	1.7	..	..	29	..	-7.3
169 Niger	2.5	-0.9	-2.5	-4.1	2.3	1.7	0.9	..	28	..	-4.8	..
170 Sierra Leone	0.9	1.1	0.7	-1.6	59.3	94.7	-2.5	-7.7	25	33	-13.2	-2.9
171 Afghanistan	..	..	0.6	..	..	..	..	..	..	..	..	..
172 Burkina Faso	2.8	4.0	1.7	1.2	3.8	-0.5	-0.4	..	20	..	0.3	..
173 Guinea	2.8	..	1.3	..	..	18.0	..	..	44	..	..	-4.2
All developing countries	3,410T	4.6	2.9	3.6	71.0	164.2	1.2	0.6	34	34	-4.0	-2.6
Least developed countries	110T	2.8	0.6	0.2	14.9	20.0	-0.5	1.2	27	30	-2.7	-1.1
Sub-Saharan Africa	260T	2.6	1.5	-1.1	14.7	24.5	-0.9	2.5	..	..	-3.7	-1.5
Industrial countries	18,140T	3.0	2.5	2.1	4.9	53.1	1.3	1.0	43	43	-4.2	-3.3
World	21,550T	3.3	2.4	3.3	15.7	68.7	1.3	0.9	42	42	-4.2	-3.2

Note: Data for industrial countries for this subject area are in table 50.

HDI rank		Life expectancy at birth (years) 1992	Maternal mortality rate (per 100,000 live births) 1988	Population per doctor 1990	Scientists and technicians (per 1,000 people) 1986-90	Enrolment ratio for all levels (% age 6-23) 1991	Tertiary full-time equivalent gross enrolment ratio Total (%) 1991	Female (%) 1991	Daily newspapers (copies per 100 people) 1990	Tele-visions (per 100 people) 1990	Real GDP per capita (PPP$) 1991	GNP per capita (US$) 1991
1	Canada	77.2	7	450	174	89	66	71	23	64	19,320	20,510
2	Switzerland	77.8	6	630	202	74	28	20	46	40	21,780	33,710
3	Japan	78.6	16	610	110	73	39	41	59	62	19,390	26,840
4	Sweden	77.7	7	370	262	70	47	55	53	47	17,490	25,180
5	Norway	76.9	4	500	231	77	62	67	61	42	17,170	24,090
6	France	76.6	13	350	83	78	39	42	21	40	18,430	20,460
7	Australia	76.7	5	440	48	71	40	43	25	49	16,680	17,120
8	USA	75.6	13	420	55	86	66	72	25	81	22,130	22,340
9	Netherlands	77.2	14	410	92	71	35	33	31	50	16,820	18,840
10	United Kingdom	75.8	11	710	90	72	26	26	40	43	16,340	16,600
11	Germany	75.6	8	370	86	73	22	24	39	57	19,770	20,510
12	Austria	75.7	11	230	21	64	29	27	35	47	17,690	20,200
13	Belgium	75.7	4	310	..	76	32	35	31	45	17,510	19,010
14	Iceland	78.1	2	350	..	81	..	..	..	32	17,480	23,230
15	Denmark	75.3	4	390	85	77	32	34	35	54	17,880	23,760
16	Finland	75.4	15	410	103	84	58	67	56	50	16,130	23,930
17	Luxembourg	75.2	2	550	..	58	..	..	38	26	20,800	31,860
18	New Zealand	75.3	18	580	253	78	39	38	32	44	13,970	12,360
19	Israel	76.2	6	350	76	73	..	..	26	26	13,460	12,110
21	Ireland	75.0	3	630	236	73	..	24	17	29	11,430	11,150
22	Italy	76.9	6	210	82	64	..	19	11	42	17,040	18,580
23	Spain	77.4	7	280	44	83	31	33	8	40	12,670	12,480
25	Greece	77.3	7	580	48	72	..	..	14	20	7,680	6,420
27	Czechoslovakia	72.1	14	310	..	67	12	12	51	41	6,570	2,700
31	Hungary	70.1	21	340	50	64	16	16	23	41	6,080	2,750
41	Malta	75.7	5	890	..	76	..	..	15	74	7,575	7,300
42	Portugal	74.4	14	490	..	66	20	24	4	18	9,450	6,180
48	Bulgaria	71.9	40	320	113	67	..	..	45	25	4,813	1,840
49	Poland	71.5	15	490	164	71	..	..	13	30	4,500	1,790
72	Romania	69.9	210	560	..	62	..	..	..	20	..	1,400
76	Albania	73.0	100	720	..	66	..	..	4	9	..	..
	Aggregates											
	Industrial	74.5	24	390	85	79	..	..	30	54	14,860	14,920
	Developing	63.0	420	6,670	9	46	..	..	4	5	2,730	880
	World	65.6	290	5,260	25	49	..	..	9	15	5,490	4,160
	OECD	76.5	11	440	84	80	47	47	31	60	19,000	20,930
	Eastern Europe and former Soviet Union	70.3	49	290	..	..	..	..	..	..	5,670	2,520
	Eastern Europe only	71.1	66	450	..	67	..	..	25	29	5,210	1,950
	European Community	76.3	9	400	81	73	29	29	25	44	16,760	17,650
	Nordic	76.5	7	410	182	76	49	55	51	48	17,230	24,380
	Southern Europe	76.9	7	290	65	72	..	25	10	37	14,100	14,410
	Non-Europe	76.6	13	480	80	82	58	62	35	72	20,780	23,100
	North America	75.8	12	420	67	86	66	72	25	80	21,860	22,160

Successor states of the former Soviet Union

HDI rank		Life expectancy	Maternal mortality	Population per doctor	Scientists	Enrolment	Total	Female	Daily newspapers	Tele-visions	Real GDP	GNP
28	Lithuania	72.6	29	220	..	..	..	..	..	..	5,410	2,420
29	Estonia	71.2	41	210	..	..	..	..	..	..	8,090	3,970
30	Latvia	71.0	57	200	..	..	..	..	..	..	7,540	3,920
34	Russian Federation	70.0	49	210	..	..	..	..	..	..	6,930	3,470
40	Belarus	71.0	25	250	127	..	..	..	29	27	6,850	3,280
45	Ukraine	70.0	33	230	20	..	..	..	25	33	5,180	2,190
53	Armenia	72.0	35	250	..	..	..	..	..	..	4,610	1,930
61	Kazakhstan	69.0	53	250	..	..	..	..	..	..	4,490	2,030
66	Georgia	73.0	55	170	..	..	..	..	..	..	3,670	1,780
71	Azerbaijan	71.0	29	250	..	..	..	..	..	..	3,670	1,240
75	Moldova, Rep. of	69.0	34	250	..	..	..	..	..	..	3,500	1,700
80	Turkmenistan	66.0	55	290	..	..	..	..	..	..	3,540	1,440
82	Kyrgyzstan	68.0	43	280	..	..	..	..	..	..	3,280	1,160
91	Uzbekistan	69.0	43	280	..	..	..	..	..	..	2,790	980
97	Tajikistan	70.0	39	350	..	..	..	..	..	..	2,180	690

Note: Data for developing countries for this subject area are in table 2.

HDI rank	Unemployment rate (%) Total 1992	Unemployment rate (%) Youth (15-24) 1991-92	Adults with less than upper-secondary education (as % of age 15-64) 1991	Ratio of income of highest 20% of households to lowest 20% 1980-91	Female wages (as % of male wages) 1990-92	Average annual rate of inflation (%) 1980-91	Average annual rate of inflation (%) 1992	Years of life lost to premature death (per 1,000 people) 1990	Injuries from road accidents (per 100,000 people) 1990-91	Intentional homicides by men (per 100,000 males) 1985-90	Reported rapes (per 100,000 women age 15-59) 1987-89	Sulfur and nitrogen emissions (kg of NO₂ and SO₂ per capita) 1989
1 Canada	11.2	17.8	24	7.1	63	4.3	1.0	9	988	2.7	23	209
2 Switzerland	2.5	..	19	8.6	68	3.8	2.3	10	436	1.1	18	39
3 Japan	2.2	4.4	33[a]	4.3	51	1.5	1.8	8	640	0.9	5	..
4 Sweden	4.8	11.5	33	4.6	90	7.4	1.6	11	263	1.7	43	61
5 Norway	5.9	13.9	21	5.9	87	5.2	-1.0	10	280	1.6	20	68
6 France	10.2	19.5	49	6.5	81	5.7	2.3	10	361	1.4	17	56
7 Australia	10.7	19.5	44	9.6	88	7.0	1.5	9	169	2.5	44	..
8 USA	7.3	13.7	17	8.9	59	4.2	2.6	11	1,398[b]	12.4	118	160
9 Netherlands	6.8	10.5	44	5.6	77	1.8	2.1	10	348	1.2	26	57
10 United Kingdom	9.9	15.4	35	6.8	70	5.8	4.5	12	605	1.6	..	105
11 Germany	4.8	5.6	18	5.7	78	2.8	5.4	12	660	1.2	26	60
12 Austria	..	..	33	..	78	3.6	4.4	11	786	1.4	27	..
13 Belgium	7.8	..	57	4.6	64	4.2	3.8	11	863	2.3	..	71
14 Iceland	3.0	..	..	..	81	30.0	3.2	..	343	0.6	..	60
15 Denmark	11.1	..	39	7.1	83	5.2	1.9	12	207	1.4	35	100
16 Finland	13.0	23.5	40	6.0	78	6.6	1.0	11	256	4.1	19	115
17 Luxembourg	1.5	..	..	..	55	4.2	2.2	..	490	1.6	..	78
18 New Zealand	10.3	18.5	..	8.8	81	10.3	1.8	11	538	2.6	..	44
19 Israel	..	..	..	6.6	..	89.0	15.6	9	..	0.5	4	..
21 Ireland	16.1	19.5	60	..	71	5.8	15.6	11	250	1.2	..	64
22 Italy	10.5	32.7	72	6.0	80	9.5	4.7	10	383	2.5	4	71
23 Spain	18.1	34.4	78	5.8	70	8.9	6.1	10	389	1.7	12	108
25 Greece	9.2	..	..	..	69	17.7	15.8	10	282	1.2	..	50
27 Czechoslovakia	..	..	27	..	71	3.5	11.2	16	..	1.3	12	239
31 Hungary	..	..	..	3.2	..	10.3	23.0	15	..	3.5	31	141
41 Malta	..	..	..	..	..	2.1	2.1	..	..	..	2	..
42 Portugal	4.1	9.4	93	..	76	17.4	12.6	12	628	2.3	5	30
48 Bulgaria	..	..	..	..	..	7.8	82.6	15	..	4.0	21	..
49 Poland	..	..	..	3.9	78	63.1	43.0	16	..	2.5	19	141
72 Romania	..	..	..	..	..	6.2	210.3	19	..	..	..	..
76 Albania	..	..	..	..	..	-0.4	226.0	..	..	..	..	..
Aggregates												
Industrial	6.5	..	..	..	..	4.9	53.1	13	..	5.4	48	..
Developing	..	..	..	..	..	71.0	164.2	49	..	..	..	..
World	..	..	..	..	..	15.7	68.7	35	..	..	..	..
OECD	7.6	14.6	34	6.8	67	4.4	3.1	10	809	5.0	51	113
Eastern Europe and former Soviet Union	3.7	..	..	..	..	..	960.9	17	..	6.9	..	..
Eastern Europe only	11.1	..	..	3.7	..	27.7	64.9	17	..	2.6	19	165
European Community	9.5	18.7	48	6.1	76	5.7	4.6	11	494	1.6	17	74
Nordic	8.1	15.4	34	5.7	85	6.6	1.1	11	253	2.1	32	82
Southern Europe	12.4	31.2	76	6.0	75	9.9	5.8	10	397	2.1	7	78
Non-Europe	6.3	11.5	23	7.3	58	3.9	2.3	10	1,094	7.9	74	164
North America	7.7	14.1	18	8.7	59	4.2	2.5	11	1,358	11.5	109	165

Successor states of the former Soviet Union

HDI rank	Unemployment rate (%) Total 1992	Youth (15-24) 1991-92	Adults with less than upper-secondary education 1991	Ratio of income 1980-91	Female wages 1990-92	Inflation 1980-91	Inflation 1992	Years of life lost 1990	Injuries road accidents 1990-91	Intentional homicides 1985-90	Reported rapes 1987-89	Sulfur and nitrogen emissions 1989
28 Lithuania	1.0	..	..	..	..	..	1,194.3	19	..	..	..	..
29 Estonia	1.9	..	..	..	..	..	1,009.0	..	..	..	..	..
30 Latvia	2.1	..	..	..	..	..	1,032.4	..	..	..	..	..
34 Russian Federation	0.8	..	..	..	..	..	1,353.0	17	..	9.0[c]	..	..
40 Belarus	0.5	..	..	..	..	..	81.2	14	..	..	..	..
45 Ukraine	0.3	..	..	..	..	..	1,445.3	16	..	..	..	..
53 Armenia	3.5	..	..	..	..	..	828.7	14	..	..	..	..
61 Kazakhstan	0.5	..	..	..	..	..	96.1	19	..	..	..	..
66 Georgia	1.0	..	..	..	..	..	150.0	15	..	..	..	..
71 Azerbaijan	..	..	..	..	..	..	..	16	..	..	..	..
75 Moldova, Rep. of	..	..	..	..	..	..	1,057.1	19	..	..	..	..
80 Turkmenistan	..	..	..	..	..	..	..	29	..	..	..	..
82 Kyrgyzstan	..	..	..	..	..	..	97.9	20	..	..	..	..
91 Uzbekistan	..	..	..	..	..	..	677.0	20	..	..	..	..
97 Tajikistan	..	..	..	..	..	..	..	24	..	..	..	..

a. 1988.
b. 1985.
c. Estimate for the former Soviet Union.

HDI rank		Prisoners (per 100,000 people) 1980-86	Juveniles (as % of total prisoners) 1980-86	Intentional homicides by men (per 100,000) 1985-90	Reported rapes (per 100,000 women age 15-59) 1987-89	Drug crimes (per 100,000 people) 1980-86	Asylum applications received (thousands) 1983-92	Divorces (as % of marriages contracted) 1987-91	Births outside marriage (%) 1985-92	Single-female-parent homes (%) 1985-91	Suicides by men (per 100,000) 1989-91
1	Canada	94	..	2.7	23	225	236	43	23	..	20
2	Switzerland	54	..	1.1	18	129	181	33	6	4	34
3	Japan	..	..	0.9	5	31	4	22	1	5	21
4	Sweden	..	..	1.7	43	..	252	48	52	6	27
5	Norway	..	..	1.6	20	116	37	45	34	..	23
6	France	40	1	1.4	17	..	318	39	32	7	30
7	Australia	60	6	2.5	44	403	24	35	16	..	21
8	USA	426	..	12.4	118	234	508	48	27	8	20
9	Netherlands	27	3	1.2	26	38	111	30	12	5	12
10	United Kingdom	77	5	1.6	..	..	139	42	31	10	12
11	Germany	77	12	1.2	26	..	1,498	33	15	8	28
12	Austria	87	..	1.4	27	77	144	36	22	..	35
13	Belgium	27	14	2.3	..	40	85	32	12	7	32
14	Iceland	..	..	0.6	..	..	..	19	..	6	22
15	Denmark	47	..	1.4	35	176	59	49	47	6	30
16	Finland	75	8	4.1	19	..	9	58	..	10	49
17	Luxembourg	..	..	1.6	..	..	2	39	13	3	25
18	New Zealand	60	..	2.6	..	..	..	38	25	8	23
19	Israel	..	32	0.5	4	25	..	19	1	..	11
21	Ireland	..	3	1.2	..	..	..	..	18	..	14
22	Italy	60	13	2.5	4	6	65	8	7	2	11
23	Spain	49	20	1.7	12	15	43	11	10	3	12
25	Greece	24	12	1.2	..	..	36	14	3	..	6
27	Czechoslovakia	..	..	1.3	12	..	3	32	..	..	30
31	Hungary	142	7	3.5	31	..	57	37	9	..	58
41	Malta	..	..	0.6	2	..	..	..	1	..	6
42	Portugal	58	12	2.3	5	13	4	13	16	6	15
48	Bulgaria	160	2	4.0	21	..	(.)	20	12	..	23
49	Poland	204	11	2.5	19	..	3	17	5	..	24
72	Romania	..	..	..	..	..	1	20	..	..	13
76	Albania	..	..	..	..	..	..	10	..	..	..
	Aggregates										
	Industrial	..	..	5.4	48	..	3,820T	34	17	..	21
	Developing	..	..	..	..	..	..	..	..	..	..
	World	..	..	..	..	..	..	..	..	..	..
	OECD	201	..	5.0	51	..	3,760T	34	20	7	20
	Eastern Europe and former Soviet Union	..	..	6.9	..	..	..	34	13	..	..
	Eastern Europe only	186	..	2.6	19	..	64T	22	7	..	26
	European Community	59	..	1.6	17	..	2,360T	28	19	6	19
	Nordic	..	..	2.1	32	..	360T	50	46	7	32
	Southern Europe	53	..	2.1	7	..	150T	10	9	3	11
	Non-Europe	370	..	7.9	74	178	770T	39	19	7	20
	North America	393	..	11.5	109	233	740T	48	27	8	20

Successor states of the former Soviet Union

HDI rank		Prisoners	Juveniles	Intentional homicides by men	Reported rapes	Drug crimes	Asylum applications received	Divorces	Births outside marriage	Single-female-parent homes	Suicides by men
28	Lithuania	..	..	..	..	..	..	36	7	..	..
29	Estonia	..	..	..	..	..	..	47	25	..	..
30	Latvia	..	..	..	..	..	..	46	16	..	..
34	Russian Federation	..	..	9.0[a]	..	..	..	42	14	..	35[a]
40	Belarus	..	..	..	..	..	..	35	8	..	..
45	Ukraine	..	..	..	..	..	..	40	11	..	..
53	Armenia	..	..	..	..	..	..	..	..	..	..
61	Kazakhstan	..	..	..	..	..	..	..	..	..	..
66	Georgia	..	..	..	..	..	..	..	..	..	..
71	Azerbaijan	..	..	..	..	..	..	..	..	..	..
75	Moldova, Rep. of	..	..	..	..	..	..	31	10	..	..
80	Turkmenistan	..	..	..	..	..	..	..	..	..	..
82	Kyrgyzstan	..	..	..	..	..	..	..	..	..	..
91	Uzbekistan	..	..	..	..	..	..	..	..	..	..
97	Tajikistan	..	..	..	..	..	..	..	..	..	..

a. Data for former Soviet Union.

HDI rank		Life expectancy at birth (years)		Tertiary full-time equivalent gross enrolment ratio (%)		Real GDP per capita (PPP$)		GNP per capita (US$)		Total education expenditure (as % of GDP)		Total health expenditure (as % of GDP)	
		1960	1992	1965	1991	1960	1991	1976	1991	1960	1991	1960	1991
1	Canada	71.0	77.2	26	66	7,758	19,320	8,300	20,510	4.6	7.4	5.3	9.9
2	Switzerland	71.2	77.8	8	28	9,313	21,780	8,910	33,710	3.3a	5.4a	3.3	8.0
3	Japan	67.9	78.6	13	39	2,701	19,390	4,990	26,840	4.9	5.0	3.0	6.8
4	Sweden	73.1	77.7	13	47	6,483	17,490	9,180	25,180	5.9a	6.5	4.7	8.8
5	Norway	73.4	76.9	11	62	5,443	17,170	7,630	24,090	4.6	7.6	3.2	8.4
6	France	70.3	76.6	18	39	5,344	18,430	6,680	20,460	3.6	6.0	4.3	9.1
7	Australia	70.7	76.7	16	40	7,204	16,680	7,770	17,120	..	..	4.8	8.6
8	USA	69.9	75.6	40	66	9,983	22,130	8,190	22,340	5.3	7.0	5.3	13.3
9	Netherlands	73.2	77.2	17	35	5,587	16,820	6,850	18,840	4.9	5.8	4.0	8.7
10	United Kingdom	70.6	75.8	12	26	6,370	16,340	4,220	16,600	3.4a	5.3	3.9	6.6
11	Germany	69.7	75.6	11	22	6,038	19,770	7,460	20,510	2.4	5.4	4.9	9.1
12	Austria	68.7	75.7	9	29	4,476	17,690	5,360	20,200	2.9a	5.4a	4.4	8.5
13	Belgium	70.3	75.7	15	32	5,207	17,510	6,830	19,010	4.8a	5.4a	3.4	8.1
14	Iceland	73.2	78.1	..	..	5,352	17,480	7,100	23,230	..	..	3.4	8.3
15	Denmark	72.1	75.3	14	32	5,900	17,880	8,030	23,760	4.0a	6.1	3.6	7.0
16	Finland	68.5	75.4	11	58	4,718	16,130	6,150	23,930	4.9	6.6	3.8	8.9
17	Luxembourg	68.2	75.2	..	..	6,970	20,800	8,430	31,860	..	..	..	..
18	New Zealand	70.9	75.3	15	39	7,222	13,970	4,590	12,360	2.2a	5.8a	4.2	7.7
19	Israel	68.6	76.2	..	..	3,958	13,460	4,080	12,110	..	..	1.0a	4.2
21	Ireland	69.6	75.0	..	..	3,214	11,430	2,670	11,150	3.0a	5.9	3.8	8.0
22	Italy	69.2	76.9	..	..	4,375	17,040	4,030	18,580	4.2a	4.1a	3.6	8.3
23	Spain	69.0	77.4	6	31	2,701	12,670	3,090	12,480	1.1a	5.6	1.6	6.5
25	Greece	68.7	77.3	..	..	1,889	7,680	2,650	6,420	2.0	3.0	2.6	4.8
27	Czechoslovakia	69.9	72.1	14	12	..	..	..	..	..	..	2.9a	5.9
31	Hungary	68.1	70.1	13	16	..	..	..	..	..	..	2.6a	6.0
41	Malta	68.5	75.7	..	..	..	..	1,700	7,300	..	..	..	..
42	Portugal	63.3	74.4	5	20	1,618	9,450	1,700	6,180	1.8a	5.5a	2.3	6.2
48	Bulgaria	68.5	71.9	..	..	..	..	..	..	..	..	2.0a	5.4
49	Poland	67.1	71.5	..	..	..	..	..	..	3.8a	4.9a	3.5a	5.1
72	Romania	65.5	69.9	..	..	..	..	..	..	2.9a	3.1a	2.0a	3.9
76	Albania	62.1	73.0	..	..	..	..	..	..	..	..	..	..
	Aggregates												
	Industrial	69.0	74.5	..	..	..	..	..	..	..	..	..	..
	Developing	46.2	63.0	..	..	..	..	..	..	..	..	..	..
	World	53.4	65.6	..	..	..	..	..	..	..	..	..	..
	OECD	69.6	76.5	19	47	6,280	19,000	6,330	20,930	4.6	5.9	4.3	9.7
	Eastern Europe and former Soviet Union	..	..	..	..	..	..	..	..	..	..	..	..
	Eastern Europe only	66.8	71.1	..	..	..	..	..	..	..	..	2.8	5.2
	European Community	69.7	76.3	12	29	5,050	16,760	5,360	17,650	3.3	5.3	4.0	8.2
	Nordic	71.9	76.5	12	49	5,770	17,230	7,960	24,380	5.4	6.6	4.0	8.4
	Southern Europe	67.6	76.9	..	..	3,390	14,100	3,400	14,410	3.3	4.5	2.9	7.6
	Non-Europe	69.3	76.6	28	58	7,470	20,780	7,150	23,100	5.2	6.3	4.5	10.7
	North America	70.0	75.8	39	66	9,780	21,860	8,200	22,160	5.3	7.0	5.3	13.0

Successor states of the former Soviet Union

HDI rank		1960	1992	1965	1991	1960	1991	1976	1991	1960	1991	1960	1991
28	Lithuania	69.1	72.6	..	..	..	..	..	..	..	..	..	..
29	Estonia	68.8	71.2	..	..	..	..	..	..	..	..	..	..
30	Latvia	69.6	71.0	..	..	..	..	..	..	..	..	..	..
34	Russian Federation	..	..	..	..	..	..	..	..	..	..	..	..
40	Belarus	..	..	..	..	..	..	..	..	..	..	..	..
45	Ukraine	..	..	..	..	..	..	..	..	..	..	..	..
53	Armenia	..	..	..	..	..	..	..	..	..	..	..	..
61	Kazakhstan	..	..	..	..	..	..	..	..	..	..	..	..
66	Georgia	..	..	..	..	..	..	..	..	..	..	..	..
71	Azerbaijan	..	..	..	..	..	..	..	..	..	..	..	..
75	Moldova, Rep. of	..	..	..	..	..	..	..	..	..	..	..	..
80	Turkmenistan	..	..	..	..	..	..	..	..	..	..	..	..
82	Kyrgyzstan	..	..	..	..	..	..	..	..	..	..	..	..
91	Uzbekistan	..	..	..	..	..	..	..	..	..	..	..	..
97	Tajikistan	..	..	..	..	..	..	..	..	..	..	..	..

a. Public expenditure only.

Note: Data for developing countries for this subject area are in table 4.

32 Human capital formation

HDI rank	Mean years of schooling (25+) Total 1992	Female 1992	Male 1992	Scientists and technicians (per 1,000 people) 1986-90	R & D scientists and technicians (per 10,000 people) 1986-89	Expenditure on research and development (as % of GNP) 1989-91	Upper-secondary graduates (as % of population of normal graduate age) 1991	Tertiary graduates (as % of population of normal graduate age) 1990-91	Science graduates (as % of total graduates) Total 1990-91	Female 1990-91	Male 1990-91
1 Canada	12.2	12.0	12.4	174	34	1.4	72.5	33.3	16	8	26
2 Switzerland	11.6	11.2	12.0	202	28	1.8	87.6	7.6	25	13	31
3 Japan	10.8	10.7	10.9	110	60	2.8	91.1	23.7	26	5	34
4 Sweden	11.4	11.4	11.4	262	62	2.8	80.2	12.0	26	13	41
5 Norway	12.1	11.9	12.2	231	49	2.0	89.3	30.8	17	8	29
6 France	12.0	12.1	11.9	83	51	2.3	75.8	16.3	27	..	..
7 Australia	12.0	11.9	12.1	48	33	1.3	..	24.4	19	11	29
8 USA	12.4	12.5	12.3	55	..	2.9	73.9	29.6	15	9	23
9 Netherlands	11.1	11.4	10.9	92	44	2.2	82.2	8.3	22	9	31
10 United Kingdom	11.7	11.8	11.6	90	..	2.3	74.4	18.4	26	14	36
11 Germany	11.6	11.1	12.2	86	47	2.9	100.0+	12.7	32	13	43
12 Austria	11.4	10.8	12.0	21	19	1.3	86.6	7.8	22	10	31
13 Belgium	11.2	11.2	11.2	..	37	1.7	..	13.3	28	25	31
14 Iceland	9.2	9.3	9.1	..	47	..	..	..	..	..	..
15 Denmark	11.0	10.9	11.1	85	50	1.6	100.0+	16.5	26	11	42
16 Finland	10.9	10.8	11.0	103	43	1.8	100.0+	17.2	33	13	52
17 Luxembourg	10.5	10.3	10.8	..	..	..	52.0	..	..	..	..
18 New Zealand	10.7	10.9	10.5	253	..	..	..	16.1	17	10	23
19 Israel	10.2	9.2	11.1	76	59	3.1	..	5.1	32	29	35
21 Ireland	8.9	9.0	8.8	236	22	1.1	78.3	16.0	29	19	37
22 Italy	7.5	7.5	7.6	82	20	1.1	50.7	9.2	17	13	21
23 Spain	6.9	6.6	7.1	44	11	0.7	64.0	7.5	16	9	25
25 Greece	7.0	6.6	7.4	48	1	0.3	..	5.3	40	32	48
27 Czechoslovakia	9.2	8.6	9.8	..	69	3.3	88.6	11.8	55	34	71
31 Hungary	9.8	9.9	9.7	50	33	2.0	87.8	6.4	51	36	72
41 Malta	6.1	5.9	6.4	..	1	(.)	..	2.1	32	21	38
42 Portugal	6.4	5.6	7.3	..	8	0.5	50.6	2.2	30	20	43
48 Bulgaria	7.0	6.4	7.6	113	69	2.7	..	6.4	38	37	39
49 Poland	8.2	7.8	8.5	164	..	1.2	..	6.6	32	29	36
72 Romania	7.1	6.7	7.5	..	4	2.6	..	2.2	68	..	..
76 Albania	6.2	5.2	7.2	..	..	..	..	1.7	30	22	39
Aggregates											
Industrial	10.0	..	..	85	41	..	..	19.2	24	13	32
Developing	3.9	..	..	9	3	..	..	1.2	28	..	..
World	5.2	..	..	25	12	..	..	3.8	24	..	..
OECD	11.1	11.0	11.2	84	41	2.5	77.5	21.3	22	10	30
Eastern Europe and former Soviet Union	8.8	..	..	..	..	..	..	..	..	..	..
Eastern Europe only	8.1	7.7	8.5	..	37	2.1	..	6.1	34	30	38
European Community	10.1	9.9	10.3	81	34	2.1	75.4	12.6	26	13	34
Nordic	11.3	11.2	11.4	182	53	2.2	90.6	17.8	25	11	39
Southern Europe	7.2	7.0	7.4	65	14	0.9	55.8	7.6	18	13	24
Non-Europe	11.9	11.9	11.9	80	..	2.7	78.4	27.6	19	8	27
North America	12.4	12.5	12.3	67	..	2.8	73.8	29.9	15	8	24

Successor states of the former Soviet Union

HDI rank	Total 1992	Female 1992	Male 1992	Scientists and technicians	R & D	Expenditure	Upper-secondary	Tertiary	Total	Female	Male
28 Lithuania	9.0	..	..	..	..	..	..	..	..	..	..
29 Estonia	9.0	..	..	..	..	..	..	..	..	..	..
30 Latvia	9.0	..	..	..	..	..	..	..	..	..	..
34 Russian Federation	9.0	..	..	..	..	..	..	..	..	..	..
40 Belarus	7.0	..	..	127	..	..	..	..	37	..	..
45 Ukraine	6.0	..	..	20	..	..	..	..	44	..	..
53 Armenia	5.0	..	..	..	..	..	..	..	..	..	..
61 Kazakhstan	5.0	..	..	..	..	..	..	..	..	..	..
66 Georgia	5.0	..	..	..	..	..	..	..	..	..	..
71 Azerbaijan	5.0	..	..	..	..	..	..	..	..	..	..
75 Moldova, Rep. of	6.0	..	..	..	..	..	..	..	..	..	..
80 Turkmenistan	5.0	..	..	..	..	..	..	..	..	..	..
82 Kyrgyzstan	5.0	..	..	..	..	..	..	..	..	..	..
91 Uzbekistan	5.0	..	..	..	..	..	..	..	..	..	..
97 Tajikistan	5.0	..	..	..	..	..	..	..	..	..	..

Note: Data for developing countries for this subject area are in table 5.

HDI rank	Life expectancy at birth (years) 1992	Average age at first marriage (years) 1980-90	Maternal mortality rate (per 100,000 live births) 1988	Secondary net enrolment ratio (%) 1990	Upper-secondary graduates (as % of females of normal graduate age) 1991	Tertiary full-time equivalent gross enrolment ratio (%) 1991	Tertiary natural and applied science enrolment (as % of female tertiary) 1990-91	Women in labour force (as % of total labour force) 1991	Administrators and managers (% females) 1980-89	Parliament (% of seats occupied by women) 1992
1 Canada	80.6	25.2	7	96	74.1	71	11	45	35	13
2 Switzerland	81.1	26.7	6	76	84.4	20	21	38	6	16
3 Japan	81.5	25.8	16	98	94.3	41	10	41	7	6
4 Sweden	80.7	30.4	7	85	82.1	55	33	48	..	33
5 Norway	80.3	27.5	4	87	79.3	67	23	45	22	38
6 France	80.7	26.4	13	85	80.1	42	24	43	9	6
7 Australia	79.9	26.0	5	79	..	43	23	42	30	13
8 USA	79.1	25.2	13	80	76.2	72	..	45	38	10
9 Netherlands	80.4	26.7	14	77	76.4	33	17	40	12	23
10 United Kingdom	78.5	25.7	11	79	76.7	26	32	43	22	9
11 Germany	78.8	25.6	8	82	100.0+	24	31	41	..	21
12 Austria	78.9	24.1	11	..	80.6	27	21	41	12	21
13 Belgium	79.0	22.4	4	88	..	35	35	42	13	10
14 Iceland	80.7	28.3	2	..	..	..	29	..	..	24
15 Denmark	78.3	28.6	4	88	100.0+	34	29	46	14	34
16 Finland	79.4	26.8	15	94	100.0+	67	42	47	19	39
17 Luxembourg	78.9	25.8	2	..	57.0	..	..	36	6	13
18 New Zealand	78.5	24.7	18	82	..	38	19	43	17	17
19 Israel	78.1	23.9	6	..	..	..	24	..	..	9
21 Ireland	77.9	25.3	3	82	85.9	24	24	32	16	12
22 Italy	80.1	23.2	6	..	54.4	19	21	37	38	8
23 Spain	80.4	24.7	7	94	70.1	33	22	35	6	16
25 Greece	80.0	22.5	7	88	..	..	30	36	15	5
27 Czechoslovakia	75.9	22.2	14	..	90.4	12	32	47	..	9
31 Hungary	74.1	22.4	21	78	..	16	15	46	..	7
41 Malta	77.9	22.2	5	80	..	..	25	25	..	2
42 Portugal	77.8	22.1	14	..	58.1	24	20	44	15	9
48 Bulgaria	75.1	21.1	40	63	..	..	42	46	29	13
49 Poland	75.9	22.8	15	80	..	..	26	45	..	9
72 Romania	72.9	21.1	210	..	..	..	..	46	..	3
76 Albania	76.3	20.4	100	..	..	..	..	41	..	6
Aggregates										
Industrial	78.0	24.5	24	..	..	..	23	43	24	10
Developing	64.5	20.8	420	..	..	..	25	35	9	11
World	67.5	21.0	290	..	..	..	24	37	12	11
OECD	79.7	25.3	11	85	80.3	47	22	42	24	12
Eastern Europe and former Soviet Union	74.5	21.8	49	..	..	..	..	..	..	8
Eastern Europe only	74.9	22.0	66	77	..	..	28	46	..	8
European Community	79.5	25.1	9	84	78.2	28	26	40	19	13
Nordic	79.8	28.7	7	88	89.5	55	32	47	18	35
Southern Europe	80.0	23.5	7	93	60.5	24	22	37	23	10
Non-Europe	79.9	25.4	13	86	81.6	62	12	44	28	9
North America	79.2	25.2	12	82	76.0	72	11	45	38	10

Successor states of the former Soviet Union

HDI rank	Life expectancy at birth (years) 1992	Average age at first marriage (years) 1980-90	Maternal mortality rate (per 100,000 live births) 1988	Secondary net enrolment ratio (%) 1990	Upper-secondary graduates (%) 1991	Tertiary full-time equivalent gross enrolment ratio (%) 1991	Tertiary natural and applied science enrolment (%) 1990-91	Women in labour force (%) 1991	Administrators and managers (% females) 1980-89	Parliament (% of seats occupied by women) 1992
28 Lithuania	77.1	..	29	..	..	..	..	..	..	7
29 Estonia	75.6	..	41	..	..	..	..	..	..	13
30 Latvia	75.5	..	57	..	..	..	..	..	..	14
34 Russian Federation	74.4	21.7	49	..	..	..	..	..	..	9
40 Belarus	75.9	21.8	25	..	..	..	..	..	..	4
45 Ukraine	75.0	..	33	..	..	..	..	..	..	..
53 Armenia	75.2	..	35	..	..	..	..	..	..	..
61 Kazakhstan	73.2	..	53	..	..	..	..	..	..	7
66 Georgia	76.3	..	55	..	..	..	..	..	..	..
71 Azerbaijan	74.8	..	29	..	..	..	..	..	..	2
75 Moldova, Rep. of	72.0	..	34	..	..	..	..	..	..	2
80 Turkmenistan	69.7	..	55	..	..	..	..	..	..	5
82 Kyrgyzstan	72.8	..	43	..	..	..	..	..	..	6
91 Uzbekistan	72.6	..	43	..	..	..	..	..	..	10
97 Tajikistan	72.1	..	39	..	..	..	..	..	..	3

Note: Data for developing countries for this subject area are in table 8.

Females as a percentage of males (see note)

HDI rank	Life expec-tancy 1992	Population 1992	Years of schooling 1992	Secondary enrolment 1990	Upper-secondary graduates 1990	University full-time equivalent enrolment 1991	Natural and applied science enrolment 1991	Labour force 1970	Labour force 1992	Unemploy-ment 1991-92	Wages 1990-92
1 Canada	109	102	97	101	105	119	65	..	81	88	63
2 Switzerland	109	105	93	93	93	63	45	52	62	136	68
3 Japan	108	103	98	102	107	..	24	64	69	108	51
4 Sweden	108	103	100	101	105	91	62	61	92	67	90
5 Norway	109	102	98	101	80	121	74	38	83	79	87
6 France	111	105	102	108	112	116	63	54	76	169	81
7 Australia	109	100	98	104	..	107	53	42	71	88	88
8 USA	109	105	102	101	106	111	..	59	82	91	59
9 Netherlands	108	102	104	103	87	74	89	..	66	178	77
10 United Kingdom	107	105	102	104	106	110	70	55	75	40	70
11 Germany	109	108	91	98	98	68	58	..	70	120	78
12 Austria	109	109	90	93	87	80	51	..	70	113	78
13 Belgium	109	105	100	104	..	76	81	42	72	203	64
14 Iceland	107	99	102	107	..	..	78	..	..	131	81
15 Denmark	108	103	98	103	115	110	74	58	87	191	83
16 Finland	111	106	98	101	143	97	68	73	89	69	78
17 Luxembourg	110	105	95	96	117	..	..	35	56	180	55
18 New Zealand	108	102	104	101	..	101	70	38	77	89	81
19 Israel	105	100	83	109	..	98	60	..	..	156	..
21 Ireland	108	99	102	105	121	90	55	36	47	71	71
22 Italy	109	106	99	107	115	95	51	..	58	219	80
23 Spain	108	103	93	109	120	109	61	24	54	187	70
25 Greece	107	103	89	102	..	107	60	..	56	176	69
27 Czechoslovakia	111	105	88	106	104	80	55	80	89	124	71
31 Hungary	112	107	102	103	..	77	52	70	85	83	..
41 Malta	106	103	92	..	..	..	64	27	33	56	..
42 Portugal	110	107	76	108	134	..	56	34	78	145	76
48 Bulgaria	109	102	84	105	..	..	88	79	85	..	..
49 Poland	113	105	93	..	..	..	65	85	82	..	78
72 Romania	109	103	89	96	..	80	..	83	85	..	..
76 Albania	109	94	71	88	..	..	..	..	69	..	..
Aggregates											
Industrial	108	104	95	99	..	..	64	..	73	118	..
Developing	104	96	55	..	..	..	..	..	58	..	..
World	105	98	74	..	..	..	..	..	62	..	..
OECD	109	105	98	102	107	103	64	55	74	122	67
Eastern Europe and former Soviet Union	107	104	..	..	..	..	..	..	..	..	..
Eastern Europe only	86	80	70	63	..	..	54	..	65	..	..
European Community	109	105	96	104	109	96	66	46	68	152	76
Nordic	109	103	99	102	111	102	68	59	88	107	85
Southern Europe	108	105	94	107	119	102	61	26	59	200	75
Non-Europe	109	104	100	102	106	111	62	60	77	93	58
North America	109	105	101	101	106	112	65	59	82	91	59

Successor states of the former Soviet Union

HDI rank	Life expec-tancy 1992	Population 1992									
28 Lithuania	113	111	..	..	..	..	..	..	..	..	..
29 Estonia	114	114	..	..	..	..	..	..	..	..	..
30 Latvia	114	115	..	..	..	..	..	..	..	..	..
34 Russian Federation	116	114	..	..	..	..	..	..	..	..	..
40 Belarus	114	114	..	..	..	..	..	..	..	..	..
45 Ukraine	114	117	..	..	..	..	..	..	..	..	..
53 Armenia	110	104	..	..	..	..	..	..	..	..	..
61 Kazakhstan	114	106	..	..	..	..	..	..	..	..	..
66 Georgia	111	111	..	..	..	..	..	..	..	..	..
71 Azerbaijan	112	105	..	..	..	..	..	..	..	..	..
75 Moldova, Rep. of	110	110	..	..	..	..	..	..	..	..	..
80 Turkmenistan	111	103	..	..	..	..	..	..	..	..	..
82 Kyrgyzstan	113	105	..	..	..	..	..	..	..	..	..
91 Uzbekistan	110	102	..	..	..	..	..	..	..	..	..
97 Tajikistan	108	101	..	..	..	..	..	..	..	..	..

Note: All figures are expressed in relation to the male average, which is indexed to equal 100. The smaller the figure the bigger the gap, the closer the figure to 100 the smaller the gap, and a figure above 100 indicates that the female average is higher than the male average. Data for developing countries for this subject area are in table 9.

HDI rank		Years of life lost to premature death (per 1,000 people) 1990	Deaths from circulatory system diseases (as % of all causes) 1990-91	Deaths from malignant cancers (as % of all causes) 1990-91	AIDS cases (per 100,000 people) 1992	Alcohol consumption (litres per adult) 1986-91	Tobacco consumption (kg per adult) 1985-91	Population per doctor 1990	Health bills paid by public insurance (%) 1991	Public expenditure on health (as % of total public expenditure) 1989-91	Total expenditure on health (as % of GDP) 1960	Total expenditure on health (as % of GDP) 1991	Private expenditure on health (as % of total health expenditure) 1989-91
1	Canada	9	32	27	3.4	10.6	2.6	450	82	14.6	5.3	9.9	27.8
2	Switzerland	10	43	27	6.8	13.5	2.9	630	91	15.7	3.3	8.0	31.7
3	Japan	8	38	25	0.2	6.3	2.4	610	87	30.7	3.0	6.8	28.0
4	Sweden	11	50	22	1.4	6.4	1.5	370	94	11.1	4.7	8.8	22.0
5	Norway	10	46	22	1.1	5.0	2.0	500	..	13.0	3.2	8.4	3.4
6	France	10	32	28	7.3	16.7	2.3	350	75	13.2	4.3	9.1	26.1
7	Australia	9	48	24	3.6	10.2	2.0	440	70	15.4	4.8	8.6	32.2
8	USA	11	44	24	19.6	9.6	2.6	420	61	14.8	5.3	13.3	56.1
9	Netherlands	10	36	27	3.1	9.9	3.0	410	71	10.4	4.0	8.7	26.9
10	United Kingdom	12	45	26	2.2	9.2	1.9	710	93	12.2	3.9	6.6	16.7
11	Germany	12	49	23	2.1	12.3	2.3	370	92	12.3	4.9	9.1	28.2
12	Austria	11	52	24	2.2	..	2.1	230	84	11.2	4.4	8.5	32.9
13	Belgium	11	40	25	1.1	12.4	2.9	310	86	12.2	3.4	8.1	11.1
14	Iceland	..	45	26	1.1	5.2	2.4	..	93	19.3	3.4	8.3	13.0
15	Denmark	12	43	26	3.8	11.6	2.6	390	85	9.0	3.6	7.0	18.5
16	Finland	11	50	19	0.5	9.5	1.6	410	82	14.7	3.8	8.9	19.1
17	Luxembourg	..	44	25	2.5	15.3	2.1	550	91	10.3	..	6.6	8.6
18	New Zealand	11	45	24	1.8	10.1	2.1	580	90	..	4.2	7.7	21.1
19	Israel	9	44	19	0.5	..	2.0	350	..	..	1.0a	4.2	..
21	Ireland	11	46	22	1.9	5.4	2.4	630	90	12.0	3.8	8.0	24.2
22	Italy	10	44	26	6.6	10.9	1.9	210	75	14.8	3.6	8.3	22.5
23	Spain	10	42	22	8.7	15.1	2.4	280	90	11.8	1.6	6.5	17.8
25	Greece	10	52	20	1.6	2.3	3.0	580	85	12.2	2.6	4.8	23.0
27	Czechoslovakia	16	57	20	..	..	2.5	310	..	..	2.9a	5.9	..
31	Hungary	15	54	21	0.2	..	3.3	340	..	..	2.6a	6.0	..
41	Malta	..	52	19	1.1	..	..	..	..	..	..	..	..
42	Portugal	12	45	17	2.5	12.2	1.9	490	..	9.8	2.3	6.2	38.3
48	Bulgaria	15	64	12	..	..	4.1	320	..	..	2.0a	5.4	..
49	Poland	16	55	17	0.1	..	3.5	490	..	..	3.5a	5.1	..
72	Romania	19	65	11	1.7	..	2.0	560	..	..	2.0a	3.9	..
76	Albania	..	..	..	..	..	..	720	..	..	..	4.0	..
	Aggregates												
	Industrial	13	45	24	7.8	..	2.4	390	..	..	4.3	9.4	..
	Developing	49	..	..	5.7	..	..	6,670	..	..	..	4.2	..
	World	35	..	..	6.7	..	..	5,260	..	..	..	8.6	..
	OECD	10	42	24	8.5	10.2	2.4	440	77	15.3	4.3	9.7	39.4
	Eastern Europe and former Soviet Union	17	..	..	..	..	..	290	..	..	..	3.7	..
	Eastern Europe only	17	58	16	0.6	..	3.0	450	..	..	2.8	5.2	..
	European Community	11	43	25	4.5	12.1	2.2	400	85	12.7	4.0	8.2	24.0
	Nordic	11	47	22	1.7	7.9	1.9	410	88	11.6	4.0	8.4	17.2
	Southern Europe	10	44	24	6.5	11.7	2.2	290	81	13.8	2.9	7.6	21.8
	Non-Europe	10	42	24	12.0	8.7	2.5	480	71	18.7	4.5	10.7	47.9
	North America	11	43	24	18.0	9.7	2.6	420	63	14.8	5.3	13.0	54.2

Successor states of the former Soviet Union

HDI rank		Years of life lost to premature death	Deaths from circulatory	Deaths from malignant	AIDS cases	Alcohol	Tobacco	Population per doctor	Health bills	Public exp.	GDP 1960	GDP 1991	Private
28	Lithuania	19	..	..	..	..	..	220	..	..	..	3.6	..
29	Estonia	..	..	..	..	..	..	210	..	..	..	..	..
30	Latvia	..	..	..	..	..	..	200	..	..	..	..	..
34	Russian Federation	17	..	..	..	..	..	210	..	..	..	3.0	..
40	Belarus	14	51	..	..	..	..	250	..	..	..	3.2	..
45	Ukraine	16	53	..	..	..	..	230	..	..	..	3.3	..
53	Armenia	14	36	..	..	..	..	250	..	..	..	4.2	..
61	Kazakhstan	19	49	..	..	..	..	250	..	..	..	4.4	..
66	Georgia	15	..	..	..	..	..	170	..	..	..	4.5	..
71	Azerbaijan	16	66	..	..	..	..	250	..	..	..	4.3	..
75	Moldova, Rep. of	19	75	..	..	..	..	250	..	..	..	3.9	..
80	Turkmenistan	29	53	..	..	..	..	290	..	..	..	5.0	..
82	Kyrgyzstan	20	49	..	..	..	..	280	..	..	..	5.0	..
91	Uzbekistan	20	55	..	..	..	..	280	..	..	..	5.9	..
97	Tajikistan	24	47	..	..	..	..	350	..	..	..	6.0	..

a. Public expenditure only.

Note: Data for developing countries for this subject area are in table 12.

HDI rank		Enrolment ratio for all levels (% age 6-23) 1991	Upper-secondary full-time equivalent gross enrolment ratio (%) 1991	Upper-secondary technical enrolment (as % of total upper secondary) 1991	19-year-olds still in full-time education (%) 1990-91	Tertiary full-time equivalent gross enrolment ratio (%) 1991	Tertiary natural and applied science enrolment (as % of total tertiary) 1990-91	Expenditure on tertiary education (as % of all levels) 1991	Public expenditure per tertiary student (PPP$) 1990-91	Total education expenditure (as % of GDP) 1960	Total education expenditure (as % of GDP) 1991	Public expenditure on education (as % of GDP) 1991
1	Canada	89	101	..	46	66	14	29.0	10,420	4.6	7.4	6.7
2	Switzerland	74	107	75	54	28	34	22.5	10,190	3.3ª	5.4ª	5.4
3	Japan	73	99	28	..	39	26	21.1	7,570	4.9	5.0	3.7
4	Sweden	70	98	73	22	47	43	18.3	8,550	5.9ª	6.5	6.5
5	Norway	77	122	60	47	62	27	19.8	7,440	4.6	7.6	6.8
6	France	78	106	54	61	39	31	17.7	5,870	3.6	6.0	5.4
7	Australia	71	91	28	..	40	33	35.9	10,930	..	5.5	4.7
8	USA	86	89	..	38	66	14	34.4	13,640	5.3	7.0	5.5
9	Netherlands	71	132	70	59	35	18	29.8	9,370	4.9	5.8	5.6
10	United Kingdom	72	100	20	21	26	39	20.7	7,960	3.4ª	5.3ª	5.3
11	Germany	73	123	80	65	22	42	22.0	6,320	2.4	5.4	4.0
12	Austria	64	120	76	..	29	31	22.7	5,030	2.9ª	5.4ª	5.4
13	Belgium	76	99	59	58	32	39	19.0	6,240	4.8ª	5.4ª	5.4
14	Iceland	81	..	..	..	..	33	..	..	..	6.0ª	6.0
15	Denmark	77	91	67	51	32	34	21.4	7,690	4.0ª	6.1	6.1
16	Finland	84	..	55	36	58	52	23.7	7,220	4.9	6.6	6.1
17	Luxembourg	58	..	69	..	..	..	..	12,240	..	5.8ª	5.8
18	New Zealand	78	79	..	28	39	23	35.0	..	2.2ª	5.8ª	5.8
19	Israel	73	..	..	..	..	32	19.0	..	..	6.0ª	6.0
21	Ireland	73	112	22	24	..	34	24.0	7,050	3.0ª	5.9	5.5
22	Italy	64	88	71	..	..	31	10.0	4,250	4.2ª	4.1ª	4.1
23	Spain	83	91	37	..	31	29	18.5	3,880	1.1ª	5.6	4.5
25	Greece	72	..	28	..	..	40	20.0	..	2.0	3.0	..
27	Czechoslovakia	67	86	54	16	12	45	16.0	..	..	4.6ª	4.6
31	Hungary	64	96	76	14	16	22	15.6	7,010	..	6.7	6.2
41	Malta	76	..	..	..	..	32	12.0	..	..	4.4ª	4.4
42	Portugal	66	79	17	31	20	28	16.6	4,450	1.8ª	5.5ª	5.5
48	Bulgaria	67	..	..	..	..	45	14.0	..	..	5.4ª	5.4
49	Poland	71	..	..	..	..	33	22.0	..	3.8ª	4.9ª	4.9
72	Romania	62	..	..	..	..	72	10.0	..	2.9ª	3.1ª	3.1
76	Albania	66	..	..	..	..	33	..	..	..	..	..
	Aggregates											
	Industrial	79	..	..	..	..	21	26	..	..	..	4.9
	Developing	46	..	..	..	..	41	19	..	..	..	3.9
	World	49	..	..	..	..	31	26	..	..	..	4.8
	OECD	78	97	49	43	47	21	26	10,800	4.6	5.9	4.9
	Eastern Europe and former Soviet Union	..	..	..	..	..	..	..	..	..	..	..
	Eastern Europe only	67	..	..	..	..	35	17	..	..	4.9	4.8
	European Community	73	104	55	50	29	34	19	6,310	3.3	5.3	4.7
	Nordic	76	102	68	36	49	40	20	..	5.4	6.6	6.4
	Southern Europe	72	88	52	..	..	..	14	..	3.3	4.5	4.3
	Non-Europe	82	92	28	39	58	17	30	12,280	5.2	6.3	4.9
	North America	86	90	..	39	66	14	34	13,340	5.3	7.0	5.6

Successor states of the former Soviet Union

HDI rank												
28	Lithuania	..	..	..	..	..	..	..	..	..	..	..
29	Estonia	..	..	..	..	..	..	..	..	..	..	..
30	Latvia	..	..	..	..	..	..	..	..	..	..	..
34	Russian Federation	..	..	..	..	..	44	..	..	..	..	..
40	Belarus	..	..	..	..	..	41	..	..	..	..	..
45	Ukraine	..	..	..	..	..	49	..	..	..	..	..
53	Armenia	..	..	..	..	..	..	..	..	..	..	..
61	Kazakhstan	..	..	..	..	..	..	..	..	..	..	..
66	Georgia	..	..	..	..	..	..	..	..	..	..	..
71	Azerbaijan	..	..	..	..	..	..	..	..	..	..	..
75	Moldova, Rep. of	..	..	..	..	..	..	..	..	..	..	..
80	Turkmenistan	..	..	..	..	..	..	..	..	..	..	..
82	Kyrgyzstan	..	..	..	..	..	..	..	..	..	..	..
91	Uzbekistan	..	..	..	..	..	..	..	..	..	..	..
97	Tajikistan	..	..	..	..	..	..	..	..	..	..	..

a. Public expenditure only.

Note: Data for developing countries for this subject area are in table 15.

HDI rank		Radios (per 100 people) 1990	Tele-visions (per 100 people) 1990	Annual cinema atten-dances (per person) 1988-91	Annual museum atten-dances (per person) 1987-91	Registered library users (%) 1987-91	Daily news-papers (copies per 100 people) 1990	Book titles published (per 100,000 people) 1988-91	Printing and writing paper consumed (metric tons per 1,000 people) 1990	Letters posted (per capita) 1991	Tele-phones (per 100 people) 1990-92	Inter-national telephone calls (minutes per capita) 1990-92	Motor vehicles (per 100 people) 1989-90
1	Canada	102	64	3.0	1.0	..	23	..	95	..	78	25	60
2	Switzerland	84	40	2.3	1.4	15.9	46	219	135	..	89	224	48
3	Japan	91	62	1.2	0.5	14.2	59	..	104	190	56	9	45
4	Sweden	88	47	1.8	1.7	..	53	137	181	..	80	79	49
5	Norway	79	42	2.5	1.4	..	61	91	54	456	46	81	45
6	France	89	40	2.1	0.2	36.8	21	76	68	379	61	41	48
7	Australia	128	49	2.4	1.0	..	25	61	83	226	55	35	54
8	USA	212	81	3.9	1.4	..	25	..	139	648	79	36	74
9	Netherlands	91	50	1.0	1.3	..	31	90	103	..	66	75	39
10	United Kingdom	114	43	1.8	..	..	40	150	87	286	48	47	41
11	Germany	90	57	1.5	1.2	14.2	39	85	135	..	59	44	41
12	Austria	61	47	1.4	2.5	57.3	35	49	156	..	64	92	47
13	Belgium	78	45	1.6	..	..	31	139	109	327	59	91	43
14	Iceland	78	32	..	..	..	..	..	35	245	48	80	52
15	Denmark	103	54	1.8	1.9	..	35	198	100	..	88	82	37
16	Finland	100	50	1.2	0.8	..	56	224	135	325	76	47	44
17	Luxembourg	63	26	1.4	0.2	..	38	137	109	378	53	..	57
18	New Zealand	93	44	..	0.1	..	32	..	50	..	72	..	52
19	Israel	47	26	..	1.5	..	26	..	36	..	47	23	19
21	Ireland	62	29	3.3	0.2	..	17	..	45	..	27	24	27
22	Italy	79	42	1.5	0.1	1.9	11	48	53	137	57	23	52
23	Spain	31	40	2.0	(.)	23.3	8	100	44	..	40	18	37
25	Greece	42	20	..	0.3	29.1	14	40	24	39	49	24	25
27	Czechoslovakia	59	41	3.2	1.0	22.3	51	59	16	..	29	7	24
31	Hungary	60	41	2.1	1.0	21.2	23	77	19	143	19	18	21
41	Malta	53	74	0.9	..	30.8	15	128	25	111	56	54	36
42	Portugal	23	18	1.0	0.4	5.5	4	65	24	76	31	14	34
48	Bulgaria	44	25	2.9	0.8	23.2	45	36	10	..	32	10	16
49	Poland	43	30	0.5	0.6	21.8	13	28	7	..	15	6	17
72	Romania	20	20	..	0.1	23.6	..	9	7	..	13	1	..
76	Albania	18	9	2.2	..	10.7	4	12	1	..	2	6	..
	Aggregates												
	Industrial	113	54	2.3	0.8	..	30	74	95	401	48	31	50
	Developing	18	6	3.0	..	..	4	5	4	13	3	..	3
	World	35	15	2.8	..	..	9	15	20	105	13	..	15
	OECD	126	60	2.4	0.9	..	31	94	106	406	64	36	54
	Eastern Europe and former Soviet Union	..	..	..	..	..	..	..	..	..	15	..	..
	Eastern Europe only	41	29	1.6	0.6	22.0	25	34	10	..	18	6	19
	European Community	81	44	1.7	0.6	18.2	25	92	82	249	54	39	42
	Nordic	92	48	1.8	1.5	..	51	161	128	..	74	73	45
	Southern Europe	55	37	1.6	0.1	11.8	10	66	45	116	48	21	43
	Non-Europe	164	72	3.0	1.1	..	35	..	122	486	71	27	63
	North America	201	80	3.8	1.4	..	25	..	135	648	79	34	73

Successor states of the former Soviet Union

HDI rank		Radios	Tele-visions	Annual cinema	Annual museum	Registered library	Daily news-papers	Book titles published	Printing paper	Letters posted	Tele-phones	Intl calls	Motor vehicles
28	Lithuania	..	..	..	..	..	..	..	..	..	22	1	16
29	Estonia	..	..	..	..	..	..	105	..	..	21	28	..
30	Latvia	..	..	..	..	..	..	..	..	..	24	..	14
34	Russian Federation	..	..	..	..	..	..	..	..	..	15	..	..
40	Belarus	31	27	..	0.5	..	29	24	..	..	16	..	..
45	Ukraine	79	33	..	0.4	..	25	11	..	..	16	..	..
53	Armenia	..	..	..	..	..	..	..	..	..	18	..	..
61	Kazakhstan	..	..	..	..	..	..	..	..	..	11	..	..
66	Georgia	..	..	..	..	..	..	..	..	..	10	..	11
71	Azerbaijan	..	..	..	..	..	..	..	..	..	10	..	..
75	Moldova, Rep. of	..	..	..	..	..	..	..	..	..	11	..	5
80	Turkmenistan	..	..	..	..	..	..	..	..	..	6	..	..
82	Kyrgyzstan	..	..	..	..	..	..	..	..	..	7	..	..
91	Uzbekistan	..	..	..	..	..	..	..	..	..	7	..	..
97	Tajikistan	..	..	..	..	..	..	..	..	..	5	..	..

Note: Data for developing countries for this subject area are in table 16.

38 Employment — Industrial countries

| HDI rank | | Labour force (as % of total population) 1991 | Percentage of labour force in | | | Future labour force replacement ratio[a] 1992 | Earnings per employee annual growth rate (%) 1980-90 | Earnings disparity: ratio of earnings of upper half to lower half of labour force | | Percentage of labour force unionized 1989-90 | Weekly hours of work (per person in manu-facturing) 1989-91 | Expenditure on labour market programmes (as % of GDP) 1990-92 |
			Agri-culture 1990-92	Industry 1990-92	Services 1990-92			1980-81	1990-91			
1	Canada	50	5	23	72	99	(.)	4.0	4.4	35	31	3.0
2	Switzerland	53	6	34	60	80	..	..	..	26	42	0.6
3	Japan	52	7	34	59	83	2.0	2.4	2.6	27	45	0.5
4	Sweden	53	3	28	69	92	0.9	2.0	2.1	85	37	6.0
5	Norway	50	6	24	70	96	1.6	..	..	55	35	2.7
6	France	43	6	29	65	100	2.2	3.1	3.0	12	39	2.8
7	Australia	49	6	24	70	104	-0.3	..	..	42	34	2.1
8	USA	50	3	25	72	106	0.7	4.8	5.6	17	34	0.8
9	Netherlands	46	5	25	70	86	1.1	2.0	2.3	25	40	3.3
10	United Kingdom	49	2	28	70	96	2.6	2.5	3.3	42	43	2.3
11	Germany	38	3	39	58	80	1.8	2.7	2.5	34	39	3.5
12	Austria	46	7	37	56	84	1.8	3.4	3.5	46	..	1.5
13	Belgium	42	3	28	69	88	0.1	2.5	2.3	53	34	3.9
14	Iceland	55	11	26	63	122	..	..	..	78	47	..
15	Denmark	56	6	28	66	82	0.6	2.1	2.2	73	..	6.5
16	Finland	51	9	29	62	92	2.8	..	..	71	..	5.5
17	Luxembourg	44	3	31	66	82	..	..	..	50	..	1.1
18	New Zealand	47	11	23	66	112	-0.7	..	..	51	39	2.7
19	Israel	39	4	22	74	159	-3.6	..	..	..	36	..
21	Ireland	38	14	29	57	135	1.9	..	..	52	..	4.4
22	Italy	43	9	32	59	79	1.0	2.1	2.1	40	..	1.5
23	Spain	39	11	33	56	90	0.9	..	..	16	37	3.7
25	Greece	39	23	27	50	91	0.6	..	..	25	..	1.2
27	Czechoslovakia	50	11	45	44	109	0.4	..	..	..	..	1.0
31	Hungary	45	15	31	54	97	2.3	..	..	..	..	2.8
41	Malta	37	3	28	69	111	..	..	..	..	..	..
42	Portugal	49	17	34	49	97	0.7	2.6	2.6	30	..	1.1
48	Bulgaria	50	17	38	45	99	..	..	..	..	..	0.8
49	Poland	49	27	37	36	122	0.1	..	..	..	..	2.8
72	Romania	47	29	43	28	114	..	..	..	..	..	1.0
76	Albania	48	56	19	25	162	..	..	..	..	..	..
	Aggregates											
	Industrial	48	9	33	58	97	1.2	..	..	..	..	..
	Developing	45	58	15	27	..	2.6	..	..	..	..	..
	World	45	13	31	56	..	2.3	..	..	..	..	..
	OECD	47	5	29	66	94	1.3	3.4	3.7	28	..	1.7
	Eastern Europe and former Soviet Union	51	21	42	37	..	..	..	..	..	..	..
	Eastern Europe only	48	24	38	38	115	0.5	..	..	..	..	1.9
	European Community	43	6	32	62	89	1.6	2.6	2.7	32	..	2.9
	Nordic	53	6	27	67	91	1.4	2.1	2.1	74	..	5.4
	Southern Europe	42	12	32	56	85	0.9	2.2	2.1	30	..	2.1
	Non-Europe	50	5	27	68	100	0.9	4.0	4.6	22	..	0.9
	North America	50	3	25	72	105	0.6	4.7	5.4	19	..	1.0

Successor states of the former Soviet Union

HDI rank		Labour force 1991	Agri-culture 1990-92	Industry 1990-92	Services 1990-92	Future labour force replacement ratio 1992						
28	Lithuania	52	10	33	57	111	..	..	..	..	..	..
29	Estonia	51	9	33	58	109	..	..	..	..	..	..
30	Latvia	55	9	33	58	..	..	..	..	..	..	..
34	Russian Federation	53	20	46	34	..	..	..	..	..	..	..
40	Belarus	53	..	..	..	..	..	..	..	..	..	..
45	Ukraine	51	..	..	..	..	..	..	..	..	..	..
53	Armenia	..	11	32	57	..	..	..	..	..	..	..
61	Kazakhstan	..	20	22	58	..	..	..	..	..	..	..
66	Georgia	37	14	30	56	..	..	..	..	..	..	..
71	Azerbaijan	..	15	21	64	..	..	..	..	..	..	..
75	Moldova, Rep. of	..	21	26	53	..	..	..	..	..	..	..
80	Turkmenistan	32	..	..	..	..	..	..	..	..	..	..
82	Kyrgyzstan	42	16	24	60	..	..	..	..	..	..	..
91	Uzbekistan	..	17	20	63	..	..	..	..	..	..	..
97	Tajikistan	..	14	19	67	..	..	..	..	..	..	..

a. Population under 15 divided by one-third of the population aged 15-59.

Note: Data for developing countries for this subject area are in table 17.

| HDI rank | | Unemployed persons (thousands) 1992 | Unemployment rate (%) | | | | | Unemployment benefits expenditure (as % of total government expenditure) 1991 | Incidence of long-term unemployment (as % of total) | | Regional unemployment disparity (25% worst regions versus 25% best) 1989 | Ratio of unemployment rate of those not completing secondary school to rate of those graduating from third level | |
			Total 1992	Total including discouraged workers 1992	Female 1990-91	Youth (15-24) 1992	Male youth (15-19) 1992		More than 6 months 1991-92	More than 12 months 1991-92		Males 1989-90	Females 1989-90
1	Canada	1,560	11.2	11.9	10.3	17.8	21.6	8.1	33	13	2.0	3.6	2.4
2	Switzerland	100	2.5	..	3.1			0.4	..	..	..	1.0	0.9
3	Japan	1,420	2.2	4.1	2.2	4.4	7.3	0.7	35	15	1.9	..	..
4	Sweden	210	4.8	7.3	3.9	11.5	12.9	0.8	26	8	2.4	2.6	2.8
5	Norway	130	5.9	7.3	5.2	13.9	17.0	2.2	41	24	1.6	5.5	2.0
6	France	2,490	10.2	10.3	13.3	19.5	16.5	3.2	58	36	1.5	..	..
7	Australia	940	10.7	12.1	9.9	19.5	25.1	4.0	59	35	1.5	3.7	1.4
8	USA	9,380	7.3	8.2	6.9	13.7	20.3	1.5	21	11	2.0	5.9	4.6
9	Netherlands	480	6.8	7.7	9.2	10.5		4.5	58	43	1.1	2.5	1.5
10	United Kingdom	2,680	9.9	10.4	5.3	15.4	14.8	1.7	46	28	1.8	4.0	2.4
11	Germany	1,810	4.8	..	5.3	5.6	4.3	3.0	63	46	2.2	4.8	1.9
12	Austria	130	3.7	..	3.9	..	..	1.8	..	..	1.3	6.9	2.0
13	Belgium	440	7.8	9.1	11.1			5.8	76	62	1.5	2.8	2.9
14	Iceland	6	3.0	..	3.4			..	..	..	..	..	..
15	Denmark	290	11.1	11.3	12.3	..		5.5	53	31	1.4	..	..
16	Finland	330	13.0	15.9	10.6	23.5	26.0	3.6	32	9	3.3	7.5	8.0
17	Luxembourg	3	1.5	..	2.1	..	..	..	57	..	..	..	..
18	New Zealand	170	10.3	11.1	9.7	18.5	23.2	..	39	21	1.3	..	..
19	Israel	210	11.2	..	14.2			..	..	..	..	..	..
21	Ireland	230	16.1	16.5	12.6	19.5	27.8	6.3	76	60	1.1	..	..
22	Italy	2,800	10.5	12.7	15.9	32.7	35.3	1.0	84	67	2.9	1.9	1.7
23	Spain	2,790	18.1	18.2	26.0	34.4	33.9	7.0	66	47	1.9	1.2	1.7
25	Greece	350	9.2	..	15.4	..	..	..	71	47	1.4	0.9	0.5
27	Czechoslovakia	550	5.3	..	5.6	..	..	..	..	..	..	..	..
31	Hungary	660	12.3	..	11.0	..	..	..	..	..	..	..	..
41	Malta	5	3.8	..	2.3	..	..	..	..	..	..	..	..
42	Portugal	190	4.1	4.5	5.1	9.4	8.4	..	58	38	2.2	..	..
45	Bulgaria	580	15.6	..	..	..	..	..	..	..	..	..	..
49	Poland	2,510	13.6	..	15.2	..	..	..	..	..	..	..	..
75	Romania	930	8.2	..	10.7	..	..	..	..	..	..	..	..
79	Albania	190	12.5	..	..	..	..	..	..	..	..	..	..
	Aggregates												
	Industrial	35,450T	6.5	..	..	..	..	..	..	..	..	..	..
	Developing	..	..	..	..	..	..	..	..	..	..	..	..
	World	..	..	..	..	..	..	..	..	..	..	..	..
	OECD	28,930T	7.6	9.0	8.3	14.6	17.6	2.9	46	30	2.0	4.1	3.0
	Eastern Europe and former Soviet Union	6,310T	3.7	..	..	..	..	..	..	..	..	..	..
	Eastern Europe only	5,420T	11.1	..	11.8	..	..	..	..	..	..	..	..
	European Community	14,550T	9.5	11.8	11.5	18.7	18.6	3.3	64	46	2.0	2.7	1.9
	Nordic	970T	8.1	10.1	7.4	15.4	17.5	3.3	38	18	2.3	5.6	5.2
	Southern Europe	6,140T	12.4	14.0	18.3	31.2	32.3	3.4	74	56	2.3	1.5	1.6
	Non-Europe	13,680T	6.3	7.4	6.0	11.5	16.8	2.4	26	14	1.9	5.4	4.1
	North America	10,940T	7.7	8.5	7.2	14.1	20.4	2.4	22	11	2.0	5.6	4.3

Successor states of the former Soviet Union

HDI rank		Unemployed persons (thousands) 1992	Total 1992										
28	Lithuania	30	1.0	..	..	..	..	..	..	..	..	..	..
29	Estonia	20	1.9	..	..	..	..	..	..	..	..	..	..
30	Latvia	40	2.1	..	..	..	..	..	..	..	..	..	..
34	Russian Federation	580	0.8	..	..	..	..	..	..	..	..	..	..
40	Belarus	30	0.5	..	..	..	..	..	..	..	..	..	..
46	Ukraine	70	0.3	..	..	..	..	..	..	..	..	..	..
53	Armenia	60	3.5	..	..	..	..	..	..	..	..	..	..
61	Kazakhstan	40	0.5	..	..	..	..	..	..	..	..	..	..
66	Georgia	20	1.0	..	..	..	..	..	..	..	..	..	..
71	Azerbaijan	..	..	..	..	..	..	..	..	..	..	..	..
72	Moldova, Rep. of	..	..	..	..	..	..	..	..	..	..	..	..
80	Turkmenistan	..	..	..	..	..	..	..	..	..	..	..	..
82	Kyrgyzstan	..	..	..	..	..	..	..	..	..	..	..	..
91	Uzbekistan	..	..	..	..	..	..	..	..	..	..	..	..
97	Tajikistan	..	..	..	..	..	..	..	..	..	..	..	..

		Real GDP per capita (PPP$) 1991	GNP per capita (US$) 1991	Share of industrial GNP (%) 1991	Income share		Social security benefits expenditure (as % of GDP) 1985-90	Total education expenditure (as % of GDP) 1991	Total health expenditure (as % of GDP) 1991
HDI rank					Lowest 40% of households (%) 1980-91	Ratio of highest 20% to lowest 20% 1980-91			
1	Canada	19,320	20,510	3.1	17.5	7.1	18.8	7.4	9.9
2	Switzerland	21,780	33,710	1.3	16.9	8.6	13.3	5.4a	8.0
3	Japan	19,390	26,840	18.6	21.9	4.3	11.0	5.0	6.8
4	Sweden	17,490	25,180	1.2	21.2	4.6	33.7	6.5	8.8
5	Norway	17,170	24,090	0.6	19.0	5.9	17.6	7.6	8.4
6	France	18,430	20,460	6.5	18.4	6.5	26.1	6.0	9.1
7	Australia	16,680	17,120	1.7	15.5	9.6	8.0	5.5	8.6
8	USA	22,130	22,340	31.5	15.7	8.9	12.6	7.0	13.3
9	Netherlands	16,820	18,840	1.6	20.1	5.6	28.7	5.8	8.7
10	United Kingdom	16,340	16,600	5.3	17.3	6.8	17.0	5.3	6.6
11	Germany	19,770	20,510	10.5	19.5	5.7	23.0	5.4	9.1
12	Austria	17,690	20,200	0.9	..	..	22.5	5.4a	8.5
13	Belgium	17,510	19,010	1.1	21.6	4.6	19.8	5.4a	8.1
14	Iceland	17,480	23,230	(.)	..	..	..	6.0a	8.3
15	Denmark	17,880	23,760	0.7	17.4	7.1	27.8	6.1	7.0
16	Finland	16,130	23,930	0.7	18.4	6.0	22.2	6.6	8.9
17	Luxembourg	20,800	31,860	(.)	..	..	18.8	5.8a	6.6
18	New Zealand	13,970	12,360	0.2	15.9	8.8	14.3	5.8a	7.7
19	Israel	13,460	12,110	0.3	18.1	6.6	13.2	6.0a	4.2
21	Ireland	11,430	11,150	0.2	..	..	19.9	5.9	8.0
22	Italy	17,040	18,580	5.9	18.8	6.0	21.6	4.1a	8.3
23	Spain	12,670	12,480	2.7	19.4	5.8	13.4	5.6	6.5
25	Greece	7,680	6,420	0.4	..	..	11.9	3.0	4.8
27	Czechoslovakia	6,570	2,700	0.2	..	..	18.4	4.6a	5.9
31	Hungary	6,080	2,750	0.2	25.7	3.2	18.2	6.7	6.0
41	Malta	7,575	7,300	(.)	..	..	..	4.4a	..
42	Portugal	9,450	6,180	0.3	..	..	10.4	5.5a	6.2
48	Bulgaria	4,813	1,840	0.1	..	..	15.4	5.4a	5.4
49	Poland	4,500	1,790	0.4	23.0	3.9	11.5	4.9a	5.1
72	Romania	..	1,400	0.2	..	..	..	..	3.9
76	Albania	..	..	(.)	..	..	..	3.1a	4.0
	Aggregates								
	Industrial	14,860	14,920	100.0	..	..	16.2	..	9.4
	Developing	2,730	880	..	..	..	2.7	..	4.2
	World	5,490	4,160	..	..	..	14.7	..	8.6
	OECD	19,000	20,930	94.8	18.3	6.8	16.3	5.9	9.7
	Eastern Europe and former Soviet Union	5,670	2,520	4.5	..	..	..	..	3.7
	Eastern Europe only	5,210	1,950	1.0	23.8	3.7	14.9	4.9	5.2
	European Community	16,760	17,650	35.1	18.9	6.1	21.7	5.3	8.2
	Nordic	17,230	24,380	3.1	19.4	5.7	27.0	6.5	8.4
	Southern Europe	14,100	14,410	9.3	19.0	6.0	18.5	4.5	7.6
	Non-Europe	20,780	23,100	55.4	17.9	7.3	12.3	6.3	10.7
	North America	21,860	22,160	34.6	15.9	6.7	13.2	7.0	13.0

Successor states of the former Soviet Union

		Real GDP per capita (PPP$) 1991	GNP per capita (US$) 1991	Share of industrial GNP (%) 1991	Lowest 40% of households (%) 1980-91	Ratio of highest 20% to lowest 20% 1980-91	Social security benefits expenditure 1985-90	Total education expenditure 1991	Total health expenditure 1991
28	Lithuania	5,410	2,420	(.)	..	..	17.2	..	3.6
29	Estonia	8,090	3,970	(.)	..	..	..	..	..
30	Latvia	7,540	3,920	(.)	..	..	..	..	..
34	Russian Federation	6,930	3,470	2.7	..	..	..	..	3.0
40	Belarus	6,850	3,280	0.2	..	..	..	..	3.2
45	Ukraine	5,180	2,190	0.7	..	..	..	..	3.3
53	Armenia	4,610	1,930	..	..	..	..	..	4.2
61	Kazakhstan	4,490	2,030	..	..	..	..	..	4.4
66	Georgia	3,670	1,780	..	..	..	..	..	4.5
71	Azerbaijan	3,670	1,240	..	..	..	..	..	4.3
75	Moldova, Rep. of	3,500	1,700	(.)	..	..	..	..	3.9
80	Turkmenistan	3,540	1,440	..	..	..	..	..	5.0
82	Kyrgyzstan	3,280	1,160	..	..	..	..	..	5.0
91	Uzbekistan	2,790	980	..	..	..	..	..	5.9
97	Tajikistan	2,180	690	..	..	..	..	..	6.0

a. Public expenditure only.

Note: Data for developing countries for this subject area are in table 18.

	Official development assistance (ODA) disbursed					Bilateral aid				Aid to least developed countries (as % of ODA)	Multi-lateral aid (as % of ODA)
	US$ millions	As % of GNP		As % of central government budget	Per capita (US$)	Social allocation ratio	Social priority ratio	Human expenditure ratio	For human priorities (%)		
HDI rank	1992	1970	1992	1991	1991-92	1989-91	1989-91	1989-92	1989-91	1992	1991-92
1 Canada	2,515	0.41	0.46	2.0	96	20.3	44.4	0.042	9.0	29	31.7
2 Switzerland	1,139	0.13	0.46	3.2	142	29.3	50.7	0.068	14.9	30	29.9
3 Japan	11,128	0.23	0.30	1.3	86	9.7	35.4	0.010	3.4	17	22.0
4 Sweden	2,452	0.41	1.03	2.8	267	5.7	51.2	0.030	2.9	32	29.4
5 Norway	1,226	0.33	1.12	2.0	281	22.9	78.2	0.200	17.9	47	37.0
6 France	7,823	0.46	0.59	3.2	262	13.1	27.4	0.021	3.6	25	22.9
7 Australia	969	0.59	0.36	1.3	59	32.0	32.9	0.038	10.5	20	27.6
8 USA	10,815	0.31	0.18	0.8	44	19.5	58.2	0.020	11.3	23	24.9
9 Netherlands	2,741	0.60	0.86	..	335	25.9	53.2	0.118	13.8	30	31.0
10 United Kingdom	3,126	0.42	0.30	1.2	110	15.4	42.8	0.020	6.6	33	45.2
11 Germany	6,952	0.33	0.36	..	171	7.9	42.5	0.012	2.1	25	32.2
12 Austria	530	0.07	0.29	0.6	67	24.3	28.4	0.020	6.9	21	23.2
13 Belgium	832	0.48	0.37	..	165	..	..	..	..	35	36.7
14 Iceland	..	..	..	..	..	..	..	..	..	..	..
15 Denmark	1,392	0.40	1.02	3.2	242	38.7	64.6	0.255	25.0	36	44.4
16 Finland	644	0.09	0.62	2.0	163	26.2	32.2	0.052	8.4	37	36.1
17 Luxembourg	36	..	0.26	1.2	98	..	..	..	..	35	..
18 New Zealand	97	0.23	0.26	0.5	30	..	..	..	..	20	..
19 Israel	-2,066	..	-3.33	..	-405	..	..	..	..	..	..
21 Ireland	69	0.16	0.16	0.6	38	..	..	..	..	33	..
22 Italy	4,122	0.17	0.34	0.7	126	21.9	38.6	0.029	8.5	27	38.0
23 Spain	1,618	0.01	0.26	0.6	34	..	..	..	..	5	..
25 Greece	..	..	..	..	..	..	..	..	..	..	..
27 Czechoslovakia	..	..	..	..	..	..	..	..	..	..	..
31 Hungary	..	..	..	..	..	..	..	..	..	..	..
41 Malta	..	..	..	..	..	..	..	..	..	..	..
42 Portugal	302	1.05	0.36	..	44	..	..	..	..	73	..
48 Bulgaria	..	..	..	..	..	..	..	..	..	..	..
49 Poland	..	..	..	..	..	..	..	..	..	..	..
72 Romania	..	..	..	..	..	..	..	..	..	..	..
76 Albania	..	..	..	..	..	..	..	..	..	..	..
Aggregates											
Industrial	..	..	..	..	..	..	..	..	..	..	..
Developing	..	..	..	..	..	..	..	..	..	..	..
World	..	..	..	..	..	..	..	..	..	..	..
OECD	60,528T	0.31	0.33	1.6	105	16.1	43.8	0.023	7.0	25	28.9
Eastern Europe and former Soviet Union	..	..	..	..	..	..	..	..	..	..	..
Eastern Europe only	..	..	..	..	..	..	..	..	..	..	..
European Community	29,013T	0.34	0.42	2.0	155	20.0	46.0	0.038	9.2	27	32.5
Nordic	5,714T	0.32	0.96	2.6	242	28.8	65.0	0.180	8.7	37	35.4
Southern Europe	6,042T	0.15	0.32	0.7	85	21.9	38.6	0.027	8.5	23	38.0
Non-Europe	23,458T	0.30	0.22	1.2	55	17.9	50.7	0.020	9.1	21	24.4
North America	13,330T	0.32	0.21	1.0	49	19.7	56.0	0.023	11.0	24	26.2

Successor states of the former Soviet Union

28 Lithuania	..	..	..	..	..	..	..	..	..	..	..
29 Estonia	..	..	..	..	..	..	..	..	..	..	..
30 Latvia	..	..	..	..	..	..	..	..	..	..	..
34 Russian Federation	..	..	..	..	..	..	..	..	..	..	..
40 Belarus	..	..	..	..	..	..	..	..	..	..	..
45 Ukraine	..	..	..	..	..	..	..	..	..	..	..
53 Armenia	..	..	..	..	..	..	..	..	..	..	..
61 Kazakhstan	..	..	..	..	..	..	..	..	..	..	..
66 Georgia	..	..	..	..	..	..	..	..	..	..	..
71 Azerbaijan	..	..	..	..	..	..	..	..	..	..	..
75 Moldova, Rep. of	..	..	..	..	..	..	..	..	..	..	..
80 Turkmenistan	..	..	..	..	..	..	..	..	..	..	..
82 Kyrgyzstan	..	..	..	..	..	..	..	..	..	..	..
91 Uzbekistan	..	..	..	..	..	..	..	..	..	..	..
97 Tajikistan	..	..	..	..	..	..	..	..	..	..	..

Note: Data for developing countries for this subject area are in table 19.

42 Resource flow imbalances

HDI rank	Export-import ratio (exports as % of imports) 1991	Export growth rate as % of import growth rate 1980-91	Trade dependency (exports plus imports as % of GDP) 1991	Terms of trade (1987=100) 1991	Net workers' remittances from abroad (US$ millions) 1991	Public debt (as % of GDP) 1984	Public debt (as % of GDP) 1991	Government net debt interest payments (as % of total expenditures) 1991	Gross international reserves (months of import coverage) 1991	Current account balance (US$ millions) 1991
1 Canada	106	73	47	105	..	59.1	77.6	11.3	1.4	-24,600
2 Switzerland	93	97	55	96	-2,060	..	..	..	6.5	10,310
3 Japan	134	70	16	99	..	67.9	68.2	1.1	2.4	84,740
4 Sweden	111	123	51	103	20	67.0	45.7	0.2	3.0	-1,640
5 Norway	133	336	56	90	-140	38.7	40.1	-3.0	3.7	6,130
6 France	92	106	37	102	-1,790	43.8	48.6	5.0	2.0	-1,200
7 Australia	96	92	26	107	..	..	26.3	3.9	3.4	-9,660
8 USA	79	57	16	102	-7,600	45.2	59.8	6.7	2.6	-24,670
9 Netherlands	106	126	89	100	-315	64.5	75.8	9.0	2.4	11,950
10 United Kingdom	88	59	45	104	..	54.4	35.4	4.9	1.5	-9,580
11 Germany	104	91	50	95	-4,210	41.7	42.0	4.5	2.3	9,980
12 Austria	81	117	56	89	367	47.9	57.0	6.7	2.7	-144
13 Belgium	..	139	..	..	-274	118.5	133.2	18.9	..	6,200
14 Iceland	90	..	..	101	..	..	..	..	..	..
15 Denmark	111	125	61	104	..	65.9	60.7	6.0	1.7	2,510
16 Finland	106	65	41	99	..	19.0	22.4	1.1	2.8	-6,000
17 Luxembourg	..	..	..	..	..	..	..	..	..	..
18 New Zealand	109	113	41	94	245	..	..	..	2.6	30
19 Israel	71	131	46	104	..	..	..	..	3.0	-5,260
21 Ireland	117	192	115	92	..	104.8	99.8	15.0	2.1	-1,760
22 Italy	95	81	30	101	779	77.4	104.0	18.1	3.3	-16,670
23 Spain	65	80	29	108	1,600	43.8	49.3	8.3	7.1	-19,810
25 Greece	40	72	52	107	2,120	49.5	95.9	24.6	3.5	-5,560
27 Czechoslovakia	..	..	73	137	..	..	..	..	3.8	961
31 Hungary	90	220	70	102	..	..	..	..	3.7	370
41 Malta	58	..	..	113	..	..	..	..	..	..
42 Portugal	62	111	66	112	4,520	..	..	18.9	10.5	-2,100
48 Bulgaria	127	..	..	..	..	..	..	..	..	-718
49 Poland	95	165	39	104	..	..	..	..	2.1	-2,190
72 Romania	75	..	..	..	..	..	..	..	2.4	-1,310
76 Albania	38	..	..	..	..	..	..	..	..	..
Aggregates										
Industrial	96	..	30	101	..	..	..	..	2.7	310T
Developing	90	..	45	99	..	..	..	..	4.3	9,030T
World	91	..	32	100	..	..	..	..	4.2	9,340T
OECD	96	88	29	100	-6,740T	53.9	60.5	7.1	2.7	8,460T
Eastern Europe and former Soviet Union	92	..	..	..	..	..	..	..	..	..
Eastern Europe only	92	..	..	..	..	..	..	..	3.1	-2,890T
European Community	95	95	44	100	2,430T	54.6	58.9	9.1	2.7	-26,040T
Nordic	114	152	52	100	-120T	51.3	43.0	1.0	2.8	1,000T
Southern Europe	79	82	32	104	9,020T	66.2	87.3	16.3	5.0	-44,140T
Non-Europe	97	66	19	102	-7,360T	53.9	62.6	5.5	2.4	20,580T
North America	84	60	19	103	-7,600T	46.4	61.4	7.1	2.4	-49,270T

Successor states of the former Soviet Union

HDI rank	Export-import ratio 1991									
28 Lithuania	..	..	..	..	..	..	..	..	..	..
29 Estonia	43	..	..	..	..	..	..	..	..	..
30 Latvia	24	..	..	..	..	..	..	..	..	..
34 Russian Federation	145	..	..	..	..	..	..	..	..	..
40 Belarus	85	..	..	..	..	..	..	..	..	..
45 Ukraine	72	..	..	..	..	..	..	..	..	..
53 Armenia	8	..	..	..	..	..	..	..	..	..
61 Kazakhstan	48	..	..	..	..	..	..	..	..	..
66 Georgia	15	..	..	..	..	..	..	..	..	..
71 Azerbaijan	43	..	..	..	..	..	..	..	..	..
75 Moldova, Rep. of	27	..	..	..	..	..	..	..	..	..
80 Turkmenistan	28	..	..	..	..	..	..	..	..	..
82 Kyrgyzstan	11	..	..	..	..	..	..	..	..	..
91 Uzbekistan	48	..	..	..	..	..	..	..	..	..
97 Tajikistan	85	..	..	..	..	..	..	..	..	..

Note: Data for developing countries for this subject area are in table 20.

HDI rank		Military expenditure (as % of GDP)		Military expenditure (as % of combined education and health expenditure)		ODA disbursed (as % of military expenditure)	Average annual exports of non-nuclear arms to developing countries		Armed forces		
							US$ millions	Percentage share	Per 1,000 people	Per teacher	Per doctor
		1960	1990-91	1960	1990-91	1992	1988-92	1988-92	1990	1990	1990
1	Canada	4.3	2.0	66	15	22	..	..	4.0	0.3	2.0
2	Switzerland	2.4	1.5	45	14	31	149	0.2	8.2	0.9	4.0
3	Japan	1.0	1.0	17	12	34	..	..	3.7	0.4	2.3
4	Sweden	2.8	2.3	30	16	44	675	0.8	..	..	..
5	Norway	3.2	3.1	48	22	27	..	..	8.9	0.9	2.6
6	France	6.3	3.5	131	29	18	6,588	7.7	5.4	0.5	2.6
7	Australia	2.4	2.4	46	24	13	..	..	3.4	0.3	1.5
8	USA	8.8	5.1	173	46	4	20,000	23.4	..	..	..
9	Netherlands	3.9	2.5	67	22	38	1,340	1.6	..	..	..
10	United Kingdom	6.4	4.2	96	40	7	6,017	7.0	14.8	1.5	9.2
11	Germany	4.0	2.8	67	29	18	2,069	2.4	9.2	0.8	2.7
12	Austria	1.2	1.0	20	9	34	..	..	2.0	0.3	1.3
13	Belgium	3.4	2.3	49	20	18	..	..	8.0	0.6	2.6
14	Iceland	(.)	(.)	(.)	(.)	..	..	..	6.2	0.6	3.2
15	Denmark	2.7	2.1	37	18	52	..	..	6.9	0.8	2.7
16	Finland	1.7	1.9	25	15	25	..	..	6.6	0.8	2.3
17	Luxembourg	1.0	1.2	19	10	33	..	..	16.1	1.8	4.9
18	New Zealand	1.4	1.9	29	16	11	..	..	..	..	..
19	Israel	2.9	8.6	85	106	..	489	0.6	3.5	0.3	1.8
21	Ireland	1.4	1.4	24	12	12	..	..	2.6	0.3	0.9
22	Italy	2.7	2.1	39	21	17	947	1.1	30.3	1.9	14.8
23	Spain	2.9	1.7	126	18	18	643	0.8	14.6	1.8	4.7
25	Greece	4.8	5.5	145	71	..	..	..	..	..	..
27	Czechoslovakia	3.8	1.6	60	17	..	1,442	1.7	8.5	0.8	3.5
31	Hungary	1.8	2.0	31	18	..	..	..	6.2	0.5	2.3
41	Malta	..	0.8	..	10	..	..	..	12.6	1.4	3.4
42	Portugal	4.2	3.1	156	32	21	..	..	..	..	..
48	Bulgaria	3.2	2.8	70	29	..	..	..	8.2	0.8	3.0
49	Poland	3.0	2.7	41	30	..	..	..	..	..	..
72	Romania	2.3	1.4	47	25	..	..	..	5.6	0.5	2.5
76	Albania	9.0	4.8	..	51	..	..	..	3.0	0.6	1.0
	Aggregates										
	Industrial	6.3	3.4	97	33	..	73,500T	86.0	8.7	0.8	3.9
	Developing	4.2	3.5	143	60	..	11,800T	14.0	4.0	0.6	18.5
	World	6.0	3.4	104	37	..	85,300T	100.0	4.7	0.7	16.1
	OECD	6.4	3.2	96	30	21	38,430T	47.3	10.2	0.9	4.8
	Eastern Europe and former Soviet Union	..	7.4	103	96	..	34,580T	38.7	6.3	0.6	2.5
	Eastern Europe only	..	2.1	47	24	..	1,440T	..	6.7	0.6	2.7
	European Community	4.7	2.9	83	28	20	17,600T	21.6	14.0	1.2	6.4
	Nordic	2.7	2.3	33	17	40	680T	..	7.4	0.8	2.6
	Southern Europe	3.3	2.1	72	22	17	1,590T	0.8	23.9	1.8	10.7
	Non-Europe	7.5	3.5	110	32	19	20,490T	..	..	..	..
	North America	8.5	4.8	163	43	7	20,000T	23.4	..	..	..

Successor states of the former Soviet Union

HDI rank		Military expenditure (as % of GDP)		Military expenditure		ODA disbursed	Average annual exports		Armed forces		
		1960	1990-91	1960	1990-91	1992	1988-92	1988-92	1990	1990	1990
28	Lithuania	..	..	..	..	..	..	..	7.0	0.8	1.9
29	Estonia	..	..	..	..	..	..	..	5.3	0.6	3.8
30	Latvia	..	..	..	..	..	..	..	6.8	0.6	5.1
34	Russian Federation	11[a]	10[a]	134[a]	132[a]	..	33,135[a]	38.7[a]	6.6	0.5	2.4
40	Belarus	..	..	..	..	..	..	..	7.5	0.6	2.4
45	Ukraine	..	..	..	..	..	..	..	7.0	1.0	3.3
53	Armenia	..	..	..	..	..	..	..	..	..	..
61	Kazakhstan	..	..	..	..	..	..	..	..	..	..
66	Georgia	..	..	..	..	..	..	..	..	..	..
71	Azerbaijan	..	..	..	..	..	..	..	..	..	..
75	Moldova, Rep. of	..	..	..	..	..	..	..	..	..	..
80	Turkmenistan	..	..	..	..	..	..	..	..	..	..
82	Kyrgyzstan	..	..	..	..	..	..	..	..	..	..
91	Uzbekistan	..	..	..	..	..	..	..	..	..	..
97	Tajikistan	..	..	..	..	..	..	..	..	..	..

a. Data for former Soviet Union.

Note: Data for developing countries for this subject area are in table 21.

HDI rank		Urban population (as % of total)			Urban population annual growth rate (%)		Population in largest city (as % of urban)	Population in cities of more than 1 million (as % of urban)	Popula-tion in cities of more than 1 million (as % of total)	Major city with highest population density	Population per km²	Population exposed to 60+ decibels of road traffic noise (%)
		1960	1992	2000	1960-1992	1992-2000	1990	1990	1990	City	1980-90	1980-90
1	Canada	69	78	79	1.7	1.0	17	42	33	Montreal	6,360	..
2	Switzerland	51	63	64	1.2	0.9	22	22	13	Lausanne	5,510	26
3	Japan	63	77	78	1.6	0.5	26	47	36	Tokyo	13,970	58
4	Sweden	73	84	86	0.9	0.3	23	35	29	Stockholm	3,050	9
5	Norway	50	76	79	1.9	0.8	..	..	..	..	..	26
6	France	62	74	77	1.3	0.7	23	31	23	Paris	20,650	34
7	Australia	81	85	86	1.9	1.2	25	71	60	Sydney	3,320	..
8	USA	70	76	77	1.3	0.9	9	55	41	New York	8,720	18
9	Netherlands	85	89	89	1.0	0.6	30	30	25	The Hague	6,390	20
10	United Kingdom	86	89	90	0.4	0.3	14	26	23	Birmingham	4,440	26
11	Germany	76	86	87	0.6	0.2	9	51	43	Munich	4,190	32
12	Austria	50	59	63	0.8	0.8	47	47	28	Vienna	3,690	35
13	Belgium	92	97	98	0.4	0.1	14	14	13	Brussels	4,160	39
14	Iceland	91	91	98	1.6	1.0	..	..	..	..	..	..
15	Denmark	74	85	88	0.9	0.3	31	31	26	Copenhagen	5,740	18
16	Finland	38	60	62	1.9	0.5	34	34	20	Helsinki	2,620	11
17	Luxembourg	59	85	87	1.6	0.5	..	..	..	..	..	..
18	New Zealand	77	84	85	1.5	0.9	..	..	..	..	..	..
19	Israel	76	92	92	3.2	1.7	45	45	41	..	..	..
21	Ireland	45	58	59	1.7	1.5	46	46	26	Dublin	4,490	..
22	Italy	59	69	72	0.9	0.5	13	41	28	Naples	10,340	..
23	Spain	57	79	83	1.9	0.9	17	28	22	Barcelona	17,430	50
25	Greece	43	64	68	1.9	0.9	55	68	43	..	..	40
27	Czechoslovakia	47	79	83	2.1	1.1	10	10	8	Prague	2,820	..
31	Hungary	40	66	68	1.6	1.0	31	31	20	Budapest	3,950	..
41	Malta	67	88	90	1.0	0.6	..	..	..	..	..	..
42	Portugal	22	36	40	1.9	1.9	48	48	16	Lisbon	9,890	30
48	Bulgaria	39	69	73	2.4	0.9	22	22	15	..	..	..
49	Poland	48	63	66	1.7	1.2	15	36	22	Warsaw	3,420	..
72	Romania	34	55	58	2.2	1.4	18	18	9	Bucharest	3,270	..
76	Albania	31	36	39	2.8	2.6	..	..	..	..	..	..
	Aggregates											
	Industrial	61	74	78	1.2	0.7	17	43	33	..	..	..
	Developing	22	35	49	4.3	4.4	18	40	14			
	World	34	44	57	3.8	3.8	18	41	21	..	..	
	OECD	68	77	79	1.2	0.7	16	45	35	..	..	32
	Eastern Europe and former Soviet Union	47	65	..	..	..	..	..	..	..	..	..
	Eastern Europe only	43	64	67	1.9	1.2	18	25	16	..	..	..
	European Community	69	79	81	0.9	0.5	17	37	29	..	..	33
	Nordic	62	77	80	1.2	0.4	28	33	26	..	..	15
	Southern Europe	54	69	73	1.4	0.7	20	38	26	..	..	45
	Non-Europe	68	77	78	1.5	0.8	15	52	40	..	..	31
	North America	70	76	77	1.3	0.9	9	54	40	..	..	18

Successor states of the former Soviet Union

HDI rank		1960	1992	2000	1960-1992	1992-2000	1990	1990	1990	City	1980-90	1980-90
28	Lithuania	39	70	75	..	..	8	16	14	..	..	..
29	Estonia	56	72	75	..	..	..	..	..	..	..	..
30	Latvia	55	72	75	..	..	48	48	34	..	..	..
34	Russian Federation	53	74	..	..	..	..	..	..	..	..	..
40	Belarus	31	67	..	1.0	..	..	..	..	..	..	..
45	Ukraine	46	68	..	0.7	..	..	..	..	..	..	..
53	Armenia	50	68	..	0.6	..	..	..	..	..	..	..
61	Kazakhstan	44	58	..	..	..	..	..	..	..	..	..
66	Georgia	42	56	..	..	..	..	..	..	..	..	..
71	Azerbaijan	48	53	..	0.4	..	..	..	..	..	..	..
75	Moldova, Rep. of	22	48	..	..	..	..	..	..	..	..	..
80	Turkmenistan	45	45	..	..	..	..	..	..	..	..	..
82	Kyrgyzstan	34	38	..	..	..	..	..	..	..	..	..
91	Uzbekistan	34	40	..	0.3	..	..	..	..	..	..	..
97	Tajikistan	33	31	..	..	..	..	..	..	..	..	..

Note: Data for developing countries for this subject area are in table 22.

HDI rank		Estimated population (millions)			Annual population growth rate (%)		Total fertility rate 1992	Fertility rates over time (1992 as % of 1960)	Contra-ceptive prevalence rate (%) 1985-92	Depen-dency ratio (%) 1992	Population aged 60 and over (%) 1992	Life expectancy at age 60 (years)	
		1960	1992	2000	1960-1992	1992-2000						Male 1989-90	Female 1989-90
1	Canada	17.9	27.4	30.4	1.3	1.3	1.8	47	73	48	16	..	..
2	Switzerland	5.4	6.8	7.2	0.7	0.6	1.6	67	71	47	20	19.1	23.9
3	Japan	94.1	124.5	128.1	0.9	0.4	1.7	81	64	44	18	20.0	24.4
4	Sweden	7.5	8.6	9.0	0.5	0.5	2.0	89	78	56	22	19.1	23.3
5	Norway	3.6	4.3	4.5	0.6	0.6	1.9	68	76	55	21	18.3	22.9
6	France	45.7	57.1	58.8	0.7	0.4	1.8	65	80	53	19	18.8	24.0
7	Australia	10.3	17.6	19.6	1.7	1.4	1.9	57	76	50	15	18.8	23.1
8	USA	180.7	255.2	275.3	1.1	1.0	2.0	58	74	52	17	18.6	22.7
9	Netherlands	11.5	15.2	16.1	0.9	0.7	1.7	53	76	45	17	18.3	23.4
10	United Kingdom	52.4	57.7	58.8	0.3	0.2	1.9	70	81	54	21	17.4	21.7
11	Germany	72.7	80.2	82.6	0.3	0.4	1.5	62	75	46	20	17.8	22.2
12	Austria	7.0	7.8	8.0	0.3	0.3	1.5	56	71	49	20	18.1	22.3
13	Belgium	9.2	10.0	10.1	0.3	0.1	1.6	63	79	50	21	17.6	22.5
14	Iceland	0.2	0.3	0.3	1.2	1.1	2.2	55	..	55	15	19.5	22.9
15	Denmark	4.6	5.2	5.2	0.4	0.2	1.7	64	78	49	20	17.5	21.7
16	Finland	4.4	5.0	5.1	0.4	0.3	1.8	66	80	49	19	17.1	21.9
17	Luxembourg	0.3	0.4	0.4	0.6	0.7	1.6	68	..	45	19	..	..
18	New Zealand	2.4	3.5	3.7	1.2	0.9	2.1	55	70	52	15	17.8	21.9
19	Israel	2.1	5.1	6.3	2.8	2.6	2.9	75	..	66	13	..	..
21	Ireland	2.8	3.5	3.4	0.7	-0.2	2.2	56	60	61	15	16.0	20.0
22	Italy	50.2	57.8	58.1	0.4	0.1	1.3	54	78	45	20	18.3	22.9
23	Spain	30.5	39.1	39.6	0.8	0.2	1.4	50	59	48	19	..	..
25	Greece	8.3	10.2	10.3	0.6	0.2	1.5	67	..	49	20	..	..
27	Czechoslovakia	13.7	15.7	16.3	0.4	0.4	2.0	80	77	52	17	..	..
31	Hungary	10.0	10.5	10.5	0.2	0.0	1.8	91	73	50	19	..	..
41	Malta	0.3	0.4	0.4	0.4	0.7	2.1	60	..	51	15	..	..
42	Portugal	8.8	9.9	9.9	0.4	0.1	1.5	49	66	50	19	18.0	22.0
48	Bulgaria	7.9	8.9	8.9	0.4	-0.1	1.9	83	76	50	20	..	..
49	Poland	29.6	38.4	39.5	0.8	0.4	2.1	70	75	54	15	..	..
72	Romania	18.4	23.3	24.0	0.7	0.4	2.2	93	58	51	16	..	..
76	Albania	1.6	3.3	3.6	2.3	1.0	2.8	48	..	60	8	..	..
	Aggregates												
	Industrial	930T	1,210T	1,400T	0.8	0.6	2.0	65	60	51	18	18.5	22.9
	Developing	2,070T	4,240T	4,930T	2.2	1.9	3.8	60	53	..	..	..	..
	World	3,000T	5,450T	6,330T	1.8	1.6	3.4	61	52	..	..	..	..
	OECD	630T	810T	850T	0.8	0.6	1.8	63	73	49	18	18.6	23.0
	Eastern Europe and former Soviet Union	290T	390T	410T	0.9	0.6	2.4	..	32	53	..	12.9	16.6
	Eastern Europe only	80T	100T	100T	0.6	0.3	2.1	80	71	52	16	..	..
	European Community	300T	350T	350T	0.5	0.3	1.6	61	75	49	20	18.0	22.6
	Nordic	20T	23T	24T	0.4	0.4	1.9	74	78	53	21	18.2	22.6
	Southern Europe	100T	120T	120T	0.6	0.1	1.4	53	70	47	20	18.3	22.8
	Non-Europe	310T	430T	460T	1.1	0.8	1.9	64	71	49	17	19.1	23.3
	North America	200T	280T	310T	1.1	1.0	2.0	57	74	52	17	18.6	22.7

Successor states of the former Soviet Union

HDI rank		1960	1992	2000	1960-1992	1992-2000	Total fertility rate 1992	Fertility rates over time	Contra-ceptive prevalence rate	Dependency ratio	Population aged 60 and over	Male	Female
28	Lithuania	2.8	3.8	3.8	1.0	0.1	2.0	80	12	51	17	13.3	17.0
29	Estonia	1.2	1.6	1.6	0.8	0.0	2.1	115	26	52	17	12.1	15.8
30	Latvia	2.1	2.7	2.6	0.7	-0.1	2.0	110	19	51	..	12.1	15.8
34	Russian Federation	118.8	149.0	155.2	0.7	0.5	2.1	..	22	49	..	12.0	15.8
40	Belarus	8.1	10.3	10.8	0.8	0.6	2.0	..	13	49	..	12.9	16.4
45	Ukraine	42.4	52.2	53.8	0.6	0.4	2.0	..	15	52	..	12.5	15.8
53	Armenia	1.8	3.5	3.6	2.1	0.4	2.6	..	12	54	..	13.5	16.5
61	Kazakhstan	9.6	17.0	18.3	1.8	0.9	3.0	..	22	61	..	12.5	16.4
66	Georgia	4.1	5.5	5.8	0.9	0.7	2.3	..	8	52	..	14.1	17.1
71	Azerbaijan	3.8	7.3	8.0	2.1	1.2	2.8	..	7	61	..	14.2	18.2
75	Moldova, Rep. of	3.0	4.4	4.6	1.2	0.7	2.6	..	..	56	..	12.5	14.7
80	Turkmenistan	1.6	3.9	4.5	2.8	1.9	4.6	..	12	82	..	12.8	15.8
82	Kyrgyzstan	2.2	4.5	5.2	2.3	1.8	4.0	..	25	72	..	13.0	16.7
91	Uzbekistan	8.6	21.5	25.2	2.9	2.0	4.4	..	19	69	..	14.1	17.1
97	Tajikistan	2.1	5.6	6.9	3.1	2.7	5.4	..	15	89	..	15.1	18.0

Note: Data for developing countries for this subject area are in table 23.

HDI rank	Land area (thousands of km²)	Population density (people per km²) 1992	Arable land and permanent cropland (as % of land area) 1990	Permanent grasslands (as % of land area) 1990	Forest and wooded land (as % of land area) 1990	Irrigated land (as % of arable land area) 1989	Internal renewable water resources per capita (1,000 m³ per year) 1990	Annual fresh water withdrawals As % of water resources 1980-89	Per capita (m³) 1980-89
1 Canada	9,980	3	5	..	49	2	109.4	2	1,800
2 Switzerland	41	166	13	32	32	6	6.5	6	500
3 Japan	378	329	12	..	67	62	4.4	20	920
4 Sweden	450	19	7	..	68	4	21.1	2	480
5 Norway	324	13	3	..	31	11	96.2	1	530
6 France	552	104	35	21	28	7	3.0	22	730
7 Australia	7,690	2	6	54	14	4	20.4	5	1,300
8 USA	9,370	27	21	26	32	10	9.9	19	2,160
9 Netherlands	37	410	28	31	10	59	0.7	16	1,020
10 United Kingdom	245	235	28	44	10	2	2.1	24	510
11 Germany	357	225	36	16	30	4	1.3	27	690
12 Austria	84	93	18	24	47	..	7.5	4	450
13 Belgium	31	322	25	20	20	..	0.9	72	910
14 Iceland	103	3	1	18	..	..	671.9	(.)	350
15 Denmark	43	120	61	..	12	17	2.2	11	290
16 Finland	338	15	8	..	77	3	22.1	3	770
17 Luxembourg	3	126	22	27	33	..	2.7	1	120
18 New Zealand	271	13	2	50	27	54	117.4	(.)	380
19 Israel	21	245	..	..	..	50	0.4	88	450
21 Ireland	70	50	14	68	..	..	13.4	2	270
22 Italy	301	192	41	17	23	25	3.1	30	980
23 Spain	505	77	41	20	31	16	2.8	41	1,170
25 Greece	132	77	31	41	20	30	4.4	12	720
27 Czechoslovakia	128	123	39	13	37	6	1.8	6	380
31 Hungary	93	113	57	13	18	3	0.6	5	500
41 Malta	(.)	1	..	..	..	8	(.)	92	70
42 Portugal	92	107	35	9	35	17	3.3	16	1,060
48 Bulgaria	111	81	..	..	..	30	2.0	7	1,600
49 Poland	313	123	48	13	29	1	1.3	30	470
72 Romania	238	98	..	..	..	32	1.6	12	1,140
76 Albania	29	115	..	..	..	..	3.1	1	90
Aggregates									
Industrial	53,620T	22	13	..	34	9	9.7	21	1,200
Developing	78,110T	54	10	..	..	22	6.8	16	520
World	131,730T	41	11	..	..	18	7.3	17	650
OECD	31,400T	26	12	37	34	10	10.7	21	1,220
Eastern Europe and former Soviet Union	22,200T	17	..	..	..	..	..	..	..
Eastern Europe only	910T	110	48	13	29	2	1.5	16	700
European Community	2,370T	146	36	24	26	14	2.4	27	790
Nordic	1,260T	19	8	..	58	8	38.2	5	500
Southern Europe	1,030T	113	39	21	28	20	3.1	30	1,060
Non-Europe	27,710T	16	11	39	34	9	15.8	18	1,710
North America	19,350T	15	12	26	41	9	19.5	17	2,120

Successor states of the former Soviet Union

HDI rank	Land area (thousands of km²)	Population density (people per km²) 1992	Arable land and permanent cropland (as % of land area) 1990	Permanent grasslands (as % of land area) 1990	Forest and wooded land (as % of land area) 1990	Irrigated land (as % of arable land area) 1989	Internal renewable water resources per capita (1,000 m³ per year) 1990	Annual fresh water withdrawals As % of water resources 1980-89	Per capita (m³) 1980-89
28 Lithuania	65	58	..	..	..	..	..	..	..
29 Estonia	45	35	..	..	..	..	..	..	..
30 Latvia	65	41	..	..	..	..	..	..	..
34 Russian Federation	17,080	9	..	..	..	..	..	..	..
40 Belarus	208	49	..	..	..	..	..	..	..
45 Ukraine	604	86	..	..	..	..	..	..	..
53 Armenia	30	116	..	..	..	..	..	..	..
61 Kazakhstan	1,720	6	..	..	..	..	..	..	..
66 Georgia	70	78	..	..	..	..	..	..	..
71 Azerbaijan	87	84	..	..	..	..	..	..	..
75 Moldova, Rep. of	34	128	..	..	..	..	..	..	..
80 Turkmenistan	488	8	..	..	..	..	..	..	..
82 Kyrgyzstan	199	23	..	..	..	..	..	..	..
91 Uzbekistan	447	48	..	..	..	..	..	..	..
97 Tajikistan	143	39	..	..	..	..	..	..	..

Note: Data for developing countries for this subject area are in table 24.

47 Energy consumption

	Commercial energy consumption				Share of world commercial energy consumption (%)	Annual rate of change in commercial energy consumption (%)		Commercial energy efficiency (energy consumption in kg of oil equivalent per $100 GDP)	
	Total (billion kg of oil equivalent)		Per capita (kg of oil equivalent)						
HDI rank	1965	1991	1965	1991	1991	1970-80	1980-91	1965	1991
1 Canada	118	256	6,010	9,390	3.6	3.5	2.0	279	50
2 Switzerland	15	27	2,500	3,940	0.4	1.2	1.4	105	12
3 Japan	146	440	1,470	3,550	6.1	2.2	2.2	145	13
4 Sweden	32	51	4,160	5,900	0.7	1.2	1.3	176	25
5 Norway	17	39	4,650	9,130	0.5	3.3	1.8	247	37
6 France	120	220	2,470	3,850	3.1	2.3	1.2	122	18
7 Australia	37	90	3,290	5,210	1.3	3.8	2.2	167	30
8 USA	1,270	1,940	6,540	7,680	27.0	1.3	1.4	173	35
9 Netherlands	39	78	3,130	5,150	1.1	2.6	1.4	191	27
10 United Kingdom	189	212	3,480	3,670	3.0	-0.2	0.7	242	24
11 Germany	188	277	2,480	3,460	3.9	1.8	0.4	176	18
12 Austria	15	27	2,060	3,500	0.4	2.0	1.4	151	17
13 Belgium	..	28	..	2,790	0.4	..	..	177	14
14 Iceland	..	..	..	..	..	..	..	..	..
15 Denmark	14	19	2,910	3,750	0.3	0.6	(.)	193	17
16 Finland	10	28	2,230	5,600	0.4	3.0	2.8	..	25
17 Luxembourg	..	..	..	..	..	..	..	..	..
18 New Zealand	7	17	2,620	4,890	0.2	2.6	5.0	121	39
19 Israel	4	9	1,570	1,930	0.1	3.0	2.3	94	15
21 Ireland	4	10	1,500	2,750	0.1	3.1	0.8	206	25
22 Italy	82	159	1,560	2,760	2.2	1.6	0.9	115	14
23 Spain	29	87	901	2,230	1.2	5.1	1.7	118	16
25 Greece	5	22	615	2,110	0.3	6.6	2.8	101	38
27 Czechoslovakia	48	73	3,370	4,680	1.0	2.8	0.6	..	222
31 Hungary	19	29	1,830	2,830	0.4	3.9	0.7	..	95
41 Malta	..	..	..	..	..	..	..	..	..
42 Portugal	5	16	506	1,580	0.2	5.1	2.9	109	24
48 Bulgaria	15	32	1,790	3,540	0.4	5.1	0.8	..	403
49 Poland	64	121	2,030	3,170	1.7	4.6	1.1	..	155
72 Romania	29	70	1,540	3,050	1.0	5.9	0.6	..	254
76 Albania	1	4	420	1,150	0.1	..	..	..	..
Aggregates									
Industrial	2,520T	4,380T	3,360	4,840	61.0	2.6	1.6	166	26
Developing	710T	2,110T	200	550	..	6.9	6.5	156	73
World	3,230T	6,490T	1,030	1,350	..	4.6	4.8	164	34
OECD	2,340T	4,040T	3,540	5,050	56.3	2.2	1.7	166	24
Eastern Europe and former Soviet Union	..	..	..	..	..	..	..	..	..
Eastern Europe only	180T	330T	2,070	3,310	4.6	4.6	0.9	..	199
European Community	680T	1,130T	2,240	3,260	15.7	2.8	1.3	161	19
Nordic	73T	140T	3,540	5,960	1.9	2.5	2.0	197	26
Southern Europe	120T	280T	1,180	2,430	3.9	3.9	1.7	115	16
Non-Europe	1,580T	2,750T	4,780	6,410	38.3	1.9	1.7	169	28
North America	1,390T	2,200T	6,490	7,850	30.6	1.7	1.5	182	36

Successor states of the former Soviet Union

28 Lithuania	..	..	..	..	..	..	..	..	..
29 Estonia	..	..	..	..	..	..	..	..	..
30 Latvia	..	..	..	..	..	..	..	..	..
34 Russian Federation	..	..	..	..	..	..	..	..	..
40 Belarus	..	..	..	..	..	..	..	..	..
45 Ukraine	..	..	..	..	..	..	..	..	..
53 Armenia	..	..	..	..	..	..	..	..	..
61 Kazahkstan	..	..	..	..	..	..	..	..	..
66 Georgia	..	..	..	..	..	..	..	..	..
71 Azerbaijan	..	..	..	..	..	..	..	..	..
75 Moldova, Rep. of	..	..	..	..	..	..	..	..	..
80 Turkmenistan	..	..	..	..	..	..	..	..	..
82 Kyrgyzstan	..	..	..	..	..	..	..	..	..
91 Uzbekistan	..	..	..	..	..	..	..	..	..
97 Tajikistan	..	..	..	..	..	..	..	..	..

Note: Data for developing countries for this subject area are in table 25.

HDI rank		City	Major city with highest concentration of SO_2 — Micro-grammes of SO_2 per m³ 1990-91	Sulfur and nitrogen emissions (kg of NO_2 and SO_2 per capita) 1989	Share of global emissions (greenhouse index) — Absolute share (%) 1989	Per 10 million people 1989	Pesticide consumption (metric tons per 1,000 people) 1985-91	Nuclear waste from spent fuel (metric tons of heavy metal per 1,000 km²) 1990	Hazardous and special waste production (metric tons per km²) 1987	Gener-ation of municipal waste (kg per capita) 1990	Population served by municipal waste services (%) 1990	Waste recycling (as % of consumption) — Paper and cardboard 1985-90	Glass 1985-90
1	Canada	Hamilton	28	209	1.68	0.61	1.2	0.1	0.7	600	100	20	12
2	Switzerland	Zurich	19	39	0.16	0.23	0.4	2.1	13.0	440	98	49	65
3	Japan	Tokyo	26	..	4.68	0.38	0.7	1.8	1.8	410	100	50	54
4	Sweden	Göteberg	12	61	0.22	0.25	0.2	0.6	1.2	370	100	43	44
5	Norway	Oslo	7	68	0.21	0.49	0.3	..	0.7	470	85	26	..
6	France	Paris	38	56	1.54	0.27	1.7	2.0	7.2	330	99	46	29
7	Australia	..	..	..	1.13	0.64	..	..	(.)	680	..	32	17
8	USA	New York	37	160	17.84	0.70	1.5	0.2	19.6	720	100	29	20
9	Netherlands	Rijnmond	24	57	0.52	0.34	1.3	0.5	30.6	500	99	50	67
10	United Kingdom	London	32	105	2.21	0.38	..	4.2	10.5	350	100	31	21
11	Germany	Leipzig	102	60	4.44	0.55	0.4	1.4	17.2	350	96	40	45
12	Austria	Vienna	22	..	0.22	0.28	0.8	..	7.4	330	99	37	60
13	Belgium	Antwerpen	32	71	0.37	0.37	1.0	4.0	27.9	340	100	36	55
14	Iceland	Reykjavik	4	60	0.01	0.38	..	..	0.1	310	..	..	..
15	Denmark	Copenhagen	19	100	0.18	0.35	0.9	..	2.5	480	..	35	60
16	Finland	Turku	14	115	0.18	0.36	0.3	0.2	1.0	620	75	41	36
17	Luxembourg	Luxembourg	17	78	0.03	0.79	..	..	1.5	450	100	..	..
18	New Zealand	Dunedin	14	44	0.15	0.43	..	..	0.4	660	..	19	53
19	Israel	..	..	..	0.14	0.27	0.4	..	1.5	..	..	21	..
21	Ireland	Dublin	26	64	0.13	0.37	0.0	..	0.3	310	..	..	23
22	Italy	..	..	71	1.60	0.28	1.6	0.0	11.0	350	..	27	48
23	Spain	Madrid	64	108	0.93	0.24	3.4	0.4	3.4	320	90	51	27
25	Greece	Athens	45	50	0.29	0.29	..	..	3.4	300	100	30	15
27	Czechoslovakia	Praha	63	239	0.74	0.47	..	..	51.3	250	65	49	..
31	Hungary	..	..	141	0.25	0.24	0.2	..	43.5	460	63	29	..
41	Malta	..	..	..	0.01	0.28	..	..	..	..	..	..	..
42	Portugal	Barriero/Sexial	69	30	0.21	0.21	2.2	..	11.3	260	88	39	30
48	Bulgaria	..	..	..	0.33	0.37	..	..	..	..	..	..	..
49	Poland	Chorzow	82	141	1.46	0.38	0.5	..	0.2	340	55	..	..
72	Romania	..	..	..	0.71	0.30	..	..	..	..	..	..	..
76	Albania	..	..	..	0.03	0.09	..	..	..	..	..	..	..
	Aggregates												
	Industrial	..	..	..	56.05	0.47	..	..	..	..	..	..	..
	Developing	..	..	..	43.95	0.10	..	..	..	..	..	..	..
	World	..	..	..	100.00	0.18	..	..	..	..	..	..	..
	OECD	..	..	113	38.93	0.48	1.3	0.3	6.8	500	98	36	33
	Eastern Europe and former Soviet Union	..	..	17.12	0.42	..	..	..	..	..	..	..	..
	Eastern Europe only	..	..	165	3.52	0.35	..	..	..	..	..	..	..
	European Community	..	..	74	12.45	0.36	1.5	1.5	9.0	350	97	38	37
	Nordic	..	..	82	0.80	0.34	0.4	0.4	1.0	470	89	38	46
	Southern Europe	..	..	78	3.04	0.26	2.3	0.2	6.4	330	91	36	37
	Non-Europe	..	..	164	25.62	0.59	1.2	0.2	6.9	620	100	34	30
	North America	..	..	165	19.52	0.69	1.4	0.2	9.8	710	100	26	19

Successor states of the former Soviet Union

HDI rank		City	Micro-grammes	Sulfur/nitrogen	Absolute share	Per 10 million	Pesticide	Nuclear	Hazardous	Municipal waste	Pop. served	Paper/cardboard	Glass
28	Lithuania	..	..	..	..	..	..	..	..	..	..	..	..
29	Estonia	..	..	..	..	..	..	..	..	..	..	..	..
30	Latvia	..	..	..	..	..	..	..	..	..	..	..	..
34	Russian Federation	..	..	..	13.60[a]	0.47[a]	..	..	..	..	..	..	..
40	Belarus	..	..	..	..	..	..	..	..	..	..	..	..
45	Ukraine	..	..	..	..	..	..	..	..	..	..	..	..
53	Armenia	..	..	..	..	..	..	..	..	..	..	..	..
61	Kazakhstan	..	..	..	..	..	..	..	..	..	..	..	..
66	Georgia	..	..	..	..	..	..	..	..	..	..	..	..
71	Azerbaijan	..	..	..	..	..	..	..	..	..	..	..	..
75	Moldova, Rep. of	..	..	..	..	..	..	..	..	..	..	..	..
80	Turkmenistan	..	..	..	..	..	..	..	..	..	..	..	..
82	Kyrgyzstan	..	..	..	..	..	..	..	..	..	..	..	..
91	Uzbekistan	..	..	..	..	..	..	..	..	..	..	..	..
97	Tajikistan	..	..	..	..	..	..	..	..	..	..	..	..

a. Estimate for the former Soviet Union.

National income accounts

HDI rank		Total GDP (US$ billions) 1991	Agri-cultural production (as % of GDP) 1991	Industrial production (as % of GDP) 1991	Services (as % of GDP) 1991	Consumption Private (as % of GDP) 1991	Consumption Government (as % of GDP) 1991	Gross domestic investment (as % of GDP) 1991	Gross domestic savings (as % of GDP) 1991	Tax revenue (as % of GNP) 1991	Central government expenditure (as % of GNP) 1991	Exports (as % of GDP) 1991	Imports (as % of GDP) 1991
1	Canada	511	..	..	..	60	21	20	19	19	24	24	23
2	Switzerland	232	..	..	..	57	14	27	29	..	..	26	29
3	Japan	3,360	3	42	55	57	9	32	34	14	16	9	7
4	Sweden	206	3	34	63	54	27	17	19	38	44	27	24
5	Norway	106	2	36	62	51	21	19	28	36	46	32	24
6	France	1,200	3	29	68	60	18	21	21	38	44	18	19
7	Australia	300	3	32	65	62	19	19	19	25	28	13	13
8	USA	5,610	..	..	..	67	18	15	15	18	25	7	9
9	Netherlands	291	4	32	64	59	14	21	26	45	53	46	43
10	United Kingdom	877	..	..	..	64	21	16	15	34	38	21	24
11	Germany	1,570	2	39	59	54	18	21	28	29	33	26	25
12	Austria	164	3	36	61	55	18	26	26	32	40	25	31
13	Belgium	197	2	30	68	63	15	20	23	43	49	60	61
14	Iceland	..	..	..	..	..	..	..	..	..	..	..	..
15	Denmark	112	5	28	67	52	25	17	23	35	42	32	29
16	Finland	110	6	34	60	56	24	21	20	28	31	21	20
17	Luxembourg	..	..	..	..	..	..	..	..	..	..	..	..
18	New Zealand	43	9	26	65	63	17	18	20	34	44	22	20
19	Israel	63	..	..	..	58	28	23	14	24	36	19	27
21	Ireland	39	11	9	80	56	16	19	28	40	48	62	53
22	Italy	1,150	3	33	64	62	17	20	20	39	50	15	15
23	Spain	527	..	..	..	62	16	25	22	30	34	11	18
25	Greece	58	17	27	56	72	20	17	8	29	60	15	37
27	Czechoslovakia	33	8	56	36	67	..	31	..	44	56	49	24
31	Hungary	31	11	34	55	67	13	19	19	47	55	33	37
41	Malta	..	..	..	..	..	..	..	..	..	..	..	..
42	Portugal	65	..	..	..	..	..	..	..	34	43	25	40
48	Bulgaria	8	13	50	37	73	13	13	15	44	..	..	..
49	Poland	78	7	50	43	58	20	21	22	..	..	19	20
72	Romania	28	19	49	32	57	14	34	29	34	37	..	..
76	Albania	..	..	..	..	..	..	..	..	..	..	..	..
	Aggregates												
	Industrial	17,000T	4	37	59	61	17	22	22	24	30	15	16
	Developing	3,100T	17	36	47	65	11	26	25	16	24	21	24
	World	20,100T	7	37	56	61	16	23	23	23	29	16	17
	OECD	16,730T	3	37	60	61	16	21	22	24	30	15	16
	Eastern Europe and former Soviet Union	..	13	48	39	48	18	34	36	..	44	..	..
	Eastern Europe only	180T	10	49	41	62	17	24	22	42	49	31	25
	European Community	6,090T	3	34	63	59	18	20	22	34	40	23	24
	Nordic	530T	4	33	63	53	25	18	22	35	41	28	24
	Southern Europe	1,800T	4	33	63	62	17	21	20	36	45	14	18
	Non-Europe	9,890T	3	41	56	63	15	21	22	17	22	9	9
	North America	6,120T	..	..	..	66	18	16	15	18	25	9	10

Successor states of the former Soviet Union

HDI rank		Total GDP (US$ billions) 1991	Agri-cultural production (as % of GDP) 1991	Industrial production (as % of GDP) 1991	Services (as % of GDP) 1991	Consumption Private (as % of GDP) 1991	Consumption Government (as % of GDP) 1991	Gross domestic investment (as % of GDP) 1991	Gross domestic savings (as % of GDP) 1991	Tax revenue (as % of GNP) 1991	Central government expenditure (as % of GNP) 1991	Exports (as % of GDP) 1991	Imports (as % of GDP) 1991
28	Lithuania	..	20	45	35	63	16	21	21	..	48	..	..
29	Estonia	..	16	40	44	65	10	29	25	..	33	..	..
30	Latvia	..	20	48	32	46	10	34	43	..	43	..	..
34	Russian Federation	..	13	48	39	41	20	39	40	..	47	..	..
40	Belarus	..	..	..	..	..	..	34	..	..	34	..	..
45	Ukraine	..	..	..	..	..	..	..	..	..	38	..	..
53	Armenia	..	..	..	..	..	..	..	..	..	36	..	..
61	Kazakhstan	..	..	..	..	54	9	26	..	..	37	..	..
66	Georgia	..	..	..	..	..	..	..	..	..	32	..	..
71	Azerbaijan	..	..	..	..	..	..	15	..	..	32	..	..
75	Moldova, Rep. of	..	..	..	..	..	..	..	..	..	35	..	..
80	Turkmenistan	..	..	..	..	..	..	..	..	..	42	..	..
82	Kyrgyzstan	..	34	28	38	50	16	34	34	..	38	..	..
91	Uzbekistan	..	..	..	..	..	..	..	..	..	46	..	..
97	Tajikistan	..	..	..	..	..	..	..	..	..	..	..	..

Note: Data for developing countries for this subject area are in table 26.

50 Trends in economic performance

HDI rank		Total GNP		GNP per capita annual growth rate (%)		Average annual rate of inflation (%)		Exports as % of GDP (% annual growth rate)	Tax revenue as % of GNP (% annual growth rate)	Direct taxes as % of total taxes		Overall budget surplus/ deficit (as % of GNP)	
		US$ billions 1991	Annual growth rate (%) 1980-91	1965-80	1980-91	1980-91	1992	1980-91	1980-91	1980	1991	1980	1991
1	Canada	560	3.1	3.3	2.0	4.3	1.0	0.4	1.2	61	59	-3.6	-2.7
2	Switzerland	229	2.2	1.5	1.6	3.8	2.3	0.9	..	15	..	-0.2	..
3	Japan	3,352	4.3	5.1	3.6	1.5	1.8	2.6	2.0	75	73	-7.0	-1.6
4	Sweden	217	2.0	2.0	1.7	7.4	1.6	-0.5	2.0	21	14	-8.2	0.7
5	Norway	104	2.5	3.6	2.3	5.2	-1.0	(.)	-0.5	30	22	-2.0	0.7
6	France	1,164	2.3	3.7	1.8	5.7	2.3	-0.3	0.4	19	20	-0.1	-1.4
7	Australia	300	2.8	2.2	1.6	7.0	1.5	1.5	2.1	68	72	-1.5	0.6
8	USA	5,677	3.1	1.8	1.7	4.2	2.6	1.6	(.)	62	55	-2.8	-4.8
9	Netherlands	285	2.1	2.7	1.6	1.8	2.1	-0.4	0.3	33	35	-4.5	-2.8
10	United Kingdom	955	2.8	2.0	2.6	5.8	4.5	0.4	1.0	43	43	-4.6	0.8
11	Germany	1,897	2.3	3.0	2.2	2.8	5.4	-0.7	0.4	19	17	-1.8	-2.5
12	Austria	157	2.3	4.0	2.1	3.6	4.4	-0.9	0.1	23	22	-3.4	-4.8
13	Belgium	189	2.2	3.6	2.0	4.2	3.8	0.8	0.2	40	36	-8.2	-5.4
14	Iceland	6	2.4	..	1.8	30.0	3.2	..	..	..	..	..	..
15	Denmark	122	2.2	2.2	2.2	5.2	1.9	-2.2	0.7	41	44	-2.7	-0.3
16	Finland	120	2.9	3.6	2.5	6.6	1.0	2.8	0.9	29	32	-2.2	0.1
17	Luxembourg	12	4.2	..	3.5	4.2	2.2	..	..	..	..	..	..
18	New Zealand	43	1.0	1.7	0.7	10.3	1.8	0.7	0.9	75	65	-6.8	1.5
19	Israel	62	3.7	3.7	1.7	89.0	15.6	5.5	-5.4	47	40	-16.1	-5.7
21	Ireland	39	2.4	2.8	3.3	5.8	15.6	-2.4	1.6	39	39	-13.6	-2.4
22	Italy	1,070	2.4	3.2	2.2	9.5	4.7	2.7	2.8	33	36	-10.7	-10.0
23	Spain	487	3.2	4.1	2.8	8.9	6.1	-0.8	2.9	25	34	-4.2	-2.3
25	Greece	65	1.6	4.8	1.1	17.7	15.8	-0.3	0.8	19	22	-4.8	-26.2
27	Czechoslovakia	39	0.7	..	0.5	3.5	11.2	..	..	..	26	..	-6.9
31	Hungary	29	0.5	5.1	0.7	10.3	23.0	..	0.1	22	21	-2.9	0.8
41	Malta	3	3.5	..	3.8	2.1	2.1	..	..	..	..	..	..
42	Portugal	59	3.2	4.6	3.1	17.4	12.6	1.6	1.4	21	26	-10.1	-5.0
48	Bulgaria	16	1.7	..	1.7	7.8	82.6	..	..	..	53	..	-9.9
49	Poland	69	1.2	..	0.6	63.1	43.0	..	..	..	..	..	-7.2
72	Romania	31	0.3	..	(.)	6.2	210.3	..	..	..	38	..	2.0
76	Albania	..	..	..	..	-0.4	226.0	..	..	..	..	..	-17.1
	Aggregates												
	Industrial	18,140T	3.0	2.5	2.1	4.9	53.1	1.3	1.0	43	43	-4.2	-3.3
	Developing	3,410T	4.6	2.9	3.6	71.0	164.2	1.2	0.6	34	34	-4.0	-2.6
	World	21,550T	3.3	2.4	3.3	15.7	68.7	1.3	0.9	42	42	-4.2	-3.2
	OECD	17,110T	3.0	2.9	2.2	4.4	3.1	11.0	1.0	43	42	-4.2	-3.3
	Eastern Europe and former Soviet Union	970T	..	..	..	..	960.9	..	..	..	..	..	..
	Eastern Europe only	180T	0.9	..	0.6	27.7	64.9	..	..	..	32	..	-4.6
	European Community	6,340T	2.5	3.1	2.2	5.7	4.6	0.1	1.2	28	29	-4.1	-3.4
	Nordic	570T	2.3	2.7	2.1	6.6	1.1	-0.1	0.9	29	25	-4.6	0.4
	Southern Europe	1,680T	2.6	4.0	2.4	9.9	5.8	1.5	2.7	30	35	-4.2	-3.3
	Non-Europe	9,990T	3.5	2.9	2.3	3.9	2.3	1.9	0.9	65	61	-4.3	-3.4
	North America	6,240T	3.1	1.9	1.7	4.2	2.5	1.4	0.1	62	56	-2.9	-4.6

Successor states of the former Soviet Union

HDI rank		US$ billions 1991	Annual growth rate 1980-91	1965-80	1980-91	1980-91	1992						
28	Lithuania	10	..	..	..	..	1,194.3	..	..	..	..	..	..
29	Estonia	6	..	..	..	..	1,009.0	..	..	..	..	..	..
30	Latvia	9	..	..	..	..	1,032.4	..	..	..	..	..	..
34	Russian Federation	480	..	..	..	..	1,353.0	..	..	..	..	..	..
40	Belarus	32	..	..	..	..	81.2	..	..	..	..	..	..
45	Ukraine	121	..	..	..	..	1,445.3	..	..	..	..	..	..
53	Armenia	7	2.9	..	..	..	828.7	..	..	..	..	..	..
61	Kazakhstan	42	2.1	..	..	..	96.1	..	..	..	..	..	..
66	Georgia	9	2.9	..	..	..	150.0	..	..	..	..	..	..
71	Azerbaijan	12	1.9	..	..	..	..	..	..	..	..	..	..
75	Moldova, Rep. of	10	..	..	..	..	1,057.1	..	..	..	..	..	..
80	Turkmenistan	6	3.2	..	..	..	..	..	..	..	..	..	..
82	Kyrgyzstan	7	4.1	..	..	..	97.9	..	..	..	..	..	..
91	Uzbekistan	28	3.4	..	..	..	677.0	..	..	..	..	..	..
97	Tajikistan	6	2.9	..	..	..	..	..	..	..	..	..	..

Note: Data for developing countries for this subject area are in table 27.

	Sub-Saharan Africa	Arab States	South Asia	South Asia excl. India	East Asia	East Asia excl. China	South-East Asia	Latin America and the Caribbean	Latin America and the Caribbean excl. Mexico and Brazil	Least developed countries	All developing countries	Industrial countries	World
Table 2: Profile of human development													
Life expectancy	51.1	64.3	58.5	55.2	70.5	70.8	62.9	67.7	68.2	50.1	63.0	74.5	65.6
Access to health services	59	88	74	74	91	100	77	88	87	54	81	..	..
Access to safe water	45	79	..	52	83	92	53	79	74	45	70	..	..
Access to sanitation	31	62	..	28	97	97	48	70	71	32	56	..	..
Calorie supply (% of req.)	92	128	103	97	113	123	113	114	107	91	109	..	..
Adult literacy rate	51	57	47	39	81	97	86	86	87	46	69	..	..
Overall enrolment	35	59	45	30	44	73	54	62	64	31	46	79	49
Newspaper circulation	1.2	3.9	2.7	1.2	5.6	28.5	3.8	9.5	11.0	0.6	4.4	30.3	9.2
Televisions	2.5	9.9	2.7	1.2	3.7	14.9	6.0	16.5	13.7	0.9	5.5	54.4	14.7
Real GDP per capita	1,250	4,420	1,260	1,600	3,210	9,510	3,420	5,360	4,650	880	2,730	14,860	5,490
GNP per capita	540	2,130	330	310	650	7,190	1,000	2,480	1,870	240	880	14,920	4,160
Table 3: Profile of human deprivation (in millions unless otherwise stated)													
Total poor	..	..	..	..	..	..	..	..	..	350T	1,300T	..	..
Rural poor	..	..	..	..	..	..	..	..	..	300T	1,000T	..	..
Refugees (thousands)	..	..	..	..	..	..	..	..	..	..	19,000T	..	..
No health services	..	..	..	..	..	..	..	..	..	250T	1,000T	..	..
No safe water	..	..	..	..	..	..	..	..	..	330T	1,300T	..	..
No sanitation	..	..	..	..	..	..	..	..	..	370T	1,900T	..	..
Illiterate adults	..	..	..	..	..	..	..	..	..	150T	900T	..	..
Illiterate females	..	..	..	..	..	..	..	..	..	100T	600T	..	..
Out-of-school children (thousands)	..	..	..	..	..	..	..	..	..	42,000T	80,000T	..	..
Malnourished children (thousands	..	..	..	..	..	..	..	..	..	38,000T	192,000T	..	..
Dying before age five (thousands)	..	..	..	..	..	..	..	..	..	400T	12,200T	..	..
Table 4: Trends in human development													
Life expectancy													
1960	40.0	46.7	43.8	43.1	47.5	54.7	45.3	56.0	56.6	39.0	46.2	69.0	53.4
1992	51.1	64.3	58.5	55.2	70.5	70.8	62.9	67.7	68.2	50.1	63.0	74.5	65.6
Infant mortality													
1960	165	165	164	161	146	83	126	105	103	170	149	35	128
1992	101	54	94	106	27	24	55	47	45	112	69	13	60
Access to safe water													
1975-80	25	71	..	27	..	70	15	60	57	21	36	..	..
1988-91	45	79	..	52	..	92	53	79	74	45	70	..	..
Malnourished children (under five)													
1975	31	25	69	62	26	..	46	17	14	46	40	..	..
1990	31	20	59	51	21	..	34	10	11	40	35	..	..
Adult literacy													
1970	28	30	33	26	..	..	67	76	81	29	46	..	..
1992	51	57	47	39	..	..	86	86	87	46	69	..	..
Overall enrolment													
1980	39	48	36	26	51	65	51	59	59	31	45	..	..
1990	35	59	45	30	54	73	54	62	64	32	46	..	..
Real GDP per capita													
1960	..	1,310	700	940	730	..	1,000	2,140	2,410	580	950	..	..
1991	..	4,420	1,260	1,600	3,210	..	3,420	5,360	4,650	880	2,730	..	..
Table 5: Human capital formation													
Adult literacy													
total	51	57	47	39	81	97	86	86	87	46	69	..	..
female	40	45	33	26	69	95	80	84	86	34	58	..	..
male	63	70	61	51	92	99	91	88	90	58	79	..	..
Literacy at age 15-19	73	79	61	50	93	100	95	94	94	59	80	..	..
Mean years of schooling													
total	1.6	3.4	2.3	2.2	5.2	8.1	4.5	5.4	6.6	1.6	3.9	10.0	5.2
female	1.0	2.2	1.2	1.1	3.9	6.2	3.7	5.2	6.4	0.9	3.0	..	..
male	2.2	4.6	3.4	3.2	6.5	10.0	5.4	5.5	6.7	2.2	4.9	..	..
Scientists and technicians	..	6.7	3.2	2.1	9.7	45.1	9.7	29.5	29.5	..	8.8	84.9	25.0
R & D scientists	..	3.5	2.4	..	..	..	..	..	4.8	..	..	..	..
Tertiary graduates	0.3	2.1	..	0.6	0.5	..	2.6	2.4	2.3	0.3	1.2	19.2	3.8
Science graduates	21	29	..	16	43	..	24	25	28	18	28	24	24

	Sub-Saharan Africa	Arab States	South Asia	South Asia excl. India	East Asia	East Asia excl. China	South-East Asia	Latin America and the Caribbean	Latin America and the Caribbean excl. Mexico and Brazil	Least developed countries	All developing countries	Industrial countries	World
Table 6: Narrowing South-North gaps (expressed as % of average for North)													
Life expectancy													
1960	58	68	63	62	69	79	66	81	82	57	67	100	..
1992	68	86	78	74	95	95	84	91	91	67	84	100	..
Adult literacy													
1970	28	30	33	26	..	..	67	76	81	29	41	100	..
1992	53	59	48	40	..	..	89	89	90	47	71	100	..
Calorie supply													
1965	74	71	71	69	70	78	70	82	81	71	72	100	..
1988-90	68	95	76	72	84	91	84	84	79	67	81	100	..
Access to safe water													
1975-80	25	71	..	27	..	70	15	60	57	21	36	100	..
1988-91	45	79	..	52	..	92	53	79	74	45	70	100	..
Under-five mortality													
1960	75	76	76	77	89	93	78	88	88	75	80	100	..
1992	85	94	89	87	98	99	94	96	96	85	92	100	..
Table 7: Widening South-North gaps (expressed as % of average for North)													
Real GDP per capita													
1960	14	21	12	16	15	17	13	37	46	9	18	100	..
1990	8	29	8	10	21	62	22	35	31	6	17	100	..
Years of schooling													
1980	17	21	25	25	54	70	39	48	57	17	38	100	..
1992	15	33	22	21	51	79	44	53	64	15	36	100	..
Overall enrolment													
1980	56	69	52	39	73	93	73	85	86	45	64	100	..
1990	46	78	59	38	58	96	71	82	84	42	61	100	..
Fertility													
1965	46	43	48	45	48	62	51	55	60	47	50	100	..
1992	29	37	45	36	86	95	57	61	57	32	59	100	..
Telephones													
1980	10	21	7	13	5	34	11	32	47	7	12	100	..
1990-92	3	11	1	1	6	60	3	19	17	1	6	100	..
Table 8: Status of women													
Life expectancy	52.8	65.4	58.7	55.2	72.2	73.7	64.9	70.6	70.9	51.0	64.5	78.0	67.5
Age at first marriage	19.0	21.3	18.7	18.6	22.1	24.7	22.0	22.0	22.2	18.7	20.8	24.5	21.0
Literacy at age 15-24	37	46	37	29	82	..	87	89	92	36	67	..	..
Primary enrolment													
net	43	82	..	60	95	100	96	81	81	47	81	..	..
gross	60	90	74	69	119	105	107	104	100	55	90	..	..
Secondary enrolment	15	47	27	15	43	84	45	55	55	12	34	..	..
Tertiary enrolment	1.1	10.7	..	1.5	1.8	24.9	5.5	15.1	22.2	0.9	4.3	..	..
Tertiary natural and appl. sciences	16	29	27	34	..	20	21	27	28	20	25	23	24
Administrators and managers	13	17	2	3	11	4	13	16	17	5	9	24	12
Parliament	6	4	6	5	20	7	11	7	8	8	11	10	11
Table 9: Female-male gaps (female as % of male)													
Life expectancy	107	104	101	100	105	109	106	109	108	104	104	108	105
Population	102	97	93	94	94	100	101	100	100	100	96	104	98
Literacy													
1970	42	36	41	36	..	..	72	91	91	38	54	..	..
1992	60	63	53	47	75	95	88	95	95	54	71	..	..
Years of schooling	40	46	33	30	60	62	67	95	96	42	55	95	74
Primary enrolment													
1960	52	57	46	36	..	..	77	95	94	44	61	..	..
1990	..	87	..	..	94	100	97	..	..	80	..	..	..
Secondary enrolment	67	73	55	48	78	96	91	110	114	60	72	..	..
Tertiary enrolment	35	63	..	33	48	49	..	93	99	30	51	..	..
Labour force	62	21	41	42	75	72	72	53	54	..	58	73	62
Table 10: Rural-urban gaps													
Rural population (% of total)	70	45	74	76	69	30	70	27	31	79	65	27	56
Rural access to health	..	75	..	..	..	100	..	..	..	..	..	..	..
Urban access to health	..	98	..	..	..	100	..	..	..	..	..	..	..
Rural access to water	31	55	..	43	80	78	46	55	46	30	62	..	..
Urban access to water	74	97	..	78	88	98	71	89	89	60	85	..	..
Rural access to sanitation	23	32	..	20	95	94	42	37	38	25	45	..	..
Urban access to sanitation	55	89	54	58	100	99	66	85	89	61	75	..	..
Rural-urban disparity													
health	..	77	..	..	..	100	..	..	..	..	..	..	..
water	42	57	..	55	91	80	65	62	52	50	73	..	..
sanitation	42	36	..	34	95	95	64	44	43	41	60	..	..
child nutrition	88	..	..	85	86	..	83	93	92	89	87	..	..

	Sub-Saharan Africa	Arab States	South Asia	South Asia excl. India	East Asia	East Asia excl. China	South-East Asia	Latin America and the Caribbean	Latin America and the Caribbean excl. Mexico and Brazil	Least developed countries	All developing countries	Industrial countries	World
Table 11: Child survival and development													
Pregnant women													
with prenatal care	64	40	64	50	..	96	64	66	63	50	62	..	..
with anemia	43	38	78	53	25	..	62	37	37	44	52	..	..
Births attended	40	54	63	37	94	96	67	63	64	31	66	..	..
Low-birth-weight babies	14	11	30	30	6	4	12	11	10	18	16	..	..
Maternal mortality	700	280	580	660	130	110	340	200	210	730	420	24	290
Infant mortality	101	54	94	106	27	24	55	47	45	112	69	13	60
Duration of breast-feeding	20	..	..	23	..	..	18	9	12	23	..	..	..
One-year-olds immunized	49	88	84	72	94	88	86	81	78	55	80	..	..
ORS access rate	56	84	77	77	27	..	84	70	62	57	63	..	..
Underweight children	31	20	59	51	21	..	34	10	11	40	35	..	..
Under-five mortality	160	75	130	150	32	27	80	60	55	160	100	15	90
Table 12: Health profile													
Years of life lost	89	36	..	62	..	10	32	23	23	92	49	13	35
Tuberculosis cases	220	77	212	188	166	160	206	93	113	220	176	..	..
Malaria cases	..	..	320	500	10	..	360	590	540	..	240	..	..
AIDS cases	9.3	..	..	..	..	..	..	3.2	2.0	10.2	5.7	7.8	6.7
Population per doctor	35,680	2,230	3,320	5,870	750	1,040	7,040	1,210	1,330	19,110	6,670	390	5,260
Population per nurse	8,190	7,970	2,960	5,100	1,450	1,240	2,020	3,610	1,880	7,430	3,390	..	..
Nurses per doctor	4.4	0.3	1.1	1.2	0.5	0.8	3.5	0.3	0.7	2.6	2.0	..	..
External aid health flows	19.9	2.2	3.9	9.6	0.4	0.2	3.4	1.2	2.7	24.9	2.2	..	..
Public exp. on health, 1960	0.7	0.8	0.5	0.5	0.9	0.2	0.5	1.2	1.5	0.8	0.9	..	..
Public exp. on health, 1990	2.5	2.9	1.4	1.7	2.2	2.4	1.0	2.4	2.4	2.0	2.2	..	..
Total exp. on health	4.4	3.9	5.4	3.4	4.8	6.4	2.9	3.9	4.1	3.8	4.2	9.4	8.6
Table 13: Food security													
Food production per capita	96	107	114	100	136	97	121	110	101	92	118	..	..
Agricultural production	21	15	31	30	18	6	15	11	13	37	17	..	..
Calorie supply per capita	2,170	3,050	2,210	2,150	2,650	2,820	2,450	2,690	2,500	2,070	2,480	..	..
Calorie supply (% of req.)	92	128	103	97	113	123	113	114	107	91	109	..	..
Food import dependency													
1969/71	6.5	29.9	4.3	7.9	3.2	..	10.0	..	..	..	6.7	..	..
1988/90	10.2	49.5	6.1	16.7	7.0	..	9.9	18.7	11.3	11.3	10.5	..	..
Cereal imports	10,440T	30,680T	3,610T	3,550T	24,630T	11,200T	9,290T	20,160T	8,400T	7,250T	99,440T	..	..
Food aid	1,270T	670T	610T	510T	43T	2T	90T	440T	400T	1,320T	3,130T	..	..
Table 14: Education flows													
First-grade intake	71	92	..	83	100	100	97	99	99	75	92	..	..
Primary enrolment													
net	48	87	..	..	98	100	98	89	83	53	86	..	..
gross	69	99	88	60	124	104	109	107	103	67	99	..	..
Primary repeaters	19	10	5	9	6	..	8	13	10	15	8	..	..
Primary completers	57	82	50	50	85	99	78	45	52	51	71	..	..
Transition to secondary	36	71	..	..	63	99	..	78	75	39	65	..	..
Primary entrants to secondary	18	58	..	..	54	98	..	..	..	17	51	..	..
Secondary enrolment													
net	..	43	..	..	..	79	42	31	36	15	33	..	..
gross	18	55	38	22	49	86	46	49	53	16	41	..	..
Secondary repeaters	..	16	..	..	2	(.)	2	7	11	14	5	..	..
Tertiary enrolment	2.0	12.4	..	3.1	2.9	35.8	12.1	17.1	23.3	2.2	6.8	..	..
Table 15: Education imbalances													
Pupil-teacher ratio													
primary	40	26	48	50	22	31	26	27	28	45	34	..	..
secondary	22	19	..	23	15	25	18	15	16	24	18	..	..
Secondary technical	6.7	10.5	1.6	1.2	9.7	17.9	7.7	18.6	23.8	5.9	7.9	..	..
Tertiary natural and appl. science	37	41	..	28	51	42	32	42	46	28	41	21	31
Tertiary students abroad	15	10	5	5	3	2	2	1	1	9	4	..	..
Education exp. as % of GNP													
1960	2.4	3.5	2.1	..	..	..	..	2.1	2.5	1.3	2.2	..	..
1990	..	5.2	3.4	2.9	2.8	3.5	4.2	4.2	3.6	3.0	3.9	4.9	4.8
as % of total public exp.	15.7	21.0	11.1	9.6	12.6	22.4	18.5	..	..	14.1	14.2	..	..
Primary/secondary educ. exp.	..	74	72	75	73	77	75	58	67	76	68	..	..
Higher educ. expenditure	..	18	17	16	15	11	17	25	21	15	19	26	26
Current exp. per tertiary student	8.2	0.7	0.9	1.0	1.9	0.1	..	0.8	0.5	5.6	1.9	..	..

	Sub-Saharan Africa	Arab States	South Asia	South Asia excl. India	East Asia	East Asia excl. China	South-East Asia	Latin America and the Caribbean	Latin America and the Caribbean excl. Mexico and Brazil	Least developed countries	All developing countries	Industrial countries	World
Table 16: Communication profile													
Radios	15	25	8	7	21	68	15	34	35	10	18	113	35
Televisions	2.5	9.9	2.7	1.2	3.7	14.9	6.0	16.5	13.7	0.9	5.5	54.4	14.7
Cinema attendances	..	1.0	4.9	..	..	4.6	..	0.9	1.1	..	3.0	2.3	2.8
Daily newspapers	1.2	3.9	2.7	1.2	5.6	28.5	3.8	9.5	11.0	0.6	4.4	30.3	9.2
Book titles	2.7	5.5	1.9	3.8	8.4	..	4.2	..	9.2	1.8	5.2	74.4	15.1
Paper consumed	1.5	3.4	1.6	0.9	5.5	25.9	3.9	9.0	7.7	0.3	4.0	95.2	20.3
Post offices	3.4	..	16.9	..	..	7.7	6.0	..	..	..	..	..	..
Letters posted	3.3	6.8	15.1	7.6	..	59.7	8.5	19.4	11.0	3.2	13.4	401.0	104.9
Telephones	1.5	5.4	0.7	0.6	3.0	30.2	1.7	9.3	8.5	0.3	3.1	47.8	13.0
Motor vehicles	2.6	5.5	0.7	0.5	..	7.5	2.4	8.8	7.8	..	3.1	50.1	15.4
Table 17: Employment													
Labour force	39	28	38	37	59	55	47	41	39	42	45	48	45
Women in labour force	37	19	28	27	43	42	41	34	34	38	35	43	37
Labour force in agriculture													
1965	79	63	72	..	..	..	..	44	42	83	72	22	57
1990-92	67	33	61	56	70	24	58	25	25	73	58	9	13
Labour force in industry													
1965	8	14	12	..	..	..	..	21	21	6	11	37	19
1990-92	8	24	12	16	15	34	14	25	23	8	15	33	31
Labour force in services													
1965	13	23	16	..	..	..	..	35	37	11	17	41	24
1990-92	25	43	27	28	15	42	28	50	52	19	27	58	56
Earnings growth rate													
1970-80	-1.5	..	..	..	..	..	..	2.0	0.6	..	1.3	2.2	1.6
1980-90	..	-4.7	3.4	3.5	3.6	7.1	5.1	0.1	-1.8	..	2.6	1.2	2.3
Table 18: Wealth, poverty and social investment													
Real GDP per capita	1,250	4,420	1,260	1,600	3,210	9,510	3,420	5,360	4,650	880	2,730	14,860	5,490
GNP per capita	540	2,130	330	310	650	7,190	1,000	2,480	1,870	240	880	14,920	4,160
Income share: lowest 40%	..	..	..	..	..	..	..	..	..	..	..	..	..
Highest 20%/lowest 20%	..	..	..	..	..	..	..	..	..	..	..	..	..
People below poverty line													
total	54	25	43	52	9	6	35	40	38	64	31	..	..
rural	65	30	47	59	13	11	40	61	58	71	37	..	..
urban	23	22	32	26	..	..	24	30	27	31	28	..	..
Social security exp.	0.9	1.4	0.7	2.1	3.4	..	2.5	3.4	3.2	1.2	2.7	16.2	14.7
Education exp.	4.6	5.4	3.4	2.9	2.8	3.5	4.2	4.2	3.6	3.0	3.9	4.9	4.8
Health expenditure, public	2.5	2.9	1.4	1.7	2.2	2.4	1.0	2.4	2.4	2.0	2.2	..	..
Health expenditure, total	4.4	3.9	5.4	3.4	4.8	6.4	2.9	3.9	4.1	3.8	4.2	9.4	8.6
Table 19: Aid flows													
ODA received	18,080T	5,280T	6,650T	4,300T	2,990T	50T	6,570T	5,290T	4,740T	16,180T	45,210T	..	..
ODA as % of GNP	10.4	1.1	1.7	4.6	0.4	..	1.7	0.5	1.4	13.6	1.3	..	..
ODA per capita	35	21	6	14	2	(.)	14	12	23	30	11	..	..
ODA per poor person	69	191	13	27	28	..	38	26	55	42	32	..	..
Social allocation ratio	22.5	16.7	19.6	22.0	14.4	27.0	27.9	23.8	24.1	23.5	22.0	..	..
Social priority ratio	52.2	77.8	57.1	60.7	18.0	7.4	45.9	51.0	51.9	56.6	56.3	..	..
Human expenditure ratio	1.221	0.143	0.190	0.614	0.010	..	0.218	0.061	0.175	1.801	0.161	..	..
Human priority aid	11.7	13.0	11.2	13.4	2.6	2.0	12.8	12.1	12.5	13.3	12.4	..	..
Table 20: Resource flow imbalances													
Total external debt	152T	145T	116T	44T	101T	41T	167T	437T	218T	88T	1,168T	..	..
as % of GNP	101	55	35	54	16	14	56	40	58	81	40	..	..
Debt service ratio													
1970	4.7	..	..	..	..	..	..	14.4	11.9	4.5	13.3	..	..
1991	25.3	32.7	26.5	19.2	9.9	7.1	18.2	30.1	29.8	25.2	21.3	..	..
Export-import ratio	120	121	79	68	71	54	90	105	113	51	90	96	91
Trade dependency	48	54	22	37	58	84	98	22	33	33	45	30	32
Terms of trade	85	87	94	86	107	105	97	106	103	92	99	101	100
Workers' remittances	..	-2.2	1.5	3.4	..	..	0.2	0.4	0.7	2.4	0.2	..	..
Gross international reserves	2.1	3.2	2.9	2.3	5.8	1.8	4.3	4.7	6.4	2.9	4.3	2.7	4.2
Current account balance	-7,740T	-260T	-1,820T	-1,820T	15,230T	2,340T	4,560T	-730T	-730T	-9,280T	9,030T	310T	9,340T

	Sub-Saharan Africa	Arab States	South Asia	South Asia excl. India	East Asia	East Asia excl. China	South-East Asia	Latin America and the Caribbean	Latin America and the Caribbean excl. Mexico and Brazil	Least developed countries	All developing countries	Industrial countries	World
Table 21: Military expenditure and resource use imbalances													
Military exp. as % of GDP													
1960	0.7	4.9	2.8	..	..	..	..	1.8	2.1	2.1	4.2	6.3	6.0
1990-91	3.0	7.0	3.5	4.6	4.1	3.1	2.8	1.7	2.7	3.5	3.5	3.4	3.4
as % of health/educ. exp.													
1960	27	129	113	320	343	273	110	55	58	..	143	97	104
1990-91	43	91	72	95	85	49	61	25	45	..	60	33	37
Arms imports, total	750T	6,190T	4,900T	2,450T	2,450T	1,220T	1,370T	850T	820T	2,120T	17,830T	..	..
as % of national imports	1.0	4.4	13.2	14.6	-0.4	..	0.7	0.7	1.6	..	2.0	..	..
Armed forces													
per 1,000 people	2.6	13.0	1.9	3.0	4.1	28.4	5.2	3.4	5.0	3.2	4.0	8.7	4.7
per teacher	1.0	1.3	0.5	0.9	0.5	2.6	0.7	0.4	0.6	1.2	0.6	0.8	0.7
per doctor	82.5	27.5	5.8	11.3	3.5	18.0	23.9	3.6	5.3	87.5	18.5	3.9	16.1
Table 22: Growing urbanization													
Urban population, %													
1960	14	34	18	19	20	36	18	49	52	9	22	61	34
1992	29	55	27	29	31	70	30	73	69	21	35	74	44
2000	38	61	34	34	82	75	37	76	73	28	49	78	57
Urban pop. growth rate													
1960-92	6.0	4.8	3.7	4.4	3.8	4.4	4.2	3.8	3.5	5.9	4.3	1.2	3.8
1992-2000	5.6	3.9	4.0	4.6	4.7	2.1	4.1	2.6	2.7	5.8	4.4	0.7	3.8
Population in cities over 1 mill.													
(as % of urban)	34	40	38	51	40	57	40	46	41	41	40	43	41
in largest city	28	28	8	21	9	37	29	24	32	37	18	17	18
in cities over 1 mill. (as % of total)	10	22	10	..	12	42	12	32	27	8	14	33	21
Table 23: Demographic profile													
Population													
1960	230T	100T	580T	130T	700T	40T	230T	210T	100T	240T	2,070T	930T	3,000T
1992	560T	260T	1,180T	300T	1,260T	80T	470T	450T	210T	540T	4,240T	1,210T	5,450T
2000	710T	320T	1,390T	370T	1,390T	80T	540T	520T	240T	670T	4,930T	1,400T	6,330T
Population growth rate													
1960-92	2.8	2.9	2.3	2.6	1.9	2.0	2.3	2.3	2.2	2.6	2.2	0.8	1.8
1992-2000	3.4	2.7	2.0	2.6	1.2	1.1	1.8	1.7	1.8	2.8	1.9	0.6	1.6
Growth rates over time	129	118	93	114	94	44	92	70	74	125	96	..	..
Population doubling date	2015	2015	2025	2020	2040	2060	2030	2030	2035	2015	2030	..	..
Crude birth rate	46	37	32	40	21	19	28	26	27	44	30	..	..
Crude death rate	15	8	11	13	6	6	8	7	7	16	9	..	..
Total fertility rate	6.5	5.4	4.4	5.5	2.2	2.0	3.5	3.2	3.4	6.1	3.8	2.0	3.4
Fertility rates over time	96	73	71	82	39	34	59	54	62	92	60	65	61
Contraceptive prevalence	15	45	39	26	83	79	47	58	53	18	53	60	52
Table 24: Natural resources balance sheet													
Land area	24,300T	11,130T	5,110T	1,820T	11,350T	1,790T	5,010T	20,430T	9,960T	19,930T	78,110T	53,620T	131,730T
Population density	22	23	232	167	111	42	93	22	21	27	54	22	41
Arable land	6.2	4.5	44.0	23.0	9.1	2.9	12.2	7.4	6.1	6.1	9.8	12.9	10.7
Pesticide consumption	0.09	0.38	0.05	0.01	0.14	0.28	0.15	0.36	0.42	0.08	0.14	..	..
Forest area	29	4	17	8	14	17	56	47	37	29	29	..	..
Production of fuel wood	34	23	26	33	17	..	24	24	23	30	23	..	..
Deforestation	0.9	1.5	0.5	1.1	..	..	0.7	0.7	0.9	0.9	0.9	..	..
Renewable water resources	7.2	1.0	3.4	6.9	..	2.2	13.8	24.0	24.8	11.4	6.8	9.7	7.3
Fresh water withdrawals													
as % of water resources	5	68	19	22	16	18	5	6	7	6	16	21	17
per capita	120	1,060	760	1,110	480	740	270	510	570	260	520	1,200	650
Irrigated land	6	27	30	51	46	42	22	9	11	12	22	9	18
Global emissions	0.12	0.11	0.04	0.04	0.08	0.18	0.16	0.24	0.23	0.09	0.10	0.47	0.18
Table 25: Energy consumption													
Commercial energy consumption													
1965	48T	..	59T	9T	140T	10T	30T	130T	76T	6T	710T	2,520T	3,230T
1991	130T	250T	330T	38T	780T	92T	130T	440T	190T	20T	2,110T	4,380T	6,490T
per capita													
1965	200	420	100	100	180	280	120	540	700	42	200	3,360	1,030
1991	280	1,160	290	140	650	1,880	380	1,030	970	52	550	4,840	1,350
Energy imports	20	..	25	23	10	12	12	10	10	31	13	..	..
Annual change in consumption													
1970-80	6.6	6.1	6.3	5.2	7.7	9.5	8.0	7.8	6.1	14.7	6.9	2.6	4.6
1980-90	3.2	10.2	7.1	6.7	5.7	7.7	6.1	3.7	3.1	6.4	6.5	1.6	4.8
Energy efficiency													
1965	..	228	159	112	182	166	139	118	115	41	156	166	164
1991	..	76	113	52	115	26	37	41	53	23	73	26	34

	Sub-Saharan Africa	Arab States	South Asia	South Asia excl. India	East Asia	East Asia excl. China	South-East Asia	Latin America and the Caribbean	Latin America and the Caribbean excl. Mexico and Brazil	Least developed countries	All developing countries	Industrial countries	World
Table 26: National income accounts													
Total GDP	230T	350T	300T	80T	720T	350T	350T	1,070T	380T	80T	3,100T	17,000T	20,100T
Agricultural production	21	16	30	30	17	6	15	11	13	37	17	4	7
Industrial production	34	36	27	22	42	41	39	36	37	20	36	37	37
Services	45	48	43	48	41	53	46	53	50	43	47	59	56
Private consumption	66	69	71	79	53	55	57	72	74	83	65	61	61
Government consumption	17	15	12	12	10	10	10	9	8	14	11	17	16
Gross domestic investment	17	22	22	17	37	39	34	19	16	15	26	22	23
Gross domestic savings	12	15	20	9	38	37	31	19	18	2	25	22	23
Tax revenue	27	..	11	12	16	16	19	16	14	..	16	24	23
Central gov't exp.	32	..	18	21	..	17	21	25	16	..	24	30	29
Exports	26	30	10	15	24	29	46	11	17	11	21	15	16
Imports	22	25	12	22	34	55	51	11	15	22	24	16	17
Table 27: Trends in economic performance													
Total GNP	260T	470T	380T	90T	800T	360T	350T	1,050T	330T	110T	3,410T	18,140T	21,550T
GNP growth rate	2.6	1.7	5.5	5.5	9.4	9.3	5.7	1.8	1.1	2.8	4.6	3.0	3.3
GNP per capita growth rate													
1965-80	1.5	3.0	1.4	1.2	4.2	5.2	2.6	3.8	2.0	0.6	2.9	2.5	2.4
1980-91	-1.1	-0.2	3.0	2.5	7.8	8.3	3.1	-0.1	-0.3	0.2	3.6	2.1	3.3
Annual rate of inflation													
1980-91	14.7	6.7	8.2	8.2	5.9	6.0	6.4	208.1	158.5	14.9	71.0	4.9	15.7
1992	24.5	17.1	9.7	8.2	7.4	6.3	6.2	442.4	25.4	20.0	164.2	53.1	68.7
Growth rate of exports/GDP	-0.9	1.4	4.3	2.1	1.3	-8.8	0.6	-0.1	0.8	-0.5	1.2	1.3	1.3
Growth rate of tax revenue/GNP	2.5	2.9	1.1	-0.3	..	-0.2	0.6	(.)	1.4	1.2	0.6	1.0	0.9
Direct taxes													
1980	..	19	21	16	..	26	49	28	47	27	34	43	42
1991	..	22	18	13	..	35	47	30	33	30	34	43	42
Budget surplus/deficit													
1980	-3.7	-11.7	-6.0	-4.5	..	-2.3	-2.9	-2.4	-1.7	-2.7	-4.0	-4.2	-4.2
1991	-1.5	-3.6	-6.5	-4.8	..	-1.7	2.1	-2.4	0.4	-1.1	-2.6	-3.3	-3.2

	High human development		Medium human development		Low human development				Low-income	
	All countries	Developing countries	All countries	Excl. China	All countries	Excl. India	High-income	Middle-income	All countries	Excl. China and India
Table 2: Profile of human development										
Life expectancy	74.1	70.5	68.0	65.4	55.8	51.9	76.0	67.3	62.0	55.1
Access to health services	..	95	88	85	..	62	..	82	80	70
Access to safe water	..	86	77	70	..	45	..	77	66	47
Access to sanitation	..	76	80	59	22	30	..	68	52	33
Calorie supply (% of req.)	..	122	109	107	99	93	..	117	106	100
Adult literacy rate	..	92	80	79	49	47	..	80	65	58
Overall enrolment ratio	71	66	50	58	42	33	75	59	44	40
Newspaper circulation	28.9	27.8	4.6	6.0	2.1	1.0	30.5	9.8	3.0	1.6
Televisions	47.5	17.7	6.6	10.7	2.4	1.5	56.3	15.1	3.0	2.9
Real GDP per capita	14,000	7,290	3,420	4,000	1,170	1,200	18,230	5,000	2,000	1,620
GNP per capita	13,790	3,830	970	1,680	330	320	19,790	2,220	360	380
Table 3: Profile of human deprivation (in millions unless otherwise stated)										
Total poor	..	..	..	..	..	..	..	..	..	..
Rural poor	..	..	..	..	..	..	..	..	..	..
Refugees (thousands)	..	..	..	..	..	..	..	..	..	..
No health services	..	..	..	..	..	..	..	..	..	..
No safe water	..	..	..	..	..	..	..	..	..	..
No sanitation	..	..	..	..	..	..	..	..	..	..
Illiterate adults	..	..	..	..	..	..	..	..	..	..
Illiterate females	..	..	..	..	..	..	..	..	..	..
Out-of-school children (thousands)	..	..	..	..	..	..	..	..	..	..
Malnourished children (thousands)	..	..	..	..	..	..	..	..	..	..
Dying before age five (thousands)	..	..	..	..	..	..	..	..	..	..
Table 4: Trends in human development										
Life expectancy										
1960	67.3	58.5	48.5	50.4	42.6	41.4	69.6	54.1	44.2	41.0
1992	74.1	70.5	68.0	65.4	55.8	51.9	76.0	67.3	62.0	55.1
Infant mortality										
1960	..	83	139	124	165	166	..	111	158	162
1992	..	30	40	51	98	104	..	49	76	95
Access to safe water										
1975-80	..	68	..	42	..	28	..	48	28	22
1988-91	..	86	..	70	..	45	..	77	66	47
Malnourished children (under five)										
1975	..	14	29	32	57	42	..	22	45	44
1990	..	10	22	23	48	37	..	16	40	37
Adult literacy										
1970	..	83	..	60	31	28	..	61	31	28
1992	..	92	..	79	49	47	..	80	65	58
Overall enrolment										
1980	..	64	51	52	37	33	..	55	43	39
1990	..	66	56	58	42	33	..	59	44	40
Real GDP per capita										
1960	..	3,140	1,010	1,680	670	740	6,310	..	700	740
1991	..	7,290	3,420	4,000	1,170	1,200	18,230	..	2,000	1,620
Table 5: Human capital formation										
Adult literacy										
total	..	92	80	79	49	47	..	80	65	58
female	..	90	70	73	35	35	..	76	53	48
male	..	93	89	85	62	59	..	85	77	68
Literacy at age 15-19	..	97	91	90	64	63	..	91	76	71
Mean years of schooling										
total	9.8	7.0	4.8	4.6	2.0	1.6	10.6	5.3	3.4	2.4
female	..	6.5	3.8	3.8	1.0	0.9	10.3	..	2.3	1.5
male	..	7.4	5.9	5.4	2.9	2.4	10.9	..	4.4	3.2
Scientists and technicians	80.3	50.7	10.7	15.4	2.9	1.7	81.2	33.4	5.8	4.6
R & D scientists	..	8.2	..	3.2	..	..	..	7.1	..	..
Tertiary graduates	15.1	2.7	1.4	2.4	..	0.3	19.9	2.7	0.5	0.6
Science graduates	29	31	29	25	19	19	24	28	29	18

	High human development		Medium human development		Low human development				Low-income	
	All countries	Developing countries	All countries	Excl. China	All countries	Excl. India	High-income	Middle-income	All countries	Excl. China and India
Table 6: Narrowing South-North gaps (expressed as % of average for North)										
Life expectancy										
1960	..	85	70	73	62	60	..	78	64	59
1992	..	95	91	88	75	70	..	90	83	74
Adult literacy										
1970	..	87	..	63	32	29	..	64	33	30
1992	..	95	..	81	50	48	..	82	67	60
Calorie supply										
1965	..	86	71	74	72	72	..	76	71	72
1988-90	..	90	81	79	73	69	..	87	79	74
Access to safe water										
1975-80	..	68	..	42	..	28	..	48	..	22
1988-91	..	86	..	70	..	45	..	77	..	47
Under-five mortality										
1960	..	92	84	86	76	77	..	89	79	77
1992	..	98	96	95	86	85	..	95	90	87
Table 7: Widening South-North gaps (expressed as % of average for North)										
Real GDP per capita										
1960	..	50	20	25	11	11	..	34	14	12
1990		48	21	25	8	8	..	33	13	11
Years of schooling										
1980	..	59	49	43	23	22	..	42	36	24
1992	..	68	47	43	22	20	..	52	33	22
Overall enrolment										
1980	..	92	73	74	53	47	..	79	62	56
1990	..	87	66	76	55	43	..	78	58	53
Fertility										
1965	..	63	48	54	47	45	..	52	47	46
1992	..	68	69	52	39	31	..	51	54	36
Telephones										
1980	..	48	10	21	8	14	..	27	5	11
1990-92	..	37	7	12	1	1	..	20	2	1
Table 8: Status of women										
Life expectancy	77.5	73.7	69.9	67.6	56.4	52.9	79.2	70.2	63.1	56.3
Age at first marriage	24.8	22.4	22.0	22.0	18.8	18.9	24.3	21.8	20.4	19.9
Literacy at age 15-24	..	..	81	80	38	34	..	84	63	54
Primary enrolment										
net	..	..	93	90	..	48	..	88	80	60
gross	..	..	111	101	68	55	..	100	87	65
Secondary enrolment	..	..	45	49	22	14	..	48	30	21
Tertiary enrolment	..	..	4.2	10.6	..	1.2	..	12.4	1.6	2.0
Tertiary natural and applied sciences	24	27	..	25	25	25	21	29	24	23
Administrators and managers	22	14	12	13	3	5	23	16	7	7
Parliament	10	6	15	8	6	6	11	7	13	8
Table 9: Female-male gaps (female as % of male)										
Life expectancy	110	109	105	105	102	104	109	107	104	105
Population	105	100	96	98	96	99	104	101	96	100
Literacy										
1970	..	90	..	59	44	45	..	74	44	46
1992	..	97	78	85	55	55	..	88	66	64
Years of schooling	91	91	63	68	36	37	94	79	48	44
Primary enrolment										
1960	..	95	..	83	50	50	..	82	50	50
1990	..	100	94	..	..	..	..	92	90	85
Secondary enrolment	..	109	80	84	59	61	..	89	67	66
Tertiary enrolment	..	85	58	..	..	34	..	84	42	36
Labour force	59	58	67	55	47	55	59	50	61	58
Table 10: Rural-urban gaps										
Rural population (% of total)	27	22	62	51	74	74	24	39	73	73
Rural access to health	..	..	..	..	..	..	..	..	..	..
Urban access to health	..	..	..	..	..	..	..	..	..	..
Rural access to water	..	70	70	51	..	33	..	55	60	37
Urban access to water	..	91	87	88	..	72	..	91	80	72
Rural access to sanitation	..	42	76	40	..	22	..	46	60	24
Urban access to sanitation	..	87	90	82	54	55	..	86	72	58
Rural-urban disparity										
health	..	..	..	..	..	..	..	..	..	..
water	..	77	80	58	..	46	..	60	75	51
sanitation	..	48	84	49	..	40	..	53	83	41
child nutrition	..	..	86	87	..	87	..	92	86	85

	High human development		Medium human development		Low human development				Low-income	
	All countries	Developing countries	All countries	Excl. China	All countries	Excl. India	High-income	Middle-income	All countries	Excl. China and India
Table 11: Child survival and development										
Pregnant women										
with prenatal care	..	70	..	57	64	59	..	59	63	58
with anemia	..	34	38	51	65	46	..	43	54	51
Births attended	..	67	78	64	55	40	..	65	66	43
Low-birth-weight babies	..	7	9	11	23	19	..	11	18	17
Maternal mortality	56	130	200	260	640	700	30	250	470	620
Infant mortality	..	30	40	51	98	104	..	49	76	95
Duration of breast-feeding	..	7	..	15	..	21	..	11	..	21
One-year-olds immunized	..	87	90	87	70	56	..	81	79	64
ORS access rate	..	81	55	83	68	61	..	75	59	68
Underweight children	..	10	22	23	48	37	..	16	40	37
Under-five mortality	..	35	55	70	150	160	..	70	110	145
Table 12: Health profile										
Years of life lost	12	13	..	29	..	83	11	24	..	70
Tuberculosis cases	..	97	155	141	213	207	..	120	193	199
Malaria cases	..	230	190	460	330	..	..	450	190	..
AIDS cases	6.9	2.7	..	..	..	9.8	8.4	3.5	..	..
Population per doctor	570	1,320	1,980	3,410	13,550	25,320	500	2,640	7,690	19,260
Population per nurse	..	1,790	2,600	3,940	4,650	7,230	..	4,220	3,210	5,860
Nurses per doctor	..	0.7	0.8	0.9	2.9	3.5	..	0.6	2.3	3.3
External aid health flows	..	0.5	1.4	1.8	9.4	16.2	..	1.2	4.9	15.2
Public exp. on health, 1960	..	1.2	0.8	0.7	0.6	0.7	..	1.0	0.8	0.5
Public exp. on health, 1990	..	2.1	2.3	2.4	1.6	1.9	..	2.2	1.7	1.4
Total expenditure on health	9.0	4.7	3.9	4.0	4.9	3.6	9.6	3.9	4.0	3.0
Table 13: Food security										
Food production per capita	..	99	118	110	109	98	..	106	122	107
Agricultural production	..	8	17	15	32	33	..	13	28	27
Calorie supply per capita	..	2,840	2,480	2,410	2,180	2,130	..	2,740	2,390	2,270
Calorie supply as % of req.	..	122	109	107	99	93	..	117	106	100
Food import dependency										
1969/71	..	19.2	6.1	12.2	5.9	8.5	..	12.7	3.7	7.0
1988/90	..	36.4	10.4	18.0	7.8	12.9	..	21.2	6.3	12.9
Cereal imports	..	20,980T	99,440T	86,010T	12,110T	12,060T	..	46,190T	35,040T	21,550T
Food aid	..	44T	3,130T	3,080T	1,850T	1,760T	..	840T	2,290T	2,150T
Table 14: Education flows										
First-grade intake	..	100	98	96	..	75	..	96	90	82
Primary enrolment										
net	..	93	95	92	..	54	..	90	84	..
gross	..	110	116	107	81	67	..	105	97	75
Primary repeaters	..	10	8	10	8	16	..	11	7	12
Primary completers	..	73	77	67	52	52	..	64	73	58
Transition to secondary	..	82	65	72	..	..	..	70	61	..
Primary entrants to secondary	..	59	54	..	..	..	..	53	49	..
Secondary enrolment										
net	..	48	..	37	..	..	..	38	..	24
gross	..	61	49	51	30	19	..	49	38	26
Secondary repeaters	..	5	5	9	..	..	..	10	3	..
Tertiary enrolment	..	22.4	7.4	13.3	2.5	2.5	..	15.1	3.2	4.3
Table 15: Education imbalances										
Pupil-teacher ratio										
primary	..	28	24	26	45	43	..	28	36	39
secondary	..	17	17	18	..	23	..	19	18	21
Secondary technical	..	17.2	10.2	11.4	2.6	4.7	..	11.5	6.6	..
Tertiary natural and applied science	26	46	40	37	..	33	23	41	41	32
Tertiary students abroad	..	1	4	4	..	10	..	4	5	5
Education exp. as % of GNP										
1960	..	2.2	2.2	2.5	2.3	2.3	..	2.4	2.0	1.9
1990	4.7	3.7	4.1	4.7	3.6	3.6	4.9	4.5	3.0	3.9
as % of total public exp.	..	..	14.0	19.3	14.1	15.7	..	20.0	12.8	14.8
Primary/secondary education expenditure	..	74	66	65	72	74	..	65	70	72
Higher educ. expenditure	24	15	21	21	17	16	24	21	18	20
Current exp. per tertiary student	..	0.2	1.6	0.7	2.3	4.6	..	0.8	2.1	4.2

	High human development		Medium human development		Low human development				Low-income	
										Excl.
	All countries	Developing countries	All countries	Excl. China	All countries	Excl. India	High-income	Middle-income	All countries	China and India
Table 16: Communication profile										
Radios	101	47	21	23	9	11	121	31	13	13
Televisions	47.5	17.7	6.6	10.7	2.4	1.5	56.3	15.1	3.0	2.9
Cinema attendances	2.2	1.6	..	1.6	3.9	..	2.4	1.3	3.0	0.4
Daily newspapers	28.9	27.8	4.6	5.0	2.1	1.0	30.5	9.8	3.0	1.6
Book titles	61.3	19.8	6.2	..	1.6	..	90.9	12.1	3.7	1.9
Paper consumed	..	16.9	4.8	5.4	1.3	0.6	19.5	8.3	2.5	1.3
Post offices	..	..	..	7.6	13.8	..	8.7	..	..	6.8
Letters posted	370.3	48.9	..	11.6	12.5	4.5	381.0	19.3	11.3	4.4
Telephones	41.6	18.7	3.5	5.8	0.7	0.5	61.2	10.0	0.9	0.7
Motor vehicles	..	11.4	..	4.8	0.7	0.6	13.1	6.9	0.8	0.9
Table 17: Employment										
Labour force	47	44	50	41	38	38	48	43	46	39
Women in labour force	41	34	39	34	31	34	41	33	36	35
Labour force in agriculture										
1965	..	28	73	53	74	75	..	53	78	77
1990-92	9	17	46	18	64	66	5	22	66	63
Labour force in industry										
1965	..	32	11	18	10	9	..	19	9	8
1990-92	32	29	25	31	10	10	29	41	12	11
Labour force in services										
1965	..	40	16	29	16	16	..	28	13	15
1990-92	59	54	29	41	26	24	66	37	22	26
Earnings growth rate										
1970-80	..	..	..	..	..	..	..	..	..	..
1980-90	0.9	-0.2	2.7	1.6	2.9	1.8	1.6	0.1	3.2	2.4
Table 18: Wealth, poverty and social investment										
Real GDP per capita	14,000	7,290	3,420	4,000	1,170	1,200	18,230	5,000	2,000	1,620
GNP per capita	13,790	3,830	970	1,680	330	320	19,790	2,220	360	380
Income share: lowest 40%	..	..	..	..	..	..	..	..	..	..
Highest 20%/lowest 20%	..	..	..	..	..	..	..	..	..	..
People below poverty line										
total	..	25	20	37	46	53	..	38	30	46
rural	..	37	23	41	52	62	..	47	36	55
urban	..	21	..	29	30	25	..	29	28	23
Social security expenditure	15.9	2.7	3.3	3.3	0.6	1.0	16.2	4.6	2.1	1.2
Education expenditure	5.8	3.7	4.1	4.7	3.6	3.6	5.9	4.6	3.0	3.9
Health expenditure, public	..	2.1	2.3	2.4	1.6	1.9	..	2.2	1.7	1.4
Health expenditure, total	9.2	4.7	3.9	4.0	4.9	3.6	9.6	3.9	4.0	3.0
Table 19: Aid flows										
ODA received	..	1,170T	18,920T	15,970T	25,120T	22,770T	..	14,650T	31,910T	26,610T
ODA as % of GNP	..	0.2	1.0	1.0	4.3	8.2	..	0.9	2.7	6.5
ODA per capita	..	4	9	16	14	26	..	16	10	23
ODA per poor person	..	23	46	53	25	45	..	40	30	50
Social allocation ratio	..	31.3	20.3	21.3	22.5	23.2	..	23.1	21.4	22.5
Social priority ratio	..	44.0	61.5	63.7	53.2	53.8	..	54.5	57.0	58.8
Human expenditure ratio	..	0.028	0.125	0.136	0.515	1.023	..	0.113	0.329	0.860
Human priority aid	..	13.8	12.5	13.6	12.0	12.5	..	12.6	12.2	13.2
Table 20: Resource flow imbalances										
Total external debt	..	293T	608T	547T	267T	196T	..	702T	423T	291T
as % of GNP	..	35	38	46	53	84	..	44	40	80
Debt service ratio										
1970	..	..	..	11.0	11.3	9.0	..	13.7	11.5	8.0
1991	..	19.0	21.0	24.5	27.8	26.2	..	25.7	20.3	27.2
Export-import ratio	72	71	108	106	88	90	79	97	99	88
Trade dependency	31	62	41	42	27	42	32	37	33	43
Terms of trade	101	103	98	94	90	84	100	100	102	92
Workers' remittances	..	0.5	..	-0.2	1.2	1.6	..	0.7	1.0	2.4
Gross international reserves	4.0	4.1	4.8	3.2	2.6	2.2	3.2	3.8	6.1	3.0
Current account balance	11,700T	10,080T	8,330T	-4,560T	-10,690T	-10,690T	8,760T	-830T	1,410T	-11,480T

	High human development		Medium human development		Low human development				Low-income	
	All countries	Developing countries	All countries	Excl. China	All countries	Excl. India	High-income	Middle-income	All countries	Excl. China and India
Table 21: Military expenditure and resource use imbalances										
Military exp. as % of GDP										
1960	6.2	1.9	6.9	2.6	2.2	2.5	5.4	7.5	6.5	3.5
1990-91	3.3	2.3	4.0	3.7	3.3	3.6	3.3	3.8	3.9	3.2
as % of health/educ. exp.										
1960	98	115	162	97	94	138	99	80	232	167
1990-91	33	39	67	54	65	65	32	55	84	63
Arms imports, total	..	1,850T	10,200T	8,970T	5,780T	3,340T	..	6,510T	7,560T	3,880T
as % of national imports	..	0.7	1.7	2.5	10.4	9.2	..	1.6	3.3	5.6
Armed forces										
per 1,000 people	8.2	5.8	5.1	7.9	2.3	3.1	10.6	7.1	2.8	3.9
per teacher	0.8	0.8	0.6	0.8	0.7	1.0	1.0	0.7	0.6	0.9
per doctor	4.5	5.7	9.4	17.1	31.6	59.2	5.9	12.4	19.4	47.9
Table 22: Growing urbanization										
Urban population, %										
1960	62	53	24	30	15	12	66	43	17	14
1992	76	78	38	49	26	26	77	62	27	27
2000	79	81	56	56	33	33	79	66	34	34
Urban pop. growth rate										
1960-92	1.9	3.8	4.0	4.3	4.6	5.7	1.7	3.9	4.3	5.2
1992-2000	1.1	2.2	4.3	3.6	4.7	5.5	0.9	3.1	4.7	5.1
Population in cities over 1 mill. (as % of urban)	45	49	40	41	38	39	46	40	38	40
in largest city	20	32	16	24	17	30	19	24	12	27
in cities over 1 mill. (as % of total)	34	38	15	20	10	10	36	24	10	11
Table 23: Demographic profile										
Population										
1960	1,000T	130T	1,190T	470T	810T	370T	670T	710T	1,620T	520T
1992	1,370T	260T	2,320T	1,040T	1,760T	880T	890T	1,340T	3,260T	1,170T
2000	1,440T	290T	2,630T	1,210T	2,130T	1,110T	960T	1,540T	3,830T	1,450T
Population growth rate										
1960-92	0.9	2.2	2.1	2.4	2.4	2.7	0.8	1.8	2.2	2.5
1992-2000	0.7	1.5	1.6	1.9	2.5	3.1	0.6	1.6	1.9	2.7
Growth rates over time	..	61	93	88	105	126	..	82	100	116
Population doubling date	..	2040	2035	2025	2020	2015	..	2025	2030	2020
Crude birth rate	..	24	25	30	37	44	..	30	30	39
Crude death rate	..	6	7	8	13	15	..	8	10	13
Total fertility rate	2.0	2.8	3.0	3.8	5.1	6.2	1.9	3.4	3.9	5.4
Fertility rates over time	62	51	48	59	79	92	62	63	61	81
Contraceptive prevalence	62	61	68	51	30	16	73	47	52	26
Table 24: Natural resources balance sheet										
Land area	58,160T	8,000T	44,160T	34,600T	29,410T	26,120T	34,020T	59,290T	38,420T	25,570T
Population density	23	32	52	33	59	33	26	22	84	45
Arable land	12.0	8.3	8.0	7.3	12.8	7.4	11.5	8.2	12.6	7.9
Pesticide consumption	..	..	0.18	0.23	0.06	0.06	..	0.32	0.10	0.08
Forest area	..	..	29	34	29	30	..	35	25	29
Production of fuel wood	..	..	20	21	29	34	..	20	25	31
Deforestation	..	..	..	0.8	0.8	0.9	..	0.9	0.9	0.9
Renewable water resources	11.2	15.8	6.6	11.2	5.8	9.4	9.9	13.4	4.7	8.9
Fresh water withdrawals										
as % of water resources	20	14	16	16	17	16	23	16	16	13
per capita	1,120	760	490	530	540	470	1,270	540	500	460
Irrigated land	10	15	25	16	22	18	10	11	28	22
Global emissions	0.43	0.24	0.11	0.16	0.07	0.10	0.46	0.20	0.07	0.09
Table 25: Energy consumption										
Commercial energy consumption										
1965	2,610T	110T	550T	420T	72T	22T	2,510T	490T	230T	44T
1991	4,690T	390T	1,430T	740T	370T	79T	4,240T	1,110T	1,140T	160T
per capita										
1965	3,020	780	240	330	87	68	3,380	740	130	85
1991	4,160	1,570	700	820	240	120	4,840	1,190	390	170
Energy imports	..	11	12	14	23	21	..	13	12	15
Annual change in consumption										
1970-80	3.0	7.5	6.7	6.4	7.2	10.2	2.4	5.9	7.8	10.2
1980-90	2.3	5.3	6.6	7.7	7.0	5.8	3.1	6.4	5.9	5.3
Energy efficiency										
1965	164	140	170	162	132	74	166	134	175	153
1991	26	41	85	56	92	40	25	64	127	48

	High human development		Medium human development		Low human development				Low-income	
	All countries	Developing countries	All countries	Excl. China	All countries	Excl. India	High-income	Middle-income	All countries	Excl. China and India
Table 26: National income accounts										
Total GDP	17,910T	940T	1,760T	1,400T	430T	210T	17,330T	1,850T	920T	330T
Agricultural production	4	8	17	14	32	33	3	13	28	27
Industrial production	38	37	39	38	26	24	37	39	35	31
Services	58	55	44	48	42	43	60	48	37	42
Private consumption	61	64	63	67	72	75	61	62	62	70
Government consumption	16	9	11	12	13	14	16	13	11	12
Gross domestic investment	22	26	27	24	21	16	21	25	29	23
Gross domestic savings	23	26	28	22	17	10	22	26	28	18
Tax revenue	24	15	19	19	12	14	24	19	15	17
Central gov't exp.	30	18	..	30	19	23	32	32	20	24
Exports	15	26	21	22	13	20	16	18	17	20
Imports	17	37	20	20	15	22	17	18	17	23
Table 27: Trends in economic performance										
Total GNP	18,900T	920T	2,110T	1,670T	540T	250T	17,750T	2,700T	1,100T	370T
GNP growth rate	3.1	4.7	4.4	3.1	4.5	3.2	3.2	2.5	6.7	4.3
GNP per capita growth rate										
1965-80	2.7	3.9	4.0	3.8	1.8	2.0	3.0	3.1	2.7	1.9
1980-91	2.0	1.5	5.1	1.5	1.9	0.2	2.5	0.5	4.4	1.2
Annual rate of inflation										
1980-91	8.5	..	87.1	110.3	10.0	12.5	4.6	121.9	9.3	14.9
1992	50.9	..	286.2	377.2	14.2	19.6	3.1	542.2	11.3	16.2
Growth rate of exports/GDP	1.0	-2.8	2.9	0.4	3.3	0.8	0.9	0.9	5.3	-0.1
Growth rate of tax revenue/GNP	0.9	-0.3	..	1.0	1.1	(.)	0.9	1.3	0.5	-0.7
Direct taxes										
1980	43	36	..	35	23	24	43	33	40	53
1991	42	37	..	35	21	25	42	33	33	44
Budget surplus/deficit										
1980	-4.1	-2.0	..	-4.6	-5.6	-4.2	-4.1	-3.8	-5.6	-4.7
1991	-3.1	0.4	..	-2.7	-6.2	-4.5	-3.3	-2.0	-5.0	-2.8

Selected definitions

Aid human expenditure ratio The percentage of a donor's GNP going to human priority areas in recipient countries or the amount of official development assistance received for human priority areas as a percentage of the recipient country's GNP.

Bilateral aid social allocation ratio The percentage of bilateral official development assistance that goes to the social sector.

Bilateral aid social priority ratio The percentage of bilateral social sector official development assistance that goes to human priority areas.

Births attended The percentage of births attended by physicians, nurses, midwives, trained primary health care workers or trained traditional birth attendants.

Budget surplus/deficit Current and capital revenue and grants received, less total expenditure and lending, minus repayments.

Contraceptive prevalence rate The percentage of married women of childbearing age who are using, or whose husbands are using, any form of contraception, whether modern or traditional.

Current account balance The difference between (a) exports of goods and services (factor and non-factor) as well as inflows of unrequited private transfers but before official transfers and (b) imports of goods and services as well as all unrequited transfers to the rest of the world.

Daily calorie requirement per capita The average number of calories needed to sustain a person at normal levels of activity and health, taking into account the distribution of the population by age, sex, body weight and environmental temperature.

Daily calorie supply per capita The calorie equivalent of the net food supplies in a country, divided by the population, per day.

Debt service The sum of repayments of principal and payments of interest made in foreign currencies, goods or services on external public, publicly guaranteed and private non-guaranteed debt.

Dependency ratio The ratio of the population defined as dependent—those under 15 and those over 64—to the working-age population, aged 15 to 64.

Direct tax Taxes levied on the actual or presumptive net income of individuals, on the profits of enterprises and on capital gains, whether realized on land sales, securities or other assets.

Discouraged workers People who leave the labour force in the face of poor job prospects or decide not to enter.

Domestic investment (gross) Outlays in addition to the fixed assets of the economy plus net changes in the level of inventories.

Domestic savings (gross) The gross domestic product less government and private consumption.

Earnings per employee Earnings in constant prices derived by deflating nominal earnings per employee by the country's consumer price index.

Education expenditures Expenditures on the provision, management, inspection and support of pre-primary, primary and secondary schools; universities and colleges; vocational, technical and other training institutions; and general administration and subsidiary services.

Employees Regular employees, working proprietors, active business partners and unpaid family workers, but excluding homemakers.

Enrolment ratio (gross and net) The gross enrolment ratio is the number of students enrolled in a level of education, whether or not they belong in the relevant age group for that level, as a percentage of the population in the relevant age group for that level. The net enrolment ratio is the number of students enrolled in a level of education who belong in the relevant age group, as a percentage of the population in that age group.

Exports of goods and services The value of all goods and non-factor services provided to the rest of the world, including merchandise, freight, insurance, travel and other non-factor services.

External debt   The sum of public, publicly guaranteed and private non-guaranteed long-term debt, use of IMF credit, and short-term debt.

Female-male gap   A set of national, regional and other estimates in which all the figures for females are expressed in relation to the corresponding figures for males, which are indexed to equal 100.

Fertility rate (total)   The average number of children that would be born alive to a woman during her lifetime, if she were to bear children at each age in accord with prevailing age-specific fertility rates.

Food aid in cereals   Cereals provided by donor countries and international organizations, including the World Food Programme and the International Wheat Council, as reported for that particular crop year. Cereals include wheat, flour, bulgur, rice, coarse grain and the cereal components of blended foods.

Food import dependency ratio   The ratio of food imports to the food available for internal distribution: that is, the sum of food production plus food imports, minus food exports.

Food production per capita index   The average annual quantity of food produced per capita in relation to that produced in the indexed year. Food is defined as comprising nuts, pulses, fruit, cereals, vegetables, sugar cane, sugar beets, starchy roots, edible oils, livestock and livestock products.

Future labour force replacement ratio   The population under 15 divided by one-third of the population aged 15 to 59.

Government expenditures   Expenditures by all central government offices, departments, establishments and other bodies that are agencies or instruments of the central authority of a country. It includes both current and capital or developmental expenditures but excludes provincial, local and private expenditures.

Greenhouse index   Net emissions of three major greenhouse gases (carbon dioxide, methane and chlorofluorocarbons), weighting each gas according to its heat-trapping quality, in carbon dioxide equivalents and expressed in metric tonnes of carbon per capita.

Gross domestic product (GDP)   The total output of goods and services for final use produced by an economy, by both residents and non-residents, regardless of the allocation to domestic and foreign claims.

Gross national product (GNP)   The total domestic and foreign value added claimed by residents, calculated without making deductions for depreciation. It comprises GDP plus net factor income from abroad, which is the income residents receive from abroad for factor services (labour and capital), less similar payments made to non-residents who contribute to the domestic economy.

Gross national product (GNP) per capita and growth rates   The gross national product divided by the population. Annual GNP per capita is expressed in current US dollars. GNP per capita growth rates are annual average growth rates that have been computed by fitting trend lines to the logarithmic values of GNP per capita at constant market prices for each year of the time period.

Health expenditures   Expenditures on hospitals, health centres and clinics, health insurance schemes and family planning.

Health services access   The percentage of the population that can reach appropriate local health services on foot or by the local means of transport in no more than one hour.

Human development index (HDI)   A composite measure of human development containing indicators representing three equally weighted dimensions of human development—longevity (life expectancy at birth), knowledge (adult literacy and mean years of schooling), and income (purchasing power parity dollars per capita).

Human priority areas   Basic education, primary health care, safe drinking water, adequate sanitation, family planning and nutrition.

Immunized   The average vaccination coverage of children under one year of age for the antigens used in the Universal Child Immunization (UCI) Programme.

Income share   The income in both cash and kind accruing to percentile groups of households ranked by total household income.

Infant mortality rate The annual number of deaths of infants under one year of age per 1,000 live births. More specifically, the probability of dying between birth and exactly one year of age times 1,000.

Inflation rate The average annual rate of inflation measured by the growth of the GDP implicit deflator for each period shown.

International reserves (gross) Holdings of monetary gold, Special Drawing Rights (SDRs), the reserve positions of members in the IMF, and holdings of foreign exchange under the control of monetary authorities expressed in terms of the number of months of imports of goods and services these could pay for at the current level of imports.

Labour force The economically active population, including the armed forces and the unemployed, but excluding homemakers and other unpaid caregivers.

Least developed countries A group of developing countries that was established by the United Nations General Assembly. Most of these countries suffer from one or more of the following constraints: a GNP per capita of around $300 or less, land-locked location, remote insularity, desertification and exposure to natural disasters.

Life expectancy at birth The number of years a newborn infant would live if prevailing patterns of mortality at the time of its birth were to stay the same throughout its life.

Literacy rate (adult) The percentage of persons aged 15 and over who can, with understanding, both read and write a short, simple statement on their everyday life.

Low-birth-weight babies The percentage of babies born weighing less than 2,500 grammes.

Maternal mortality rate The annual number of deaths of women from pregnancy-related causes per 100,000 live births.

Mean years of schooling Average number of years of schooling received per person aged 25 and over.

Military expenditures Expenditures, whether by defence or other departments, on the maintenance of military forces, including for the purchase of military supplies and equipment, construction, recruit-ing, training and military aid programmes.

Official development assistance (ODA) The net disbursements of loans and grants made on concessional financial terms by official agencies of the members of the Development Assistance Committee (DAC) of the Organisation for Economic Co-operation and Development (OECD) to promote economic development and welfare, including technical cooperation and assistance.

ORS access ratio The proportion of the population with a regular supply of oral rehydration salts (ORS) in their community.

Population density The total number of inhabitants divided by the surface area.

Poverty line That income level below which a minimum nutritionally adequate diet plus essential non-food requirements are not affordable.

Primary education Education at the first level (International Standard Classification of Education—ISCED—level 1), the main function of which is to provide the basic elements of education, such as elementary schools and primary schools.

Primary intake rate Number of new entrants into first grade, regardless of age, expressed as a percentage of the population of official admission age for the first level of education.

Primary school completion rate The proportion of the children entering the first grade of primary school who successfully complete that level in due course.

Purchasing power parities (PPP) See *Real GDP per capita*.

Real GDP per capita (purchasing power parities, or PPP) The method of using official exchange rates to convert the national currency figures to US dollars does not attempt to measure the relative domestic purchasing powers of currencies. The United Nations International Comparison Project (ICP) has developed measures of real GDP on an internationally comparable scale using purchasing power parities (PPP) rather than exchange rates as conversion factors, which is expressed in PPP dollars.

Rural-urban disparity A set of national, regional and other estimates in which all the rural figures are expressed in relation to the corresponding urban figures, which are indexed to equal 100.

Safe water access The percentage of the population with reasonable access to safe water supply, including treated surface waters, or untreated but uncontaminated water such as that from springs, sanitary wells and protected boreholes.

Sanitation access The percentage of the population with reasonable access to sanitary means of excreta and waste disposal, including outdoor latrines and composting.

Science graduates Tertiary education graduates in the natural and applied sciences, including medicine.

Scientists Persons with scientific or technological training—usually taken to mean completion of third-level education in any field of science—who are engaged in professional work in research and development activities, including administrators and directors of such activities.

Secondary education Education at the second level (ISCED levels 2 and 3), based on at least four years' previous instruction at the first level, and providing general or specialized instruction or both, such as middle schools, secondary schools, high schools, teacher training schools at this level and vocational or technical schools.

Secondary technical education Education provided in those second-level schools that aim at preparing the pupils directly for a trade or occupation other than teaching.

Social security benefits Compensation for loss of income for the sick and temporarily disabled; payments to the elderly, the permanently disabled and the unemployed; family, maternity and child allowances and the cost of welfare services.

South-North gap A set of national, regional and other estimates in which all figures are expressed in relation to the corresponding average figures for all the industrial countries, indexed to equal 100.

Technicians Persons engaged in scientific research and development activities who have received vocational or technical training for at least three years after the first stage of second-level education.

Terms of trade The ratio of a country's index of average export prices to its index of average import prices.

Tertiary education Education at the third level (ISCED levels 5, 6 and 7), such as universities, teachers colleges and higher professional schools—requiring as a minimum condition of admission the successful completion of education at the second level or evidence of the attainment of an equivalent level of knowledge.

Trade dependency Exports plus imports as a percentage of GDP.

Transition from first- to second-level education Number of new entrants into secondary general education, expressed as a percentage of the total number of pupils in the last grade of primary education in the previous year.

Under-five mortality rate The annual number of deaths of children under five years of age per 1,000 live births averaged over the previous five years. More specifically, the probability of dying between birth and exactly five years of age times 1,000.

Underweight (moderate and severe child malnutrition) The percentage of children, under the age of five, below minus two standard deviations from the median weight-for-age of the reference population.

Unemployment The unemployed comprise all persons above a specified age who are not in paid employment or self-employed, are available for paid employment or self-employment and have taken specific steps to seek paid employment or self-employment.

Water sources, internal renewable The average annual flow of rivers and aquifers generated from endogenous precipitation.

Years of life lost to premature death The sum of the years lost to premature death per 1,000 people, conveying the burden of mortality in absolute terms.

Classification of countries

Countries in the human development aggregates

High human development
(HDI 0.800 and above)

Argentina	Uruguay
Armenia	USA
Australia	Venezuela
Austria	
Bahamas	
Barbados	
Belarus	
Belgium	
Brunei Darussalam	
Bulgaria	
Canada	
Chile	
Colombia	
Costa Rica	
Cyprus	
Czechoslovakia	
Denmark	
Estonia	
Finland	
France	
Germany	
Greece	
Hong Kong	
Hungary	
Iceland	
Ireland	
Israel	
Italy	
Japan	
Korea, Rep. of	
Kuwait	
Latvia	
Lithuania	
Luxembourg	
Malta	
Mexico	
Netherlands	
New Zealand	
Norway	
Panama	
Poland	
Portugal	
Russian Federation	
Singapore	
Spain	
Sweden	
Switzerland	
Trinidad and Tobago	
Ukraine	
United Kingdom	

Medium human development
(HDI 0.500 to 0.799)

Albania	Samoa
Algeria	Saudi Arabia
Antigua and	Seychelles
Barbuda	South Africa
Azerbaijan	Sri Lanka
Bahrain	Suriname
Belize	Swaziland
Bolivia	Syrian Arab Rep.
Botswana	Tajikistan
Brazil	Thailand
China	Tunisia
Cuba	Turkey
Dominica	Turkmenistan
Dominican Rep.	United Arab
Ecuador	Emirates
Egypt	Uzbekistan
El Salvador	Viet Nam
Fiji	
Gabon	
Georgia	
Grenada	
Guatemala	
Guyana	
Honduras	
Indonesia	
Iran, Islamic Rep. of	
Iraq	
Jamaica	
Jordan	
Kazakhstan	
Korea, Dem. Rep. of	
Kyrgyzstan	
Lebanon	
Libyan Arab Jamahiriya	
Malaysia	
Maldives	
Mauritius	
Moldova, Rep. of	
Mongolia	
Morocco	
Nicaragua	
Oman	
Paraguay	
Peru	
Philippines	
Qatar	
Romania	
Saint Kitts and Nevis	
Saint Lucia	
Saint Vincent	

Low human development
(HDI below 0.500)

Afghanistan	Togo
Angola	Uganda
Bangladesh	Vanuatu
Benin	Yemen
Bhutan	Zaire
Burkina Faso	Zambia
Burundi	Zimbabwe
Cambodia	
Cameroon	
Cape Verde	
Central African	
Rep.	
Chad	
Comoros	
Congo	
Côte d'Ivoire	
Djibouti	
Equatorial Guinea	
Ethiopia	
Gambia	
Ghana	
Guinea	
Guinea-Bissau	
Haiti	
India	
Kenya	
Lao People's Dem. Rep.	
Lesotho	
Liberia	
Madagascar	
Malawi	
Mali	
Mauritania	
Mozambique	
Myanmar	
Namibia	
Nepal	
Niger	
Nigeria	
Pakistan	
Papua New Guinea	
Rwanda	
São Tomé and Principe	
Senegal	
Sierra Leone	
Solomon Islands	
Somalia	
Sudan	
Tanzania,	
U. Rep. of	

Countries in the income aggregates

High-income *(GNP per capita* *above $6,000)*	*Middle-income* *(GNP per capita* *$651 to $6,000)*		*Low-income* *(GNP per capita* *$650 and below)*
Australia	Albania	Paraguay	Afghanistan
Austria	Algeria	Peru	Bangladesh
Bahamas	Angola	Philippines	Benin
Bahrain	Antigua and Barbuda	Poland	Bhutan
Barbados	Argentina	Romania	Burkina Faso
Belgium	Armenia	Russian Federation	Burundi
Brunei Darussalam	Azerbaijan	Saint Kitts and Nevis	Cambodia
Canada	Belarus	Saint Lucia	Central African Rep.
Cyprus	Belize	Saint Vincent	Chad
Denmark	Bolivia	Samoa	China
Finland	Botswana	Senegal	Comoros
France	Brazil	Seychelles	Djibouti
Germany	Bulgaria	Solomon Islands	Egypt
Greece	Cameroon	South Africa	Equatorial Guinea
Hong Kong	Cape Verde	Suriname	Ethiopia
Iceland	Chile	Swaziland	Gambia
Ireland	Colombia	Syrian Arab Rep.	Ghana
Israel	Congo	Tajikistan	Guinea
Italy	Costa Rica	Thailand	Guinea-Bissau
Japan	Côte d'Ivoire	Trinidad and Tobago	Guyana
Korea, Rep. of	Cuba	Tunisia	Haiti
Kuwait	Czechoslovakia	Turkey	Honduras
Luxembourg	Dominica	Turkmenistan	India
Malta	Dominican Rep.	Ukraine	Indonesia
Netherlands	Ecuador	Uruguay	Kenya
New Zealand	El Salvador	Uzbekistan	Lao People's Dem. Rep.
Norway	Estonia	Vanuatu	Lesotho
Oman	Fiji	Venezuela	Liberia
Portugal	Gabon	Zimbabwe	Madagascar
Qatar	Georgia		Malawi
Saudi Arabia	Grenada		Maldives
Singapore	Guatemala		Mali
Spain	Hungary		Mauritania
Sweden	Iran, Islamic Rep. of		Mozambique
Switzerland	Iraq		Myanmar
United Arab Emirates	Jamaica		Nepal
United Kingdom	Jordan		Nicaragua
USA	Kazakhstan		Niger
	Korea, Dem. Rep. of		Nigeria
	Kyrgyzstan		Pakistan
	Latvia		Rwanda
	Lebanon		São Tomé and Principe
	Libyan Arab Jamahiriya		Sierra Leone
	Lithuania		Somalia
	Malaysia		Sri Lanka
	Mauritius		Sudan
	Mexico		Tanzania, U. Rep. of
	Moldova, Rep. of		Togo
	Mongolia		Uganda
	Morocco		Viet Nam
	Namibia		Yemen
	Panama		Zaire
	Papua New Guinea		Zambia

Countries in the major world aggregates

Least developed countries

Afghanistan
Bangladesh
Benin
Bhutan
Botswana
Burkina Faso
Burundi
Cambodia
Cape Verde
Central African Rep.
Chad
Comoros
Djibouti
Equatorial Guinea
Ethiopia
Gambia
Guinea
Guinea-Bissau
Haiti
Lao People's
  Dem. Rep.
Lesotho
Liberia
Madagascar
Malawi
Maldives
Mali
Mauritania
Mozambique
Myanmar
Nepal
Niger
Rwanda
Samoa
São Tomé and
  Principe
Sierra Leone
Solomon Islands
Somalia
Sudan
Tanzania
Togo
Uganda
Vanuatu
Yemen
Zaire
Zambia

All developing countries

Afghanistan
Algeria
Angola
Antigua and
  Barbuda
Argentina
Bahamas
Bahrain
Bangladesh
Barbados
Belize
Benin
Bhutan
Bolivia
Botswana
Brazil
Brunei Darussalam
Burkina Faso
Burundi
Cambodia
Cameroon
Cape Verde
Central African
  Rep.
Chad
Chile
China
Colombia
Comoros
Congo
Costa Rica
Côte d'Ivoire
Cuba
Cyprus
Djibouti
Dominica
Dominican Rep.
Ecuador
Egypt
El Salvador
Equatorial Guinea
Ethiopia
Fiji
Gabon
Gambia
Ghana

Grenada
Guatemala
Guinea
Guinea-Bissau
Guyana
Haiti
Honduras
Hong Kong
India
Indonesia
Iran, Islamic Rep. of
Iraq
Jamaica
Jordan
Kenya
Korea, Dem.
  Rep. of
Korea, Rep. of
Kuwait
Lao People's
  Dem. Rep.
Lebanon
Lesotho
Liberia
Libyan Arab
  Jamahiriya
Madagascar
Malawi
Malaysia
Maldives
Mali
Mauritania
Mauritius
Mexico
Mongolia
Morocco
Mozambique
Myanmar
Namibia
Nepal
Nicaragua
Niger
Nigeria
Oman
Pakistan
Panama

Papua New Guinea
Paraguay
Peru
Philippines
Qatar
Rwanda
Saint Kitts and
  Nevis
Saint Lucia
Saint Vincent
Samoa
São Tomé and
  Principe
Saudi Arabia
Senegal
Seychelles
Sierra Leone
Singapore
Solomon Islands
Somalia
South Africa
Sri Lanka
Sudan
Suriname
Swaziland
Syrian Arab Rep.
Tanzania, U.
  Rep. of
Thailand
Togo
Trinidad and
  Tobago
Tunisia
Turkey
Uganda
United Arab
  Emirates
Uruguay
Vanuatu
Venezuela
Viet Nam
Yemen
Zaire
Zambia
Zimbabwe

Industrial countries

Albania
Armenia
Australia
Austria
Azerbaijan
Belarus
Belgium
Bulgaria
Canada
Czechoslovakia
Denmark
Estonia
Finland
France
Georgia
Germany
Greece
Hungary
Iceland
Ireland
Israel
Italy
Japan
Kazakhstan
Kyrgyzstan
Latvia
Lithuania
Luxembourg
Malta
Moldova, Rep. of
Netherlands
New Zealand
Norway
Poland
Portugal
Romania
Russian Federation
Spain
Sweden
Switzerland
Tajikistan
Turkmenistan
Ukraine
United Kingdom
USA
Uzbekistan

Countries in the regional aggregates

Sub-Saharan Africa

Angola
Benin
Botswana
Burkina Faso
Burundi
Cameroon
Cape Verde
Central African Rep.
Chad
Comoros
Congo
Côte d'Ivoire
Djibouti
Equatorial Guinea
Ethiopia
Gabon
Gambia
Ghana
Guinea
Guinea-Bissau
Kenya
Lesotho
Liberia
Madagascar
Malawi
Mali
Mauritania
Mauritius
Mozambique
Namibia
Niger
Nigeria
Rwanda
São Tomé and Principe
Senegal
Seychelles
Sierra Leone
Somalia
South Africa
Sudan
Swaziland
Tanzania, U. Rep. of
Togo
Uganda
Zaire
Zambia
Zimbabwe

Arab States

Algeria
Bahrain
Egypt
Iraq
Jordan
Kuwait
Lebanon
Libyan Arab Jamahiriya
Morocco
Oman
Qatar
Saudi Arabia
Syrian Arab Rep.
Tunisia
United Arab Emirates
Yemen

Latin America and the Caribbean

Antigua and Barbuda
Argentina
Bahamas
Barbados
Belize
Bolivia
Brazil
Chile
Colombia
Costa Rica
Cuba
Dominica
Dominican Rep.
Ecuador
El Salvador
Grenada
Guatemala
Guyana
Haiti
Honduras
Jamaica
Mexico
Nicaragua
Panama
Paraguay
Peru
Saint Kitts and Nevis
Saint Lucia
Saint Vincent
Suriname
Trinidad and Tobago
Uruguay
Venezuela

East Asia

China
Hong Kong
Korea, Dem. Rep. of
Korea, Rep. of
Mongolia

South-East Asia and Oceania

Brunei Darussalam
Cambodia
Fiji
Indonesia
Lao People's Dem. Rep.
Malaysia
Myanmar
Papua New Guinea
Philippines
Samoa
Singapore
Solomon Islands
Thailand
Vanuatu
Viet Nam

South Asia

Afghanistan
Bangladesh
Bhutan
India
Iran, Islamic Rep. of
Maldives
Nepal
Pakistan
Sri Lanka

OECD

Australia
Austria
Belgium
Canada
Denmark
Finland
France
Germany
Greece
Iceland
Ireland
Italy
Japan
Luxembourg
Netherlands
New Zealand
Norway
Portugal
Spain
Sweden
Switzerland
United Kingdom
USA

Eastern Europe

Albania
Bulgaria
Czechoslovakia
Hungary
Poland
Romania

Successor states of the former Soviet Union

Armenia
Azerbaijan
Belarus
Estonia
Georgia
Kazakhstan
Kyrgyzstan
Latvia
Lithuania
Moldova, Rep. of
Russian Federation
Tajikistan
Turkmenistan
Ukraine
Uzbekistan

Nordic countries

Denmark
Finland
Iceland
Norway
Sweden

Southern Europe

Greece
Italy
Malta
Portugal
Spain

European Union

Belgium
Denmark
France
Germany
Greece
Ireland
Italy
Luxembourg
Netherlands
Portugal
Spain
United Kingdom

Non-European countries

Australia
Canada
Israel
Japan
New Zealand
USA

North America

Canada
USA

Human Development Report Office
Occasional Papers

1. Human Development in a Changing World
    Mahbub ul Haq, New York, 1992

2. Globalization and the Developing World: An Essay on the International
    Dimensions of Development in the Post–Cold War Era
    Keith Griffin and Azizur Rahman Khan, New York, 1992

3. Developing Countries in the International Economic System: Their Problem
    and Prospects in the Markets for Finance, Commodities, Manufactures and
    Services
    Dragoslav Avramovic, New York, 1992

4. Global Governance for Human Development
    Paul Streeten, New York, 1992

5. Disarmament as a Chance for Human Development.
    Is There a Peace Dividend?
    Herbert Wulf, New York, 1992

6. Towards a Human Development Strategy
    Keith Griffin and Terry McKinley, New York, 1993

7. Human Development: From Concept to Action
    A 10-Point Agenda
    Inge Kaul and Saraswathi Menon, New York, 1993

8. Sustainable Human Development: Concepts and Priorities
    Sudhir Anand and Amartya Sen, New York, forthcoming

9. New Perspectives on Human Development
    Mahbub ul Haq, New York, forthcoming

Human Development Report Office
United Nations Development Programme
336 East 45th Street, 6th Floor
New York, NY 10017
USA